Public Sector Shock

Public Sector Shock

The Impact of Policy Retrenchment in Europe

Edited by

Daniel Vaughan-Whitehead

Senior Economist, International Labour Office, Geneva, Switzerland and Professor, Sciences Po, Paris, France

Edward Elgar
Cheltenham, UK • Northampton, MA, USA

International Labour Office
Geneva, Switzerland

Published by
Edward Elgar Publishing Limited
The Lypiatts
15 Lansdown Road
Cheltenham
Glos GL50 2JA
UK

Edward Elgar Publishing Inc.
William Pratt House
9 Dewey Court
Northampton, MA 01060
USA

In association with

International Labour Office
4 route des Morillons
1211 Geneva 22
Switzerland
ISBN 978-92-2-126568-9 (paperback)

A catalogue record for this book
is available from the British Library

Library of Congress Control Number: 2012948851

This book is available electronically in the ElgarOnline.com
Economics Subject Collection, E-ISBN 978 1 78195 535 2

MIX
Paper from
responsible sources
FSC® C018575
FSC
www.fsc.org

ISBN 978 1 78195 534 5 (cased)

Typeset by Servis Filmsetting Ltd, Stockport, Cheshire
Printed and bound by MPG PRINTGROUP, UK

Contents

Contributors

Szilvia Altwicker-Hámori Fellow, Centre for Health Sciences, ZHAW Zurich University of Applied Sciences, Winterthur, Switzerland.

José-Ignacio Antón Lecturer in Economics, University of Salamanca, Spain.

Dominique Anxo Professor of Economics and Director of the Centre for Labour Market Policy Research, School of Management and Economics, Department of Economics and Statistics, Linnaeus University, Sweden.

Gerhard Bosch Economist and sociologist, Professor at the University of Duisburg-Essen and Director of the Institut Arbeit und Qualifikation (Institut for Work, Skills and Training), Germany.

Kerly Espenberg Vice-Director of Applied Research Centre of the EuroCollege, University of Tartu, Estonia.

Vojmir Franičević Professor of Economics and Political Economy, Faculty of Economics, University of Zagreb, Croatia.

Jérôme Gautié Professor of Economics, University of Paris I Panthéon-Sorbonne; Director of the Institut des Sciences Sociales du Travail; Researcher at the Centre d'Économie de la Sorbonne, Paris, France.

Damian Grimshaw Professor of Employment Studies and Director of EWERC (European Work and Employment Research Centre), Manchester Business School, University of Manchester, United Kingdom.

János Köllő Scientific Advisor, Institute of Economics of the Hungarian Academy of Sciences, Budapest, Hungary.

Jaan Masso Senior Research Fellow, Faculty of Economics and Business Administration, University of Tartu, Estonia.

Teo Matković Assistant Professor of Social Policy, Faculty of Law, University of Zagreb, Croatia.

Yannis Monogios Head of the Fiscal and Monetary Policy Research Department, Centre of Planning and Economic Research (KEPE), Athens, Greece.

Rafael Muñoz de Bustillo Professor of Applied Economics, University of Salamanca, Spain.

Philip O'Connell Director of the Geary Institute and Professor of Applied Social Science, University College Dublin, Ireland.

Helena Rato Senior Researcher and Director of Research and Consultancy Department, Instituto Nacional de Administraçao, Lisbon, Portugal.

Jill Rubery Professor of Comparative Employment Systems and Co-director of the European Work and Employment Research Centre, Manchester Business School, University of Manchester, United Kingdom.

Wiemer Salverda Professor of Labour Market and Inequality and Director Emeritus of the Amsterdam Institute for Advanced Labour Studies at the University of Amsterdam, the Netherlands.

Zafiris Tzannatos Senior Adviser for Employment Policy and Macroeconomics, ILO Regional Office for the Arab States, Beirut, Lebanon.

Valentina Vasile Professor of Economics, Senior Researcher and Scientific Director, Institute of National Economy, Romanian Academy of Sciences, Bucharest, Romania.

Daniel Vaughan-Whitehead Senior Economist, Conditions of Work and Employment Branch, International Labour Office, Geneva, Switzerland and Professor, Sciences Po, Paris, France.

Foreword

This volume and the research project that led to its publication are important in at least two respects. First, because it marks the continuation of what I think is a very important cooperation between the International Labour Organization and the European Commission. I was able to take part in the 2011 meeting on work inequalities in the crisis, and in some ways this is a follow-up to that. Second, because of the substantive issues involved. In the various chapters of the present volume, what strikes me most is how they explore behind some of the headline slogans that tend to dominate political discourse and policymaking. When it comes to the confrontation between austerity and growth and jobs, nobody loves austerity and everybody loves growth and jobs, but unfortunately it is slightly more complicated than that. In this volume the authors look into the complexities and the realities of what is taking place in European labour markets and particularly in the public sector, thus circumventing the sterility of the general discussion and focusing on the actual problems facing governments – also governments as employers – working people and, by extension, our societies. I think the ILO's input at the G20 and everywhere else, needs to be based on high-quality evidence of the kind presented in this volume.

The themes addressed in this volume take us very much to the heart of the crisis. The point of departure for discussion in Europe about public sector adjustment is explicit acceptance of the importance of the state as provider and protector, and the importance of high-quality public services and services of general interest (as reflected in both the Lisbon Treaty and the Charter of Fundamental Rights). Another key consideration is the extent to which economies and societies throughout the world regard as one of Europe's greatest assets its well-established public sectors and state administrations: whatever their shortcomings and need for reform, they are social assets which many countries covet. We must therefore do our best to ensure that they are not squandered.

The discussion of public sector adjustments in the context of the crisis is also part of a longer-running story. Consideration of the role of the state in the public sector in our societies did not start the day that Lehman Brothers collapsed. In many countries, over the past 30 years at least, the public sector, industrial relations and the appropriate size and role of government in our societies have been keenly debated. Over the past 20 or 30 years, perceptions of the employment opportunities provided by the public sector and its role in the provision of services have developed considerably and this comes out very strongly in the case studies presented in this book. There have also been processes of structural reform in the public sector driven by a range of considerations, including the recognition that sometimes the state sector does need to get smaller, but also that there is a need for efficiency in public services. Another issue has been the future of the welfare state. However, the crisis has not simply accelerated an ongoing process but rather has brought us to an intersection, at which the discussion of structural reform encounters what is called here 'quantitative change', and whose circumstances and motives are quite different. For 20 or 30 years, in a number of countries structural reform processes have not been a conscious and independent policy choice of governments. Employers' and workers' organizations have been involved in all this with varying degrees of success, enthusiasm, resistance and so on.

But the current crisis has introduced quite a different set of circumstances to the ongoing debate. As emphasized in this volume, there is perceived to be a need for immediate ad hoc reactions in the face of pressure from financial markets and the extreme state of public finances. These new pressures are quite distinct from the public sector reform process and we are struggling with the way these two phenomena are interacting. It is probably no coincidence that some countries that have not engaged in longer-term structural reform of the state sector are now feeling the pain most acutely. Other countries which took up this job earlier on seem to be doing rather better. This point is emphasized in several chapters of this volume.

A second key element which needs to be emphasized in our current circumstances is social dialogue. However, in situations of extreme urgency, when decisions of fundamental importance have to be taken literally overnight under financial duress, social dialogue can be extraordinarily difficult. Sometimes governments expect the social partners simply to turn up to be informed of decisions already set in stone and to do no more than sign them off as 'agreements'. Indeed, social dialogue has been stress-tested to breaking point in many countries.

But it is not a matter of pointing the finger. Rather the fact is that some of the basic institutions of social dialogue are suffering severe damage, at the same time as the social partners' input is needed in decision-making on expenditure cuts and revenue raising, as well as in the appropriate mix in processes of fiscal consolidation. It is a worry that not only has social dialogue frequently been suspended, but that in some instances it has simply ceased. One has to fear for the long-term survival of well-established labour market institutions which, once lost, are extraordinary difficult to restore.

The ILO should not simply be a commentator on events in labour markets, but rather an actor, as well as an assistant to other actors. Historically, the ILO has not often been – at least in the countries represented in this book – a direct actor. In the current crisis, the ILO tends to get called in as a fire brigade or ambulance service, trying to pick up the pieces once decisions have been taken. This volume can play a part in a wider reflection on how the ILO can deepen its role in the relevant countries: it is the ILO's duty to help its tripartite constituents, and that applies with particular force in Europe right now. If there is sufficient demand from constituents, the ILO needs to be ready to upgrade its role there.

When I was growing up, the public sector offered something of a safe choice: if you couldn't get a job in the private sector, the state would pick you up. Many of my schoolmates picked up a job in the civil service, nobody was unemployed, there were safety nets and full employment and everything was pretty comfortable. You would also get a pension, and probably earlier than workers in the private sector. That is all gone, however. The state also played a key social role. I grew up in a region with a very high level of dependency on the state. Today this dependency is even higher with regard to public sector employment. The regional aspect developed in this volume is also very interesting, including the issue of the public sector wage premium and the so-called 'wage penalty'. These are issues on which the ILO can do a lot more. I believe very strongly in the public sector: as employer – indeed, as a *good* employer – as a provider in society and as a key element in social justice.

Guy Ryder
Director-General
International Labour Office, Geneva

1. Public sector shock in Europe: Between structural reforms and quantitative adjustment

Daniel Vaughan-Whitehead

1. INTRODUCTION

The public sector has always been considered a cornerstone of European societies and, as such, also an essential lever for economic growth and political stability. It is also considered to be an essential element of the European Social Model, with many EU provisions serving as a useful framework for the good functioning of the public sector in EU member states. The public sector also represents a priority for public budgets. It is certainly also because of its central role that the public sector has been the constant object of reforms and restructuring over recent decades. All European countries have gone through a series of restructurings and reforms of their public sector and public expenditure.

However, of late we have experienced what we might call a 'public sector shock'. The budget deficits with which most European countries find themselves – and which have been aggravated, even provoked and fuelled by the latest financial and economic crisis, which started in 2008 – have plunged the public sector into a wave of 'adjustments', unprecedented not only in terms of their pace but also the scale of the attendant cuts in expenditure, employment and wages.

The magnitude of these adjustments has motivated the comparative work that we present in this volume. Its aim is precisely to document the nature, type and size of the adjustments being carried out in European countries and to provide concrete evidence on their effects. The aim is not to contest the objectives and any foreseen advantages of such adjustments – especially their immediate impact on the budget through curbing expenditure and making savings. Our aim is rather to document their social effects in the longer term, mainly with regard to the quality of jobs and working conditions in the public sector, but also throughout the economy, as well as – although this was not our primary objective –

their effects on the future quality of public services. A group of high-level national experts have tried to explain the 'public sector adjustments' story in their country based on information at national level that they have complemented and illustrated with case studies. These concrete examples are aimed at illustrating such adjustments in a particular sector – for instance, education, health or public administration – or to shed light on a specific issue or impact helpful for extending our knowledge of current public sector adjustments and their effects. We cover here 15 countries: 14 countries from the EU27 and one candidate country.

By producing a comparative panorama, we hope to enlarge the perspective of current public sector adjustments, help to identify some important policy elements or ingredients and cast some light on the best policy mix to reform the public sector efficiently. This could lead to positive outcomes not only on the budgetary side, but also in other policy areas, thereby enhancing the social, economic, political and general welfare of European citizens. The role of the actors shaping the process and final outcomes is an object of particular concern.

In this introductory chapter we summarize the main features of public sector adjustments and reforms before summarizing the most important findings on their effects. Chapter 2 explores the importance of the public sector for gender issues and thus analyses in detail the potential effects of such adjustments for women.

Subsequent chapters present the public sector adjustments in particular countries, each following a similar structure. Each starts with a brief introduction defining the public sector and its extent in terms of employment and activities, followed by a presentation of the adjustments/reforms recently introduced and some evidence of their effects, notably through a series of case studies. Each chapter also presents policy considerations and recommendations on public sector adjustments and reforms.

2. PUBLIC SECTOR ADJUSTMENTS ALL OVER EUROPE

2.1 Definition of the Public Sector across Europe

2.1.1 Diversity in definition

One of the difficulties of this comparative work consists in defining the public sector. It obviously comprises different activities and occupations in different countries. For instance, in Romania and Portugal but also France, the public sector traditionally includes state-owned enterprises, while in others it does not. To avoid such differences, we confined our

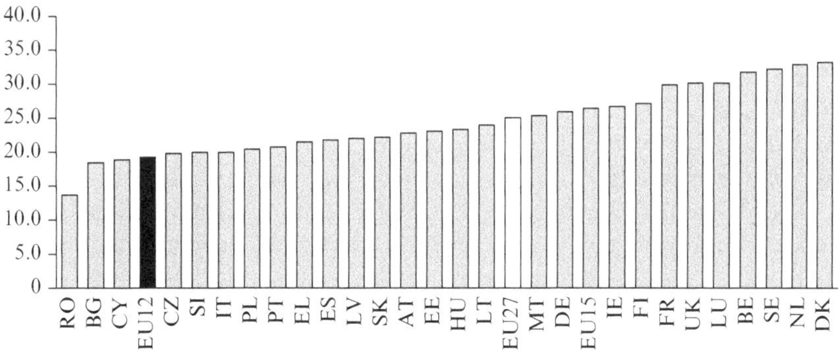

Note: This figure should be interpreted with caution since Eurostat does not draw a distinction between organizations in the private and those in the public sector; the figures above can thus just be used as a proxy of the size of the public sector.

Source: Eurostat.

Figure 1.1 Employment in public sector (NACE sectors), EU27, 2010 (as percentage of total)

analysis to the 'core' public sector, that is, excluding state-owned enterprises but including the three main public sectors (also following the Eurostat NACE (Nomenclature générale des Activités économiques dans les Communautés européennes) distinctions): (i) public administration (or general government employment); (ii) education; and (iii) health care and social services. Figure 1.1 presents the extent of employment in these sectors[1] in the EU, including the 15 countries covered in this study.

2.1.2 The public sector and European (and national) social model(s)

Since the Single Act was adopted in 1986, the EU has implemented liberalization in the public sector, transport and energy in an attempt to boost efficiency in areas often supposedly adversely affected by the domination of local, regional or national monopolies. But it has also progressively strengthened its commitment to good-quality services in these important areas. It has defined objectives of general interest in the relevant sectors and has set up a number of monitoring mechanisms and control agencies. More generally, EU institutions have committed themselves to services of general economic interest (SGEI) and have put in place a range of regulations to govern them.

The Treaty of Lisbon, Protocol No. 26 on Services of General Interest (EU 2009: 307) and Article 36 of the European Charter of Fundamental Rights (EU 2009: 204) clearly underline the importance of services of general interest in the EU, and set out principles to guide the EU approach to these services.

Protocol No. 26 on Services of General Interest imposes on the EU and the member states a shared responsibility for 'a high level of quality, safety and affordability, equal treatment and the promotion of universal access and of user rights' in public services, including public administration.

The Protocol also establishes, for the first time at primary law level, the fundamental principles which apply to services of general interest. The Treaty thus creates the possibility for the Union to legislate in this field by laying down the principles and conditions – particularly economic and financial conditions – which enable them to fulfil their missions, using regulation and the ordinary legislative procedure. At the same time, it acknowledges that the organization, delivery and financing of such services are primarily for member states to decide at national, regional or local level.

The Charter of Fundamental Rights also includes the right to good administration, while the 2001 White Paper on European Governance has set out major principles of good governance, which is relevant also for the public sector (openness, participation, accountability, effectiveness and coherence; EC 2001). More recently, the European Commission has issued a 'quality framework' for social services of general interest (SSGI) to ensure that citizens have access to essential services. It will review the situation on a regular basis and promote quality initiatives, in particular for social services that address particularly important needs (EC 2011). At the same time, it aims to increase clarity and legal certainty with regard to the EU rules that apply to these services, especially with regard to the current trends addressed in this volume.

Such basic principles and conditions have been enshrined in national legislation, including a strong and high-quality public service as part of the national social model. Other European directives also apply to the public sector. For instance, the European Community (EC) Directive on fixed-term work was agreed by the European Council in 1999 to prevent fixed-term employees from being less favourably treated than similar permanent employees, and to limit the use of repeated fixed-term contracts.

The right to strike is also laid down in the European Social Charter and has been adopted in some countries, such as the Netherlands since the 1980s. Some public sector employees still do not benefit from the right to strike, however, such as civil servants in Germany.

2.2 Context of the Crisis and Fiscal Deficits

Over the past few years, most EU governments have implemented various measures to overcome the economic crisis and kick-start economic recovery. While many initiatives were taken to sustain economic growth and create jobs – especially in the first period in 2007–09 – many governments have also realized the need to introduce reforms to address rising debts. In fact, government measures to rescue the financial sector, to sustain the economy during the crisis and to minimize social costs – notably through the use of automatic social stabilizers, such as social assistance and unemployment benefits – combined with sharply reduced revenues have left governments with sizeable deficits. These deficits, combined with low economic growth, have sharply increased debt levels in many countries, which in some cases were also present before the crisis. On average, debts in OECD countries increased from 55.6 per cent of GDP in 2007 to 74.2 per cent of GDP in 2010 (OECD 2011a, 2011b).

In this context, fiscal consolidation has become the cornerstone of the current policy debate across Europe, especially in those countries where the debts are most severe, such as Greece, Ireland and Portugal.

Within this fiscal consolidation, there have been policy debates on public expenditure, especially in the public sector, and more generally on what should be the appropriate role of the government in the economy and in society as a whole. While most EU countries had already started public sector reforms before the crisis, the slowdown of economic growth and increased public debt accompanying the crisis has suddenly called into question the relative stability of public sector jobs and wages. A series of adjustments and reforms have been proposed and rapidly implemented. It is this process that the present volume proposes to document in 14 EU countries and one candidate country (Croatia), while also providing evidence on their short- and long-term effects.

2.3 Diversity in the Timing and Nature of the Reforms

It is first essential to distinguish the *timing* of public sector adjustments. Some reforms started well before the crisis and have merely been continued in recent years without much influence from the crisis, as in Sweden and Germany. In the Netherlands, many public sector adjustments had already taken place in the 1980s and 1990s, including significant wage and employment cuts. Consequently, until early 2012 no wage and employment adjustments had been undertaken in the Netherlands. These may come later, however, as from 2013. In other countries, it is the crisis that has generated or accelerated the need for reforms in the public sector, as is evident in Greece, Portugal and Romania.

There is also a distinction to be made concerning the *nature* of these adjustments, especially between *structural reforms* and *quantitative adjustments* (see Table 1.1).

Table 1.1 Adjustments/reforms in the public sector, selected countries, 2000–2010

Structural reforms / Quantitative adjustments	Low	Middle	High
Low	Croatia	Netherlands*	
Middle	Latvia Lithuania	Estonia Germany	France Sweden**
High	Greece Hungary Romania	Ireland Portugal Spain	United Kingdom

Note: * Quantitative adjustments carried out in the 1980s–90s. ** Structural reforms had already taken place in Sweden during the 1990s with employment downsizing that continued in the 2000s.

Source: Compiled by the author.

In some countries, significant public sector reforms are being carried out, notably to improve productivity and overall efficiency, while other countries are implementing mainly quantitative adjustments, notably with regard to employment, wages and public expenditure in general. The latter type of adjustment seems to be a common feature in the current period, especially within the framework of austerity packages aimed at reducing budgetary and fiscal deficits. The following chapters will show that this type of adjustment currently prevails in Greece, Hungary, Ireland, Portugal, Romania, Spain and the United Kingdom.

Other countries had already started significant reforms of their public sector even before the crisis, such as Sweden and the Nordic countries in general, but also France, Germany and the United Kingdom, although in very different ways.

Some countries are characterized rather by a mix of public sector structural reforms and quantitative adjustments, such as Estonia, the Netherlands and Portugal. While these can reinforce each other, they can also conflict. As emphasized by Helena Rato in Chapter 11 on Portugal, the quantitative adjustments imposed during the crisis may have halted the reform process already under way in the public sector.

Quantitative adjustments generally lead to significant cuts or freezes in public expenditure, wages and employment. Current plans in most European countries focus on reducing programme expenditure. This generally consists of reducing spending on, for example, social benefit systems, health care, old-age pensions or development aid – and reducing compensation costs, through either staff reductions or wage and benefit cuts. Government can also be reorganized through across-the-board efficiency cuts or overall spending freezes. The reforms also generally aim at reducing pension costs, a reform that also concerns future retirees in the public sector.

There are also different types of structural reforms that we have regrouped under four major headings.

Among the structural reforms, most countries have engaged, first, in *decentralization* of political power and spending responsibilities to regional or municipal governments. This was the case in Sweden, but also Spain, Germany and many other European countries.[2]

A second institutional change consists in reforming *human management practices* in order to improve employees' job satisfaction and efficiency. This can incorporate skills strategies and redesign of work, and also the introduction of pay systems related to performance, alongside evaluation systems rather than seniority. We shall see in this volume that most European countries have adopted one or the other or all of these measures.

A third type of structural reforms consists in merely *adjusting (generally downsizing) operations* to maximize economies of scale, a trend particularly implemented in the education and health-care sectors.

This may also be related to a fourth institutional change, which is the *shifting of part of the activities previously carried out by the state to the private sector*, through either privatization, or outsourcing and agentification. Although there is a general trend in this direction in most European countries, the United Kingdom has exemplified this move both in the 1980s and in the most recent period. This involves a radical redesign and streamlining of service provision or, at the extreme, withdrawal from areas of provision. The other possibility is to carry out quantitative adjustments, that is, reductions in spending involving employment or wage cuts.

Obviously, the effects of such changes in the public sector – which we investigate in the next section – may differ greatly according to the relevant policies.

We shall see throughout this volume that this overview of types of public sector adjustments could help us to better define the *drivers of such policy changes*. Why are such changes currently taking place in the public sector? Distinguishing between the different motives is useful: first, there is a primary budgetary motive, with the need to cut public expenditure; second, an economic motive with the aim of making public services more modern and efficient, also with greater mobility between the public and private spheres; third, a political motive within the debate on redesigning the role and size of the state and privatization/outsourcing of public utilities; and finally, we might mention a demographic motive given the emerging population pressures. Other drivers may also be discerned. The global context and the role in particular of international organizations, such as the International Monetary Fund (IMF) but also the EU and the European Central Bank (ECB) should also be taken into account and may explain national differences currently observed throughout Europe.

In a number of countries public sector adjustments have been imposed by the budgetary situation, while in others they intervened under various constraints. Distinctions can be drawn between countries such as Greece, Romania and Ireland, and those in which the budgetary situation had been consolidated before the crisis, such as Sweden, the Netherlands and, to some extent, also Croatia. We should also distinguish between countries in which some adjustments had already taken place, such as outsourcing in the United Kingdom, Germany and Sweden, the high percentage of public sector employees already under temporary contracts, as in Sweden and Spain, or the abolition of the wage indexation system for public sector employees, as in France. All these changes made before the crisis may explain its more modest impact on public sector adjustments, although in Spain and the United Kingdom quantitative adjustments have been drastic, despite previous reforms.

Table 1.1 shows the different mixes of structural and quantitative changes. The objective of such a combination of quantitative adjustments and more structural reforms in the public sector is to 'do more with less' (in France, 'do better with less'), on the assumption that cuts and rationalization of spending and human and financial resources may lead to better and not lower quality of public services. The aim of this volume is to attract the reader's attention to the risks of seeing this set of adjustments – also depending on their scale and nature – as leading to 'doing less with less', or even, if the adjustments are not well thought through, to end up 'doing less with more' because of the budgetary implications of the reforms and their unexpected long-term social and economic costs.

2.4 Diversity in the Implementation of Reforms/Adjustments

Not only the nature of the adjustments may differ between European countries, but also the manner in which they are implemented.

2.4.1 Implementation or not of prior reviews and cost–benefit analyses

First, the reforms may be the result of a complete series of reviews or be implemented without prior review. In principle, any reforms in the public sector should be preceded by evidence and data on decision-making and measure all the likely benefits, costs and effects of government decisions and policies. Evidence in countries such as Sweden in the 1990s shows that the implementation of programme reviews, value-for-money assessments and cost–benefit analyses have helped to identify how much is being spent, what is being produced and with what outcomes for different parts of society. This has served to define the best ways to generate savings while not losing efficiency (see OECD 2011a, where the example of Canada is also presented).

Chapter 7 on Greece highlights that no such reviews had been carried out before imposing serious public sector adjustments. Other chapters in this volume – for instance, Rafael Muñoz de Bustillo and José-Ignacio Antón for Spain (Chapter 13), in relation to health sector reform – also highlight a lack of pre-reform measures of performance, which can serve as a baseline against which to measure reform progress.

2.4.2 Existence or lack of an institutional framework

Second, reforms may be laid down once and for all and be subject to a long-term implementation programme, or, at the other extreme, be changed frequently with no particular road map or clear direction. The existence of a strong institutional framework for decision-making – in particular a medium-term expenditure framework – helps to ensure that governments stick to the reforms, while giving investors and businesses confidence in its capacity to manage public finances (Schick 2010). In contrast, many EU governments have modified their initial framework and plans several times, often within the same year, thus creating confusion, lack of transparency and confidence.

This was the case in Greece where a new plan and new measures on employment and wage cuts were announced – generally increasing the magnitude of adjustments – every few months. We shall see that Romania (Chapter 12) has also been characterized by incessant sets of new reforms/adjustments in the public sector, with several changes of direction.

2.4.3 Unilateral or negotiated

Reforms can be the result of a long process of negotiations at national and, sometimes, local level, or they may be the result of hasty decision-making. They may have involved a number of actors in the process – in particular, workers' representatives – or they may have been decided by the government unilaterally. Communication with regard to reforms helps to build credibility, keep civil servants and citizens informed and thus eventually increase people's sense of 'ownership' of reforms. A lack of communication, combined with a lack of government assessment of the potential impact of regulations, can only lead to loss of trust and discontent.

The role of communication and social dialogue is thus also investigated in this volume. Has there been sufficient communication around public sector adjustments? Have they been discussed or negotiated with the trade unions and employers' representatives?

Clearly, public sector adjustments have been decided without much prior consultation or negotiations in countries such as Greece, Portugal, Romania, Spain and many others. In contrast, there were negotiations on public sector reforms in Sweden and Ireland.

The same country may also be characterized by different methods in different periods. While the first years of the crisis in Ireland did not lead to many negotiations on the anti-crisis policy responses, which were decided mainly by the government alone, a tripartite agreement was signed in 2010 to determine reforms in the public sector until 2015.

Generally, however, the various chapters in this volume conclude that the most recent adjustments in the public sector have been decided fairly quickly, without involving the social partners, something that trade unions in the public sector have denounced and which has fuelled waves of protest in these countries. Similarly, according to the OECD (2011a), 'social dialogue has been insufficiently used in current public sector reforms'.

Among the three Baltic states (Chapter 3), only Estonia seems to have been making use of extensive tripartite consultations between government and social partners on public sector reforms. This has helped to limit wage cuts and seems to have led to a more coordinated and balanced approach – and also fewer strikes. By contrast, reforms in Lithuania have focused mainly on wage cuts unilaterally decided by the government, leading to immediate protests by the trade unions and the general public. However, more consultation has helped rather than impeded Estonia in designing rapid policy responses to the crisis, including a fairly strict austerity package.

2.4.4 Differentiated roles of international actors

Finally, some countries have been subject to the influence of international actors more than others. Current public sector policies in Croatia – as in Romania or Bulgaria a few years ago – have been influenced by the forthcoming EU accession, which requires strong administrative capabilities to take on board the Community *acquis*, while also managing EU structural funds. Other countries are receiving direct assistance from the IMF, such as Hungary and Romania, which have signed Memorandum agreements with the IMF, but also Greece, which is under the direct monitoring of a 'Troika' composed of the IMF, the EU and the ECB.

For instance, the macroeconomic motivations behind the fiscal policies of the three Baltic countries were also quite different, dominated by the need to satisfy the Maastricht criteria to join the Eurozone in the case of Estonia and to satisfy the loan conditionalities of the IMF in the case of Latvia, while Lithuania, under less international pressure, has managed to increase its deficit during the crisis.

2.5 Recent Focus on Quantitative Adjustments

Most governments across Europe have announced workforce reduction measures and/or cuts to salaries and benefits in the public sector.

2.5.1 Employment: non-replacement, job cuts and changed work contracts

We see in this volume that a number of countries – such as France, Croatia and Portugal but also many others – have set replacement ratios (usually one for two) to fill the gaps left by employees leaving for retirement. This has often been complemented by cuts in the labour force, sometimes on a massive scale. The new coalition government in the United Kingdom, partly driven by an ideological belief that this will lead to more efficiency in public services, has applied massive and unprecedented employment cuts and a pay freeze across all areas of the public sector for 2011–13. At the other extreme, Nordic countries, such as Sweden, as shown by Dominique Anxo (Chapter 14), have not announced any employment or wage cuts in the crisis – although employment in the public sector has fallen in the 1990s and 2000s in Sweden. They have also been limited so far in the Netherlands, Croatia and Germany.

The reduction of public sector employees can be done progressively or rapidly: several countries covered in this volume have chosen the latter option. The nature of employment adjustments can also take various forms: dismissals, reduced working hours, outsourcing, privatization, changes in work contracts, for instance from permanent to temporary or from full- to part-time. The size and features of such adjustments, which we document in the various chapters, often depend on the initial size of public sector employment in individual countries. In Spain and Romania, for example, the public sector is considered too large. Similarly, employment cuts may not have the same effects if they take place in a large state and public sector, as in France, or in an already small state and public sector, as in Ireland. Finally, employment cuts in the public sector must also be considered in the context of a serious fall in employment in the private sector because of the crisis.

In this volume our aim is to document employment changes in the public sector by segments – ministries and other national administrations, local/regional administration, hospitals and so on – but also by gender, skills or qualifications and also central/local level. We also try to distinguish between public sector employment reductions due to the crisis (in 2008–10) and longer-term employment reductions (since 2000).

Quantitative adjustments have also been accompanied and often preceded by more structural adjustments in the composition of employment, mainly due to various trends such as the recourse to more fixed-term contracts and also the outsourcing of a number of public service jobs. The number of temporary contracts in the public sector has increased rapidly throughout Europe. The highest increase has been observed in Spain (up to 24 per cent), but other countries have seen significant increases, such as Sweden since the early 1990s, with temporary contracts accounting for 18 per cent of jobs in the public sector, 16 per cent in central administration and nearly 19 per cent in local administration. In France, such employment increased by nearly 14 per cent between 2005 and 2009, thus representing a share of 15 per cent of employment in the public sector. In Germany, such jobs increased from 10 per cent in 2002 to 15 per cent in 2010.

Countries such as Portugal have also modified the status of public sector employees, allowing fixed-term contracts to develop. By contrast, fixed-term contracts in Croatia, although introduced in public administration – where they represent 8 per cent of total employment – have not developed much in the public sector as a whole. The situation is similar in Romania.

Another way to gain flexibility and also to reduce spending is to replace jobs previously carried out in the public sector by new jobs in the private sector through outsourcing and privatization of public services. Governments' use of outsourcing has also rapidly increased in OECD countries, from 8.7 to 10.3 per cent between 2000 and 2009. This process has been implemented on a large scale in the United Kingdom, but also in Germany, as shown in this volume.

This has led to a reduction in the share of government expenditure and also public sector employment, for instance in Germany. The trend is thus leading to reduced expenditure. It is important to look at the potential risks of this approach.

2.5.2 Wages: cutting basic wages, bonuses and benefits

Almost all European countries have announced plans to freeze or cut public sector wages. Only in the Netherlands, so far, have both employment and wages continued to slowly increase in 2008–11, which is explained by the quantitative adjustment already carried out in the decades before the crisis.

This volume shows that the reforms in the public sector have completely transformed both the wage levels and the wage structure of public sector employees.

According to OECD data, wages represent 80 per cent of total compensation. The rest can take the form of performance-related pay. There are also thirteenth- or fourteenth-month payments for public sector employees. In addition, the government contributes to retirement plans or pensions, as well as private health insurance costs or other social contributions. Table 1.2 summarizes the changes identified in the 15 countries covered in this volume. It shows that there have been significant cuts and that they have been implemented in various ways, either through a basic wage freeze or cut in Estonia, Ireland, Latvia, Lithuania, Romania and many others, or through the abolition of bonuses previously enjoyed by public sector employees, such as the thirteenth-month payment in Hungary and the thirteenth- and fourteenth-month payments in Greece.

Interestingly, public sector wages have not fallen in the Netherlands during the crisis, for a number of reasons. First, because wage cuts already took place in the 1980s and 1990s. Second, because of this past experience the government decided this time to focus less on pay reductions and tried to find other adjustment measures (see Chapter 10 on the Netherlands). This trend may already have stopped, however. While nominal wages continued to increase in 2008–11, they were allowed to lose some ground with regard to inflation, with a 1.1 per cent decrease in the public sector real wage in 2011. Job growth also ceased in all three major public sectors, education, health and public administration. New measures announced in mid-2012 seem to confirm this change of direction.

The magnitude of the wage cuts in 2009–11 varied by country, from no cuts in Germany (except the Christmas bonus), the Netherlands (just a slight decrease in real terms) and Sweden, to 5–10 per cent in Croatia, Estonia and the United Kingdom, 10–15 per cent in Lithuania and Portugal and as much as 25 per cent in Latvia. The most significant reductions, however, have been in Greece (15–20 per cent in 2010 alone, with 15 per cent more cuts announced for 2012), Romania (25 per cent in 2010) and Hungary (37 per cent for unskilled workers).

While some countries have cut wages across the board by the same amount along the wage scale – as in Hungary and Romania – others have implemented a regressive cut, with reductions proportionally higher for higher-income employees and lower for low-income employees. We shall see in the next section that the impact on wage inequality is obviously different in the two cases.

A number of non-monetary benefits have been abolished, such as for housing or meals in Portugal and Romania or for sick leave in Spain. Pension entitlements have also been cut in countries such as Greece and Spain, but also others.

Table 1.2 Adjustments to wages and employment, selected European countries

Case study	Employment	Wage cuts and structure
Croatia	New recruitment frozen	–6% in 2009; return to 2008 level; then freeze –15% for state officials
Estonia	–1% in 2008–09	Cuts concerned 71% of public sector employees –10% in public administration and –3% in education in 2009–10
France	–7% in 2008–12 in central government public service Staff reductions in hospitals	About 10% real loss for starting wages in many jobs in 2000–10 due to across-the-board wage increases and an 'index point' lower than inflation Increase in the social contribution pension equal to a 3.5% loss in net wages Wage individualization
Germany		Performance-related pay up to 8% of total wage bill Increase in low paid New lower pay scale to avoid outsourcing Christmas bonus reduced; reduction of yearly bonus
Greece	First target of –20% by 2015 modified to –26%, mainly through cuts in fixed-term contracts Already –15% by 2011	–15–20% in 2011 (–21% for military personnel) Abolition of thirteenth- (paid in December) and fourteenth- (Easter and summer) month payments New cuts in 2012 (–15%)
Hungary	Downward trend until 2008, then an increase of 4.7% in 2008–10; and slight decrease by –1.7% in 2010–11	Abolition of thirteenth-month payment in 2009 and of subsidies for housing, heating and travel Cuts between –37% for unskilled and –13% for high skilled in 2008–10
Ireland	No layoffs so far but no replacement of retirees and no renewal of many temporary contracts –5.2% in 2009–11	Wage cuts introduced in December 2009 from –5% (for lowest wage) to –15% (for highest wages) –4.7% on average in 2010
Latvia	–4.3% in 2008–09	–25% in public administration and –20% in education in 2009–10
Lithuania	–1.1% in 2008–09	–15% in public administration in 2009–10

Table 1.2 (continued)

Case study	Employment	Wage cuts and structure
Netherlands	Continued to increase in 2008–10 (by 6%) especially part-time Significant cuts planned up to 2014	Wage cuts progressive in the 1980s Real wage decline in 2010–11 by –1 to 2% (by –2% in public administration to –2.5% in education)
Portugal	–9.5% in public administration in 2005–10 Public sector unemployment growth of 20%	–2.5% of real wage in public administration in 2010 Further cut of 3.5–10% in 2011 In 2012 suspension of thirteenth- and fourteenth-month payments (for holiday and Christmas bonuses); corresponds to –16% for most skilled
Romania	–9.5% in 2008–11 Further cuts in 2012	–25% in 2010 Cut of thirteenth-month pay and abolition of most bonuses –10% in 2011 despite some attempts to compensate for former cuts Wage freeze in 2012
Spain	–18,000 in 2010 in public administration No new recruitment in 2012	–5% in 2010 Frozen in 2011 and 2012 Result: –10% real wages in 2010–11 Same in autonomous regions
Sweden	Previous reduction of 17.7% in 1991–2007 Cut by 1.4% in 2008–10 (95% of them short-term contracts) Also cuts in part-time employment. Higher cuts at local level	Similar wage growth as in private sector (3.3% in 2005–09)
United Kingdom	–10% planned over 5 years (2010–14); largely exceeded in 2010–11 (–6.1%) so double cut may be forecast by 2014 In 18 months (2010–11) already –9% in public administration, –4% in education and –3% in health	Wage freeze in 2010–12 has led to –5% real wage in 2010–11 1% cap on basic wage rises in 2013–14

3. EFFECTS OF SUCH ADJUSTMENTS: SHORT AND LONG TERM

One of the aims of the project reflected in this volume was to identify some of the effects already observed or expected from current public sector adjustments. Since the public sector reforms are still in process it was too early to benefit from a comprehensive database. We have tried to cope with this data deficit by giving concrete examples from each country and also carrying out a number of case studies to report on the changes already observed at local level (Table 1.3). These case studies are aimed at illustrating the nature of public sector adjustments in each country and document all their effects (either already observed or expected).

As previously indicated, the adjustments in the public sector mainly follow budgetary objectives which certainly need to be achieved. But while we do not question these objectives and the positive effects they may bring for macroeconomic outcomes, we try to attract the reader's attention to some of the risks of such a policy in terms of social conflicts,

Table 1.3 Case studies carried out in 2011–2012 in the selected European countries (see individual chapters)

Case study	Case study 1	Case study 2
Croatia	Upper secondary education	Wage moderation process in 2008–11
Estonia	Health-care services	Rescue sector
France	Public sector reform process	Education
Germany	Public procurement	Local budgetary adjustments in the city of Duisburg
Greece	Health care	Education
Hungary	Health sector: doctors' situation	Education
Ireland	Services to the unemployed	Education
Netherlands	Effects of past wage moderation	Health-care wage regulation
Portugal	Health	Education (two schools)
Romania	Education	Wage reforms in the public sector
Spain	Health system	Education
Sweden	Elderly care in Växjö municipality	Local public employment agencies
United Kingdom	Job search services to the unemployed	Local government

as already witnessed by the waves of strikes all over Europe, but also new wage dynamics that could increase the proportion of low-paid workers and inequalities, lower-quality jobs and working conditions in the public sector, with further risks of lower motivation and increased migration, which could ultimately lead to a fall in the quality of public services.

3.1 Widespread Waves of Protest

More than ever before, the latest series of reforms and adjustments in the public sector has provoked an unprecedented wave of protests and even riots in a number of European countries, which we document systematically in each national chapter of this volume, which all provide a table on public sector strikes/demonstrations from 1998 to mid-2012. The protests were most extensive in countries in which the most restrictive policies were implemented, such as Greece, Portugal, the United Kingdom and Spain, but also in countries where the adjustments have been less severe, such as France and Croatia.

Not only have there been demonstrations at national level, in many cases well beyond the public sector, but also at local level and in specific sectors or professions. Besides demonstrations by employees in health (doctors, nurses) or in education (teachers) we have observed for the first time demonstrations by occupations generally little inclined to demonstrate or organize strikes, such as the police (for instance, in France, Greece and other countries).

This chain of demonstrations throughout Europe was the most immediate and striking effect of the adjustments implemented in the public sector, whose implications and costs – high both socially and economically – have yet to be evaluated. They have had a direct impact on public sector employees' motivation and productivity, and on the overall quality of public services. Interestingly, a rapid deterioration of the social climate seems to have been avoided in the countries where the government has managed to organize tripartite consultations, as in Estonia, as distinct from Latvia and Lithuania, and in Ireland over the most recent period, from the agreement concluded in 2010.

3.2 New Wage Dynamics

Wage moderation in the public sector started before the financial crisis in most European countries. For instance, the abolition in the 1980s or 1990s of public sector pay inflation indexation mechanisms in some countries – for instance, France – were aimed at progressively reducing the public sector wage bill. However, the recent decision to freeze or even cut wages in the public sector in a more systematic and significant way – we have seen all components of the wage structure, such as basic wage, bonuses and benefits affected – in almost all European countries has rapidly modified wage dynamics in the public sector and their position with regard to private sector wages.

3.2.1 From a 'wage premium' to a 'wage penalty' for public sector employees?

There is generally scant evidence on wage differences between the public and the private sectors. We have tried in this volume to present the available evidence and to try as far as possible to decompose the differences that might be due to different qualifications or positions, and those due to intrinsic differences pertaining to the public sector.

Generally, there is a recognition that public sector wages should be higher than in the private sector since it generally attracts the most educated labour force. Because of this higher educational level, together with longer seniority (greater length of service), a wage premium is to be expected in the public sector and has generally been confirmed by the available data. For instance, in the United Kingdom half of the public sector premium is associated with the higher share of professionally qualified and higher-skilled employees in the public sector (see Bozio and Disney 2011 for the United Kingdom). In Germany the premium is due to a higher skill level, but also because many high- and medium-level activities, such as education, the judiciary or tax offices are concentrated in public services. Higher pay for the low skilled and for nearly all public sector groups are also found in eastern Germany because of the generally low wage levels in the private sector there.

We have also generally observed throughout Europe a wage premium which is higher for the low skilled and which becomes negative compared to the private sector for the most-skilled and highest-income deciles.

It is obviously difficult to compare average wages in the public and private sectors because of the different labour force characteristics. The possible impact of compositional effects should be particularly highlighted. For example, increasing the outsourcing of low-skilled public sector activities in order to cut public sector expenditure may artificially increase average wages in the public sector (also in comparison to the private sector) without reflecting an improvement of the wage situation of remaining employees. At the same time, the failure to replace those – generally more highly skilled and better paid – who are retiring may lead to an artificial increase in the average wage in the public sector, despite cuts in the wages of those remaining and lower wages for new recruits.

The comparison made in Table 1.4 should thus be treated with caution

Table 1.4 Public/private pay gap, selected European countries

	Public/private sector pay gap	Part of public sector
Croatia	From +34% in 2000 to 24% in 2008 and 31% in 2010	+17% in health, 10% in public administration and 1% in education in 2011
Estonia	From –4% in 2006 to +2% in 2010 For low paid, from +8.5% in 2001 to 0% in 2007	
France	N.A.	
Germany	Public sector wages slightly lower than in private sector except for unskilled and women, and most East Germans	
Greece	11% public sector premium has fallen since 2010 and may have disappeared	
Hungary	From 15% in 2004 to –12% in 2009	In 2008–10 wages of doctors in public sector fell from 90 to 70% of doctors' wages in private sector In 2008–10, wages of public sector teachers fell from 43 to 38% of the private sector wage
Ireland	According to benchmarking body it has fallen behind private sector wages Wage premium in public sector of 26% in 2006, according to various studies. Has fallen since then to 22% (2009)	
Latvia	From +21% in 2006 to +9% in 2010	
Lithuania	From +23% in 2006 to +15% in 2010	
Netherlands	Public sector wages scales were strongly reduced relative to the private sector in the 1980s. Controlling for workforce composition	Rates for government and education lagged behind the private sector by 19%, health care by 11% in the 1990s

Table 1.4 (continued)

	Public/private sector pay gap	Part of public sector
	public sector pay is 2% below the private sector (2011)	The current pay penalty pay in the public sector (controlled by skills composition) is 9–16% for education, 4% for government and nil for health care
Portugal	In 2000–09 real wages fell by –3.6% in the public sector compared to +9.4% in the private sector	
Romania	From +44.5% in 2009 to –15.6% in 2010 (a loss of 60.1 percentage points)	
Spain	From +17% in 2009 to +7% in 2011 (gap reduced by 60%)	
Sweden	Wage premium in the public sector declined slightly in 2000–10	Convergence of wage levels in the public sectors towards those in the private sector
United Kingdom	Wage premium in the public sector declined in 2010–12	

since it generally refers to average wage figures. This is also why we complement this gross comparison whenever possible with more detailed analysis that allows us to decompose what differentials might be due to skill differences and what might be due to employment in one or the other sector.

Despite its limitations, a comparison over time of average wages in the two sectors provides a number of instructive elements illustrative of trends.

The evidence collected so far is fairly clear. We have witnessed over recent years a radical transformation in the hierarchy of wage levels between the public and the private sector.

The most important new dynamic is the freezing or cutting of public sector wages, which has brought about a decline in comparison to private sector wage dynamics. The trend is dramatic in countries in which the wage premium that prevailed before the crisis has been converted over the course of two or three years – but sometimes even less – into a wage penalty for those working in the public sector. This is the case in Romania, where the advantage of 45 per cent in 2009 was converted into a loss of 15 per cent – that is, a loss of more than 60 percentage points – by the end of 2010. In Hungary, the premium of 15 per cent in 2004 was transformed into a penalty of 12 per cent, which has increased even further in 2010–12. If it continues, the trend towards a reduction of the wage premium – as shown in Table 1.4 – may also lead to a wage penalty in other European countries in the near future, in 2013.

In the Netherlands this disappearance of the wage premium in the public sector has occurred over a long time, from a 21 per cent premium in 1979 right down to 1 per cent in 1996 and even –0.4 per cent in 2004. This shift was most significant in education, where employees gradually lost their wage premium of 21 per cent in 1979 to reach a disadvantage of –6 per cent in 2004.

In a few countries, such as Portugal and Romania, the minimum wage in the public sector has been set below that in the rest of the economy, illustrating the new wage dynamics generated by recent public sector adjustments and austerity measures.

Croatia is one of the only countries here where the public sector premium has continued to increase rather than decrease, from 24 to 31 per cent between 2008 and 2010.

3.3 Inequalities and Vulnerable Groups

Wages have traditionally been found to be more compressed in the public sector, with lower wages being generally higher than in the private sector, and then a progression along the wage scale, however, with wage levels generally less generous for the most-skilled occupations than in the private sector.

The different chapters of this book confirm that wage disparity between the top and the bottom is smaller in the public sector than in the private sector – for instance in Croatia, Germany, Spain, Sweden and the United Kingdom. In Sweden, for instance, the wage dispersion is lower for both state and local authorities compared to the private sector.

On this basis, what have been the effects of recent public sector adjustments on wage inequality in the public sector? Not only the magnitude of wage cuts, but even more the distribution of those wage cuts across the wage scale has influenced the outcome.

As the OECD has recently remarked, across-the-board wage cuts may be inefficient and less likely to lead to permanent cuts in expenditure (OECD 2011a: 50). In addition, they can affect segments of the population unevenly, for instance those at the bottom of the wage scale. The effects on inequality in the public sector thus depend on the progressivity of across-the-board wage adjustments.

In certain countries, wage cuts were implemented at the same rate across the board. This was the case in Romania where a cut of 25 per cent was imposed in 2010 uniformly on all public sector employees. In other countries, such as Portugal, the wage cuts have been progressive, thus increasing along the wage scale and contributing to reducing wage inequalities between the top and the bottom.

Public recognition in Romania that the uniform reduction of 25 per cent was a mistake (see Chapter 12 on Romania) led to some readjustments in 2012.

In France, the traditional 'index point' has not been sufficiently adjusted to inflation and has thus led to a loss in purchasing power for several occupations (of approximately –10 per cent for the 2000–10 period). This was accompanied by some compensation, with plans to redistribute 50 per cent of the wage savings due to employment cuts to remaining employees.

This volume shows that the impact of wage cuts has been different by country according to the type of cuts implemented. Where the cut was progressive along the wage scale, the impact on inequality was lower. Where the cut was uniform across occupations and skill levels, this had the effect of disadvantaging low-income groups. The abolition of bonuses, such as thirteenth- or fourteenth-month payments, corresponds to a uniform cut and has produced increased inequality, as in Hungary where the cut of the thirteenth-month payment led to a 12 per cent decline in the public sector wage and a 37 per cent fall among the low skilled, but only a 13 per cent fall among the most skilled.

Increased inequalities because of adjustments have also come from the different work contracts and different pay and working conditions proposed to new employees. Lower pay levels for new recruits in Ireland, for instance, have increased inequalities and brought a sort of dual market in the public sector. Similarly in France the decrease of starting wages in real terms in many occupations de facto leads to intergenerational inequality. Germany also has a strong internal labour market with lifelong employment, but at the same time an increasing number of peripheral employees with temporary contracts.

In most European countries – Spain being the most extreme case – the increase in the proportion of temporary workers who do not enjoy the same working conditions (especially in terms of job stability) is also creating increasing inequality among the public sector labour force.

Another way of looking at inequality is also to identify whether the adjustments are having disproportionate effects on certain categories of workers, especially those considered the most vulnerable. No doubt, certain categories of workers have been more affected by public sector adjustments. Lower employment prospects will directly hit those categories that tend to work in the public sector, especially women, young people and migrant workers for some professions.

The chapter on gender by Jill Rubery (Chapter 2) provides the reasons why women will be harder hit than men by the current public sector adjustments. Women represent a major part of public sector employees, but the public sector also traditionally provides women greater access to highly skilled positions and better pay: the gender pay gap documented in the various chapters of this book is traditionally lower in the public sector. There are also more flexible working-time arrangements and work–family life reconciliation practices. These disproportionate effects of public sector adjustments on women require a dedicated chapter, taking a transversal and cross-country approach.

3.4 Impact on Low Pay and Poverty among Public Sector Employees

The cuts in employment and wages have had some impact on security among public sector employees, for a number of reasons, including their difficulty in getting re-employed in either the public or the private sector; their shift to part-time and temporary contracts, as in Greece; and the cut or abolition of overtime payments. The cuts in pension benefits also increase poverty rates: a 10 per cent increase in public pension expenditure is associated with a 1.5 percentage point increase in older people's relative income (OECD 2009).

The most dramatic development has been in Hungary where the abolition of the thirteenth-month payment has led to a rapid increase of low-paid employees in the public sector. As documented in Chapter 8 on Hungary, low pay affected 31 per cent of public sector employees with less than secondary education in 2008, but 55 per cent in 2010. This means that more than one unskilled public sector employee out of two had fallen below the poverty threshold by May 2010.

Severe wage cuts in Lithuania also led to an immediate increase in low-paid employees in the public sector. Specifically, female jobs seem to have been hit by the increased proportion of low paid, for example, teachers.

In Romania, although there are more low-paid employees in the private than in the public sector, the dramatic fall in wages in the latter suddenly increased the proportion of employees below the poverty threshold (see Chapter 12 on Romania). A minimum wage lower in the public sector than in the rest of the economy has further contributed to this, with a similar trend in Portugal.

In Germany, the increase of casualization (fixed-term, part-time) in the public sector has led to a rapid increase of low-paid workers, as documented by Gerhard Bosch in Chapter 6 on Germany, also in the case studies at the municipal level. At the same time, outsourcing and low wages in the private sector have also contributed to a race to the bottom in terms of wages and work contracts. Typically in Germany in order to avoid outsourcing lower entry wages for low skilled were decided in the public sector. The author concludes that 'the state has increasingly become a major driver in the expansion of a low-wage sector as a result of outsourcing and privatization and also as a contracting authority'.

Similarly in the United Kingdom, the shift of many public sector employees from full-time to involuntary part-time has led to an increased proportion of low-paid workers among public sector employees.

3.5 Indirect Effects on Working Conditions

Reductions in employment and wages have also had indirect effects on working conditions, summarized in Table 1.5. First, labour force reductions combined with the same volume of services to be delivered will obviously lead to increased workloads and higher work intensity. This has also led to a greater number of working hours in countries such as Estonia, Germany, Greece and Spain. The problem is that this increased number of working hours has often been accompanied by a reduction in the hourly overtime rate, as in Greece, Hungary and Portugal. One of the most important changes in working conditions for public sector employees in Portugal – apart from significant wage cuts – was the reduction of overtime rates that clearly affected those working longer, with also those working at night suddenly losing their premium compared to those working during the day.

Overtime payments have even been abolished, as in the education sector in Estonia, or for all public sector employees in Romania, where they are now compensated with free time. There are similar restrictions in Croatia and Estonia.

While for some countries, working hours have been increasing in the public sector, often alongside a decrease in hourly overtime rates, some other countries have reduced working hours in the public sector as an adjustment mechanism in the crisis, notably through the shift from full- to part-time contracts. In the three Baltic countries, working hours' adjustments were lower than in the private sector.

Finally, training has also been allowed to decline, with lower career progression, frozen in a number of countries.

Case studies in individual chapters provide a number of illustrations of these trends, for instance in education and health care.

In France, lower resources including less employment have led to an intensification of work: the remaining employees have to work harder to

Table 1.5 Effects on working conditions and social dialogue, selected European countries

	Working conditions	Social dialogue
Croatia	Restrictions on overtime	
Estonia	Training cuts by 60% Non-paid overtime in education	Fewer strikes than in the other two Baltic states
France	Work intensification in many services due to job cuts	Lack of social dialogue in the reforms
Germany	New working conditions arrangements in the new generation of collective agreements: working-time flexibility, performance-related pay, prolongation of weekly working hours	Fragmentation of social dialogue: decentralization from national to many local agreements
Greece	Increase in working hours and reduction in overtime rates Freeze of automatic progression New payroll grid and job-ranking system Lower pension entitlements	Continuous waves of general protests and strikes but also for all public sector occupations and sectors
Hungary	Reduction in the number of working hours and also of hourly rates	Lack of social dialogue in the reforms Dismantling of the previous tripartite structures Reduced use of collective bargaining in public sector
Ireland		Pay increase scheduled in national agreement cancelled in March 2009. Disputes and protests against wage freeze and pension levy in first half of 2009 Public sector agreement 2010–14 in March 2010 for some public sector reforms, but no further wage cuts and no compulsory redundancies. Industrial peace maintained
Latvia		Several protests and strikes Softening of the rules of collective bargaining

Table 1.5 (continued)

	Working conditions	Social dialogue
Lithuania		Unilateral wage cut in June 2009 without consultation, followed by strikes and national agreement in October 2009
Netherlands		From central agreement to 8 subsector wage agreements already in 1993, and subsequently to 14 agreements
Portugal	Cut of overtime pay rates Additional supplements for housing, meals, travel, unhealthy activities frozen Progression criteria tightened Career progression frozen in 2011 Pay progression by merit also stopped in 2011 Fall in vocational training by 50%	Series of strikes/protests both at national and public sector level
Romania	No payment of overtime but compensation by free time Abolition of previous compensations (for meals etc.) Decrease in vocational training	New law on social dialogue in 2011 that brings a number of changes, such as an increased representativeness threshold, abolition of national collective contract and reduction of automatic extensions previously used at sectoral level
Spain	Increase in weekly hours Abolition of employees' pension funds (–0.3% of total wage) Abolition of wage complement for sick leave in region of Madrid (–40% of previous wage in case of sick leave); same in regions of Valencia and Galicia	2010 agreement on wage increase in public sector broken by government Increased conflicts Reduction of role of trade unions and social dialogue in public sector Reduction of hours employees released to perform trade union activities in many regions

Table 1.5 (continued)

	Working conditions	Social dialogue
Sweden	Little impact from the crisis High share of short-term contracts in public sector (17–18%) Working time slightly increased in the crisis Slight decrease in training	Negotiated flexibility leading to individualization and differentiation of wages
United Kingdom	Increased workload alongside significant job cuts	Protests in the public sector

meet demand which is often increasing rather than decreasing, as shown in the examples on education and health care provided by Jérôme Gautié in Chapter 5 on France. In Spain, public sector employees have experienced not only abolition of the job stability principle – along the systematic issuing of fixed-term contracts for new recruits – but also longer working hours and larger workloads, and wage levels have been allowed to fall below private sector wages in a number of sectors.

A case study on elderly care in a municipality in Sweden (Chapter 14) also shows some intensification of work for employees in this sector.

In Germany (Chapter 6), the state and the *Länder* unilaterally increased the weekly working hours of civil servants to 42 hours (Bavaria and Thuringia), while weekly working hours were also increased by collective agreements for the non-civil servant public employees. The cut of the Christmas bonus was applied to all.

Increased workload and increased working hours (above 12 hours a day) among doctors and nurses is well documented in Chapter 8 on Hungary, while those on France (Chapter 6) and Portugal (Chapter 11) describe the same problem for teachers. A case study in two schools in Portugal (Chapter 11) clearly shows the increased workload on teachers alongside employment cuts, mainly through the non-renewal of fixed-term contracts, with increased stress, excessive class sizes and lower motivation, which have adversely affected the quality of the education provided. The same process is described in Croatia (Chapter 4) and other countries.

This trend towards deteriorating working conditions has been aggravated by changes in the functioning of collective bargaining, also described in Table 1.5, notably with the abolition of previous extension clauses in Romania (Chapter 12) and the reduced recourse to social dialogue in the public sector in Hungary (Chapter 8), where tripartite institutions were also modified.

3.6 Effects on Human Capital and Long-term Quality of Jobs and Pay

The reduction in training but also lower expenditure on human capital in general bring long-term risks of human capital losses in the public sector.

Training was reduced by a record 50 per cent in Portugal in terms of both total number of training hours and number of trainees. In Croatia, training, which is traditionally higher in the public sector, has plummeted since 2008 to private sector levels. Training expenditure was also reduced by 60 per cent in the Baltic states over the past few years. Vojmir Franičević and Teo Matković for Croatia (Chapter 4) show how investment in human capital has decreased in the public sector, especially in education, leading to a lack of professionals and skills in a number of schools.

Alongside cuts in expenditure in human capital, more difficult career progressions due to austerity programmes may also have an impact. Career development was frozen in Portugal and the United Kingdom, with career services even dismantled in the latter. Similarly in Greece, career progression has become more difficult due to the obstacles hindering public sector employees from moving up the ranking scale even if all their performance evaluations are successful.

Lower career prospects combined with cuts in wages and benefits risk affecting the public sector's ability to attract and retain staff, with high performers leaving to pursue higher-paid opportunities with private companies or abroad. Such effects are already observable and reported in the various chapters.

One case study in the United Kingdom (Chapter 15) shows how outsourcing unemployed services to private providers has led to a loss of previously qualified employees in this area.

Jaan Masso and Kerly Espenberg in Chapter 3 on the three Baltic countries (Estonia, Latvia and Lithuania) show how long tenure in the public sector has made possible a significant accumulation of job-specific human capital, while shortened tenure due to fiscal consolidation measures has started to reduce such capital, with the most experienced employees leaving, especially in education and public administration.

In Germany (Chapter 6), the case study of the municipality of Duisburg highlights the difficult budgetary situation of, in particular, old industrial cities that have to finance a large part of the costs of long-term unemployment even though their revenues are shrinking. As a result, they are highly indebted and must cut basic services, while lowering pay and working conditions in the public sector.

In the Netherlands (Chapter 10), experience in the 1980s illustrates the negative effects that a significant deterioration in pay and working conditions can have on public sector attractiveness. It has significantly reduced the willingness of young well-educated people to work in education. Key civil servants report that an 'area of tension' has developed between the existing public wage structure and wage cuts motivated by budgetary problems (BZK 2011). Especially the combination of labour force ageing – in 2008, 35 per cent were aged 50 and over – and unattractive labour conditions is likely to discourage younger employees, leading to an expectation that 70 per cent of all employees in government and education (30 per cent retirement, 40 per cent mobility) will leave and need replacing by 2020.

In Portugal (Chapter 11), the retirement of public employees is most detrimental with regard to the highest-qualified staff, who are not replaced or are replaced by less-skilled employees, a process that has also led to a lowering of human capital.

Chapter 7 on Greece also documents the reduction in the number of higher-ranking public sector officials, from 30,000 to 10,000.

From these examples, we can thus expect that the magnitude of current public sector adjustment together with decreasing public expenditure – notably on training – will lead to significant changes in the skill composition of public sector employees.

3.7 Transformation of the Public Sector's Image

To date, the public sector has been regarded as an important element of the European Social Model. However, the image of the public sector has changed radically over the past few years. As shown in this volume, public sector employees have been the target of campaigns aimed at depicting them as almost parasites of the labour market, enjoying strong trade unions and unjustified better pay and working conditions – despite their reported 'low productivity' – which allegedly have contributed to the huge budget deficits that most European states now face.

Certain professions have come under particular attack, such as public administration, but also education and health care.

This type of campaign has focused on public sector advantages – especially in the context of the economic crisis – and seems to have influenced the image of the public sector in public opinion, as shown in Spain and other countries, thus facilitating acceptance of radical adjustments and reforms. The change of image and perceptions of the role of the public sector has in fact been much more radical in the countries facing the biggest budget deficits. The image of public sector employees is today radically different in, say, Greece compared to that in Sweden.

While such denigration of public sector jobs and conditions may be partly explained by the current economic context, it will have a long-term impact on the public's perception of the public sector.

Such a deterioration of the public image and prestige of public employees – combined with their deteriorating working conditions – will have a negative impact on the recruitment of young qualified people, the motivation of its existing labour force and the quality of services produced.

Denigration of public sector occupations may also progressively undermine the guiding role that the public sector has played in progress on workers' rights and entitlements in general. Most labour improvements and equity arrangements – for instance, for reconciling work and family life or part-time arrangements – were generally first introduced in the public sector and then extended to the private sector. This was also the case with pension and health insurance. By removing such a pilot function, one important lever for improving working conditions might progressively disappear in Europe, and the public sector will tend to copy labour conditions in the private sector.

3.8 Migration

Worsening wages and working conditions in several occupations in the public sector has also led to waves of emigration. This volume provides evidence on doctors from countries such as Hungary and Romania, but the same movement has been reported in the Czech Republic and Poland. In Romania, almost 10 per cent of doctors have emigrated since 2007 (Holt 2010). In Hungary, as reported by Szilvia Altwicker-Hámori and János Köllő (Chapter 8), 500 to 600 doctors left every year between 2004 and 2008 compared to 750–800 graduates per year, a figure which has since been on the rise. In 2011, 100 doctors per month applied for a certificate of goodwill required for working abroad.

This situation has led to a series of protests in these countries. In 2011, thousands of Czech, Slovak, Hungarian and Polish doctors deposited notices of resignation as a sign of protest and also went on strike. A case study in the chapter on Hungary describes this doctors' revolt and its effects. Evidence of emigration of public sector employees from the Baltic states is also provided, in occupations such as doctors, police and armed forces, and rescue workers, with a case study on this important occupation. A case study on the deteriorating pay and working conditions of doctors in Estonia is also presented, with their immediate effects, including emigration to Finland. Emigration of nurses and health sector employees in general has also been reported by trade unions.

3.9 Industrial Relations

The types of reform selected for the public sector may lead to differentiated use of social dialogue. Negotiations and consultations with the social partners seem to have been rare in the face of significant quantitative adjustments to reduce the budget deficit, generally carried out hastily.

According to the OECD (2011a: 35), 'while consultation processes on proposed regulations have improved, consultation in the area of procurement is not as widespread', with only one-third of OECD member states involving citizens at some point in the procurement process, most often to monitor the integrity of the award process or to monitor implementation.

This assessment is confirmed for EU countries where social dialogue has generally been poor. In a series of countries initial tripartite agreements have not been respected. This was the case in Spain, for example, where the agreement for 2010 not to cut wages was broken by the government, which then unilaterally imposed a 5 per cent reduction. Zafiris Tzannatos and Yannis Monogios in Chapter 7 on Greece also show how social dialogue was completely excluded from the negotiations on rescue and austerity packages. This neglect of dialogue in the reform process has certainly contributed to the mushrooming of protests and strikes as an alternative outlet.

At the same time, the process of radical adjustments and reforms seems to have had an impact on collective bargaining, especially where the reforms themselves have modified the functioning of collective bargaining mechanisms and rules.

In Latvia, the crisis has led to a weakening of the rules on collective bargaining. In Croatia, attempts to reduce the scope of collective agreements led to trade union mobilization and withdrawal of proposed changes (see Chapter 4 on Croatia). In Romania, the new Law on Social Dialogue abolished the collective agreement at national level, but also tightened up the representativeness conditions, thus rendering trade unions action more difficult, and also dismantled the automatic extension of collective agreements at sectoral level, which will limit the scope of collective bargaining.

Similarly, in Greece the contents of collective agreements were not respected, which led to a high-level mission by the ILO in 2011 (ILO 2011b). In Hungary, the new Labour Code not only dismantled the tripartite council, which had some say in minimum wage fixing and wage recommendations, but also modified collective bargaining provisions.

This current period has contributed to lowering trade unionization in the public sector, as documented here and there in this volume, for example, in the three Baltic states.

This trend will be further aggravated by the structural shifting of collective bargaining in many European countries away from nationally fixed agreements to decentralized agreements by subsectors, as had already happened in Sweden and the Netherlands in the 1990s, but more recently in Germany and Romania. This fragmentation of collective bargaining in Germany to the 16 federal states has led to a lower trade union impact on local working conditions. There are also more similarities in Germany between private industry and public sector industrial relations than there were in the past (Keller 2011).

The current austerity packages have contributed to undermining collective bargaining in the public sector in different ways. First, by the abolition of extension clauses – as in Romania and Greece – or the non-renewal of collective agreements, or the reduction of hours made available for trade union activity, as in Spain.

This trend is to be seen as an important loss for public sector employees. Evidence in this volume shows that wages and working conditions can be better protected where workers are represented by strong trade unions and benefit from comprehensive collective agreements.

Countries with strong trade unions in the public sector, such as France, have managed to limit wage cuts while the absence or weakening of trade unions has led to higher wage cuts. A tradition of collective bargaining in Sweden has also allowed a high degree of flexibility and efficiency gains at local level. The very low trade unionization in countries such as Estonia – in both the private and public sectors – may also explain why the wage rates of the two sectors have progressively converged.

3.10 Potential Effect on Service Quality: Lower Quality and Fewer Resources

The examples in this volume show that in many cases it has not been possible to achieve the aim of most of the reforms, as indicated by the OECD (2011a), namely to 'improve efficiency . . . using fewer resources'. The examples show that resources have certainly fallen, but that this has also brought a deterioration in performance and service quality.

The case studies on the health sector show that there is often a decrease in efficiency with a deterioration of inputs. As shown in the case of France in both education and health care, this has led to a mismatch between demand and supply, and the cuts and reforms could not be achieved without sacrificing quality. A case study in Estonia shows a rapid increase in medical waiting lists and a rapid decrease in the number of doctors, technical equipment and operating theatres.

In Croatia, workers' satisfaction and motivation in the public sector have decreased, as shown in the case studies presented.

One of our case studies in Romania shows restricted access for teachers and the impossibility of career advancement. This has also led to a lower number of qualified employees, with a direct impact on the quality of services provided.

The different case studies on services to the unemployed show some of the adverse effects of outsourcing in the United Kingdom: the interests of the service providers do not always coincide with the public interest. In Germany as well, underspending and underinvestment are expected to affect the efficiency of the public sector and also to make many local municipalities incapable of delivering proper public services.

The chapters on the United Kingdom (Chapter 15) and Ireland (Chapter 9) also show how lower resources in the public sector have disproportionately affected disadvantaged groups. Cuts in the budget and quality of education in Ireland have hit lower-income families who have no other choice than the state system. Similarly, government spending cuts have affected families in the lowest-income regions in the United Kingdom. A case study in Germany reveals the impact of cuts in one low-income region. Similarly in Hungary spending cuts in education have led to poorer services for low performers, so that their dropout rate has increased. Selection by social background has also increased. Similarly, all programmes for improving the integration of Roma children into the education system were either interrupted or significantly reduced.

This volume offers many instances of falling quality in public services: cuts in security services leading to increased insecurity; longer delays in judicial decision-making, along with pay reductions, leading to increased corruption; lack of skills, including IT, in the public sector due to reduced investment; lower services also in health care, including the closure of emergency centres; and in education larger class sizes and fewer teachers in France, Romania and many other countries.

3.11 Detrimental Effects on Longer-term Reforms in the Public Sector?

The examples presented in individual chapters also highlight that quantitative cuts are often presented as necessary for restructuring the public sector, but in some cases may contradict or impede structural reforms needed to improve overall efficiency.

For example, the efficiency of reforms aimed at encouraging and facilitating mobility between institutions to better allocate human resources – implemented in most EU countries, including France – may be frustrated and even penalized by more recent adjustments aimed at using mobility as a door to exit the public sector, as in Portugal. In this country, the new special mobility status decided under budgetary pressure and to avoid redundancies in the public sector is not really encouraging the mobility sought before the crisis to improve public sector efficiency.

Similarly, all measures aimed at facilitating career progression and better recognition of skills, performance and merit – also alongside new public management (NPM) changes and more performance-related pay – have been undermined by recent measures to stop or limit career advancement and progression. The greater recourse to fixed-term employment contracts may also reduce employees' willingness to move from one institution to the other due to the risk of losing their job. In Germany, recent changes in the public sector do not seem to have been much influenced by concepts of NMP (Keller 2011).

Structural reforms of pay in the public sector may also be halted by immediate wage cuts or freeze.

In Romania, the structural reform of introducing a simpler and unified wage scale – with fewer grades – clashed directly with the 25 per cent across-the-board wage cuts and a lower minimum wage in the public sector.

Similarly, performance-related pay cannot be used if possible wage increases are frozen, a conflict that occurred recently in Portugal.

Interestingly, in some cases public sector wages have declined during the crisis as a result of the reduction of profit-sharing bonuses that have fallen automatically, thus acting as a buffer to avoid employment cuts. This has happened in Estonia, where it can partly explain why pay adjustments were higher than in the private sector, but also why employment cuts were also lower in the public sector. This type of downward adjustment – of course with a need to limit their negative impact on lower incomes – may be more efficient than wage cuts across the board. This type of effect might legitimate increased recourse to these schemes in public sector reforms in a number of European countries – as they started in France – not only as a tool to motivate performance in the public sector, but also to allow some wage flexibility in an economic downturn. Of course, one key condition is to introduce such performance-based pay not in a period of crisis but rather in a period of growth so that employees can first see the advantages of these schemes and not associate them with wage cuts. It is typically a structural reform in pay systems that should be dissociated from quantitative adjustments, in other words, wage cuts.

The case study on education in Romania highlights the permanent tensions between structural reforms and quantitative adjustment in education.

The efficiency of some of the structural reforms themselves could be questioned. Outsourcing as a structural solution to increase public sector efficiency and reduce costs – for instance, by taking advantage of expertise outside the public sector – remains unproven. While this move is expected to produce cost savings but also productivity gains through better leveraging and utilization of market knowledge, past experiences for instance in the United Kingdom have shown the limits of this model in terms of accountability, transparency, efficiency and effectiveness of service delivery. The efficiency of the process also very much depends on the monitoring and guidance of the state. In this volume, the subcontracting to private agents of job search services to the unemployed seems to be very different in Sweden and in the United Kingdom. While it is based only on cost minimization in the United Kingdom, the contracts are given to private providers in Sweden only on the basis of the quality of services provided. The outcome of the process will thus be radically different in those two cases. Similarly, the reform of civil service status or the development of temporary contracts with the emergence of a dual market, as in France and Germany, can also have long-term implications for the quality of public services. Decentralization can also have its drawbacks.

4. POLICY CONSIDERATIONS: FOR A BETTER POLICY MIX?

4.1 More Predictable and Gradual Adjustments

The negative effects of wage cuts on inequality could also be reduced if such cuts were more progressive along the wage scale and if they were applied gradually over time, as shown by Philip O'Connell in the case of Ireland (Chapter 9). As pointed out by the OECD (2011a), 'most successful consolidation plans involve progressive and multi-year adjustments'.

In this respect, we shall see that the example of the Netherlands is instructive. Because they had already adjusted through significant wage cuts in the past with limited success – it led to distortions by converting the previous public sector premium into a wage penalty and contributing to a reduction in human capital there – they decided not to adjust through wage moderation in the 2008–10 crisis. Interestingly, the Hungarian government is currently trying to provide compensation to public sector employees at the bottom of the wage scale after the abolition of their thirteenth-month payment hit them disproportionately hard, plunging many of them below the poverty threshold. Similarly in Romania, as reported by Valentina Vasile (Chapter 12), there was political recognition in 2011 that the uniform 25 per cent wage cut for all public sector employees implemented in 2010 had been a mistake that the government in Romania is now trying to put right (in 2012 the basic wage in the public sector was increased in nominal terms by 8 per cent in June and 7 per cent in December), a process which is also visible in Hungary and a few other countries.

This indicates a policy lesson, namely that if wage reductions are to be implemented, they need to be progressive and not across the board.

4.2 More Negotiated Reforms

The evidence presented in this volume tends to show that transparency in public sector adjustments can help build trust and enables employees and the public to judge the relative effects of these plans on specific income or skills categories, sectors or regions. This requires that reforms be discussed and possibly negotiated with the trade unions. This would also reduce conflicts of the kind that recently paralysed most European countries and have contributed to undermining the economic recovery.

The method by which the adjustments were decided and implemented often explains the unsatisfactory outcomes and general discontent found in this volume about public sector adjustments. In particular, there was an impoverishment of social dialogue in this process at a moment when we would have needed an enrichment of it. But far from it, evidence is provided that social dialogue and collective bargaining institutions have been dismantled in a number of countries and that it would be important first to stop this process, and second to start rebuilding social dialogue. The case of Ireland also showed that only a national agreement made it possible to continue public sector reforms without major social conflicts, and that it even helped to start focusing on more structural reforms while minimizing quantitative adjustments. Reforms in the public sector in Europe will thus have to be carried out in the coming years in a more sound, transparent and negotiated way, and involve all actors directly and indirectly concerned.

4.3 Better Combination of Quantitative Adjustment and Structural Reforms

As indicated by the OECD, public sector adjustments within fiscal consolidation plans should normally aim at doing more with less. If they clash with other policy goals, however, they may end up doing less with less, or even doing less with more. Overall efficiency may be undermined. This volume presents several examples of how public sector reforms may lead to a lower quality of human capital and skills, poorer working conditions and, ultimately, a decrease in the quality of public services, due to a mismatch between demand and supply. We saw in particular that fiscal and budgetary goals should not be attained at the expense of other public sector reforms.

We also underline the need not to forget more structural reforms in the public sector: too large and too rapid quantitative adjustments – especially if they impede any career or system reforms – may hinder the attainment of reforms aimed at improving public sector efficiency. Resource rationalization must be weighed against service delivery in attempts to achieve savings.

Reforms should thus take into account cost rationalization in the long term rather than attempt simply to make quick savings in the public sector, thereby leading to higher costs in the future. It might be very costly, for example, to re-open hospitals or schools at a later date, as happened in previous reforms in the Netherlands but also other European countries.

4.4 Reforms Should Not Call into Question the Traditional Role of the Public Sector for Society

Reforms in the public sector can be implemented without questioning its importance for society as a whole. The government and media campaigns aimed at denigrating certain public sector occupations, reported here for individual countries are not healthy and gain nothing in terms of productivity and efficiency. In any case, public sector reforms cannot be achieved against the employees but with them, and they should be involved in the process.

Moreover, in these public debates on the public sector little is said about its contribution to employment and wage conditions, not to mention social developments: we have seen how public sector developments with regard to working conditions often lead the way for the rest of the economy. The public sector also has an important role in generating economic growth.

It is because of its experience of the adverse effects of wage cuts on demand during the public sector reforms in the 1980s that the Netherlands has partly resisted further wage and employment cuts more recently: indeed, employment increased by 6 per cent in 2008–11. Wiemer Salverda (Chapter 10) shows that this has helped to mitigate the effects of the recession so far. One of the case studies on health care shows the interaction between public consumption and economic growth.

Damian Grimshaw in Chapter 15 on the United Kingdom also shows how the cuts in spending and wages in the public sector have contributed to reducing a major source of demand in regions where the public sector usually drives economic growth.

4.5 Raising Revenues as well as Cutting Expenditure

As emphasized by the OECD (2011a: 39), 'two-thirds of fiscal consolidation has been weighted so far towards spending cuts and one-third [towards] revenue enhancements'. We may question whether this structure is balanced. First, we have seen that cutting expenditure may be counterproductive and does not always lead to efficiency gains. Second, we have seen that public sector reforms based on cuts alone may not ultimately achieve improvements in public services. Revenues can be increased by fighting tax evasion, but also by raising taxes. In the latter case, however, it is important to evaluate the impact of different taxes in terms of equality: flat rate taxes and increased consumption taxes disadvantage lower incomes, but also affect employment since such taxes reduce consumption and thus employment across the board.

4.6 For a Monitoring Process

More generally, the results of this comparative volume highlight the need to put in place a better monitoring or assessment process of both the short- and long-term effects of all types of public sector adjustments, in terms of efficiency and quality of service delivery, but also in terms of the quality of work, inequality and the costs and outcomes for the states' budget. This assessment does not seem to have been carried out systematically in most European countries despite the magnitude of public sector adjustments and reforms. This monitoring process, if it is to be effective, should be carried out by an independent body but then lead to a general consultative exercise involving the social partners.

5. CONCLUSION

While it is difficult to offer conclusions on a process that is still going on in most European countries, the comparative work on public sector adjustments we present here should be seen as a contribution to a better understanding of the nature and extent of such adjustments in different European countries, making it possible to identify some of their effects.

First, significant diversity was found between European countries. This may concern the nature and extent of these adjustments, their timing or the policy mix. Such differences might be explained by whether the individual country has already experienced significant public sector adjustments in the past, like the Netherlands or Sweden. The scale of adjustment may also depend on whether it takes place in countries with large-scale public sector employment or not. We should also distinguish between countries in which the burden of the adjustments has fallen mainly on public sector employees – as in Greece – and those where the burden was redistributed more equally among all sectors/actors, as in Ireland.

Another key factor in diversity is clearly identified in this book: whether the country is under budgetary pressure so that large-scale adjustments seem unavoidable in the face of the public deficit. Countries that had healthier public finances before the crisis, such as Sweden but also to a lesser extent Germany, have been less under pressure to cut public expenditure. They have been in an even better position if they had already started both public sector reforms and adjustments in an earlier phase, as was the case with Sweden and, in a different way, the Netherlands. By contrast, the public sector has come under most pressure in the countries with the largest budget deficits, namely Greece, Portugal, Spain, Romania, Hungary, Ireland and a few others. Finally, we have also seen that public sector retrenchment can reflect an ideological belief that the private sector operates more efficiently and at lower cost than the public sector, as in the United Kingdom.

This volume also shows that this immediate and urgent pressure to make savings and reduce public expenditure tends to favour quantitative adjustments, mainly cuts in expenditure, jobs and wages in the public sector. While in some cases these adjustments could efficiently complement structural reforms in the public sector, we have also seen that they can limit the effects of these institutional reforms and even halt them, as in some cases in Portugal and Romania. Clearly, more consideration is required for the reconciliation of quantitative adjustments and structural reforms when designing and before implementing policy changes in the public sector.

At the same time, the need to reduce current deficits should not be the only consideration when deciding on the type and extent of public sector adjustments in Europe today. Evidence collected in this volume shows that a disproportionate focus on quantitative adjustment brings a number of risks and leads to adverse effects in the social and economic spheres.

The wages and working conditions of public sector employees are obviously being modified by the magnitude of the changes involved. In a number of countries, public sector employees have lost the wage premium they traditionally had over the private sector, which was empirically justified by higher education levels in the public sector.

Not surprisingly, such dynamics may now lower skills and human capital levels in public sector occupations. At the same time, uniform wage cuts along the wage scale have hit lower grades harder and thus have contributed to increasing wage inequalities, while plunging many workers below the poverty threshold. Gender inequality has also been fuelled by public sector adjustments, as a result of the traditional importance of the public sector for women's employment, access to higher positions and more flexible time and work and family arrangements.

Job losses in the public sector have also contributed to increasing the workload of the remaining public sector employees and their working hours, while payment rates for overtime have been reduced, even frozen in a number of countries. The simultaneous reduction in expenditure has also reduced the human and material resources available for carrying out public services, which generally remain the same or even increase – as in health care and education.

The neglect of social dialogue in the reform process and the abolition of a number of provisions that encouraged collective bargaining in the public sector have also contributed to lowering working conditions in the public sector. The public sector has also lost its role as a model employer with job security, collective bargaining, codetermination and good pay and working conditions, instead converging with private sector practices.

These changes and the way they have been implemented have triggered an immediate and massive wave of demonstrations and strikes by public sector employees – often joined by other social groups – throughout Europe. Beyond the immediate economic costs of such protests, the worsening social climate in the public sector must be seen as ringing an alarm bell concerning the future.

As we have seen, the future prospects for human capital and job quality in the public sector are also under threat. Not only have deteriorating wages and working conditions in the public sector compared to those in the private sector led to significant emigration – especially among doctors and nurses, but also teachers – but the public sector has stopped attracting the quantities of young qualified graduates which hitherto have been its lifeblood.

Examples provided in the various chapters of this book also highlight that all these changes – especially when resulting in an increasing mismatch between greater demand and falling supply – cannot be neutral for the future quality of public services. This is already to be observed in education and health care, but also threatens in public administration.

The aim of this work, under the auspices of the European Commission and the ILO, and following a first project on inequalities in the crisis (Vaughan-Whitehead 2011), was to monitor the public sector reform process currently being carried out in Europe and to provide evidence on its effects. There is an obvious need to continue such monitoring, especially since it will be possible to evaluate the effects of the current reforms in more detail only as more data become available in the course of time. A number of conditions can already be highlighted on the basis of this comparative work, however. First in terms of method, the evidence provided highlights the need to use social dialogue as a reform tool and to involve workers' representatives in this process more closely. Second, in terms of timing, it also points to the need to consider more gradual and progressive adjustments rather than carrying out all employment and wage adjustments over one or two years. Third, in terms of the nature of the adjustments, this work points to the need to promote a more balanced combination between quantitative adjustments and structural reforms in the public sector, but also a better mix between fiscal and other important considerations, such as equality, social dialogue, employment prospects, working conditions and the future efficiency and quality of public services. Only under these conditions could public services in Europe continue to provide an important source of both social cohesion and economic growth.

The slightly new perspectives put forward in early May 2012 by the ECB President, Mario Draghi, on the need 'to put growth back at the centre of the agenda' and to 'sustain Global Demand',[3] and some European leaders' requests for more growth-enhancing policies, rather than just austerity packages, might constitute the right opportunity to reconsider public sector adjustments and reforms in a more balanced, negotiated and thorough way, so that they not only help to reduce budget deficits, but also contribute fully and effectively to the models of economic growth and welfare that the European Union would like to follow in the longer term.

NOTES

1. With regard to these sectors unfortunately Eurostat does not draw a distinction between organizations operating in the private sector and those operating in the public sector. These figures can thus only be an approximation or proxy of the size of the public sector (individual chapters provide a more detailed portrayal). While public administration includes mainly public employees, the education and health-care sectors can also include private sector organizations and employees.
2. In some cases, however, responsibilities for financing services have been decentralized without adequate additional funding. This was clearly the case in Germany which might have been a way to force the municipalities and the *Länder* to cut expenditure.
3. European Central Bank meeting, Barcelona, 4 May 2012. See: 'Europe should put growth at centre of agenda: ECB President Mario Draghi', *The Economic Times*, http://articles.economictimes.indiatimes.com/2012-05-03/news/31559093_1_fiscal-consolidation-ecb-president-mario-draghi-euro-zone See also: http://www.eurofora.net|newsflashes/news/ecbheaddraghireplytosarkozycall.html.

REFERENCES

Bozio, A. and R. Disney (2011), 'Public sector pay and pensions', The IFS Green Budget, February, Institute for Fiscal Studies, London. Available at: www.ifs.org.uk.

BZK (2011), *Trendnota Arbeidszaken 2011* (Trend Note Labour Matters 2011), Ministry of the Interior, The Hague, The Netherlands.
EIRO (2008), *Industrial Relations in the Public Sector*, prepared by L. Bordogna, 11 December, EIRO: Dublin.
European Commission (2001), *European Governance – A White Paper*, 25 July, COM(2001) 428, Brussels: European Commission. Available at: http://ec.europa.eu/governance/white_paper/en.pdf.
European Commission (2011), 'A quality framework for services of general interest in Europe', Communication from the Commission to the European Parliament, the Council, the European Economic and Social Committee and the Committee of the Regions, 20 December, COM(2011) 900 final, Brussels: European Commission. Available at: http://ec.europa.eu/commission_2010-2014/president/news/speeches-statements/pdf/20111220_1_en.pdf.
European Union (2009), *The Lisbon Treaty*, The Consolidated Reader-Friendly edition of Treaty on European Union (TEU) and the Treaty on the Functioning of the European Union (TFEU), as amended by the Treaty of Lisbon (2007), 3rd edn, Foundation for EU Democracy. Available at: http://en.euabc.com/upload/books/lisbon-treaty-3edition.pdf.
Holt, E. (2010), 'Doctors in Eastern Europe prepare to walk out over pay', *The Lancet*, **376** (9737), 24 July, 221–2.
Hood, C. (2010), 'Reflections on public service reform in a cold fiscal climate', Report for the 2020 Public Services Trust.
International Labour Office (ILO) (2011a), *Manual on Collective Bargaining and Dispute Resolution in the Public Service*, Geneva: ILO.
International Labour Office (ILO) (2011b), 'Report on the High Level Mission to Greece', Athens, 19–23 September, Geneva: ILO. Available at: http://www.ilo.org/wcmsp5/groups/public/---ed_norm/---normes/documents/missionreport/wcms_170433.pdf.
Keller, B. (2011), 'After the end of stability: recent trends in the public sector of Germany', *International Journal of Human Resource Management*, **22** (11), 2331–48.
Lamo, A., J.J. Pérez and L. Schuknecht (2012), 'Public or private sector wage leadership? An international perspective', *Scandinavian Journal of Economics*, **111** (1), 228–44.
OECD (2005), *Modernizing Government: The Way Forward*, Paris: OECD.
OECD (2009), *Ageing and Changes in Public Service Delivery*, Paris: OECD.
OECD (2011a), *Government at a Glance*, Paris: OECD.
OECD (2011b), *Restoring Public Finances*, Public Governance and Territorial Development Directorate, Paris: OECD.
Schick, A. (2010), 'Post-crisis Fiscal Rules: Stabilising Public Finance while Responding to Economic Aftershocks', *OECD Journal on Budgeting*, 2010/2, Paris: OECD.
Vaughan-Whitehead, D. (ed.) (2011), *Work Inequalities in the Crisis: Evidence from Europe*, Cheltenham, UK and Northampton, MA, USA: Edward Elgar and Geneva: ILO.

2. Public sector adjustment and the threat to gender equality

Jill Rubery*

1. INTRODUCTION

From the Second World War onwards the public sector played a highly significant if variable role in integrating women into wage employment and promoting gender equality (Kolberg 1991; Whitehouse 1992; O'Connor 1993; Gornick and Jacobs 1998; Pillinger 2004; Mandel and Semyonov 2005, 2006; Mandel and Shalev 2009). A large public sector has been associated with better employment opportunities and conditions for lower-skilled women but also with higher levels of gender segregation. Differences in the size of public sector employment reflect the development of the welfare state and the importance attached to services rather than transfers. In Central and Eastern European countries under the previous socialist regimes, women were overrepresented in areas such as education and health, but these professional-type jobs offered lower pay and status than comparable jobs in the West (Healy and McKee 1997; Brainerd 2000; Pollert 2003; Pillinger 2004). In the transition period these jobs have remained primarily in the public sector, and public sector employees have lost out on the rising wages, at least at the top end, in the emerging private sector (True 1999).

Up until the financial crisis of 2008, the long-term expectation within Europe has been that public services would at least be maintained and even grow as more and more states responded to new social needs for childcare and expanded education, health and elderly care. However, the economic crisis and public expenditure adjustment have confounded these expectations, with pressure now towards service contraction. Moreover, optimism that the public sector would be a vehicle for promoting greater gender equality in both quantity and quality of employment experience has been replaced by fears of privatization and that a shrinking welfare state will reduce the quantity and quality of jobs available to women and restrict the services that women rely on to enter employment in both public and private sectors.

The contribution of the public sector to gender equality in employment is multidimensional. To explore these different dimensions in the 14 member states and one candidate country (Croatia) covered in this volume, the chapter is divided as follows. In Section 2 we consider the employment contribution to gender equality, including access to higher-level and professional jobs. In Section 3, we consider the contribution to pay and pensions. In Section 4, contributions to gender equality policies through work–life balance policies and specific equality commitments are assessed. Each section considers the contribution before the crisis and the potential implications of austerity policies for gender equality, drawing on examples from the country chapters. Finally, Section 5 summarizes the variations across countries in the public sector contribution to gender equality and outlines the core dangers for gender equality that lie in current discourses on the public sector and in the actual plans for public sector adjustment.

2. EMPLOYMENT IN THE PUBLIC SECTOR AND GENDER EQUALITY

2.1 Women's Representation and Concentration in Public Sector Employment

The public sector is not only a major source of employment in areas associated with women's employment but also provides many jobs for highly qualified women (Kolberg 1991; Whitehouse 1992; O'Connor 1993; Gornick and Jacobs 1998; Mandel and Semyonov 2005, 2006; Mandel and Shalev 2009). While the concentration of quality jobs for women in the public sector may exacerbate gender segregation, in the context of recession and austerity the key concern is that planned contractions in public services may not only damage long term the society's well-being and competitiveness but may also lead to a decline in quality employment for women which cannot be immediately replaced if at all by private sector quality employment.

To examine the employment opportunities provided by the public sectors in the 14 selected member states and one candidate country, we use the European Labour Force Survey (ELFS), taking the NACE sectors public administration, education and human health and social work as a proxy definition for the public sector. Table 2.1 reveals that the representation of women in these three combined sectors is both high and relatively uniform across our 15 selected countries, with the female share varying from 65 to 76 per cent compared to a female share of all NACE sectors of

Table 2.1 Female shares of public sector NACE, EU27 and 15 selected European countries (2nd quarter 2011 ELFS data)

	Female share all NACE	Female % public administration NACE O	Female % education NACE P	Female % human health and social work NACE Q	Female % All public sector NACE O+P+Q
EU (27 countries)	45.6	53.4	71.5	78.4	69.2
Germany	46.3	51.1	69.3	77.4	68.1
Estonia	50.4	50.8	87.5	83.8	76.2
Ireland	47.2	51.8	74.9	80.9	73.0
Greece	40.4	64.8	66.0	64.6	65.2
Spain	45.0	57.7	66.1	78.0	67.2
France	47.5	48.4	66.2	79.0	66.0
Latvia	50.9	42.5	79.7	83.3	69.1
Lithuania	51.5	51.9	81.2	87.1	75.0
Hungary	46.0	51.2	76.8	78.3	68.3
Netherlands	46.6	60.7	63.2	83.4	73.9
Portugal	47.6	62.7	77.5	82.2	74.8
Romania	44.8	60.9	74.7	79.6	71.2
Sweden	47.6	44.7	72.7	82.3	72.1
United Kingdom	46.6	49.8	72.0	78.2	70.1
Croatia	45.1	53.3	76.3	78.4	68.7

Source: Eurostat.

40.4 to 51.5 per cent. National data on actual public sector employment reveal a similar level of overrepresentation, with female shares normally above 60 per cent. More variation in female shares is found within the subsectors: for example, for public administration the female share in Greece is 64.8 per cent compared to an EU average of 53.4 per cent and for education, Estonia has a very high female share at 87.5 per cent compared to 71.5 per cent EU average.

In contrast to the rather similar female share of the public sector, the concentration of women's employment in the public sector shows more variation among the 15 states, from 22.5 to 49.1 per cent of total female employment (see Figure 2.1), reflecting both differences in the public sector NACE share of total employment and the extent of women's integration in the private sector.

These variations are primarily explained by the concentration of women in health and social work (NACE Q) which shows much greater variation (over 21 percentage points) than that in education or public

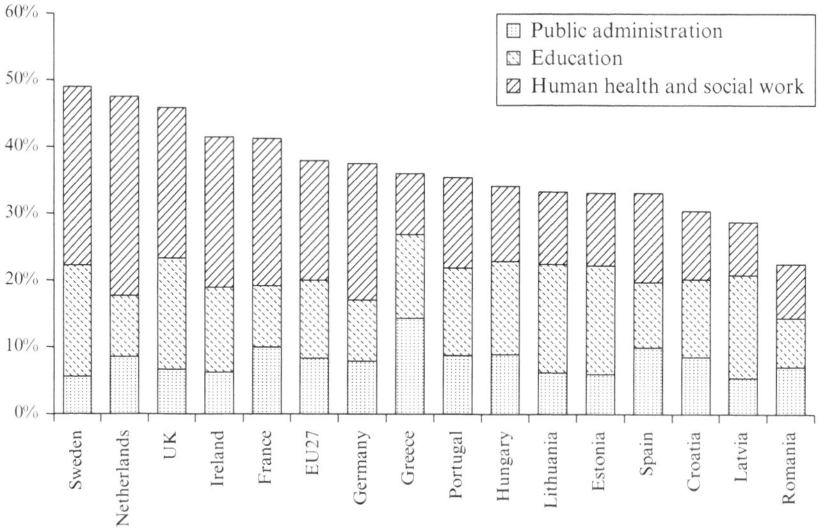

Source: Eurostat.

Figure 2.1 Concentration of female employment in public administration, education, and human health and social work, EU27 and 15 selected European countries (2nd quarter 2011 ELFS data)

administration (8 to 9 percentage points) among the selected countries (see Figure 2.1). All the northern old member states have 20 to 29 per cent of women employed in NACEQ compared to 8 to 13 per cent in all the selected Central and Eastern and Southern European countries. These lower concentrations largely reflect lower shares in social work. These data suggest a polarization between welfare states in the development of the health- and social-care sector but one that does not follow a simple neoliberal versus continental European classification as the highly neo-liberal United Kingdom, together with Ireland, have high employment concentration in this sector. Some countries have high concentrations in education (the Baltic states, Hungary, Portugal and Greece) and there is a well-above-average concentration in public administration for Greece and somewhat above average for Spain.

While in some countries the majority of the health sector may be in the private sector (for example, Germany), employment in education and health, whether within or outside the public sector, is everywhere strongly influenced by trends in public spending.

2.2 Gender Differences by Administrative Organization and Employment Status

Women's presence within the public sector varies according to both occupational gender segregation and the administrative organization. For example, in both Spain and Sweden women are more strongly represented at the regional level due to this level of government taking responsibility for health and education. In contrast, in Portugal education and health are under central government. In some countries, for example Estonia and the United Kingdom, social-care work may be largely financed by the public sector but the primarily female workforce is employed by the private sector. Even in Sweden there is some outsourcing of elder-care services (Anxo, ch. 14 in this volume) although in this case the incentive is not to pay lower wages, unlike in Estonia and the United Kingdom (Rubery et al. 2011).

Within the public sector there are inequalities arising from differences in employment status between civil servants and other employees, where these status divisions take on significance. In some countries, the long-term shift from civil to non-civil servants has been associated with an increasing feminization of total public sector employment (Gautié, ch. 5; Bosch, ch. 6). In Germany, women now account for 46 per cent of all civil servants but in the federal state they account for only 25 per cent, even though their share has grown strongly, from a fifth to a quarter between 2002 and 2008. In France, women also have higher representation among the growing share of non-civil servants (78.4 per cent) but account for two-thirds overall of public sector employment (see Gautié, ch. 5). In Estonia women's share of civil service positions declined from 68 to 64.5 per cent between 2006 and 2010, while their share of non-civil service posts rose from 66.9 to 71.8 per cent (Masso and Espenberg, ch. 3).

With the prime exception of Spain where there is a large gender gap in the share on fixed-term contracts (Muñoz de Bustillo and Antón, ch. 13), women as well as men have benefited from the job security in the public sector with tenure in public sector jobs for both sexes longer than in the private sector. Women's tenure in the public sector may even equal men's (for example, 15 years in Sweden for both sexes; Anxo, ch. 14) or indeed exceed men's (11.4 to 9.4 years in Hungary; Altwicker-Hámori and Köllő, ch. 8).

2.3 The Public Sector and Access to Professional and High-skill Jobs

The public sector in all countries provides a high share of educated women's employment, particularly in education and health. Figure 2.2 shows that these public sector NACE sectors in 2010 accounted for 42 to 66 per cent of female higher education graduates employed in all NACE

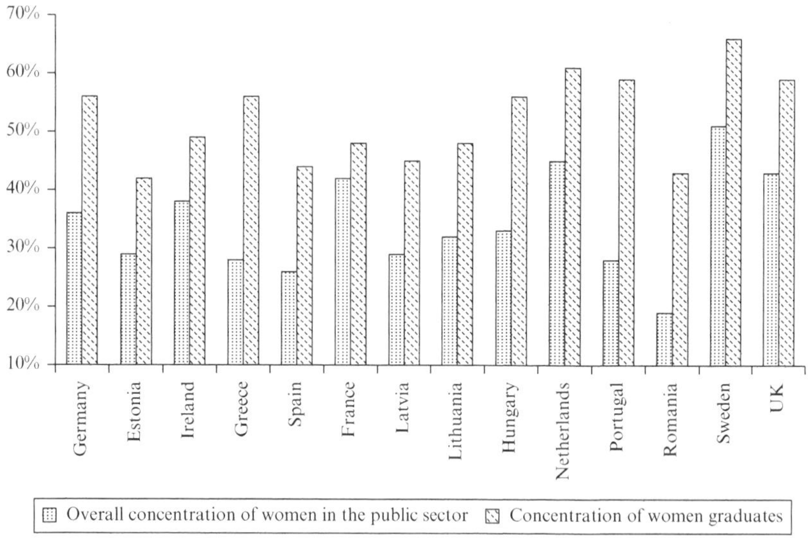

Source: Eurostat.

Figure 2.2 Concentration of all female employment and of all women higher-educated graduates in public administration, education, and human health and social work, 14 selected EU countries (2010 ELFS data)

sectors (no data for Croatia). These concentrations are even higher than those for all women; double or more in the cases of Greece, Portugal and Romania and at least 50 per cent higher in a further five countries. This high share of the tertiary educated translates into a higher share of women in skilled jobs in the public sector than in the private sector; for example, in the United Kingdom 28 per cent of women are all classed as high skilled in the public sector compared to 18 per cent in the private sector.[1] In Lithuania, 72.6 per cent of women and 63.6 per cent of men are in managerial, professional and associated professional jobs in the public sector compared to 36.9 per cent of women and 30 per cent of men in the private sector. While women have traditionally been nurses in all countries they are also increasingly the dominant group among doctors, and took up a higher proportion of health professional posts and teaching at a much earlier stage in the Central and Eastern European countries (Lane 1983; Healy and McKee 1997) than in Western economies.

Women have been better represented in professional than in either management or even higher-level civil service work, but according to Table 2.2 this share has increased for the EU27 from under a quarter in 2003 to 31.7

Table 2.2 Gender balance among senior administrators at national and European level, EU15 and EU27

	Proportion of women among the highest-ranking civil servants (levels 1 and 2 combined)		
	2003	2007	2009*
National administrations EU15 average	20.7	30.5	28.5
National administrations EU27 average**	24.8	32.9	31.7
European institutions	13.9	19.5	23.4

Note: * 2009 data not fully comparable with previous years ** 2003 data based on 2004 for Czech Republic, Greece, Lithuania, Malta and Poland; 2007 data based on 2006 for the Netherlands; 2009 data level 2 missing for Finland.

Source: EU (2010).

per cent in 2009, slightly down on the 2007 figure. The female shares of these higher grades are particularly low in Germany and Ireland, at well under 20 per cent (EU 2010: figure 3) but are above or close to 40 per cent in Lithuania, Sweden, Latvia, Romania and Portugal. In Germany, women's share of managerial positions is only 29 per cent in the public and 23 per cent in the private sector (Bosch, ch. 6). In France, women account for the majority of higher-grade public sector jobs but have a relatively low representation among managerial jobs at only 22.2 per cent in 2009 (Gautié, ch. 5). Various countries have introduced measures to try to improve women's success in promotion systems. In France there now has to be gender parity on recruiting committees and in Sweden at least one woman must be included in all shortlistings for managerial posts (OECD 2011). For federal appointments in Germany the 2001 Federal Equal Opportunity Act requires both equality in representation of candidates for posts where women are underrepresented and gender parity in the appointments panels, together with preference for the underrepresented sex. However, these strong measures exist in a context where women's representation is almost at the lowest for the EU.

2.4 Significance of Public Sector Job Opportunities and Associated Risk from Adjustment

Table 2.3 classifies the 15 countries according to the importance of these NACE sectors for women's employment and the extent to which the public sector provides women with access to higher-level jobs (indicated

Table 2.3 Importance of job opportunities in public sector for gender equality, 15 selected European countries

	Employment concentration % 1 <30%; 2 >30<40; 3 >40	Share of women among higher-level administrators %	Combined scores for employment concentration and vertical segregation High >3; Medium >2<3; Low <2.5
Germany	37.6 (2)	<25 (0)	2 (L)
Estonia	33.1 (2)	>35 (1)	3 (M)
Ireland	41.5 (3)	<25 (0)	3 (M)
Greece	36.0 (2)	>25<35 (0.5)	2.5 (M)
Spain	33.1 (2)	>25<35 (0.5)	2.5 (M)
France	41.2 (3)	>25<35 (0.5)	3.5 (H)
Latvia	28.7 (1)	>35 (1)	2 (L)
Lithuania	33.3 (2)	>35 (1)	3 (M)
Hungary	34.1 (2)	>25<35 (0.5)	2.5 (M)
Netherlands	47.4 (3)	<25 (0)	3 (M)
Portugal	35.5 (2)	>35 (1)	3 (M)
Romania	22.5 (1)	>35 (1)	2 (L)
Sweden	49.1 (3)	>35 (1)	4 (H)
United Kingdom	45.8 (3)	>25<35 (0.5)	3.5 (H)
Croatia	30.5 (2)	>25<35 (0.5)	2.5 (M)

Source: Compiled by author from all contributions to this volume.

by the share of women in higher-level civil service jobs). This vertical segregation measure is intended to capture the potential for the public sector to 'normalize' women's integration in higher-level jobs and management. The intention here is to capture those countries where there is most risk of a major displacement of women due to public sector cutbacks but one shortcoming is that this approach does not address the lower integration of women into employment where public service development is limited.

These scores indicate that women in Sweden, the United Kingdom, France, Ireland and the Netherlands have the most to lose in any shrinkage of the public sector due to their high dependence on the public sector for employment opportunities. However, in two of these countries – Ireland and the Netherlands – women still make up less than a quarter of higher-level civil servants, while those with the highest shares of women in these roles offer more limited employment opportunities as measured by volume – for example, Romania, Lithuania, Latvia and Estonia. These high female shares of the higher grades may reflect the relatively low status of the public services historically in these countries.

2.5 Public Sector Adjustments and Gender Effects

In the initial phase of the financial crisis, men's employment in the private sector suffered most. However, more recent changes, particularly in countries that either have been forced or have chosen to implement extensive cutbacks in the public sector are towards a greater loss of jobs among women (for example, the United Kingdom, Spain, Portugal, Greece, Latvia, Hungary, Romania and Ireland). These gender effects reflect women's higher share of public sector jobs rather than any disproportionate displacement of women. In many contexts there is no clearly thought-through plan of adjustments, more an across-the-board cut as, for example, in Greece. As the introductory chapter makes clear, there is a range of country experiences with some having made more significant structural or quantitative adjustments in the past and some not planning or not yet implementing significant employment cuts. More than proportionate reductions in women's employment may reflect the mode of adjustment: for example, in Spain the particularly heavy cuts in education and health (Muñoz de Bustillo and Antón, ch. 13), in Latvia in health (Masso and Espenberg, ch. 3) and in the United Kingdom in local government (Grimshaw, ch. 15), all areas of high female employment. The displacement of temporary employees clearly has a disproportionate impact on women where they have a higher share than men, for example in Spain.

Where the adjustments are more structural than financial, the effect on women's employment has been mixed. Shifts from civil service to more standard employment contracts, often on less-favourable terms and conditions, have been associated in most cases with an increasing feminization. Where modernization has led to outsourcing, this has often involved female-type jobs including ancillary functions such as cleaning and sometimes more core functions such as care work, but also some male job segments such as IT services or maintenance work. Where the current adjustments are leading to a new phase of outsourcing, women are likely to be most affected due to their higher share of overall employment. The United Kingdom has the most explicit policy of increasing private sector involvement in public service delivery. Countries such as Sweden and Germany have relatively high use of outsourcing of services but are not planning major adjustments. Other countries such as Greece are mainly planning full-scale privatization of public enterprises which may affect men as much as women. As outsourcing affects mainly lower-skill jobs, a skill upgrading of the remaining public sector employment can be expected, but such compositional change should not be interpreted as signalling improvements in public sector job quality. Some adjustment policies, including decisions to freeze career advancement, for example in Spain, Romania and Portugal, will also freeze the current level of gender inequality in job positions and prevent equalization of women's career chances. As more qualified women are making their career in the public service this will also impact negatively on women's careers relative to men's in the labour market as a whole. One may also anticipate an increase in female unemployment or underemployment, particularly if job opportunities dry up in areas for which women have specialist and non-transferable training, such as teaching, nursing or medicine.

3. PAY AND REWARD IN THE PUBLIC SECTOR

3.1 Pay Compression and Gender Equality

Research on Western developed countries suggests that a large public sector tends to reduce the gender pay gap and increase women's contribution to household income (Whitehouse 1992; Estévez-Abe and Hethey 2010). These benefits arise from the public sector in Western welfare states adopting a higher minimum floor to wages, in effect reducing gender pay discrimination, particularly in countries with low or non-existent floors to wages in the private sector. However, the advent of competitive tendering for public service provision has put this practice into question; for example, in Germany the new integrated collective agreement in the public sector in 2005 introduced a lower minimum rate of pay to facilitate effective competition between public and private sector workers (Bosch, ch. 6) in a country where there is no minimum floor in the private sector and thus large scope for discriminatory rates of pay.

Moreover, even though in most Western European welfare states the public sector reduces the average gender pay gap and raises pay for the lower skilled, salaries for higher-qualified workers may fall below those in the private sector. This pay compression reflects the use of regulation to set pay in the public sector, whether through collective bargaining or by administrative decree, thereby limiting flexible and variable pay particularly at the top end. The outcome for gender equality is thus mixed as Mandel and Shalev (2009: 1881) argue:

> As a result, we hypothesize that in restraining class inequality, the public sector has an ambiguous effect on gender wage inequality. Its relatively high wage floor narrows gender differentials at the low end of the class structure

> while its restricted wage ceiling widens them at the top. The two-sided impact of the welfare state as an employer on women's representation and intra-class inequality leaves us with no specific prediction. (Mandel and Shalev 2009)

These effects may be exacerbated if the state acts as a monopsonistic employer, seeking to depress wages in professions that are not found in the private sector or only under contract to the public sector. This argument has been made to explain, for example, relatively low earnings in the care sector for both lower-skilled care workers (Machin and Manning 2004; Rubery et al. 2011) and higher-skilled nurses (Nowak and Preston 2001). These tendencies may also in part explain the often very low wages enjoyed by professionals in public services – including teachers, nurses and doctors – in many Central and Eastern European welfare states (for example, Hungary, Estonia, Latvia, Lithuania and Romania in this volume). These are in part a reflection of long-term low valuation of these public service jobs, which may be linked to the early employment of high shares of women in these occupations under the previous socialist regimes (Healy and McKee 1997; Brainerd 2000; Pollert 2003; Pillinger 2004).

The current policy interest in 'market testing' wages in the public sector against the private sector by competitive tendering and policies to reduce public–private wage gaps presumes that wages in the private sector provide the appropriate benchmark. This ignores the almost universal findings of continuing wage discrimination against women which remains despite women's more continuous careers and investments in human capital. Thus higher pay in the public sector may be interpreted as the effect of not applying a discrimination discount rather than as 'overpayment'.

3.2 Public–Private Wage Differentials and Gender Pay Equality

In most Western economies average public sector pay is higher than in the private sector reflecting in part the more-skilled work although there are variations within this pattern. Where a premium is found, further analysis controlling for skill or education and broken down by gender tends to reveal higher premia for the lower than the higher skilled/educated and for women compared to men. These higher premia for women are in relation to lower pay for women compared to men in the private sector; men's public sector pay still tends to be higher than that of women, even within skill categories (Arulampalam et al. 2007).

A recent study of public–private pay differentials using SILC data for the European Central Bank (Giordano et al. 2011) covered six of our country sample and found the public–private sector premium to be always positive, after controlling for a set of individual characteristics, and to be higher for women (Table 2.4). Beyond that some significant differences emerge: of the six countries, Germany has the largest gender gap in the premium (2.7 per cent for men compared to 19.4 per cent for women) and France the smallest (3.9 and 6.5 per cent, respectively) but in this case for both sexes the premium is modest. In contrast, Spain, Portugal and Ireland have small gender gaps but high premia for both sexes (23.3 and 26.2 per cent in Spain, 19 and 22.1 per cent in Portugal, 16.2 and 20.2 per cent for Ireland). Greece has a gender gap of 9.3 percentage points but also sizeable premia for both sexes: 16.6 per cent for men and 25.9 per cent for women. Premia tend to decline at the higher ends of the income distribution and Germany, Greece and France have steeper declines for men, particularly in Greece where the female premium remains high throughout the distribution. In Spain, Ireland and Portugal men also faced declining premia but the female premium peaks at mid-range.

This comparative study for the most part confirms other studies based on more reliable national data. For Germany, Melly (2005) found a positive premium for women but a negative one for men, but positive premia are found for men as well as women in Eastern Germany throughout most or all of the wage distribution (Bosch, ch. 6). Bargain and Melly's (2008) study of France confirms that long-term pay levels are roughly similar in the public and private sectors, although Beffy and Kamionka (2010) suggest that lower-skilled men may face a negative premium. In Spain, Muñoz de Bustillo and Antón (ch. 13) find that observable characteristics explain all but 5.4 percentage points of the male hourly wage public sector premium of 17 per cent but 19.2 percentage points of the female premium of 29.5 per cent remain unexplained. Moreover, as human capital characteristics fail to explain the gender pay gap in Spain, the public sector premium may be modifying discrimination.

In Portugal, Campos and Pereira (2009) found a rising public sector premium, up from 10 per cent in 1996 to 15 per cent in 2005, and Strauss and Maisonneuve (2007) found Portugal to have one of the highest public–private wage gaps by international standards. In Ireland, the introduction of benchmarking for public sector pay from 2003 onwards led to a major rise in the public sector pay premium from 9.7 to 21.6 per cent in three years (2003–06), particularly for men (5.3 to 22.5 per cent compared to a rise from 13.8 to 21.4 per cent for women) although proportionally more women benefited due to their higher public sector presence (Kelly et al. 2009). The premia are said to be underestimated due to more generous public sector pensions and greater job security, but the study does not consider whether the wages paid to women in the private sector, the benchmark used to assess 'overpayment', are depressed by discrimination.

Table 2.4 *Estimates of the public–private wage premium, six selected EU countries*

	Germany	Spain	France	Greece	Ireland	Portugal
Men						
Public	0.027**	0.232***	0.039***	0.166***	0.162***	0.190***
Obs.	15,028	23,789	17,309	8,421	8,379	7,985
R^2	0.431	0.4	0.221	0.439	0.38	0.459
F	363.7	356.6	92.5	409.5	344.0	422.0
Women						
Public	0.194***	0.262***	0.065***	0.259***	0.202***	0.221***
Obs.	14,715	17,473	16,168	6,066	8,371	7,274
R^2	0.251	0.423	0.177	0.477	0.395	0.567
F	170.7	312.0	87.2	337.8	244.1	616.6

Note: *** Significant at 1%, ** significant at 5%.

Source: Giordano et al. (2011, Table 4).

Among the three Northern European countries not covered by the SILC study, only the United Kingdom has a significant positive pay differential, reflecting the relatively low pay for women, particularly part-timers, in the private sector, concentrated around the national minimum wage. Estimates vary with Emmerson and Jin (2012) finding raw premia of 20.2 and 27.5 per cent for men and women, respectively, reduced to 8.9 and 15.5 per cent after controlling for education, while Dolton and Makepeace (2011) find a 0 per cent premium for men and a 6 per cent premium for women after controls. Chatterji et al. (2007) find that while the male gap can be largely explained by individual characteristics, much of the female gap is unexplained.

In the Netherlands and Sweden it is less clear that public sector employment commands a pay premium even for women. In Sweden, the absence of a clear premium reflects the relatively low overall gender pay gap in the economy, such that women and the lower skilled fare better in the private sector than in most Western economies. Moreover, it is municipalities, where many of the lower-skilled women are concentrated, that provide an exception to the general trend towards widening differentials in the rest of the public sector and the private sector. In the Netherlands, wages in the public sector for women do not seem to command a premium, although only men face a negative premium. However, these results also control for working part-time which is both more common in the public sector and attracts less of a penalty than in the private sector, although this may be because it involves more high-skilled work (Salverda, ch. 10).

In the Central and Eastern European countries public–private pay differentials are much less likely to be positive and also sometimes vary dramatically over time, reflecting frequent and large swings in economic policy and political priorities both during transition and since the financial crisis. In Latvia and Lithuania there has been a persistent if varying average positive pay differential in the public sector (Masso and Espenberg, ch. 3) although further breakdowns fail to find a positive differential in education and health, in line with reports of very low pay by EWCO (2010) with respect to professionals in Lithuania in health, education, research and social establishments and by EPSU (2010) with respect to health and social-care workers in Latvia. Even at the aggregate level in Estonia working for the public sector is not always advantageous overall or for women, in part because of major fluctuations in the public–private differential. A 2003 study (Leping 2005) found that women benefited more, or lost less from working in the public sector than men but Masso and Espenberg found that both sexes lost in 2005–07 with women facing a negative premium of –7.1 per cent compared to –1.9 per cent for men. By 2009, men had regained a positive public sector premium at 5.3 per

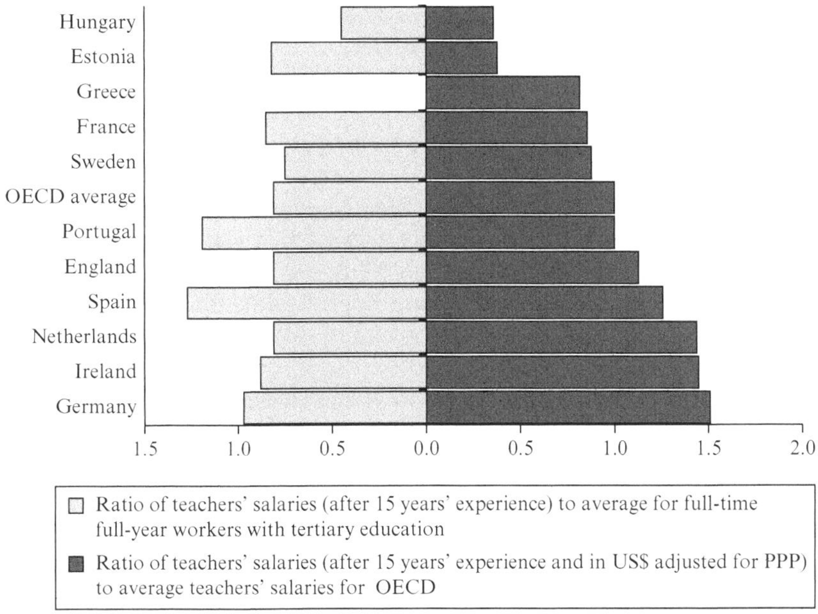

Note: First ratio not available for Greece.

Source: OECD (2011: chart D3.1).

Figure 2.3 Comparisons of teachers' salaries (i) relative to full-time full-year employees with a tertiary education (ii) in US$ adjusted for PPP, OECD average and 11 selected EU countries

cent but that for women was still negative at –2.1 per cent. This outcome reflects the low wages for some highly feminized job areas such as teaching where Estonian teachers receive almost the lowest pay in all OECD countries (see Figure 2.3) and have the highest feminization rate of the 15 countries considered here (see Table 2.1).

Hungary in fact has the lowest pay for teachers both in purchasing power parity (ppp) and relative to other tertiary qualified people. The general problem of low pay in the public sector is even more acute for health and education professionals most of whom are women (see Altwicker-Hámori and Köllő, ch. 8). Hungary has also experienced rapid fluctuations in the public–private wage differential and a one point reduction in this differential results in a 0.36 per cent increase in the gender pay gap (ibid.). Information on Romania (Vasile, ch. 12) suggests that pay in the public sector has been low in parts of the public sector – particularly education and health – for some time, and a 2008 World Bank survey found that this had created problems in attracting good-quality staff (EWCO 2009), problems that have no doubt been exacerbated by the recent dramatic 25 per cent cut in public sector pay. Average pay in the public sector in Croatia is higher than in the private sector and women in the public sector on average earn more than men in the private sector. However, Nestić (2010) shows that the gender pay gap in Croatia is underestimated due to women's high qualifications, with many of these high-qualified women working in the public sector for low wages. Franičević and Matković (ch. 4) suggest that low pay is again acute in education but health professionals may be somewhat better paid than in some other Central and Eastern European countries.

3.3 Public–Private Pension Differentials and Gender Equality

With respect to pensions, the advantages of being employed in the public sector vary among countries. These advantages are particularly strong in the United Kingdom and Ireland where national pension provision is on a flat rate basis and the more generous defined benefit occupational pensions provided by private capital have closed, leaving public sector workers as the main groups with access to defined benefit pensions. There are major public debates over whether these benefits should be curtailed or wages lowered/contributions increased to compensate for these differential benefits. In 2008–09 around five million employees in the United Kingdom were in defined benefit pension schemes in the public sector compared to under two million in the private sector (Bozio and Disney 2011) but women have always had less access to private sector company pensions in the United Kingdom. In Ireland, three-quarters of both male and female public sector employees are in an occupational scheme (Kelly et al. 2009), but in the private sector only 38 per cent of women belong to one, compared to 55 per cent of men (O'Connell, ch. 9). In Germany, civil servants benefit from contribution-free improved pensions, available to other public sector employees through modest contributions. Moreover, the large gender gap in coverage of occupational pensions in the private sector is not found in the public sector. In Estonia there is also better pension provision for civil servants but not for all public sector employees, while Romania from 2011 has eliminated all specific provisions for certain public sector employees. In France, public sector workers pay lower contributions and have a higher minimum pension entitlement which tends to benefit women with shorter work histories and lower pay. In Greece, female public sector employees had possibilities of early retirement. In the Dutch and Swedish public sectors there are relatively generous collectively agreed top-ups to national pensions but comparable to provisions in some

Table 2.5 Importance of public sector pay and pensions for gender equality, 15 selected European countries

	Public sector pay premium	Public sector pensions	Combined scores for public sector pay and pensions premium
Germany	Positive (1)	Partially better (0.5)	1.5
Estonia	Negative (–1)	Partially better (0.5)	–0.5
Ireland	Positive (1)	Better (1)	2.0
Greece	Positive (1)	Partially better (0.5)	1.5
Spain	Positive (1)	Neutral (0)	1.0
France	Neutral (0)	Partially better (0.5)	0.5
Latvia	Neutral (0)	Neutral (0)	0
Lithuania	Neutral (0)	Neutral (0)	0
Hungary	Negative (–1)	Neutral (0)	–1.0
Netherlands	Neutral (0)	Partially better (0.5)	0.5
Portugal	Positive (1)	Neutral (0)	1.0
Romania	Negative (–1)	Neutral (0)	–1.0
Sweden	Neutral (0)	Partially better (0.5)	0.5
United Kingdom	Positive (1)	Better (1)	2.0
Croatia	Neutral (0)	Neutral (0)	0

Source: Compiled by author from all contributions to this volume.

other sectors and large organizations, so that good pension provision is less exclusively found in the public sector than in the United Kingdom, Ireland and to some extent Germany.

3.4 Significance of Public Sector Pay and Rewards and Associated Risk from Public Sector Adjustment

Table 2.5 classifies the 15 countries by the pay and pensions offered in the public sector to women compared to the private sector. A score of 1 is given for a positive overall pay premium for the public sector, zero where pay in both sectors is roughly the same or there is very mixed evidence, and –1 where there is evidence of a negative premium (Hungary and Romania). The pay differential in the public sector may be more likely to be positive where the private sector is deregulated with high wage inequality, and likewise the public sector may provide only marginally better or similar conditions to the private sector where the latter has stronger gender equality policies and more egalitarian wage structures, as in Sweden. This scoring may underestimate the public sector influence on gender equality as it does not capture its role as a benchmark for gender equality for the private sector in some contexts. In other contexts, a neutral outcome may indicate relatively poor gender equality in both sectors, and in the case of the Central and Eastern European states evidence of very low pay for professionals in sectors such as education even where there is an overall pay premium. Where the score is minus, the implication is not that deterioration in pay and conditions in the crisis matters less as many women are employed in this sector and are already 'undervalued'. The only implication is that any shrinkage of the public sector or downgrading of pay will not lead to the loss of a positive example for gender equality. Many countries have a national pension system applying to both the public and the private sectors, thereby justifying a score of zero. Where the public pension provides some benefits over a private sector pension, particularly for women, a score of 0.5 or 1 is given depending on the extent of public sector advantage and the impact of a shrinkage of the public sector or a downgrading of its pension provision on gender equality.

3.5 Public Sector Adjustments to Pay and Rewards and Gender Equality

Public sector adjustment through declining relative or real earnings in the public sector poses major risks for gender equality because of both the high female concentration in the public sector and the positive wage premium that may partially compensate for widespread pay discrimination in the private sector. The first type of risk applies to all countries, such that even in Hungary where there is a negative wage premium in the public sector, the gender pay gap at the aggregate level is found to follow directly the public–private wage differential. The higher premium for women puts women's jobs more in the front line for wage cuts although the policies pursued so far with respect to which jobs are vulnerable has varied between countries.

The significance of recent nominal or relative pay cuts needs to be put in the context of longer-term trends. Some countries had embarked on longer-term policies of public sector relative wage cuts before the onset of the financial crisis – for example, Germany, Portugal and France. In contrast, public sector pay in Ireland rose markedly in the 2000s. For some countries, the public–private differential had remained stable while in others there is a history of swings towards and away from the public sector, particularly in Hungary. Overlaid on these divergent trends are the differences in timing and form of the economic crisis and the focus on fiscal consolidation and public sector cost reduction as the resolution.

Thus to date Sweden, Germany, the Netherlands and Croatia have not made major adjustments to public sector pay in response to the crisis. In contrast, as shown in the introductory chapter of this volume, all the

Eurozone countries facing sovereign debt crises (Ireland, Greece, Spain and Portugal) plus many of the new member states (Romania, Estonia, Latvia, Lithuania and Hungary) have imposed very significant nominal wage cuts and/or cuts to thirteenth- and fourteen-month salaries, with the highest cuts in Romania (25 per cent) and Greece (20 per cent in 2011 and a further 15 per cent planned for 2012). This has led to a large rise in low-paid public sector workers – for example, in Hungary and Romania – many of whom are women. In the Baltic states the high share of performance pay facilitated widespread reductions in nominal pay that significantly reduced the pay premium in Latvia and Lithuania. Cuts have been targeted on higher earners in Portugal and Ireland, but have been made across the board in Romania. In Spain, the 19 per cent public sector premium in 2009 is predicted to decline to 7 per cent by 2011 (Muñoz de Bustillo and Antón, ch. 13). The United Kingdom and France have frozen pay, although in France this is offset by some compensation funded through job cuts.

In Greece, women have lost rights to early retirement in the public sector and contribution years have increased from 37 to 40, which will affect women more with their interrupted careers. In France, rights to early retirement for those with an interrupted career due to children have also been curtailed, and contribution rates for pensions are to be equalized upwards for public sector workers by 2020. In Ireland the focus has been on increasing contributions for public sector pensions, thereby adding to the wage cuts, while in the United Kingdom there have been wide-ranging changes, including added contributions, increases in retirement age and changes from final salary to career average pension schemes.

4. GENDER EQUALITY AND WORK–LIFE BALANCE POLICIES

4.1 Working Time and Work–Life Balance

The importance of the public sector for women's employment also arises out of the opportunities it provides for women to have continuous careers through provisions for paid leave, childcare, flexible working and part-time or regular hours. The reasons for greater opportunities in the public sector include:

- the greater stability of public sector employment (and the larger scale of public sector organizations) – as small organizations or those undergoing rapid change claim difficulties in accommodating leave;

- the greater likelihood that statutory rights to leave and flexible working will be enforceable in the public sector;
- the greater likelihood that the public sector offers provision over and above the statutory;
- the higher share of women in higher-level jobs, which may increase feelings of entitlement for leave taking or flexible working; and
- the more limited market pressures to work long and unpredictable hours (though in sectors such as health other factors may lead to non-standard and variable hours).

The significance of the public sector for these reasons may vary according to:

- the level of statutory entitlements and their enforceability in the private sector;
- the extent of additional provisions in the public sector (which may reflect the statutory provision);
- the commitment of public sector employers to gender equality; and
- the importance of flexible working or part-time work opportunities for combining work and family life – according to the national pattern of women's integration in the wage economy and social norms in relation both to employment organization and women's and mothers' roles in the household.

The influence of national norms and practices is revealed by the highly variable shares of part-time work in the public sector NACE sectors that largely conform to the average part-time work shares for all NACE combined (see Figure 2.4). Thus female part-time work accounts for 7 to 80 per cent of all female employees in the three public sector NACE, but expressed as a proportion of the country average part-time share for all NACE these vary only from 68 to 106 per cent. The public sector part-time share is somewhat below the country average in Spain, Greece and Hungary but for the others the ratios range from 90 to 106 per cent. Public administration uses less part-time work than health or education where the ratios are often above the country average, particularly in health for the Netherlands and Sweden. The only exception was Hungary where the part-time share was 12.2 per cent compared to an all NACE average of 9.2 per cent, and interestingly this proportion had tripled in the 2008–11 period, up from 4.1 per cent, suggesting a form of work sharing (see Altwicker-Hámori and Köllő, ch. 8). Shares of men working part-time tend to be higher in the public sector than for all NACE combined, but still tend to be less than half those for women and often closer to only a

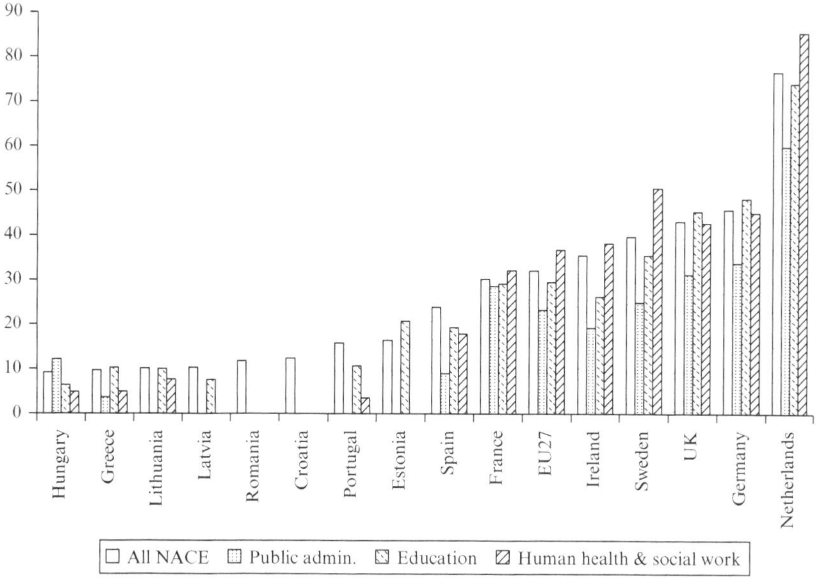

Source: Eurostat.

Figure 2.4 Share of part-time in female employment in public administration, education, human health and social work relative to all sectors, EU27 and 15 selected European countries (ELFS data 2nd quarter 2011)

third of the female rates, with Hungary again the only country where men have a higher share.

Although the actual part-time shares are in line with those for the labour market as a whole, the European Company Survey (ECS) found that part-time work in public administration is primarily organized to meet employee needs while in education and health and social work the main driver was the needs of the company (Anxo et al. 2007a: 33), due in part to the high incidence of unsocial hours and night work in health and the difficulty of adapting working time in education (ibid.: 34). Evidence supporting the idea that the public sector offers part-time for reconciliation rather than flexibility reasons is found in the greater use in the public sector of part-time involving fixed daily schedules or other fixed cycles and more restricted use of variable hours for part-time workers compared to the private sector (ibid.: 44).

Enhanced rights to flexible working or part-time work are also provided in the public sector in some countries (Table 2.6). In Germany, all public service employees have rights to work part-time for family reasons and to

Table 2.6 Work–life balance options offered by the public sector relative to the private sector, 15 selected European countries

Country	Options
Germany	The 2001 Federal Equality Act for the Public Sector gives all public service employees including managers the right to work part-time for family reasons and to return to full-time work. There are opportunities for a flexible distribution of hours and for combining part-time work with the parental leave allowance
Estonia	Limited to some provisions for parental leave and some protections during pregnancy
Ireland	Public sector workers are more likely to receive supplementary payments for maternity leave. Civil servants also have opportunities to take unpaid leave, previously restricted to term-time working but now open for general flexibility
Greece	Public sector employees are regulated by different systems with the main difference rights to nine months' paid childcare leave after maternity leave compared to four months for private sector employees. Childcare leave is an alternative to working-time reductions which are also more generous in the public sector. Unpaid leave can be for up to 60 months in the public sector, 19 in the private sector
Spain	Extra six free days plus rights to continuous working with shorter lunch breaks, leave for adult care, rights to work shorter hours until child is 12, flexible working rights, paternity leave, rights to add holidays and breastfeeding breaks to leave
France	Right to work 50 to 90 per cent time and for those on 50 per cent time to be paid at 60 per cent. Also the right to return to full-time work. Maternity leave is paid in full without a ceiling unlike the private sector. Entitlements to 12 days rather than three days for care of sick child
Latvia	No differences known
Lithuania	No differences known
Hungary	Public employees have right to work two hours less per day until the child is two and one hour less until the child is four while private sector mothers only have the two-hour reduction for one year and a one-hour reduction for another six months but few mothers exercise these rights due to long parental leave
Netherlands	Work and Care Act 2001 implemented universally in public sector with more paid leave opportunities; more variable implementation in private sector

Table 2.6 (continued)

Country	Options
Portugal	Right to work continuous days with a 30-minute break, thereby reducing working time to 6.5 hours per day only for women in public sector who are civil servants or on permanent contracts or members of a union
Romania	No specific policies
Sweden	Collective agreement in public sector since 1989 has provided top-ups to parental leave pay; this influences particularly the take-up by fathers of parental leave
United Kingdom	Widespread practice of additional maternity leave pay (31 per cent of public sector establishments and 57.5 per cent of large public sector establishments compared to 11 per cent in private sector), opportunities for job sharing and flexitime and greater likelihood to grant request for part-time or flexible hours
Croatia	No specific policies but women return to workplace sooner from parental leave, probably due to better reconciliation/ fewer unsocial hours working

return to full-time work. They can also seek a flexible distribution of hours and may combine part-time work with parental leave. In France, all civil servants have the right to work part-time – from half-time up to 90 per cent and those on half-time receive 60 per cent of the full-time wage. These rights do not extend to contracted employees in the public sector. In the United Kingdom, a survey found that 79 per cent of public sector employees had access to part-time work options compared to 65 per cent in the private sector (Hooker et al. 2007: 36) and a higher share of public sector workers (61 to 52 per cent in the private sector) felt that they would be able to work reduced hours on a temporary basis, work flexible hours and have job-share options. A parallel survey of employers found that 36 per cent of public sector compared to 11 per cent of private sector workplaces offered job sharing and flexi-time was available in 31 per cent of public compared to 24 per cent of private workplaces. The United Kingdom has introduced a general right for parents to ask to work flexibly (extended now from young children to children 16 and under and for carers of adults). Survey results suggest that public sector workplaces are more likely to receive requests (59 per cent of public compared to 37 per cent of private sector workplaces had received requests) and are more likely to allow those returning from maternity leave to change to part-time hours (65 per cent willing compared to 56 per cent) (Hayward et al. 2007). In Portugal there is little evidence of an explicit demand for part-time work, but in the public sector civil servants since 1998 and more recently permanent employees have the option to work a continuous day, that is with only a 30-minute break and thereby only spend 6.5 hours at work per day under a full-time contract, reducing time spent at the workplace by 1.5 hours.

According to the ECS, in some countries public entities are at the forefront of offering flexible working (among our sample Germany, Ireland, Latvia and Sweden) (Riedmann et al. 2006). In Sweden this is in part evident in the much greater post-maternity leave reduction in working time in the public than the private sector (43 per cent compared to 34 per cent cut in working time for female professionals; EWCO 2006), suggesting a greater sense of entitlement in the public sector.

The ECS also revealed the public sector in some countries (Greece, France and Hungary among our sample) to be lagging behind the private sector in flexible working (Riedmann et al. 2006) but this may be due to less employer-oriented flexibility in the public sector. Additional leave entitlements and more regular working hours may also compensate for lack of flexible working. For example, in Spain there is robust evidence that public employees are more satisfied with working-time arrangements, even though part-time work is relatively limited. This satisfaction may be due to the provision of six extra free days per year, and to the work–life balance policy (the 2005 *Plan Concilia*) which provides for more continuous working with shorter lunch breaks, rights to add holidays and to convert breastfeeding breaks to extend parental leave, paternity leave, rights to reduce working hours until the child is 12 and rights to return to work if taking leave to care for adults (EIROnline 2006). In Hungary the public sector provides for more hours reductions and for longer for new mothers in the public compared to the private sector, but only 12.5 per cent of mothers return to work before the child is two including fewer than 15 per cent of higher-skilled mothers, thereby reducing the practical significance of these entitlements. In Croatia there is a much lower tendency in the public sector (except for health) to work Saturdays, Sundays and in the evening, and while in the private sector the incidence of such work patterns is similar for men and women, in the public sector women are less likely than men to work unsocial hours.

Public sector organizations have also been found to be more likely to have experience of staff taking parental leave, supporting the notion that staff have a greater sense of entitlement in the public sector (Anxo et al. 2007b: figure 3). The incidence in the public sector exceeded that in the private sector by a large margin in Greece, Germany, Latvia, the United Kingdom, Ireland, the Netherlands and Portugal, but only by a small margin in Sweden and Spain (but with Sweden having the highest overall incidence and Spain the lowest). In France and Hungary, the incidence was higher in the private sector. In some countries access to leave is also extended in the public sector; for example, in Greece, public sector employees have longer paid childcare leave (Kazassi 2011) and in the United Kingdom most public sector employers provide much longer paid leave than the statutory provision (Hayward et al. 2007). In Ireland, research has also found that workers in the public sector NACE categories are more likely to receive additional payments for maternity leave (Russell et al. 2011). In Sweden, public, sector employers provide 90 per cent of pay instead of the statutory 80 per cent, and remove the statutory ceiling to compensation so that even higher-paid workers are almost fully compensated when on leave, which accounts for the higher take-up of leave among fathers in the public sector (Haas et al. 2011), although some similar agreements exist in parts of the private sector. In the Netherlands, statutory parental leave after maternity leave is part-time and compensated through tax allowances equivalent to half the statutory minimum wage, but employers through collective agreements can allow more flexibility in how leave is taken and provide paid leave up to 75 per cent of normal earnings. Some 79 per cent of public sector and health sector employees are found to have a paid parental leave compared to 25 per cent in the private sector (Groenendijk and Keuzenkamp 2011). In France, the public sector pays for maternity leave at 100 per cent of salary with no upper ceiling, while only large private employers do not apply the statutory ceiling. Also public sector employees are entitled to 12 days' unpaid leave a year to care for a sick child compared to three in the private sector (Fagnani and Boyer 2011).

In Croatia, women return from parental leave at an earlier stage, particularly in education and public administration where only two-thirds are using leave when the child is between six months and one year compared to around 85 per cent in the private sector and in health. When the child is aged between one and two years the shares fall to 8 to 9 per cent compared to 20 per cent in the private sector and 13 per cent in health, suggesting that unsocial hours are a deterrent in these two sectors. Data show a much lower incidence of unsocial hours working in the public sector outside health, particularly for women (Franičević and Matković, ch. 4).

Public sector employers are also more likely to provide assistance with childcare: 6 per cent of establishments in the public sector had their own kindergartens compared to 2 per cent in the private sector, according to the ECS, and in the United Kingdom 10 per cent of public sector establishments provided childcare in the workplace compared to 2 per cent of private sector establishments (Hayward et al. 2007). Other leave

Table 2.7 Alternative forms of work–life balance offered by the public sector; examples from selected European countries

Work–life balance policy	Public sector advantage type 1	Public sector advantage type 2
Working time	Regular compared to longer hours in private sector *Examples*: Portugal, Croatia, Romania	Flexible (employee preference) compared to either regular/ standard hours or flexible (employer preference) in private sector *Examples*: Netherlands, United Kingdom, France, Germany
Maternity and parental leave	Shorter length of leave taken due to return to work more feasible (very long paid leave in private sector) *Example*: Croatia	Longer paid leave (short paid leave in private sector) *Examples*: United Kingdom, Greece, Ireland

opportunities not related to childcare (Anxo et al. 2007b: figure 22) are also more frequent in the public sector.

The type of advantages offered by the public sector may differ depending on conditions prevailing in the private sector (Table 2.7). Thus where the private sector requires long and irregular hours then the public sector work–life balance advantage may stem from the offer of regular working time. This seems to be the case, for example, in Portugal, Croatia and Romania, examples of Southern European and Central and Eastern European economies where there is limited tradition of and a lack of demand for part-time work but where public sector hours for full-timers are shorter and more regular. In contrast, where, as in France and the Netherlands, full-timers in the private sector have more-regulated and shorter hours but part-time work is primarily organized to meet employer flexibility needs, the main advantage offered by the public sector is that of flexible working to meet employee needs. In Germany there are also fewer mini jobs among part-time workers in the public compared to the private sector. In the United Kingdom, the private sector requires both long and irregular hours for full-timers, and part-time work is oriented towards employer flexibility, such that the public sector contributes to work–life balance by offering both more regular hours and employee-oriented flexible working. A parallel set of differences can be found in respect of leave arrangements: where statutory paid leave in the private sector is long, as is found in most Central and Eastern European countries, the public sector may offer the same leave but its working-time and other arrangements may facilitate an earlier return to work (found, for example, in Croatia although not in Hungary). Where instead statutory paid leave in the private sector is very short, the public sector may offer longer paid leave and a delayed return to work, as, for example, in the United Kingdom or Greece.

4.2 Equality Policies and the Public Sector

The public sector may also be more likely than the private sector to make an overt commitment to gender equality and introduce policy programmes to implement gender equality. This is far from a universal characteristic and the motivation may be the need to start to tackle deep-rooted gender inequalities within the public sector. However, the public sector may still provide more fertile ground for the development of gender equality policies than the private sector. In this section we consider examples (see Box 2.1) where gender equality is a general and mainstreamed principle in the public sector. The United Kingdom and Germany have both introduced a duty on public sector organizations to promote equal opportunity and to report on the outcomes. France has also introduced a general requirement for gender parity in recruitment committees and in 2008 adopted a charter for gender equality in the public sector, which resulted in some ministries developing action plans for gender equality. The 2007 Gender Equality Act in Spain included a clause on promoting gender equality in the public sector, on top of its reconciliation policy of 2005. Sweden requires both private and public sector organizations to undertake gender audits and develop gender equality plans. In the Netherlands the 2001 Work and Care Act required all employers to facilitate combining work and care, but the public sector has taken the lead in a more comprehensive implementation (Remery 2001 quoted in Van der Lippe and Van Dijk 2002; Remery et al. 2003). All the policies reported in Box 2.1 are relatively recent and except for Sweden arguably weakly embedded in the public sector and national culture; as such there may be questions over the commitment to these goals under austerity. No such commitments to promoting gender equality within the public sector were found in the remaining countries.

Evidence of trade union campaigns for gender equality in the public sector is also confined to a limited number of countries (Box 2.2). In the United Kingdom, trade unions have lodged many equal pay claims for women, such that employers have agreed to introduce single pay spines for the whole sector – for example, in health, local government and universities – to reduce the risks of future claims. In Germany the new pay system in the public sector was brought about in part by the trade union

BOX 2.1 MAIN STREAMING GENDER EQUALITY: EXAMPLES FROM SELECTED EU COUNTRIES

In *Germany* the Federal Equality Act for the Public Sector that applies to the federal and state levels requires: gender-neutral job adverts; equal numbers of women and men invited to job interviews for jobs in which women are underrepresented and equal gender representation in selection committees; preferential consideration of the underrepresented sex in recruitment and promotions; interruptions of work for family reasons, partner's income to be disregarded in recruitment and promotion decisions; an obligatory equal opportunity plan, actions to increase female share which should not decrease even in a job freeze or planned redundancies; family-friendly working hours and conditions; opportunities offered to move from part- to full-time with no discrimination on grounds of part-time, telework etc.; involvement of an equal opportunity appointee; and regular reporting.

In the *United Kingdom* since 2007 all public organizations have a duty to promote gender equality – known as the gender duty. The 2010 Equality Act introduced a single equality duty with the requirement to eliminate discrimination, harassment and victimization, advance equality of opportunity and foster good relations between people who share a characteristic and those who do not. Public organizations with more than 150 employees should publish information on the effect of their policies and practices on employees, service users and others from the protected groups including evidence of analyses undertaken. Employers should ensure that their pay system is designed to achieve equality between men and women and are recommended to undertake an equal pay audit for gender. This is not mandatory but over 40 per cent of public bodies are reported to be auditing their pay systems for sex bias (EHRC 2011).

France after 2001 introduced a progressive move towards gender parity in recruitment committees in the public sector. In central government these committees must include at least one-third women and the female share increased from 36.1 per cent in 2001 to 47.6 per cent in 2006, but progress in local authorities and the public health sector was more limited. In 2008 following adoption of a charter to promote equality in the public sector some ministries adopted 'action plans' with quantitative targets, especially for top executive levels, and committed to promoting gender-friendly working-time arrangements (Gautié, ch. 5).

In *Sweden* each organization in both the public and private sectors must have a gender equality plan (gender pay monitoring) and examine whether there are unexplained gender wage differences and take measures if there are such differences (Anxo, ch. 14).

In the *Netherlands* the 2001 Work and Care Act placed responsibility on employers to facilitate the combination of work and care, but there is scope within the legal regulations for widespread variations in the form of provision including the provision of paid leave (Remery et al. 2003). The main exception to such variation is public administration where comprehensive regulations reflect the tendency for the public sector to take the lead in this area (Remery 2001 quoted in Van der Lippe and Van Dijk 2002).

In *Spain* the 2007 Gender Equality Act included a clause requiring the promotion of equality in the public sector with respect to employment and training, gender balance in recruitment committees, gender equality monitoring etc. (Muñoz de Bustillo and Antón, ch. 13).

objective of introducing more gender-sensitive pay grading, although this goal has not yet been achieved due largely to employer opposition. German trade unions have also been active in gender equality initiatives at the local government level.

4.3 Significance of Public Sector Gender Equality and Work–Life Balance Policies and Associated Risk from Public Sector Adjustment

Table 2.8 provides a further classification of the public sector contribution to gender equality, this time with respect to their gender equality and work–life balance policies. For work–life balance a score of 1 is given for significantly better policies in the public sector, often due to rather weak statutory policies. We limit our approach to formal policies rather than

BOX 2.2 SOCIAL PARTNER OR STATE INITIATIVES TO IMPROVE WOMEN'S PAY IN THE PUBLIC SECTOR: EXAMPLES FROM SELECTED EU COUNTRIES

In *Estonia*, in 2005 the public service union Rotal concluded a minimum salary agreement for social care staff working in residential care for children. These mainly female workers had been working below minimum wage levels (EPSU 2010).

In *Germany*, the trade union ver.di sought to develop an integrated collective agreement for all public sector employees, based on a gender-neutral job evaluation system. Although in 1998 the union established an 'upgrading commission' to draw up concrete proposals for 'gender fair' job evaluation within the public sector, little progress has been made, in part because employers' associations have threatened to walk away from the collective agreements. The fragmentation of health and social care pose particular problems, and although some collective agreements have been negotiated to cover both public and private sector social care providers, other organizations are not covered and church providers are specifically exempted. The lack of a national minimum wage has led to some very low pay; for example one social enterprise, operating in cooperation with a Hungarian care company, was paying only €2 per hour (ibid.).

In *Ireland* in 2002 a Public Services Benchmarking Body was established to review public sector pay against that in the private sector, in response to unions' arguments that private sector pay had risen much faster in the booming economy. However, the benchmarking exercise did not seek to address the undervaluation of women's work. The first exercise evaluated 109 grades, and pay rises were awarded to health- and social-care staff – for example, nurses' pay increased between 8 and 16 per cent. The second benchmarking exercise in 2007 only increased senior managers' pay within health and social care (15 of the 109 grades examined) (ibid.).

In *Latvia* the government introduced a new remuneration system in 2004 based on equality principles, with wages for civil servants to be based on job evaluation and qualifications. In 2005 regulations were introduced for a single payment system for all public sector workers and a new agreement was signed between the Ministry of Health and the trade unions on wage increases, but these have not been implemented fully in practice. Moreover, the health-care system has long faced funding shortages, leading to low wages and staff shortages, compensated in part by overtime so that doctors and nurses work the equivalent on average of 1.4 full-time jobs while being paid for a single full-time job. Despite strikes and government commitments to resolve low pay and working hours, little improvement has occurred in practice. As in Estonia and Hungary, salaries are subsidized by additional payments from clients but many professionally qualified health employees are leaving Latvia to work elsewhere (ibid.).

In *Sweden* the Trade Union Confederation (LO) in 2007 promoted the use of 'equality pools'. These were taken up in the municipality sector along with other sectors so that those areas with a mainly female workforce benefited, particularly assistant nurses. However, concerns were raised that this neglected the interests of female workers in male-dominated sectors and the equality pool has been transformed into a 'low-income pool' to give larger wage increases to low-income workers in general. This benefits women in general but with less specific effects on the public sector (EIRO 2011).

In the *United Kingdom* trade unions have been very active in pressing for change to public sector pay grading and have brought a large number of legal cases. Consequently employers have been willing to introduce single pay spines based on gender-sensitive job grading to reduce the basis for future claims in local government, the NHS and universities. The implementation of the local government agreement has proved extremely difficult as the operation of no-win–no-fee lawyers in the sector has led to problems in reaching compromises with the unions in case this leads to yet more individual law suits for backdated pay (Perkins and White 2010).

Table 2.8 Importance of work–life balance policies and gender equality policies, 15 selected European countries

	Work–life balance policies	Gender equality policy	Combined score work–life balance and gender equality policy	Combined score pay and conditions (Table 2.5 plus Table 2.8) High ≥3; Medium >1<3; Low <1.5
Germany	Better (1)	Specific policy (1)	2	2 + 1.5 = 3.5 (H)
Estonia	No difference (0)	No specific policy (0)	0	0 + –0.5 = –0.5 (L)
Ireland	Partially better (0.5)	No specific policy (0)	0.5	0.5 + 2 = 2.5 (M)
Greece	Better (1)	No specific policy (0)	1	1 + 1.5 = 2.5 (M)
Spain	Better (1)	Specific policy (1)	2	2 + 1 =3 (H)
France	Better (1)	Specific policy (1)	2	2 + 0.5 = 2.5 (M)
Latvia	No difference (0)	No specific policy (0)	0	0 + 0= 0 (L)
Lithuania	No difference (0)	No specific policy (0)	0	0 + 0 = 0 (L)
Hungary	No difference (0)	No specific policy (0)	0	0 + –1 = –1 (L)
Netherlands	Partially better (0.5)	Specific policy (1)	1.5	1.5 + 0.5 = 2 (M)
Portugal	Partially better (0.5)	No specific policy (0)	0.5	0.5 + 1 = 1.5 (L)
Romania	No difference (0)	No specific policy (0)	0	0 + –1 = –1 (L)
Sweden	Partially better (0.5)	Specific policy (1)	1.5	1.5 + 0.5 = 2 (M)
United Kingdom	Better (1)	Specific policy (1)	2	2 + 2 = 4 (H)
Croatia	No difference (0)	No specific policy (0)	0	0 + 0 = 0 (L)

Source: Prepared by author.

the general benefits from working in a public sector with more regulated and standardized working hours, even though this may contribute significantly to work–life balance. A score of 0.5 is awarded where the policies are somewhat better, either due to limited public sector policies or because the private sector or statutory policies are strong so that the public sector provides only marginal improvement or better implementation. Zero is given where there is no evidence of significant policy differences. The scoring for gender equality policies has been done on a slightly different basis: here we award a score of 1 wherever there is a specific requirement for public sector employers to promote gender equality or aspects of gender equality in a fairly comprehensive way even where private sector organizations face the same requirements. The reason is that it is reasonable to suppose that even where the requirement is general, public sector employers may implement it more conscientiously.

4.4 Effects of Public Sector Adjustments on Gender Equality and Work–Life Balance Policies

Public sector adjustment is primarily having an indirect effect on work–life balance and equality policies rather than leading to an explicit policy rollback. These effects are no less important because of being indirect and reinforce the importance of a gender mainstreaming approach to all forms of public policy. Three main types of policy can be identified as affecting work–life balance: increases in working hours, increases in work intensity as a consequence of cuts, and unpaid leave or reduced working hours. Spain, Greece and Germany (although varying by *Land* and by part of public service) have all increased standard working hours in the public service in order to save costs, but without assessment of the gender equality impacts of longer full-time hours. In addition, teaching hours have increased in Spain, Romania, Ireland and Portugal (through reduction in hours for preparation). This is in an occupation which is predominantly female in all countries. Several country chapters report increases in unpaid overtime hours as a consequence of reduced staffing (for example, Portugal, France, Estonia and Romania). Romania took a decision not to pay for any supplementary hours and Portugal made payments more restrictive. In some contexts the main changes have been enforced cuts to working hours, either though movement to part-time jobs or through pressure to take unpaid leave periods (for example, in Greece, Latvia and Hungary). These policies may herald a new stage of flexible working where employers no longer commit to providing year-round standard hours employment even in the more-regulated public sector. In the United Kingdom, the employment cuts have led to a very reduced share of full-time employees in local government. In some other countries, for example Croatia, changes to working time associated with public sector adjustment have been more limited. Whichever adjustment form is used, the outcome is a trend towards more employer-determined working time, where staff are required to work more or fewer hours than their preferred or originally contracted hours. Moreover, these changes may set up diverse challenges for gender equality. In some contexts more flexible and shorter hours to cut labour costs may be relatively easy to introduce and opportunities for full-time work may be more difficult to secure. In other contexts the consequences of replacing only a fraction of any staff who leave may reduce the scope for negotiating working-time arrangements to fit family commitments, and may convert regular and standard working time into requirements for long and unpredictable hours as the remaining staff struggle to cope with demands. Where unpaid leave is used, this may be increasingly designed to meet employer needs rather than the more family-friendly term-time working where leave coincides with school holidays. Ireland has extended its term-time working for parents to a short working time policy for all to facilitate unpaid leave.

So far there has been no repeal of gender equality policies in the public sector. However, the fact that some of these measures were introduced only shortly before or even during the crisis, has undoubtedly limited their potential to change policy and practice. In Spain, the ambitious Gender Equality Act was introduced only in 2007 and set up a new equality ministry which was abolished just two years later in 2010 (Gago and Serrano 2011). In the United Kingdom, the Equality Act was passed only shortly before the change in government in 2010 and although it was subsequently enacted, an important clause to require private sector companies to undertake equal pay reviews has not been activated. This has reinforced the importance of the public sector in monitoring for equal pay.

5. SUMMARY AND CONCLUSIONS

5.1 Varying Importance of the Public Sector in Promoting Gender Equality

Table 2.9 summarizes the variable role of the public sector in promoting gender equality as analysed in the previous sections. The contributions of the public sector to employment opportunities is separated from that to improving job quality: that is, we have used the employment scoring in Table 2.3 to categorize employment opportunities for women in the public sector as high, medium or low which is then compared to the combined

*Table 2.9 Importance of public sector for gender equality, 15 selected European countries**

Advantage in public sector working conditions (pay, pensions, work–life balance and gender equality)	Importance of employment in public sector (quantity and vertical segregation)		
	High (3.5–4)	Medium (2.5–3)	Low (2)
High (3–4)	United Kingdom	Spain	Germany
Medium (1.5–2.5)	France Sweden	Ireland Greece Netherlands Portugal	
Low (0 to –1)		Estonia Lithuania Hungary Croatia	Latvia Romania

Note: * See Tables 2.3, 2.5 and 2.8 for details of scoring. Actual distributions of scores indicated.

scores on working conditions as presented in the final column of Table 2.8 (based on Tables 2.5 and 2.8). Although each dimension has the same maximum score of four, the distribution of the countries varies, reflecting in part the negative scoring for pay in two countries and somewhat different score cut-offs are used to classify countries with high, medium or low premia in pay and working conditions in the public sector. What we can derive from this table is that, for example, women in the United Kingdom have the most to lose potentially from either a shrinkage of the public sector or a deterioration in relative working conditions. This follows in part from the comparison to the poor private sector conditions but also from the gender duty in the United Kingdom on public sector organizations. Spain and Germany also have better working conditions but women's employment dependence is only medium and low, respectively. Six countries have a medium differential in working conditions and these divide into two high – Sweden and France – and four medium – Ireland, Greece, the Netherlands and Portugal – employment dependency countries. The interpretation behind these positions can vary even within the same category. Thus Sweden and the Netherlands end up with medium differential working conditions because of requirements on the private sector to promote gender equality, while France is in the medium category because in the public sector there are strong work–life balance and equality policies but low pay differentials, and the opposite is more the case in Greece, Ireland and Portugal. The significance of the public sector for gender equality may be equally high in practice in, for example, Sweden, as the relatively small differentials in conditions reflect the spread of good practice from the public to the private sector and any reversal of commitment to gender equality in the public sector could negatively affect commitment in the private sector.

All the Central and Eastern European countries have low differentials in working conditions between public and private sectors, reflecting low and often variable pay differentials and a general absence of positive gender equality and work–life balance policies. This means that if the private sector grew relative to the public sector there may be no major immediate deterioration in gender equality, but in reality any rebalancing would be likely to occur not through growth but through downsizing of the public sector which of course would mainly displace women from employment. If austerity leads to further deterioration in working conditions, gender equality would decline but in a context where the public sector instead of ameliorating discrimination is reinforcing such tendencies. Furthermore, even where the public sector scores poorly on pay levels and formal work–life balance policies, it may still offer advantages to women in the form of regular working time which may be undermined by more flexible working involving pressure for unpaid overtime. It should also be remembered that the low female employment concentration in the public sector reflects a low level of public services in these countries which both constrains the demand for female labour and provides poor support for care responsibilities.

5.2 Prospects for Gender Equality under Austerity: Impact of Public Sector Adjustment

The variable role of the public sector in promoting gender equality suggests that what is at stake in this period of public sector adjustment may differ. In some countries it is the loss of a good employment sector that is at risk, but in others the key risk is of a further downward spiral of poor employment conditions in female-dominated jobs, both lower skilled and professional. To date not only the extent but also the form of adjustment has varied, ranging from employment loss, to cuts to nominal wages or paid hours and to increased hours and work intensity. Some adjustments relate to longer-term restructuring, associated with privatization and new public management, with planned implications often for both service and job quality, while others are simply financial adjustments to deal with the immediate crisis. Despite these variations there are common longer-term risks for gender equality arising out of the current crisis and the associated pressure on the public sector. These risks stem in part from the growing discourse that treats any premium paid above that in the private sector (in the form of pay or more-favourable conditions) as illegitimate. This is to ignore the widespread evidence of continuing gender discrimination in pay and the dominance of the male lifecourse in shaping working time and work organization in the private sector. Instead of pressing for reform of private sector conditions, policymakers are holding them up as a benchmark against which to judge conditions in the public sector. This approach provides little optimism that any long-term amelioration of gender discrimination is on the agenda. A second long-term risk has always been present but has now been made manifest, and that is the power of the state to change unilaterally the terms and conditions of employment in the public sector, in particular for groups such as teachers and nurses where there are limited private sector alternatives. These are professions for which women have trained in good faith and where in several countries the right to progress along a career path has simply been frozen. The final risk is perhaps the most important of all and that is the discourse that denies the feasibility of public support for care in the future. The notion that support for care is a luxury good is predicated on the availability of women's unpaid labour as the default option. Cutting back the public sector has direct implications for the roles that women are expected to play in European society. However, it is far from clear that women will be able or willing to take on caring needs that are left unmet by public services, thereby leaving open whether the long-term consequence of public sector adjustment will be a further transition towards a more fragmented European society where the core risk is that no-one takes care of those who need and deserve support.

NOTES

* I am grateful to Wiemer Salverda and Jennifer Whillans for advice and assistance with the data.

1. See: http://www.ons.gov.uk/ons/rel/lmac/public-and-private-sector-earnings/2012/estimating-differences-in-public-and-private-sector-pay.html#tab-Differences-between-the-public-and-private-sectors.

REFERENCES

Anxo, D., C. Fagan, M. Smith, M.-T. Letablier and C. Perraudin (2007a), *Part-time Work in European Companies*, Establishment Survey on Working Time 2004–2005, European Foundation for the Improvement of Living and Working Conditions.

Anxo, D., C. Fagan, M. Smith, M.-T. Letablier and C. Perraudin (2007b), *Parental Leave in European Companies*, Establishment Survey on Working Time 2004–2005, European Foundation for the Improvement of Living and Working Conditions.

Arulampalam, W., A. Booth and M. Bryan (2007), 'Is there a glass ceiling over Europe? Exploring the gender pay gap across the wage distribution', *Industrial and Labor Relations Review*, **60** (2), 163–86.

Bargain, O. and B. Melly (2008), 'Public sector pay gap in France: new evidence using panel data', Discussion Paper Series, IZA DP, No. 3427.

Beffy, M. and T. Kamionka (2010), 'Public–private wage gaps: is civil-servant human capital sector specific?', INSEE document de travail.

Bozio, A. and R. Disney (2011), 'Public sector pay and pensions', IFS Green Budget, February 2011, available at: http://www.ifs.org.uk/budgets/gb2011/11chap7.pdf (accessed 18 October 2012).

Brainerd, E. (2000), 'Women in transition: changes in gender wage differentials in Eastern Europe and the former Soviet Union', *Industrial and Labor Relations Review*, **54** (1), 138–62.

Campos, M.M. and M.C. Pereira (2009), 'Wages and incentives in the Portuguese public sector', *Economic Bulletin*, Banco de Portugal, Summer, 57–77.

Chatterji, M., K. Mumford and P. Smith (2007), 'The public–private sector wage differential: gender, workplaces and family friendliness', University of Dundee Discussion Paper No. 202.

Dolton, P. and G. Makepeace (2011), 'Public and private sector labour markets', in P. Gregg and J. Wadsworth (eds), *The Labour Market in Winter: The State of Working Britain*, Oxford: Oxford University Press, pp. 272–88.

EHRC (2011) 'Equality information and the equality duty: a guide for public authorities', available at: http://www.equalityhumanrights.com/advice-and-guidance/public-sector-equality-duty/guidance-on-the-equality-duty/ (accessed 18 October 2012).

EIRO (2011), 'Employment and industrial relations in the health care sector', available at: http://www.eurofound.europa.eu/docs/eiro/tn1008022s/tn1008022s.pdf (accessed 18 October 2012).

EIROnline (2006), 'Agreement on work–life balance in the public sector', available at: http://www.eurofound.europa.eu/eiro/2006/02/feature/ES0602104F.htm (accessed 18 October 2012).

Emmerson, C. and W. Jin (2012), 'Public sector pay and pensions', IFS Green Budget, February, available at: http://www.ifs.org.uk/budgets/gb2012/12chap5.pdf (accessed 18 October 2012).

EPSU (2010), *Pay and the Gender Wage Gap in Health and Social Care*, Report on EPSU study on pay in the care sector in relation to overall pay levels and the gender pay gap in different countries in the European Union, available at: http://www.epsu.org/IMG/pdf/FINAL_REPORT_ON_PAY_IN_HEALTH_AND_SOCIAL_CARE.pdf (accessed 18 October 2012).

Estévez-Abe, M. and T. Hethey (2010), 'Women's work, family income and public policy', paper presented at conference on 'Inequality and the Status of the Middle Class: Lessons from the Luxembourg Income Study', University of Luxembourg, 28–30 June, available at: http://www.lisproject.org/conference/papers/estevez-abe-et-al.pdf (accessed 18 October 2012).

EU (2010), *More Women in Senior Positions*, Directorate-General for Employment, Social Affairs and Equal Opportunities, Luxembourg: Publications Office of the European Union.

EWCO (2006), 'Working time after parental leave', 24 March, available at: http://www.eurofound.europa.eu/ewco/2006/03/SE0603NU04.htm (accessed 18 October 2012).

EWCO (2009), 'Survey finds major differences in public sector earnings', 16 March, available at: http://www.eurofound.europa.eu/ewco/2009/01/RO0901019I.htm (accessed 18 October 2012).

EWCO (2010), 'Remuneration of public sector employees', 10 September, available at: http://www.eurofound.europa.eu/ewco/2010/05/LT1005019I.htm (accessed 18 October 2012).

Fagnani, J. and D. Boyer (2011), *France*, available at: http://www.leavenetwork.org/fileadmin/Leavenetwork/Country_notes/france_02052011.pdf (accessed 18 October 2012).

Gago, E. and C. Serrano (2011), 'Women, gender equality and the economic crisis in Spain', paper presented at Pantheon University conference on 'Women, Gender Equality and the Economic Crisis', 1–2 December.

Giordano, R., D. Depalo, M.C. Pereira, B. Eugène, E. Papapetrou, J.J. Perez, L. Reiss and M. Roter (2011), 'The public sector pay gap in a selection of euro area countries', European Central Bank Working Paper Series No. 1406, December.

Gornick, J.C. and J.A. Jacobs (1998), 'Gender, the welfare state, and public employment: a comparative study of seven industrialized countries', *American Sociological Review*, **63** (5), 688–710.

Groenendijk, H. and S. Keuzenkamp (2011), *The Netherlands*, April, available at: http://www.leavenetwork.org/fileadmin/Leavenetwork/Country_notes/netherlands_09062011.pd (accessed 18 October 2012).

Haas, L., A.-Z. Duvande and A. Chronholm (2011), *Sweden*, April, available at: http://www.leavenetwork.org/fileadmin/Leavenetwork/Country_notes/sweden_02052011.pdf (accessed 18 October 2012).

Hayward, B., B. Fong and A. Thornton (2007), *The Third Work – Life Balance Employer Survey: Main Findings*, BMRB Social Research for the Department for Business, Enterprise and Regulatory Reform Employment Relations Research Series No. 86.

Healy, J. and M. McKee (1997), 'Health sector reform in Central and Eastern Europe: the professional dimension', *Health Policy and Planning*, **12** (4), 286–95.

Hooker, H., F. Neathey, J. Caseborne and M. Munro (2007), *The Third Work – Life Balance Employee Survey: Main Findings*, Institute for Employment Studies for the Department for Business, Enterprise and Regulatory Reform Employment Relations Research Series No. 58.

Kazassi, E.H. (2011), *Greece*, available at: http://www.leavenetwork.org/fileadmin/Leavenetwork/Country_notes/greece_02052011.pdf (accessed 18 October 2012).

Kelly, E., S. McGuinness and P. O'Connell (2009), 'Benchmarking, social partnership and higher remuneration: wage settling institutions and the public–private

sector wage gap in Ireland', *Economic and Social Review*, **40** (3) (Autumn): 339–70.
Kolberg, J.E. (1991), 'The gender dimension of the welfare state', *International Journal of Sociology*, **21** (2), 119–48.
Lane, C. (1983), 'Women in socialist society with special reference to the German Democratic Republic', *Sociology*, **17** (4), 489–505.
Leping, K.-O. (2005), 'Public–private sector wage differential in Estonia – evidence from quantile regression', Faculty of Economics and Business Administration Working Paper No. 39, University of Tartu.
Machin, S. and A. Manning (2004), 'A test of competitive labour market theory: the wage structure among care assistants in the south of England', *Industrial and Labor Relations Review*, **57** (3), 371–85.
Mandel, H. and M. Semyonov (2005) 'Family policies, wage structures, and gender gaps: sources of earnings inequality in 20 countries', *American Sociological Review*, **70** (6), 949–67.
Mandel, H. and M. Semyonov (2006), 'A welfare state paradox: state interventions and women's employment opportunities in 22 countries', *American Journal of Sociology*, **111** (6), 1910–49.
Mandel, H. and M. Shalev (2009), 'How welfare states shape the gender pay gap: a theoretical and comparative analysis', *Social Forces*, **87** (4), 1873–912.
Melly, B. (2005), 'Public–private sector wage differentials in Germany: evidence from quantile regression', *Empirical Economics*, **30** (2), 505–20.
Nestić, D. (2010), 'The gender wage gap in Croatia – estimating the impact of differing rewards by means of counterfactual distributions', *Croatian Economic Survey*, **12** (1), 83–119, available at: http://hrcak.srce.hr/file/80210 (accessed 18 October 2012).
Nowak, M. and A. Preston (2001), 'Can human capital theory explain why nurses are so poorly paid?', *Australian Economic Papers*, **40**, 232–45.
O'Connor, J. (1993), 'Gender, class and citizenship in the comparative analysis of welfare state regimes: theoretical and methodological issues', *British Journal of Sociology*, **44** (3), 501–18.
OECD (2011), *Education at a Glance*, Paris: OECD.
Perkins, S.J. and G. White (2010), 'Modernising pay in the UK public services: trends and implications', *Human Resource Management Journal*, **20** (3), 244–57.
Pillinger, J. (2004), *Closing the Gender Wage Gap*, EP SU/PS I Equal Pay Survey.
Pollert, A. (2003), 'Women, work and equal opportunities in post-communist transition', *Work Employment Society*, **17**, 331–57.
Remery, C. (2001), 'Organizations, equal opportunity policies, and the position of women: the case of the Netherlands', in T. Van der Lippe and L. Van Dijk (eds), *Women's Employment in a Comparative Perspective*, New York: Aldine de Gruyter, pp. 85–105.
Remery, C., A. van Doorne-Huiskes and J. Schippers (2003), 'Family-friendly policies in the Netherlands: the tripartite involvement', *Personnel Review*, **32** (4), 456–73.
Riedmann, A., with H. Bielenski, T. Szczurowska and A. Wagner (2006), 'Working time and work–life balance in European companies', Establishment Survey on Working Time 2004–2005, European Foundation for the Improvement of Living and Working Conditions.
Rubery, J., G. Hebson, D. Grimshaw, M. Carroll, L. Smith, L. Marchington and S. Ugarte (2011), 'The recruitment and retention of a care workforce

for older people', Report for the Department of Health as part of its Social Care Workforce Initiative, available at: http://www.kcl.ac.uk/sspp/departments/sshm/scwru/dhinitiative/projects/ruberyetal2011recruitmentfinal.pdf (accessed 18 October 2012).

Russell, H., D. Watson and J. Banks (2011), 'Pregnancy at work: a national survey', HSE Crisis Pregnancy Programme and The Equality Authority.

Strauss, H. and C. Maisonneuve (2007), 'The wage premium on tertiary education: new estimates for 21 OECD countries', OECD Economics Department Working Paper No. 589, Paris.

True, J. (1999), 'Expanding markets and marketing gender: the integration of the post-socialist Czech Republic', *Review of International Political Economy*, **6** (3), 360–89.

Van der Lippe, T. and L. Van Dijk (2002), 'Comparative research on women's employment', *Annual Review of Sociology*, **28**, 221–41.

Whitehouse, G. (1992), 'Legislation and labour market gender inequality: an analysis of OECD countries', *Work, Employment and Society*, **6** (March), 65–86.

3. Early application of fiscal austerity measures in the Baltic states

Jaan Masso and Kerly Espenberg

1. INTRODUCTION

The economic recession in 2008–09 had a strong negative effect on the public sector in the Baltic states. Unlike the rest of the EU, where public sector reforms to cope with the challenges arising as a result of the crisis started in 2010–11 and were related to the debt crisis, in the Baltic states the public sector was heavily consolidated as early as 2009 and in Estonia significant budget cuts were introduced in February 2009. Thus, for the Baltics there should be comparatively more evidence on the effects of public sector cuts on the economy, the labour market and the quality of public services. The Baltic states' experience of the crises might also provide some lessons for the rest of Europe: hopefully some positive, but also some concerning the possible negative consequences of public sector adjustments.

Adjustment in the course of crises without exchange rate devaluation through so-called 'internal devaluation' (wage cuts restoring international competitiveness) has sometimes been described as fairly successful (for example, due to the relatively rapid recovery since 2010), and was introduced on the basis of quite a strong consensus among both politicians and the general public (for example, according to Eurobarometer, the approval ratings for the government increased from 38 per cent in summer 2009 to 53 per cent in spring 2010 (OECD 2011a) and without major protests. However, the policy choice was also simply chosen by local conditions (the private sector's large euro-denominated debt burden), and thus exchange rate devaluation would have ended up with the insolvency of many households and enterprises.

Labour market developments in the public sectors of the Baltic states are also an interesting object of study for other reasons. Estonia in particular has been characterized by a strong commitment to the balanced budget rule. The political rhetoric of the right-wing parties has implemented the idea of the 'lean state'. The Estonian public sector has been known for improving its services through the use of highly innovative ICT solutions and products, such as digital receipts, web-based tax declarations, e-voting, digital signatures and e-government (paperless government), to name but a few.

While this chapter focuses mainly on Estonian experience, where possible we also try to cover the most important developments and features of the public sectors in Latvia and Lithuania. While there are important differences between the countries, factors such as similar historical background, level of economic development and highly correlated business cycles facilitate joint study.

2. GENERAL GOVERNMENT REVENUES, EXPENDITURES AND DEBT

Compared to the EU average, the government sector in the Baltic states is relatively small, on average (as indicated, for example, by the share of government expenditure in GDP: see Table 3.1). The Estonian government is in fact one of the smallest in the OECD. During the post-independence

Table 3.1 Overview of public finances in the Baltic states, 2006–2010

Country	2006	2007	2008	2009	2010
Primary balance, % of GDP					
Estonia	2.6	2.6	−2.7	−1.8	0.4
Latvia	0.0	0.0	−3.6	−8.2	−6.8
Lithuania	0.3	−0.3	−2.6	−8.2	−5.3
EU27	1.2	1.8	0.4	−4.3	−3.9
Government consolidated gross debt, % of GDP					
Estonia	4.4	3.7	4.5	7.2	6.7
Latvia	10.7	9.0	19.8	36.7	44.7
Lithuania	17.9	16.8	15.5	29.4	38.0
EU27	61.5	59.0	62.5	74.7	80.1
Tax revenues, % of GDP					
Estonia	30.8	31.5	31.8	35.8	34.3
Latvia	30.8	30.8	29.7	27.0	27.5
Lithuania	29.6	29.9	30.4	29.7	27.4
EU27	40.7	40.6	40.4	39.7	39.6
Changes in tax revenues, %					
Estonia	20.0	22.9	2.5	−4.4	−1.0
Latvia	29.5	31.7	4.8	−26.4	−1.0
Lithuania	18.5	20.5	14.9	−19.9	−4.4
EU27	6.9	5.8	0.1	−7.6	4.2

Source: Eurostat.

period the Baltic states have mainly been governed by right-wing parties and the principle of limited government has been constantly followed. The relatively low share of government expenditures as a share of GDP also reflects the lower GDP per capita in these countries (Staehr 2010). Compared to Central European economies (Poland, Hungary), the Baltic states have introduced fairly small public sectors with basic service provision.

In Estonia, the primary balance was positive during the boom years, which was related to higher than expected revenues and conservative fiscal policy. However, even in 2009, which marked the deepest point of the crisis, Estonia met the Maastricht criteria and the fiscal balance had again turned positive by 2010 (thanks also to some one-off revenues). These numbers do not show that there was less need for austerity measures, but rather that the relatively low deficit figures were achieved thanks to the budget cuts. The fiscal policy outcomes were also influenced by the quality of the fiscal policy institutions (in preparation, authorization and implementation): fairly high in Estonia (highest among the Central and East European (CEE) countries), but lower in Latvia and Lithuania (Fabrizio and Mody 2008).

The crisis clearly had a negative influence on the Baltic states' public finances. The sovereign debt that has traditionally been low – for example, thanks to the high growth trend (Staehr 2010) – increased during the crisis but has remained one of the lowest in the EU27 (for example, Estonia has no outstanding government bonds). It was possible to maintain low indebtedness in Estonia thanks to the fiscal reserves accumulated during the boom years (around 10 per cent of GDP). Unlike Estonia, however, Latvia had no fiscal reserves to support the economy during the deep recession. It is noticeable that Latvia's financing problems emerged in 2008 when the sovereign debt was just 20 per cent of GDP.[1] Latvia and Lithuania have increased their indebtedness to more-average levels during the crises.

During the boom period of 2006–07, total government revenues and expenditures increased considerably. At the beginning of the crisis, all three countries experienced problems in reacting to the difficulties they faced. Tax revenues decreased in all three Baltic states. In Estonia, where the share of tax revenues is the highest, the fall in tax revenues was lower than the EU average and much lower than in Latvia and Lithuania. The cyclical volatility of public finances was affected, on the one hand, by deliberate decisions – there were tax cuts during 2006–07 and tax increases in 2009 (OECD 2009) – but also by the somewhat more limited role of automatic fiscal stabilizers (such as the fact that the income tax system is proportional rather than progressive; for earlier evidence, see Kattai et al.

2003). In Estonia, tax revenues as a percentage of GDP actually increased in 2010 due to revenue-enhancing policies.

It can be argued that choosing budget cuts instead of other measures – such as financing a higher deficit with borrowing – was the right way of adjusting to the crisis because the GDP decline was longer lasting rather than temporary; – for example, in Estonia the 2007 GDP level will not be exceeded, according to Ministry of Finance forecasts, earlier than 2015 (Rahandusministeerium 2012) – and at least in early 2009, one could sell sovereign bonds in the market only at fairly high interest rates, if at all. The latter was also reflected in the high spreads of the credit default swaps (it was quite expensive to insure oneself against default by the Baltic states).

While generally the direct effect of the crisis on the public finances of the CEE countries was modest (Staehr 2010), the one exception was Latvia, which had to bail out its largest domestic bank (Parex Bank). The Baltic states managed their public finances differently during the crises: Latvia turned to the IMF and its fiscal policies were designed to satisfy the loan conditionalities; Estonia ran tight fiscal policies in order to satisfy the Maastricht criteria to join the Eurozone; and Lithuania managed to run substantial deficits during the crisis without turning to the IMF (ibid.). These different contexts have also influenced the public sector adjustments: in Estonia, for example, the less severe austerity measures were mostly of a cost-saving type and in Latvia much stronger budget consolidation – also involving structural changes – was needed.

Three supplementary state budget cuts passed in Estonia in 2009 accounted for 9.3 per cent of GDP. Compared to other countries undergoing fiscal consolidation, the government relied relatively strongly on non-tax measures (additional dividends from state-owned enterprises). Concerning the major consolidation measures, operational measures (mostly wage cuts) constituted around 0.73 per cent of GDP, adjustments in pensions (reducing the pension increase and suspending contributions to the second pillar) in total 1.2 per cent of GDP, decreased transfers to local governments (0.28 per cent) and other social security (0.72 per cent). In 2009, revenue measures were less important (2.7 per cent of GDP, increased VAT, unemployment insurance contributions and excise duties), while in 2010 revenues and expenditures were more balanced (1.3 versus 1.6 per cent of GDP). Generally, with these proportions Estonia was close to the OECD average. The state budget strategy has foreseen the restoration of fiscal balance by 2014 with gross debt stabilizing at around 14 per cent of GDP, which is still a fairly low number (OECD 2011b). Thus in Estonia about half of the budget cuts were achieved by the suspension for two years of contributions to the funded pension scheme, which perhaps made the cuts less painful, but later they will have to be made up by higher pension contributions.

In Estonia, while cuts were generally in expenditure and so far have not concerned structural changes (as they were implemented very fast), this has led to further discussions of the sustainability of the public finances – for example, the sustainability of the social insurance system (Praxis 2011) – and structural changes (centralizing support functions, looking at possibilities to merge institutions, such as schools, and analysing the delivery of public services with the aim of reducing red tape – OECD 2011b). In the case of Estonia the need for territorial administrative reform – including reducing the current relatively large number of local governments and increasing the average size of municipalities – is a long-debated issue, but has not been implemented due to opposition from the largest party of the previous ruling coalitions (the Reform Party).

Another factor that fostered successful implementation of the reforms was Estonia's better institutions: along with Slovenia, Estonia has been assessed as the least corrupt country among the new EU member states. Also, Estonians have higher trust in national political institutions (parliament, government, parties) than Latvians and Lithuanians (based on Eurobarometer surveys; Kuokštis and Vilpišauskas 2010), which enabled a more rapid reaction to the crisis in Estonia and prevented tax revenues from declining too much (the growth of the shadow economy was more modest). In the new EU countries, the fiscal situation has also been improved by the EU structural funds, amounting to about 2–3 per cent of GDP during 2010–13 (Staehr 2010). It could also be because the budget amendments in 2009 and 2010 were agreed on a tripartite basis by government, unions and employer organizations (Aslund and Dombrovskis 2011). Kuokštis and Vilpišauskas (2010) indicate that the severe internal devaluation was possible thanks to domestic consensus between policymakers and people about the commitment to fixed exchange rates, but also due to flexible labour markets. There was in any case very little contestation of fiscal austerity measures.

Estonia has managed to cope with the crisis more effectively than the other two Baltic states and the EU in general. Although during the economic downturn (2008–09) general government expenditures exceeded revenues, unlike many other countries, Estonia did not borrow heavily and instead decided to cut spending. The fiscal consolidation is believed to have contributed to the strong recovery. In 2011, Estonia showed the highest growth rate in the EU, although to some extent, the rapid growth rates experienced in 2010 resulted from the former drastic fall. Nevertheless, it is clear that the Estonian economy was capable of adjusting rapidly to the new situation and possibilities. This is certainly due to the small size of the economy and its openness to international markets. The latter also benefited from the stimulus packages introduced by other countries (Statistics Estonia 2010).

3. EMPLOYMENT IN THE PUBLIC SECTOR

3.1 Public Sector Employment Dynamics

Figure 3.1 gives a short overview of employment in Estonia's public sector. More than one-third of public sector employees are employed in local government institutions and about a quarter in state institutions. Other central units employ about 15 per cent and social security funds and other public sector units about 16 per cent of all public sector employees. Although the share of social security institutions is marginal in relative terms, the number of employees has increased significantly during the past five years: while in 2006 there were 254 employees, in 2010 the total was

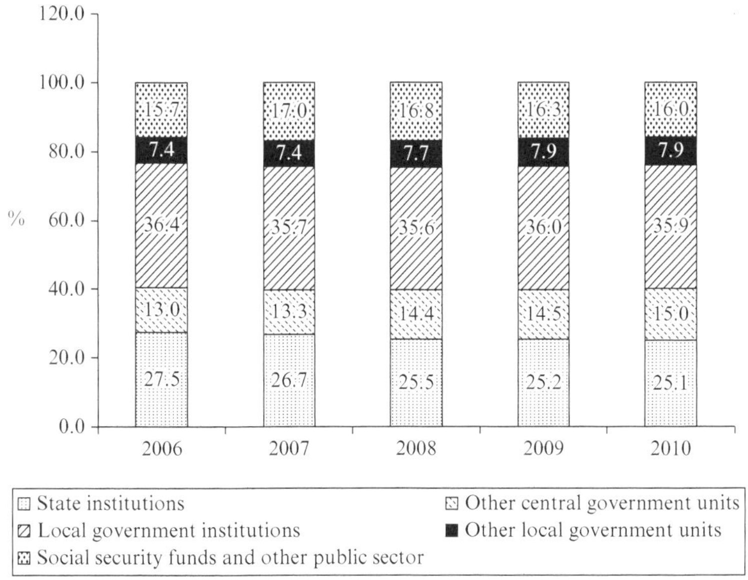

Note: State institutions: state institutions and constitutional institutions.

Source: Ministry of Finance.

Figure 3.1 Public sector employment by type of institution, Estonia, 2006–2010

712. In state and local government institutions the number of employees decreased during 2006–10, while in other central and local government units the increase was fairly stable during the period. In other public sector units employment increased during the boom period of 2006–07 and decreased during the recession (2009–10).

When considering public sector employment as the sum of employment in public administration, health care and nursing care (which is actually not entirely correct, given that in the last two sectors there are both privately and publicly owned entities), the share of public sector employment in total employment is similar to the EU27 average in the Baltic states, in Latvia and Lithuania about 25 per cent and in Estonia 28 per cent (EU27 average was 25.8 per cent). Among OECD countries, despite a relatively small government sector, Estonia's share of employment in general government and public corporations is above the OECD average (in 2008, 18.7 and 15 per cent, respectively). One reason is that, similar to the Nordic countries, Estonia relies relatively less on non-profit institutions or private enterprises for the provision of public services. Outsourcing – 80 per cent of which is in the form of intermediate consumption – is used relatively less and government employees more for the delivery of public services.

The Estonian public sector is female dominated. For instance, in 2009 36.1 per cent of employed women worked in the public sector, compared to 16.5 per cent of males. The gender composition of public sector employees has changed significantly during the past ten years. At the beginning and end of the period the distribution of employees by gender is similar: the share of females is approximately 52 per cent and of males 48 per cent. However, during the recovery from the Russian crisis (at the beginning of the new millennium) and period of strong growth (mid-2000s to 2008) the share of females increased considerably and decreased again thereafter (data from the Government Office Yearbook, 2007–10). Therefore, we can conclude that the share of females among public employees has been pro-cyclical.

The crisis had a clear negative influence on the Baltic states' labour markets, although it varied considerably between them (see Table 3.2). In Latvia, private sector employment increased most during the boom period of 2005–07. Unlike in Estonia, public sector employment decreased in Latvia and remained unchanged in Lithuania. During the crisis (2008–09) the total employment change was highest in Latvia, followed by Estonia and Lithuania. In all three countries most of the employment reduction came from the private sector. In 2010, which marked the start of the recovery, total employment decreased in all the Baltic states, but the changes were smaller and more similar across countries than in 2008–09.

Table 3.2 Changes in employment during boom (2005–2007), recession (2008–2009) and recovery (2010), public and private sectors, Baltic states (%)

Time period	Estonia			Latvia			Lithuania		
	Total	Private	Public	Total	Private	Public	Total	Private	Public
2005–07	7.9	8.7	5.8	8.0	13.4	−6.4	4.1	5.6	0.1
2008–09	−9.2	−12.3	−0.9	−12.2	−15.1	−4.3	−6.8	−8.8	−1.1
Percentage of job losses	100.0	97.5	2.6	100.0	91.0	9.2	100.0	96.2	3.9
2010	−4.2	−6.3	1.1	−4.6	−11.1	−2.0	−5.1	−6.1	−2.5

Note: Public and private sectors are defined here based on NACE sectors: in other words, the public sector includes public administration, education, health care and social work.

Source: National statistical offices.

While in 2008 employment in Estonia even increased a little compared to 2007, which marked the peak of the boom period, the increase was driven by the private sector. In the public sector, employment decreased by 7,200 during 2006–08. In 2009, in contrast, when private sector employment fell notably, in the public sector employment increased by 3,100 and was quite stable during 2010, too. While in the private sector the number of employed fell by almost 90,000 during 2008–10, in the public sector the increase was 2,200. As a result, the public sector employment share increased from 23.7 per cent in 2008 to 27.6 per cent in 2010.

Employment cuts have been a much less important adjustment measure in the public sector compared to the private sector (for more details, see Masso and Krillo 2011). In 2009, when comparing the reasons for leaving their last job, personnel cuts was indicated as the reason by 30 per cent of the non-employed whose last job was in the private sector and by 14 per cent of those whose last job was in the public sector. The most frequent reasons for quitting for former public sector employees were illness, retirement and maternity leave (that is, voluntary quits). Concerning those whose employment was terminated due to employer-related reasons (enterprise closure or reorganization, personnel cuts), the public and private sectors show similar patterns, with the percentage of males experiencing job loss increasing during the recession (in the private sector from 51 per cent in 2006 to 66 per cent in 2009; in the public sector from 20 per cent in 2006 to 34 per cent in 2009), probably because employment reductions were concentrated in the male-dominated parts of the public sector.

One possible outcome of public sector adjustments – for example, wage cuts – is that people may try to find a job in the private sector. However, job-to-job analysis shows that this is not the case in Estonia; in fact, during the crisis the trend has been rather the reverse. The job-to-job flows between sectors are quite common in Estonia, especially in the public sector. In 2008, 55 per cent of people who changed job started work in the private sector. The change of sector was much more frequent in the case of previous employment in the public sector, possibly indicating higher investment in job-specific human capital. The figures converged in 2009 and 2010, which may indicate relatively worse opportunities for getting a new job in the public sector. Similarly, administrative records show that during the crisis the percentage turnover of Estonian public sector employees decreased considerably: while in the growth period the turnover rate was about 14–15 per cent, in 2009 (the deepest crisis year) the figure was less than 7 per cent (Government Office Yearbook, 2007–10).

Flows out of unemployment (Table 3.3), are generally somewhat higher for former public sector employees, indicating their higher competitiveness in the labour market. That applies especially to males: in other words, males with past public sector employment have quite a high probability, even during the crisis, of re-entering employment. For females, however, this applies only prior to the crisis period, while during the crisis their employment re-entry rate was a lot lower, which is astonishing given the recession affecting male-dominated sectors. This could be due to the higher average level of education in the public sector, while private sector job losses were greatest in sectors – such as construction – with many blue-collar jobs. Those made unemployed in the public sector had a higher average level of education and thus more competitiveness in the labour market.

Related to labour market flow analysis is that concerning job tenure in the public and private sectors. Long tenure may be related to and important for the accumulation of job-specific human capital, while shortened tenure due to fiscal consolidation measures may threaten the quality of public services, if the most experienced employees leave. As expected, according to the Labour Force Survey (LFS) data the average job tenure is almost twice as high in the public as in the private sector (6 versus 11 years). During the crisis, if there is any change, it is rather increasing (for males in the public sector from 10.3 years in 2008 to 10.9 years in 2010). Thus during the crisis, employees with lower tenure have been leaving, although that does not exclude problems in some areas. Concerning sub-branches of public services, job tenure has decreased in public administration and increased in health care and education. Furthermore, the departure of younger employees may cause future problems when the average age of the workforce is high, for example, in the case of teachers

Table 3.3 Flows between labour market states, private and public sectors, Estonia, 2008–2010

Group	Year	Employment to employment (EE)	Job change (Ee)	Employment to inactivity (EO)	Employment to unemployment (EU)	Unemployment to employment (UE)	Share of flows between sectors in all Ee flows
Private, total	2008	90	8	7	2	52	11
	2009	82	8	9	9	52	12
	2010	76	8	11	13	25	25
Private, males	2008	92	9	6	3	48	7
	2009	82	9	7	11	48	7
	2010	74	9	9	17	19	6
Private, females	2008	89	8	9	2	56	16
	2009	81	8	12	7	57	21
	2010	79	7	13	9	35	50
Public, total	2008	91	5	8	1	67	55
	2009	88	3	10	2	51	41
	2010	88	2	8	4	36	33

Table 3.3 (continued)

Group	Year	Employment to employment (EE)	Job change (Ee)	Employment to inactivity (EO)	Employment to unemployment (EU)	Unemployment to employment (UE)	Share of flows between sectors in all Ee flows
Public, males	2008	94	4	6	0	67	67
	2009	87	4	9	4	80	58
	2010	87	6	10	3	49	31
Public, females	2008	90	5	8	2	71	49
	2009	88	3	10	2	36	28
	2010	88	1	7	4	27	37
All	2008	91	7	7	2	50	17
	2009	83	7	9	7	46	16
	2010	80	6	10	10	26	26

Note: The letters E, U and O denote the three labour market states of employment, unemployment and inactivity, respectively. Over a given period, for instance, EU denotes movement from employment to unemployment; we also use EE to denote constant employment with the same employer and Ee job-to-job mobility. For non-employed persons their last job is used to determine their sectoral affiliation. The public sector is defined as public administration, education and health care.

Source: Authors' calculations based on Estonian LFS; 2010 includes only the first quarter.

(in 2008, 49 years versus the national average of 42 years among private sector employees). Additional evidence on this issue from Ministry of Finance administrative records on public employees shows that during 2008–10 the share of officials with length of service of 1–5 years' average job tenure increased from 32 to 37 per cent, the share of those with 5–10 years fell from 23 to 20 per cent and that of those with 10–20 years rose from 29 to 33 per cent. The decreasing share of those with a service length of up to one year shows that during the crisis new hires fell significantly (if someone left the organization, then a new employee was not hired for the position).

3.2 Public Sector Employees Migrating Abroad

The other problem is that the high level of uncertainty about job losses and wage cuts may induce workers to look for work abroad. While temporary migration (or return migration) may have positive effects for the sending country (knowledge transfer from abroad or income transfers), permanent migration may mean the loss of a skilled workforce that may limit growth during a recovery. These issues have been particularly hotly debated in connection with a number of public sector occupations (doctors, police officers, rescue workers and armed forces). In the public sector, it is easier to move abroad due to the higher percentage of employees with a good education, language skills and so on. Estonian doctors and other medical staff, for example, are highly valued in Finland (see also Case Study 1).

Concerning the available evidence, there are no recent data to estimate the incidence of working abroad by sectors. However, surveys on migration intentions show that in 2006 the public sector had both a lower number of people with work experience abroad during the past five years (15 per cent in the private sector versus 10 per cent in the public sector) and a higher share of people without migration intentions (69 versus 63 per cent – the survey included 1,505 people). The much larger database of CV-Keskus (data on the employment histories of about 15 per cent of Estonian workers, around 50,000 employees) indicates that 10 per cent of private and 6 per cent of public sector employees have foreign work experience.

The official migration statistics indicate that during the crisis, emigration rose sharply in Latvia and Lithuania (in 2007–09 by 77 and 55 per cent, respectively), but not so much in Estonia (just 6 per cent during 2007–09; Philips and Pavlov 2010). However, the numbers may be greatly underestimated, especially in Estonia, because people working in Finland often do not change their place of residence, are hired by Estonian companies and their taxes are paid in Estonia. The evidence from the Estonian

LFS indicates that the number of people working abroad rose from around 15–20 thousand in 2007 to 20–30 thousand in 2009 (Eamets 2011).

In Estonia, the health-care sector was hit hard by the crisis (redundancies and wage cuts[2]) caused by the cutting of the funding for health-care services. The sector has been covered by a sectoral agreement on minimum wages (the current one was set on 1 January 2008) extended to all employers (the agreements have not covered other issues). Although there are no reliable estimates on how many Estonians work abroad (such statistics are not collected), trade unions in the health sector have pointed out that the migration of nurses and care workers to other countries was a result of the cuts, and was also due to uncertainties and increased workload. Also, many other benefits with regard to training have been cut as a result of the crisis (Osila and Nurmela 2011). The issue of emigration may also be important in other parts of the public sector, for example, there is anecdotal evidence of defence personnel leaving, for example, to work for security companies abroad.

4. WAGES IN THE PUBLIC SECTOR

The recession has strongly affected public sector wages in the Baltic states. Wage cuts and unpaid leave were used extensively to balance state budgets (see Masso and Krillo 2011). Public administration was the only area in which working time did not decrease significantly, as adjustment was carried out rather by wage cuts (and in Latvia also by employment cuts related to the need for much more extensive austerity measures). The widespread implementation of wage cuts was also facilitated by the weakness of trade unions and widespread performance-related pay. In many sectors the latter constitutes up to 30 per cent of wages, which makes it possible to keep base wages lower, while in the old EU countries performance-related pay usually constitutes only a small share of total pay (Eamets 2011).[3] In the public sector various wage components (basic wages, bonuses, fringe benefits) were reduced, but in different institutions different adjustment strategies were used (see Case Studies 1 and 2 in this chapter and the police case study in Masso and Krillo 2011); however, due to the lack of survey data we cannot provide aggregate data on the relative importance of these various measures.

As can be seen from Table 3.4, the share of those whose wages were cut increased considerably during the crisis. It is also important to note that for all periods the share of workers whose wages were cut has been higher in the public sector, but the discrepancies have increased substantially during the crisis. Concerning other evidence from surveys of firms,

Table 3.4 Proportion of workers whose nominal hourly wages decreased over the year, Estonia, 2006–2010 (%)

Indicator/group	2006	2007	2008	2009	2010Q1
All employees	22	14	17	45	45
Public sector	29	22	25	61	71
Private sector	21	13	16	40	44

Source: Authors' calculations based on Estonian LFS data.

Fabiani et al. (2011) reported that in 2009 in Estonia 44 per cent of private firms made wage cuts (3 per cent in a total sample of nine countries). We may note that even before the crisis a large percentage of people in the LFS data were experiencing wage decreases. That can be considered as a kind of regression to the mean: people had a temporary pay increase in one year – for example, some bonuses – that were not repeated the following year, showing up in the data as a wage decrease.

4.1 Public Sector and Private Sector Progressively Converging in the Three Baltic States

Public administration wages were hit hard in all three Baltic states (with wage cuts ranging from 7.6 per cent in Estonia to 18 per cent in Latvia; see Table 3.5), reflecting cuts in the budgets of both national and local government. In Latvia, wages were reduced considerably in the public sector, particularly government institutions, while wages in Lithuania and Estonia fell relatively evenly across the board, with the wage decrease in the construction industry being the sharpest (Masso and Krillo 2011). This explains why private sector wages slightly lost out compared to the public sector: in Estonia the indicator decreased from 106 to 96 in 2008–09 and from 88 to 84 in Lithuania (see Table 3.6). In Latvia, at the beginning of the recession average public wages were substantially higher than private wages, but by the end of 2009 the difference was insignificant (9 per cent in Table 3.6). On 1 July 2009, wages below LVL 300 were cut by 15 per cent and those above LVL 300 by 20 per cent (Curkina 2009). Similar wage cuts were implemented in Lithuania and Estonia (8–10 per cent) (see Glassner 2010). As a result, private sector wages as a percentage of public sector wages increased from 78 per cent in 2008 to 91 per cent in 2010 in Latvia. As in the private sector the public sector wages were cut: in Estonia the indicator decreased from 106 to 96 in 2008–09 and from 88 to 84 in Lithuania (see Table 3.6). While all the above information applies

Table 3.5 Annual wage changes by economic sector in the Baltic states, 2008–2010 (%)

Industry	Estonia			Latvia			Lithuania		
	2008	2009	2010	2008	2009	2010	2008	2009	2010
Total economy	13.8	−4.6	1.1	20.6	−4.0	−3.3	19.3	−4.4	−3.9
Primary	17.7	−7.4	7.1	17.2	−4.6	5.8	23.4	−7.8	−2.6
Industry	11.5	−3.5	5.5	13.4	−4.0	2.9	17.5	−4.2	−0.1
Manufacturing	10.8	−3.9	5.2	19.8	−2.1	0.2	17.5	−4.4	−0.1
Energy	17.0	6.8	5.2	5.6	−5.0	5.2	15.9	−0.1	1.0
Construction	8.3	−13.4	3.6	19.0	−1.1	−5.1	10.3	−21.1	−8.3
Business services	12.3	−4.2	−0.9	21.0	−1.8	−1.5	18.8	−5.2	−4.6
Public services	17.4	−4.5	−1.0	20.2	−10.1	−6.7	22.0	−11.3	0.8
Public administration	15.7	−7.6	−2.7	16.1	−18.0	−8.5	23.1	−9.7	−5.5
Education	20.4	−2.5	−0.7	23.4	−9.9	−10.5	25.9	7.8	−5.0
Health	20.1	−2.4	−3.5	19.2	−9.9	−4.3	20.9	−2.0	−4.5

Source: National statistical offices of Estonia, Latvia and Lithuania.

Table 3.6 Wages in the public sector relative to the private sector and economy average in the Baltic states, 2006–2010 (%)

	2006	2007	2008	2009	2010
Private sector wage/ public sector wage					
Estonia	104	108	106	96	98
Latvia	79	76	78	86	91
Lithuania	87	93	88	84	85
Public administration/ total economy					
Estonia	123	127	129	125	121
Latvia	142	148	142	122	115
Lithuania	95	96	97	99	99
Education/total economy					
Estonia	85	83	88	90	88
Latvia	97	99	101	95	88
Lithuania	81	77	77	79	78
Health/total economy					
Estonia	97	98	104	106	101
Latvia	99	103	102	95	94
Lithuania	91	86	88	80	84

Source: Authors' calculations based on data from Eurostat, national statistical offices and Estonian LFS. The private and public sector wages for Latvia and Lithuania are from the national statistical offices, the data for Estonia are calculated from the LFS data.

to gross wages, net wages were further reduced in Latvia due to the reduction of the tax-free allowance and the introduction of progressive income taxation. Aslund and Dombrovskis (2011) argue that in Latvia the real wage reduction was probably larger in the private sector than shown by official statistics due to the abandoning of the fringe benefits (that did not enter official statistics). Table 3.6, however, tends to show that private and public sector wages have been converging over the past few years.

It is noticeable that the wage gap was initially in favour of the private sector in Estonia, while in Latvia and Lithuania it favoured the public sector. Latvia's higher public sector wages pertain first of all to public administration, but to a lesser extent also to education and health. For all countries we can note that public administration has relatively higher, and both health and education relatively lower wage rates. Concerning the public–private gap in health and education, in Latvia the public sector had higher wages during 2006–08, but during the crisis the private sector had higher wages. The numbers reflect the tendency observed elsewhere that the public sector suffered from the crisis relatively more in Latvia.

The private–public[4] sector pay gap in Estonia has been analysed in more detail by Leping (2005). The study showed that the dynamics of public and private sector wages have been quite similar in Estonia. At the end of the Soviet period and during the early transition, wages were higher in the private sector than in the public sector (something similar was found by Adamchik and Bedi (2000) for Poland in 1996). Later the wage differences between the two sectors decreased. Public sector wages exceeded private sector wages in 1999 when the Baltic states were hit by the Russian crisis. From 2002 to 2005 wages were higher in the private sector. Leping (2005) also analysed the wage differences with quintile regressions. The results showed that in the case of low-wage employees the potential wage level is similar in both the public and the private sectors, but in the case of high-wage employees, the private sector offers much better wage opportunities. The wage premium from working in the public sector for low-wage employees (10th percentile) declined from 8.5 per cent in 2001 to zero in 2004. The wage penalty from working in the public sector for high-wage employees (90th percentile) increased from 4 per cent in 2001 to 11 per cent in 2004. Our analysis reveals a private sector pay penalty for those with a higher education.

Table 3.6 reveals that the period after the one analysed by Leping (2005) is characterized by wage dynamics closely following macroeconomic fluctuations. While in 2005 public sector wages were higher, during 2006–08 wage growth in the public sector was unable to keep pace with the rapid wage growth in the private sector. The recession in 2009 turned the gap in favour of the public sector again (although there were wage cuts both in the private and the public sectors). The recovery in 2010 tends to move the balance more in favour of private sector again because there are signs of wage pressure there. It has been declared in Estonia's State Budget Strategy that public sector wages will not increase before 2014. This has increased tensions (see Section 6 on industrial relations). Thus we may conclude that wage dynamics have rather been led by the private and public sectors responding to pressures, rather than the public sector wage increases creating an upward pressure on wages in the private sector.

4.2 A High Gender Pay Gap

Especially in Estonia the gender pay gap deserves attention due to its size: it is one of the largest in Europe. Econometric analysis using LFS data for 2000–08 showed that the gender pay gap was 23 per cent in the public sector and 31 per cent in the private sector. In the private sector the gap was higher in foreign-owned than in domestic enterprises (38 and 29 per cent, respectively), and the same applied to the unexplained part of the wage gap (18, 23 and 31 per cent, respectively, of private sector wages). To a certain extent that is explained by the generally higher wage inequality in the private sector. The gender pay gap was smaller for trade union members (Anspal et al. 2010). The lower wages of women are attributable to the fact that certain relatively low-paid occupations are female dominated. In most OECD countries teachers and nurses tend to earn less than the average university-educated adults, and Estonia is even further below the OECD average on this indicator.

4.3 Low Pay Dynamics in the Public Sector

As we saw, the public–private sector wage gap may be less informative as it does not reveal the wage distributions within the public and private sectors, for instance the share of low-paid employees. For example, while in general in Lithuania wages have been higher in the public sector, at the same time the Lithuanian public sector also has a group of extremely low-paid public sector employees (health-care professionals, cultural and artistic workers; EWCO 2010). The story seems to be that even within the public sector, wage inequality is quite large. The numbers from Estonian LFS data in Table 3.7 reveal that the increase in the share of low-paid employees during the crisis years can be attributed rather to the private sector, while in the public sector the share is actually declining. While generally the share of low-wage employees is lower in the public sector, similar to the private sector the proportion is twice as high among women,

Table 3.7 Share of low-wage employees in the public and private sectors, Estonia, 2005–2010

Sector	2005	2006	2007	2008	2009	2010
Private sector	0.29	0.28	0.28	0.27	0.32	0.33
Private sector, females	0.39	0.39	0.41	0.40	0.44	0.41
Private sector, males	0.19	0.18	0.17	0.15	0.21	0.26
Public sector	0.23	0.27	0.29	0.30	0.27	0.25
Public sector, females	0.29	0.33	0.34	0.36	0.32	0.28
Public sector, males	0.10	0.13	0.17	0.15	0.14	0.16
All	0.27	0.28	0.28	0.28	0.31	0.31

Source: Authors' calculations based on Estonian LFS data.

illustrating again the importance of considering gender issues when discussing the public sector labour market.

4.4 Higher Wage Compression in the Public Sector

Naturally, we would expect the wage distribution to be more compressed in the public sector, where wages are more regulated (defined pay scales). Thus it would be helpful to look at the wage gap by percentiles (Table 3.8). For males, working in the public sector seems to be more beneficial for low-wage earners, while among high-wage earners in most periods the gap has favoured the private sector. Among females, the gap has been in favour of the public sector among both low- and high-wage earners, while it is higher among high-wage earners: in other words, the picture is the opposite of that of males. Part of the story could be Estonia's high gender wage gap, which is a lot lower in the public sector. But generally these results seem to be well in line with evidence from other countries. In Estonia, the impact of the unions is low in both the private and public sectors. Collective bargaining has been more widespread in sectors such as health care and education, which are mostly part of the public sector, and also in transport, energy and mining, which belong both to the public and private sectors (Masso and Eamets 2007). Thus the low unionization in Estonia should reduce the importance of the wage gap between private and public sectors (Leping 2005).

One factor contributing to inequality is that the Estonian government has a delegated system of human resource management and a strong performance orientation (performance-related pay). Concerning wage inequality in the public sector, the OECD (2011c) notes that in public services it should be similar to other countries (middle managers earn 1.5

Table 3.8 Wage inequality: net hourly wages in the public and private sectors, Estonia, 2005–2010

Group	Sector	Statistic	2005	2006	2007	2008	2009	2010
Females	Private	p10	14.12	16.37	19.49	23.71	23.54	22.74
	Public	p10	15.30	16.82	19.68	23.71	23.87	25.39
	Public/ private	p10	1.08	1.03	1.01	1.00	1.01	1.12
	Private	p90	41.19	50.58	59.05	71.14	74.11	73.82
	Public	p90	51.49	54.37	63.97	77.07	82.42	73.82
	Public/ private	p90	1.25	1.07	1.08	1.08	1.11	1.00
Males	Private	p10	15.89	18.91	24.41	29.64	26.68	24.61
	Public	p10	19.84	23.14	24.80	29.64	29.64	27.05
	Public/ private	p10	1.25	1.22	1.02	1.00	1.11	1.10
	Private	p90	58.85	72.69	91.53	106.71	107.90	112.20
	Public	p90	58.85	65.00	76.77	94.86	100.78	118.11
	Public/ private	p90	1.00	0.89	0.84	0.89	0.93	1.05

Note: P10 and p90 denote, respectively, the 10% and 90% quintiles of the wage distribution.

Source: Authors' calculations based on Estonian LFS data.

times more than economists). On the other hand, unlike in most OECD countries, in Estonia the wages of public sector workers are made public, which should contribute to transparency and leave less room for discrimination (such as gender inequality).

High intersectoral labour mobility (see Table 3.3), on the one hand, could lower the monopsony power of public sector employers, which should increase wages in the public sector, but on the other hand, the low geographical mobility of labour decreases public sector wages, especially in peripheral regions (Leping 2005).

4.5 Some Econometric Findings on the Public Sector–Private Sector Wage Gap

As a final step in the analysis of the public–private sector wage gap, we ran quintile regression models. We estimated the wage gap for the 10, 25, 50, 75 and 90 percent quintiles, and as a robustness check we also estimated the usual mean OLS regression. The list of explanatory variables includes the usual ones deployed in wage equations: age, tenure, firm size, education, occupational categories, dummy part-time employees, gender and location. The results presented in Table 3.9 show again that the public sector compresses the wage distribution: working in the public sector increases the wages of low-wage employees, but lowers the wages of high-wage employees. For 2005–07, the estimated wage gap was on average –3.8 per cent, with +6.9 per cent in the lowest percentile and –10.4 per cent in the highest percentile. In 2009, the three numbers for the gap were just +1.6, +7.8 and –4.6 per cent, in other words, the effect of changing the balance in favour of the public sector was felt in both the lower and upper parts of the wage distribution.

Employees with a university degree benefit from working in the public sector in the case of lower quintiles (+6.7 per cent in the lowest 10 per cent), but lose out in the case of higher quintiles (–11.2 per cent in the highest 10 per cent), which is a result similar to Leping (ibid.). What is potentially worrying is that the gap in the highest 10 per cent has even widened (although generally the public sector has become more attractive during the crisis). Workers with secondary-level education, on the other hand, lose out from working in the public sector in the highest quintiles (although many of the estimates are statistically insignificant, especially during the crisis). The results for employees with primary-level education could also be driven by the relatively small number of employees in this group. The issue remains whether the public sector offers other non-wage advantages (fringe benefits, more stable job relationships) that compensate for wages.

With regard to gender, Leping (2005) found for 2003 that women benefit more, or actually lose less, from working in the public sector than men in the case of most quintiles. In our data, however, the contrary emerges: working in the public sector is more to the benefit of males: for mean regressions the wage gaps for 2005–07 were –7.1 and –1.9 per cent, respectively, and in 2009 –2.1 and 5.3 per cent. It seems that there are some specifically female-oriented jobs that are relatively low paid (such as teachers). Thus the public sector is in this sense effectively not contributing enough to decreasing Estonia's high gender wage gap.

It should be reasonable to assume that in the public sector organizations personnel practices are based more on rules than in the private sector. However, case studies in the public sector organizations (Kallaste et al. 2010) indicate that the use of job evaluation means that bureaucratic regulations do not necessarily reduce subjectivity in wage determination. Vertical segregation seems to be important as well (there are more males in the top leadership), while in the private sector horizontal segregation was also quite important (males and females working in different occupations).

Table 3.9 Estimated size of the public–private sector wage gap from OLS and quintile regressions, Estonia

Quintile	Specification	2005–2007		2008		2009	
		Wage gap	*T*-stat.	Wage gap	*T*-stat.	Wage gap	*T*-stat.
OLS	All	−0.038	(−3.86)***	−0.061	(−4.12)***	0.016	(1.36)
OLS	Females	−0.071	(−5.48)***	−0.079	(−3.93)***	−0.021	(−1.47)
OLS	Males	−0.019	(−1.28)	−0.054	(−2.47)**	0.053	(2.41)**
OLS	Primary education	−0.071	(−3.84)***	−0.091	(−2.41)**	0.042	(1.30)
OLS	Secondary education	−0.044	(−2.96)***	−0.056	(−2.86)***	0.013	(0.80)
OLS	Higher education	−0.035	(−1.78)*	−0.089	(−3.03)***	−0.000	(−0.02)
q10	All	0.069	(5.34)***	−0.012	(−0.43)	0.078	(3.80)***
q10	Females	0.023	(1.66)*	−0.056	(−2.21)**	0.037	(1.27)
q10	Males	0.095	(4.65)***	−0.016	(−0.52)	0.117	(5.45)***
q10	Primary education	0.026	(0.94)	−0.057	(−0.86)	0.069	(1.68)*
q10	Secondary education	0.057	(2.37)**	−0.043	(−1.39)	0.063	(2.52)**
q10	Higher education	0.067	(1.71)*	0.017	(0.33)	0.103	(2.11)**
q25	All	0.009	(0.83)	−0.050	(−2.56)**	0.038	(2.25)**
q25	Females	−0.003	(−0.22)	−0.064	(−4.16)***	0.014	(0.96)
q25	Males	−0.002	(−0.12)	−0.042	(−1.27)	0.083	(3.71)***
q25	Primary education	−0.012	(−0.96)	−0.085	(−2.45)**	0.054	(1.58)
q25	Secondary education	0.006	(0.27)	−0.059	(−3.10)***	0.023	(1.44)
q25	Higher education	−0.044	(−2.71)***	−0.050	(−1.46)	0.037	(0.98)

q50	All	−0.043	(−10.09)***	−0.059	(−3.35)***	0.007	(0.60)
q50	Females	−0.052	(−5.24)***	−0.054	(−2.55)**	−0.026	(−2.69)***
q50	Males	−0.039	(−2.88)***	−0.048	(−1.60)	0.030	(1.15)
q50	Primary education	−0.063	(−3.54)***	−0.134	(−3.73)***	−0.019	(−0.61)
q50	Secondary education	−0.046	(−3.56)***	−0.054	(−2.20)**	−0.007	(−0.35)
q50	Higher education	−0.050	(−1.75)*	−0.098	(−3.23)***	0.005	(0.15)
q75	All	−0.074	(−8.57)***	−0.079	(−3.46)***	−0.032	(−2.70)***
q75	Females	−0.094	(−7.06)***	−0.112	(−4.68)***	−0.073	(−4.31)***
q75	Males	−0.063	(−5.25)***	−0.047	(−1.42)	0.026	(0.98)
q75	Primary education	−0.113	(−4.38)***	−0.084	(−1.09)	0.007	(0.15)
q75	Secondary education	−0.059	(−3.45)***	−0.053	(−2.00)**	−0.019	(−0.77)
q75	Higher education	−0.084	(−2.53)**	−0.184	(−5.49)***	−0.055	(−2.24)**
q90	All	−0.104	(−6.67)***	−0.089	(−4.92)***	−0.046	(−1.73)*
q90	Females	−0.146	(−8.11)***	−0.142	(−3.18)***	−0.130	(−5.59)***
q90	Males	−0.066	(−3.31)***	−0.051	(−1.26)	0.011	(0.32)
q90	Primary education	−0.151	(−4.09)***	−0.063	(−0.59)	0.048	(0.59)
q90	Secondary education	−0.102	(−3.84)***	−0.045	(−1.19)	−0.025	(−0.88)
q90	Higher education	−0.112	(−2.99)***	−0.192	(−3.75)***	−0.199	(−4.37)***

Note: Reported are the parameter estimates from the quintile regressions on the hourly log wage. The list of other explanatory variables in the regressions includes age, age squared, tenure, tenure squared, four dummies for firm size groups, three dummies for education, eight dummies for one-digit occupational categories, dummies for part-time employees, gender and location (capital region). * Significant at 10%; ** significant at 5%; *** significant at 1%.

Source: Authors' calculations based on Estonian LFS data.

Wages are determined by two systems supporting each other (legal acts, such as the Public Service Act, versus organizations' internal salary administration), that may make wage determination non-transparent for employees (another problem could be that the evaluation of occupations is carried out only for a subset of jobs). In practice, the statutory wage components (such as for workers with degrees, wages, tenure) were adjusted to make total pay correspond to the internal pay schemes without breaking the law. As a result, bureaucratic legislation does not necessarily reduce the gender pay gap automatically and the more equal pay in the public sector is rather due to internal job evaluation. Also, the positive example of the public sector could help to reduce the problem in the private sector (ibid.). Similarly, the study on the remuneration of public sector employees in Lithuania found that in the case of centralized remuneration, pay conditions could still vary greatly across the institutions as the remuneration of public sector employees is governed by a large number of different legal documents (EWCO 2010).

5. ADJUSTMENTS IN OTHER WORKING CONDITIONS DURING THE CRISIS

Compared to other adjustment mechanisms (wages and employment), adjustment through working time (mainly part-time employment and reduced hours) has been less important in the Baltic states, and the same applies for the public sector. However, at least in Estonia it has been quite substantial (from 2008 to 2009 average hours decreased by 3.8). In 2009–10 unpaid vacation leave was used to cut labour costs (see Masso and Krillo 2011). In public administration, working hours remained largely the same in 2008–09. One can see some reduction in hours in the health sector in all three Baltic countries and education in Estonia and an increase in part-time employment in Latvia (Table 3.10).

In addition to wages, the cuts in public expenditure also affected training. In sum, total training expenditure in all branches of the civil service decreased in 2009 by almost 60 per cent on average, but recovered in 2010 thanks to the more active use of foreign aid (EU funds, Avaliku teenistuse aastaraamat 2011). Training expenditure as a share of payroll decreased in the ministries from 2.5 per cent in 2008 to 1.5 per cent in 2009 and then increased again to 2.1 per cent in 2010. According to the Estonian LFS, the proportion of those who had participated in some kind of training during the past four weeks in 2008 was 2.8 per cent in the private and 7.7 per cent in the public sector; in 2009 both numbers increased somewhat. Thus, we would say that compared to the private sector the public sector

Table 3.10 Adjustment in working time in the public and private sectors, Baltic states, 2008–2009

Country	Industry	Average working hours at main job			Share of part-time employees		
		2008	2009	Change 2008–09	2008	2009	Change 2008–09
Estonia	Public admin.	39.4	39.2	−0.2	2.9	2.2	−0.7
	Health	38.3	37.9	−0.4	14.1	11.8	−2.3
	Education	35.6	34.9	−0.7	12.7	13.1	0.4
	Total	39.1	37.6	−1.5	7.2	10.5	3.4
Latvia	Public admin.	39.0	39.1	0.1	3.7	4.2	0.5
	Health	39.1	38.5	−0.6	7.6	10.1	2.5
	Education	36.3	36.3	0.0	9.0	8.4	−0.6
	Total	39.4	38.8	−0.6	6.3	8.9	2.6
Lithuania	Public admin.	40.0	39.9	−0.1	2.3	1.6	−0.6
	Health	39.3	38.4	−0.9	5.1	5.9	0.9
	Education	35.6	35.5	−0.1	11.0	9.7	−1.3
	Total	39.2	38.6	−0.6	6.7	8.3	1.6
EU27	Public admin.	36.8	36.7	−0.1	12.9	12.9	0.0
	Health	33.9	33.9	0.0	31.4	31.6	0.2
	Education	32.0	31.9	−0.1	25.2	25.7	0.5
	Total	37.3	36.9	−0.4	18.2	18.8	0.5

Source: Eurostat, Authors' calculations.

suffered less from training cuts as the private sector did not have a similar possibility of funding training expenditure from structural funds.

The Estonian LFS in 2007–08 also includes questions about the work environment. Generally, in the public sector satisfaction with different aspects of working conditions (work safety, intensity, health, work environment) is higher than in the private sector: in general the share of employees rating working conditions good or very good was 10 percentage points higher in 2007–08. Concerning unequal treatment at work (information was gathered only in 2008), during the past five years with regard to all aspects in the public sector fewer employees had experienced unequal treatment; the differences were greatest concerning the distribution of work or shifts (2.7 per cent in the private versus 1.2 per cent in the public sector), but perhaps somewhat surprisingly the percentage with experience of discrimination was quite low for all aspects. A more important issue in the public sector seems to be unpaid overtime (in 2008, 0.7 per cent in the private and 1.7 per cent in the public sector), especially in the education sector. Unfortunately due to lack of data for later years it is not possible to see, for example, the influence of public sector cuts on these issues.

6. INDUSTRIAL RELATIONS DURING THE CRISIS

In Estonia, in which the level of unionization is generally low, the public sector is significantly more unionized than the private sector, especially in education and health care where the union membership rates are above 20 per cent (see Table 3.11). As also indicated in previous studies (Osila 2011), union membership is much lower in the public administration. For comparison, the public administration in Latvia is characterized by very high coverage of collective agreements of more than 80 per cent, with sectoral unions (Curkina 2011). In Latvia it has been observed that the economic crisis has led to the softening of the rules of collective bargaining. While there are some estimates on unionization rates, it is difficult to estimate collective bargaining coverage; in Estonia the estimate from ROTAL[5] was that the agreements in force in 2008 covered 4,080 employees (7 per cent of employment). During the crisis, union membership has remained fairly stable in Estonia.

Unlike many other European countries, wage cuts did not lead to large-scale protests in the public sector in Estonia. The government declared that public sector wage cuts are necessary to balance the state budget and to avoid heavy state borrowing and massive lay-offs. Therefore, wage cuts were accepted by public sector trade unions and employees without major opposition. Wage reductions were seen as a better solution than the other alternative (massive lay-offs).

On 25 June 2009, the Estonian government approved the draft acts to cut the wages of many public sector workers. The changes were

Table 3.11 Union membership in the public and private sectors, Estonia, 2005–2010 (%)

Industry	2005	2006	2007	2008	2009	2010
Total economy	9	8	8	6	8	9
Public sector	21	21	20	17	19	20
Private sector	4	4	3	2	3	4
Public administration	4	4	4	4	6	5
Education	26	25	20	19	21	19
Health care	22	24	24	16	22	29

Source: Authors' calculations based on Estonian LFS.

implemented quite easily and without hostile reactions on the part of trade unions. Teachers' wages were decreased by 4 per cent, back to 2008 levels. Minimum wages of prosecutors were decreased by 6 per cent, and the wages of police and border guards by 8 per cent. Support for recruits was decreased by 8 per cent, and the wages of members of the armed forces that exceeded the minimum wage were cut by 8 per cent.

Unlike in Estonia and Latvia, where the governments were able to implement measures unfavourable to public sector employees quite easily (in Latvia several protest actions followed the government decision to implement budget cuts and wage reductions in the education sector: see Curkina (2009) for more details), Lithuanian trade unions reacted to the government plans more actively. At the beginning of 2009 the trade unions (both public and private sector) organized a protest action in response to the government's unwillingness to discuss on a programme that the unions found to be inadequate in light of the economic and labour market situation. As no satisfactory response came from the government, on 16 January 2009 trade unions organized a general protest action in which 5,000–7,000 people participated (Blaziene 2009a). The next strong reaction followed in July 2009 in response to the government decision on 17 June 2009 to cut the basic nominal monthly wage in the public sector without consulting the trade unions.

The basic weekly wage[6] was to be reduced from LTL 128 (about €37) to LTL 115 (€33) in the public sector. The pay cut was planned to enter into force on 1 August 2009 and would have affected about 230,000 public sector employees, most of whom were relatively low paid. The Lithuanian Trade Union Confederation (LPSK) reacted by adopting a 'Declaration regarding the inconsiderate and unreasonable policy implemented by LRV' on 19 June. As the government ignored LPSK's warning, a hunger strike was organized on 2 July 2009 in Independence Square in front of the parliament buildings. The government and LPSK agreed that, while a cut in public sector wages was unavoidable, the biggest burden should be assumed by the highest-paid public sector employees. In the end, it was agreed with the trade union representatives that the government would cancel its decision to reduce the basic monthly wage with effect from 3 July. As a result, LPSK stopped the hunger strike action on 3 July. As promised, the main burden of the salary decrease was placed on the highest-paid public sector employees, including lawyers and state officials. Pay rises for civil servant qualification grades were cut on a temporary basis from 1 August 2009 to 31 December 2010: more specifically, by 10–15 per cent for the third (lowest) qualification rating and by 30–50 per cent for the first (highest) qualification rating (Blaziene 2009b). In October 2009, four sectoral trade unions and the Pensioners' Party simultaneously launched five protest actions near the parliament and four government ministries. The protests arose due to dissatisfaction with the government's policy of seeking to match budget revenue with expenditure, which resulted in significant wage cuts for public sector employees.

In Lithuania, in response to the trade union actions, a national agreement was signed by the government and national peak social partner organizations at the end of October 2009. In the agreement, economic, administrative and social commitments were stipulated (for more details, see Blaziene 2009c). From the public sector perspective the most important issue was job losses. The national agreement was widely criticized by independent experts and opponents, who argued that the accord was void and that it met the interests only of its signatory parties rather than those of the public. At the beginning of 2011 a discussion was initiated to renew the agreement. Among other things, employers criticized the government for delays in reducing the number of civil servants.

It may be surprising that in Estonia no strikes were called during the crisis when austerity measures were introduced, but took place later during the recovery. Although the State Budgetary Strategy for 2012–15, approved in late April 2011 by the government, prescribes zero growth in the operating costs of state institutions for the next four years, in light of the recovery, union pressure to increase wages has strengthened. Since independence Estonia has had only a few strikes and the teachers' strike in March 2011 was the most widespread in the country's post-war history. The reason for the strike was the refusal by the Ministry of Education and Research to raise basic wages by 20 per cent in 2012. The three-day strike involved about 15,000 education workers. The support strikes were organized in several other sectors, such as medicine, transport, road workers and power plants. The strike drew attention to the longstanding problems of teachers' relatively low wages and high workload, including unpaid overtime. The ministry's position is that funds for the pay increase should be found from the education system due to Estonia's already relatively high level of education expenditure as a share of GDP (in 2008, 5.67 per cent of GDP, versus 5.07 per cent in the EU27), for example, through reforming the school network and closing those with fewer pupils.

The recent State and Local Government Authorities Industrial Relations Study (Praxis, University of Tartu 2011) covered many aspects of the public sector industrial relations system in Estonia. Seventy-two interviews with different target group representatives (employers, trade union representatives, employees' representatives, trade union confederations and employers' confederation) were carried out during the study. Interviews showed that the fact that trade unions largely just accepted government pressure to cut wages and implement unpaid leave also indicated to people that the unions are weak as regards protecting their members' interests. Several interviewed trade union representatives also emphasized that their bargaining power to resist the crisis measures was weaker than that of the employers (see Table 3.12). Although the wage cuts and unpaid leave were clearly not in workers' interests, the employees' representatives agreed to them because the alternative proposed/considered (lay-offs) by the employers would have been even worse. On the other hand, in some state agencies where problems were especially acute during the crisis (for example, the Estonian Rescue Board) workers decided to join forces to demand a pay increase and improvements in other working conditions (see Case Study 2, below).

In the interviews the trade union representatives also pointed out that one negative side-effect that influenced union membership during the crisis was the union membership fee. As wages decreased and the ability of the trade unions to protect their members' interests remained weak, it persuaded people to withdraw from the trade union.

Another interesting impact of the crisis was the fact that the employers – that is, the heads of public sector institutions – admitted that their ministry had pressured them during the crisis to abandon the collective agreement in force before the crisis. There were several cases in which the collective agreement was terminated because the ministry had forced the head of the institution to take that step. Several heads and employees' representatives of public sector institutions admitted in interviews that it was not possible to provide employees with the benefits laid down in the collective agreement during the crisis. In some institutions the changes were made to the collective agreement, while in others changes were agreed orally between employers and employees' representatives.

7. IMPACT ON THE PROVISION OF PUBLIC SERVICES

The economic crisis has also affected the accessibility of health-care services. Thus it is the topic of Case Study 1 (Section 8.1). Figure 3.2 presents data from the Estonian social survey on the self-reported numbers of people not receiving medical aid. The figure indicates that while for family doctors the more or less continuous improvement came to a halt in 2010, in the case of specialists (consultants) the situation became even worse.[7] Furthermore, own estimates of health were quite stable during 2005–10; among those below the poverty line they actually improved (the percentage of people considering their health good or very good increased during 2008–10 from 32 to 45 per cent). Concerning other countries, in Latvia

Table 3.12 Unionization of Estonian, Latvian and Lithuanian public sectors

Sector	Estonia	Latvia	Lithuania
Unions with membership			
Public administration	Estonian Employees' Unions' Confederation (TALO) – in the sector 167, total 11,729	LAPA – Latvian United Trade Union of Police workers – 1,700; Trade Union of Employees of State Institutions – 4,620; Trade Union of Employees of Local Governments – 1,352	Lithuanian Trade Union of Civil Servants (LVTPS) – 3,180; Lithuanian Trade Union of Constables and Police Employees (LVRSRPS) – 3,000
Education	Estonian Education Personnel Union (EEPU) – 10,538; Association of Intellectuals – 1,500; Federation of the Estonian Universities, Institutions of Science, Research and Development – 1,247	Latvian Education and Science Workers' Trade Union (LIZDA) – 35,844 (2010)	Lithuanian Teachers' Trade Union (LMPS) – 1,800; Lithuanian Education Employees' Trade Union (LŠDPS) – 12,000; Christian Trade Union of Education Workers (KŠDPS) – 1,040; Federation of Lithuanian Education and Science Trade Unions (LŠMPSF) – 7,479
Density			
Density in education, 2008	22.4%	48.3%	15.4%
Density in public administration, 2008	0.4%	8.9%	3.0%

Density in hospitals, 2006	78.0%	57.0%	3.0%
Bodies to refuse the conclusion of collective agreements	Several ministries, local governments	Police	Ministry of Interior; organizational level in education (school principals reluctant to recognize unions)
Collective bargaining coverage			
Public administration	ROTAL ca 7%	No data	Enterprise-level agreements ca 10% of civil servants
Education	Difficult to estimate due to different levels, but high	93% of LIZDA members covered by collective agreement	Organizational level, no valid sectoral level
Levels of bargaining			
Public administration	Sectoral, multi-employer, enterprise level	Organization level	Enterprise level only
Education	Sectoral, multi-employer, enterprise level	Organizational (universities), sectoral level	About 20–30% (estimate)

Source: Authors' compilation based on data from EIROnline.

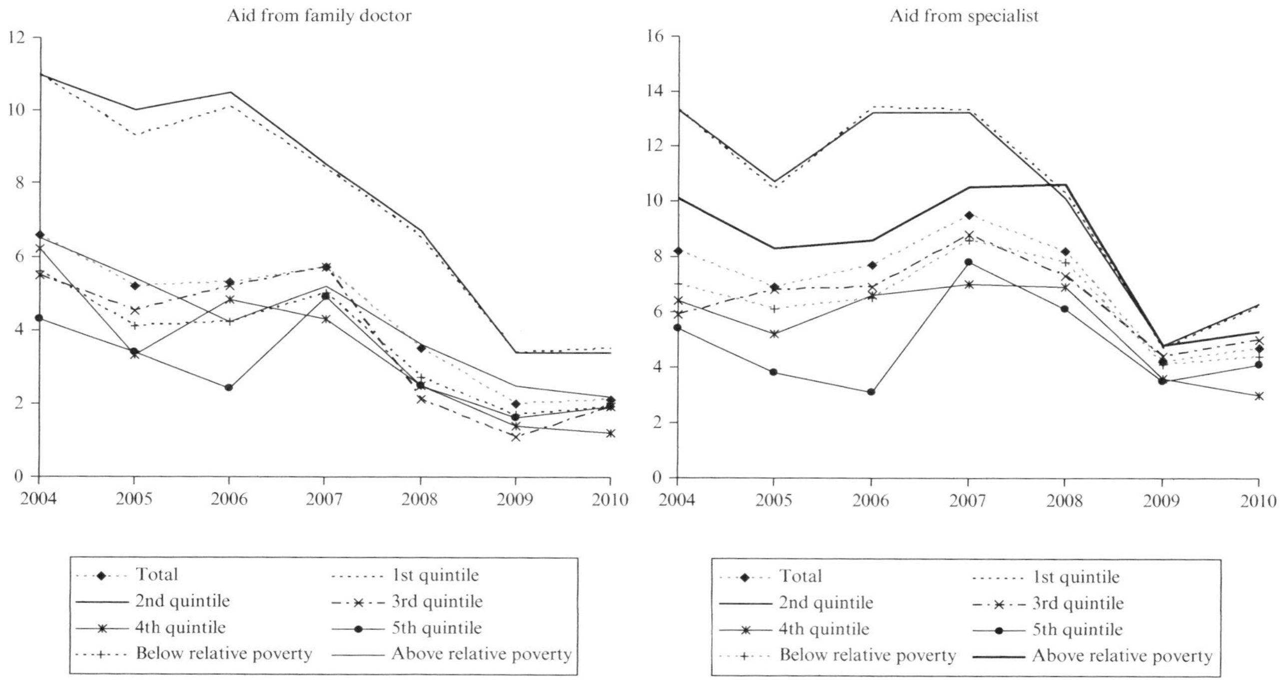

Source: Statistics Estonia, based on Estonian social survey. Availability of medical aid: the people not receiving medical aid are those who during the past 12 months needed medical aid, but for some reason did not get it.

Figure 3.2 Percentage of people not receiving medical aid, Estonia, 2004–2010

the situation somewhat worsened in 2009 (from 6.9 to 8.1 per cent due to excessive costs); generally Latvia seems to have by far the highest values on this indicator (in Estonia and Lithuania the figures are just 0.8 and 0.7 per cent of surveyed individuals, respectively).

One interesting example illustrating the negative effects of the crisis on the provision of public services is the programme 'A kindergarten place for each child', which was halted by the Estonian government in 2009. The programme started in 2007 and was aimed at helping local governments to solve the problem of lack of kindergarten places. According the Pre-school Child Care Institutions Act (passed 18 February 1999), a rural municipality or city government will provide all children from one to seven years of age whose residence is in the administrative territory of the given rural municipality or city and whose parents so wish, the opportunity to attend a childcare institution in the catchment area.

In 2008, €14.4 million was budgeted for the programme, €9.6 million of which was distributed to local governments (75 million EEK for improving the educational environment and €4.8 million for wages if the minimum wage of a kindergarten teacher who had a higher education was equal to a municipal junior school teacher's minimum wage and the minimum wage of a teacher with vocational education was equal to at least 85 per cent of the junior pedagogue's minimum wage); €4.8 million was project-based support for local governments that started building a new kindergarten facility or to renovate the existing building so that new kindergarten places were developed. Before halting the programme, five kindergartens were built with state support (Peterson 2010). Nevertheless, despite the fact that the programme was frozen in 2009, it was still possible to increase the number of kindergarten places because local governments can get support for this activity from structural funds. However, since the crisis severely hit the revenue base of local governments, it has been difficult to provide the necessary self-financing and therefore the goal has not been reached. The issue has been on the media agenda because of the government's decision to halt the programme, but so far no steps have been taken to restart it.

Concerning education, given that pupil/teacher ratios and average class sizes were at relatively low levels before the crisis in Latvia and Lithuania (but not so in Estonia, see Table 3.13) caused by declining birth rates, it is more difficult to find arguments that the employment cuts worsened the situation in education. The other issue concerns the wages of teachers. Similarly, in the health sector the number of hospital beds per 100,000 inhabitants in Estonia was at the level of other EU countries, while Latvia and Lithuania exceeded it considerably. Thus, one may find some arguments here that there was indeed room for consolidation in the Latvian health-care sector without threatening the provision of health care at the required level.

Table 3.13 Education and health sector indicators, Baltic states, 2006 and 2009

Country	Beds per 100,000 inhabitants		Ratio of students to teachers, ISCED 1–3		Average class size, ISCED 1		Average class size, ISCED 2	
	2006	2009	2006	2009	2006	2009	2006	2009
Estonia	565.3	550.9	13.3	16.3	19.3	18.1	23.1	20.1
Latvia	690.7	543.9	11.2	10.6	14.8	15.1	18.0	16.3
Lithuania	758.6	682.4	9.0	8.0	14.8	14.9	21.7	20.6
Hungary	792.1	715.0	10.9	11.4	20.0	20.7	21.4	21.7
Poland	647.5	665.0	12.1	11.4	20.1	18.7	24.7	23.3
France	704.7	660.5	14.2	14.6	22.5	22.7	24.3	24.5
Germany	829.1	822.9	17.2	16.6	22.1	21.7	24.7	24.7
UK	356.8	330.2	15.6	15.8	24.5	24.5	22.4	19.6

Source: Eurostat.

The Latvian government carried out significant reorganization in health care, with large-scale job losses, reduced services and merging institutions. The government decided to close several hospitals and closed about a hundred schools, with 2,400 teachers laid off (thereby bringing the pupil/teacher ratio to more reasonable levels: Aslund and Dombrovskis 2011).[8] The number of civil servants was reduced by 8,000 and half of the 75 state agencies were closed down. It was easier to implement administrative reforms as most people supported the idea of fewer bureaucrats. The positive impact of the austerity measures was that because the cuts needed to be selective, the macroeconomic crisis accelerated reforms, for example, in health care, education (too many institutions of higher learning) and local government (ibid.). The very difficult situation in Latvia made it easier to undertake reforms, some of which, like the one pertaining to local government, have still not been undertaken in Estonia for political reasons.

8. CASE STUDIES

8.1 Case Study 1: Changes in the Accessibility of Health-care Services as a Result of the Crisis

8.1.1 Introduction

The Estonian health-care system has undergone significant changes since independence in 1991. In 1990, Estonia had about 120 hospitals with about 14,000 acute care beds. In the early 1990s, the main aim of the health sector reform was to move away from a Semashko-type – a radically supplier-oriented system financed by the state budget and controlled by the state by central planning, with no private suppliers – health-care system to a decentralized and market-forces-driven system. During the second half of the 1990s the changes were more incremental. The legal environment was rearranged to increase efficiency and transparency. An important milestone in hospital sector reform was the development of the Hospital Master Plan 2015 (adopted in 2003) to make projections about future hospital capacity. The plan suggested that the number of acute in-patient beds be reduced by two-thirds and that acute in-patient care be concentrated in larger hospitals, decreasing the total number of hospitals through mergers and other types of restructuring, by three-quarters (from 68 to 15[9]) by 2015 (Habicht et al. 2006).

According to the Health Care Services Organization Act that entered into force in 2001, all public hospitals had to be incorporated in private law as foundations or joint-stock companies. As a result, all public hospitals began to act under private law, having full managerial rights over assets and access to financial markets, but at the same time giving them full residual claimant status. In addition, the Estonian Health Insurance Fund (EHIF) was established through special legislation as a public independent legal entity with seven regional departments and replaced the previous system of regional and central sickness funds (EHIF 2011).

Today, Estonian health insurance is based on social insurance and the system relies on the principle of solidarity: the EHIF covers the cost of health services required in case of illness regardless of the amount of social contributions paid. The Fund also uses the social contributions paid by the working population to cover the cost of health services provided to persons with no employment income. For the health services provided to the persons benefiting from insurance cover, the EHIF pays the health-care institution on the basis of the reference price fixed by the government and indicated in the Fund's list of health services (ibid.).

Nevertheless, the implementation of health sector reform has been prolonged and therefore criticized. The National Audit Office 2010 audit concludes that the active treatment hospital network set out in the hospital network development plan is too big and unsustainable, because not all hospitals will have enough patients, qualified doctors or money for hospital improvements in the future. The audit criticizes the ministry, saying that the lack of clear decisions by the Minister of Social Affairs on the hospital network required has damaged the interests of the state as well as hospital managers (National Audit Office 2010). In the overview of the use and preservation of state assets in 2010, the National Audit Office emphasizes that although the Minister of Social Affairs admitted at the time that the hospital network is not optimal or sustainable in the use of both human and financial resources, the minister has not taken any significant steps to reform the hospital network after the audit. The government's action programme for 2011–15 approved in spring 2011 does not mention reforming the hospital network at all. The main conclusion is that the hospital network needs reform and the GP system needs development (National Audit Office 2011).

8.1.2 Study design

When designing the case study, the research team used data from the EHIF, interviews and media analysis. Interviews[10] were done with representatives of the following institutions: the EHIF as an institution responsible for funding decisions in the health-care sector; the Estonian Hospitals' Association as the union established for representing common interests in health-care matters and arranging cooperation between hospitals;[11] and one large and two smaller hospitals[12] to cover the hospitals' side as well.

Interview plans for the EHIF and the Estonian Hospitals' Association were more general than those for hospitals. In the former the questions were asked at societal level; in the latter the focus was on measures implemented by hospitals to cope with the negative effects of the crisis. The questions asked focused on the following issues: the most important measures taken during the crisis (2009–11), reasons why those measures were chosen and which other alternatives were considered and whether it would have been possible to achieve the necessary cost savings more effectively with other measures.

8.1.3 Decreasing the amount of services provided

To cope with the negative effects of the crisis, the EHIF made the following decisions:

- in March 2009 the EHIF increased the maximum allowed duration of waiting time for ambulatory specialized medical care (excluding day-care surgery) from four to six weeks (the four-week period had been stable from 2002 when the time limit was first set);
- in 2009 the quantity of planned stationary services (for example, operations that can be planned for a longer period ahead) was decreased by 4 per cent; and
- in 2010 the reference price of all health-care services was decreased by 6 per cent.

Hannes Danilov, the head of the EHIF, commented that in the difficult budgetary situation the first measure was necessary to keep the level of services at the same level: 'This year [2009] we cannot increase the number of treatment cases due to the stringent budget, but it is likely that the demand increase will continue and therefore we are forced to increase the length of waiting lists' (Board of the Estonian Health Insurance Fund 2009). The increase in the maximum allowed waiting time helped to save funds as less medical treatment was provided. According to Danilov, the second measure was used because until 2008 access to the service was rather good (waiting period was 1–1.5 months) and the decrease did not reduce accessibility considerably. Due to the development of technology and improvements in treatment methods it is increasingly possible to provide such services as ambulatory or in the form of day care. Reference prices were cut because lower costs were planned for health insurance in the state budget. In the opinion of Danilov the steps taken were the best choices when taking into account the difficult situation faced. Accessibility to health-care services decreased somewhat, but not drastically and most important health-care functions – such as emergency medical care – are at a decent level.

8.1.4 Hospitals' strategy of reducing staff costs

The changes undertaken directly influenced the revenue base of the hospitals. Hospital representatives admitted in their responses that in terms of fixed costs efficiency has been achieved long ago and there was no room to decrease those costs in order to cut costs during the recession. To some extent it was possible to do things more cheaply; however, this meant a decrease in service quality because it was more uncomfortable for the patient and more labour intensive for hospital staff. Control over the procurement and use of medical equipment was strengthened. In some hospitals, investments in construction work and repair were postponed until the recovery.

Another fairly extreme option would have been to close down less-profitable departments; however, this option was not used (at least not in hospitals included in the survey) because there was a general feeling that it would be very difficult to open them again when times got better, for several reasons (staff would leave and it would be difficult and costly to rehire and retrain good specialists; clients would get used to using the services of other service providers; EHIF contracting policy is based on previous policy and therefore it would be difficult to make a fresh start).

Therefore, staff costs were the main source of cutting costs. Hospitals included in the survey used different strategies to cut staff costs. In one of the largest hospitals in Estonia there were no lay-offs. Since the base wages of the medical staff are regulated in the collective agreement signed by the government, the Estonian Hospitals' Association, the Estonian Nurses' Union and the Federation of Estonian Healthcare Professionals' Unions and in most cases minimum levels are paid (see Masso and Krillo 2011 for more details), it was not possible to decrease basic wages. Therefore, mostly bonuses were decreased. On the average, wages were reduced by 9 per cent for all employees. The hospital management of the large hospital therefore decided not to use part-time work and non-paid leave because the resulting cost savings would have been modest. In one smaller Estonian hospital wages were decreased by at least 10 per cent, mainly by cutting bonuses and minimizing overtime. To decrease the basic wage, changes in individual employment contracts were made in 2010. Therefore, the strategies used were similar to the larger hospital in this case. However, another smaller hospital laid off pension-aged staff, optimized the use of overtime and, where possible, used unpaid leave in 2010. In this hospital wages were not decreased.

8.1.5 Turnover and emigration in response

The reactions of medical staff to the budget cuts varied. According to hospital representatives, the most important trends that emerged during the recession were as follows. First, working in other medical institutions increased. The head of one smaller hospital admitted that a very important reason for the worsening of accessibility to medical services was the lack of medical staff (especially doctors) who quit on their own initiative. Second, the representative of a large hospital said that doctors who could speak Finnish started to look for jobs in Finland. This trend emerged approximately a year after the start of the recession and peaked in 2011 (for example, in this hospital approximately 2.5 per cent of doctors left to work in Finland). Unfortunately, there are no national-level data available to enable us to estimate how many Estonian doctors have emigrated during the recession.

8.1.6 Decreases in service accessibility

The number of persons on the waiting list for doctors' appointments has increased considerably in recent years, even before the crisis (see Table 3.14). This applies to all kinds of services: specialized medical care, health care and dental care. During the 2005–11 period, the number of persons on waiting lists increased by almost 70 per cent. The increase was particularly high in ambulatory specialized care and ambulatory medical rehabilitation. It is important to note that in most services the trend has not reversed during the crisis, the exceptions being day-care surgery and procedures where the number of people on waiting lists decreased during the boom and has increased in recession time; and in-patient health care and orthodontia which have shown a pro-cyclical trend. In ambulatory medical rehabilitation, the number of persons on waiting lists has also

Table 3.14 Number of persons on waiting lists for medical care, Estonia, 2005–2011

	2005	2008	2009	2010	2011	Change 2005–11 %	Change 2005–07 %	Change 2008–11 %
Total	171,746	224,563	249,921	259,227	289,077	68	30	29
Specialized medical care								
Ambulatory specialized medical care	128,882	179,132	207,761	218,979	244,997	90	41	37
Day-care surgery and procedures	3,699	3,213	3,041	3,428	3,801	3	−11	18
In-patient medical treatment	12,414	12,365	11,972	9,603	9,098	−27	−28	−26
Ambulatory medical rehabilitation	2,545	3,799	3,292	4,048	5,740	126	6	51
In-patient medical rehabilitation	1,236	1,356	1,413	1,308	1,645	33	14	21
Health care								
Ambulatory health care	306	492	591	496	776	154	23	58
In-patient health care	620	992	748	715	877	41	24	−12
Dental care								
Persons with a child under 1 year or who are engaged in day-time studies	16,646	17,041	16,155	15,886	17,118	3	7	0
Orthodontia	5,398	6,173	4,948	4,764	5,025	−7	28	−19

Source: Estonian Health Insurance Fund.

Table 3.15 Number of persons on waiting lists for medical care, by reason, Estonia, 2005–2011

Reason for waiting list	2005	2008	2009	2010	2011	Change 2005–11 %
Total	171,746	224,563	249,921	259,227	289,077	*68*
Within permitted waiting period (that is, waiting no longer than permitted period)	115,023	130,825	154,372	151,310	174,888	*52*
Due to lack of financial resources*	1,347	54	1,998	1,244	2,002	*49*
Due to lack of capacity*/**	6,561	4,227	2,453	3,047	1,406	*−79*
Due to special requests of the patient (certain doctor or date of appointment)*	27,419	56,325	50,121	51,732	57,629	*110*
Due to follow-up inspection*	20,641	30,344	37,652	47,179	50,673	*145*
Other reasons*	755	2,788	3,325	4,715	2,479	*228*
Share of those who get an appointment time within the permitted waiting period	*67.0*	*58.3*	*61.8*	*58.4*	*60.5*	

Note: * Marked only if a person has waited longer than the maximum permitted waiting period; ** Lack of doctors and other staff, rooms, technical equipment and so on.

Source: Estonian Health Insurance Fund.

increased considerably during the recession compared to the period of economic growth.

The number of people who have to wait longer than the maximum period set by the EHIF has also increased during the crisis (see Table 3.15). While in 2005 two persons out of three got an appointment within the permitted waiting period (four weeks), in 2008–11 the share was about 58–60 per cent.

8.1.7 Lack of doctors leading to lower capacity to respond to demand

The number of people who had to wait longer than the maximum waiting period set by the EHIF due to financial stringency increased by 37 times during the crisis and the problem has remained relevant during the recovery period. In 2011, the EHIF carried out two inspections of local and central hospitals, focusing on the specialist areas in which waiting periods are longest. The aim of the inspections was to ascertain the reasons for long waiting times in ambulatory specialized medical care and to find solutions. The results indicate that in August the main problem was lack of capacity due to a lack of doctors and unavailability of technical equipment and rooms. The staff problems were partly caused by the holiday season but partly they were permanent. In some hospitals there were problems with a lack of specialists. This problem was highlighted in both August and October. The heads of the hospitals where there were problems with staff indicated to the EHIF that they are actively seeking doctors but it is difficult to find good specialists. Another problem emphasized by the hospitals in October was the lack of financial resources. As a result, the EHIF and hospitals started negotiations to increase funding in those specialities. Another conclusion was that, as a rule, the number of doctors' hours for which patients must pay is significantly lower than hours that are free of charge (in other words, paid by the EHIF). This is despite the fact that appointments can be obtained much more quickly if one pays (EHIF 2011).

8.1.8 Conclusion

Facing a difficult situation and the need to cut costs in order to keep the budget balanced, the EHIF decreased the quantity of planned stationary services by 4 per cent and the reference price of health-care services by 8 per cent, and also increased the maximum allowed waiting time for ambulatory specialized medical care from four to six weeks. These measures had immediate negative effects on hospital budgets because the vast bulk of their revenues comes from the EHIF.

Inevitably, these developments meant that accessibility to health-care services has worsened during the crisis. The number of persons on waiting lists and who have to wait longer than the maximum period set by the EHIF has increased. Hospitals have used various adjustment mechanisms: some have reduced staff costs by wage cuts, some by laying off personnel of pensionable age. Hospital managements admit that one effect of the crisis that has negative effects both now and during the recovery is doctors leaving to find positions elsewhere. The interviews indicate that in smaller hospitals doctors leave to work in larger hospitals and large hospitals face the situation that doctors move abroad (mainly to Nordic countries).

The question is whether better measures could have been taken to cope with the crisis. Hannes Danilov, head of the EHIF, believes that the options chosen were the best, all things considered. Hospital representatives thought that a better hospital network would have helped to alleviate outcomes. However, this would have required clear policy decisions on hospital reform. In Danilov's opinion the health-care system should be better defended against economic cycles and the state should borrow from abroad if necessary to maintain services (again, it was emphasized that all these steps require reform).

8.2 Case Study 2: Estonian Rescue Services Hit by Public Sector Adjustments

8.2.1 Introduction

In Estonia, the provision of rescue service is coordinated by the Estonian Rescue Board. Until the end of the 1990s there was a fairly widespread network of volunteers (similar to many other EU countries today) but at the beginning of the new millennium it was decided that rescue service should be provided by the state in a centralized way. In total, there are about 2,500 Rescue Board employees, 1,800 of them in rescue stations.

The crisis has hit Estonian rescue workers hard,[13] probably more than many other public service providers in Estonia. During the crisis years the budget of the Rescue Board has been cut by 20 per cent, which has had direct consequences for workers' wages and other working conditions, as well as for the quality of rescue services.

Interviews were conducted with Alo Tammsalu, deputy director general of the Estonian Rescue Board, and with Toomas Suigusaar, representative of the Estonian Rescue Sector Workers' Trade Union. The focus of the interviews was twofold: first, the effects of the crisis on Rescue Board employees; second, the effects on service quality and accessibility. An extensive media analysis was also carried out.

8.2.2 Developments during the crisis – effects on workers

On 29 June 2009, the government and the State and Local Government Workers' Trade Union Confederation (ROTAL) reached agreement to reduce the basic wage of rescue workers at all levels by 8 per cent from 1 July 2009. The negotiations between the government and ROTAL were very intense and only a couple of days before the agreement was reached (25 June) the government threatened that unless workers' representatives agreed a wage cut, 193 rescue workers would have to be laid off at the beginning of July. Fearful of redundancies, workers' representatives agreed to the demand. As a result of the agreement, the government promised not to lay off rescue workers in 2009.

Toomas Suigusaar, representative of the Rescue Workers' Trade Union, admits that during the negotiations the employer clearly had the upper hand: the decision was basically made by the management without asking the opinion of the trade union because it was clear that the budget needed to be cut. The trade union had to choose whether to accept the heavy lay-offs or cut the wages of all rescue workers by 8 per cent. Facing such pressure, the trade union decided to change the collective agreement and accept wage cuts. At that time (2009) there were only 250 trade union members working for the Rescue Board.

Basic wages were cut by 8 per cent for all employees – rescue workers as well as management and office workers. However, due to the other measures applied (analysed in detail below), the total wage decrease was on average 20–25 per cent, according to Alo Tammsalu. He said that employees whose wages were higher before the crisis experienced higher income decreases during the recession. In other words, the crisis measures were not uniform across different employee categories.

Tammsalu admitted in the interview that the management of the Rescue Board had faced a very difficult situation in 2008 when the economic downturn began. Due to the very stringent budget, at the beginning of 2009 it was decided that rescue workers could not do overtime.[14] Although workers' representatives demanded 24-hour shifts in collective agreement negotiations at the end of 2008, finally they agreed to the employer's demand that only 22 hours of a 24-hour shift would be remunerated. In 2010, 24-hour shifts were restored.[15] However, due to lack of resources the income of rescue workers did not increase. 'Since we had no money, we gave a free day for the rescue workers and each rescue worker worked a month less a year as a result', commented Tammsalu in the media.

At the beginning of the crisis, the additional remuneration and other benefits were also decreased considerably due to the lack of funds. It was decided not to use holiday bonuses other than statutory holiday pay, no Christmas bonuses were paid and the use of official cars and telephone expense payments was cut. According to Tammsalu, the 8 per cent wage cut was one of the last measures used when it was clear that the budget had to be balanced. Unlike many other state and private organizations, unpaid leave days could not be used in the Rescue Board – at least in the case of rescue workers – because it was simply not possible to close rescue stations for a couple of days a month and no extra human resources were available (overtime was not allowed).

In 2010, the wages of rescue workers remained at the same level as 2009. Negotiations between the government and employees' representatives were very intense and the final agreement for 2010 was not reached before mid-December 2009. Although at the beginning of the negotiations the Rescue Board said that it would be necessary to lay off 110 workers, finally about €1 million extra funding was found, so the number of lay-offs was decreased to 40. The lay-offs concerned mainly rescue workers and support staff (for example, repair staff), and were based on medical examinations and evaluations. In addition to lay-offs, it was decided that no new employees would be hired in positions that become vacant due to voluntary departures. Therefore, during 2010–11 the number of job positions in the Rescue Board decreased by approximately 100 (that is, 4 per cent).

Although the measures implemented were not in favour of the employees and hit their income hard, few people left the organization voluntarily. The main reason was the difficult labour market situation in general. Another interesting effect of the crisis is the 'contrariwise career system'. Since during the good times (2007–08) the wages of low-paid employees (mainly rescue workers) in the Rescue Board increased more than those of higher-paid employees, and during the crisis, on the contrary, wages fell proportionally more for those whose wages were higher and less for those at the lower end of the wage scale, office workers have begun to prefer to work as rescue workers. Tammsalu sees several further reasons for that. On the one hand, there is less responsibility, but on the other the shifts are more flexible (rescue workers currently have one 24-hour shift followed by 72 hours' leisure time in which many take a second job). Tammsalu also said that the workload of office staff is considerable and they have to do overtime without receiving extra pay.

8.2.3 Immediate effects on service provision

Wage cuts and decreases in paid working time had clear negative effects on life rescue capabilities. In autumn 2009, trade union representative Andres Reinberg commented that in many places lay-offs have led to a situation in which only three or four men respond to an emergency call instead of six men previously. According to him, four men is the minimum acceptable level to fight a fire. Tammsalu agrees with that and also admits that the decision to abolish overtime in 2009 led to a situation in which the ability to provide life rescue services was reduced.

In October 2011 it was announced that the Rescue Board would close more than 10 rescue stations because of lack of funds. There were at that time 16 rescue stations out of 82 that were not capable of providing life rescue services at all and 20 rescue stations that could do so only occasionally. Therefore, the main aim of the restructuring was to merge rescue stations to guarantee life rescue capability.

Finally, at the beginning of February 2012 the Rescue Board decided to close nine rescue stations in rural areas that did not have life rescue capabilities. It is hoped that the gap will be partially covered by volunteers (Tammsalu claims that there are more than 1,000 voluntary rescue workers in Estonia). However, he admits that state support for volunteers is weak. As always, there are losers from the changes, but according to Tammsalu, the gains should exceed the losses. As a result of the reform, the service quality for 121,000 citizens in areas with higher population density will increase and it will decrease for 20,000. As a result of the reform, the location of rescue stations will be better in accordance with demographic changes over the past decade. It is estimated that to guarantee life rescue capabilities in all rescue stations, approximately €6 million would have been needed.

Due to its lack of resources the Rescue Board does not have the funds to renew equipment. For example, while it has been agreed that every five years personal protective clothing and equipment should be renewed, during the crisis this has not been possible. Repair work and services have been cut to a minimum.

Both Tammsalu and Suigusaar said that it is agreed that all those working in rescue stations to be closed will be offered a job in other rescue stations. The 80 persons concerned will be distributed between rescue stations that remain after the reform (72 rescue stations in total). Moreover, it is likely that new employees will be needed partly because of this restructuring (to provide life rescue services, a minimum of three men have to respond) and partly because of the educational reform. Since the beginning of 2012, at least a general secondary education has been needed to work for the Rescue Board and new professional requirements have been implemented. This is the final stage of the training reform that has lasted about ten years.

8.2.4 Service provision during the crisis

Table 3.16 reports the number of deaths due to fire. As can be seen, until 2010 in Estonia the number of deaths per 100,000 inhabitants due to fire decreased significantly. Within a five-year period (from 2006 to 2010) the death rate decreased by about 2.6 times in Estonia, much more than in Latvia, Lithuania and Finland. However, in 2010–11 we can see a slight increase in the death rate.

8.2.5 Conclusion

The difficult decisions made during the crisis in the Estonian rescue services have not been easy for the management. From 2008 to 2011 the

Table 3.16 *Number of deaths due to fire in Estonia and neighbouring countries, 2006–2011*

Year	Number of deaths				Deaths by 100,000 inhabitants			
	Estonia	Latvia	Lithuania	Finland	Estonia	Latvia	Lithuania	Finland
2006	164	207	297	90	12.2	10.2	8.9	2.3
2007	132	163	270	102	9.8	9.0	8.6	1.7
2008	89	145	203	104	6.6	7.1	7.9	1.9
2009	63	148	233	80	4.7	6.4	6.6	2.0
2010	69	122	137	67	5.1	6.5	7.0	1.5
2011	73	207	297	90	5.4	5.5	4.2	1.2

Source: Estonian Rescue Board.

budget of the Rescue Board was cut by 20 per cent, resulting in lay-offs, wage cuts, unpaid overtime and restructuring of rescue stations. The number of rescue workers was also cut by voluntary departures and some rescue stations now have only three employees or fewer. Therefore, large-scale reform is in process to restructure the whole system so that life rescue capability is secured.

One side-effect of the tensions was an increase in unionization. While in spring 2009 there were 250 trade union members, at the beginning of October the number was already 700 and it increased to more than 1,000 by 2011. According to the trade union representatives, the main reason for increased unionization was the heightened sense of insecurity.

Regarding the latest trends, in September 2011 the government announced that it had found an extra €2.1 million (€1.4 million for wages and €0.7 million for other spending, such as equipment). This will be used to pay for overtime work, redundancy payments for rescue workers whose rescue stations will be closed and do not want a job in other rescue stations and to compensate those who lose out as a result of the reform.[16]

Tammsalu admits that today the situation is more difficult from the Rescue Board side because the government has announced that its budget will not be increased until at least 2016. The problem is particularly topical because of the recent sharp increase in fuel prices. Since fuel consumption is an important part of Rescue Board costs, the administration must find ways of cutting spending. Dissatisfaction among employees is increasing and it is likely that the voluntary departure rate will increase as the economy recovers. On the negative side, Tammsalu says that whereas the 2009 wage cuts applied to all rescue sector workers uniformly, the wage increase will apply to rescue workers, which means that the inequalities within the Rescue Board will rise and this may cause tensions. Currently, the average wage of rescue workers is €600–700 (national average wage was about €860 in Estonia in the second quarter of 2011).

The crisis has clearly had a negative impact on both Rescue Board workers and the quantity and quality of service. Tammsalu concludes: 'We did not have scope to "let out air" from our budget. Before this 20 per cent decrease we already had to work very efficiently. Therefore, we [the management of the Rescue Board] had no other choice but to cut services'.

Looking back at developments in 2009–11, the question is, what could have been done differently? Suigusaar, the trade union representative, thinks that the Rescue Board should have been firmer during the crisis. In his opinion political considerations exert too much influence, which creates destabilization and fosters tensions. Tammsalu, the employer's representative, sees developments in recent years as partly forced, but still necessary to guarantee that the rescue system develops to match demographic trends. On the positive side he finds that much has been achieved in terms of preventive measures, even during the crisis. He sees preventive work and monitoring as the main mechanisms helping to save funds to ensure an adequate response.

9. CONCLUSIONS AND POLICY ISSUES

Estonia's fiscal situation has generally been regarded as relatively healthy due to the limited sovereign debt burden and strong commitment to a balanced budget, thus there is no direct need to consolidate public sector expenditure to cope with a debt crisis. Estonia has had a relatively small public sector, due to the dominance of right-wing parties in government and relatively low revenues. The Estonian public sector underwent adjustment during the early crisis (2009–10), mostly to address the Maastricht criteria and make it possible for Estonia to join the Eurozone. While these adjustments were more mechanical and did not entail structural changes, naturally the crisis has led to further discussions on the sustainability of public finances and structural changes. Due to the limited revenue increase it is hard to meet the growing wage claims due to the recovery in the private sector. This chapter outlines a number of negative effects that the Baltic states have experienced during the crisis, such as the decrease in public sector wages, labour mobility to the private sector, and migration abroad (especially among health sector employees). The case studies of rescue workers and health care further illustrate the negative effects of fiscal consolidation.

In terms of social dialogue, against a background of relatively low general union density in the public sector unionization has increased, although the adjustments during the crisis demonstrate trade union weakness. As indicated by surveys and our case studies, trade unions generally just gave in to pressure from the government to introduce austerity measures. Wage cuts did not lead to large-scale protests, but in the course of the recovery dissatisfaction has been increasing (teachers' strike in March 2012). The breakdown of tripartite dialogue due to the employers' representatives leaving the board of the Unemployment Insurance Fund and the Health Insurance Fund (the disagreements were about the unemployment insurance contribution and administration of the reserves of the two funds) also indicates a failure of tripartite dialogue (Osila 2012). We can see some indications of increasing union density (as in rescue services), thus the question remains whether in the future we shall see more changes in collective labour relations in the public sector.

Compared to Latvia and Lithuania, the Estonian public sector was probably in a better situation due to previous reforms. Nevertheless, in several areas (rescue sector, health care, education) stakeholders argued that the unfinished structural reforms were the reason for the more painful adjustment during the crisis and must be addressed if Estonia is to solve its challenges. However, this depends very much on political will.

NOTES

1. This may bear some resemblance to the 'debt intolerance' phenomenon noted by Reinhart et al. (2003).
2. The funding for health care also decreased in Lithuania and uncovered existing inefficiencies. The health-care system was streamlined with job cuts among nurses (Blaziene 2011). The health sector was in fact too large, for example, in terms of hospital beds per population, and consequently also underfunded.
3. That argument is based on the fact that while according to Fabiani et al. (2011) cutting flexible wages was the major adjustment strategy for 9.8 per cent of surveyed European firms, cutting base wages was only important for 1.2 per cent of firms, with Estonia the only country where cutting base wages was the main adjustment strategy for a substantial number of firms (14 per cent of all firms).
4. Public sector was defined in his study as all organizations where central governments or local governments owned more than 50 per cent of the share capital.
5. Riigi-ja Omavalitsuse Töötajate Ametiühingute Liit (Confederation of Trade Unions of the State and Self-Government Institution Workers).
6. The basic monthly wages are applied as a reference to determine the wages of public sector employees such as tutors, social workers, librarians and cultural workers.
7. We have excluded dentists as people mostly have to pay for dental services themselves. However, in the case of dentists similar tendencies can be observed (the situation improved until 2009 and worsened in 2010).
8. In Latvia, public financing of health care decreased by 21 per cent in 2009, which, may increase household spending on health care. There have been some criticisms of the cutbacks, but it is an open question what their effects will be (Curkina 2009).
9. Later it was increased to 19.
10. A telephone interview was conducted with a representative of the Estonian Hospitals'

Association. The head of the EHIF, Mr Hannes Danilov, and representatives of the hospitals (one large and two smaller) preferred to provide answers in written form.
11. The Estonian Doctors' Association as the union representing the rights of doctors was also asked to participate in the study, but did not respond.
12. The large hospital is one of the biggest in Estonia, while one of the smaller hospitals participating in the study is located in southern and the other in northern Estonia.
13. 'Rescue workers' means those directly involved in rescuing people, not Rescue Board employees in general.
14. In Estonia, rescue workers are subject to the total working-time regulation. According to the Employment Contracts Act, in calculating total working time, overtime means work exceeding the agreed working time at the end of the calculation period.
15. Under Estonian legislation, the employer must provide a 30-minute break for every eight hours worked, which is not calculated as part of working time. Since rescue workers cannot leave the scene during the break, it was agreed that rest time would be calculated as part of working time.
16. As a result of the reform, first-level commands will be closed and men will move to second- and third-level commands. As a result, their wages will increase.

REFERENCES

Adamchik, V.A. and A.S. Bedi (2000), 'Wage differentials between the public and the private sectors: evidence from an economy in transition', *Labour Economics*, **7**, 203–24.

Anspal, S., L. Kraut and T. Rõõm (2010), *Sooline palgalõhe Eestis: empiiriline analüüs*, Research report, Eesti Rakendusuuringute Keskus CentAR, Poliitikauuringute Keskus PRAXIS, Sotsiaalministeerium.

Aslund, A. and V. Dombrovskis (2011), 'How Latvia came through the financial crisis', Special Report, Peterson Institute for International Economics, Georgetown University.

Avaliku teenistuse aastaraamat 2010 (2011), Tallinn: Rahandusministeerium. Available at: http://www.avalikteenistus.ee/?id=11199 (accessed 14 November 2011).

Blaziene, I. (2009a), 'Unions organise protest actions against cuts in the public sector pay', European Industrial Relations Observatory. Available at: http://www.eurofound.europa.eu/eiro/2009/07/articles/lt0907029i.htm (accessed 14 November 2011).

Blaziene, I. (2009b), 'Trade union hunger strike averts public sector pay cut', European Industrial Relations Observatory. Available at: http://www.eurofound.europa.eu/eiro/2009/10/articles/lt0910019i.htm (accessed 14 November 2011).

Blaziene, I. (2009c), 'National agreement to combat economic downturn finally signed', European Industrial Relations Observatory. Available at: http://www.eurofound.europa.eu/eiro/2009/11/articles/lt0911019i.htm.

Blaziene, I. (2011), 'Lithuania: industrial relations in the health care sector', European Industrial Relations Observatory. Available at: http://www.eurofound.europa.eu/eiro/studies/tn1008022s/lt1008029q.htm.

Board of the Estonian Health Insurance Fund (2009), Press release. Available at: http://www.haigekassa.ee/haigekassa/uudised?news=haigekassa-noukogus-kinnitati.

Curkina, I. (2009), 'Trade union protests against education cuts and reforms', European Industrial Relations Observatory. Available at: http://www.eurofound.europa.eu/eiro/2009/08/articles/lv0908029i.htm.
Curkina, I. (2011), 'Latvia: Representativeness study of the European social partner organisations – Public administration sector'. Available at: http://www.eurofound.europa.eu/eiro/studies/tn0912027s/lv0912029q.htm.
Eamets, R. (2011), 'Employment, labour market flexibility and the economic crises in the Baltic States', in *Estonian Human Development Report 2010/2011*, Tallinn: Estonian Cooperation Assembly, pp. 74–81.
Estonian Health Insurance Fund (EHIF) (2011), 'Availability of health care services in local and central hospitals in August 2011'. Available at: http://www.haigekassa.ee/haigekassa/uudised?news=tervishoiuteenuste-kattesaada.
EWCO (2010), *Remuneration of Public Sector Employees 10-09-2010*. Available at: http://www.eurofound.europa.eu/ewco/2010/05/LT1005019I.htm.
Fabiani, S., A. Lamo, J. Messina and T. Rõõm (2011), 'Firm adjustment during the times of crises', paper presented at the 23rd Annual EALE Conference, Cyprus, 22–24 September. Available at: http://www.eale.nl/Conference2011/Programme/papers%20sessie%20B/add159466_FHG2LIoH4K.pdf (accessed 10 November 2011).
Fabrizio, S. and A. Mody (2008), 'Breaking the impediments to budgetary reforms: evidence from Europe', IMF Working Paper No. 08/82, Washington, DC.
Glassner, V. (2010), 'The public sector in the crisis', ETUI Working Paper 2010.07, European Trade Union Institute, Brussels.
Habicht, T., A. Aaviksoo and A. Koppel (2006), 'Hospital sector reform in Estonia', PRAXIS 2006. Available at: http://rahvatervis.ut.ee/bitstream/1/1143/1/Praxis2006.pdf.
Kallaste, E., M. Karu, L. Kraut and P. Turk (2010), *Sooline palgalõhe Eestis: juhtumite uuringud*, Research report, Eesti Rakendusuuringute Keksus CentAR, Poliitikauuringute Keskus PRAXIS, Sotsiaalministeerium. Available at: http://www.sm.ee/fileadmin/meedia/Dokumendid/Sotsiaalvaldkond/kogumik/3_raport.pdf.
Kattai, R., A. Kangur, T. Liiv and M. Randveer (2003), 'Automatic fiscal stabilisers in Estonia: the impact of economic fluctuations on the general government budget balance', Bank of Estonia Working Paper No. 11/2003, Tallinn.
Kuokštis, V. and R. Vilpišauskas (2010), 'Economic adjustment to the crises in the Baltic states in comparative perspective', Vilnius University, mimeo.
Leping, K.-O. (2005), 'Public–private sector wage differential in Estonia – evidence from quintile regression', Faculty of Economics and Business Administration Working Paper No. 39, University of Tartu.
Masso, J. and R. Eamets (2007), 'Macro-level labour market flexibility in the Baltic States', in T. Paas and R. Eamets (eds), *Labour Market Flexibility, Flexicurity and Employment: Lessons of the Baltic States*, Hauppauge, NY: Nova Science, pp. 101–42.
Masso, J. and K. Krillo (2011), 'Mixed adjustment forms and inequality effectts in Estonia, Latvia and Lithuania', in D. Vaughan-Whitehead (ed.), *Work Inequalities in the Crises: Evidence from Europe*, Cheltenham, UK and Northampton, MA, USA: Edward Elgar and Geneva: ILO, pp. 38–102.
National Audit Office (2010), *Sustainability of the Hospital Network* (in Estonian), Tallinn: National Audit Office of Estonia.

National Audit Office (2011), *Overview of the Use and Preservation of State Assets in 2011*, Auditor General's summary of observations made in the year, Tallinn: National Audit Office of Estonia.

OECD (2009), *OECD Economic Surveys: Estonia*, Paris: OECD.

OECD (2011a), *The Call for Innovative and Open Government. An Overview of Country Initiatives*. Available at: http://dx.doi.org/10.1787/9789264107052-en.

OECD (2011b), *Restoring Public Finances*, Special Issue of the OECD *Journal on Budgeting*, Vol. 2011/2, Paris: OECD.

OECD (2011c), *Government at a Glance 2011. Country Note: Estonia*, Paris: OECD.

Osila, L. (2011), 'Estonia: representativeness of the European social partners' organizations – public administration sector'. Available at: http://www.eurofound.europa.eu/eiro/studies/tn0912027s/ee0912029q.htm (accessed 19 October 2012).

Osila, L. (2012) 'Government refuses to reduce unemployment insurance premiums', European Industrial Relations Observatory. Available at: http://www.eurofound.europa.eu/eiro/2011/12/articles/ee1112019i.htm.

Osila, L. and K. Nurmela (2011), 'Estonia: industrial relations in the health care sector'. Available at: http://www.eurofound.europa.eu/eiro/studies/tn1008022s/ee1008029q.htm.

Peterson, T. (2010), 'The programme "A kindergarten place for every child" was halted as a result of the economic crisis' (in Estonian), *Õpetajate Leht*, 30 April: 4. Available at: http://www.opleht.ee/?archive_mode=article&articleid=3470.

Philips, K. and D. Pavlov (2010), 'Estonia', in A. Platonova and G. Urso (eds), *Part 1: Migration and the Labour Markets in the European Union (2000–2009)*, Brussels: IOM, pp. 93–103.

Praxis (2011), *Eesti sotsiaalkindlustussüsteemi jätkusuutliku rahastamise võimalused* (The possibilities to sustainably finance the Estonian social insurance system (Eesti sotsiaalkindlustussüsteemi jätkusuutliku rahastamise võimalused), Tallinn: Praxis.

Praxis, University of Tartu (2011) State and Local Government Authorities' Industrial Relations' Study. Available at: http://www.sm.ee/fileadmin/meedia/Dokumendid/Toovaldkond/uuringud/Kollektiivsete_töösuhete_uuring_analyysiraport.pdf (in Estonian) (accessed 19 October 2012).

Rahandusministeerium (2012), '2012. aasta kevadine majandusprognoos'. Available at: http://www.fin.ee/?id=263.

Reinhart, C., K.S. Rogoff and M.A. Savastano (2003), 'Debt intolerance', *Brookings Papers on Economic Activity*, **34** (1): 1–74.

Staehr, K. (2010), 'The global financial crisis and public finances in the new EU countries from Central and Eastern Europe', Bank of Estonia Working Paper No. 2/2010, Tallinn.

Statistics Estonia (2010), *Yearbook 2010*, Tallinn: Statistics Estonia.

4. Croatia: Public sector adaptation and its impact on working conditions

Vojmir Franičević and Teo Matković

1. INTRODUCTION

Croatia's public sector is the focus of public debate and confrontation. Two arguments dominate public debate: first, there is an overgrown but inefficient state (see Jafarov and Gunnarsson 2008; Bađun et al. 2011); second, there is overemployment in the public sector, coupled with advantages over private sector workers with regard to working conditions. The fact that the public sector is highly vulnerable, but hard to reform became clear with the recession starting in 2008. So far, however, stability has prevailed in the public sector, with modest employment adjustments, minor changes in working conditions and wage freeze but no major cuts. This outcome is due primarily to the particular political and social context, and to a lesser extent to the prevailing economic conditions (a stable banking system and relatively low fiscal deficit at the start of the recession, allowing for public debt increase). However, with worsening economic performance (including Croatia's main trading partners) in 2012, after zero growth in 2011, stability and moderate adjustments will be much harder to sustain.

This chapter considers only general government sector employment until June 2012. It is organized as follows. Section 2 deals with the public sector's size, structure and dynamics. Section 3 covers public sector structural reforms and adjustment policies, as well as crisis dialogue. Section 4 deals with the effects of crisis adjustments on public sector working conditions. Section 5 presents two case studies to illustrate adjustments in secondary education (Case Study 1), and conflicts and dialogue concerning public sector wage adjustments in the economic and political context of the period (Case Study 2). In the concluding section we discuss forthcoming challenges.

2. PUBLIC SECTOR: SIZE, STRUCTURE AND DYNAMICS

Croatia's public sector comprises general government and state-owned companies. The latter are a matter of great concern, but will not be dealt with here. General government includes central government (ministries, offices, state agencies and other budgetary organizations and extra-budgetary funds, including the bulk of health care and education) and local (429 municipalities, 126 cities and 21 counties) entities.[1]

We shall focus on general government and institutions that depend on it. Inside that 'core', we differentiate between public services and public administration. This is due to their different regulatory treatment and separate collective bargaining, but also differences in dynamics and the challenges they are facing.

A legacy of the late 1990s' expansion, general government expenditures reached 48.8 per cent of GDP in 1999 (EBRD data). After efforts at fiscal stabilization, the early 2000s brought fairly stable general government revenues and expenditures relative to GDP, with a decreasing negative fiscal balance, primarily due to increasing revenues from persistent growth. However, from 2009, due to the recession, the fiscal deficit has been increasing, as has public debt as a proportion of GDP (Table 4.1). Issues of fiscal stability and public sector viability are coming to the fore, particularly if high foreign debt is also taken into account. With negative trends continuing (and forecasts expect a fall in GDP in 2012 by about 1.5 per cent) reducing public sector employment and the wage bill is again the preferred policy course.

2.1 Size and Structure of Public Sector Employment

Due to the lack of a functional state employment register, in what follows we resort mainly to Labour Force Survey (LFS) data (Figure 4.1). Since 2000, the total number of employees increased steadily until 2008, while the share of employees in state-owned organizations declined steadily, from 64 per cent in 1997 to 37 per cent in 2008. However, total employment in the general government sector (GGS) remained stable at about 250–260 thousand.[2] A modest decline in the GGS share in waged employment from 25 per cent in 2000 to 20 per cent in 2008 was due to employment growth in the private sector. The recession swept away about 8 per cent of private sector waged employment in 2009 and 2010, while the core public sector employment numbers remained stable, leading to a rebound in the share of employees in the public sector.

The three core general government sectors maintained a fairly steady

Table 4.1 Selected macroeconomic data, Croatia, 2005–2011

	2005	2006	2007	2008	2009	2010	2011
GDP change rate	4.3	4.9	5.1	2.1	–6.9	–1.4	0.0
Consolidated general government expenditure (as a percentage of GDP)	41.1	40.1	41.0	40.1	42.2	42.3	41.3
Consolidated general government fiscal balance, (as a percentage of GDP)	–3.5	–3.4	–3.0	–2.1	–4.6	–5.4	–5.4
Public debt (as a percentage of GDP)*	38.2	35.4	32.9	29.3	35.8	42.1	46.7
With government guaranteed debt	45.5	42.9	41.3	42.3	51.3	60.3	64.6
Foreign debt (as a percentage of GDP)	72.1	74.8	77.7	85.0	101.0	103.6	101.8
Unemployment rate – ILO	12.7	11.2	9.6	8.4	9.1	11.8	13.5
Unemployment rate – administrative	17.9	16.6	14.9	13.2	14.9	17.4	17.8
Public sector wage bill as a percentage of GDP (general state)	10.0	9.7	9.8	9.8	10.7	10.7	10.7

Note: * Government Finance Statistics (GFS) 2001 including debt to pensioners.

Sources: Based on Croatian Bureau of Statistics (CBS), Croatian National Bank (CNB) and Ministry of Finance data (as of June 2012).

number of employees throughout the period. The public administration and defence workforce had declined from 114,000 to 98,000 in 1997–10, but the number of employees in central government administration remained stable at about 16,000 persons, and on average another 16,000 were employed in local administration. Employment decline was mainly due to the demobilization in the early 2000s of the large military force built up during the 1990s' war. The number of public employees in education had increased from 72,000 to 85,000, particularly in tertiary education. Private institutions and the education workforce increased from 3 to 5 per cent during the period. Starting at about 83,000 in 1997–98, public employment in the health and welfare sector dropped by about 10,000 employees in the late 1990s, while the share of private employment in the sector increased from 6 per cent in 1997–98 to 15 per cent in 2009–10. After 2000, the number of public employees in the health-care system was

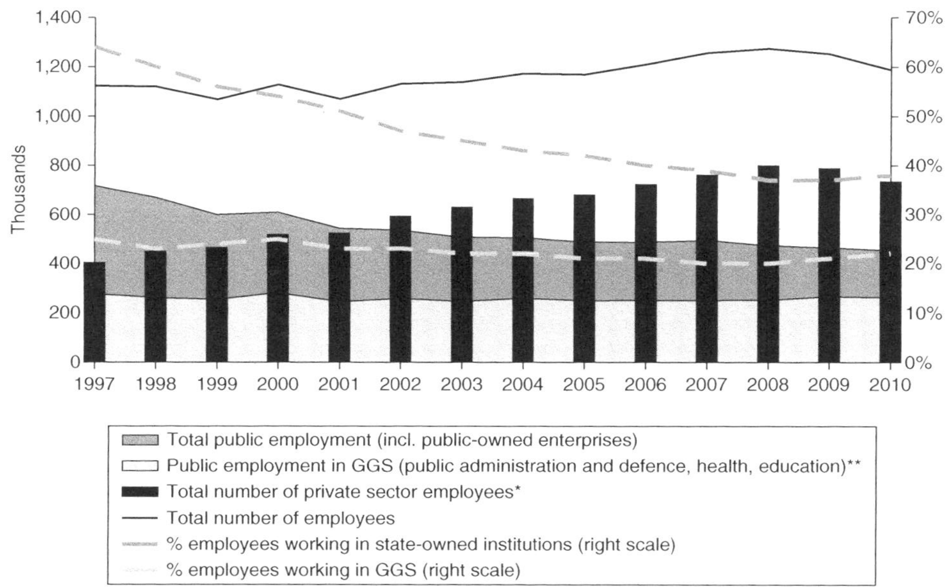

Note: * Includes employees in companies in process of privatization; this segment declined in number from 57,000 in 1997 to 6,000 in 2010.
** The number is lower than that provided by the LABORSTA estimate, as the private sector workforce in the health and education sector is not included here.

Source: LFS.

Figure 4.1 Persons in waged employment, by sector of ownership, and in general government sector, Croatia, 1997–2010

stable at about 71,000, and there was considerable expansion just as the recession was gaining ground, growing to 81,000 in 2009–10.

As for the educational structure of the public sector, the most marked change involved upgrading. While the share of tertiary educated employees increased from 13 to 15 per cent in the private sector, in all three general government sectors the level is considerably higher and upgrading faster. The educational structure improved most in public administration and defence (from 25 to 37 per cent), while in health and education the upgrading was more modest (from 72 to 77 per cent and from 33 to 35 per cent, respectively) and the improvements took place in 2009–10, coinciding with the crisis.

With regard to the *age structure*, the general government workforce has aged considerably between 1998 and 2010. The mean age of employees has increased. Ageing was least evident in education (4.6 years), as the workforce was fairly old in the first place and there was a major expansion during the decade. In health and welfare the average age rose by 5.9 years. Persons employed in public administration and defence in the mid-1990s were as young as those in the private sector. However, as the army was downsized, the average age increased by 8.0 years in only 12 years.

With regard to the gender structure, in 2010 women made up about 66 per cent of the core public sector workforce, up from about 60 per cent at the turn of the century. This is substantially higher than in the private sector, where the share of women declined from 48 per cent in the late 1990s to 43 per cent in the mid-2000s, and has remained at that level since. There is variation between sectors. In health and welfare, about four-fifths of employees are female. In education, the process of feminization continued throughout the period. Pre-school and primary education is overwhelmingly feminized. The public administration and defence sectors used to employ more males than females, but parity was reached by the reduction of the armed forces, feminization of the judiciary (70 per cent) and compulsory insurance (77 per cent). Evidently, adjustments in the public sector are affecting women disproportionally.

3. PUBLIC SECTOR STRUCTURAL REFORMS AND CRISIS ADJUSTMENTS

3.1 Structural Reforms: Under the Impact of International Financial Institutions (IFIs) and Future EU Membership

Several IFI-inspired public sector reforms were enacted in the 1990s (for example, in the health system in 1993 and in the pension system in 1999), but in the 2000s it was the Europeanization process that became most influential. IFI influence has remained strong, and mainly complementary to EU accession demands. While paper reformism produced a large number of strategies, as well as state agencies (some barely functional), the reformist efforts suffered from limited capacities to enforce and monitor changes. Despite this, in the process, the public sector landscape and rules have changed in many respects. The impact of reforms on public sector employment and working conditions is mainly invisible from aggregate data, but many employees have experienced substantive changes in their job, with regard to content, skill demands and intensity.

3.1.1 Public administration between delayed core reforms and outsourcing at the periphery

During the 2000s, the public administration was the focus of reform efforts. The 2001 Law on State Civil Servants and Employees, in an effort at modernization, replaced 'the former career system . . . with classification according to job complexity' (Koprić 2009: 12) with the intention of introducing human resource management through new payroll and personnel systems. However, even a decade later 'the current reward system remains fragmented and too compressed to provide performance incentives to staff' (World Bank 2009), while neither a public sector employment registry nor a new Law on Public Administration Salaries is in place.

Throughout the 2000s reform of the pay system was particularly high on the IFIs' agenda. Despite the first draft of the new wage law written in 2005, it was submitted to the parliament only in 2008, and after the first reading it has never returned. Most controversial (and calling forth a protest petition from the public administration unions in 2008) was the change from pay based on tenure to pay based on efficiency and quality of work, in relation to measured performance and grading. While grading was introduced in public administration in 2001 its impact on promotion and pay has remained very limited. Grading is still being applied as a formality – high grades prevail and unsatisfactory ones were below 1 per cent in 1995–2000 and almost non-existent in 2002–05 (Ratković 2010).

Efficiency-led policies are focused on cost cutting, including privatization and outsourcing (Box 4.1). They have been applied unevenly and hesitantly, often contested by unions due to numerous irregularities. However, it seems that the new government will intensify the application of such practices with regard to health, education, prisons and the like.

3.1.2 Health care: reforms focused on overspending

The health sector that developed in the 1990s was characterized by centralization and 'dirigiste' privatization of primary health care (Box 4.2)

BOX 4.1 OUTSOURCING IN PUBLIC ADMINISTRATION: BOTH REFORM AND CRISIS ADJUSTMENT POLICY, CROATIA

Outsourcing peripheral activities in public administration is among the World Bank's favourite cost-cutting strategies. The process started in the early 2000s as a reform measure, but became part of the government's anti-recession policies (2010 Economic Recovery Plan). The government's December 2010 report shows that most ministries and other government bodies either fully or partially outsourced auxiliary activities: mainly cleaning, food and drink, security and maintenance. Also, jobs in accounting and IT were at risk (interview with Petar[3] from SDLSN union – trade union of state and local government employees). While the total number of affected civil employees in 2010 was not given, there were still 1,725 to be replaced by outsourcing with demands that the process 'be continued'. An SDLSN document (November 2010) says that there are '2,794 employees whose jobs in state bodies the government intends to ... subcontract'. However, the law so far puts a ceiling on expenditure on such services at 2 per cent of the institutions' wage bill. By the beginning of 2011, the SDLSN was campaigning for changes in the Law on Civil Servants in order to protect cleaning jobs from being wiped out and subcontracted to private firms.

Working conditions in most cases of subcontracting activities 'have worsened' and rights 'decreased' (Petar). Nowadays, he adds: 'this is mostly a completed process'. He mentioned a case of outsourcing in one ministry in 2003, which the union reported to the state attorney under suspicion of corruption due to the 'extremely detrimental contract' that was signed (working rights were decreased and about half the workers whom the contractor 'inherited' were dismissed). The media often reports on contracts given to 'connected persons' or politicians'/political party cronies. Petar also reported on a good-practice model at the Ministry of Defence when a state-owned firm was established to which in-house activities (cleaning, catering and so on) were subcontracted and took over hundreds of redundant employees. A collective agreement was signed with the firm.

While scope for further outsourcing of 'typical' occupations in public administration is limited, it seems that much more is to be expected, particularly in the health sector.

BOX 4.2 PRIMARY CARE DOCTORS: INCREASED PRESSURE AND UNCERTAINTY, CROATIA

Substantial primary care reform in the 1990s forced a large number of doctors and nurses into private practice but existentially dependent on public financing through contracts with HZZO (public insurer). Most remained located in the health centres where they were employed before, leasing the premises. Some work on their own premises and some engage in additional private services – for example, simple surgery and diagnostics, as Boris does. With the 2010 reform, doctors became concessionaries (at county level a fixed number of concessions is offered – and paid to local government).

The 2010 reform offered a possibility for primary care staff in health centres to return to public employment. So far there has been only a modest return, despite calculations showing that doctors relying solely on HZZO contracts would have inferior earnings in comparison with public employment. A 2011 survey by the Medical Chamber showed that only about one-third of respondents were considering re-employment. Boris explains this by 'savings' made on different items, included in their capitation fees (uniforms, sanitary materials and so on), but also the desire to be one's 'own boss'. Even if the capitation fee does not cover all expenditure ('doctors often pay themselves lower wages than are paid to the nurses', who are protected by the collective agreement), explains Marija, they have opportunities for additional earnings (non-contracted services). However, Boris's wife, a concessionary at a local health centre, is considering a return to public employment. And Marija, currently a health centre employee (before moving to Zagreb she used to be a lessee), is cautious: for her colleagues with concessions, things changed for the worse – she is waiting; but is positive about the potential of private 'group practices' with greater capacity to invest and serve patients better.

Among the main complaints are the increased administrative pressure (largely caused by HZZO monitoring and regulations, but also incompatibility with regard to the software used), uncertainty in the case of sickness (it is up to them to organize replacements; 'those with concessions seldom take sick leave or holidays', Marija) and lack of funds to invest in the equipment that HZZO presses them to buy. Those in health centres, while no longer paying rent, have to pay running costs (water, electricity and so on), often far above what is included in their capitation fees, which is causing a lot of dissatisfaction.

There are considerable differences between primary care providers not only concerning status and security (private in own premises vs. private in public premises vs. those employed by health centres and covered by a collective agreement), but also concerning the number and composition of patients:[4] it is preferable for capitation purposes to have a larger share of very young and/or elderly patients. But for many, working time has become longer (for Marija by 1.5 to 2 hours daily; she makes home visits out of working time), intensity has increased, as has stress, while satisfaction has decreased ('I don't see my patients for months, they just call the nurse for prescriptions'), while the worsening of working conditions is 'evident', she complains. The workload of many nurses has increased, too: while they are protected by collective agreements, computerization – 'copy and paste medical practice', as Boris put it – has led to more duties falling on nurses in many practices.

On a couple of occasions protests have been organized by primary care provider associations against unfavourable HZZO regulations and demands (leading to increased workloads but also unfavourable financial conditions). Generally, there is a lot of dissatisfaction with the state of primary medicine: while it should be responsible for some 70 per cent of the health system, in reality it is 30 per cent (with specialists and hospitals being overburdened). Primary medicine seems ripe for major reform once again.

and liberalization of private practices (Zrinščak 2008: 130–33).[5] The main concerns of health-care reforms in the 2000s were overspending, too little private participation and 'distorted incentives' (for example, concerning referrals to specialists or drug prescriptions) embedded in the 'system of flat fees per patient' (Mihaljek 2007). This made the system's financial sustainability questionable. The aims were to lower the first and increase the second, but reform attempts typically united providers and clients in opposition to restrictions and cuts in public health provision.

Reform efforts in 2008–11 coincided with recession, and included:

financial stabilization, hospital reorganization and reductions in non-health personnel. However, health care's share of expenditure increased from 7.2 per cent of GDP in 2008 to 7.8 per cent in 2010 (Švaljek 2012). This explains why so far reform has not resulted in a noticeable worsening of working conditions in public health establishments. Yet, the 2012 budget, with its substantial decrease in health funding (by some 730 million HRK less than in 2011), together with a decrease in the contribution rate from 15 to 13 per cent of the gross wage, may signify the beginning of more radical changes.

Hospitals have been particularly targeted. Significant savings are expected 'after staff rationalization and central procurement are implemented'. This should include 'rationalization of non-medical services across hospitals' (World Bank 2011: 44). The new health minister confirmed this (Ostojić 2012). In view of a 0.9 per cent increase in employment in hospitals from the start of 2009 to the end of 2010, and an additional 1.1 per cent in 2011 (HZZO data) and their high deficits, coupled with the reduced health budget, it is likely that in years to come outsourcing will increase. Particularly vulnerable to this will be (mostly feminized) cleaning, laundry and food services. So far, outsourcing has been modest: it started in the early 2000s with laundry services in some hospitals. Out of 500 people affected, some were transferred to other jobs – as in the hospital where Iva worked previously – and some were taken on by the private employers winning the contract. Currently, some 14,000 people are at risk of outsourcing (if all non-health personnel in hospitals are counted). While cost considerations may prevail, Iva is concerned by the risk of falling hygiene standards in hospitals and doubtful about alleged cost savings. However, she warns: 'they cannot proceed with this without the unions; and we shall contest it'.

For medical staff, the harmonization of working time in line with European Directive 2003/88/EC is particularly important. Its provisions require treating all kinds of work as working time (duty and work on-call) with a 48-hour weekly limit, longer working time being possible only with the signed consent of the employee ('opt-out'). Based on government regulations of August 2011, from 2012 such work will be considered overtime, which is financially beneficial in comparison to the previous system, particularly when fully applied in 2013. This change highlighted a lack of doctors in hospitals (Marko). However, Iva warns that, particularly in major centres, doctors' working time is underused, while many are simultaneously working for private establishments. Opt-outs may cause additional problems if not universally adopted, as those who opt out will find themselves disproportionally burdened with duty hours and on-call work. On the other hand, for those who stick to the 48-hour limit, it will take fewer days than before to fully comply with working hours requirements, potentially leading to many problems once the new system is fully applied in 2013.

3.1.3 Education: uncertainty as expansionary structural reform push loses momentum

A set of structural reforms in the 2000s introduced a number of changes in all segments of the education system, leading to some decentralization and increasing standardization. The acceptance of major EU education-related documents was enshrined in the Education Sector Development Plan 2005–2010, which scheduled a major expansion and comprehensive reforms. Between 2003 and 2009 basic laws regulating all levels of education were adopted, creating several regulatory and oversight agencies, a performance evaluation framework and standardized final exams in upper secondary education, substantially increasing performance pressure on teachers. Several surveys (Krištof et al. 2011; Prijić-Samaržija et al. 2011) indicated decreased autonomy and increased work intensity in tertiary education due to the introduction of an additional year of study and the more demanding standards of the Bologna reform package.

However, the crisis caused a funding contraction in 2010, as total education expenditure from central government decreased by 2.4 per cent and local government education expenditure declined by 4.4 per cent. Consequently, several reforms have lost their momentum, such as the implementation of national pedagogical standards improving pupil/teacher ratios and introducing one-shift schools, while promotion and training opportunities for teachers have shrunk (see Case Study 1). The crisis has hit job security particularly hard in tertiary education, where in the mid-2000s expansion was largely founded on hiring large numbers of non-tenured assistants. Budgetary constraints emerging from the crisis, coupled with the sheer volume of recruitment in the mid-2000s (total number of assistants in the system grew by 29 per cent in the two years prior to 2009), meant limited promotion opportunities and many assistants were offered only temporary post-doctoral posts (senior assistants). Anxieties are increasing as those contracts will shortly expire, and not many tenured positions are being offered.[6]

3.2 Crisis Adjustments in the Public Sector: 2009–2012

By autumn 2008 the recession was coming. While no cuts in public expenditure were made in the 2009 budget – spending was increased by 6 per cent – a hard landing came quickly: three months later, the first budget revision was necessary and others followed. The context has changed, favouring policies that reduce expenditure while postponing or slowing down financially demanding reform projects. Measures targeting public sector employment, wages and benefits were imposed and/or negotiated with public sector unions during 2009 and renegotiated in 2010 and 2011. The base wage was cut by 6 per cent in May 2009 (effectively negating the 6 per cent increase in January 2009) and frozen later on, while reductions in other benefits were modest (withdrawal of the 2010 Christmas supplement and restrictions on travel allowances) (Table 4.2).

In addition, some groups were targeted with token restrictions just to increase the government's popularity (for example, cuts in public officials' wages and ceilings on managers' wages in state-owned companies). Measures restricting employment included a hiring freeze in public administration (2009), which was replaced by a 'one-for-two' system in 2010, allowing for one new employee to replace two leaving employment (primarily due to retirement). Data on the effects of 'one for two' are not available, but evidence is accumulating that it was not adhered to firmly.

Another avenue of public sector adjustments is achieved indirectly through the reduction of non-wage budgetary items. Reductions in investment, materials and services for budget-financed organizations have affected the working conditions of certain employee groups (see Case Study 1).

As of 2012, there is, a renewed sense of urgency as registered unemployment has been growing quickly (peaking at 343,000 in February, a number expected to be surpassed once the tourist season ends), while the economic outlook for 2012 and 2013 is bleak. The new government is under conflicting pressures: to stop fiscal degeneration and avoid a rating downgrade, but also to avoid a deepening of the recession and social conflicts, including with public sector unions.

Second phase adjustments are taking place. The first nominal cut in the state budget (by 3.4 billion HRK) was made in the 2012 budget, followed by measures to increase revenues (a VAT increase from 23 to 25 per cent). Its regressive impact is, similar to the 2009 VAT increase, somewhat corrected by income tax changes, which have become increasingly progressive. This will adversely affect the wages of senior civil servants and professionals (in particular, in health and higher education), while increasing income compression. In addition, some measures with respect to employment practices were announced. First, reductions in public sector employment through cuts in temporary service and fixed-time contracts, affecting younger people (for example, trainees) and former employees (now retired) engaged on service contracts. Second, an early retirement scheme for some 5,000 employees in the public sector is being considered, but not realized yet. Altogether this would amount to some 10,000 (4 per cent) job cuts in

Table 4.2 Crisis adjustment measures and public sector employees, Croatia, 2008–2012

Policy area	Measures	Implementation	Objectives	Reach	Impact on public sector employees
Public expenditure	Budget revisions	2009, 2010	Fiscal consolidation and stability; ensuring social expenditure	State 'clients' and employees, public procurement actors from private sector	Differential, nominal wage cuts avoided after May 2009
	Budget – spending reduced by 3.4 billion HRK	February 2012	Fiscal stability, preventing rating downgrade		
	Cost cutting in ministries and state/public companies	2009–12	Reducing expenditure		Working conditions negatively affected (e.g., training funds)
Revenue	Solidarity tax on wages, pensions and other income, with exemptions and two rates (2 and 4%)	Aug 2009 (until July/Nov 2010)	Increasing revenues	Universal – all incomes	Negatively affecting wages and incomes
	VAT increase from 22 to 23%	Aug 2009			Negative, regressive
	VAT increase from 23 to 5%	2012			
Employment measures	Freezing of new employment in public administration	2009	Efficiency/savings	Public administration and public companies	Minor effects
	Downsizing by 5%; 'one-for-two' system	Sept 2010			

	Outsourcing	2000s, with a push in 2010		Public administration, health	Mostly negative, inferior working conditions
	Restrictions on overtime, temporary service contracts and fixed-time contracts	February 2012		Public administration	Negative on those affected, so far minor effects on expenditure
Wage measures	Cuts by 6%, return to Dec. 2008 level, freeze	May 2009 (extended Dec. 2011	Reducing expenditure	Public sector (core)	Negative, but further nominal wage cuts avoided
	Cuts by 10%	April 2009	… and increasing legitimacy	State officials	Minor effects
	Cuts by 5%	July 2009		Management in public companies	
	Ceiling put at 3.2 × April average net wage	July 2009			
	Tenure supplement reduction (from 0.5 to 0.3%), and no 2.2% supplement in education for 2012 (currently under negotiation)	June 2012	Expenditure	Public sector (core)	Negative, particularly with regard to senior employees
Cuts in benefits	Christmas bonus; some restriction in travel allowance	2010	Expenditure	Public sector (core)	Negative, particularly the low paid
	Christmas, tenure and holiday bonus for 2012/13; daily travel allowance reduction (under negotiation)	June 2012			

Source: Prepared by the authors from multiple sources.

the public sector (*Jutarnji list*, 11 April 2012). Furthermore, restrictions on overtime payments hurt earnings, particularly in public administration where it was an important tool to 'stimulate' the underpaid skilled workforce. Also, budget cuts in education (by some 0.3 billion HRK) and health (by some 0.7 billion HRK) will increase pressure in the direction of outsourcing (in health care) and force all those reaching the age of 65 out of higher education (so far, an extension to 70 was widely applied). Reduction of the disposable workforce and service contracting will likely increase intensity of work in the public sector. However, by the end of June 2012, it seemed that the government's savings plans had failed to catch on at the implementation level. While the employees' compensation reduction for 2012 was set at 2 billion HRK (a reduction of 6.5 per cent), in the first five months of 2012 it actually increased by 170 million HRK compared to 2011. This prompted the government, which was firmly dedicated to the announced savings benchmarks (including a 21.6 billion HRK wage bill ceiling; and reducing government expenditure to 37 per cent of GDP by 2014), to attempt to negotiate revisions of collective agreements in the public sector, with the possibility (but also the threat) of taking some drastic and unilateral (for example, changing pay coefficients and/or base wage; cancelling collective agreements) measures if negotiations fail. Importantly, in the proposed collective agreement changes, sent to unions in June 2012, the government included pulling out of commitments to wage increases promised in the 2009 agreement and the 2011 addition to it. (See Case Study 2.) After the first two rounds of negotiations, there is no sign of a new agreement – the unions seem ready to accept one-off cuts in benefits only, conditional on future compensation (information provided by a union leader over the phone). The trade unions are dedicated to opposing cuts in the tenure supplement (from 0.5 per cent a year to 0.3 per cent[7]) and the 2.2 per cent supplement for employees in education; but it is this measure's fiscal effect that is the biggest. The unions have threatened strikes and legal action in response to any unilateral measures. Despite pronounced differences between unions, it is likely that they will remain united in defending wages and previous favourable agreements. However, the government seems dedicated to making cuts, to avoid otherwise necessary budget revision and a rating downgrade to 'junk' status (compromising fiscal stability and pro-growth investment plans). In the face of that, unions' readiness to compromise on cuts in various benefits may vary.

Fiscal problems are increasing in 2012 at local level, too, leading to pressures on employees in local administration and locally funded public services. Decreases and late payment of salaries and benefits, also employment cuts, are spreading, as a number of counties, municipalities and cities find themselves in a fiscally unviable position (due to decreasing revenues and/

or high indebtedness). By June 2012, the City of Zagreb was on the brink of cancelling the collective agreement for 10,500 city employees, after two rounds of failed negotiations with unions on reducing wages and benefits. Also, the City holding company (including local utilities) is deadlocked over similar management attempts. As at national level, conflicts with unions, including strikes, are increasingly likely.

3.3 Crisis Dialogue

Both the public sector reforms of the 2000s and crisis adjustments are played out in a formally consolidated institutional setting. While social dialogue in the private sector has characteristically been weak (Franičević 2011: 170–72), in the public sector formal bargaining has been a major avenue for negotiations. In addition, informal bargaining and deals made with relevant ministries have also been important (for example, concerning pay coefficients and various supplements). Despite a frequently confrontational discourse and major difficulties in pursuing dialogue, the formal institutions of dialogue constrained both sides in their actions. Although interwoven with conflicts, it was the negotiation process between PSE (public service) unions and the government/ministries that led to the 2009 May agreement on a wage freeze and its renewal in 2011, as well as to the basic collective agreement in the PSE (October 2010). During the crisis period collective agreements protecting most benefits were agreed in public administration (2008 with amendments in 2010), health care (October 2011) and education (primary in April 2011, secondary in December 2010, higher and science in October 2011 – detailed in Case Study 2).

Behind this outcome is the strength of the public sector unions. Trade union density in the public sector is about 60 per cent (Bagić 2010), with a high concentration of membership in strong national unions. The falling share of the private sector in total trade union membership – down to about 30 per cent (ibid.) – has negatively affected their ability to influence policies towards more austerity in the public sector, also advocated by employers. Moreover, the PSE unions' mobilization capacity, including massive strikes, is much stronger, particularly in education, than in the private sector. Finally, regulations concerning renewal and cancellation of collective agreements in the Labour Code proved to be quite favourable for public sector unions, enabling unlimited extension of rights after a collective agreement's expiry. This is about to change, as the new government has sent to the parliament the new law[8] that would make further adjustments easier by limiting the duration of collective agreements to three months after expiry and by changing the trade union representativeness criteria (but also that of the employers). A new area of conflict (including between unions and their federations) is emerging. Some PSE unions see the draft law as an attack on their unity, by privileging unions in particular professions (Josip, PSE union leader); others see it as privileging the 'big players'; the big confederations differ on local representativeness criteria. Certainly, with the new law enacted, both the incentives that actors are facing and the rules of social dialogue will change, with effects that remain unclear.

Three major protest actions have been crucial for understanding the period's dynamics and outcomes: the 2006 and 2009 strikes in public services, and the mass signing of the referendum petition organized by five national trade union confederations in summer 2010 (as detailed in Case Study 2) (Table 4.3). The rare occurrence of autonomous and locally based strikes and other protests during the period could be attributed to centralization of bargaining[9] and very modest recession adjustments in the public sector. However, several localized protest actions have emerged in various parts of the public sector as the crisis has unfolded.

Some protest actions were related to reforms. In 2008, public administration employees signed a petition against pay reform, demanding that tenure remains a factor in pay determination. In higher education a student movement against tuition fee increases in 2009 caused mobilization leading to the creation of the alternative union Academic Solidarity which was at the forefront of resistance against proposed reforms in higher education and science that were seen as paving the way for marketization and privatization. Industrial action escalated into strikes and lockouts in several faculties and institutes in July 2011. In primary health care doctors engaged in protest action, too.

Some actions emerged from unfavourable wage developments in certain niches, such as the October 2011 public protest by uniformed police against regulations on pay coefficients, and the strike of foreign-language readers at Zagreb University, March 2011 due to the deterioration of pay coefficients. Both managed to fulfil most of their goals.

While the largest public sector trade unions did not go beyond verbal support for the wave of public discontent in spring and autumn 2011, manifested in large civic protests and 'town walks', a few unions (including two from the public sector)[10] have actively participated, albeit with only modest member attendance (Kunac 2011).

Will the coming period see a new wave of protests and strikes in the public sector? Three factors point in that direction: (i) unions' discontent with the new government's attitudes towards social dialogue (too many 'messages' and 'spin' in the media instead of dialogue); (ii) there is a lack of mutual trust and a failure to build a partnership around policies and

Table 4.3 Strikes and protests, Croatia, 2009–2011

When	Who	What	Organized by	Cause	Demands	Participation	Outcome
2009							
May	Public service employees	Strike	PSE unions	6% wage cut	Restoring wages after recession ends	Support and turnout above 80%	Agreement on PSE wages
2010							
June	Citizens, union members	Referendum initiative	Five union confederations	Changes to the Labour Code's provisions on collective agreements	To prevent that change	Massive: more than 700,000	Government withdrew the amendment
2011							
March/April	Citizens, some unions' members	Citizens' protests	Citizens' groups (few unions took active part)	Dissatisfaction with the government and conditions in the country	Diverse, economic, social and political	Between a few hundred and about 10,000 on different days	Strong media impact, some impact on political actors
March–May	Foreign-language readers, Zagreb University	Strike	NSZ union (independent union of research & higher education employees)	Low pay coefficients, degradation	Increase in coefficients; injustice undone	About 60	Coefficients increased

Table 4.3 (continued)

When	Who	What	Organized by	Cause	Demands	Participation	Outcome
2011							
July	Students and faculty	Lock-out/ strike	Academic Solidarity	Proposed laws on higher education and science	Abolition of reforms	Several faculties	Laws were not put in front of parliament
October	Citizens' groups, union members	Citizens' protest	Citizens' groups with unions support	Dissatisfaction (as above)	Broad and diverse	4,000 in Zagreb, 1,000–1,500 in Split and 300 in Rijeka	Very limited
October	Police employees	Protest on Zagreb main square	Police union	Decrease of wages for 2,800 employees due to proposed coefficient changes	To prevent wage decrease and job degradation	About 1,000 uniformed employees	Compromise, regulation cancelled

reforms; and (iii) inherent difficulties in agreeing on cuts to wages and benefits that are presently being discussed by two sides.

4. EFFECTS OF ADJUSTMENTS: WORKING CONDITIONS IN THE PUBLIC SECTOR, 2000–2010

4.1 Job Security and Contractual Arrangements

It is worth examining whether there have been any crisis-related changes in job security and unemployment risks. The tenure structure in the public sector is indicative of high stability. The proportion of general government employees working in their current job for more than 10 years increased from 40 per cent in 1997–98 to 62 per cent in 2006–07 and 66 per cent in the crisis years of 2009–10. Through the 2000s average job tenure has been increasing slightly in the private sector, but significantly faster in the public sector (Table 4.4).

An increase in the proportion of 'high tenure' employees seems not to be a result of layoffs of 'recent arrivals' or limited input of fresh workforce in the public sector during the crisis. The extent of recent recruitment, approximated by the proportion of employees with fewer than two years' job tenure, actually increased since the mid-2000s in all public subsectors and has not declined in the crisis period (unlike in the private sector). This would not be the case if the employment ban (or one-for-two replacement) within the public administration was being imposed consistently. Furthermore, there was a noticeable increase in recruitment into the health-care sector just as the crisis stuck.

Job exit indices (Table 4.5) confirm stability. Through the 2000s, only about 5–6 per cent of the short-term unemployed were formerly employed

Table 4.4 Average tenure duration (in years) and share of short-tenure employees (in %), Croatia, 2003–2010

	Private employees		Public administration and defence		Education		Health	
	Average tenure	<2 yrs	Average tenure	<2 yrs	Average tenure	<2 yrs	Average tenure	<2 yrs
2003–04	7.7	29	11.0	7	14.8	11	15.3	9
2006–07	8.1	28	12.6	10	15.1	11	16.3	8
2009–10	8.7	22	14.3	11	15.1	10	17.5	10

Table 4.5 Share in short-term unemployment stock, flows into unemployment and private sector employment, Croatia, 2003–2010 (%)

	2003–04	2006–07	2009–10
(A) Former public sector employees among the short-term unemployed	6.1	5.8	5.8
(B) Short-term unemployed who used to work in the public sector as a percentage of total public sector employment	1.9	1.2	1.3
(C) Short-term unemployed who used to work in the private sector as a percentage of total private sector employment	7.9	4.8	6.1
(D) Job shifters from the public sector	0.6	1.2	0.5

in the public sector, with no noticeable increase in 2009–10 (A). The relative risk of losing one's job is approximated as a ratio of short-term unemployed and total sectoral employment. In mid-decade the number of short-term unemployed that used to work in the public sector decreased to about 1.2 per cent of the public sector workforce, and there has been no substantial increase since (B). In the private sector this ratio is much higher and strongly contingent on the economic cycle (C).

However, recent unemployment register data (Table 4.6) show increased turnover and insecurity with regard to public sector entry. While the number of unemployed recruited to the public sector increased greatly between 2009 and 2011 in all three subsectors (A), there was also a large increase in outflow into unemployment from the public sector (C). This turnover mostly affected young people, as increasingly recruiting was done through fixed-term contracts (B), while persistently about 90 per cent of persons who entered unemployment from the public sector had less than three years' tenure in total (D). Therefore, the increase in the 0–2 years' tenure category from LFS might indicate the emergence of a secondary labour market segment within the public sector, disfavouring new entrants.

In the early 2000s job shifts from the public to the private sector were very low: less than 1 per cent of public sector employees annually made this shift (Table 4.6, row D). During the boom period (2006–07), such shifts doubled, but diminished substantially again during the crisis. As public-to-private transition is about twice as high among secondary educated and intermediate occupations, this indicator might primarily stand for outsourcing of auxiliary services to the private sector providing some

Table 4.6 Registered entry to and exit from public sector, Croatia, 2009–2011

		Public administration	Education	Health
(A) Left unemployment register for employment in the sector	2009	3,026	8,736	4,252
	2010	3,891	9,854	5,493
	2011	6,835	11,280	6,733
(B) Share employed via fixed-term contract, %	2009	89	88	84
	2010	95	91	87
	2011	95	92	87
(C) Entered unemployment from the sector	2009	3,095	8,719	5,221
	2010	5,356	10,021	5,689
	2011	7,334	11,997	7,331
(D) Share of entrants to unemployment with less than 3 years' tenure, %	2009	87	89	69
	2010	69	90	84
	2011	88	87	80

Note: Education and health sectors include private employment.

Source: Public employment service.

numerical support for examples (see Box 4.1) of subcontracting affecting public sector employment.

There was a substantial decline in job change intentions (Figure 4.2): in 2009–10 it is the lowest on record, which points to increased risk aversion stemming from the crisis. However, this change is only a continuation of a long-term declining trend, in both the private and public sectors. Nevertheless, tertiary educated workers in the public sector seem increasingly dissatisfied with their job during the crisis. While the intention to change job all but disappeared among public sector employees without tertiary education, among the tertiary educated the share of those who sought another job had not declined since 2005. In fact, there was a 1–2 per cent reversal in declared intention to change job in 2009–10. This is consistent with findings on wage compression in the public sector, but also shows that perception of job-loss risk is much higher for those with lower education.

4.1.1 Limited flexibility in public sector employment

In view of the recent increase in the proportion of people with short tenure in the public sector it is worth examining whether the core workforce has been fenced with auxiliary temporary or fixed-term employees (Figure 4.3).

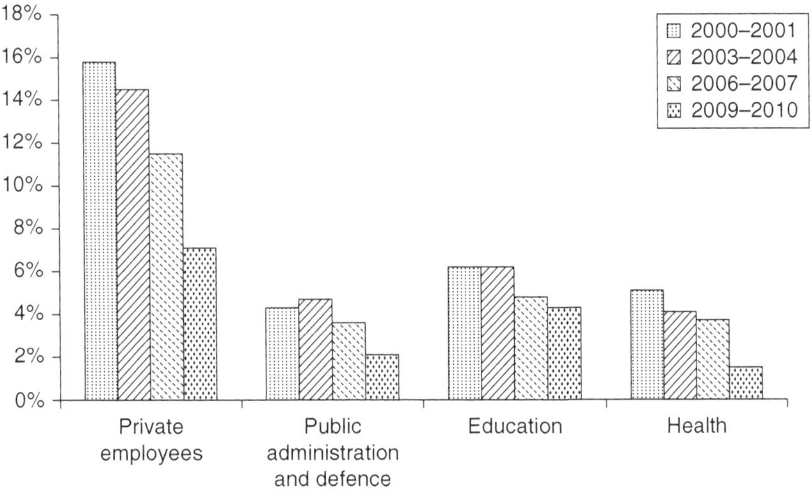

Figure 4.2 Reported intention of job change, Croatia, 2000–2010 (%)

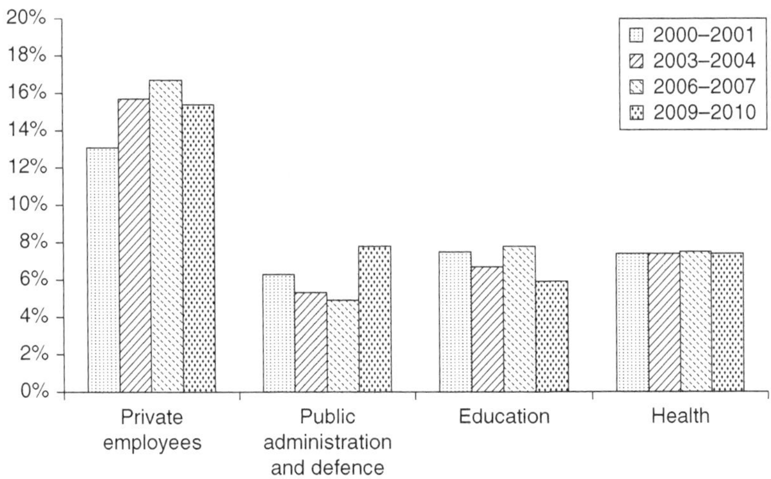

Figure 4.3 Temporary contracts in private and public sector employment, Croatia, 2000–2010 (%)

The LFS data provide evidence for this only in the public administration, where the share of fixed-term workers increased from the pre-crisis 4.9 per cent to 7.8 per cent. The growth of temporary contracts (including trainees) in public administration is also visible from administrative employment statistics, increasing from 6.2 per cent in 2007 to 7.3 per cent in 2010. However, such an increase in temporary work arrangements has not been observed in education (decline from 8 to 6 per cent) or the health-care sector (stable at 7–8 per cent). In general, neither pre-crisis reforms nor early crisis adjustment caused a major push towards the use of fixed-term contracts in the public sector in general; but employment register data (see Table 4.6) indicate that such arrangements are common for new entrants, and as of recently often lead back to unemployment. Substantial cuts in fixed-term contracts announced by the government in February 2012, if carried out as planned (about 5,000 workplaces) would decimate this peripheral (mostly young) segment of employees and endanger the common recruitment route, but even if carried out, the total room for reducing the public sector workforce through this channel is very limited.

While private sector employees are twice as likely to work on fixed-term contracts, temporary employment had not really caught on in the public sector prior to the crisis, apart from a traineeship mechanism with the implicit promise of upgrading to a permanent contract. As the crisis emerged, however, the situation deteriorated somewhat, as return to unemployment became a more likely outcome for public sector fixed-term employees (and trainees) than progress to a permanent contract (Table 4.6; also see Subsection 3.1.3 for non-tenured positions in higher education). However, such flexibility at the periphery so far affects only a minor part of the workforce, as work on a secure permanent contract has remained a standard.

4.2 Wages

Public sector wages[11] are based on job complexity coefficients, introduced by the 2001 Law on Wages in Public Services. The base wage is subject to collective negotiations. If no agreement is reached, the government can decide unilaterally. Negotiations are commonly preceded by union pressure and strikes. Importantly, coefficient values are determined by government regulations.

This has focused the sectoral unions' efforts on (re)negotiating various supplements to coefficients and supplements for working conditions or tenure, as well as various benefits, mostly formalized through collective agreements. Coefficients and supplements have also been a subject of public pressure and informal lobbying, leading to their frequent changes: in education this happened 13 times and for state employees 20 times during the 2000s (Frane, union expert). All this resulted in a complex and non-transparent web of supplements to wages and coefficients,

Table 4.7 Real wage trends in main industrial sectors, Croatia, 2001–2011

	2001	2002	2003	2004	2005	2006	2007	2008	2009	2010	2011
Total	2.6	3.2	4.0	3.7	1.5	1.9	2.2	0.8	0.2	–0.5	–0.4
Manufacturing	6.5	4.3	4.5	2.1	2.6	3.2	1.6	0.8	–1.2	–0.1	–0.6
Construction	6.5	10.8	6.4	1.7	–0.6	2.9	4.5	0.5	–1.5	–3.8	–0.6
Trade	4.9	7.5	4.9	3.4	1.4	1.5	2.3	0.8	–1.7	0.6	–0.6
Real estate, renting and business services*	0.7	1.4	4.9	4.8	3.2	3.5	0.3	0.5	–0.2	–3.6	–2.6
Public administration	–6.1	0.1	5.0	1.0	–0.3	1.3	4.4	3.1	1.9	–0.7	–0.7
Education	1.7	0.6	4.3	3.3	–0.5	0.7	3.1	1.6	0.7	–0.3	0.1
Health	–0.9	–1.2	2.6	2.7	3.5	0.8	2.7	0.3	0.0	–1.2	–1.5

Note: * ISIC 3 (up to 2008): K, ISIC 4 (2009 to 2011): 63, 64, L,M,N. Incorporated businesses only.

Source: CBS.

differentiating remuneration far beyond what is laid down in the law. Disentangling this is currently a policy focus.

4.2.1 Real wages: public sector catching up and holding on

Table 4.7 illustrates trends of real net wages by selected ISIC sectors. Until 2007, real wage growth in the public sector was slower except for election years (2003 and 2007). However, between 2007 and 2009 the trend was reversed, in line with the 2006 Agreement. With basic wages raised by 6 per cent at the beginning of three consecutive years (in 2007, 2008, 2009), the public sector 'was faring better than manufacturing' (Nestić 2010), and most business sectors. Despite the 2009 cut and consequent freeze of the base wage in the public sector, the impact of the recession was much stronger and earlier in the private sector (Matković 2010). Consequently, LFS data indicate that the public–private sector net wage gap increased from 24 per cent in 2008 to 30 per cent in 2009 and remained at this level in 2010.

However, incorporated business data (Table 4.7) indicate that in 2010 and 2011 wage moderation was slightly more pronounced in the public sector, as real wages decreased faster there than in manufacturing or trade. The exception of the education sector is to be understood by a negotiated annual supplement increase (2.2 per cent) still in force. The relative improvement in wages of public sector workers is to be understood

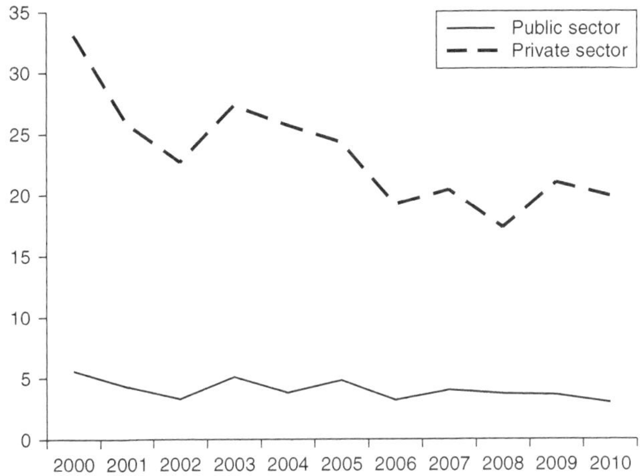

Source: LFS, full-time employees.

Figure 4.4 *Share of employees reporting income below 60% total mean, Croatia, 2000–2010 (%)*

via belated application of wage brakes in 2009 and the ability of public sector trade unions to negotiate against further wage cuts by settling for increased taxation of all employees (see Case Study 2).

4.2.2 On a different path: income inequality and low pay in the public and private sectors

The occurrence of low pay is far lower in the public sector. There is a major difference between the private and public sectors in the shares of employees earning below 60 per cent of the mean wage (Figure 4.4). This is consistent with the estimate of Nestić and Bakarić (2012: 12), which shows that only 2 per cent of full-time employees in the core public sector were receiving the minimum wage in 2008, but 11 per cent in the private sector. The gap had narrowed between 2000 and 2008, but increased again with the onset of the recession. As the crisis emerged, the share of employees with low pay increased in the private sector, but in the public sector it became even less prevalent.

The estimation of the Gini coefficient (Figure 4.5) in the public and private sectors yields consistent findings. First, wage inequality in the public sector is significantly lower. Second, a long-term gentle decrease in inequality is evident in the private sector while in the public sector inequality remained stable throughout the period. Third, a slight increase in inequality emerged within both the public and private sectors as the crisis struck.

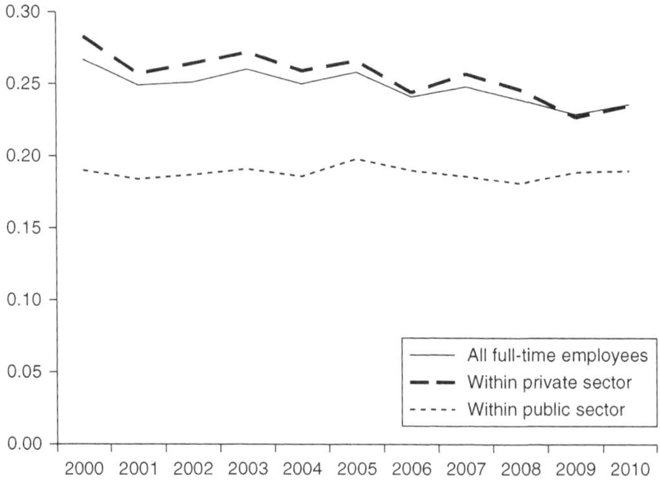

Source: LFS, full-time employees.

Figure 4.5 Gini coefficients for public and private sectors, Croatia, 2000–2010

Low-income inequalities have been a major argument in favour of pay reforms in the public sector, in particular in public administration, founded on claims that high wage compression adversely affects people's motivation (Budak 2011). Such an adverse effect should be particularly strong among those with considerable human capital, as they can expect low rewards under the current system. The wage premium of academically educated employees over their peers with only an upper secondary education is fairly low in the public administration (57–62 per cent through the past decade) and in education (46–49 per cent). Only in the health sector is the premium for tertiary educated employees (91–96 per cent) comparable to the private sector. Those differences are reflected in Gini coefficients over the 2000s, which were lowest in the education sector (16–18), followed by public administration (17–20) and highest in health care (20–23). Not much change in within-sector compression is evident through the 2000s, either from LFS or administrative data.

However, the public–private differences in remuneration of the tertiary educated had emerged from high within-sector compression, coupled with lagging of public sector wages in the early 2000s. By 2006, academically educated employees in public administration earned 3 per cent less, and in education even 28 per cent less than their tertiary educated peers in the substantially similar business services sector. Discontent in 2006, resulting

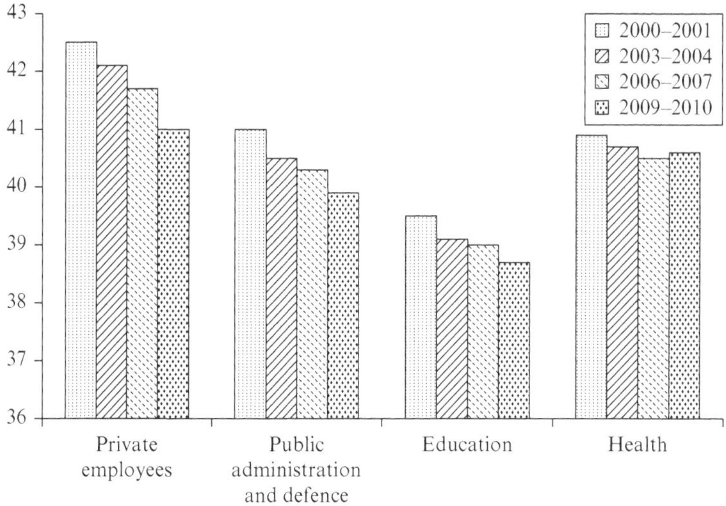

Figure 4.6 Average reported working hours, Croatia, 2000–2010

in a massive strike starting from the education sector was therefore not surprising. However, the attractiveness of wages in public administration and education for the tertiary educated is likely to have improved since then,[12] due to the catch-up of public sector wages both in the boom (from negotiated public sector wage growth in 2007–08) and at the outset of the recession (from earlier and stronger downward adjustment of wages in the private sector).

4.3 Workplace Conditions

4.3.1 Steady decline of number of hours worked and no recourse to part-time work

Average reported working hours (Figure 4.6) have declined slightly during the crisis, but this development does not depart from the long-term trend, as the number of weekly working hours has fallen steadily in both the public and private sectors since the late 1990s. As the austerity measures of 2012 have set a target of doing away with overtime compensation, it is likely that the trend of working-hour reductions in the public sector will continue.

Part-time work is very uncommon in the public sector (at about 1 per cent) and declining except in education, where such arrangements are stable at about 5 per cent. The crisis has not changed this pattern.

Institutional failure to facilitate such employment is constraining opportunities for improving the work–life balance of public sector employees.

With the exception of the health sector, in which weekend and night shifts are common, the public sector offers better opportunities than the private sector for work–life balance with regard to working unsocial hours. Within the public sector, female employees in all subsectors are less likely to work unsocial hours or weekends than their male peers, in particular in public administration and defence. However, working from home is an infrequent arrangement, in both the public and private sectors with only about 2–3 per cent of employees reporting it everywhere except in education (where about 10 per cent report at least sometimes working from home). During the crisis, the share of employees reporting working from home had declined by about a third, but as initial levels were very low, this is unlikely to affect work–life balance in general.

4.3.2 Training participation as the first victim of austerity

The level of Croatian workforce training participation is persistently among the lowest in Europe. Some improvement was evident between 2004 and 2006 – as LFS-reported participation in training during the last month increased from 0.8 to 2.0 per cent in the private sector, from 0.8 to 3.3 per cent in public administration, 3.2 to 5.1 per cent in education and 1.8 to 2.4 per cent in health care. However, as the crisis developed, among both public and private sector employees it became the lowest on record (only 0.6 per cent in the private sector, 0.7 per cent in public administration and 0.9 per cent in health and education). Before the crisis, participation in training was more common among public sector employees (very much related to EU accession demands and training funding), but since 2008 it has plummeted to levels observed in the private sector. As nothing much had happened with respect to wage compression through the period, it is likely that lack of training opportunities (and funds) is more important for understanding the scope of training participation in Croatia than (de)motivation due to wage level.

5. CASE STUDIES

5.1 Case Study 1: Structural Change and Austerity Pain in Vocational Secondary Education

This case study portrays the crisis-related development of working conditions at a technical secondary school located in a less-affluent county. It is based on examination of sector-based reforms and indicators, and interviews with trade union officials and employees.

5.1.1 Cuts in expenditure and coping strategies

Between 2002 and 2008 public upper secondary education expenditure was stable, wavering between 0.87 and 0.93 per cent of GDP. In reaction to the crisis, the education budget was severely limited. In 2010, central government budget expenditure on education decreased by 22 per cent in services, by 67 per cent in furniture and equipment and by 52 per cent in software. Moreover, local government expenditure for upper secondary education stagnated in 2009 and then declined by 15 per cent in 2010. Schools were ordered to cut their operational expenditure by 10–30 per cent. Consequently, in many schools headteachers imposed strict rationing of office resources and expenditure for teacher training. Secondary schools can also collect their own income through courses, renting facilities or other activities, but not much is generated in that fashion.

The school we visited has managed to make ends meet so far. Much refurbishment and equipment renewal was done before the recession. As payments from the county got reduced and delayed, non-critical acquisitions were put on hold and essential purchases were arranged via instalments. No major hindrances in daily work were noted by the teachers, apart from rationing of training travel allowances and arrears in reimbursements. Some resources and equipment were acquired through donations, projects and EU funds. The struggling business sector in the region is not in a position to help the school, as was the case in 'better times'. At the beginning of 2012 all finances had to be transferred to the County Treasury (and the school bank account closed). There is a lot of uncertainty with regard to this move, undermining schools' operational autonomy, possibly leading to stringent rationing.

5.1.2 Negative impact on human capital and career development

There has been a reduction in human capital investment at the national level as education agencies have decreased the number of places in courses and seminars for teachers. There has been a slowdown in professional promotion procedures towards the status of teacher-mentor or adviser (accompanied by 7 or 12 per cent wage increases, respectively), with about 2,000 candidates waiting from 2008 to 2010. Such restrictions were also felt in the school we visited, with increased rationing and delays in reimbursements.

5.1.3 Cuts in wages and persistent personal indebtedness

The wage reduction of 2009 and weak growth since has hit the living standards of school employees. There is a sense of personal stagnation concerning income and training. However, employees are aware that they are more fortunate than most in a region with low average wages and high unemployment. Hardship is more serious among younger and middle-aged teachers, many of whom took out loans (especially mortgages) during better times. There are several coping strategies through additional earning: by mentoring pupils for their final vocational project or tutoring for state final exams, within the school; or by engaging in adult education, provision of IT or language courses within firms (although this has dried up due to the crisis), and informal private tutoring.

5.1.4 Is segmentation emerging?

Once they have obtained a permanent employment contract, teachers' job security is assured. The majority spend their entire career in the school ('when I became a teacher here, 80 per cent of my colleagues were my teachers when I was a pupil') and interviewed teachers do not see lucrative job alternatives at the moment. Several new teachers were employed on permanent contracts during 2011 (some part-time) as old teachers reached retirement age.

Administration and maintenance personnel feel replaceable and less secure. In the case at hand, accounting was made largely redundant with the introduction of a county treasury, prompting the accountant to re-qualify as a vocational teacher for business subjects in the same school. Ideas on outsourcing cleaning services in education predate the crisis, and cleaners are well aware of their precarious position. They try to cope by being 'on good terms' with decision-makers (thus not participating in strikes), putting in extra effort when told and performing additional duties (such as making coffee).

5.1.5 Defensive position prevails

In line with the secondary education unions' militant legacy, the school participated in both the 2006 and the 2009 public service strikes and is highly unionized. However, the trade union does not play a major role in the school's day-to-day affairs, as most issues are resolved through informal consultations. At the beginning of 2012, there was a nominal readiness to participate in further strikes but most interviewees expressed scepticism that there is anything to be gained, as general austerity gets under way. A defensive position prevails: the best interviewees hoped for was that things remain as they are.

5.1.6 No way forward: peripheral cuts and core anxieties

In this particular case the impact of the crisis is not yet overwhelming, reflecting the broad patterns discussed earlier. Opportunities for training and advancement have become limited. Since the 2009 wage cut, there have been no major income setbacks and some wage increment was maintained, but debts incurred during the boom are a major concern to many teachers. However, job insecurity is mounting in the auxiliary workforce and those with non-permanent contracts, without much attention from the trade unions. Cuts in local funding have reduced procurement and maintenance capabilities, as well as the financial autonomy of schools. Despite employees' active coping practices, many are facing real financial constraints and there is pessimism about future wage and working conditions.

Underinvestment in human capital, promotion, equipment and maintenance, coupled with the prospect of outsourcing non-core workers and reducing the influx of teachers might have negative mid-term effects on working conditions, school community cohesion and education quality. Maintaining non-wage expenditure – too heavy a burden for impoverished local governments alone – training, recruitment and advancement pathways, as well as promoting the interests of 'non-essential' workers should be given at least the same priority in social dialogue as wage issues and benefits – so far the unions' main focus – if the education system is to overcome its structural challenges.

5.2 Case Study 2: Moderation on Wages and Benefits in Public Services: Between Conflict and Cooperation

This chapter will not focus on recession period adjustments *per se*, but the relative lack of them: a largely unplanned outcome of actors' conflicts and dialogue on wages and benefits within the particular political context. It is based on interviews, documentation and media reports.

5.2.1 Prologue: relative wages and fairness coming to the fore

In November 2006, PSE unions demanded negotiations on the base wage increase, due to a relative fall in wages in the previous period ('our policy is exclusively based on relative values, we are interested in dignity and status', explains Josip, a union leader). After negotiations failed the unions organized a three-day strike. It was a big success as 80,000 members participated. The agreement was reached about increasing the base wage (by 6 per cent each January over three years), as well as additions to coefficients in education and science by 2.2 per cent a year from 2007 to 2013. The three education unions are the backbone of the public sector action, with the ability to ensure particular advantages for their members.

5.2.2 Rocky road to sharing the burden of the crisis

In autumn 2008, when the global crisis struck, the prime minister asked the public sector unions to accept a freeze on the third tranche of the 6 per cent wage increase. The unions rejected this demand; public sector employees should not be shouldering the crisis burden alone. While public sector employees received their scheduled January 2009 rise, very soon budget revision became necessary. PSE unions, faced with demands for wage cuts, raised the issue of fairness again, demanding guarantees that wages will be restored once recovery sets in. Unions rejected the government's offer that wage cuts will be annulled after GDP increases by 2 per cent for two consecutive quarters: 'We didn't want to accept an ultimatum without knowing what would happen to our wages once we are out of recession' (Josip). In response, the new Law on Basic Wages was passed unilaterally, resulting in a 6 per cent wage cut. The unions denounced this as an assault on the institutions of social dialogue.[13]

It was critical to restore credibility among membership and the public: unions chose to react with a strike in the week before the May 2009 local elections. The strike started with an 80 per cent turnout, strengthening unions' bargaining power amid dramatic three-day negotiations. The key to the agreement reached was the prime minister's decision to cut a deal before the strike was joined by tens of thousands of others and prevent a massive protest scheduled in Zagreb's main square a day before the election. The government committed itself to (i) increasing the base wage by inflation by January 2010; (ii) restoring public/private sector 2008 wage parity (existing before the 6 per cent cut) even in the absence of GDP growth by 31 December 2011; and (iii) in order to improve the public sector's relative standing, convergence to a new target level by 2016.[14] Criteria for revision were defined, in case the economic situation continues to deteriorate.

Both sides claimed victory but Luka, a government official, felt it untenable to link a freeze with an obligation to achieve parity and convergence, when 'we don't know what will happen tomorrow', but ministers said that they 'must sign'. While the government happily turned to local elections, a new crisis broke in June 2009 – budget revision became necessary again. The government asked for a further 6 per cent wage cut and withdrawal of Christmas and holiday bonuses. This was supported by employers and private sector unions. But this time the government – led by Jadranka Kosor after Ivo Sanader had surprisingly stepped down – faced confident unions threatening lawsuits and strikes: 'we have already made our contribution . . . and have a sacrosanct agreement' (Josip in the media). The government could not afford a major conflict. The trade union position that everybody should take on their fair share of the burden prevailed:

a progressive 'solidarity tax' was imposed on all but the lowest incomes, and VAT was increased by 1 per cent. Employers and private sector unions were dissatisfied and economists pointed to the negative effects. However, measures contributed to fiscal stability and regular payouts to public sector employees and clients.

5.2.3 From major conflict to pragmatic compromise: moderation consolidated

Since no recovery was in sight, in March 2010, public sector unions were asked to agree to cuts in Christmas and holiday bonuses and gifts for children. The finance minister exclaimed: 'all rights from collective agreements are on the table'. However, the unions once again raised the thorny issue of fairness. In May, both sides were still locked-in and the government turned to the Labour Code changes to undermine the PSE unions' comfortable bargaining position. Namely, the Labour Code stipulates that after expiry, rights laid down in collective agreements last until a new collective agreement has been agreed (in practice, this may go on for years). The proposed changes would make it possible to cancel basic collective agreements for the public administration (signed until 2012), and to disable invoking the extended rights clause when the PSE basic collective agreement expires, which was due in June 2010.

While aimed at PSE employees, this move galvanized all trade union confederations into fighting against reductions in employees' rights, whether in the private or the public sector. The unions decided to initiate a referendum on the proposed law change, making it a political issue. For both sides the stakes increased enormously. Significantly, over the summer of 2010, negotiations on changes to the law, basic collective agreement and revisions to the May 2009 agreement went on in parallel with the referendum initiative.

In two weeks of June 2010, more than 720,000 citizens had signed the petition (well above the necessary 450,000) turning it into a 'referendum on the government'. This gave the unions a major boost but an ambiguous mandate. The government's attempt to deny its legality provoked public outrage, further weakening its bargaining position. The government backed off and withdrew the proposal from the parliament. In such a context a favourable new basic collective agreement for PSE was reached in October, guaranteeing continuation of most rights for the next three years. Concessions were modest: no Christmas bonus for 2010 and withdrawal of rights to a commuter supplement for those living less than 1 kilometre from their workplace. Clearly, the government lost, at high political and reputational cost. However, it was not a clear victory for the unions: the political mandate given by the referendum was beyond the unions' basic agenda and deemed too risky a path to follow.

This emerged clearly in October 2010 when the Constitutional Court decided that the referendum could not be held. The unions' first reaction was hostile: threats of strikes, protests and early elections; 'this was a shot in democracy's chest' (one union leader in media). However a readiness to negotiate on compensation will soon prevail: 'knocking down the government is not our role', explained Josip. Indeed, in November the following was agreed: (i) a 'referendum on referendums' (to reduce the number of necessary signatures to 200,000); (ii) the establishment of labour courts; (iii) the cancellation of collective agreements only in the case of fundamentally changed economic conditions (and one year extended application after expiry); (iv) the abolition of firms' work regulations[15] (the last two points call for changes in the Labour Code). Negative reactions were widespread. Some commentators had seen the compromise as proof of the power of social dialogue, but disappointed ones saw it as opportunistic support for the failing government whose public approval ratings were sliding. Frane states openly: 'in the end, this has destroyed the unions' political power'. What remains were understandable attempts to capitalize on government weakness in the election year of 2011 to protect the working conditions of public sector employees.

In 2011, both sides initiated talks on revision of the 2009 agreement. Parliamentary elections were an important part of both sides' strategy (Josip and Luka confirm 'political calculation'). Indeed, throughout the campaign the ruling party 'boasted about keeping fiscal stability without cutting wages' (Josip) (while the opposition led by the Social Democratic Party was promising not to cut wages and employment in the public sector; a promise that lost its credibility just a couple of months later). Finally, in October 2011 'changes and additions' to the 2009 agreement brought: (i) a continuation of the wage freeze to December 2012; (ii) no inflation indexation; and (iii) more favourable convergence criteria. If all unions signed, those additions would have become legally enforceable about two weeks before the December elections. However, a major health sector union declined to sign. This led to arbitration, which gave the green light to the agreement, making it legally enforceable, but too late for the outgoing government to benefit from it politically.

5.2.4 Social dialogue matters

Stability of employment, moderate wage adjustment and one-off cuts in some benefits were the dominant effects of conflicts and negotiations during 2009–11. Stjepan recalls the education unions' conference in Warsaw: some 'looked upon us as heroes'. Indeed, public sector employees in Croatia have suffered much less than many of their peers in other countries. How can this outcome be explained in the face of prolonged recession? Why has the government backed off at critical junctures? One answer is the public sector unions' strength. The public sector unions' strike capacity is considerable. Furthermore, there was a more specific hindrance on the government side as a public governance crisis (due to corruption scandals involving the government) struck at the same time as recessionary effects on the budget had to be dealt with (summer 2009). Also, the political cycle, with 2009 local and 2011 parliamentary elections was influencing actors' behaviour, increasing the government's readiness to compromise. One could add the weaknesses of the state as a 'party to collective agreements' (Potočnjak 2010: 18), due to contradictory incentives that sectoral ministers typically have as negotiators. However, all this would hardly have been possible if Croatia had not had, on the eve of recession, quite a comfortable fiscal situation regarding public debt and fiscal balance (Table 4.1), giving the government room to manoeuvre. Yet, in 2012 this room is much smaller.

Policy choices are inherently political, leading sometimes to unstable yet contested 'equilibria'; particularly when they touch upon redistribution issues. The functioning social dialogue institutions are thus especially important in periods of conflict, encouraging compromise solutions and providing more stability and legitimacy to the choices made over inherently painful social dilemmas. In addition, while this case shows the importance of fairness in sharing the burden of adjustment policies, the policies of fairness turned out to be a matter of conflicting interpretations, as the 2009 conflicts over the crisis tax show.

5.2.5 Can moderation last?

Is the public sector's status cemented and beneficial moderation set to last? Hardly so, as the economic situation has changed for the worse since 2011, both at national and European levels. Thus there is much greater and urgent pressure on both sides to devise both viable and fair solutions. Josip believes that the unions' moderation will be sustained, as the 2011 amendment to the agreement 'is signed and legitimate', but hard to revise if economic conditions do not deteriorate dramatically. 'So far, the May 2009 agreement has not inflicted any costs . . . which puts the new government in a more comfortable position', explains Luka. However, he agrees that the 'hot potato' is only delayed by one year. Attacking benefits and rights in collective agreements may necessitate (inherently controversial) labour law changes but also lead to new rounds of social dialogue with public sector unions. Could the long, hot summer of 2010 be repeated? The political strength and unity of the PSE unions has been weakened. The atmosphere in society has changed, too, in favour of more radical cuts in the public sector (as public opinion surveys attest). However, the unions' capacities are still high and the education unions in particular are determined to fight for fair distribution of the burden once again, threatening protest actions and strikes, as in 2009, if unilateral cuts are enforced. While it is still unlikely that the new government will turn its back on social dialogue and resort to one-sided austerity measures, risking open conflicts with unions and public sector employees – it is not impossible. Structural, fiscal and ideological pressures, as well as IFI recommendations all call for more radical changes in employment and working conditions. Again, the key to the policies chosen will reside in actors' relative powers, incentives and bargaining skills, opening up considerable scope for unintended effects.

6. CONCLUSIONS

The public sector in Croatia has not experienced dramatic changes in recession years. So far, stability and moderation have prevailed. This was in major part due to the successful efforts of the public sector unions. Reforms, modernization and Europeanization in the public sector seemed to have a limited impact on job content and intensity, but were hard to discern at aggregate levels. However, the government has not seriously challenged basic employment and working conditions, even when such a course was strongly advised by IFIs. Several potentially far-reaching reforms so far have been ineffectual, because they were partial, delayed or withdrawn (public administration reform, recent higher education and science reform). However, some reforms did have important effects on working conditions (including unintended ones), such as the 'Bologna' reform and primary health-care reforms.

Public sector employees have avoided strong austerity measures so far, while their unions have signed a number of agreements protecting existing working conditions and committing the government to future improvement. But with prolongation of the recession, pressures to impose austerity, much beyond the wage freeze (at the 2008 level) enacted since 2009, are on the increase again, and previous commitments are called into question by the current government. However, so far – and probably in times to come – it is employees exposed to subcontracting and privatization of non-core activities in the public sector (for example, cleaning and food services), as well as those on various sorts of non-permanent contract, who have turned out to be particularly vulnerable. While the public sector has been vital for preserving female employment security and income, this might not remain so, as a continuation of austerity may reduce training and advancement prospects (already visible) and early career transitions to permanent posts.

After the pre-electoral intermezzo of 2011, and further economic deterioration, is a new phase of austerity unavoidable? The future is uncertain, despite pre-election promises (of the former opposition) that public sector wages and employment will not be cut. This commitment is vacuous and not credible, as the new government's declarations and moves attest. The possibility of much deeper cuts is increasing. However, the effect of austerity on the relative wage level of public sector workers is uncertain, as deepening of the private sector crisis may put downward pressure on its wages as well.

Finally, the crisis is also creating a 'window of opportunity' for deeper reforms in the public sector, putting social dialogue and actors' credibility to their greatest test. Public administration reform is the most imminent, but also the most challenging; as is pay-system reform in the public administration and PSE, at both national and local levels, to which the current government has committed itself. New regulations are currently being negotiated on unions' and employers' national representativeness and on a radical shortening of collective agreements' validity after expiration, opening a new arena for contestation and protest. They may significantly change the playing field for social dialogue, making it substantially different from the present one. While the reform tasks seem formidable, public opinion surveys show a high level of readiness for public sector reforms. However, it is questionable how long this support will last after reforms start to affect livelihoods at a personal level. Once the winners and losers of the reforms start to emerge the political field might become more contested, and policy manoeuvring more complex. Stalling strategies might lead to the waste of another opportunity to find a fair and efficient solution. Weathering the reforms is a challenge, with uncertain consequences for both public sector employees and Croatian society itself.

NOTES

1. Local government units have a certain autonomy over communal activities, education, pre-school, culture and so on. However, the 2001 move towards decentralization remained partial (Rogić-Lugarić 2011: 63). For example, primary and secondary education employees' wages and benefits are financed from the state budget, while material expenses and capital investments fall upon local budgets.
2. In terms of public sector employment, Croatia is not a European outlier. The exception is employment in state-owned companies, which stands at 12 per cent of total employment, twice the EU average (Bejaković et al. 2010).
3. The identities of all the interviewees were substituted with generic Croatian names.
4. According to Poslovni.hr (1 December 2010), in practices with a large number of

patients, between 60 and 110 patients are dealt with a day; and only such practices tend to be profitable. Marija confirms that after e-medicine was introduced she deals daily with a workload of 80, sometimes up to 120, patients. She finds it 'terrible'.

5. We interviewed Marko from the Croatian Medical Chamber; Iva from the health union; Vinka a hospital internist; Boris a primary health-care doctor active in the private doctors' association; and Marija a primary health doctor.
6. Nevertheless, many higher education institutions contract out a substantial part of the teaching workload via civil contracts to professors employed in other institutions. In 2010, up to 44 per cent of professors working via an employment contract had such teaching stints.
7. A high-ranking government official explained this change in an e-mail communication. In addition to its fiscal effects, it also corresponds to Croatia's commitment (in the EU negotiations) to reform the tenure-based pay system.
8. In order to avoid changes in the Labour Code the government prepared a separate law, which some find controversial in legal terms.
9. In local administration and pre-school education, dialogue and bargaining take place at local level, but very much informed by the outcomes of national dialogue.
10. This was a sign of increasing disputes inside the major PSE union confederation: two unions left Matica during the summer of 2011 (social care and health).
11. We thank Jurica Zrnc for assistance with wage data.
12. In 2010, compared to academically educated employees in business services, their peers in public administration had a 7 per cent higher wage and those in education a 20 per cent lower one.
13. However the public administration unions agreed in March on a 6 per cent decrease, and their collective agreement was left intact. Petar, from the major public administration union, explains the union's weakness: (i) low strike capacity ('we strike directly against our employer and chief . . . most members have secondary education and low labour market competitiveness'; (ii) the government 'has direct instruments to put us in order; ministers are harsh on their employees, but not so on their constituencies'; (iii) 'it is hard to get public support for PA . . . only those in uniforms get any sympathy'. And there was a 'secret agreement' struck: 'it guaranteed that if PSE eventually gets more, it will be granted to PA as well' (SK). This defensive and subdued position is typical of most public administration unions, their arrangements being largely dependent on PSE unions.
14. Parity was defined in terms of ratio between gross wage for an academically educated beginner in public services and average gross wage in the country. Target level for 2016 was set up as 92:100, up from 85:100 in 2008.
15. A company document that employers use to regulate in-firm work organization and conditions. Unions, however, complain that many employers use it as a substitute for collective bargaining over working conditions.

REFERENCES

Bađun, M., V. Pribičević and M. Deskar Škrbić (2011), 'Utjecaj veličine, strukture i efikasnosti državne potrošnje na ekonomski rast Hrvatske', 'Dijagnostika rasta' project, mimeo, pp. 1–46.

Bagić, D. (2010), 'Sustav industrijskih odnosa u Republici Hrvatskoj: hrvatski sindikati između društvene integracije i tržišnog sukoba', PhD dissertation, University of Zagreb.

Bejaković, P., V. Bratić and G. Vukšić (2010), 'Employment in the public sector: international comparisons', *Newsletter*, No. 51, August, Institute of Public Finance, Zagreb.

Budak, J. (ed.) (2011), *Deset tema o reformi javne uprave u Hrvatskoj*, Zagreb: Economic Institute Zagreb and Friedrich Ebert Stiftung in Zagreb, pp. 1–37.

Franičević, V. (2011), 'Croatia – Prolonged crisis with an uncertain ending', in D. Vaughan-Whitehead (ed.), *Work Inequalities in the Crisis: Evidence from Europe*, Cheltenham, UK and Northampton, MA, USA: Edward Elgar and Geneva: ILO, pp. 143–97.

Jafarov, E. and V. Gunnarsson (2008), 'Efficiency of government social spending in Croatia', *Financial Theory and Practice*, **32** (3): 289–320.

Koprić, I. (2009), 'Contemporary Croatian public administration on the reform waves', IPSA XXI World Congress of Political Science, Santiago, Chile, 12–16 July, pp. 1–32.

Krištof, M., K. Pisk and I. Radeka (2011), *Primjena bolonjskog procesa na hrvatskim sveučilištima*, Zagreb: Sindikat znanosti i visokog obrazovanja.

Kunac, S. (2011), 'Neočekivani rezultat zagrebačkih protesta – korak ka omasovljenju i artikulaciji građanskih zahtjeva?', *Političke analize*, **6** (2): 29–33.

Matković, T. (2010), *Utjecaj ekonomske krize na tržište rada*, Zagreb: UNDP Hrvatska.

Mihaljek, D. (2007), 'Health care policy and reform in Croatia: how to start dealing with the causes rather than the symptoms of problems' *Newsletter*, No. 31, Institute for Public Finance, Zagreb.

Nestić, D. (2010), 'Plaće u Hrvatskoj: Trendovi, problem i očekivanja', mimeo, Zagreb.

Nestić, D. and I.R. Bakarić (2010), 'National Report Croatia', EC project – Minimum Wage Systems and Changing Industrial Relations, September.

Ostojić, R. (2012), 'Stanje zdravstvenog sustava', Okrugli stol časopisa Banka: Krvna slika zdravstvenog sustava, 6, veljače, PPT prezentacija.

Potočnjak, Ž. (2010), 'Collective agreements in the Republic of Croatia: current regulations and proposed changes', background paper for the World Bank, Zagreb.

Prijić-Samaržija, S., D. Pavletić, A. Deluka Tibljaš, S. Smovjer-Ažić, V.Katičić and M. Bajšanski (2011), *Uspješnost provedbe Bolonjskog procesa na Sveučilištu u Rijeci*, Rijeka: Sveučilište u Rijeci.

Ratković, K. (2010), 'Razvoj sustava ocjenjivanja državnih službenika u Hrvatskoj', *Hrvatska javna uprava*, **10** (1): 13–34.

Rogić-Lugarić, T. (2011), 'Financiranje jedinica lokalne i regionalne (područne) samouprave', in J. Kregar, V. Đulabić, Đ. Gardašević, A. Musa, S. Ravlić and T. Rogić-Lugarić (eds), *Decentralizacija*, Zagreb: Centar Miko Tripalo, pp. 63–83.

Švaljek, S. (2012), 'Posljednja zdravstvena reforma: potraga za dodatnim sredstvima ili još nešto?', Okrugli stol časopisa Banka: Krvna slika zdravstvenog sustava, 6, veljače, PPT prezentacija.

World Bank (2009), 'Program document for a proposed loan', Report No. 55111-HR, Washington, DC.

World Bank (2011), 'Program document for an economic recovery development policy loan', Report No. 58226-HR, Washington, DC.

Zrinščak, S. (2008), 'Zdravstvena politika', in V. Puljiz (ed.), *Socijalna politika Hrvatske*, Zagreb: Pravni fakultet Sveučilišta u Zagrebu, pp. 119–62.

5. France: The public service under pressure

Jérôme Gautié*

1. INTRODUCTION

In France, the crisis that started in 2008[1] erupted in a context in which significant reforms had been introduced recently, affecting both the size and the organization of the public service, which plays a crucial role in France as it employs about one-fifth of the total workforce. This raises a methodological issue, as it may become difficult to disentangle, in the changes undergone by the public sector, what is due to reforms introduced before the crisis and what results directly from measures induced by the crisis.

France is a good example of a mix of structural reforms and quantitative adjustments in the public service which raises the issue of how they are combined or when and where they may reveal inconsistencies. The issue is complex because if some structural changes result directly from policies intended to reform the public sector, others may also be induced by the quantitative adjustments themselves, such as job cuts, for instance, which may impact on public service organization and delivery.

The consequences of public sector adjustments can first be assessed in terms of their impact on public employees – concerning employment level and status,[2] wage level and structure, but also work organization and working conditions. The second set of consequences that must be taken into account concerns the labour market. As the public service is a significant employer of well-educated school-leavers and of women, these categories may be more affected by the freeze on hiring and/or job cuts. Finally, one needs to investigate the consequences of the adjustments for public service delivery, in both quantitative and qualitative terms.

Section 2 focuses on the main features of the adjustments in the French public sector, beginning by mapping the background, before presenting the main measures. Section 3 focuses on consequences in terms of pay, employment and public service activities. Section 4 introduces two case studies to illustrate both the modalities of adjustment and their effective and potential impacts. Section 5 summarizes findings and offers some concluding remarks on the policy issues raised by these adjustments.

2. PUBLIC SERVICE ADJUSTMENTS BEFORE AND AFTER THE CRISIS

2.1 The French Public Service: Between Uniformity and Segmentation

Figure 5.1 gives an overall picture of the French public sector, introducing a distinction between public sector in the broad sense, public administrations and public service (in the strict sense). The last, the *Fonction Publique* (FP), on which we shall focus in what follows, covers central government

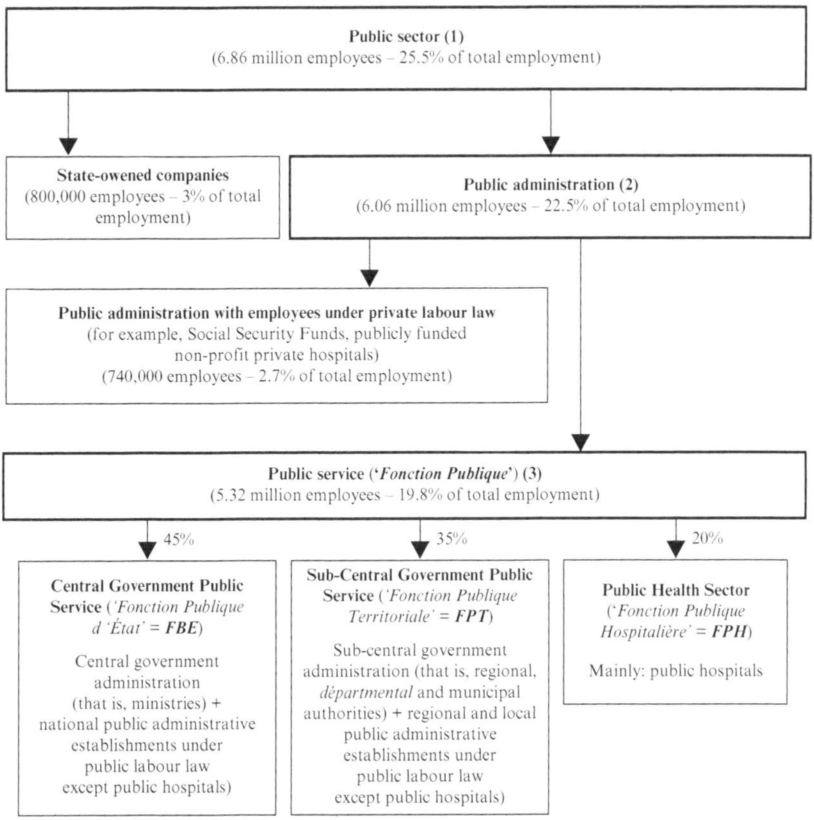

Figure 5.1 Public sector, public administration and public service in France, 2008

administrations (FPE), sub-central government administrations (FPT) and the public health sector, mainly public hospitals (FPH). At the end of 2008, the number of employees in the three branches of the public service amounted to about 5.32 million (in other words, about 19.8 per cent of total employment in France). Among them, about 45 per cent were in the FPE,[3] 35 per cent in the FPT and 20 per cent in the FPH.

Since the Napoleonic period, the French public service (*Fonction Publique*, as defined above) may be considered a good illustration of the typical Weberian state bureaucracy, with a highly centralized structure, and a specific and strong employment status, coupled with a deeply entrenched 'public service identity'. Common rules are fixed at the central level and tend to apply to all employees.[4] This applies particularly to the grading system associated with a unified pay scale, the so-called public service wage grid (*grille de la Fonction Publique*). This scale defines the index of basic wages for all employees, from the lowest level (index level 295 in 2011) to the highest (the maximum index of the scale is 1501). The 'index point' is worth a given amount in euros. Since July 2010, the value of the index point has been €55.5635; this means, for instance, that the annual gross basic wage of an employee whose wage is at index 295 will amount to €295 × €55.5635 = €16,391, that is, about €1,366 a month.

On top of the basic wage come specific allowances (family and housing allowances mainly), as well as bonuses and premiums, which depended until recently only on the work post and/or the position held (or the specific administration in which one works), and not on performance. In this system, pay progression is mainly seniority based: the employee's wage index increases automatically every two or three years until reaching the highest wage index available in his or her grade in his or her occupational category, the so-called '*corps*' (for instance 'second class university professor' – 'second class' being the grade, university professor being the occupational category). Length of tenure is also a criterion taken into account for promotion to a higher grade in one's occupational category (for instance, to move from second to first class). Note that all the occupational categories (*corps*) are classified in one of the three broad occupational groups: 'C' for the low-skilled occupations, 'B' for middle-skilled occupations/middle management staff and 'A' for high-skilled occupations/upper management.

Despite its apparent high degree of centralization and uniformity, the French FP, in many respects, is quite a fragmented system. One has to keep in mind that there is not only one but three public services, as detailed in Figure 5.1. The sub-central government administrations (regional and local authorities), the FPT, have a high degree of autonomy concerning human resource management, especially hiring. It means that policy decisions taken by the central government on downsizing, for instance, will not apply to the FPT. Concerning pay, within each branch of the public service, the share of bonuses can vary a lot from one administration to another: for instance, bonuses are much higher in the Ministry of Finance administrations than in the education system, but it is almost impossible to obtain detailed data and the precise distribution of bonuses across the different administrations is one of the best kept secrets.[5] Within each branch of the FP, the *corps* act as sub-internal labour markets (specific entry competition with *numerus clausus*, specific seniority rules, specific bonuses and so on).

Another important source of diversity is employment status. There is a crucial difference in France between statutory and contractual employment. The first covers regular civil servants – about 85 per cent of all public employees. Contractual ('non-established' or 'non-civil servant') public employees are mainly workers on fixed-term contracts, recruited to meet temporary manpower shortages and/or to replace civil servants on sick or maternity leave (especially teachers, see Subsection 4.2). But a small proportion of contractual workers benefit from open-ended contracts.[6] Contractual employees do not benefit from seniority-based career advancement rules and their pay (basic wage as well as bonuses, if any) is also lower compared to regular civil servants for similar jobs (see Case Study 2, the example of teachers – Subsection 4.2). But there is a high degree of heterogeneity here, as contractual employment may also be used to recruit some highly qualified workers from the private sector with a higher wage than civil servants.

2.2 Fiscal Consolidation and Public Service Adjustments

2.2.1 Delayed fiscal consolidation

France's public budget has never been balanced during the past 30 years. As a consequence, concerns about the public deficit had emerged well before the crisis. Changes in public service wage policy to curb public spending date back to the early 1980s,[7] but with very limited success in restoring the balance and reducing the public debt. Since the beginning of the 2000s, with the return of right-wing governments, especially from 2002, the 'state productivity narrative' (Cole 2010) emerged, with a move towards New Public Management. The objective was to improve the allocation of public resources, but also, clearly, to cut public spending, because of persistent public deficits (see Subsection 3.2).

Nevertheless, during the five years preceding the crisis (2003–07), the budget deficit (according to the Maastricht definition) never fell under 2.3 per cent of GDP, and the public debt increased slightly during the period,

Table 5.1 Public budget and public debt, France, 2003–2010 (% of GDP)

	2003	2004	2005	2006	2007	2008	2009	2010
Public spending	53.4	53.3	53.6	53.0	52.6	53.3	56.7	56.6
Public earnings	49.3	49.6	50.6	50.6	49.9	49.9	49.2	49.5
Public deficit*	–4.1	–3.6	–2.9	–2.3	–2.7	–3.3	–7.5	–7.0
Public debt*	63.3	65.2	66.8	64.1	64.2	68.2	79.0	81.7

Note: * According to the Maastricht Treaty definitions of 'public administrations'.

Source: INSEE.

remaining higher than the 60 per cent of GDP threshold imposed by the European Stability and Growth Pact (see Table 5.1). At the end of 2005, an influential report[8] written by a commission headed by Michel Pébereau, CEO of BNP-Paribas, warned that public finances had to be restored and public debt curbed. In line with this report, restoring public finances was at the top of the agenda of the newly elected (in 2007) President Nicolas Sarkozy. But if priority was given to cutting public expenditure, in particular by downsizing the public service (see below), at the same time, resources were reduced as a result of tax reductions.[9]

Since 2008, the crisis has deeply affected public finances: the public deficit has almost tripled, from 2.7 per cent of GDP in 2007 to 7.5 per cent in 2009, and was still 7.1 per cent in 2010, while the public debt jumped from 64.2 per cent in 2007 to 82.3 per cent of GDP in 2010.

The huge deficits in 2009 and 2010 due to the increase of the share of public expenditure in GDP show that, in the first years, the choice was made to let the automatic stabilizers work – and even to add some discretionary new expenditure – and therefore to postpone strong fiscal consolidation. According to an OECD survey (2011b) conducted at the end of 2010 on member countries' 'fiscal consolidation plans', France turned out to be among the countries where (strong) consolidation was needed,[10] but no substantial consolidation plan has been announced so far.

It is only with the 'sovereign debt' crisis that broke out in the second quarter of 2011 that fiscal consolidation was considered inevitable by many actors. Two plans were announced within a four-month period, the first in August, the second in November, aimed at saving about €17.5 billion in 2012–16 or about €7 billion as soon as 2012, equivalent to about 0.35 per cent of annual GDP, a fairly modest amount.

Overall, the fiscal consolidation directly resulting from the crisis was adopted relatively late compared to many other countries, and remained relatively moderate up to the beginning of 2012 (when this chapter was written). Moreover, it occurred in a context in which some public service adjustments were already in place, as we shall see.

2.2.2 Quantitative adjustments and restructuring in the public service

As mentioned in the previous section, the public service adjustments to curb public expenditure by decreasing the wage bill started in 2007, after the election of President Sarkozy – in other words, before the crisis.

The first important measure was the 'one-for-two replacement ratio' rule for retiring public employees. The objective was clearly to reverse the long-term trend of increasing public service staff. Note that this rule was supposed to apply only to central government administrations (FPE), whereas local governments (FPT) were still free in their hiring policy. Public hospitals were also not supposed to suffer from job cuts – health being a priority – but at the same time, they were also required to restructure (closure of small hospitals, introduction of regional health agencies to govern the health supply chain at regional level). But in 2007, a new plan was launched urging the hospitals to achieve a balanced budget by 2012. As a consequence, many of them had to implement a consolidation plan (*plan de retour à l'équilibre*), cutting costs by outsourcing and staff downsizing.

The one-for-two replacement rule was a perfect illustration of the 'state productivity narrative' (as labelled by Cole 2010), as half the money saved by these job cuts was supposed to be used to increase the wages of the remaining civil servants in order to foster motivation and reward higher productivity, the other half being allocated to reducing the public deficit. But above all, following here, too, the recommendations of the Pébereau report, increasing state productivity was pursued by not only quantitative but also qualitative adjustments, relying on deep restructuring and the introduction of New Public Management methods and procedures. In 2007, a new law was introduced (the General Public Policy Review, *Révision Générale des Politiques Publiques*: RGPP), aiming at 'identifying the reforms that will enable the reduction of public spending, while improving the efficiency of public policies'. If it was supposed to entail reform of all 'public policies', it has been mainly about reorganizing central public administrations (FPE). Note that the official aim of the RGPP was to reorganize the public service to improve productivity, but not to redesign the perimeter of public service activity nor redefine its missions. 'Optimizing', 'rationalizing', 'merging' and 'modernizing' were key words of the government communication plan. But as it was associated with staff downsizing and budget cuts, some trade unions consider that the RGPP is only about public service retrenchment (see Case Study 1, Subsection 4.1).

To facilitate restructuring by promoting internal and external flexibility some public service internal market rules have also been reformed, with the adoption in 2009 of the law on mobility and professional careers (*loi sur la mobilité et les parcours professionnels*): the rules regulating internal mobility within the FP are eased, but the law also facilitates the reallocation of employees if their service or job is suppressed, as well as the recruitment of temporary workers, in particular by legalizing the use of temporary agency workers, which previously was prohibited.

Table 5.2 presents an overview of the main measures and their potential impact, which will be presented in the next section.

Overall, what is the result of all these measures in terms of fiscal consolidation? The net expected cumulative budgetary impact of the whole public service adjustment process amounts to €5.5 billion in 2009–11 (three years), the equivalent of about 0.28 per cent of GDP, which may appear quite a small amount compared to many other European countries. About 24 per cent resulted from reductions in the wage bill (following the one-for-two replacement ratio rule, and with 50 per cent of the wage bill of non-replaced retirees redistributed to the remaining public employees), 29 per cent from cuts in other running costs and the remaining 47 per cent from cuts in programme expenditure (including investments).

3. THE EFFECTS OF PUBLIC SERVICE ADJUSTMENTS

Compared to many other countries, the impact on wages of public service adjustments and reforms may appear fairly limited (Subsection 3.1), even though they may induce increasing differentiation and increasing inequalities among public employees. The adjustments were more severe in term of staff downsizing, in particular in the FPE, with also potential negative impacts on the labour market outcomes of skilled young people and women (3.2). The adjustments also significantly affected public service activity, in term of both working conditions and public service delivery (3.3).

3.1 Limited Impact on Wages but with Increasing Differentiation

3.1.1 Freeze on index points and increase in pension contributions

The annual wage increase mechanism was profoundly transformed at the beginning of the 1980s (Meurs 1993) in order to fight inflation and better control growth of the public service wage bill. Despite strong trade union opposition, it was decided in 1983 to cancel the automatic indexation of

Table 5.2 Overview of public service adjustments and reforms since 2007, France

Type of adjustment and reform	Measures adopted	Impacts
Quantitative adjustments in employment (job cuts)	*One-for-two replacement ratio of public employees leaving for retirement*	The expected decrease in the FPE staff during 2008–12 is estimated at –7%
	Introduced in 2007 to reduce the public sector wage bill; applies only to central government administrations (FPE); the effective replacement ratio depends on the relevant ministry and occupational group (it was higher for high-skilled occupations/upper management)	Work intensification in some services; degradation in both quantitative and qualitative terms of public service delivery in some services Increase in dualism as in some activities (for example, education) contractual employees on temporary contracts were hired to compensate partially for the decrease in the number of civil service employees
Quantitative adjustments in remuneration	*Freeze of the index point*: the basic wage of every public employee is fixed by its wage index level in the common wage grid (*grille de la Fonction Publique*); basic wage index levels range from 295 to 1,501; every index point worth about €55.5 in 2011. This index point has been frozen since 2010	For a majority of public employees, there are still increases in the basic wage resulting from seniority-based automatic increases or from promotion ('career effect'); those hardest hit are those who have reached the top wage level of their 'grade' where there are no more seniority increases Introduction of a compensation measure: the individual purchasing power guarantee (*Garantie Individuelle de Pouvoir d'Achat*) The public employees whose individual wage had increased (including the career effect) less than the consumer index price during the four-year period (2004–07) received a bonus to fill the gap between the two. The scheme was maintained for 2008–12
	Increase in pension contributions (from 7.85% to 10.55% of gross wage).	This will be implemented progressively and will lead to a 3.5% loss in wages net of social contributions in 2020

Table 5.2 (continued)

Type of adjustment and reform	Measures adopted	Impacts
Other quantitative adjustments	*Reduction in operational and investment budgets.* This applies to the FPE but also to public hospitals with budget deficits. Since 2007, but became stricter with the crisis	Deterioration in both quantitative and qualitative terms of public service delivery in some services Some public hospitals have had to reduce staff since 2009 (with the same potential consequences as depicted above)
Restructuring and other structural reforms	*General Public Policy Review (Révision Générale des Politiques Publiques), RGPP*. Adopted in 2007. Global reform which intends to introduce New Public Management and to reorganize the public service. It is conceived as the complement of the quantitative adjustments (in particular, job cuts), 'doing better with less' being the motto of the RGPP	Restructuring of numerous administrations (reduction in the number of central divisions, and in particular the reorganization of the Ministry of Finance and the decentralized administrations of central government). Top-down process, lack of social dialogue and lack of accompanying measures led to dissatisfaction among public employees
	Reforms of human resource management, 2008–09. Facilitation of internal mobility, but also the use of temporary workers; rationalization of the system of bonuses and premiums with the introduction of a unified premium (*prime de fonction et de résultat, PFR*) based on the function held, for one part, and on individual performance, for the other	This is a step further in the individualization of wage fixing in the public service. The freeze on index points means that across-the-board wage increases tend to be replaced by wage increases restricted to some categories or individuals. Skilled employees and in particular managers may benefit more from the PFR premium – therefore men more than women, senior workers more than young people and new entrants

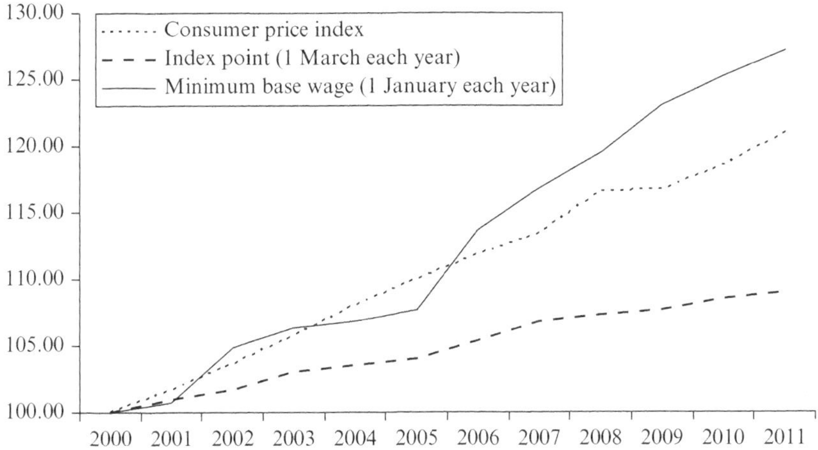

Source: Author's calculation based on DGAFP and INSEE data. For the definition of the index point see Subsection 2.1. Since July 2010, the value of the index point has been €55.5635. The 'monthly minimum basic wage' is the minimum gross monthly wage a full-time civil servant can be paid. It is indexed to the legal minimum wage in the private sector (SMIC).

Figure 5.2 Evolution of the index point of basic wages and of the minimum monthly wage in the FP compared to the evolution of the consumer price index, France, 2000–2011

index points (the reference unit of the wage grid – see Subsection 2.1) to inflation, and instead to adopt as a target a given increase in the total public service wage bill. The first result of this new wage policy was that the real value of the index point started to decline. Recently, for instance, while prices increased by 19.2 per cent between 1998 and 2008, the value of the index point increased by only 9.3 per cent (Figure 5.2). Nevertheless, it is worth mentioning that the lowest wages were not affected by this trend, as the public service has a minimum basic wage (*traitement minimum*) defined in monthly terms for full-time workers, which is indexed to the national minimum wage (SMIC), and which increased by more than 30 per cent during the period.[11]

The across-the-board wage increases were hardly affected during the first years of the crisis. If the index point annual nominal increase was slightly lower during 2008–10 than during 2003–07 (about 0.7 per cent against 0.9 per cent), its annual change in real terms was in fact higher because of lower inflation, but still negative (–0.8 per cent against –1.0 per cent). It is only at the end of 2010 that a complete freeze on the index point was decided for 2011 and 2012. Note that a freeze on the value of the index point does not necessarily imply a freeze of the basic wage (and thus a loss in purchasing power) at individual level, as automatic increases due to seniority still apply (see below).

Another policy measure may also have a significant impact but in the medium term: reform of the rules of the public employees pension system, which is a pay-as-you go system run by the state. This reform, adopted in 2010, can be considered part of the fiscal consolidation process. It was decided to progressively increase public employees' pension contributions from 7.85 per cent of gross wages in 2010 to 10.55 per cent in 2020. This means that in 2020 the wage (net of social contributions) should be about 3.5 per cent lower that it would have been without the reform. And for both the public and the private sectors, it was decided to increase the minimum retirement age from 60 to 62 years old.

3.1.2 Some compensation measures and other wage system reforms

As the value of the index point rose less than the price index, public employees who had not benefited from a career advancement during the period – whether due to an automatic seniority-based increase, which happens only every two or three years or even more, depending on the *corps* and the length of service, or to promotion – should have lost purchasing power (except for the lowest wages – see above). In 2008, the government decided to introduce a specific bonus, the 'individual guarantee of purchasing power' (*Garantie Individuelle de Pouvoir d'Achat*: GIPA) as a compensation measure. Public employees whose individual wage had increased less than the consumer index price during the past four years (2003–07) received a bonus filling the gap between the two. The measure was renewed for 2008–12.

As for central government public administrations (FPE), because the RGPP reform was supposed to increase productivity, as noted above, the government committed itself to redistributing among the remaining employees 50 per cent of the wage bill of non-replaced retirees. In fact, during the three first years of implementation, more than 50 per cent was redistributed, and the redistribution rate was higher in some ministries than in others – in 2010, for instance, about 65 per cent of the wage bill of public employees leaving for retirement was redistributed to the remaining employees in the Ministry of Finance, as against only 30 per cent in the Ministry of Agriculture.

This redistribution took the form of specific measures for some occupational categories – such as an increase in starting wages (for teachers, see below, Subsection 4.2); an occupational skill upgrading (for nurses, who were transferred from the 'B' to the 'A' occupational group, with a resulting increase in their index level); an increase in the promotion rate and so on.

Another important reform of pay and career advancement may appear more connected to the introduction of New Public Management processes than to the objective of reducing the total public service wage bill. The old system of an annual evaluation of employees was replaced from 2007 by a new individual assessment process, which is supposed to play a much greater role in promotions. Along the same lines, individual and collective merit bonuses began to be introduced in 2008–10. The objective was to rationalize and make more efficient the very complex bonuses and premiums system. The latter is to be partially and progressively replaced from 2009 by a unified premium (*prime de fonction et de résultat*) based on the function held, for one part, and on individual performance, for the other. This is a step further in the individualization of wage fixing in the public service, and may be seen as complementary to the lesser role of across-the-board and global wage policy.

3.1.3 Assessing overall impact on compensation

Once automatic wage increases due to seniority and wage increases due to promotions are included (in addition to the increase in the index point, see above), the average individual wages in the public service increased more than the price index since the mid-1990s, including in 2007–09 (see Figure 5.3 for the FPE), and the increase in purchasing power is even more significant if the 'adjusted average wage' is taken into account, to neutralize the composition effect resulting from labour turnover during the year. But this is an average: deviations may be important at the individual level.[12]

The (unadjusted) private–public wage ratio has been declining since the mid-1990s, although it started to increase slightly again in 2008–09 (see Figure 5.4 for the case of FPE). Of course, these evolutions have to be taken cautiously, as no data are available after 2009, and as many compositional effects may be at play here.

The freeze of the index point associated with the indexation of the minimum wage base to the SMIC (see Figure 5.2, above) may have contributed to the compression of wage dispersion in the public service,[13] but also to the flattening of wage profiles at low wage levels: in the lowest grades of the lowest occupational categories, such as unskilled clerks (classified in the 'C' occupational group – see above), in 2011 the difference between the wage level of an employee with 10 years of tenure and the starting wage amounted to a maximum of 3.3 per cent, whereas it amounted to about 39 per cent in the lowest grade of the top occupational categories such as university professors (A+ occupational group).

The loss of purchasing power of the index point particularly hurts new entrants (overwhelmingly young people and women) because entry wages of the majority of occupations remained unchanged in terms of index

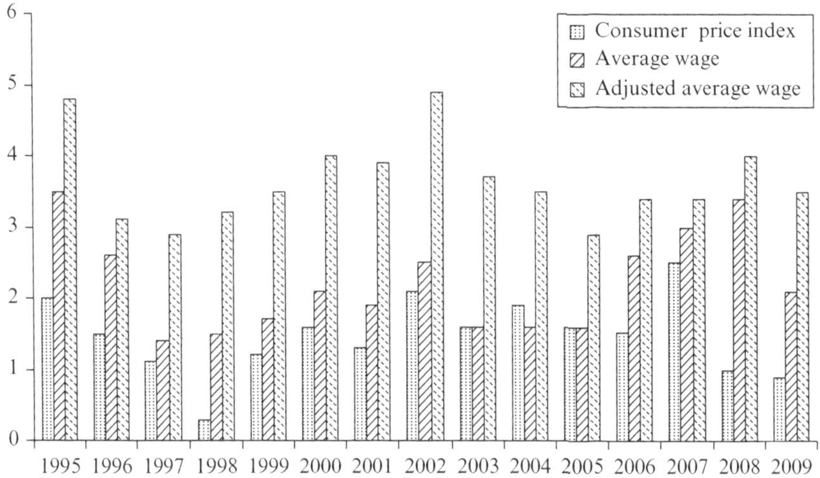

Note: The consumer price index does not include the price of tobacco. The adjusted average wage is calculated here holding staff constant from one year to another: in other words, taking into account in the calculation of the average wage for year n only the employees already present in year $n - 1$.

Source: DGAFP.

Figure 5.3 Annual increases of consumer price index, average wage and adjusted average wage in the FPE, France, 1995–2009 (%)

level. In those occupations, in terms of cumulated wage during the whole career, for a given occupation, a civil servant who entered public service in 2010 should earn about 10 per cent less (all other things being equal) than his or her colleague who entered in 2000, and even less if the increase in the pension contribution, which was introduced progressively from 2010, is taken into account.

Eventually, as already mentioned, the index point freeze also means that across-the-board wage increases tend to be replaced by increases targeted at particular categories or individuals. The introduction of the *Prime de Fonction et de Résultat* (PFR) should also increase wage differentiation within and between different occupations. Skilled employees and, in particular, managers may benefit more from the PFR premium – therefore men more than women (as women are underrepresented among managers – see next section), and senior workers more than young people and new entrants.

Note: Full-time workers (*salariés à temps complet*). Author's calculations for 2009. Scope: Central public service – see Figure 5.1.

Source: DGAFP.

Figure 5.4 Unadjusted private–public wage ratio (average wage in the private sector over average wage in the central public service), France, 1980–2010

3.2 Impact on Employment and the Labour Market

3.2.1 Decreasing number of public employees, increasing dualism

In order to obtain a medium-term view of the evolution of the number of jobs in the FPE, and to assess the specific impact of the crisis, one may refer to the annual budget laws adopted in parliament, which every year fix the maximum number of jobs created (net of abolished jobs). There was clearly a policy turnaround from 2003, after the election of right-wing president Jacques Chirac (Figure 5.5). The balance between authorized job creations and job cuts became negative (in other words, the number of new entrants was lower than the expected number of civil servants leaving, mainly retirement). But the impact of the crisis is also very clear: the negative balance tripled from –11,200 in 2007 to –33,700 in 2010 and –31,600 in 2011.

The one-for-two replacement rule for retiring public employees adopted in 2007 (see above) was put in place progressively. The effective replacement ratio averaged about 59 per cent in 2009, and about 52 per cent in 2010. Some ministries were hit much harder than others, in particular

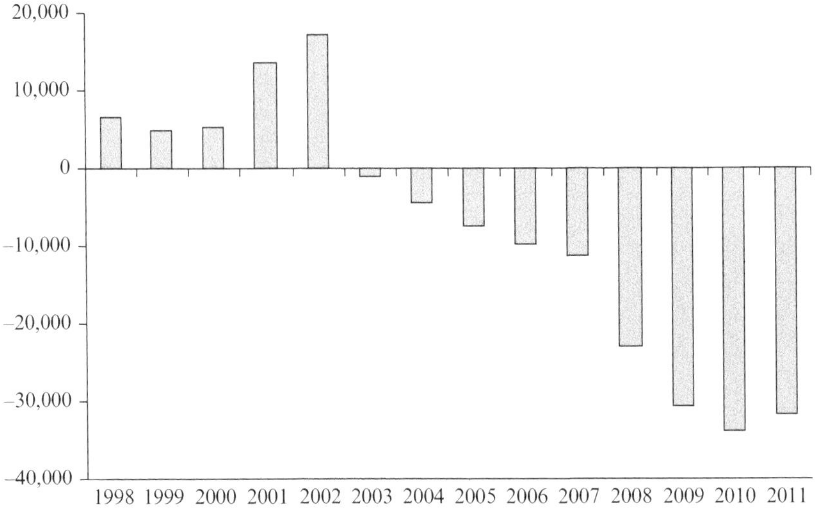

Note: These are 'annual equivalent' jobs: that is, a job created in the ninth month of the year is counted as one-quarter of a full job. Transfers of jobs to the regional and local public service (FPT) are not counted among job cuts.

Source: DGAFP.

Figure 5.5 Annual authorized (by budget law) job creations net of job cuts for the central public service (FPE), France, 1998–2011

the ministries of Defence and Foreign Affairs (Table 5.3), whereas others were sheltered, such as Tertiary Education and Research, and even more Justice, where the number of staff even increased during the period.

If the Ministry of Education (Primary and Secondary) benefited from a higher replacement ratio than average, it has been a major contributor to staff reductions because of its high share in public employment. Overall, about 87,000 jobs were lost during 2009–11, the ministries of Education and Defence alone contributing for 46.5 per cent and 26.7 per cent, respectively, of the total. Overall, for the five years 2008–12 the reduction in FPE staff as a whole is estimated at about 7 per cent.

It is worth noting that job cuts are not distributed equally across occupational skill categories. Indeed, the less skilled, the harder hit. In the ministries of the Economy and Finance, for instance, between 2008 and 2012, if the replacement ratio of the highest-skilled/upper management staff ('A' occupational group) was about 92 per cent, it was zero for the least-skilled occupational group ('C' group) (Cornut-Gentile and Eckert 2011: 28).

Whereas the number of civil servant employees decreased in the FPE,

Table 5.3 Replacement ratio of public employees in the FPE leaving for retirement and its impact on the number of employees, France, 2008–2012 (%)

Ministry	Replacement ratios average 2008–12	Evolution of employment 2008–12*
Defence	11	–11.9
Culture	66	–4.1
Finance	39	–9.3
Economy, Industry, Employment	55	–7.5
Foreign Affairs	14	–6.8
Agriculture	37	–7.4
Interior, Internal Affairs	55	–5.2
Primary and Secondary Education	60	–6.3
Tertiary Education and Research	98	–0.1
Labour and Social Affairs	36	–8.2
Justice	147	+5.8
All	na	–7.0

Note: Between 2008 and 2012, in the Ministry of Defence, only 11 per cent of public employees leaving for retirement were replaced by new recruitments, and employment decreased by 11.9 per cent. * For 2011 and 2012: estimates.

Source: RGPP, *6ème conseil de modernisation des politiques publiques, note de synthèse*, p. 2.

between 2005 and 2009 the number of contractual workers continuously increased (14.3 per cent) and therefore also their share in public service employment (from 12.3 per cent in 2005 to 15.1 per cent in 2009 (Table 5.4). This may have resulted at least partially from a substitution process between statutory and contractual (mainly temporary) employment (as we shall see in the case of the education system – Case Study 2, Subsection 4.2), indicating an overall decline in average job quality.[14]

As already mentioned, the 'replacement ratio' fixed at the central government level was supposed to apply only to FPE: FPH were supposed to be sheltered. But as the government also imposed budget consolidation on public hospitals and the wage bill represents about 70 per cent of their running costs, many had no other choice but to reduce staff. According to the estimates of the Association of Public Hospitals (*Fédération Hospitalière de France*), the number of staff (other than doctors) started to decrease from 2007. Even if the figures may appear fairly low[15] (–0.06 per cent in 2008, –1.29 per cent in 2009), the trend is increasing, whereas the burden on hospitals continues to increase because of population ageing. Part of this decline may be due to outsourcing some activities (such as

Table 5.4 Evolution of the share of non-civil servant (that is, 'contractual') employees in the public service, France, 2000–2009 (%)

	2000	2002	2004	2005	2006	2007	2008	2009
FPE	12.6	13.5	12.2	12.3	12.7	13.4	14.3	15.1
FPT	20.3	20.3	20.4	20.2	20.9	20.8	20.2	19.7
FPH	13.3	13.7	14.0	13.8	14.4	15.1	16.0	15.9
Total	14.9	15.5	15.0	15.0	15.6	16.1	16.6	16.8

Note: FPH = Public hospitals; FPT = Regional and local public services; FPE = Central public services (see Figure 5.1).

Source: DGAFP, *Rapport annuel sur l'état de la Fonction Publique*, vol.1, 2011.

catering and cleaning), but figures are not available. As in the FPE, it is worth mentioning that the share of non-civil servant employees has increased in public hospitals since the mid-2000s (from 13.8 per cent in 2005 to 15.9 per cent in 2009 – see Table 5.4).

As for the third branch of the FP – the local government administrations and public establishments (FPT) – until 2011 it was relatively sheltered in employment terms. If the number of employees continued to (slightly) increase in 2008 and 2009 it is mainly due to the transfers of staff from the FPE. The number of contractual employees decreased in 2009 (by 1.9 per cent in municipalities, 5.5 per cent in *département* governments and up to 23.9 per cent in regional governments). This may indicate some cutting of temporary jobs. Because of their high debt level and also because of the decrease in the central government financial contribution to their budget, as well as tax reform, many regions, *départements* and municipalities will have to implement budget consolidation from 2011 to 2012.

3.2.2 Cuts in recruitment and their negative impact on the skilled youth labour market

The public service (FP) plays a lesser role as employer of young people than of the working-age population as a whole (see Figure 5.6). In 2010, only 16.1 per cent of employed young people were working in the public sector, against 20 per cent of all workers. Moreover, among the young people employed in the public service, about 26 per cent were on temporary contracts[16] (against about 15 per cent of all public service employees).

Nevertheless, if we focus on skilled young people, the picture may appear quite different. Recruitment in the public service plays a very important role for the highly qualified labour market entrants. For

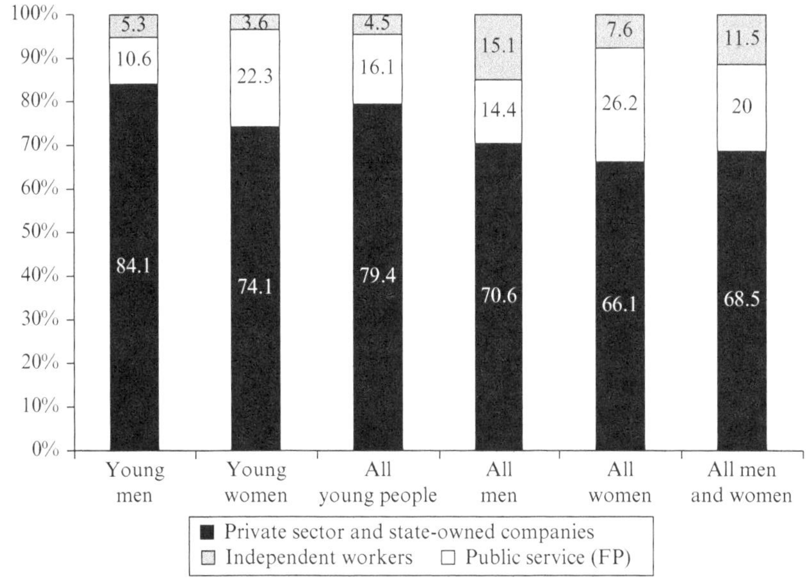

Source: DARES, Ministry of Labour.

Figure 5.6 Distribution of employment across sectors, young people (15–29) and all workers, France, 2010

instance, among the cohort that left the education system in 2004, at the beginning of 2007 about 40 per cent of those who held a PhD (*Doctorat*) or a college degree from university (*Licence*) worked in the public service (Figure 5.7). This is due of course to the recruitment of teachers and researchers in the public service.

3.2.3 Labour market impact on women

To date, job cuts in the whole FP do not seem to have impacted women more than men, globally. On the contrary, the share of women slightly increased from 60.5 per cent in 2007 to 61.9 per cent in 2010 (according to the Labour Force Survey). Concerning the FPE, which was harder hit, note that if the share of women is higher than average in the Ministry of Education, the Ministry of Defence, which has also been severely affected by job losses, is male dominated.

In a wider perspective, the public service downsizing and, more widely, the privatization and/or marketization of services previously publicly provided, may have a significant impact on women in the labour market. Indeed, in 2010, about 26 per cent of all employed women were working

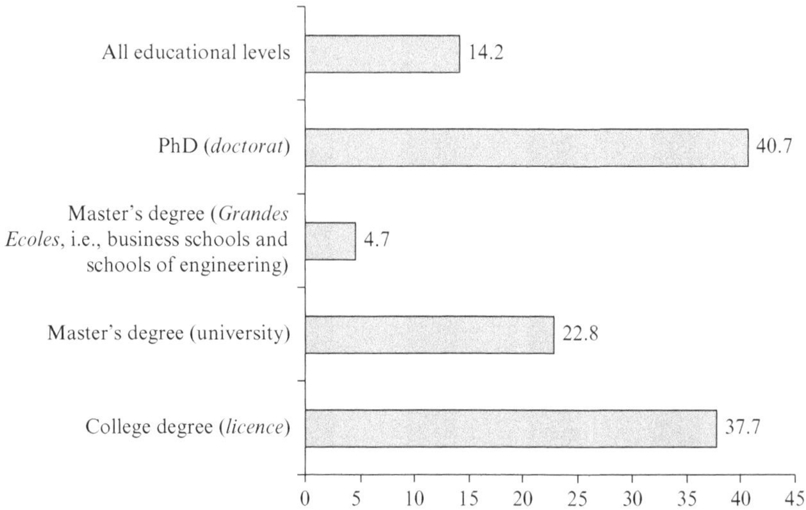

Source: DGAFP, based on CEREQ *Génération 2004* survey.

Figure 5.7 Share of the 2004 cohort of those leaving education employed in the public service at the beginning of 2007, France

in the public service, against less than 15 per cent of all employed men (see Figure 5.6, above).

But the labour market role of the public service for women must not be considered only in quantitative terms (number of jobs). Wage inequalities tend to be lower in the public than in the private sector. In 2007, the D9/D1 decile ratio amounted to 2.92 in the private sector as against 2.26 in the FPE, 2.03 in the FPT and 2.34 in the FPH. This may be one factor explaining why the lower (unadjusted) wage gap between men and women tends to be lower in the public service (FP) than in the private sector (Figure 5.8), except in FPH, where occupational segregation plays a significant role (nurses, nurse assistants and ancillary staff are highly feminized occupations – 80 per cent are women – whereas about 58 per cent of doctors are men). In both the FPE and the FPT, occupational segregation is lower, but there is an important 'glass ceiling' concerning women's access to top management: their proportion of top executives (*encadrement et direction*) was only 22.2 per cent in 2009 in the FPE. Moreover, women are overrepresented among non-civil servant public employees, especially in the lowest occupational categories.

Once the composition effect resulting from occupational segregation has been adjusted for (as well as individual characteristics, such as

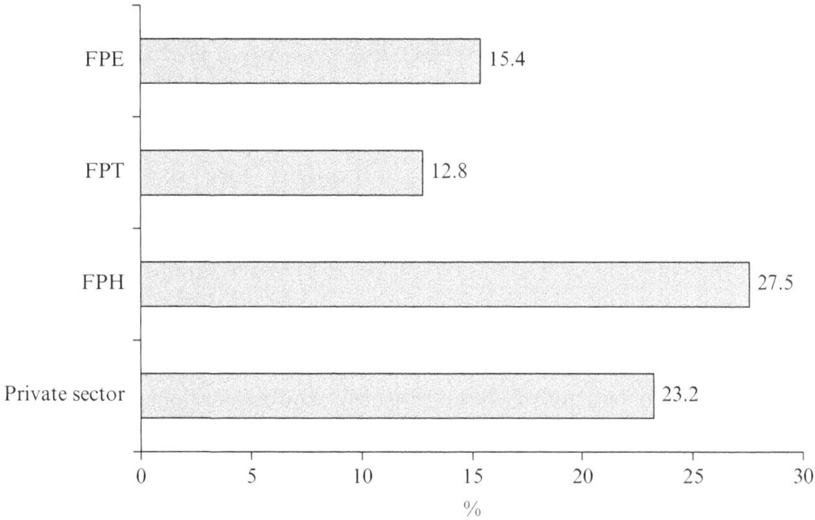

Notes: Gender pay gap = [(men's average wage – women's average wage)/women's average wage], in per cent. FPH = Public hospitals; FPT = Regional and local public services; FPE = Central public services (see Figure 5.1). Composition effects (due to occupational skills, age and so on) are not adjusted for.

Source: Author's calculation from DGAFP data.

Figure 5.8 Unadjusted gender pay gap, monthly wages net of social contributions, for full-time workers in 2007, France (%)

qualifications, length of service and so on), one can try to measure the remaining wage gap between men and women. Because of the general and impersonal pay rules in the public sector, one can assume that wage discrimination should be lower than in the private sector, but the empirical evidence is less clear.[17] Nevertheless, occupational segregation remains probably the main factor driving the gender wage gap in the different public service subsectors.

In order to assess the potential impact of public service retrenchment (in favour of the private sector), it is also relevant to analyse the gender wage differential between the public and the private sector. The unadjusted public pay premium is positive in France (see above Figure 5.4 for comparison of the average wage in the private sector and in the FPE). When controlling for workers' individual and job characteristics, the public wage premium remains on average positive, for both women and men. But the premium is decreasing along the wage distribution and even becomes negative for men in the highest deciles. According to Lucifora and Meurs

(2006), the gap between women's and men's public pay premium is increasing along the wage distribution in France (as in Italy), whereas the reverse is the case in the United Kingdom.[18] As a result, one could induce that, in relative terms, highly qualified/highly paid women would lose the most in the case of a hiring freeze in the public service.

But pay is not the only factor in job quality. One major difference between the public and private sectors relies on the fact that public jobs remain on average much more 'family friendly'. All public employees (even if they are non-civil servants) can benefit from a 'family wage bonus' ('*supplément familial*') which comes on top of the universal family allowances. It ranges from €73 to €110 per month for two children, and from €182 to €281 for three children (only one member of the couple can receive it if the two partners are public employees). Another important feature is that the working-time arrangements are, on average, much more favourable to work and family reconciliation in the public service. Civil servants (but not, in general, 'contractual' employees) have the right to choose to work part-time (from 50 to 90 per cent of full-time), and the reduction in their wage is less than proportional to the reduction in their working-time. For instance, a 50 per cent part-time employee will receive 60 per cent of the full-time wage. Moreover, the employee can choose at any time to get back to full-time working. Furthermore, whereas in the private sector up to one-third of part-time work is involuntary, the proportion is much lower among civil servants, as, except in small municipalities, statutory employment is offered on a full-time basis. Of course, the downside is that involuntary short working times are transferred to non-civil servants (contractual) employees – in other words, working-time arrangements are a major factor in the job-quality gap between civil servants and non-civil servant public employees. Another advantage is that some leave is more important in the public sector; for instance, a public employee can benefit from up to 12 days off a year to take care of a sick child, whereas the Labour Code which applies to the private sector stipulates a five-day maximum for such leave, unremunerated, unless the collective agreement says otherwise. Leave for other family events (marriage, adoption and so on) is also more generous in the public sector. The annual number of paid vacation days is supposed to be restricted to 25 days a year (five weeks), but in many services, the effective number of days-off is higher.

In addition to these rules which facilitate work–life balance, specific human resource policies have been adopted since the early 2000s to promote gender equality. Gender parity tends to be mandatory for recruitment committees (*jurys de concours*).[19] In 2008, a statement in favour of gender equality ('*Charte pour la promotion de l'égalité dans la fonction publique*') was adopted. It focuses mainly on discrimination and was drafted in collaboration with the High Authority against Discrimination (HALDE). Some ministries were more ambitious, such as the Ministry of Foreign Affairs and the Ministry of Finance, which adopted 'action plans' with quantitative targets to promote gender equality, especially among top executives. The objectives of these action plans also concern the improvement of work–life balance by promoting friendly working-time arrangements.

Overall, on average, the public sector (especially civil servants) tends to be significantly more 'women friendly' than the private sector. As a consequence, a downsizing of public employment and/or an increase of its dualism would have a negative impact on women's labour market prospects, in particular well-qualified women.

3.3 Impact on Public Service Activities

3.3.1 Overview of the issues at stake

As mentioned above, almost all public service activities were supposed to be maintained and even improved by the reform process, 'doing better with less' ('*faire mieux avec moins*') being the big motto of the RGPP. Meanwhile, staff downsizing and cuts in operational budgets ('resetting') may have had some negative impact on the delivery of public services, in both quantitative and qualitative terms. In other words, de facto withdrawal may be the (officially) unintended consequence of quantitative adjustments. Indeed, a 'beggar-your-own-services' policy may be another vector (different from privatization and outsourcing) of public service retrenchment.

In this case, the negative impact on public service delivery may be closely connected to the degradation of the work and employment conditions of the (remaining) public service employees. These conditions cover both employment status and working conditions. If statutory civil servants tend to be replaced by contractual employees, lower paid and/or less trained and skilled, this could have an impact on public service activities. The same may be true if cuts in staff and operational budgets worsen the working conditions of remaining employees (work intensification, increased stress and so on) and decrease both the level and the quality of the service delivered.

Concerning the latter, we have evidence from polls conducted to analyse public employees' perceptions of reform. It seems that, globally, public employees think that the ongoing reforms have had a negative impact on both their working conditions and public service delivery. In a poll conducted among public employees in November 2010,[20] 69 per cent of respondents considered the reforms 'unfair'. A majority also thought that the ongoing reforms would have a negative impact on all dimensions of their work and employment conditions (autonomy, content of work activity, work intensity, compensation, career prospects, relation between managers and subordinates). Another poll was conducted in April 2011 among managers.[21] Strikingly, their opinion appeared even more negative: 80 per cent declared that the reform had worsened their working conditions and 78 per cent thought that it had had a negative impact on service delivery. This results from the fact that managers were in the frontline to implement the reform which was supposed to maintain or even ameliorate activities, but with reduced resources. In fact, they were often obliged to implement painful trade-offs, leading to the de facto withdrawal or deterioration of the service, without any guidelines from above, as pointed out by many trade union representatives (see Cornut-Gentile and Eckert 2011, annex 1).

Assessing the exact impact of the reform process on the activities of public service employees and the delivery of public services is beyond the scope of this chapter. One major difficulty is that the RGPP reform has been a comprehensive process affecting all branches, and nearly all public service entities (except for local government administrations). It would be necessary to assess its impact very precisely at the micro level. We shall try in what follows to highlight some trends that seem to be emerging and to present some issues raised by different actors in the field concerning the effects of public service adjustments. As it is not possible to cover the whole range of public service activities, we shall focus here on some key sectors: security, employment, social services and health.

3.3.2 Some consequences for regalian functions: security

Restoring security has been put forward as a matter of the highest priority by Nicolas Sarkozy, as Minister of the Interior (2002–04) and after being elected president from 2007. Nevertheless, the corresponding administrations were not sheltered from downsizing and restructuring. According to the detailed report of the National Court of Accounts (Cour des Comptes 2011), the number of police employees has decreased by 2.3 per cent at national level (–1.6 per cent in the *Police Nationale*, and –3.4 per cent in the *Gendarmerie*). Operational budgets[22] other than staff and programme expenditure have decreased by 10.6 per cent during the same period, sometimes with dramatic consequences for working conditions.[23]

In order to compensate for the staff cuts, overtime has increased by almost 80 per cent during the past six years, meaning a sharp increase in workload. In some cases, retirees had to be called back to help their colleagues. The number of low-skilled, low-paid contractual staff has also increased, such as the *gendarmes adjoints volontaires*, recruited for a maximum of five years with no requirements in terms of diploma, and remunerated at the minimum wage level. As the number of national policemen and -women (including *gendarmes*) appears insufficient, many municipalities have introduced and developed municipal police forces. Between 2002 and 2010, the number of municipal police staff increased by 35 per cent. But inequalities between municipalities may be important, as resources are very unequal. The municipality of Cannes, for instance, dedicated 8 per cent of its budget to security (against less than 1 per cent in the poorest municipalities) and hired 191 municipal policemen and -women, almost as many as the 219 national policemen and -women appointed in the municipality. An increasing number of municipalities also outsource the security of municipal buildings or local events to private agencies.

Safety and security are not only about the police, but also health and sanitary controls, for instance in the food processing sector (including restaurants and food markets). Cuts in inspection staff have been high since 2007 (about –8.3 per cent in 2011 alone). This has significant consequences. In some *départements*,[24] the number of restaurant inspections has declined dramatically and it has been calculated that restaurants would be inspected on average only once every 10 years. In 2009, the European Commission threatened to ban the export of French poultry, because it discovered that many slaughterhouses had insufficient sanitary controls (FO 2011: 87–8).

3.3.3 Impact on social and health services: some examples

The employment and social services are also interesting when it comes to assessing the impact of public service adjustment. One important public sector reform launched in 2007 was the merger between the local branches of the Public Employment Service (ANPE) and the Unemployment Benefit System (ASSEDIC), to create a new entity, *Pole Emploi*, offering an integrated service to the unemployed and making economies of scale. With the crisis, however, the number of unemployed rose significantly. In some local agencies, the number of unemployed in each local agent's 'portfolio' jumped to almost 300. The working conditions of local agents have profoundly deteriorated during the crisis period (work intensification, stress due also to increasing disputes with benefit claimants). Many employees have complained about insufficient training to cope with their increasing number of tasks due to the merging of two different occupations (job search assistance and unemployment benefit case management). Between 2009 and 2010, the number of sick leaves increased by 40 per cent for those of less than five days' duration and by 32 per cent for those of more than eight months. A report published in 2011 highlighted 'increasing suffering at work, due to management led by financial considerations and relying mainly on quantitative criteria' (ibid.: 29). Even though the unemployment rate has not decreased, about 1,800 jobs were to be cut in 2011 (but new recruitments were decided at the beginning of 2012). The unions denounced the further worsening of work conditions and the correlated degradation of public employment service delivery. Another consequence is the increasing outsourcing of activities to private organizations which, according to some evaluations, are not as efficient as the Public Employment Service in helping the unemployed find a job.

Beyond the public sector proper, private non-profit organizations play a crucial role in social services (child and elderly care, but also the social and labour market integration of young people, the disabled, immigrants and other more or less vulnerable groups). Most of them survive because of public programmes, whether directly by receiving public subsidies or indirectly, because households receive financial help (public allowances or tax exemptions) earmarked for the social services these organizations provide. At the fringe of the 'public administrations' *stricto sensu*, these non-profit organizations (*associations*) constitute a 'quasi-public' sector which may be directly affected by fiscal consolidation, but plays a crucial role in maintaining social cohesion. Indeed, cuts in programme expenditure at both national and local levels have hit the whole sector hard in recent years. For instance, the number of staff in the home-provided social-care sector – which covers all occupations whose task is to help people overcome physical, mental, environmental or lifestyle difficulties – is estimated to be about 230,000 employees. According to the head of the UNA (*Union Nationale de l'Aide, des Soins et des Services à Domicile*),[25] the first network of organizations in the sector, about 10,000 jobs were lost in 2010, and the number is likely to be more or less the same or even higher in 2011 – in other words, about a 9 per cent decrease in total employment within two years – whereas the need for social care continues to increase, in particular because of the increase in the number of elderly dependent persons.

The case of public hospitals is quite specific as restructuring began in the 1990s. Since then, there have been many reforms to try to curb public health spending. But as already mentioned, the pressure has increased since 2007 with the objective of cutting hospitals' budget deficits. Staff feel pressured by the intensification of their work, especially nurses. As one put it, 'I can't bear it any more! We are asked to do more with less . . . We have to do everything too fast, at the expense of the patients. My work ethic and my sense of public service [*sens du service public*] are being challenged'. This is quoted by Agostini et al. (2011: 26), who conducted a comprehensive survey on a panel of hospitals undergoing restructuring and found that this feeling was widespread. According to a survey carried out in 2011 by the CFDT trade union in 492 establishments, between 60 and 77 per cent of the respondents among nurses, assistant nurses and housekeepers declared that their working conditions had worsened during the past five years, with increasing workloads and work intensification being mentioned particularly often.

4. CASE STUDIES

In line with the developments described in the previous section, in this section we assess the modalities and consequences of public sector adjustments by focusing on two case studies.

The first case concerns the role of social dialogue in the public service adjustments. Indeed, the way in which a reform is implemented is a key explanatory factor with regard to its impact on both public service employees and public service delivery. Has social dialogue played any role in the implementation process?

We then study a key sector which has experienced significant adjustments in recent years, the education system, which provides a good illustration of the various issues raised by public service adjustments.

4.1 Case Study 1: The Role of Social Dialogue in the Public Service Adjustments

4.1.1 Bargaining about wages and employment status

Wage fixing has been a controversial issue and a cause of disputes between governments and unions over the past 25 years, especially since the end of the indexation of the index point to inflation in the mid-1980s (see Subsection 3.1). The majority of unions are still strongly in favour of across-the-board increases through index point rises. Beyond the purchasing power issue, trade union opposition to government wage policy also results from attachment to one of the pillars of the career-based public service system. As one leader of one of the most representative unions in the public service (UNSA) stated, to increase the purchasing power of public employees by relying only on the career effect – in other words, individual wage increases due to seniority and promotions – can be considered a 'denial of the right to career advancement'. Up to 2010, unions were able to limit the impact of wage moderation via the GIPA scheme to protect individual purchasing power (see Subsection 3.1). An agreement was signed in 2008 for 2004–07 and the scheme was extended for 2008–11 and by obtaining a higher increase in the value of the index point in 2009 than initially expected. But they were not able to avoid the total freeze from mid-2010 (maintained in 2011 and 2012).

Another important trade union concern has always been the defence of civil service employment status and the correlative fight against the expansion of contractual jobs. As we have seen in Subsection 3.2, their number has increased notably since the mid-2000s, in particular in the FPE and the FPH. Following trade union mobilization, a national agreement (*protocole d'accord*) was reached in March 2011 and a new law was adopted at the beginning of 2012 to facilitate the move from contractual to statutory employment and, within non-civil servant status, from fixed-term to open-ended contracts.[26]

Overall, social dialogue did have some influence on wage fixing (up to 2010) and on the limitation of increasing dualism. But the story was quite different concerning quantitative adjustments of employment (job cuts) and, beyond that, the RGPP reform process as a whole.

4.1.2 The RGPP reform process: top-down reforms with almost no social dialogue

The General Public Policy Review has been a very important reform process since 2007 (see Subsection 2.2). In the new structure created to govern the RGPP process, the Council for the Modernization of Public Policies (CMPP), there were no union representatives. This is symptomatic. Indeed, all the unions of public service employees were unanimous in complaining about the absence of social dialogue, from decision-making to implementation.[27] As summarized by a leader of one of the public service unions, 'The method used to implement the RGPP . . . was characterized by the total absence of social dialogue at any level. . . . neither the unions nor the organizations of the users of public services were consulted'.[28] In particular, unions complained that there were very few debates in the existing consultative committees, and that when there were, the opinions and ideas they put forward were almost never taken into account in the decision-making.[29] Overall, many had the feeling that social dialogue was considered rather as an obstacle and that, in the mind of decision-makers, it needed to be circumvented if the reform process was to succeed.

The lack of dialogue, information and accountability was also highlighted by the parliament. In their report on the RGPP (Cornut-Gentile and Eckert 2011), members of the National Assembly noted in particular that the information provided by the government did not make it possible to assess the relevance of the diagnosis and of the decisions made.[30]

Overall, the reform was perceived by many as a top-down process with very little dialogue and consultation. Moreover, it often appeared brutal because of the lack of accompanying measures – in particular in terms of training – to help public employees cope with restructuring. As pointed out by one union leader,[31] there was a paradox here as the state often acted worse than any large corporation, which is obliged by law to negotiate in the case of restructuring. That has to be qualified, as the scope and magnitude of accompanying measures varied from one administration to another. There were some accompanying measures in the ministries of Defence and Finance, which were among those hardest hit by restructuring. But in many other cases, the accompanying measures (if any) were restricted to increases in compensation for some categories to facilitate acceptance of the reform by public employees.

4.1.3 Individual discontent and social mobilization

Overall, however, these measures were insufficient, as is generally indicated by the perceived negative impact of the reform on the part of public employees (see Subsection 3.3). The absence of dialogue and the top-down and arbitrary character of the process may have been an important explanatory factor (in addition to work intensification and the lack of resources because of cost cutting). In the November 2010 poll mentioned above, 79 per cent of respondents felt that they were not well informed about ongoing state and public service reform, and the same proportion had the feeling that public employees had not been sufficiently involved in the reform process (in terms of decision-making and implementation).

Even if the majority of managers supported the idea of reform when the RGPP was launched, four years later, as we noted above (April 2011 poll – see Subsection 3.3), their opinion of the process and its consequences in terms of both working conditions and service delivery had become fairly negative. One reason, as already mentioned, is that they were in the front-line in making painful choices and trade-offs, most of the time without guidelines from above, to try to deal with the consequences of cuts in staff and operational budgets. The objective of 'doing better with less' often appeared impossible to meet.

Discontent also translated into social mobilization. The number of strike days increased dramatically in 2010 (see Figure 5.9). The reform of the pension system, which put back the legal retirement age from 60 to 62 years old (in both public and private sectors) was the main motive, as was the previous reform in 2003. But many strikes were also connected with dissatisfaction concerning pay, job cuts, restructuring and its impact on working conditions. Mobilization in the Ministry of Finance offers a good illustration. The two main directories were merged (to create the *Direction Générale des Finances Publiques*, DGFiP), affecting about 125,000 employees throughout France and only about one in three civil servants leaving for retirement were replaced. To facilitate the merger, there were significant increases in the compensation of some categories

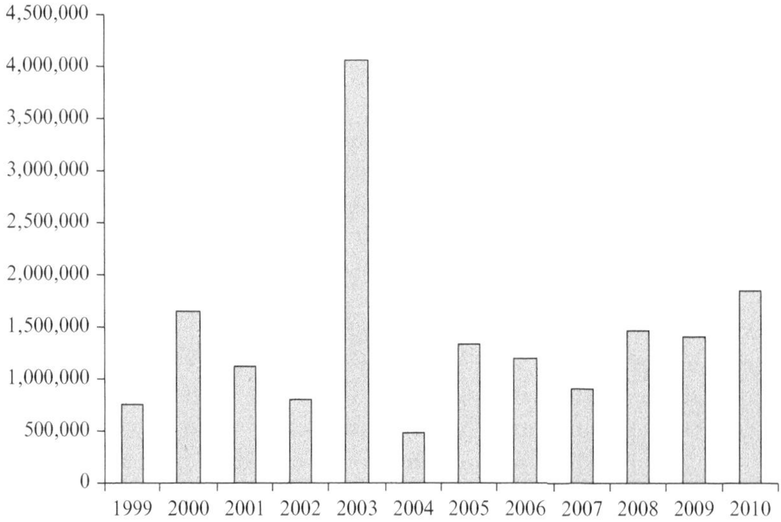

Source: DGAFP.

Figure 5.9 Number of strike days in the FPE, France, 1999–2010

of employees and, as a consequence, the total wage bill almost did not decrease. But it was far from being enough to compensate for the discontent of the great majority of employees, who complained about a significant deterioration in their working conditions. Several national strikes have taken place since 2009 with relatively high participation rates among DGFiP employees (almost 35 per cent on 27 May 2010 and more than 27 per cent on 2 February 2012). Overall, social tensions within the public service were high in 2009–12.

4.2 Case Study 2: Adjustments in the Education System – Nature and Effects

There are several good reasons to focus on the adjustments in the education system (primary and secondary schools) to get a more in-depth view of the public service adjustments. First, because of its role in economic growth and social cohesion, this is a key sector of public service delivery. Second, as mentioned briefly above (see Subsection 3.2), the education system has been a major victim of job cuts and has even become the most obvious example of these cuts for the general public. Every year, the number of retiring teachers that were not replaced was highly publicized by both the government (as a sign of its commitment to budgetary rigour) and the unions, as proof of the ongoing dismantling of the public service. Third, adjustments in the education system were not supposed to be a matter only of cutting costs, but also of 'doing better with less', a key aspect of the 'state productivity' narrative put forward by the government. Fourth, the education system is highly feminized (more than two-thirds of teachers are women), and therefore provides a good illustration of the potential impact of public sector adjustments on women. After presenting the justifications of these adjustments, we shall turn to their modalities and their consequences.

4.2.1 Was it only about cutting costs?

As for the other sectors of the public service (see Subsection 4.1), a group of experts (including some from the private sector) was put in place in 2007. The objective was clearly to analyse possibilities for cutting staff numbers. But this was only one dimension of the objectives put forward by the government, as the reform was also justified by a harsh diagnosis of the French education system.

Under left-wing governments (up to 2002), the public budget allocated to the education system had increased notably, with the strong backing of unions. In the mid-2000s, as compared to 1990, the number of teachers had increased by more than 30,000, whereas the number of pupils had decreased by about 500,000. Meanwhile, the results in terms of education system performance were mediocre. According to successive waves of the OECD Programme for International Student Assessment (PISA) survey, the French ranking among OECD countries was not only mediocre but also declining – from fourteenth in 2000 to seventeenth in 2006 and twenty-second in 2009 in reading; and from thirteenth in 2000 to seventeenth in 2006 and twenty-second in 2009 in mathematics. For the new government of 2007, this was a striking illustration that increasing the budget was not a solution and that always spending more in terms of means without implementing structural reforms was a mistake. On the contrary, the government was convinced that in the education system it was possible to 'do better with less', according to the RGPP motto.

Moreover, redistributing a share of the savings from staff cuts to the remaining employees by increasing compensation, which was another key aspect of the RGPP, also appeared important for the education system. As compared to the majority of other OECD countries, both in absolute and relative terms, French teachers were poorly paid, especially with regard to the starting wage.[32]

The adjustments implemented in the education system not only fit particularly well with the general objectives of the RGPP, but were also a good illustration of its implementation process, as depicted in Subsection

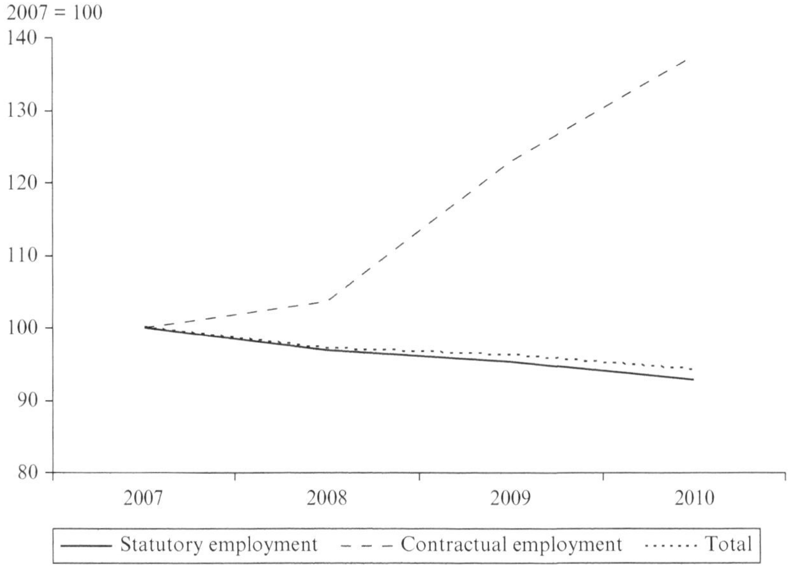

Source: Ministère de l'Éducation Nationale.

Figure 5.10 Number of teachers in secondary education, France, 2007–2010

4.1, in particular in terms of 'top-down' decisions and lack of social dialogue. There was almost no discussion with the unions concerning the reforms, as they were strongly opposed to any job cuts.

4.2.2 Quantitative adjustments: reducing staff and other costs

According to the annual budget laws (*lois de finance*) voted in parliament, the decrease in the number of staff of the Ministry of (Primary and Secondary) Education for the five-year period from 2008 to 2012 should have amounted to 70,600 full-time equivalent, mainly teachers (96.3 per cent). But the effective job cuts have been less because the number of teachers retiring had been overestimated by the government (Foucaud and Haut 2011). In primary schools, the number of teachers decreased by 1.9 per cent between 2007 and 2011, while the number of pupils increased slightly. The decline was significantly higher in secondary schools, however, amounting to 5.9 per cent during 2007–10 (see Figure 5.10), a much higher decrease than the decline in the number of pupils (about 2 per cent). It is worth noting that the decrease in the number of teachers had begun before 2007 (the peak number of teachers had been reached in 2005 in primary schools and in 2002 in secondary schools).

One consequence was that the decrease in the number of statutory employees had to be partially offset by an increase of contractual employees, in particular on fixed-term contracts. Whereas their share among teachers remained very low in primary education (less than 0.1 per cent), their number increased significantly in secondary education (by 37.5 per cent between 2007 and 2010), to reach the share of 4.4 per cent of all teachers in 2010. If the increasing trend had started previously, it accelerated notably from 2008. The first negative impact was in terms of increasing dualism, as the terms and conditions of employment (in particular concerning job security and wages) of contractual employees are much less favourable than those of statutory employees.[33] Among contractual employees, there is also a high degree of segmentation, with at least four different types of employees: those on permanent contracts (open-ended contracts, but non-civil servants), those with a one-year contract (from September to the end of August), those with shorter fixed-term contracts (from one week to several months) and those (the '*vacataires*') paid on an hourly basis, which is illegal in many cases.[34] Since 2008, according to the trade unions, the share of *vacataires* has increased the most (but there are no published statistics on the topic – and, in particular, *vacataires* are not taken into account in the figures on contractual employees that appear in Figure 5.10).

At the end of 2011, social mobilization of contractual employees in the education system emerged and a 40-page 'black book' was posted on the internet to denounce their employment conditions. The second negative impact is in terms of quality of teaching. Instead of hiring well-trained teachers on a statutory basis or contractual employees with some experience, many directors of high schools had to recruit people who had never taught before, sometimes in an emergency, organizing 'job dating' sessions with local public employment service agencies (see FO 2011).

Another way to partially offset the decrease in the number of teachers was a sharp increase in incumbents' overtime hours: they increased by 9.5 per cent between 2008–09 and 2010–11. This means increased earnings for teachers (one aspect of the government's 'insider'-oriented policy). This may have contributed to the widening of the wage gap between men and women, as on average, male teachers do twice as much overtime as female teachers.

If the primary schools were on average less affected, the impact of reducing staff was more concentrated in specific segments. This applies particularly to kindergartens for two-year-olds. Their school attendance rate decreased from 20.9 per cent in 2007 to 11.6 per cent in 2011.[35]

Although the desirability of school attendance for very young children is still debated, empirical results tend to show that it has a positive impact on later school performance, especially for children from low-educated, low-income households, particularly immigrants (DEP 2003). This decline in school attendance may therefore have a negative impact in terms of increasing inequalities in the long run. But another negative consequence is in terms of gender equality and work–life reconciliation, as pre-elementary state schools are the cheapest available childcare facilities.

It should also be noted that job cuts were not equitably distributed between the public and the 'private' education system. In France, most private schools have an agreement with the state (they are part of the *secteur privé sous contrat*). If they can select their pupils and have tuition fees – whereas state schools are free – they have to implement the same educational programme as the state schools and most of their teachers are paid by the state and therefore considered public employees. As a consequence, private schools were also affected by cuts in public employment. But whereas in 2011–12 their share in the number of secondary school pupils amounted to 17.2 per cent, their share in public job losses (full-time equivalent) was only about 9.8 per cent (Foucaud and Haut 2011). This also raises an issue of equity and inequality, as the children of low-income families usually do not have access to private schools.

Staff reductions are not the only quantitative adjustments. Other running costs or operational expenses have also been affected. Grants for pupils decreased by 6.8 per cent between 2011 and 2012, and 'social funds' for needy pupils by 4.4 per cent. There was also a severe cut (of 32 per cent) in the subsidies to non-profit organizations dedicated to extra-curricular educational activities, such as help in doing homework for children with low-skilled, low-income parents, cultural activities and so on. Once again, pupils from low-income families were probably the most affected.

4.2.3 Other aspects of the reform

Doing better with less requires that quantitative adjustments be accompanied by more structural reforms.

One of the most controversial reforms in the education system since 2007 was the big change in the recruitment of teachers in secondary education. To obtain statutory employment as a teacher, one had to have at least a college degree (*Licence*) and to enter a national competition, with a limited number of vacancies in each disciplinary field (history, mathematics and so on). Once successful, applicants became salaried interns for one year, attending training courses and practising teaching some hours a week under the supervision of a teacher in statutory employment. With the reform, the one-year salaried internship has been abolished. Candidates are required to have a master's degree and when they progress through the national competition, they immediately become full teachers with no specific training, under the supervision of a mentor (a more experienced teacher). As the requirements concerning new teachers in terms of educational level were raised, the reform was presented by the government as a way of increasing teacher quality. But the unions were opposed to the reform, claiming that the consequence would be exactly the reverse, as new entrants would no longer receive specific training. In their view, the only motive of the reform was to cut staff costs by suppressing the first year of salaried internship paid at a teacher's starting wage.[36]

As in other sectors, measures to accompany staff reductions mainly consisted of increased compensation. A new 'career contract' ('*pacte de carrière*') for teachers was introduced. The starting (nominal) wage was increased by 18 per cent between 2007 and 2012. The wages of other teachers with up to seven years' experience were also increased. Compensating premiums for specific activities (such as tutorship of new teachers, tutorship of disabled pupils) were introduced or increased. A new scheme for further training of teachers has also been introduced, as well as a systematic interview with a human resource manager after two years (and another after 15 years) of service.

But overall, in terms of funding, these measures remain modest. They amounted to about 0.5 per cent of the total teacher wage bill. According to the RGPP reform (see Subsection 3.1), remaining public employees were supposed to receive 50 per cent (in terms of increased compensation) of the funds corresponding to the reduction in the wage bill due to job cuts. In the Ministry of Education, the corresponding rate was only 39 per cent.

To conclude, in terms of both objectives and processes, the adjustments in the education system can be considered a good illustration of the whole public service reform adjustment process, and raise the same kinds of issues. Will these adjustments negatively impact the provision of education as a public service? As we have seen, the increasing share of contractual employees, even though so far it remains marginal (less than 5 per cent, but without taking into account the *vacataires*), not only induces increasing dualism in term of employment status and remuneration, but may also degrade the quality of teaching, in particular in the poorest areas where absenteeism is high among permanent teachers and therefore the use of temporary staff more important. The fact that the (semi-)private education system (which employs mainly teachers paid by the state) was less hit by reductions in staff, also raises the issue of increasing inequality of access to good education, as well as the sharp decline in the school attendance of two-year-old children.

5. POLICY ISSUES AND CONCLUSIONS

Adjustments in the French public sector cannot be considered a direct consequence of the crisis that hit France, along with the rest of Europe from 2008. The most important measures – such as the 50 per cent replacement ratio of public employees leaving for retirement in central government administrations or the RGPP reform process – were adopted just before the crisis, in 2007, following the election of President Nicolas Sarkozy. Following the 'state productivity' narrative, the reform process summarized by the 'doing better with less' motto, may appear a matter of improving efficiency by introducing New Public Management reforms, and not only as a consequence of fiscal consolidation, which indeed, until 2011, remained modest compared to many other European countries. Nevertheless, from the beginning – that is, before the significant deterioration of public finances induced by the crisis – reducing public spending in the medium term by reorganizing the public service and reducing its staff was a key objective.

One important aspect is that even though some measures were affecting (net) wages – such as the freeze of the index point of basic wages or the increase in pension contributions – overall public employees' remuneration was not hit hard, and we saw that some compensatory measures were adopted to protect the purchasing power of (almost) all public employees.

Overall, quantitative adjustments were mainly staff reductions, concentrated on the central government administrations (an estimated 7 per cent decrease between 2007 and 2012), and other operational costs.

In a way, the whole adjustment process may therefore appear to be an 'insider'-oriented policy as, on average, 50 per cent of the savings from the staff cuts was redistributed to the remaining employees. Some categories (such as newly hired teachers, nurses or some employees in the Ministry of Finance administrations which underwent deep restructuring) even benefited from non-negligible increases in compensation. Increasing dualism in some sectors is another aspect of this 'insider/outsider' story, as illustrated by the consequences of staff reduction in the education system (see Case Study 2). On the one hand, civil servant teachers could benefit from an increase in their overtime hours (not subject to income tax thanks to a recently adopted law), but with a higher workload. On the other hand, the number of contractual teachers rose significantly, and in particular, the number of those on the most precarious employment contracts.

But many alleged 'insiders' did suffer from the adjustments. In many services, reductions in staff and budgets induced work intensification and a deterioration of working conditions. This is particularly the case in services where public employees are directly in contact with 'consumers' and for which the demand has not decreased, or has even increased notably with the crisis, such as hospitals, police stations, public employment service agencies and so on.

Discontent and distrust among public employees have also been fuelled by the fact that social dialogue was often weak or even non-existent at all levels of the RGPP reform process, from (central) decision-making to implementation (see Case Study 1). This raises an important policy issue: as emphasized by many union leaders, as an employer, the public service acted worse in terms of social dialogue and accompanying measures than many (large) private companies. As we have seen in Case Study 1, there has been some social dialogue concerning wages – but with limited success, as the unions did not manage to avoid the freeze of across-the-board increases – and also concerning the limitation of increasing dualism, with the adoption of a new law in 2012 to facilitate access to civil servant status or open-ended contracts for temporary contractual employees. But the lack of social dialogue and, more generally, of discussions with stakeholders was almost total with regard to job cuts and restructuring.

At local levels, managers were particularly under stress (and we saw that, according to some polls, they therefore had developed a negative opinion of the reform process), as they were responsible for implementing the 'doing better with less' policy. But in many cases, they could not avoid doing less and/or worse in terms of public service delivery. As a consequence, some 'retrenchment' of public service was a de facto consequence of the adjustments implemented, even if it was not presented as an explicit objective of the reform process. But for some union leaders, this retrenchment was in fact the hidden agenda pursued by what could be labelled an implicit 'beggar-your-own-services' strategy. Overall, as privatizations were almost non-existent and as outsourcing remained apparently modest (but lamentably, there were no data available at the time this chapter was written), the adjustments in the public service induced a retrenchment 'at the margin', which may have hit particularly the most vulnerable users of public services, namely those who need the more public education, public health, job search assistance and so on. This may have long-term consequences in terms of human capital (if the education and health systems are affected, as seems to be the case), but also in terms of social cohesion.

NOTES

* I would like to thank Philippe Bezès, Vincent Lombard and Pascal Pavageau for providing me with helpful information and comments.

1. There were in fact two successive crises: the financial crisis in 2008–09, with a slow

recovery in 2010, and then the 'sovereign debt crisis' from the second quarter of 2011. The unemployment rate, which had jumped from 7.5 per cent at the beginning of 2008 to 10 per cent at the end of 2010, had slowly begun to decrease to 9.5 per cent in the second quarter of 2011, but started to increase again from then on, to reach 9.5 per cent at the end of 2012.

2. It is all the more important that, as we shall see, there are different kinds of contractual arrangements in the French public sector.
3. Note that teachers and academics alone, as employees of the Ministry of Education and the Ministry of Higher Education and Research, accounted for 35.6 per cent of all FPE employees in 2008 (about 858,000 employees).
4. Note that according to the OECD composite index, the delegation of the management of the public service in central governments is the lowest in France among OECD countries except Turkey (OECD 2008: 82).
5. Only very aggregated data are available; in 2008, the share of bonuses in total pay (including overtime hours) amounted to about, 15.5 per cent in FPE, 17.4 per cent in FPT and up to 23.4 per cent in FPH. Some data are also published concerning different occupations (at an aggregate level). The share of the bonus in the total wage amounted, for instance, to up to 65 per cent for top civil servants, 37 per cent for police officers, but only 10 per cent for teachers (mainly overtime hours in this case, which are included in the 'bonus and premiums' category).
6. This is mainly because since 2005, a law implementing the European directive on fixed-term contracts (European Directive 1999/70/CE, adopted 28 June 1999) requires that public administrations transform fixed-term contracts into open-ended contracts after an uninterrupted six years' service (that is, a continuous succession of fixed-term contracts during the period).
7. To prevent the public service wage bill from increasing too rapidly, rather than curbing the number of staff, the choice was made to reform the wage-fixing mechanism by cancelling the automatic indexation of the index point of the (base) wage grid to inflation (see Subsection 3.1).
8. 'Des finances publiques au service de notre avenir – rompre avec la facilité de la dette publique pour renforcer notre croissance économique et notre cohésion sociale' ('Public finance for our future – breaking with the easy solution of public debt, to foster growth and social cohesion'), Report of the Commission headed by M. Pébereau.
9. Including tax reductions on the highest incomes (by introducing a 'tax shield' – '*bouclier fiscal*' – to limit direct taxes to 50 per cent of income); income tax and social contributions (for both employers and employees) exemptions for all overtime hours; and a reduction in VAT (from 19.6 to 5.5 per cent) for restaurants.
10. According to OECD estimates, at the end of 2010, the required improvement in the underlying primary balance as a percentage of potential GDP in order to reach the 60 per cent gross debt to GDP ratio in 2025, was as high in France as in Greece and Portugal, and higher than in Spain and Italy (OECD 2011a: 19).
11. In terms of index points, the minimum wage in the FP increased from index 233 in 1998 to index 295 in 2011 – see also below.
12. Note that a belief that they were losing purchasing power was widespread among public employees. According to a survey conducted in early 2011, 55 per cent of them declared that they had not benefited from any across-the-board increase in their wage during the past five years and moreover, up to 66 per cent thought that their purchasing power had decreased during the same period (only 9 per cent declared that it had increased).
13. In the FPE, for instance, the decile ratio of annual compensation D9/D1 decreased from 2.5 to less than 2.3 between 2000 and 2007, but compositional effects may also have played a part, as the share of employees in low-skilled occupations decreased.
14. Note the figures available at the time this chapter was written were published in December 2011 and the last year covered was 2009.
15. Note that these figures are contested by the government, whose figures (source:

DGAFP, the central directorate in charge of the public service) show no decrease in the number of staff, and even a slight increase.

16. The others being on statutory employment or on contractual employment but with open-ended contracts.
17. Using European Community Household Panel (ECHP) survey (Wave 2011), when controlling for workers' individual and job characteristics, Meurs and Ponthieux (2009) found that the unexplained gender wage gap is (slightly) higher in the public sector than in the private one in France, whereas it tends to be the reverse in other European countries, such as Denmark, Germany, Italy, Spain and the United Kingdom.
18. As the authors put it 'In other words, if we had to interpret these patterns in terms of male to female wage differences, the evidence seems to suggest that females are relatively (much) better off being in the public sector – with respect to men – at the lowest deciles in Great Britain, whilst the opposite is true (i.e. they are relatively better off at the highest deciles) in France and Italy' (p. 57).
19. Civil servants are recruited in France by competitive recruitment procedures (*concours de la Fonction Publique*), with predetermined quotas for successful candidates (corresponding to the number of job vacancies to be filled). Candidates are selected and ranked by ad hoc committees.
20. On a representative sample of 803 public service employees (computer-assisted web interviewing).
21. Sample of 234 public service employees of Category A (computer-assisted web interviewing).
22. The 'operational budget' covers the expenditure required to maintain the functioning of the organization. It includes material and labour costs and the costs of providing the corresponding services.
23. Cour des Comptes (2011, p. 43). The *Force Ouvrière* union, in its publication dedicated to the consequences of the RGPP (FO 2011), presents several testimonies and anecdotes to illustrate the negative impact of such cuts. According to the director of the *Police Nationale*, because of cuts in investment budgets (almost 60 per cent), the life expectancy of each police vehicle should amount to 28 years. In a police station in Paris, employees were encouraged to look for furniture left in the street after garage sales (*vides-greniers*) to replace furniture in their office. In other police stations, employees were asked to bring their own toilet paper.
24. France's metropolitan area is divided into 22 regions and about 90 *départements*.
25. Emmanuel Verny, interview in *L'Humanité*, Tuesday, 31 August 2011, p. 3.
26. In particular, many contractual employees should be able to obtain civil servant status by just passing a professional exam, instead of going through the very selective process of national competition (*concours*); for the employees on fixed-term contracts, the conditions in terms of employment record in the public service required to get an open-ended contract are eased.
27. For more details, see the round table organized with the unions at the National Assembly, presented in the report by the National Assembly on the RGPP, Cornut-Gentile and Eckert (2011: 110–13 and 279–304).
28. Emmanuel Pailluson, secretary-general of Solidaires Concurrence Consommation, Répression des fraudes.
29. According to one trade union leader we interviewed (Pascal Pavageau, FO), one explanatory factor is that those committees are at the ministerial level, whereas many key decisions were taken at a more centralized level (the CMPP council, and even more often, the Office of the President), the ministers themselves having no other choice than to implement measures they did not adopt themselves and, in some cases, did not even support.
30. The reform began with a process of auditing, with mixed committees (civil servants and employees of private consulting agencies). But the results of the auditing were never published. The CMPP Council published short reports (six between 2007 and the end of 2011), but the members of the National Assembly complained about the 'insufficient

technical content and high degree of political marketing' of these reports (Cornut-Gentile and Eckert 2011: 78–9).
31. Laurence Laigo of the CFDT, quoted by Cornut-Gentile and Eckert (2011: 110).
32. According to the OECD (2011b), the starting wage of teachers with minimum training amounted to only to US$26,100 in 2008 in France, as compared to about US$28,100 in Italy, US$29,000 in Sweden, US$30,500 in the United Kingdom, US$36,000 in the Netherlands, US$40,700 in Spain and US$48,000 in Germany.
33. A contractual teacher on permanent contract (open-ended contract, 'CDI') may be fired if the number of pupils decreases. Moreover, his/her cumulated earnings throughout the whole career are about 30 per cent lower than the cumulated wage of a civil servant teacher. Note that employees on permanent contracts are a minority among contractual teachers, most of whom are on temporary (fixed-term) contracts (see also note 34).
34. According to the *Conseil d'État*, the highest administrative court, the use of *vacataires* in the public service is restricted to 'one-off services' and should remain exceptional. The use made by the education system is often illegal as some *vacataires* are employed for a whole year to provide a very small number of weekly hours. Note that the *vacataires* do not benefit from social security. However, many of them are also students and therefore benefit from social security.
35. In this case, too, the declining trend had already started as the school attendance rate was 34.5 per cent in 2000. One must remember that France has a near 100 per cent school attendance rate for three-year-old children.
36. According to some estimates, the hours of teaching provided before the reform by first-year (paid) teachers during their internship period, and since then provided by students during their unpaid internship, were the equivalent of more or less 18,000 full-time teachers.

REFERENCES

Agostini, M., F. Lavril and J.-C. Vaslet (2011), 'Les restructurations dans les hôpitaux publics', *HesaMag*, 2nd semester, No. 4.

Cole, A. (2010), 'State reform in France: from public service to public management?', *Perspectives on European Politics and Society*, **11** (4), 343–57.

Cornut-Gentille, F. and C. Eckert (2011), 'Rapport d'information sur l'évaluation de la révision générale des politiques publiques (RGPP)' (Comité d'évaluation des politiques publiques), no. 4019, Assemblée Nationale.

Cour des Comptes (2011), 'L'organisation et la gestion des forces de sécurité publiques', Thematic public report.

Direction de l'Evaluation de la Prospective (Ministère de l'Education Nationale) (DEP) (2003), 'Faut-il développer la scolarisation à deux ans?', *Education et Formation*, No. 66 (July–December).

Force Ouvrière (FO) (2011), *Le livre noir de la RGPP*, Paris.

Foucaud, T. and C. Haut (2011), 'Annexe 3: Enseignement scolaire', in *Rapport général de la commission des finances sur le projet de loi de finances pour 2012* (Vol. III), Sénat.

Lucifora, C. and D. Meurs (2006), 'The public sector pay gap in France, Great Britain and Italy', *Review of Income and Wealth*, **1**, 43–59.

Meurs, D. (1993), 'The rationale for, and implications of, centralised pay determination systems in the public sector', Chapter 4 in OECD, *Pay Flexibility in the Public Sector*, PUMA–Public Management Studies, Paris: OECD.

Meurs, D. and S. Ponthieux (2009), 'Public and private employment and the gender wage gap in eight European countries', in ETUI (ed.), *Privatisation and Marketisation of Services: Social and Economic Impacts on Employment, Labour Markets and Trade Unions*, Brussels: ETUI-REHS.
OECD (2008), *The State of the Public Service*, Paris: OECD.
OECD (2011a), *Restoring Public Finance*, Paris: OECD.
OECD (2011b), *Government at a Glance*, Paris: OECD.

6. Public sector adjustments in Germany: From cooperative to competitive federalism

Gerhard Bosch

1. INTRODUCTION

Although the German economy experienced its most severe slump since the Second World War in 2008–09, employment did not fall and unemployment did not increase. The effects of the recession were absorbed by firms mainly internally, despite massive declines in orders in manufacturing industry. This German 'job miracle' was made possible by two stimulus packages together totalling some €70 billion and temporary reductions in working hours through short-time working, the use of working-time accounts, reductions in overtime and increases in part-time work (Bosch 2011). The German economy recovered quickly because of the strong increase in exports, mainly to East Asia and the BRIC (Brazil, Russian Federation, India, China) countries, which were less affected by the financial crisis. Output reached and then overtook its pre-crisis level in 2011 and exports grew to a new record level of over €1 billion. This smooth landing in the crisis and the fast recovery reduced pressures on the public sector. The stimulus packages were mainly used to fund public investments, which temporarily relieved the budgets of the highly indebted municipalities, which are the main public investors in Germany. Tax revenues increased to a new record level, substantially reducing the government budget deficit in 2011.

However, substantial adjustments, such as reductions in employee numbers, pay freezes or cuts and reductions in pension entitlements, have been made gradually over the past 20 years, with important cumulative effects. Thus the share of the public sector in GDP has been reduced and today the German public sector is relatively small compared to those of other OECD countries. Because of the privatization of public companies and the outsourcing of activities, the number of public sector employees started to decrease in the early 1990s. The decrease accelerated after 2000 because of shrinking tax revenues following substantial tax cuts. In this 'decade of denationalization' (Bofinger 2008), collective bargaining in the public sector became increasingly difficult and more fragmented. It seems that after a brief pause staff reductions will continue in the years to come. In 2009, the so-called 'debt brake', which limits public debt, was enshrined in the constitution. Future German governments will only have a choice between tax increases or cuts in public expenditure. The German 'debt brake' is becoming the model for all Eurozone countries, which makes careful analysis of its possible consequences even more important.

Because of the good economic and employment performance, no special adjustment programmes for the public service in and after the financial crisis could be economically or politically justified. Therefore to understand adjustments in public sector employment our analysis has to cover a longer period starting in the 1990s and looking forward to the impact of the debt brake and the future budget plans of the Ministry of Finance.

This chapter begins with an analysis of macroeconomic indicators of public finance, which are compared with those in other EU member states (Section 2). The structure and development of public sector employment are then investigated (Section 3). This is followed by an examination of industrial relations and collective bargaining (Section 4) and a comparison of pay levels in the private and public sectors (Section 5). In Section 6, two case studies are presented. In the first, the new prevailing wage laws for public procurement, recently introduced by some *Länder* governments in order to reduce wage competition in public tendering, are outlined. In the second, local adjustment programmes in highly indebted municipalities – taking the example of Duisburg – that have lost their budget autonomy and ceded control to the *Regierungsbezirk* (the primary administrative division of a *Land* or federal state) and its chief administrative officer (*Regierungspräsident*) are analysed. The final section concludes.

2. THE 'DECADE OF DENATIONALIZATION' – PUBLIC FINANCE IN GERMANY

In order better to understand the extent to which the state in Germany has shrunk, it is helpful to examine the evolution of government expenditure in the years before the financial crisis, after which such expenditure was boosted by stimulus packages and increased spending on labour market policy, especially short-time working. Between 1999 and 2007, nominal total government expenditure in Germany increased only slightly and real total government expenditure actually fell (Table 6.1). In all other EU countries and the United States, government expenditures grew in real terms and contributed to economic growth. The main reasons for

Table 6.1 Government expenditure in selected countries, 1999–2007 (average annual growth rate in %)

	Nominal	Real*		Nominal	Real*
EU27	4.3	1.7	United States	6.1	3.3
EU15	4.1	2.0	Hungary	10.2	3.2
EWU16	3.7	1.6	Slovenia	8.8	3.2
EWU12	3.7	1.6	Poland	7.2	3.2
Latvia	14.2	9.2	Malta	5.1	2.7
Romania	31.0	8.4	Portugal	5.6	2.6
Estonia	11.9	7.6	Netherlands	4.8	2.4
Ireland	11.0	7.4	France	4.0	2.2
Cyprus	8.9	6.2	Finland	3.6	2.0
Iceland	9.6	5.8	Sweden	3.5	1.9
Lithuania	7.4	5.5	Belgium	3.8	1.8
Bulgaria	11.5	5.0	Italy	3.6	1.3
United Kingdom	6.6	5.0	Denmark	3.1	1.1
Luxembourg	7.4	4.5	Austria	2.8	1.0
Greece	7.7	4.3	Slovakia	6.5	0.1
Norway	5.9	4.0	Germany	1.3	–0.3
Czech Rep.	6.4	4.0	Japan	–1.6	–1.3
Spain	7.2	3.9			

Note: * Adjusted for inflation with the (harmonized) consumer price index (CPI).

Source: Horn et al. (2010: 9; AMECO-database of the European Commission (as of 20 April 2010); calculations by the IMK-Düsseldorf).

this uniquely German development were major tax cuts. The tax reforms introduced by the Red–Green coalition in the early 2000s had the greatest impact. Among the many changes, particular mention should be made of the lowering of the marginal rate of income tax from 51 to 42 per cent and of corporate tax from 25 to 20 per cent. In 1995 the wealth tax was declared unlawful by the Federal Court because of its unequal treatment of different forms of wealth (houses, land, shares, cash deposits) and has not been reintroduced since then. These tax reforms, and not the negative impact of the economic crisis of 2003–05 on the government budget, were the reason why Germany did not meet the Maastricht criteria between 2002 and 2005. The Maastricht criteria were incorporated into the 1992 Treaty on European Union, which led to the introduction of the euro, mainly because of pressure from Germany. The biggest ever increase in VAT, from 16 to 19 per cent, introduced in 2007 could not compensate for the revenue lost to the earlier tax cuts. If the tax laws had remained as they were in 1998,

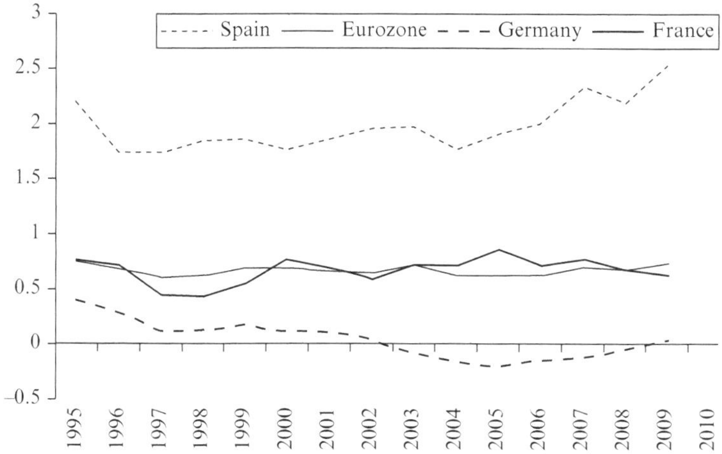

Source: Dullien and Schieritz (2011): 459 (AMECO).

Figure 6.1 Net state investment as a percentage of GDP, Germany in comparison to France, Spain and the Eurozone, 1995–2010

government revenues would have been €51 billion greater in 2011, which equates to 2.1 per cent of GDP and 9 per cent of annual tax revenues (Truger 2011: 20).

These unsustainable tax cuts increased public debt and were used to justify expenditure cuts to bring the debt rate down. Through severe budget control, the government reduced the annual budget deficit from –3.3 per cent of GNP in 2005 to –0.1 per cent in 2008 before the financial crisis. The stimulus packages and the strong impact of the built-in stabilizers on the government budget brought the deficit up again to –3.2 per cent in 2009 and –4.3 per cent in 2010. In 2010 the Maastricht criteria were met again with a deficit rate of –1.3 per cent and the government plans to reduce the deficit to 0.34 per cent in 2013.

The substantial impact of this austerity policy on employment and public sector pay will be analysed in detail later in this chapter. Here it should be mentioned that the public investment rate, which as early as the 1990s was already below the average level in the Eurozone, declined even further. The investment gap compared to the Eurozone average widened and net investment actually became negative (Figure 6.1). This policy of public disinvestment, together with a rigorous policy of wage moderation, damped down domestic demand and made the German economy completely dependent on export growth. The underinvestment in education and infrastructure might weaken economic growth in the long term.

In 2009 Germany amended its constitution to incorporate a debt brake that requires the federal government to eliminate its structural deficit by 2016. New structural debt is to be capped at 0.35 per cent of GDP after a transitional period that ends in 2016. Exceptions can be made in the event of specific emergencies that are beyond the government's control and place a great strain on its budgets. Additional borrowing will only be possible if the economy is weak. The structural target allows deficits to rise when output falls below its potential. These deficits should then be offset with surpluses during upswings.

The basic idea is that upswings and downswings follow symmetrical trajectories, which they mostly do not. The brake mechanism is not as automatic as it seems. The structural deficit has to be calculated by estimating the elasticity of government spending and revenues, that is, how much expenditure and tax revenues fluctuate over the economic cycle. Moreover, it must be ascertained whether the economy is in an upswing or a downswing. This is done by calculating the difference between actual and potential GDP – both of which are frequently revised. Model calculations have shown that, depending on the scenario used, consolidation requirements for the federal government may vary between €27.6 and €43.5 billion in 2016 (Jaecker 2010).

Moreover as from 2020, the *Länder* governments will no longer be allowed to run structural fiscal deficits at all. The losses caused by the tax cuts reduced the revenues of the *Länder* by about €25 billion, which equates approximately to their accumulated budget deficits. Transitional assistance totalling €800 million per year is planned for the particularly highly indebted states of Berlin, Bremen, Saarland, Sachsen-Anhalt and Schleswig-Holstein. In return, these five states must steadily reduce their structural deficits from their 2010 levels. The other states must aim to comply with the new provisions from 2020 onwards (Deutsche Bundesbank 2011: 18). Distinguishing between 'structural' and 'cyclical' deficits and operationalizing specific emergencies are as difficult for the *Länder* as for the federal government. The debt breaks the golden rule of public finance, namely that investments with future returns can be financed by loans, and reduces incentives for public investments. Instead, it creates incentives for the short-term consolidation of public budgets by privatization or sale-and-lease-back operations, which help to shift expenditures into the future. Since most of the *Länder* expenditures are used to pay employees in basic services such as the police, schools and universities, budget consolidation seems to be impossible without major cutbacks in basic services unless taxes are increased.

3. EMPLOYMENT IN THE PUBLIC SECTOR

3.1 Level of Employment

The public sector comprises the direct and the indirect public service. The direct public service includes employees of the federal state, the *Länder*, the municipalities and joint municipal authorities (for waste disposal, water supply and so on). The indirect public service includes institutions under public law, such as the central bank, the social insurance funds and the employment offices. Some statistics include the number of employees in enterprises under private law but under public control (more than 50 per cent of shares owned by the state).

The public service is rather decentralized. In 2009, the federal state spent only 19.2 per cent of all public expenditures compared to 45.8 per cent in the OECD31 (OECD 2011b). Part of the federal state's revenues is redistributed, mainly to the social insurance funds and, via the *Länder*, to the municipalities. Most labour-intensive services are assigned by the constitution to the *Länder* and the municipalities, which explains their high shares in public sector employment.

Table 6.2 shows that the number of employees in the public sector went

Table 6.2 The evolution of employment in the civil service (civil servants and non-civil servants), Germany, 1991–2010 ('000)

Year	Total	Direct public service					Indirect public service
		Total	Federal state	States	Municipalities	Other*	
1991	6,737.8	6,412.6	652.0	2,572.0	1,995.9	1,192.8	325.1
2000	4,908.9	4,420.9	502.0	2,273.3	1,502.2	143.4	488.0
2005	4,599.4	3,947.1	481.4	2,076.9	1,277.8	111.0	652.4
2006	4,576.0	3,897.9	477.0	2,054.5	1,261.2	105.2	678.2
2007	4,540.6	3,761.2	474.2	1,948.2	1,235.1	103.6	779.4
2008	4,505.1	3,714.7	462.2	1,929.1	1,220.4	103.0	790.4
2009	4,547.6	3,719.8	460.4	1,921.5	1,235.3	102.5	827.8
2010	4,586.1	3,741.5	457.3	1,940.7	1,241.5	102.0	844.7
Changes in %							
1991–2000	–27.71	–31.36	–23.00	–11.61	–24.75	–87.98	50.11
2000–2005	–6.30	–10.72	–4.10	–8.64	–14.94	–22.59	33.69
2005–2010	–0.29	–5.21	–5.01	–6.56	–2.84	–8.11	29.48

Note: * Post, railways, joint authorities.

Source: Destatis (2011a: 100); author's calculations.

down between 1991 and 2010 by more than 2 million, from 6,737,800 to 4,586,100.

In 2010, about 1 million employees were working in private companies under public control. Most of them, such as employees of the German Post, Telecom, Railways and hospitals, had belonged in the past to the public service. The shift from the direct to the indirect public service signifies a restructuring of the public service itself, with many activities being concentrated in institutions under private law. The reduction in public sector employment mainly took place in the 1990s, when many public utilities were privatized. Since the early 2000s, the rate of reduction has slowed down but the decline continues as a result of privatizations, mainly in the health sector, recruitment bans and early retirement schemes in the direct public sector. Just before the financial crisis and up to 2010, public sector employment started to grow slowly again.

A more detailed analysis of the impact of privatization and outsourcing shows that a staff reduction of about 11 per cent since 1991 can be attributed to rationalization strategies intended to make the public sector leaner (Vesper 2012: 13). The overwhelming share is the result of outsourcing and privatization, whose impact on the German public service has been greater than on average in the OECD as a whole. The share of the total production costs of government-produced and -funded goods and services in GDP is below the average for OECD33. In addition, the private sector is more heavily involved than on average in the OECD33 in producing public services and goods. The private sector's share grew between 2000 and 2009, due mainly to payments for health services. Since gross and net investment declined, it is not surprising that fixed capital costs are also below the OECD33 average (Figure 6.2). Consequently, the share in total government expenditure of expenditure on employee compensation (OECD 2011a) and the share of government employment in the total labour force are below the levels of most other OECD countries (Figure 6.3).

3.2 Composition of Public Sector Employment

3.2.1 Civil servants and non-civil servants[1]

Germany has a long tradition of employing civil servants, not only in core government functions, such as government ministries, public administration, the armed services and the police force but also in education and the social insurance funds. Even most employees in public enterprises, such as post offices and public transport, were employed as civil servants. Most civil servants have lifelong employment and cannot be dismissed.[2] Under German law, civil servants do not have an employment

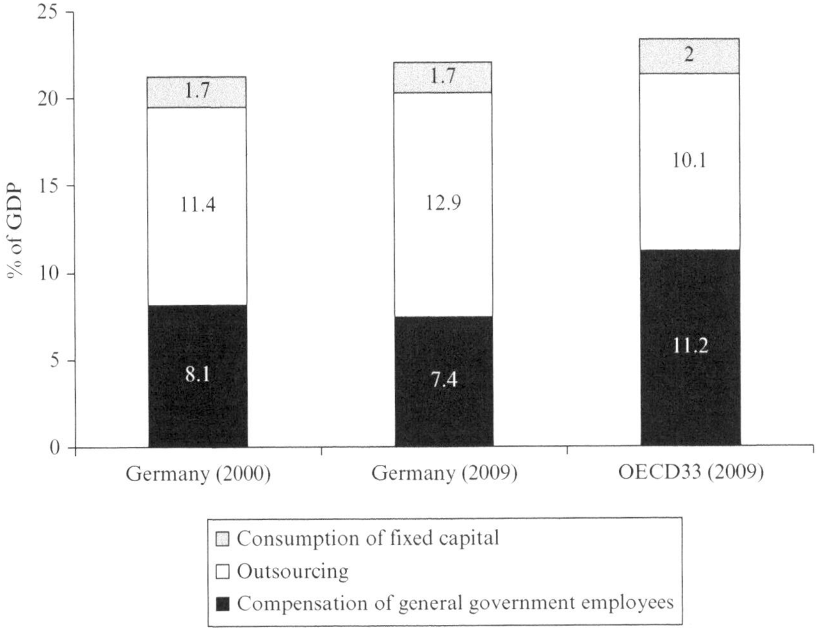

Source: OECD (2011b).

Figure 6.2 Production costs: cost of government-produced and -funded goods and services, Germany, 2000 and 2009

contract. They are nominated by the state. They are expected to be loyal to their employer and do not have the right to strike. Pay and other working conditions are not negotiated but are unilateral determined by the state. In return, the state is obliged to pay salaries that guarantee an adequate living standard ('alimentation' or maintenance principle). This includes allowances for children and spouses as well as sickness, accident, disability and old-age benefits. Civil servants do not have to pay social insurance contributions but receive support directly from the state. If the state reduces pay or benefits, the only recourse for civil servants is to go to court and claim that the alimentation principle has been infringed. The Federal Court has declared some wage and benefit cuts for civil servants to be unlawful. A recent decision (14 February 2012) concerns the new pay scale for university professors. Starting salaries were to be reduced by up to 25 per cent, while seniority increases were to be abolished and replaced by performance bonuses. The Federal Court declared these starting salaries to be infringements of the alimentation

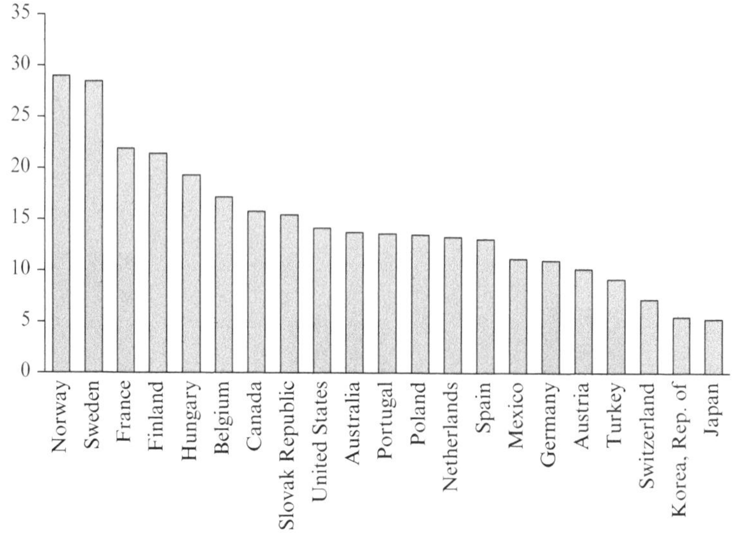

Source: OECD (2011a).

Figure 6.3 Government employment as a percentage of the labour force, Germany, 2005

principle, because the cuts were not necessarily fully compensated for by performance bonuses, and thus an adequate living standard was no longer guaranteed.

Most of the burden of job cuts since 1991 has been borne by non-civil servants, whose number went down from 4.6 million in 1991 to 2.7 million in 2009. The number of civil servants (including military personnel) fell only slightly, from 2.1 million in 1991 to 1.85 million in 2010 (Destatis 2011a: 100). The reason for this decrease in the number of civil servants was mainly the privatization of public utilities. The federal state, the *Länder* and the municipalities actually increased the number of civil servants in their employment because they are cheaper in the short run and working and employment conditions, such as pay cuts and increases in working hours can be decided unilaterally. The state does not have to pay employers' contributions to the social insurance funds (about 20 per cent of gross income). However, costs have been shifted into the future, since pensions will eventually have to be paid directly out of annual budgets and civil servants' pension entitlements are higher than those of non-civil servants.

3.2.2 Lifetime and temporary employment: increasing dualization

The German public sector is still the very model of a strong internal labour market with lifelong employment, albeit now with an increasing number of peripheral employees on temporary contracts. The internal labour market has entry positions at four different skill and task levels, with clearly defined career ladders for civil servants and non-civil servants. Access to the 'higher service' (*höherer Dienst*) normally requires a university degree. The 'higher middle service' (*gehobener Dienst*) is designed for graduates from special public service academies and the 'middle service' (*mittlerer Dienst*) is reserved for those with vocational training qualifications. The 'lower service' (*einfacher Dienst*) is open to unskilled and semi-skilled workers. For many occupations, such as teachers and judges, as well as at middle levels for inspectors or tax officers, a preparatory or training period (*Vorbereitungsdienst*) is prescribed, which ends with an examination. Only those who pass the examination have access to lifetime employment as a civil servant or are eligible for a permanent contract as a non-civil servant. Promotion used to depend mainly on seniority, a rule that has only recently been changed (see Section 4).

The average skill level is higher in the public service than in private industry because many high- and intermediate-level activities, such as education, the courts and revenue collection (tax offices), are concentrated in the public sector. This is reflected in the composition of the workforce, with some differences between civil and non-civil servants. In 2010, most civil servants were employed in the higher, higher-middle and middle service and only very few in the lower service. Since 2002, when these detailed statistics were first compiled, the skill composition has not much changed, with only a slight increase in the higher service being observed. The skill composition of the non-civil servants is somewhat different. The middle and lower service is much more densely populated with non-civil servants than with civil servants (Figure 6.4). Many of the activities at these levels are subject to outsourcing, which is obviously much easier with employees who do not enjoy guarantees of lifetime employment.

It was commonplace for civil servants to be employed on temporary contracts during the preparatory period. Since the mid-1980s, however, the possibilities for recruiting staff on temporary contracts have been extended considerably and those parts of the public sector in which lifetime employees are concentrated have made more intensive use of them than the private sector. The share of temporary employees increased between 2002 and 2010 from 10 to 14.7 per cent, a much sharper increase than in the private sector and a share now far above the average for

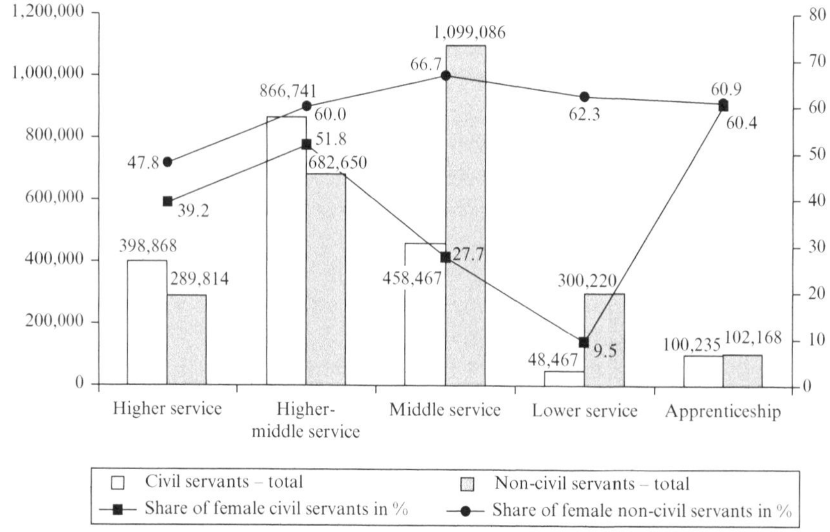

Source: Destatis (2011a); author's calculations.

Figure 6.4 Number of civil servants and non-civil servants by skill level and share of women, Germany, 2010 (%)

the economy as a whole, which was 8.9 per cent in 2010 (Table 6.3). Temporary contracts are increasingly being used to cope with shortages without increasing the number of permanent staff and endangering the goals of future staff reductions. The strict limitation of the number of core workers in the public budgets on the basis of a head count, irrespective of working hours, also requires a higher share of temporary contracts in order to make up for the hours lost by voluntary part-time employment.

The share of voluntary notices of termination is very low (0.4 per cent in the public compared to 1.9 per cent in the private sector). Labour turnover in the public sector is much lower than in private industry (6.3 per cent compared to 10.5 per cent in the first half of 2008). Turnover in the public service is highly concentrated among temporary staff (Ellguth and Kohaut 2011: 22). The high level of employment protection enjoyed by permanent employees and their low voluntary mobility explains why the burden of numerical flexibility has been shifted on to temporary employees. It also helps to explain why temporary contracts in the public sector are more often a trap than a bridge into permanent employment. A lower share of temporary workers in the public sector subsequently obtain a permanent contract than in the private sector (ibid.: 24–5).

Table 6.3 Share (number) of temporary employees in the public service by gender and total employment, Germany, 2002–2010

	2002	2005	2007	2009	2010
% of women in public sector on temporary contracts	9.2 (166,662)	9.6 (159,031)	11.2 (182,243)	13.0 (214,588)	14.0 (232,789)
% of men in public sector on temporary contracts	11.3 (128,826)	11.0 (116,690)	12.2 (127,340)	14.7 (151,742)	16.0 (166,494)
% of all employees in public sector on temporary contracts	10.0 (295,558)	10.1 (275,721)	11.6 (309,583)	13.6 (366,330)	14.7 (399,283)
% of all employees in Germany on temporary contracts*	6.6 (1,931,000)	8.3 (2,394,000)	8.8 (2,659,000)	8.6 (2,640,000)	8.9 (2,761,000)

Note: * 15–65 years, excl. apprentices and students.

Source: Destatis (2011a, different years).

3.2.3 Women in the public service

In the past decade, the number of women employed in the public service has remained virtually constant, while men's employment went down by about 9 per cent. Consequently, women's share increased and, at 53.8 per cent, was about 8 percentage points higher in 2010 than their share in total employment (Table 6.4). The public sector offers jobs for highly skilled women in particular. The share of such women in the public service, at 43 per cent, was 14 percentage points higher than in the private sector. The share of women in management positions is higher in the public service than in the private sector (29 versus 23 per cent) (Table 6.5). However, only 14.5 per cent of jobs in the upper echelons of the higher service (civil servants only) are held by women, while in the entry positions of the higher service the share of women is 65.6 per cent (Destatis 2011a: 35).

Table 6.4 Key indicators of women's employment in the public service, Germany, 2002–2010 (%)

	2002	2005	2007	2009	2010
% of women (numbers) in total employment	43.5 (15,924,000)	44.9 (16,431,000)	45.3 (17,273,000)	45.8 (17,690,000)	45.9 (17,890,000)
% of women (numbers) in total public sector employment	51.4 (2,476,614)	52.0 (2,390,782)	52.5 (2,385,172)	53.4 (2,429,354)	53.8 (2,467,162)
Total public sector employment as % of all employment	12.3 (4,809,090)	11.8 (4,599,425)	11.5 (4,540,600)	11.3 (4,547,586)	11.3 (4,586,100)
% of women in employment who work in the public sector	15.6 (2,476,600)	14.6 (2,390,800)	13.8 (2,385,200)	13.7 (2,429,400)	13.8 (2,467,200)

Sources: Destatis (2010, 2011a).

Table 6.5 Share of women among employees in the public and private sectors by skill level, Germany, 2009 (%)

	Public sector	Private sector
Management positions	29	23
High skill	43	29
Intermediate skill	56	39
Low skill	58	50
Total	53	46

Source: Ellguth and Kohaut (2011: 25) and Destatis (2011a) (total female employment rates).

3.2.4 Full- and part-time work

The number of full-timers fell from 5,571 million in 1991 to 3,107 million in 2010. At the same time, the number of part-timers increased from 1,066 million in 1991 to 1,427 million in 2010, which meant that the share of part-timers increased from 15.8 to 32.3 per cent. More than 80 per cent of the part-timers are women.

The expansion of traditional part-time working before retirement took place in the 1970s and 1980s. In accordance with the alimentation principle, civil servants are generally full-time employees. They have, however, the right to work part-time for family reasons as long as they have children under 18 or care responsibilities in the family. They can also ask to work part-time without such reasons. Such a request has to be accepted unless the employer has good reasons to refuse. Voluntary part-time employment should not involve less than 50 per cent of normal working hours. Since part-time work is the result of employees asserting their right to work part-time temporarily with the option to return to full-time work at some stage, it can be assumed that most of the 400,000 civil servants working part-time are doing so voluntarily. The non-civil servants have similar rights, but they may also be working part-time because they were recruited for a part-time job. In the private sector, full-timers have the right under federal law to work part-time, but there is no corresponding right to go back to full-time work.

In the traditional German male breadwinner system, with half-day school and a lack of public childcare, many women opt for part-time work. In 2010, 36 per cent of full-timers and 81 per cent of part-timers in the public service were women (Destatis 2011a). An analysis based on a panel of companies with employees subject to social insurance contributions (excluding public service companies that employ civil servants only) shows that the public service has a higher share of part-timers (27 per cent) than the private sector (22 per cent). The composition of part-timers also differs. Most part-timers in the public service (24 per cent of the workforce) are insured and only 3 per cent are working in a marginal part-time job, the so-called 'mini-jobs', which are not subject to social insurance contributions (private industry 10 to 12 per cent) (Ellguth and Kohaut 2011: 24). This reflects the impact of the regulations requiring substantial part-time work involving at least 50 per cent of normal full-time hours.

Two-thirds of the additional part-timers between 2002 and 2010 were older workers who opted to go part-time prior to retirement. This scheme was made attractive because participants received about 85 per cent of their former net income but had to work only 50 per cent of their previous hours. In practice only a few actually worked part-time. The others opted for a so-called 'block model' in which they worked normal full-time hours for the first two and a half years and zero hours for the second two and a half years. Since these part-timers were mostly not replaced in their so-called 'passive phase' and in many cases not after retirement either, this scheme resulted in an intensification of work for the remaining employees and also contributed to the reduction of overall staff numbers. The scheme has now been replaced by a less generous one, with a maximum quota of 2.5 per cent of older part-timers in each organization.

4. INDUSTRIAL RELATIONS AND COLLECTIVE BARGAINING IN THE PUBLIC SECTOR

Industry-wide bargaining is still common in the public sector. The highly standardized national agreement, which covered the whole public sector, has been replaced by a multitude of collective agreements. The interests of the actors on both sides have become more heterogeneous, which in turn has led to a decentralization and fragmentation of collective bargaining. Ninety-three per cent of employees in the direct public service are covered by a collective agreement compared to 57 per cent in the private sector. However, there are no areas of the public service without collective agreements as there are in the private sector. In addition, the collective agreements are not being eroded from within as they are in many private companies. Collective agreements are generally complied with by employers. Ninety-three per cent of public sector employees are represented by a works council or its equivalent, the employee council (*Personalrat*), compared to 40 per cent in the private sector (Ellguth and Kohaut 2011). The employee councils, together with the unions, monitor and enforce the collective agreements much more effectively than in the private sector. The state is no longer the model employer guaranteeing better working conditions than in the private sector, but it is still a model employer in the sense that it complies with the agreements which its representatives have signed and that it tries to intimidate 'inconvenient' employee representatives only in exceptional circumstances.

4.1 Employers' Organizations and Unions

The employers in the public sector are organized differently at local, state and federal levels. At local level there is a strong employers' organization (*kommunale Arbeitgeberverbände* or KAV). The members are drawn from 16 organizations from the municipalities, *Landkreise* (the intermediate administrative level between *Länder* and *Gemeinde*), public savings banks and other regional public organizations. The KAV has eight committees for specific public subsectors, such as savings banks, hospitals, port authorities, airports and local transport. At national level, the KAV is responsible for negotiating collective agreements. The KAV provides many services for its members who are not specialists in collective bargaining. At the *Land* level, the organization is more loosely structured. The 16 *Länder* have special departments with experts on collective bargaining and are less dependent on the expertise of an employers' organization. They coordinate their collective bargaining in a working partnership (*Tarifgemeinschaft deutscher Länder* or TDL) with minimum staff. The *Länder* are represented in the TDL by their ministers of finance. At national level, there is no employers' organization. The minister of internal affairs together with the minister of finance coordinates collective bargaining for the federal government. The constitution of the KAV and the TDL requires all its members not only to follow the collective agreements but also not to improve the agreed standards, which is usually allowed by employers' organizations in the private sector. Consequently, there is no wage drift at establishment level as in the private sector.

For many decades the federal, *Land* and local employers of the public service had a joint bargaining committee. The common goal was to negotiate a single national collective agreement for the public service. At the end of 2003, the TDL left the joint bargaining committee. The 16 *Länder* wanted to negotiate working hours and annual bonuses individually. The *Länder* have the highest shares of wage costs in their budgets, since they are responsible for highly paid public services such as education and research. The share of employee compensation in total expenditures was 36.7 per cent in 2006, compared with 10.1 per cent for the federal state and 25.9 per cent for the municipalities (Keller 2010: 29). One state (Hesse) even left the TDL in 2005. Another exception is Berlin. It was excluded from collective bargaining in 1994 because it was paying western salaries in the eastern part of the city, contrary to the agreements. Since 2003 Berlin has wanted to become a member of the TDL again.

Compared to the private sector, the unions in the public sector are fragmented. In the German Trade Union Federation (DGB), three unions represent employees in the public service: ver.di (2,071,990 members),[3] the teachers' union (GEW, 263,129 members) and the police union (GDP, 171,709 members). In addition, there is a strong union of civil servants (Deutscher Beamtenbund, DBB) with 1,265,720 members, which also organizes non-civil servants. In the past the DGB unions negotiated jointly and cooperated with the DBB. Today DGB and DBB form a joint negotiating committee which, however, does not include all DBB unions. Train drivers, pilots, doctors and air traffic controllers defected from joint bargaining and negotiated separately. In recent years, they have succeeded in improving their members' pay, in some cases after successful strikes.

4.2 Employee Representation

The German dual system of representation also exists in the public service. Collective agreements are negotiated by unions and at the company level employee councils (*Personalvertretung*) represent all employees. They have strong rights of codetermination and the right to negotiate company agreements in areas not covered by a collective agreement. The employee councils differ from works councils in the private sector. They have fewer rights to information on economic issues than their counterparts in the private sector, since it is argued that this would interfere with the rights of parliaments at the various levels to set their own budgets. The employee councils' rights to consultation and codetermination vary because all 16 *Länder* have their own employee council laws. The employee councils are strengthened by a high union density, which at 60 per cent is much higher than in the private sector (ibid.: 83).

The position of the employee councils in regulating the internal labour markets is usually very strong, since the workforce is protected against dismissals. The classification of employees is the main area of contention and disputes have often been settled only after many court decisions. The courts have now delivered such detailed judgments that most disputes between the social partners have been resolved. At the company level, however, there is still some interpretative leeway on employee classification. Strong employee representatives are using this leeway to support employees in their requests for promotion and are often successful. Employers can also take advantage of this leeway to recruit specialists from the private sector, which is becoming increasingly difficult. In this way substitutes for wage drift can be created, whether to increase employee motivation or to assist recruitment in a tight labour market.

4.3 Collective Bargaining

Until 2003, unions and employers negotiated jointly at national level. The national pattern agreements covered all blue- and white-collar non-civil servants at national, state and local levels. Shortly after the national negotiations, civil servants' pay and working hours used to be adjusted to the level of the new agreement. The main provisions of the national agreements were also adopted by the social partners in public companies (post, railways and so on). Most charity organizations as well as private service providers also followed the agreement. Thus the central public sector agreement served as a pattern agreement even beyond the public service.

Today, collective bargaining in the public sector is more decentralized than in the past. Working hours and pay differ between the federal state, the 16 *Länder* and the municipalities. The 'turning point' in public sector collective bargaining was the negotiations on the new framework agreements that started in 2003. The job descriptions in the old agreements dated back to the early 1960s and contained many jobs which had long ceased to exist (such as keypunching). There were still separate agreements for blue- and white-collar workers, while in other industries these status differences had already been abolished. The unions wanted to reduce discrimination by introducing a gender-neutral job evaluation system. They also wanted to simplify the increasingly complex system, with its more than 17,000 job descriptions, and to reduce the incentives for outsourcing. The employers had less clear goals. Their main priority was cost-neutrality. Because of the cost pressures traditional employer goals like the expansion of performance pay became clearly less important. Obviously the different goals were not compatible. Re-evaluation of traditional female jobs conflicted with the goal of cost neutrality. Moreover, both sides were pursuing goals that were themselves contradictory. Reducing wages for unskilled jobs in order to avoid outsourcing was not compatible with the union goal of reducing gender discrimination. The employers were also pursuing contradictory goals. Higher wages for specialists to make the public sector more attractive was in conflict with the employer goal of cost-neutrality.

Because of the cost pressures after the tax cuts in early 2000, the negotiations were more pressured than previously and did not end with a new single national agreement. The *Länder* refused to sign the new framework agreement because they wanted cuts in annual bonuses and longer working hours. The municipalities only continued negotiations under the 'most-favoured-treatment clause', whereby compromises subsequently agreed in the separate negotiations with the *Länder* would also apply to them. In the end, two slightly different national framework agreements were signed in 2005 by the federal state and the municipalities and in 2006 for the *Länder* with the exception of Hesse, which had its own agreement.

This 'reform of the century' signified a change in the basic assumptions about the functioning of the labour market in the public sector of the future: mobility between private and public companies should be encouraged by abolishing pay elements that exist only in the public sector, such as seniority pay increases and family allowances. Promotion should be based on efficiency instead of tenure, and performance pay should be extended. Divisive status differences between blue- and white-collar workers should be reduced in order to improve cooperation and team work. Internal flexibility should be improved by working-time flexibility and by temporary and probationary management positions. The public service should be made more attractive by raising starting salaries and reducing promotions. A main driver of the reform, finally, was the intention to simplify a wage system that over decades had become increasingly complex and bureaucratic. Losers in the new agreements were to be protected by an acquired rights clause.

The most important changes (Table 6.6) were:

- abolition of the different statuses of blue- and white-collar workers;
- joint pay grid with 15 pay grades with six experience promotions (instead of 12 seniority promotions);
- lower starting pay for low-skill workers to avoid or reduce outsourcing;
- extension of performance pay; and
- abolition of family allowances.

Set alongside these worthy objectives, the actual outcomes were much more modest. The social partners did not succeed in agreeing on new job descriptions. They decoupled these negotiations from the other parts of the collective agreements and extended the validity of the old job descriptions. It took until 2012 before new job descriptions were negotiated which, with 16,500 job descriptions, remained as complex as before. Both sides had obviously underestimated the complexity of public sector jobs.

The negotiations with the *Länder* proved to be more conflictual (see Appendix 6A: Strikes in the public service), since the employers demanded so-called 'opening clauses' with a view to introducing longer working hours and reductions in the Christmas bonus. Due to the lengthy negotiations there was a transitional period when, for the first time since the Second World War, no valid collective agreement was in force. This meant that existing employees were still protected by the old agreement since collective agreements in Germany remain in force until they are replaced by a new agreement. However, new employees had to work 42 hours per week and their Christmas bonus was lowered. Strike action proved to be not very effective, since strikes by *Länder* employees, such as school or kindergarten teachers, have fewer direct effects on the economy than strikes by train drivers or refuse collectors. The unions finally signed a new agreement. After the state of Hesse left the employers' organization, they were afraid of further fragmentation and accepted a new collective agreement with opening clauses for working hours and the Christmas bonus. The *Länder* used these opening clauses and extended working hours from 38.5 hours to between 38.7 and 39.7 hours. The Christmas bonus was substantially cut, whereby the cuts were lower for the middle- and lower-wage groups. The increase in working hours was translated directly into staff reductions. The unions clearly lost the 38.5-hour week, which they

Table 6.6 Comparison of the new and old collective bargaining legislation, Germany

	New collective bargaining legislation	Old collective bargaining legislation
Manual/ white-collar relationship	Same legislation covers all (TVöD – Collective Agreement for Public Sector Employees)	Separate collective bargaining arrangements for white-collar and manual workers
Working time in eastern and western Germany	Single working-time of 39 hours per week	Working time of 38.5 hours per week in West German Collective Bargaining Area and 40 hours per week in East German Collective Bargaining Area
Working-time flexibility	Working-time flexibilization: balancing period up to 2 weeks (working time 'corridor'/ bandwidth)	Narrower 'corridor' for balancing out overtime worked (maximum 1 week)
Differentiation of pay rates	15 pay scales in one collective agreement, all employees moved to the new system	49 wage and salary scales in various collective agreements
Seniority principle	Increase in attractiveness through improved pay at the beginning of working life	Age-related pay (up to 15 increments)
Performance-related pay	In future, up to 8% of employer's total wage bill as variable performance-related pay (starting in 2007 with 1%)	No variable performance-related components in pay
Promotion criteria	Promotion to a higher pay scale dependent solely on function (not after mere passage of time)	Promotion to higher wage scales depends on length of service and/or completion of probation (irrespective of performance)
Child/family supplement	Marital status and number of children no longer play any part in determining pay	Pay also dependent on marital status and number of children
Special payments	Introduction of a new annual special payment, paid on a sliding scale depending on pay grade, but from 2007 at a reduced rate compared with previous arrangements	Christmas bonus (82.14% West/61.6% East) Holiday allowance (€255.65/€332.34)

Table 6.6 (continued)

	New collective bargaining legislation	Old collective bargaining legislation
Classification	New regulations significantly reduce classification criteria after trials end of 2006	Opaque classification regulations: about 17,000 classification criteria
Low pay grades	New lower pay scale introduced in order to reduce outsourcing	Outsourcing/privatization of least complex activities
Filling of management positions	Introduction of 2 new instruments: fixed-term (up to 12 months) and probationary (up to 2 years) management positions	Management functions had to be assigned on a permanent basis

Source: Keller (2010: 101).

had agreed in 1990, and working hours are nearly back to 40 hours. The federal government and the employers' organization of the municipalities (KAV) demanded under reference to the most-favoured-treatment clause an increase of weekly working hours. The unions refused this prolongation of working hours. The administration court of Berlin rejected the claim of the employers, saying that picking out single clauses from a generally different agreement is unlawful.

Both framework agreements were supplemented by specific agreements for different occupational groups or subsectors such as hospitals, care, local transport and so on. The specific agreements always have priority over the general agreement. The specific agreement for doctors was negotiated after a long strike by a doctors' union that had left the former joint negotiating committee and achieved higher wage increases for its constituency. Since hospitals are subject to strict cost controls, these wage concessions were partly financed by staff reductions for other occupational groups.

The implementation of the new framework agreements is still ongoing. Surprisingly, model calculations of the impact of the new framework agreement on lifetime income are not available. It seems that neither the unions nor the employers want the long-term effects of the agreement on the incomes of different groups to be known, because this might cause all kinds of conflicts. The increased possibilities for performance pay are not being fully used, partly because the employee councils have blocked them and partly because the employers have not yet developed reliable performance indicators or assessment systems. A survey among employee councillors in North-Rhine Westphalia showed that in 32 per cent of municipalities the new low-wage group was used for newly recruited employees. In most cases it was used for cleaning. About 9 per cent of the employee councillors interviewed answered that the new wage group helped to avoid outsourcing or promoted insourcing (Schmidt et al. 2011: 254). Some of the employee councillors, however, were afraid of negative secondary effects caused by a general decrease in starting wages as previously well-rewarded activities were reclassified as 'simple'.

4.4 Consultation with Civil Servants

As compensation for the lack of a right to strike and negotiate working conditions, there are longstanding institutionalized joint consultation procedures with the unions representing civil servants (ver.di and DBB). The unions have to be consulted on all new laws concerning the status and the working conditions of civil servants. In addition, top-level talks between the ministry of the interior and the unions have to be held twice a year (Keller 2010: 127).

In the past, consultations mainly took place at national level, since civil servants' working conditions were regulated by national legislation. With the reform of the federal system in 2006, responsibility for working conditions was devolved to the *Länder*. Since then, working conditions, which used to be highly standardized, have become increasingly differentiated. The richer states in the South (Bavaria and Baden-Württemberg) are already offering higher wages to attract teachers and scarce specialists from other *Länder*. The northern states agreed to coordinate their civil servant pay policy in order to avoid wage increases as a result of mutual overbidding. A comparison of the annual wages of a civil servant in one wage group of the higher service, in which for example many teachers are classified (A 13), shows that annual salaries in Western Germany range between €52,216.81 (Bavaria) and €48,290.75 (West Berlin) and in Eastern Germany between €47,094.00 in Saxony and €44,949.04 in East Berlin. The federal government pays the highest salary at €52,915.49 (Kammradt 2009: 105).

In the past, improvements in working conditions laid down in new collective agreements were directly transferred to civil servants. This process of harmonizing working conditions went in both directions. Civil servants were granted similar rights to partial retirement or part-time work as non-civil servants and the unions achieved nearly the same job security for non-civil servants, who cannot be dismissed once they have completed 15 years of service. Since early 2000, this quasi-automatic connection between the working conditions of the two groups has evaporated. To save money, employers started to increase the wages of civil servants only after a period of time. They also underlined their demands for concessions with unilateral decisions to increase working hours and reduce the Christmas bonus for civil servants. Civil servants now have working hours between 40 (Berlin, Hamburg), 41 (federal state, North-Rhine Westphalia) and 42 (Bavaria, Thuringia) hours a week. The higher job security of civil servants is used to justify this deterioration in their working conditions compared to non-civil servants.

4.5 From a Single Contract to a Plurality of Agreements

Industrial relations still differ substantially between the private and public sectors. Coverage by collective agreements is close to 100 per cent in the public sector, due to strong employee councils and the state's responsibility for ensuring that its own regulations are enforced. The old homogeneous system, with its joint national agreement for the core public sector that served as a pattern agreement for the indirect public sector, for civil servants and for charity organizations, has now been replaced by a fragmented system of competing agreements.

Depending on the parties in power at any one time, there might be some recentralization. Berlin will join the TDL again and the new government in Hesse might follow suit. The dominant trend, however, is towards a gradual differentiation, especially in working hours and annual bonuses, between *Länder* and municipalities and between civil and non-civil servants. The formerly homogeneous system based on cooperative federalism is being replaced by a new system based on competitive federalism, with increasingly diverging standards. For the unions, the system's running costs have increased substantially. They have had to create new representational structures for civil servants in all 16 *Länder* and to coordinate the now fragmented collective bargaining. The increasing use of 'opening' or derogation clauses and of performance pay will shift more responsibility on to the employee councils, which in many cases are not yet prepared for such tasks. They will require support from the unions, although their limited resources mean that only partial support will be provided. Research on the use of opening clauses in other industries (engineering and chemical industries) showed that such decentralization also offers opportunities for unions to increase member participation, strengthen shop-floor organization and recruit new members (Lehndorff and Haipeter 2011).

5. PUBLIC SECTOR PAY AND PENSIONS

5.1 Pay

In the past decade, collectively agreed pay increases in the public sector fell behind those agreed in most private industries (Figure 6.5). Because of the tax cuts already mentioned, pressures on pay were very high in the public service. Increases in hourly rates were partly offset by a reduction in annual bonuses or increased working hours. A recent analysis of total labour costs per working hour, which include annual bonuses and employers' contributions, confirm this picture. Total labour costs in the German public sector increased between 2000 and 2010 by only 1.1 per cent per year compared to 1.7 per cent in the German private sector and much higher rates in some other EU countries, such as 4.3 per cent in the United Kingdom, 4.3 per cent in Belgium and 3.3 per cent in the Netherlands (Niechoj et al. 2011: 7).

In 2010, hourly labour costs in the private sector were €29.1, compared to €28.6 in the public sector (Niechoj et al. 2011). Average pay in the public sector is slightly above that in the private sector for full-time women employees and slightly below for male full-timers. Part-timers of both sexes

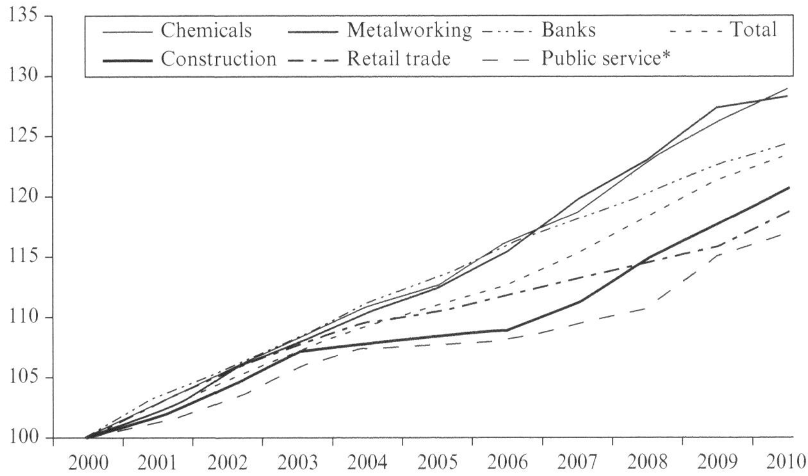

Note: * From 2005 federal state.

Source: WSI-Tarifarchiv, 31 December 2010.

Figure 6.5 Evolution of collectively agreed pay by industry, 2000–2010 (West Germany 2000=100)

Table 6.7 Gross earnings per hour, month and year of men and women in the private and public sectors, full-time (part-time), Germany, 2010*

	Paid weekly working hours		Hourly pay		Monthly pay		Annual	
	Private	Public	Private	Public	Private	Public	Private	Public
Women	38.2	39.3	17.90	18.13	2,973	3,097	35,673	36,679
	(23.8)	(24.9)	(15.23)	(16.49)	(1,585)	(1,889)	(19,015)	(22,671)
Men	38.6	40.0	22.54	21.41	3,780	3,725	45,358	44,702
	(25.2)	(25.8)	(15.61)	(18.90)	(1,709)	(2,118)	(20,507)	(25,420)
Gender gap	0.4	0.7	20.6%	13.3%	22.5%	16.9%	21.4%	17.9%
	(1.4)	(0.9)	(2.3%)	(12.8%)	(7.3%)	(10.8%)	(7.3%)	(9.4%)

Note: * Only non-civil servants, non-market services (includes charity organizations).

Source: Destatis (2011c).

are better paid in the public sector (Table 6.7). The main reason for this is the low proportion of marginal part-timers (mini-jobbers), many of whom in the private sector receive lower rates of pay than other part-timers (Voss and Weinkopf 2012). However, public sector pay is more compressed than in the private sector. Women and those in intermediate and highly skilled positions are the particular winners in this wage structure.

A recent, more detailed analysis of pay in the public and private sectors based on the Socio-Economic Panel compared the distribution of hourly gross and net wages of employees in the public and private sectors in 1995 and 2007 (Tepe and Kroos 2010). Figures 6.6 and 6.7 show the wage differences between public and private sectors for men and women in East and West Germany by percentiles. In West Germany, public sector wages in the lower percentiles are slightly higher than private sector ages for men and substantially higher for women. In the higher percentiles, the difference narrows and eventually becomes negative. In East Germany in spite of lower collectively agreed public sector wages, the positive wage gap for the lower percentiles is greater than in the West. In addition, the wage gap is also positive for the middle and higher incomes, only becoming negative for men in the very high percentiles. Because of the relative decline in private sector wage levels in East Germany, the positive wage gap increased for men and women up to the high percentiles.

For low-skilled workers, the wage gap with the private sector is positive for both men and women (Figures 6.8 and 6.9). Highly skilled men, however, earn more in the public service only in the low percentiles. For highly skilled women, there was a positive wage gap until the middle percentiles.

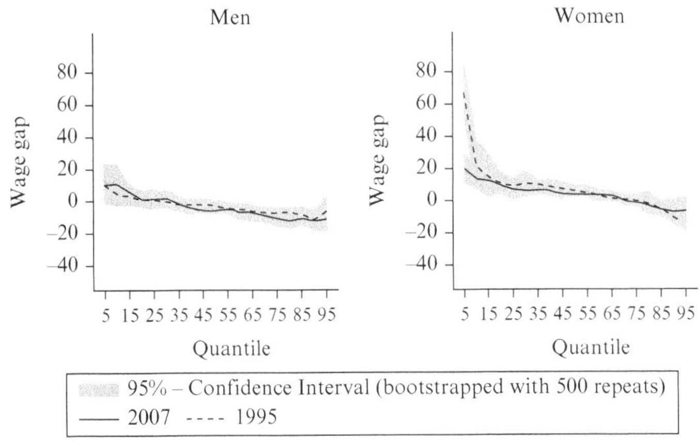

Source: Tepe and Kroos (2010: 5).

Figure 6.6 Wage gap between public service and private sector, western Germany, 1995 and 2007 (%)

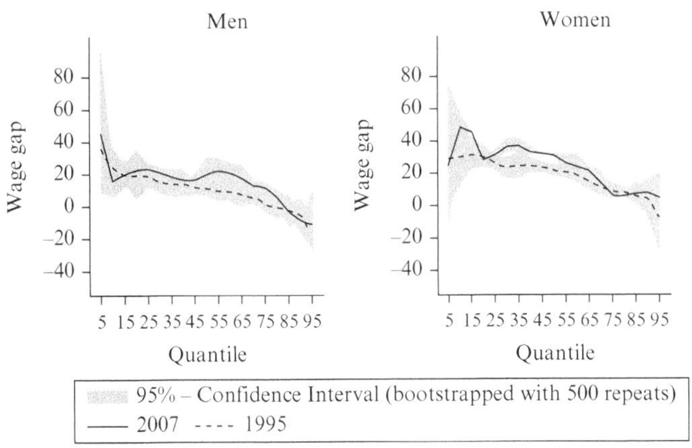

Source: Tepe and Kroos (2010: 5).

Figure 6.7 Wage gap between public service and private sector, eastern Germany, 1995 and 2007 (%)

5.2 Pensions

The status of civil servant (*Beamte*) is a lifetime status that does not end with the transition from work into retirement. German civil service law

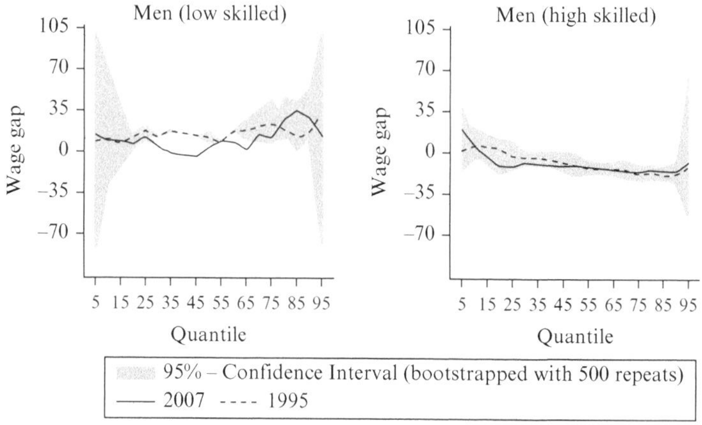

Source: Tepe and Kroos (2010: 7).

Figure 6.8 Wage gap between public service and private sector by skill level, men, Germany, 1995 and 2007 (%)

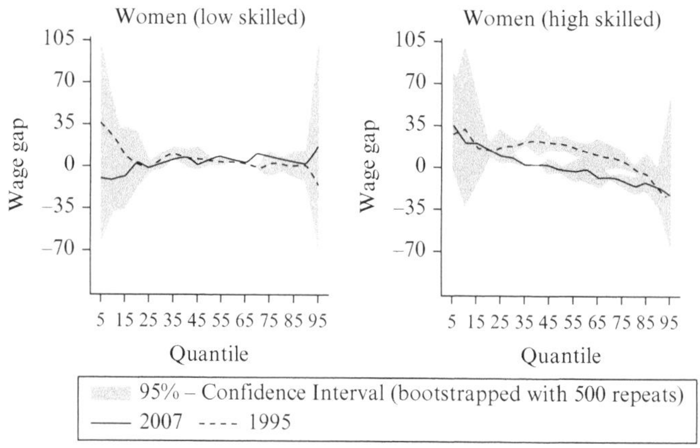

Source: Tepe and Kroos (2010: 7).

Figure 6.9 Wage gap between public service and private sector by skill level, women, Germany, 1995 and 2007 (%)

regards retirement only as the end of active service; according to the above-mentioned alimentation principle, the state remains obliged to guarantee an appropriate standard of living even for a retired *Beamte*. The pension system for civil servants is a one-pillar system with a pension paid directly by the state out of its annual budgets without any contributions from civil servants.

The pension system for non-civil servants is a two-pillar system. Like all other employees, they pay contributions to the national pension scheme. The second pillar is an occupational pension scheme for the public sector. It was agreed upon in a national collective agreement and is quasi-mandatory because virtually 100 per cent of the non-civil servant workforce is covered by this agreement. The contributions to this scheme amount to 7.86 per cent of monthly gross pay, of which the employers pay 6.54 per cent. The intention was to raise the pensions of non-civil servants to the more generous level of the pensions paid to *Beamte*.

The pensions of public sector employees are generally higher than those of employees in the private economy because the second pillar is not mandatory in the private sector and civil servants' pensions are substantially more generous than state pensions. In recent years, pension levels in the national pension system have been lowered because of the ageing of the population. The pensions of civil servants have been adapted to these decreases. Now early retirement is possible only with deductions. Between 2003 and 2009, the maximum pension level was gradually reduced from 75 per cent of the former gross income to 71.75 per cent. As early as 1992, it was decided that the maximum level could be reached only after 40 years of service instead of the 35 years previously required (Färber et al. 2011: 101–3). Because of these changes, actual pension levels decreased from 72.8 per cent of the former gross income in 1994 to 69 per cent in 2011. In subsectors with more turnover and shorter service in the public sector, such as the Post Office, it declined even further, from 72.1 to 65.6 per cent (Destatis 2011b: 81).

Comparison of the pension levels of former public and private sector employees is difficult since no statistic captures the accumulated effects of the first and second pillars. Table 6.8 shows that civil servants' pensions are far higher than state pensions. However, they have to be taxed, while pensions from the national pension system are tax free. It can be assumed that the average pensions of non-civil servants in the public sector are higher than private sector pensions, since the second, occupational pension, is mandatory, while only 21 per cent of private sector employees receive an occupational pension. The traditional male breadwinner model, in which women tend to have discontinuous employment histories, is reflected in lower pensions for women in all categories. In the private sector, women are more likely than men to be employed in industries and companies with no occupational pensions. Because of the mandatory second pillar, they are much better off in the public sector.

Table 6.8 Income sources and coverage of the population aged 65 and over, western Germany 2007

	Coverage (%)			Gross pension per month (€)		
	Total	Men	Women	Total	Men	Women
State pension	90	89	90	958	1,219	767
Occupational pension private sector	21	31	12	403	490	239
Occupational pension public sector	11	11	12	322	432	266
Civil servant pension	8	11	6	2,165	2,577	1,640

Source: http://www.sozialpolitik-aktuell.de/tl_files/sozialpolitik-aktuell/_Politikfelder/Alter-Rente/Datensammlung/PDF-Dateien/abbVIII55a.pdf.

6. CASE STUDIES

6.1 Case Study 1: Prevailing Wages to Limit Wage Competition in Public Procurement

The German public service is very lean because services have been increasingly outsourced. The value of services and goods, bought by the government in 2009 equated to 12.9 per cent of GDP, compared to 11.4 per cent in 2000. This is 2.8 percentage points above the OECD33 average (10.1 per cent in 2009) (Figure 6.2). Public procurement offers the state not only efficient allocation of its resources but also the realization of other important goals, such as the promotion of innovation, environmental protection, reduction of CO_2 emissions, equal treatment of men and women or compliance with local labour standards as required by the ILO Labour Clauses (Public Contracts) Convention, 1949 (No. 94).[4] Germany has not ratified this convention. Under European regulations, selection criteria can be extended to include environmental and social criteria (European Union 2004). The German Federal Constitutional Court confirmed the state's right to introduce prevailing wage laws and underlined the legitimacy of the goals of stabilizing the social security and collective bargaining systems (Schulten and Pawicki 2008: 186). The introduction of prevailing wages with outsourcing and subcontracting was aimed at setting minimum wage thresholds within the framework of public procurement.

In the past, it was not regarded as necessary to include such protection clauses in the public procurement laws. Until the mid-1990s, the state used to be a model employer not only for its own employees but also for workers providing outsourced services, who were paid according to collectively agreed standards. In the past two decades, the state has increasingly become a major driver in the expansion of a low-wage sector as a result of outsourcing and privatization and also as a contracting authority. Increasingly, the more than 30,000 procurement bodies in the public service have awarded contracts on the basis of price alone, although the procurement laws leave it to the procurement body to combine price and quality criteria in order to determine the most advantageous offer. Prevailing wages have emerged in response to these new needs.

Berlin was the first federal state to introduce a prevailing wage law. The SDP–Green coalition's draft legislation on a federal prevailing wage law was never enacted, since it was not passed by the second chamber (the *Bundesrat*), in which the opposition had a majority. Subsequently, some *Länder* introduced their own legislation and most others followed suit or plan to do so (Figure 6.10). In some states, such as North-Rhine Westphalia, the prevailing wage law introduced by the SDP–Green coalition was repealed by the incoming CDU government and re-introduced following the most recent elections. In 2008, the prevailing wage law in Lower Saxony was declared unlawful by the European Court of Justice.[5] Afterwards, some *Länder* (for example, Hesse) repealed their laws, while others amended them. The laws in the various *Länder* differ but there are some common trends. The early laws included only the construction industry, then local transport, security services and cleaning were included and now in Bremen all services and in Berlin all public contracts are covered. The sphere of application within the public service also differs. Some states include the municipalities, others only the state itself. Some states include all public contracts, others only those above a defined threshold value (between €10,000 and €50,000). The sanctions for non-compliance also differ. Some states exclude companies that violate the law from participation in tendering for up to three years, some allow cancellation of the contract without notice. The general contractor is always held responsible for complying with the law. In three states, the public procurement body has to agree to the selection of subcontractors. Hamburg set up its own control authority.

The first generation of prevailing wage laws required only compliance with local standards. Since Germany does not have a national minimum wage and these local standards are often very low, the latest legislation combines the prevailing wage laws with minimum wages for public procurement (Figure 6.11). The level of the minimum wage more or less corresponds to the lowest wage level in the public service in the relevant state (Schulten and Pawicki 2008: 189). The argument is that the state should not underbid itself.

Source: WSI Tarifarchiv (2011).

Figure 6.10 Prevailing wage laws for public procurement, Germany 2011

Not much is known about the implementation and impact of the prevailing wage laws. The two evaluation studies in Hamburg and in North-Rhine Westphalia are based on expert interviews and company surveys (Stefaniak and Vollmer 2005; Hamburger Senat 2007). They both show that more than 80 per cent of companies (84 per cent in North-Rhine Westphalia and 97 per cent in Hamburg) support the law and that companies do not report cost increases. The companies in Hamburg supported

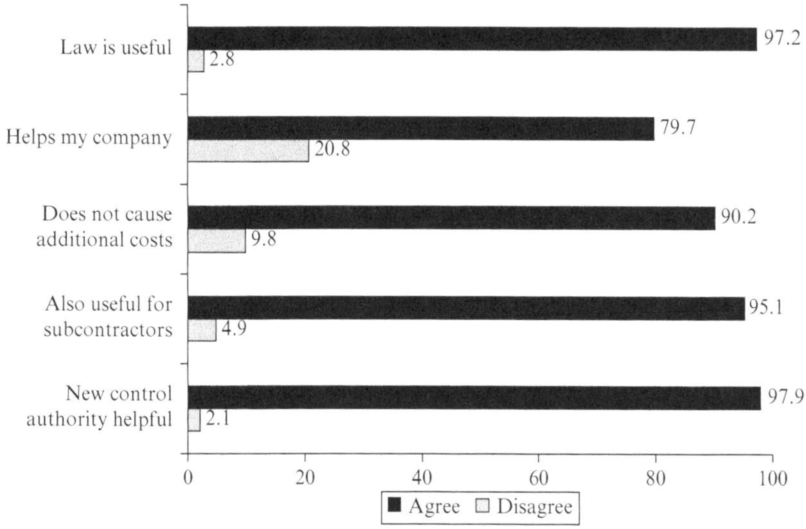

Source: Hamburger Senat (2007: 15).

Figure 6.11 Evaluation by construction companies of the Hamburg prevailing wage law as a percentage of answers (N=143)

monitoring by the state. In North-Rhine Westphalia the lack of monitoring was criticized.

All German prevailing wage laws were carefully checked to ensure compliance with European law. The experts, however, still see these laws as under threat because of the restrictive decisions of the European Court of Justice.

6.2 Case Study 2: Adjustment in the Highly Indebted City of Duisburg and Effects on the Public Service

Many German municipalities are structurally underfinanced. They suffered income losses after the tax cuts in early 2000 while having to increase expenditure on social welfare. The municipalities are formally autonomous and responsible for their budgets. However, the state parliament may impose new duties and obligations on the municipalities without providing any additional funds that may be needed. In spite of considerable efforts to consolidate budgets, deficits have increased over the past decade (Figure 6.12). These efforts included staff reductions and cuts in investment, which decreased even in nominal terms from €24 billion in 2001 to €23 billion in 2010. The main reason for the budget deficits was

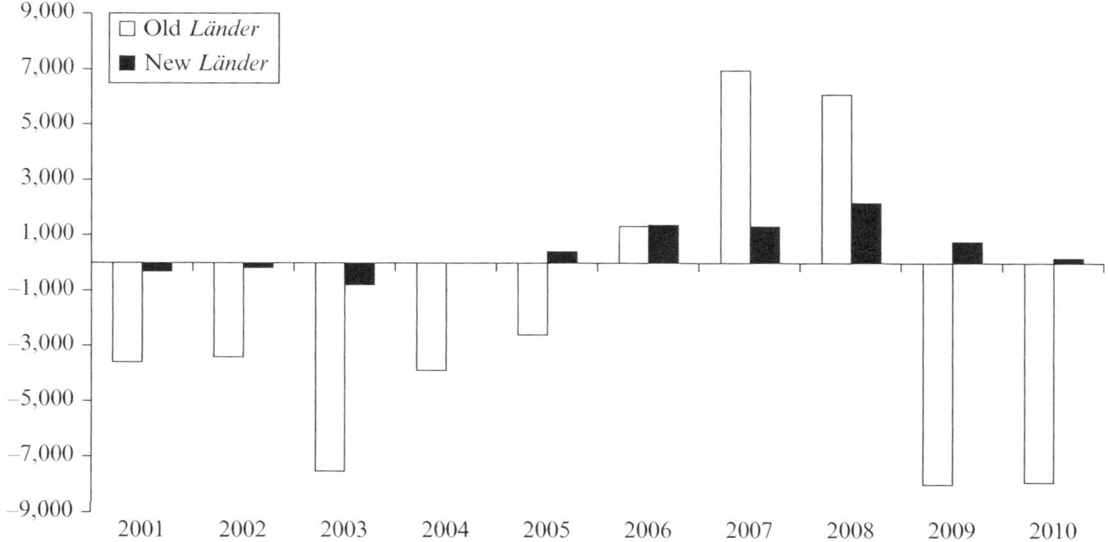

Note: * Berlin, Hamburg and Bremen.

Source: Federal Ministry of Finance (2011).

Figure 6.12 Budget surpluses and deficits of municipalities (€m), Germany, 2001–2010 (excluding city states)*

increased expenditure on social welfare, up from €27 billion in 2001 to €42 billion euros in 2010. These transfers included expenditures for the newly established childcare facilities for children between 0 and 3 years,[6] housing for the unemployed, welfare payments for older people with no or low pensions, care assistance and youth welfare services.

Some of the municipalities hardest hit by budgetary problems are those in West Germany that have seen many jobs lost in declining industries. These municipalities have especially high expenditures on the unemployed and disadvantaged children and young people, and the demand for care services is above average because the share of older people is higher than in expanding cities. At the same time, their revenues are stagnating and in spite of their financial problems they still have to contribute to the so-called 'solidarity pact' (*Solidarpakt*), through which money is transferred from western to eastern German states, transfers that will continue until 2019. Many of the municipalities with severe budget problems are in the Ruhr area, where heavy industry is concentrated. Most cities in the Ruhr area have budget deficits and their budgets are under the control of the *Regierungspräsident* (see above). They have to consolidate their budgets, their budgets need the approval of the *Regierungspräsident* and in principle they are allowed to spend money only as required to fulfil their statutory obligations.

Duisburg is a prime example of an industrial city in western Germany with increasing structural budget problems. Because of extensive job losses and high unemployment rates, revenues increased only slowly at a time when expenditures on social transfers were increasing particularly fast. The city tried to reduce the deficit by cutting investments and staffing levels, but without much success. Since 1992, its debts have been increasing continuously. By 2010, the city's debts were greater than its assets (Kambeck and Rappen 2010: 8) and the deficit had risen to €1.6 billion (Stadt Duisburg 2010: 3), which corresponds to about 133 per cent of its annual revenues.

The local government code stipulates that a city with negative equity should have surpluses until the equity becomes positive. In 2008 the *Regierungspräsident* required the city to draw up a consolidation plan. In 2010 the city council decided on a consolidation plan for 2010 to 2013 that would reduce the deficit but not achieve a balanced budget (Figure 6.13). The city council declared that a balanced budget could be reached only with financial help from the *Länder* or the federal government (ibid.: 8).

The consolidation plan envisaged, first, increasing revenue by putting up various local taxes and raising fees for most services, including libraries and theatres. Second, non-statutory benefits and services were to be cut. For example, a theatre and some swimming pools were to be closed and

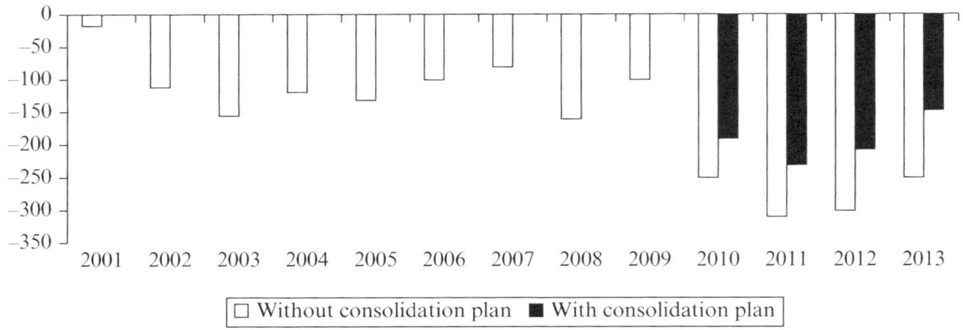

Source: Stadt Duisburg (2010: 4).

Figure 6.13 Evolution of budget deficits with and without consolidation plan, Germany, 2001–2013

subsidies for sport clubs, youth clubs and so on reduced or withdrawn completely. Third, because of the ageing of the population and smaller cohorts of children, schools were to be closed. Fourth, investments would take place only if absolutely needed. Fifth, the city's wage bill was to be reduced. The plan contained 245 individual cost-reduction measures, the most important of which was a planned staff reduction of about 10 per cent (400 employees), to be achieved by 2013. Since the city agreed with the unions not to dismiss employees, the main instrument to be used was turnover with retiring employees not being replaced. In order to control staff reductions, human resource policy is now centralized. The district president has to approve all new recruitments. Promotions are no longer being approved. An internal placement service has been put in place to assist employees in redeployment. Staff reductions through early retirement, voluntary severance or working-time reductions are being actively encouraged. Rationalization measures such as the centralization of purchasing departments should also contribute to reductions in staff requirements.

The human resource policy seems to have become so restrictive that a recent evaluation of the city's consolidation plan of the city mandated by the Chamber of Commerce warns that the public service is becoming less attractive. The report also notes that the internal placement service will only work effectively if redeployed employees are not harassed and downgraded and if the promises to promote further training are actually kept (Kambeck and Rappen 2010: 43).

7. CONCLUSIONS

Contrary to most other EU countries, employment in the German public sector was not reduced after the financial crisis. The number of public employees and also wages even increased after a long period of staff reductions and wage restraint. Considerable adjustments had taken place in previous decades, however, with substantial cumulative effects (Table 6.9). The main driver of public sector adjustments was tax cuts which caused high budget deficits and obliged the state to shrink. The number of public employees fell by nearly one-third, from 6,738,000 in 1991 to 4,586,000 in 2010. Since the share of part-timers increased from about one-sixth to about one-third of all employees in the same period, the decrease in the volume of paid hours was even higher than in the headcount. Further staff reductions are facilitated by an increase of temporary employees who do not benefit from the high level of employment protection in the public sector.

Table 6.9 Summary of main public sector adjustments, Germany, 1991–2010

Decrease of real public expenditures	1999–2007 real public expenditures per year –0.3% (EU27 +1.7%)
Staff reductions 1991–2010	1991–2010 reduction of public sector employment by nearly a third (31.9%)
Opening clauses in the collective agreement with the *Länder* 2005	Increase of weekly working hours for non-civil servants from 38.5 to 38.7 to 39.7 hours, reductions of holiday and Christmas bonuses
Unilateral changes in working conditions of civil servants	Increase of weekly working hours from 38.5 to 40 to 42 hours, reductions of holiday and Christmas bonuses
Decentralization of wage determination of civil servants	Increasing differences of annual wages between the *Länder* – system change from cooperative to competitive federalism
Wage restraint in the public sector	2000–10 increase in total labour costs in the public sector 1.1% compared to 1.7% per year in the private sector because of lower increases in agreed wages, which were, in addition, partly financed by increases in working hours and cuts in annual bonuses
Low-pay grades	Introduction of low-pay grades through the agreements in 2005 to reduce cost pressures for outsourcing
Increase of temporary employment	Above-average increase of temporary employment (from 10% in 2002 to 14.7% in 2010) which facilitates staff reductions
Outsourcing	11% of public sector staff reductions since 1991 due to outsourcing, mainly into the growing private low-wage sector
Reduction of pension levels	Between 2003 and 2009 reduction of maximum pension level for civil servants from 75 to 71.5% of former gross income
	1999 introduction of copayment for occupational pension of non-civil servants of 1.25% of gross income, which has been increased to 1.41%
Budget control of highly indebted cities through the district president	No promotions, new recruitments only by way of exception, reduction of number of apprentices

Today the German public sector is one of the smallest in the OECD. The debt brake, which was amended in the Constitution in 2009, leaves German politicians in the coming decade only the choice between further employment cuts or tax increases. The present strategies of the federal state to shift the financial responsibilities for new services such as childcare and social welfare payments to the municipalities, especially for the long-term unemployed, are not sustainable. Without additional transfers from the federal state, many municipalities will not be able to reduce their debts and the goal fixed in the German Constitution to guarantee equal living conditions in all regions will not be achieved.

The state tried to benefit from expanding the share of low-wage work in the private sector by outsourcing well-paid public sector jobs. To avoid only defensive reactions such as the introduction of new low-pay grades, as in the public sector agreements of 2005, proposals of a proactive re-regulation of the labour market were developed. Besides the introduction of minimum wages in some industries many *Länder* have introduced prevailing wage laws to take wages out of competition in public procurement by setting minimum wage thresholds. First evaluations show high acceptance by local employers and no negative impacts on costs.

The budget constraints made collective bargaining more difficult for public sector unions. On the union side, small unions organizing professionals with strong bargaining power, such as doctors, train drivers or pilots defected from joint bargaining and negotiated their own better conditions. On the employers' side, the *Länder* defected from the joint bargaining committee in 2005. The former national single agreement covering all public sector non-civil servant employees was replaced by a multitude of agreements. The two main agreements covering the *Länder*, on one hand, and the federal state and the municipalities, on the other, however, still cover the majority of the non-civil servant employees. In the past decade pay increases in the public sector were lower than in the private sector. Opening clauses in the collective agreement with the *Länder* allowed working-time increases and reductions of the Christmas bonus, as well as pay differentiation between the *Länder*. To finance the wage increases weekly working hours were increased and the Christmas bonus was reduced in all *Länder*. In addition, wages are increasingly differing between the richer and the poorer *Länder*. This encourages strategies in the richer states of poaching skilled employees from the poorer *Länder*. Cooperative federalism is slowly being replaced by competitive federalism, with diverging working conditions.

Despite strained industrial relations the unions managed to negotiate a new framework agreement which abolished seniority pay, traditional family allowances and different pay scales between blue- and white-collar workers. In exchange, the unions had to accept the expansion of performance-related pay and the introduction of low-pay grades to avoid outsourcing into the growing private low-pay sector. First evaluations show that the goal of reducing the complexity of public sector pay was not reached. The low-wage grades are partly used to reduce outsourcing of partly sector jobs. To date, performance-related pay has not been used on a large scale because employers seem to have difficulties developing appropriate indicators and human resource strategies.

In the past, improvements in the new working conditions of non-civil servants were directly transferred to civil servants. Since 2000 this quasi-automatic connection has disintegrated. Wages of civil servants are increasingly, if at all, adjusted after a time span. In addition, working hours were increased to up to 42 hours a week (Bavaria, Thuringia) and are generally above the level of non-civil servants. The maximum level of the still generous pensions for civil servants has been reduced from 75 to 71.75 per cent of the former gross income between 2003 and 2009. These possibilities for unilateral determination of the working conditions of civil servants might be one reason why most of the workforce reduction since 1991 has fallen upon non-civil servants. Some of these unilateral wage cuts obviously went too far and were declared unlawful by the Federal Court because they violate the alimentation principle which obliges the state to guarantee an adequate living standard.

NOTES

1. The distinction in the German public service between *Beamte*, with their very specific employment status, and *Angestellte*, whose employment status is similar to that of any regular employee, is not adequately captured by the English terms 'civil servant' and 'non-civil servant'. More specific translations would be 'career public servant' for *Beamte* and 'ordinary government employee' for *Angestellte*. However, for the sake of consistency across chapters dealing with other countries, 'civil servant' and 'non-civil servant' are retained here, despite their ambiguity.
2. The status of temporary civil servant (*Beamte auf Zeit*) exists for employees who are elected for a certain period, such as mayors, or employed on temporary contracts (soldiers, junior professors and so on).
3. In March 2001 five unions (DAG, DPG, HBV, IG Medien, ÖTV) merged to form the multi-branch union ver.di, which represents employees in public and private services. Ver.di is the second biggest union in Germany with 2,138,200 members in 2009. Only 8 per cent of the members are civil servants. Since 2001, membership has been shrinking continuously (from 2,806,500 in 2001 down to 2,071 in 2011). In contrast, membership of the DBB increased from 997,700 in 1990 to 1,265,720 in 2011 (Source: DGB and DBB).
4. Article 2 of ILO Convention 94 requires: '1. Contracts to which this Convention applies shall include clauses ensuring to the workers concerned wages (including allowances), hours of work and other conditions of labour which are not less favourable than those established for work of the same character in the trade or industry concerned in the district where the work is carried on (a) by collective agreement or other recognised machinery of negotiation between organizations of employers and workers representative respectively of substantial proportions of the employers and workers in the trade or industry concerned; or (b) by arbitration award; or (c) by national laws or regulations' (http://www.ilo.org/ilolex/cgi-lex/convde.pl?C094).

5. In the so-called *Rueffert* case the European Court of Justice ruled that member states may not adopt legislative measures which limit contractors for public works contracts to those undertakings which, within their tender submission, agree to pay their employees at least the rate set by a collective agreement which was not declared as generally binding based on the posted workers' directive (EUROFOUND http://www.eurofound.europa.eu/areas/industrialrelations/dictionary/definitions/ruffertcase.htm).
6. Until 2013 all municipalities are obliged to offer public childcare for at least 35 per cent of all children between 0 and 3 years. From 2013 all children above the age of 1 year have entitlements to public childcare.

REFERENCES

Bofinger, P. (2008), 'Das Jahrzehnt der Entstaatlichung', *WSI Mitteilungen*, **7**: 351–7.

Bosch, G. (2011), 'The German labour market after the financial crisis: miracle or just a good policy mix?', in D. Vaughan-Whitehead (ed.), *Work Inequalities in the Crisis: Evidence from Europe*, Cheltenham, UK and Northampton, MA, USA: Edward Elgar and Geneva: ILO, pp. 243–77.

Destatis (2010), *Mikrozensus: Bevölkerung und Erwerbstätigkeit Stand und Entwicklung der Erwerbstätigkeit in Deutschland 2010*, Fachserie 1, Reihe 4.1, Wiesbaden.

Destatis (2011a), *Finanzen und Steuern. Personal des öffentlichen Dienstes*, Fachserie 14, Reihe 6, Wiesbaden.

Destatis (2011b), *Finanzen und Steuern. Versorgungsempfänger des öffentlichen Dienstes*, Fachserie 14, Reihe 6.1, Wiesbaden.

Destatis (2011c), *Verdienste und Arbeitskosten*, Fachserie 16, Reihe 2.3, Wiesbaden.

Deutsche Bundesbank (2011), 'The debt brake in Germany – key aspects and implementation', Monthly Report, October, pp. 15–39.

Dullien, S. and M. Schieritz (2011), 'Die deutsche Investitionsschwäche: Die Mär von den Standortproblemen', *Wirtschaftsdienst*, No. 7: 458–64.

Ellguth, P. and S. Kohaut (2011), 'Der Staat als Arbeitgeber: Wie unterscheiden sich die Arbeitsbedingungen zwischen öffentlichem Sektor und der Privatwirtschaft?', *Industrielle Beziehungen*, **18** (1–2): 11–38.

European Union (2004), Directive 2004/18/EC of the European Parliament and of the Council of 31 March 2004 on the coordination of procedures for the award of public works contracts, public supply contracts and public service contracts, *Official Journal of the European Union*, L 134.

Färber, G., M. Funke and S. Walther (2011), 'Nachhaltige Finanzierung der Beamtenversorgung', Ökonomische Perspektiven und rechtliche Gestaltungsmöglichkeiten, Berlin.

Hamburger, Senat (2007), 'Evaluierungsbericht zum Hamburgischen Vergabegesetz (HmbVgG)', Mitteilung des Senates an die Bürgerschaft, Bürgerschaft der Freien und Hansestadt Hamburg, Drucksache 18/7388, November.

Horn, G.A., T. Niechoj, S. Tober, T. van Treeck and A. Truger (2010), 'Reforming the European Stability and Growth Pact: Public debt is not the only factor, private debt counts as well', IMK Report, No. 51, Düsseldorf. Available at: http://www.boeckler.de/pdf/p_imk_report_51e_2010.pdf.

Jaecker, C. (2010), 'Germany: Austerity package, debt brake and structural deficit', BHF Bank Frankfurt. Available at: http://www.consensuseconomics.

com/News_and_Articles/Germany_Austerity_and_Debt_Brake512.htm (accessed 12 February 2012).
Kambeck, R. and H. Rappen (2010), 'Duisburger Haushalt vor dem Kollaps? Eine Analyse des Haushaltsplanentwurfs 2010 und des Haushaltssicherungskonzeptes der Stadt Duisburg', RWI Essen. Available at: http://www.ihk-niederrhein.de/downloads/ihk/RWI_Haushaltsanalyse_Duisburg_Endfassung.pdf (accessed 7 March 2012).
Kammradt, N. (2009), 'Zur Besoldungsentwicklung in Bund und Ländern: Unterschiede nehmen zu', *Personalrat*, **26**: 105–6.
Keller, B. (2010), *Arbeitspolitik im öffentlichen Dienst. Ein Überblick über Arbeitsmärkte und Arbeitsbeziehungen*, Berlin: Edition Sigma.
Lehndorff, S. and T. Haipeter (2011), 'Negotiating employment security: innovations and derogations', in S. Hayter (ed.), *The Role of Collective Bargaining in the Global Economy: Negotiating for Social Justice*, Cheltenham, UK and Northampton, MA, USA: Edward Elgar and Geneva: ILO, pp. 20–46.
Niechoj, T., U. Stein, S. Stephan and R. Zwiener (2011), 'Deutsche Arbeitskosten: Eine Quelle der Instabilität im Euroraum Auswertung der eurostat-Statistik für 2010', IMK-Report 68, Düsseldorf. Available at: http://www.boeckler.de/pdf/p_imk_report_68_2011.pdf (accessed 7 March 2012).
OECD (2011a), *Government at a Glance*, Paris: OECD.
OECD (2011b), *Government at a Glance. Country Note: Germany*. Available at: http://www.oecd.org/dataoecd/59/48/48213695.pdf (accessed 17 February 2012).
Schmidt, W., A. Müller and N. Trittel (2011), *Der Konflikt um die Tarifreform des öffentlichen Dienstes: Verhandlungsprozesse und Umsetzungspraxis*, Berlin: Edition Sigma.
Schulten, T. and M. Pawicki (2008), 'Tariftreueregelungen in Deutschland – ein aktueller Überblick', *WSI-Mitteilungen*, No. 4: 184–90.
Stadt Duisburg (2010), *Haushaltssicherungskonzept 2010 der Stadt Duisburg*. Available at: http://www.duisburg.de/static/hhplan10/PDF/Massnahmen_HSK.pdf (accessed 7 March 2012).
Stefaniak, A. and H. Vollmer (2005), *Evaluierung Tariftreuegesetz Nordrhein-Westfalen – Endbericht*, Sozialforschungsstelle Dortmund, February.
Tepe, M. and D. Kroos (2010), 'Lukrativer Staatsdienst? Lohndifferenzen zwischen öffentlichem Dienst und Privatwirtschaft', *WSI-Mitteilungen*, No. 1: 3–10.
Truger, A. (2011), 'Für eine Neuausrichtung der Steuerpolitik – Aufkommenssicherung und Verteilungsgerechtigkeit als Richtschnur', *spw*, **5**: 18–24.
Vesper, D. (2012), 'Finanzpolitische Entwicklungstendenzen und Perspektiven des Öffentlichen Dienstes in Deutschland', IMK Study 25, Düsseldorf.
Voss, D. and C. Weinkopf (2012), 'Niedriglohnfalle Minijob', *WSI-Mitteilungen*, **65** (1): 5–12.

APPENDIX 6A

Table 6A.1 Strikes in the public service, Germany, 1990–2012

	Industry	Subject of conflict	Type of strike and duration	Participants	Result
1990	German Post	Intensification of work	10 days	50,000	Additional break time
1992	German Railways, German Post	Wage increases	11 days	400,000	Wages + 5.4% and 200 DM additional holiday bonus
1998	Public service	Wage increases	Warning strikes	n.a.	Wages + 1.5%; increase of wages in eastern Germany to 86.5% of western German level; agreement on partial retirement
2000	Public service	Wage increases, equalization of east German wages	Warning strikes	ca. 100,000	400 DM lump sum; + 2% from August 2000, + 2.4% from September 2001, eastern Germany to 90.5% of western Germany by January 2002
2005	University hospitals Baden-Württemberg (without doctors)	Introduction of the new framework agreement for the public service	8 days	n.a.	€390 lump sum for 2005, €300 lump sums for 2006 and 2007; new wage grid, from 2006, 88% of monthly salary as annual bonus

Table 6A.1 (continued)

	Industry	Subject of conflict	Type of strike and duration	Participants	Result
2006	Municipalities (Hamburg, Lower Saxony, Baden-Württemberg)	Demand for longer weekly working hours from employers	Strike (16 days, 4.5 and 9 weeks)	n.a.	Increase of working hours from 38.5 hours per week to 38 to 40 differentiated by age
	Länder (without Hesse and Berlin) and university hospitals	Introduction of new framework agreement of federal state and municipalities	14 weeks	n.a.	New framework agreement similar to agreement for federal state and municipalities, weekly working hours between 38.7 (Schleswig-Holstein) and 39.73 (Bavaria), special regulations for university hospitals and doctors
	Doctors in university hospital and hospitals in the *Länder*	Own collective agreement for doctors' union (Marburger Bund)	13 weeks	14,000	Own agreement for doctors
	Doctors in local hospitals	Own collective agreement for doctors' union (Marburger Bund)	8 weeks	17,500	Own agreement for doctors

2007	German Railways Transnet (DGB)/ GDBA	7% wage increase	Warning strikes	n.a.	€600 lump sum + 4.5% from January 2008
	German Railways Train Drivers' Union (GDL)	Own collective agreement for train drivers	10 days	n.a.	Own collective agreement for train drivers but obligation to cooperate with competing unions Transnet/GDBA
2008	*Land*, Berlin	Adoption of new public sector agreement for other *Länder* plus wage increases	Warning strikes	n.a.	After 35 months without wage increases unilateral decision to pay a lump sum of €300 for 2008, from June 2006 wage increase of €65 for everybody
	Federal state and municipalities	Union demand of wage increase 8.0% (minimum €200 per month)	Warning strikes	430,000	Flat rate of €50 + 3.1% from January 2008, 2.8% from January 2009 + lump sum of €225; municipalities in western Germany increase of working hours from 38.5 to 39 hours per week
2009	*Länder* (without Hesse and Berlin)	Union demand of wage increase 8.0% (minimum €200 per month)	Warning strikes	ca. 180,000	€40 lump sum for January and February, + 3% from March 2009, + 1.2% from March 2010

Table 6A.1 (continued)

	Industry	Subject of conflict	Type of strike and duration	Participants	Result
	Hesse	Union demand of wage increase 8.0% (minimum €200 per month)	Warning strikes	6,900	+ 3.0% from April 2009, + 1.2% from March 2010, €500 lump sum June 2009; new unified wage grid for white- and blue-collar workers from January 2010
	Municipalities: social workers and nursery school teachers	Wage increases and working conditions	Warning strikes	150,000	Improvement of work health promotion, improvements in wage classification
	Local transport (Bavaria)	Wage increases of 9.5% (minimum €250), increase of shift supplements	Warning strikes	4,000	€40 per month from January 2009, + 3.1% from May 2009, increase of shift supplements
2011	*Länder* (without Hesse and Berlin)	Wage increases of €50 per month + 3.0%	Warning strikes	88,000	€360 lump sum, + 1.5% from April 2011, + 1.9% from January 2012
	Land Hesse	Wage increases of €50 per month + 3.0%	Warning strikes	2,300	€360 lump sum, + 1.5% from April 2011, + 2.6% from April 2012
2012	Federal state and municipalities	Wage increase + 6.5%; for 2 years (minimum €200)	Warning strikes	300,000	Wage increases + 3.5% from March 2012, + 1.4% in January 2013 and August 2013

Source: WSI-Tarifarchiv; Statistik: Streik und Aussperrungen; Ausgewählte Arbeitskämpfe (http://www.boeckler.de/wsi-tarifarchiv_37623.htm).

7. Public sector adjustment amidst structural adjustment in Greece: Subordinate, spasmodic and sporadic

Zafiris Tzannatos and Yannis Monogios*

1. INTRODUCTION

This chapter reviews the post-2009 public sector adjustment measures in Greece. Unlike many public sector reforms in democratic countries, where checks and balances in the system lead to adjustment before dysfunctionality reaches alarming proportions, the ongoing and planned public sector adjustment in Greece is subordinate to a massive fiscal and structural adjustment programme driven by the public debt crisis: public debt was 126 per cent of GDP in 2009 and has now (June 2012) reached approximately 170 per cent.

Although Greek debt accounts for merely 1 per cent of global debt, the possibility of a sovereign default has endangered the survival of the euro and with it the world economy due to the interconnectivity of the global financial system. If this were to happen, it would be the first such default for a high-income economy in more than 60 years. Under these conditions a quick response to avoid a disorderly default and save the global economy in the short term was deemed by the lenders to carry more weight than an orderly adjustment that would put Greece on a sustainable course in the long term with lower social costs.

The structural adjustment measures constituted more a spasmodic fiscal adjustment programme than a carefully designed economic adjustment programme. The initial programme (May 2010) was frontloaded with too many measures to be implemented quickly (2010–13) without the benefit of prior expenditure, functional or social impact reviews. This knee-jerk reaction was associated with massive underperformance of that programme that consistently missed its targets.[1] Greece was drawn into a deep recession (expected 20 per cent loss in GDP by end-2012 from its

2008 level). A second programme followed (February 2012) that not only intensified fiscal measures and accelerated reforms in the public sector but also kept adding new measures in a sporadic way, notably targeting labour relations and employment in the private sector.

As of today, the picture is still changing on a daily basis[2] but, as this chapter discusses, the indications so far are that the part of the structural adjustment programme that referred to the public sector could have been better conceptualized and designed. The structure of the chapter is as follows. Section 2 provides a short overview of the Greek economy and debt. It shows that the need for public sector adjustment was clear in terms both of size and efficiency. Section 3 presents the structure and evolution of the public sector, while Section 4 discusses the public sector adjustment measures and their consequences in terms of employment size, pay, benefits and pensions. Section 5 examines in more depth reforms in the cases of the two largest government sectors, namely health and education. Section 6 summarizes and assesses several effects of the reforms including their social impact. Section 7 concludes by comparing the Greek experience, so far with lessons from international experience, and provides some policy recommendations.

2. OVERVIEW OF THE GREEK ECONOMY AND DEBT

At the end of the dictatorship in 1974, the debt-to-GDP ratio stood at 18 per cent. The restoration of democracy was followed by Greece joining the EU in 1981, ahead of Spain and Portugal, and getting access to generous structural European funds, whose use could hardly be described as prudent. Excessive government borrowing that took place in the next couple of decades and accelerated after Greece joined the euro in January 2001 enabled the government to borrow at practically zero 'spreads'.

Debt-financed economic growth followed. Focusing on the decade prior to the onset of the crisis (2009), the economy averaged annual real GDP growth close to 4 per cent, making Greece one of the best performers in the European Monetary Union (EMU). This buoyant growth largely reflected a domestic demand boom, high real wages, low interest rates, rapid credit expansion and loose fiscal policy. Greece reached a high standard of living, among the top 30 countries in the world in terms of per capita income. It was ranked 22nd according to the UNDP's Human Development Index (UNDP 2010), as well as The Economist's quality-of-life index (*The Economist* Intelligence Unit 2005). In 2008, the per capita gross domestic product (GDP) in Greece in purchasing power parity

(PPP) stood at US$30,076, which corresponded to 95 per cent of the EU average (Eurostat 2009).

The boom proved to be unsustainable. Public funds were not channelled into investments with high social returns. Public expenditures kept increasing and were driven by clientelism, nepotism and populism that are now generally admitted to have prevailed during most of the periods when the alternating governments of Conservatives and Socialists were in power since 1974. The public sector became bloated and was in need of adjustment in terms of size, structure and performance. However, the alarm bells rang only when the debt-to-GDP ratio exceeded 120 per cent in 2009 and the budget deficit reached nearly 16 per cent of GDP (against the then officially reported figure of only about 6 per cent).

Due to the unsustainable debt dynamics (Monogios and Korliras 2012), Greece became both illiquid and insolvent. However, the initial adjustment programme in 2010 treated Greece mainly as illiquid, that is, unable to meet its current debt repayment obligations. It did not (as it should) treat Greece as insolvent, that is, unable to repay its debt in the long run. The 'long run' came as early as within a year (by the end of 2011) by which time the adjustment programme was 'readjusted'. The financial markets kept panicking despite attempts to 'ring-fence' Greece. The most generous debt forgiveness package in world history that followed in February 2012 seems to have averted a European crisis (at least, at the time of writing) though the final outcome is still uncertain amidst emerging concerns about Spain and Italy (Tzannatos 2012).

3. THE STRUCTURE AND EVOLUTION OF THE PUBLIC SECTOR

The Greek public sector comprises two main components: general government and public enterprises/organizations. In turn, general government comprises central government, local government and social security entities. Central government is further divided into central administration, legal entities of private law and legal entities of public law. The central administration is made up of the presidency, ministries (offering central and decentralized services), independent authorities and decentralized authorities (Figure 7.1). The composition of the public sector is indicated in Figure 7.2.

Statistics on the size and composition of budgetary allocations, as well as on the total number of public sector employees, remain elusive. Only recently, and as part of the ongoing adjustment, has the government begun to undertake a census of its employees, a comprehensive spending

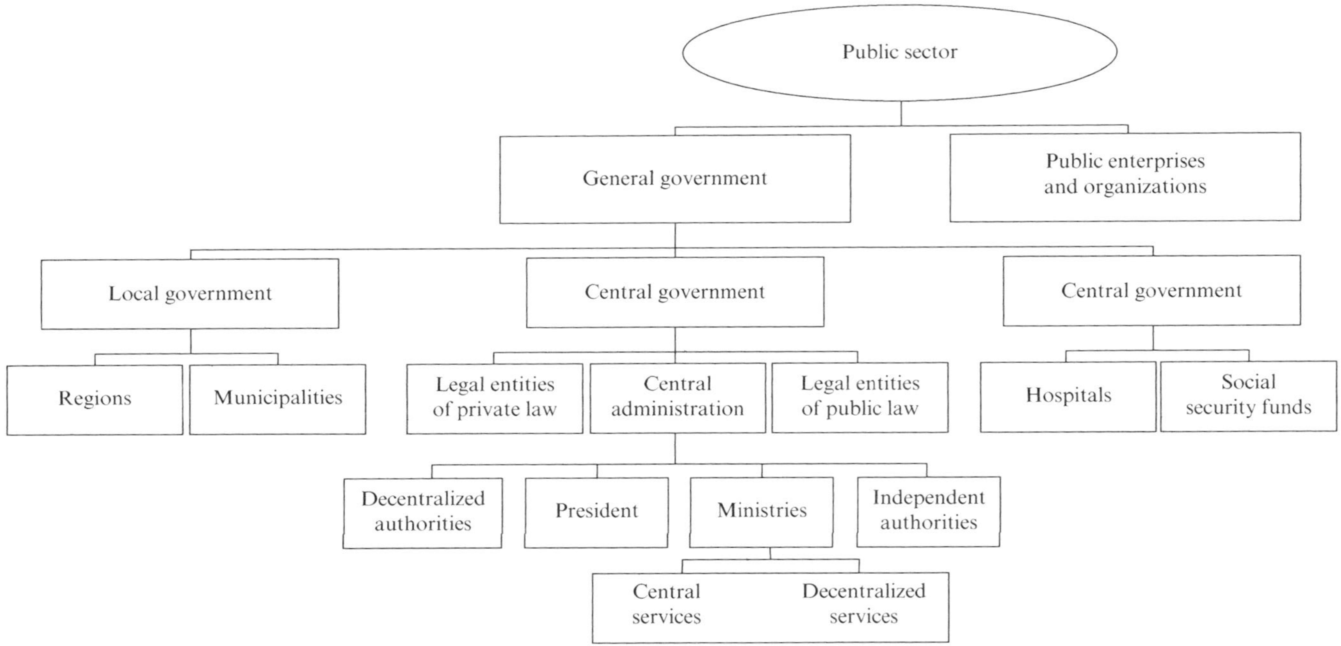

Source: OECD (2011a).

Figure 7.1 Structure of the Greek public sector

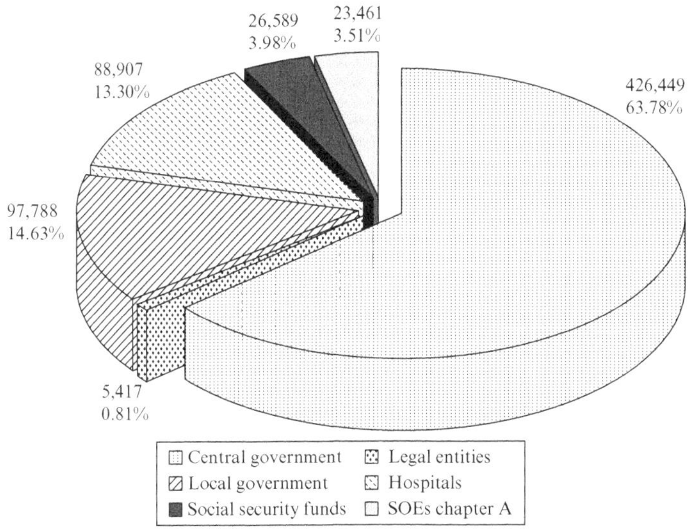

Note: SOEs (state-owned enterprises) include only those where the government has majority of shares (Chapter A).

Source: General Accounting Office.

Figure 7.2 Composition of general government permanent employment by sector, Greece, 2010 (number and as a percentage of total employment)

review, a review of social programmes and a functional review of public administration. According to some sources, public employment in all its forms had reached nearly 1 million by 2009.[3]

Based on official data, employment in the public sector increased from 264,000 in 1970 to 824,000 by 2009, equivalent to 3 per cent per annum. During that four-decade period, employment in the private sector increased by only 30 per cent, from 3 million to 3.8 million – an annual growth of less than 1 per cent. Self-employment remained practically unchanged at around 1.7 million, still a sizeable number. Specifically during the decade that preceded the crisis, Greece was at the top among OECD countries in terms of employment growth in the public sector (Figure 7.3).

The uncontrolled expansion of employment in the public sector had implications for its internal structure, which was transformed to satisfy personal ambitions more than operational needs. The organizational sprawl of the Greek public sector over the years can be seen with reference to the Ministry of Labour during the period from 1991 to 2008 when its

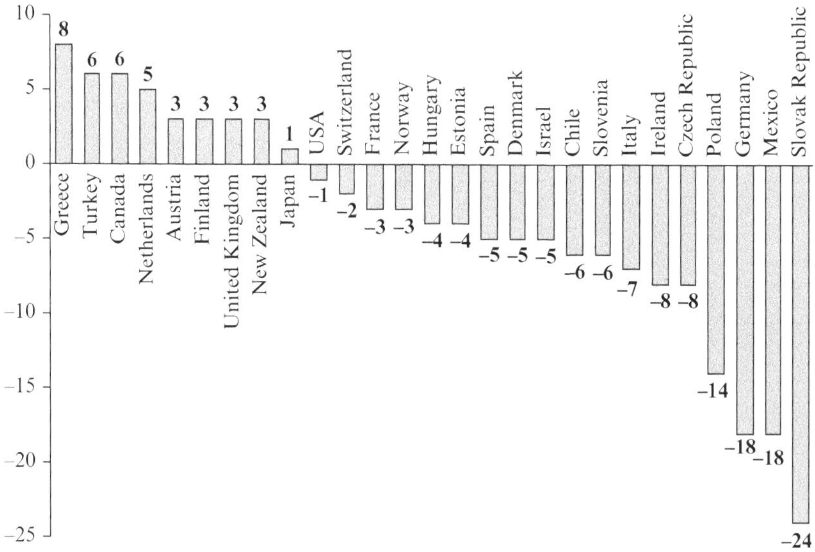

Source: International Labour Organization (ILO), LABORSTA database.

Figure 7.3 Employment growth (%) in central government and public corporations, OECD, 2000–2008

departments increased from 31 to 45 after no less than 15 ad hoc 'generations' of laws and decrees.[4]

More generally, individual ministries ended up, on average, with 439 internal structures. As many as 20 per cent of departments are staffed by only one employee while the number of persons in managerial positions is far too large compared to the number of employees under their supervision: more than half of departments have three or fewer subordinates, and more than 90 per cent of all departments have fewer than 20 employees (Figure 7.4). The majority of departments do not have the critical size to be efficient as they are at times created to satisfy the career progression of individuals rather than national objectives. The prevailing culture and procedures in the central administration encouraged a ministry-based silo vision of governance, leaving little room or inclination for cooperation and operational development (OECD 2011a).

Moreover, organizational sprawl affects the supervisory role of government for the private sector and the quality of public services. The resulting practices focus on the fulfilment of inward-looking narrow competencies as set out in the law and hundreds of legal texts. The use of performance assessments in personnel decisions in central government was minimal,

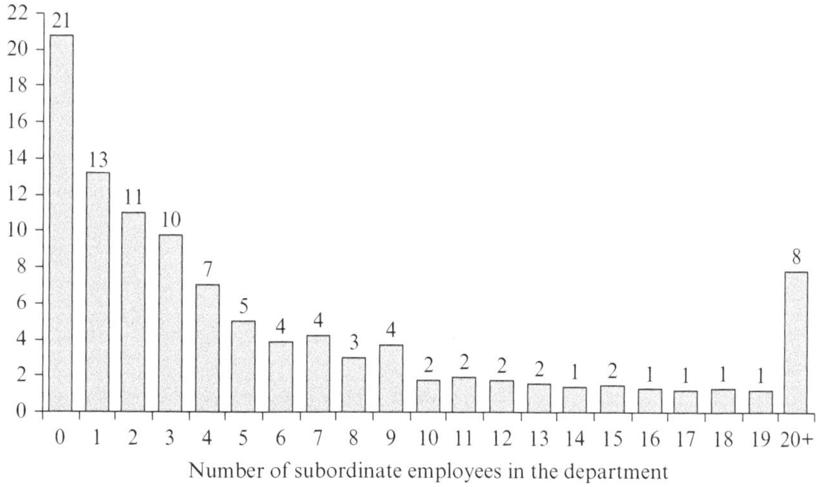

Source: Ministry of Administrative Reform and e-Governance.

Figure 7.4 Distribution of government departments according to size, Greece, 2010

while working hours were among the lowest in the OECD compared to the private sector.[5] Salary levels in the government sector were primarily a reflection of time in service rather than performance. The end result has been little room or inclination for policy coordination across and even within ministries. This has also created ample space for discretionary behaviour by officials through favours or extortion.[6]

Compensation of government employees as a percentage of GDP was practically the same in Greece in 2001 as in the euro area, at around 10.5 per cent. By 2009 the Greek share had gone up to 13.4 per cent, while it remained practically the same in the euro area. 'Special wage' regimes in Greece, such as those for judges, the military, doctors, academics and employees in state-owned enterprises (SOEs), accounted for one-third of the public sector wage bill (Mnemonio 2, February 2012).

In terms of individual wages, average monthly earnings of public sector employees were higher than those in the private sector, although they have increased less over time (Table 7.1). The public/private differential was 41 per cent for women and 27 per cent for men in 2000. This differential had declined to 34 per cent for women and 24 per cent for men by 2009, which is a typical change when governments overexpand for political reasons. However, some part of this differential is justified as the education attainment of public sector employees is higher than that of private sector

Table 7.1 Monthly earnings by sector and gender, Greece, 2000–2009 (€)

Sector	Gender	2000	2009	Total change (%)
Public	Women	754	1,171	55.3
	Men	834	1,276	52.9
Private	Women	535	871	62.9
	Men	655	1,033	57.6

Source: Labour Force Surveys.

workers. According to one source, the adjusted public/private differential was reported to be 'about 11 per cent'.[7]

All in all, the expansion of the public sector was delinked from the social objectives one would expect to find in an accountable government; recruitment was not based on merit; rewards were not aligned to performance; and social services were not commensurate with the needs and incomes of the population. Increases in public spending, other than those needed to sustain relatively high salaries and growing employment, were used for obscure procurements that served the interests of rent-seeking officials as well as those of their collaborating counterparts in the private sector. For example, as shown below in Case Study 1 (Section 5) on health care, expenditure on pharmaceuticals increased from €2.2 billion in 2001 to €6.8 billion in 2009 compared to public expenditure on hospitals of only €1.5 billion in 2009.

To summarize, Greece entered the crisis with an economy unable to sustain its public debt. The rise in the budget deficit needed to fund an insatiable public sector since the 1980s reached its limits by 2009 as government revenues as a percentage of GDP started falling and declined from more than 40 per cent in 2000 to just over 36 per cent in 2009. At the same time, public expenditure rose from 43 per cent to more than 50 per cent during the same period. Fiscal consolidation was necessary. The issue becomes what needs to be cut, how and when. The next section reviews the reform measures.

4. PUBLIC SECTOR REFORMS AND THEIR EFFECTS

The scope of the adjustment programme has left untouched practically no area of economic, labour and broader social policy. An attempt to count the measures enacted by the government by November 2011 under the first adjustment programme initiated in May 2010 returned some 72. Another

79 prior actions were included/enacted in Mnemonio 2 by February 2012 (Monogios and Tzannatos forthcoming). This section reviews the many measures that affected public sector employment and wages directly. Later on, it discusses pensions, which represent one of the most important entitlements from employment and, in the case of Greece, the largest single component of GDP.

Practically all ministries and agencies have reduced wages and employment in an attempt to bring the public wage bill from 13.4 per cent of GDP in 2009 closer to 9 per cent.[8] This was to be done through various measures, including the following:

- wage and salary cuts as well as ceilings on benefits and high pay;
- increase in the number of weekly working hours (from 37.5 to 40) and reductions in overtime payments;
- introduction of part-time public sector employment and unpaid leave;
- reduction in benefits for various activities (for example, reductions in the number of remunerated committees and councils; reduction in other additional compensation, allowances and bonus schemes);
- temporary freeze of automatic progression and the introduction of a new payroll grid and job-ranking system;
- reduction in total public sector employment and fixed-term contracts – including in SOEs, as well as in the number of 'highly ranked' officials;
- introduction of a 'one hiring for every 10 departures' rule for 2011 and 'one hiring for every five departures' rule for 2012–15;
- transfer of excess staff to a labour reserve paid on average at 60 per cent of their wage (excluding overtime and other extra payments) for up to 12 months and a cut in the productivity allowance by 50 per cent;
- reduction in the number of admissions to the military and police academies;
- reduction in benefits for SOEs (for example, the Public Electricity Company);
- reduction in the number of municipalities and subsidies for local government; and
- cuts in defence spending.

These measures were initiated in May 2010 and aimed to quickly reduce the budget deficit. Many of them missed the targets for 2011: for example, retrenchments were slower than expected while the primary budget continued to be in deficit against a projected surplus. In February 2012 the measures were intensified accordingly.

It must be noted that neither the May 2010 measures nor those up until February 2012 were based on prior functional review of public administration, a review of social spending programmes or a general expenditure review. Reviews in these areas were initiated only at the beginning of 2012 and were to be completed between July and December 2012. As discussed below (Section 6), there has been practically no social dialogue. Instead, on one hand, the government has unilaterally changed the industrial relations system and, on the other, there has been massive strike activity.

4.1 Public Sector Employment Cuts

As mentioned earlier, although the cross-border debate on Greek public sector employment is characterized by 'a lack of real data and much stereotyping' (Ammerman 2011; see also *The Economist* 2010), the Greek public sector has undoubtedly been overstaffed. Overstaffing was considered to be around 50 per cent, at least in some government organizations and agencies (OECD 2011a).

Public employment was initially envisaged to decline by about 20 per cent from its 2009 level by 2015. This was to be done through a combination of reductions in contract employment, attrition policies and involuntary exits, in addition to redundancies for the closure or merging of some public entities. The biggest reductions were to take place among temporary employees (more than 75 per cent of the 89,000 in 2009) and those working in local government (by 50 per cent of the 21,000 in 2009).

The planned reduction in total public sector employment was to be around 60,000 in 2010, half of which would come from temporary employees. Another 30,000 'surplus personnel' among those with permanent contracts aged over 60 years from about 150 state organizations and agencies were also expected to be placed on 'labour reserve', that is, they would be retained and be paid 60 per cent of their basic salary until 2012 and, if not reallocated to another job by then, they will be subsequently dismissed.[9] These planned reductions in employment fell short of the projections made in the first adjustment programme (Mnemonio 1, May 2010).[10]

According to revised targets in the second adjustment programme (Mnemonio 2, February 2012: 9), the total reduction in public sector employment by 2015 should be 150,000 (or 26 per cent for total employment or be reduced to 600,000 by 2015). Those on labour reserve were originally planned to be dismissed within two years but this period was cut to one year.[11] The possibility of re-employment is of course very limited given the 'one hiring for 10' rule (for 2011) and 'one hiring for five' rule (from 2012 to 2015) and the intensity of the recession.

4.2 Public Sector Pay Cuts

While it can be debated whether the pay difference between the public and private sectors is justified, the system of allowances that evolved over time is indicative of the clientelistic behaviour of the state.

Although there is no complete account of what benefits were paid to whom, the following highly selective list is illuminating. There was a monthly allowance of €690 paid to 420 employees in the Greek Telecommunications Organization for 'warming up car engines'. Another allowance of €420 was paid to 1,987 employees in the National Railways Organization for 'washing their hands'. A 'propeller allowance' of €840 was paid to 653 coastguards. The 'antenna bonus allowance' of €1,120 was paid to 329 employees at the Athens-Piraeus Electric Railway Company. A 'folder transferring allowance' of €290 was provided to 6,800 office workers. A 'bus handing over' allowance of €450 was paid to 1,100 workers. An allowance for 'timely handling of cases' of €595 was provided to employees at the Ministry of Justice, and a 'fax services allowance' of €870 to 657 employees at the Electrical Power Corporation. An 'annual canteen allowance' of €120 was paid to all staff at the Greek Petroleum Group, although there was an in-house restaurant where food was provided free of charge. It is said that there was even a provision for an allowance 'for not getting any other allowances'.

The reforms aimed to bring the wage and benefit structure in the public sector closer to the private sector. To do so, the reforms included pay cuts, a new and unified salary grid for the public sector and reductions in benefits. An immediate reduction in the wage bill came through the elimination of two monthly payments of the 14 customary payments paid in a year.[12] This and other reforms are included in Table 7.2, while the new salary grid is described in more detail below.

Containment of the wage bill is expected to be reinforced less directly – and with a view to increasing efficiency – through a new public sector payroll system, expected to be enacted in November 2011 (Table 7.3). The new system imposes a monthly salary cap of €2,200. It provides for six ranks and 12 subgrades instead of the current five ranks and 18 subgrades. Payments under the new scheme would be linked to productivity through the introduction of 'incentive performance payments' that could augment pay by up to 25 per cent, following a positive evaluation. For those evaluated negatively, there will be a wage freeze of up to 50 per cent.

The new evaluation system based on performance criteria will make it more difficult for a civil servant to move up through the whole ranking scale. Even if all performance evaluations are successful, it has been estimated that 100 per cent of civil servants will make it from rank F to rank

Table 7.2 Summary of pay reforms, Greece, 2010–2012 (€)

Job ranking	New pay per level of education (years of rank in parentheses)			
	Elementary	Secondary	Polytechnic*	University
A	–	–	1,992	2,096
B	–	1,497	1,811 (6 years)	1,906 (4 years)
C	1,134	1,248 (6 years)	1,509 (4 years)	1,588 (4 years)
D	986 (10 years)	1,085 (6 years)	1,312 (4 years)	1,381 (4 years)
E	858 (10 years)	943 (6 years)	1,141 (4 years)	1,201 (4 years)
F	780 (2 years)	858 (2 years)	1,037 (2 years)	1,092 (2 years)
Total no. of years	22 years	20 years	20 years	18 years

Note: * Further education.

Source: Authors' estimates based on official documents.

Table 7.3 New payroll system and job ranking in the public sector, Greece, 2011

Reduction in annual pay	14.5 per cent cut in basic salary via the elimination of 13th and 14th monthly wages
Rationalization of benefits	Abolition of all benefits except for dangerous work, work near national borders, large family allowances and national days. Added allowances for high responsibility posts, motivation, fiscal objectives (for example, tax collection) and personal attainments
Reduction in wage bill	Number of 'higher rank' officials to be reduced from 30,000 to 10,000
Lowering unit costs	Increase in weekly working hours from 37.5 to 40 hours
Pensions	Main pensions exceeding €1,200 per month cut by 20 per cent (and for those below the age of 55 years by 40 per cent); supplementary pensions above €150 per month cut by 15–30 per cent (depending on the fund); end-of-service lump-sum payment cut by an additional 10 per cent (on top of those already decided)
Level of basic salary and salary grid	Expected reduction in pay of regular employees by 17 per cent
Special wage regimes	12 per cent cut (for example, for diplomats, doctors, judges, professors, political appointees, police, armed forces)

Source: Official sources.

E, 90 per cent from rank E to D, 80 per cent from D to C, 60 per cent from C to B and only 20 per cent from B to A. Accordingly, the number of 'higher-ranking' public sector officials (estimated at 30,000 today) is expected to be reduced to some 10,000 following the new payroll and job-ranking system.

The new scale for civilian personnel provides for more or less uniform decreases in the 10–15 per cent range for the lower paid but leaves unchanged or even increases pay for the two top grades (Table 7.4). In terms of its likely effects, given the current distribution of public sector employees, pay for the majority of civil servants (about 78 per cent) is expected to remain the same. Although there are no estimates of the likely distributional impact of the new payroll and job-grading system, it is likely that some or even many civil servants will find themselves in lower grades with no allowances and lower pension entitlements than before.

Already, cuts in wages and benefits have had a significant effect on take-home pay. Following the first wave of reforms, public sector pay was reduced by 15 per cent in 2011. The reduction in the pay of those working in SOEs has been 30 per cent.

Nevertheless, not all pay reforms have been implemented while further reductions are planned. According to the IMF, the new salary grid for public sector employees introduced in November 2011 will reduce the average salary of regular public sector employees by a further 17 per cent (IMF 2011b: 83), on top of the previous cuts of about 15 per cent as a result of the elimination of two monthly wages of the 14 previously paid annually.

The overall impact on average wages in the public sector has not been estimated formally. However, based on budget figures for the total compensation of employees in 2009 and 2012 (€31 and €24 billion, respectively) and the number of public sector employees (824,000 and 693,000, respectively), the average reduction is 22 per cent. Another estimate of the reduction in public sector employees' incomes is provided by the civil service union (ADEDY). According to union estimates, the reduction has been of the order of 38–40 per cent (ILO 2011: 34).

4.3 Pensions

There are about 2.9 million pensioners in Greece in 2012 (against an employed labour force of around 4 million). Of these, 2.3 million were previously workers in the private sector (or their survivors). This compares to 3.2 million private sector workers. The number of pensioners who were former civilian workers in the public sector comes to nearly 300,000 in November 2011 while that of former military personnel comes to nearly

Table 7.4 Changes in public sector salaries based on the new system, Greece, 2010–2011 (€)

Category	Previous payroll system (valid until 30.10.2011)				New payroll (effective 01.11.2011)				Change in salaries	
	Basic salary (1)	Performance incentive (2)	Allowances (3)	Total monthly salary (4)=(1)+(2)+(3)	Basic salary (1)	Performance incentive (2)	Allowances (3)	Total monthly salary (4)=(1)+(2)+(3)	€	%
B-level newly hired	711	28.50	143	882.50	780	0	0	780	−102.50	−11.61
B-level 5 years	798	28.50	143	969.50	832	0	0	832	−137.50	−14.18
U-level 5 years	1,105	50	136	1,291.00	1,201	0	0	1,201	−90.00	−6.97
P-level 3 years	1,015	45	230	1,290.00	1,106	0	0	1,106	−184.00	−14.26
P-level 13 years	1,207	45	242	1,494.00	1,255	0	0	1,255	−239.00	−16.00
U-level 17 years	1,345	50	401	1,796.00	1,588	0	0	1,588	−208.00	−11.58
U-level 9 years	1,185	50	129	1,364.00	1,201	0	0	1,201	−163.00	−11.96
P-level 33 years	1,589	45	230	1,864.00	1,992	0	0	1,992	128.00	6.87
U-level 33 years	1,666	50	379	2,095.00	2,096	0	0	2,096	1	0.05

Note: B = Basic education level, P = Polytechnic level (further education), U = University level.

Source: Data processed by ADEDY (Greek Civil Servants' Confederation).

150,000. By 2012 the ratio of active civil servants in general government to pensioners was down to almost 2:1.

Pensions and broader social security-related payments constitute the single most important component of the government budget: contributions to insurance funds (including health expenditure) absorb 24 per cent of the budget (in 2010) of which one-third (8 per cent of the budget) goes to pensions paid to former government workers. Given the relative size of the private and public workforces, public pensions are on average 2.6 times higher than private pensions, with the highest pensions paid to military employees.

Rationalizing pensions was one of the main priorities of the adjustment programme. At the top end, workers in the public sector, especially some privileged parts of it, can and do take advantage of early retirement provisions and others end up with pensions practically exceeding their salary. Others have to make do with sub-poverty pension levels. The system is also subject to abuse, with disability pensions being almost 50 per cent higher than the other EU countries (more than 14 per cent compared to 10 per cent), as are pensions paid for those in what are sometimes generously defined as 'arduous occupations'.

One of the activities undertaken to this end was to try to account for the number of pensioners. In an attempt to identify whether there were any 'ghost' pensioners, a census of pensioners and cross-checking of personal data with full implementation of social security ID number was completed in October 2011,[13] which left 55,000 pensioners unaccounted for. If this figure accurately reflects fraud, its annual cost may be up to €700 million per year. In February 2012 the government announced that it had discovered another '60,000 ghost beneficiaries' whose alleged fraudulent claims totalled approximately €460 million per year.[14]

The pension reforms include simplification, consolidation, indexation, compliance and monitoring and apply to both public and private schemes:

- immediate reductions in pension levels for current beneficiaries (loss of two out of 14 monthly payments a year);
- parametric changes for future pensioners (increase in pensionable age, less generous determination of pension levels);
- reductions in pension among those who voluntarily retired early; and
- improved targeting.

The statutory retirement age for women was raised to 65 years, in line with men. The required years of contribution for a full pension were raised from 37 to 40 years. Early retirement penalties were increased: benefits will

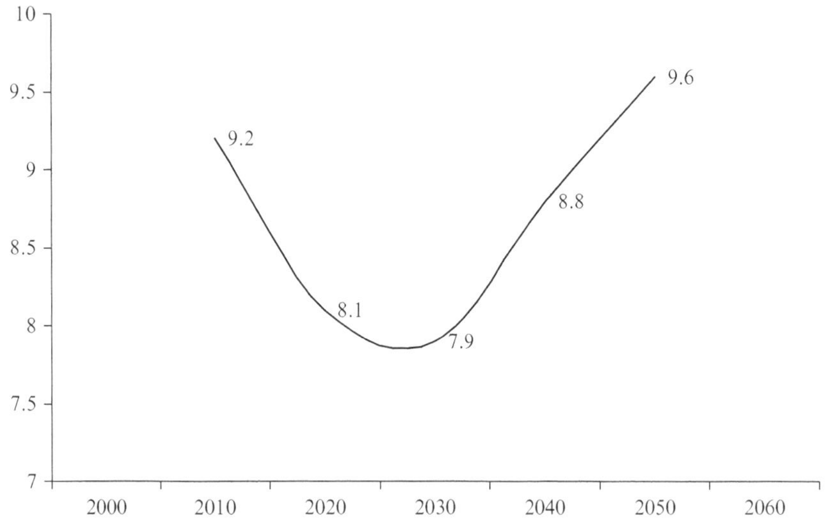

Source: Ministry of Finance (2011).

Figure 7.5 Expected pension expenditure after reforms, Greece, 2000–2050 (% of GDP)

be reduced by around 6 per cent per year of early retirement before the age of 65 without 40 years of contributions. Pension benefits will become more aligned to lifetime contributions instead of being based on final salary or wages in the last few years of employment. All voluntary exit plans from the public sector have been abolished. There is also an adjustment in supplementary pension schemes, a freeze in pension levels through 2015 and imposition of an upper cap on pensions, as well as on the end-of-service indemnity (lump sums) paid to some civil servants, sometimes at extremely high levels. The disability pension system is being reformed with the aim of reducing the number of disability pensions to 10 per cent of overall pensions by 2015. The list of arduous professions entitled to early pension rights is being restricted, which will reduce their share in total employment from 14 per cent in 2007 to about 8 per cent. The reduction in the value of pensions has applied *pro rata* to all current and future workers since the beginning of 2011. It applies to basic, contributory and supplementary pensions and any other related scheme, including indemnities (lump sums) paid at the time of retirement.

The expected course of the total pension bill according to the adjustment programme is presented in Figure 7.5. The effects will be front-loaded, with practically all savings taking place by 2020. The savings will come not only from cuts in the (high) pensions in the public sector, but also from (low) pensions such as those paid to farmers. Savings are also expected to come from changes in both the coverage ratio and the benefits ratio. As argued below, pensions in Greece constitute the most potent measure for poverty reduction and the ongoing and planned changes in the pension bill are bound to increase poverty.

The ability of the pension funds to meet future payments has been adversely affected by the recent private sector involvement (PSI) in public debt restructuring. This involved a voluntary 'haircut' in the face value of Greek government bonds. The haircut resulted in a significant loss to the social security funds of 54 per cent of the €24–30 billion they held in government bonds.

Although the effective decline in average pensions is not yet clear, it is estimated to range between 20 and 30 per cent. A further reduction in main and supplementary pensions by 15 per cent (on average) is envisaged for 2012. Moreover, there may be additional reductions in pensions to the extent that the fiscal targets for 2013 and 2014 do not materialize (Figure 7.5).

5. CASE STUDIES

5.1 Case Study 1: Ill-designed Reform Programmes in Health Care

The health sector in Greece is large and its 89,000 employees falling under the public budget are second only to those under the Ministry of Education (190,000) which are on a par with the Ministry of Defence. The health sector was among the most prominent of those included in the adjustment programme from the very beginning, with explicit expenditure cuts and detailed reform measures.

This subsection argues that there was significant room for cost reductions in the area of pharmaceuticals. However, the programme included many institutional changes despite the absence of technical studies of what should be addressed, how and over what time horizon as health sector reforms are complex and face powerful groups of health sector workers who benefit from a sizeable black economy consisting of significant moonlighting by doctors and large private under-the-table payments (ESDY 2006, 2011).

5.1.1 Profile and benchmarking of health care

Health care has been an ailing sector in Greece. The centralized nature of the system has led to corruption rather than improved allocation and performance. Planning, coordination, managerial and administrative capacity, mechanisms for assessing needs and setting priorities were all underdeveloped and weak. There were no explicit funding criteria. Sickness funds faced high and increasing budget deficits over time.

There is an oversupply of doctors and an undersupply of nurses.[15] With regard to doctors, there was an even greater oversupply of specialists (at the expense of general practitioners) who, in combination with a dysfunctional referral system, obscure procurement, irrational pricing and opaque reimbursement mechanisms deprived health care of both efficient delivery and effective prevention and treatment of the population at large.[16] The fact that pharmacists are a closed profession and the attempt to open it up was the only measure that the parliament backed off from enacting in the draconian measures introduced in February 2012, is indicative of the deep-rooted rent-seeking nature of the sector. The list of misspent finances, inefficiencies and inequitable outcomes in health care is lengthy, but it can all be summarized by saying that quality has been low and the effectiveness of public funds allocated to the health sector could improve.

Turning to funding issues, total spending on health in Greece was 9.7 per cent of GDP before the crisis, in 2008, compared to the OECD average of 9 per cent. One feature masked by this aggregate statistic is that total spending in Greece includes one of the lowest shares of public funding among OECD countries (5.9 per cent of GDP).[17] Another feature is that per capita growth in health spending in Greece was one of the fastest among the OECD economies during the10 years before the crisis.[18]

The main reason for the rapid increase in public expenditure on health spending over time was pharmaceutical costs. Per capita spending on drugs in Greece increased from €192 in 2000 to €682 in 2008, the fastest increase among 20 EU countries covered in a recent study (OECD 2011b). In 2011, spending on drugs as a percentage of total health spending in the EU ranged from 10 per cent in Denmark (lowest) to 25 per cent in Greece (highest). Obviously, pharmaceuticals are a promising area both for rent-seekers in the private sector and obliging officials in the public sector. This is yet another manifestation of lack of government accountability and corruption.

5.1.2 The measures

An obvious focus of the adjustment programme was the reduction and consolidation of the health-care budget. According to the adjustment programme, this was to be achieved not just by focusing on expenditure on pharmaceuticals (Table 7.5).

Expenditure on pharmaceuticals is a low-hanging fruit and justified in the context of fiscal adjustment. The explosion in pharmaceutical

Table 7.5 Social budget for hospitals and drugs, Greece, 2011 and 2015 (€bn)

	2011	2015
Hospitals	3.0	2.3
Drugs	3.1	1.7
Total	6.1	4.0

Source: National Budget 2012.

expenditure ought to be reduced. Overpricing was one issue. The other was that generic drugs in Greece account for barely 13 per cent of all drugs compared to 50 per cent according to international norms. A price reduction of over 90 per cent for some generic drugs has been largely achieved (Ministry of Health 2011). Further reductions in the price of medicines, creation of a negative list (drugs not to be included in medical coverage plans), expansion of the list of pharmaceuticals that do not require prescriptions, full implementation of e-prescriptions, a reference price system, enhanced purchasing and procurement mechanisms, and centralized purchasing of medical supplies are under way (European Commission 2011; Ministry of Finance 2011).

However, the adjustment programme did not stop at regulating and rationalizing pharmaceuticals. It included raising user charges as well as many structural and institutional reforms whose immediate payback in terms of fiscal savings is less evident. Moreover, as international experience suggests, health reforms require good prior technical analysis and time to work, while it would be redundant to mention that the government did not have any consultation with the stakeholders (medical personnel and users). Among the other reforms, the following were included:

- imposition of charges to the uninsured seeking medical treatment in public hospitals;
- reductions in operating costs of public hospitals;
- implementation of a new 'health map' and associated reduction in hospital expenditure, along with a re-evaluation of mandate and expenses of non-hospital supervised entities;
- an increase in copayments by insured persons for medical expenses and drugs;
- provision of unified/uniform medical services by all social insurance funds;

- payments for outpatient visits, medical tests and care by the insured and migrants;
- contract agreements between public hospitals and private health insurance companies;
- reduction in the services provided to the non-insured (gate-keeping function); and
- relaxation of smoking restrictions in public places – if a levy is paid.

5.1.3 Implementation

Public expenditures on health were reduced on average by 30 per cent (year-on-year) in the first quarter of 2011, despite an increase in the number of patients (see below). Taken together, the adjustment programme aims to create savings of more than €2 billion by 2015. However, due to the overall failure of the first wave of adjustment measures to improve the budgetary situation in 2011, additional cuts in the budget of the Ministry of Health were included for 2012.[19] According to Mnemonio 2, the government will intensify 'measures to achieve savings in the purchasing of outpatient medicines of close to €1 billion in 2012 compared to 2011' (2010: 12).

The contracts between health insurance funds and doctors are being revised. A new payment mechanism started for each new contract since 2011 based on a minimum number of patients per doctor. The new system will lead to a reduction in the overall compensation cost (wages and fees) of physicians by at least 10 per cent in 2011 compared to the previous year, and by an additional 15 per cent in 2012.

As an indication of what this means in practice, there has been a 40 per cent reduction in hospital budgets. Ten major hospital units (out of 134) were merged, with more mergers planned. Spending on mental health decreased by 45 per cent, despite much greater need as a consequence of the crisis (Economou et al. 2011). According to one study, 26,000 public health workers (including 9,100 physicians) have lost their jobs (Triantafyllou and Angelopoulou 2011).[20]

5.1.4 Effects

Although the effects of adjustment on health care usually take time to surface, some early evidence is already available. An early comparative study of 10 European countries estimated a standardized increase in suicides in Greece by 17 per cent already in 2010 (Stuckler et al. 2011a).[21] More recent data quoted in parliament confirmed that suicides increased by 25 per cent in 2010 (compared with 2009) (Avgenakis 2011), while the Minister of Health reported a 40 per cent increase in the first half of 2011 (compared with the same period in 2010) (Loverdos 2011). Media reports indicate that the inability to repay high levels of personal debt might be a key factor in the increase in suicides (Tsimas 2011). The national suicide helpline reported that 25 per cent of callers faced financial difficulties in 2010 (Katsadoros et al. 2011).

On the demand side, another study found a significant increase in people reporting that they did not go to a doctor or dentist despite feeling that it was necessary (Kentikelenis et al. 2011). The number of people able to obtain sickness benefits has declined since the crisis began as the adjustment programme has explicitly eliminated or reduced the value of practically all sickness and disability benefits (except for the totally disabled).

On the supply side, the 40 per cent cuts in hospital budgets following the implementation of the adjustment programme has resulted in understaffing and reported shortages of medical supplies as well as increased bribes to medical staff to jump queues in overstretched hospitals (Telloglou and Kakaounaki 2011). There was a 24 per cent rise in admissions to public hospitals in 2010 and a further 8 per cent in the first half of 2011. Greater recourse to public services has been the result of the inability of poorer citizens to seek private care. One study reported a decline in the order of 25–30 per cent in admissions to private hospitals (Hellastat 2010). Those in need are increasingly unable to see doctors. Neighbourhood clinics are closing down or, as a result of staffing cuts, have reduced opening hours. Nevertheless, the proportion of Greeks seeking medical attention from street clinics is reported to have increased from below 5 per cent before the crisis to about 30 per cent.

Along with reduced access to health care and increased suicide rates, homicide and theft rates have at least doubled since the crisis. The prevalence of heroin use reportedly rose to 24,000 cases in 2010 compared to 20,200 in 2009, a 20 per cent increase. However, budget cuts have resulted in the loss of one-third of street-work programmes (European Monitoring Centre for Drugs and Drug Addiction 2010).

HIV infections rose by an astonishing 52 per cent in the first half of 2011, due largely to increases in both commercial sex work and injection drug use: there was a 12.5-fold increase in HIV among injection drug users. This may be related to a rise in the number of new HIV infections as half of the increase has been attributed to infections among intravenous drug users: there were 922 new cases in 2011 versus 605 in 2010. Greek non-governmental organizations report being able to meet less than one-fiftieth of the demand for needle exchange (Stuckler et al. 2011b). In a round-up of more than 100 homeless by the police in the centre of Athens in March 2012, two-thirds of the homeless were found to be HIV positive.

5.1.5 Discussion

The capture of health care by the system's insiders – from medical personnel to pharmacists and those involved in procurement – is undeniable. Striking examples include the excessive costs of drugs, both through overpricing or bypassing generics, as well as the proliferation of departments and directors in hospitals.

However, Greece remains an average spender among OECD countries in terms of public health expenditures (Vaughan-Whitehead, Chapter 1, this volume), while such expenditures cannot be viewed solely as a cost to be cut, especially without prior assessment of the effects. Expenditure cuts in the health sector should not be dictated by the failure of the adjustment programme to close the deficit because it wrongly emphasized raising revenues. In any case, a good public system reduces the incentives for tax avoidance and evasion.

While the adjustment programme rightly focused on the case of pharmaceuticals, the attempt to address too many structural and institutional problems too quickly is likely to have significant adverse effects on health outcomes. Moreover, given that the solutions to structural and institutional problems require not just careful technical analysis but also social consensus, the reform measures are only by chance likely to lead to desirable and sustainable outcomes.

All in all, while the diagnosis has been correct, the programme seems to be ill-designed and likely to be poorly implemented. It is ill-designed at least in terms of including too many frontloaded reforms without prioritizing them and sequencing them. The prime focus of the adjustment programme was on cost savings and cost recovery. As an example, the programme relaxed the ban on smoking in public places through exemptions to be granted after the payment of a special levy of €200/m^2 in about 3,000 commercial undertakings with an area of more than 300m^2 such as restaurants, bars, night clubs and casinos. The levy is expected to fetch annually just €40 million. This is picking up pennies in front of a steam roller.

5.2 Case Study 2: Consensual Reforms in Education

Like health care, the education system in Greece has reached a point at which reforms were a necessity. Unlike in the case of health, a substantial reform was initiated that was home grown and enacted during the crisis (Law 4009 of 2011) by an unprecedented parliamentary majority without outside pressure. It is presented in this chapter as an example of reforms based on a prior assessment of the situation based on social dialogue and aimed at long-term structural problems.

The education system in Greece in 2010 was based on a law enacted in 1982 (Law 1268). Following that law there was an unprecedented but uncoordinated expansion of the education system serving insiders' interests more than those of the nation – like the rest of the public sector. Focusing henceforth on tertiary education, the handful of institutions of higher learning that existed in the 1970s were augmented by the creation of KATEs. These were initially institutions that offered further education. They subsequently evolved into Higher Technological Educational Institutes (TEIs) and, through Law 2916/2001 were subsequently upgraded to university status.[22] Whether they could act as universities, not least because of the quality of their teachers, was not taken into account. However, this upgrading well served the interest of the insiders along with the uncritical creation of new universities. Today, in a country of 11 million people, there are 24 universities (consisting of 260 departments) and 16 TEIs offering 81 specializations and consisting of 195 departments located not only in major cities but also scattered across islands, some with only a few thousand inhabitants.

With some notable exceptions, teachers resembled largely underemployed civil servants using their institution mainly as a base for moonlighting. Students were happy to take on light teaching loads serving the credentialist purpose of finding a public sector job. This unholy alliance continued in the form of many long strikes for various reasons by either students or teachers (usually when the students did not strike). A high degree of political penetration/polarization was present, as reflected in visible rival factions among faculty and student alliances in line with clear party political lines. The standards and learning outcomes of the system fell behind those internationally expected amidst conditions of increasing European integration, if not globalization.[23]

Higher education governance was weak, if not chaotic. Centralized control and fragmented organizational structures in tertiary education mirrored those of the broader public sector. Lack of capacity and/or willingness to align the system with universal principles and the demands of citizens perpetuated barriers that prevented the Greek education system from becoming internationally competitive. The 'evolution' of tertiary education in Greece made the country an international negative outlier. This is shown in Figure 7.6, which ranks 18 EU countries as well as the United States and Japan in terms of a composite 'supply indicator' that takes into account flexibility, selection of students, budget autonomy, staff policy, output flexibility, accountability, evaluation and funding rules (Martins et al. 2009).

By the time of the debt crisis, the tertiary education system in Greece was out of touch with reality. On one hand, it had the most centrally

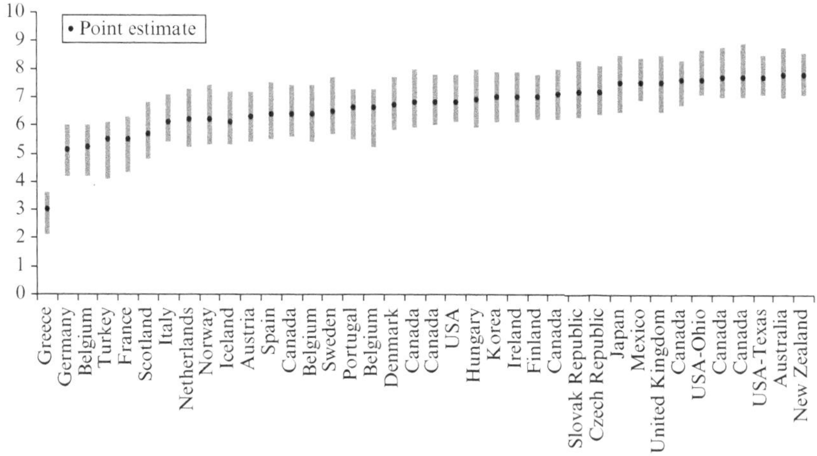

Figure 7.6 Composite supply indicator of tertiary education, Greece, 2005–2006

planned educational system among OECD countries (OECD 2011c). On the other, it had a very decentralized decision-making process serving the narrow interests of those already employed in local institutions. The alignment with EU structures was piecemeal and cosmetic. It was motivated by external funding prospects rather than an integrated vision (ibid.: 14). Effective evaluation mechanisms were lacking, as well as accountability – like other areas of public administration. All in all, Greece has failed to engage in structural reforms in the area of education for decades, which would have integrated its system with those of its European counterparts.

Leaving aside the perennial issue of accuracy and timeliness of Greek data, the higher education system was in need of reform irrespective of its fiscal implications. Its internal efficiency was low with completion rates among the lowest in the OECD with average time taken to complete a four-year course of 7.6 years. In terms of salary cost per student, the Greek figure of US$3,170 is nearly 40 per cent higher than the OECD average. In terms of external efficiency, though much depends on aggregate labour demand conditions, Greece has the highest unemployment rates among 25–29-year-olds with a tertiary degree (13.2 per cent) compared to those for the rest of the OECD countries (average of 5.7 per cent). According to data from the Labour Force Survey, no group of graduates from any university course faced an unemployment rate below 10 per cent as many as five years after graduation (Mitrakos et al. 2010). Long-term unemployment is also prevalent: 7.5 per cent of Greek graduates are unemployed for more than six months compared to the OECD average of only 3 per cent. Moreover, the Greek Constitution explicitly states that tertiary education is to be provided free of charge and exclusively by the public sector. As a result, private funding for tertiary education comes to only 6 per cent compared to, on average, 14.5 per cent for the OECD countries. But only part of the limited private sector involvement is due to the absence of student fees: the tertiary education system has very weak links with the private sector of the economy, particularly as regards joint research projects (OECD 2008). Furthermore, the centralized nature of the system in terms of budgets, ultimate appointments of elected officials and so on implies that the administrative burden of the Ministry of Education includes the processing of almost 1,000 academic requests per week.

5.2.1 Reforms[24]

The new Law 4009/2011 on restructuring the higher education system was the result of a year-long multi-layer consultation process with significant representation of stakeholders (political parties, academia, civil society) that showed political maturity, at least by Greek standards.[25] In terms of numbers, the law passed by an overwhelming parliamentary majority (260 out of 300).[26]

The new legal framework governing the higher education system repeals hundreds of pages of previous legal texts and simplifies the structure at a regulatory level. Its effects are not yet known but the right areas were addressed, including governance, the internationalization of programmes and funding mechanisms. The law expanded the role of the Hellenic Quality Assurance and Accreditation Agency and introduced evaluation mechanisms aiming to improve the overall effectiveness and efficiency of the higher education system.[27]

From the perspective of public sector governance, the law establishes a new body, the Council of the Higher Education Institute, whose typical 15-person membership will be made up of professors (7), external members (7 who would be elected by a supermajority of 80 per cent among the professors – thus avoiding very narrow political or other alliances) and students. The rector will enjoy enhanced managerial responsibilities and will be elected by the majority of professors instead of a broader constituency that previously included students. Institutions will have the right to create internal statutes and regulations as well as to define their baseline and future strategies. There will be a more 'checks and balances'-based management system which is expected to lead to more transparent and effective administration.

At the level of human resources, the law introduced what are deemed to be transparent mechanisms (such as open web-based procedures, public access to databases, and clear criteria) for the promotion of professors and other teaching staff. It also provides for obligatory evaluation of teaching staff every five years.

5.2.2 Discussion

Drafted along lines compatible with the Bologna process, the tertiary education reform law offers Greek tertiary education an opportunity to break with the past and increase its effectiveness and efficiency in a way that would better meet the challenges of the emerging national labour market and, more broadly, the economy. It can also help the system to become better integrated with European and international environments.

Whether this will materialize (and when) remains an open issue for many reasons. One is that the implementation of the law would require a series of enabling decrees and regulations that may not be forthcoming – as the experience with the overall adjustment programme so far indicates. It is not known how the reforms will be met (or avoided) by existing professors, the majority of whom were appointed under and benefited from the old system. Giving them greater autonomy may perpetuate old habits unless the other governance reforms the law sets in motion become binding and do so quickly.

The likely effects of the reforms are therefore not known. But this is not the point in the context of this chapter. The point is that the necessity of the reforms was felt, like the case of the 170 per cent debt-to-GDP ratio, and was addressed outside the partisan climate that has been created since the successive failures of the structural adjustment programme, as evidenced from the latter's successive revisions and reorientation.

6. ASSESSMENT

Public sector adjustment has been long drawn out in Greece. However, the public sector measures described in the previous sections are part of a massive and hurried fiscal adjustment programme to address the immediate liquidity problems of Greece and, with it, avoid a pan-European and global crisis.

The reform programme has followed 'first principles' and includes 'too much' to be implemented 'too soon'. It was effectively (a) a fiscal adjustment programme, not an economic one, and (b) an emergency programme for avoiding a disorderly default that would endanger the euro, instead of setting Greece on a sustainable path for economic recovery and creating an efficient and effective public sector in the medium term.

Changes in the public sector were hasty and designed without prior functional reviews to establish what is required to achieve the vision of different units, without an expenditure review to see what areas of public sector need to be rationalized more or less, and without social impact reviews.

The repeated re-evaluations and reorientation of the programme cannot be described as ordinary processes of monitoring and evaluation. The changes in magnitude, mix and course of the overall adjustment programme are so large that they suggest that efforts 'to keep Greece afloat to avoid endangering the rest of Europe in the short-run and until mechanisms are developed to safeguard the euro' were given more priority than coming up with a longer-term plan that would suit Greece better and put it on a sustainable path in the long term. What the right balance should have been is a matter of debate. There is also a dilemma between the responsibilities of and price to be paid by an individual member of any coalition (in this case the Euro club) *vis-à-vis* the collective interests of others (solidarity versus responsibility).

With these comments in mind, this section examines – selectively – what is known about or can be expected in terms of the social impact of the public sector reforms, as well as the continuing recession.

6.1 Unemployment, Social Protection and Pensions

Unemployment has grown massively as a consequence of the recession. Although an estimate of no more than 70–80,000 public sector employees have left the service so far (mainly through retirement), the total number of unemployed has increased by more than 600,000, reaching nearly 1.2 million and nearly 23 per cent in April 2012 (compared to less than 8 per cent in 2008). The 150,000 reduction expected in the public sector until 2015, the increase in the 'inactive' population by another 100,000 since 2009 and the closure of 368,000 businesses in 2010–11 and another 172,000 predicted to follow in 2012 paint a bleak picture of the labour market and overall economic situation in Greece for many years ahead.

Much of social protection in Greece took the form of employment in the public sector, including relatively high pensions and early retirement, especially for some groups, such as high-ranking civil servants, the military, judges and employees of SOEs. However, less generous pensions for most other workers, who work long hours and retire after a long working life,[28] constituted a major avenue for reducing poverty. This comes across clearly from Table 7.6. In Greece, other than pensions, the many forms of benefits found in other countries contribute very little to poverty reduction.[29] The effect of pensions on poverty reduction is highest in Greece, behind only Italy and Germany. This finding is confirmed in the latest report (2012)

Table 7.6 Contribution of benefit type to poverty reduction, Greece, 2000s

Country	Pensions	Family benefits	Sickness/ disability/ unemployment	Social assistance	Other
Belgium	−15.6	−4.7	−4.9	−0.1	−0.5
Denmark	−11.5	−2.2	−5.1	−0.3	−2.9
Germany	−18.2	−4.9	−4.1	−0.5	−0.5
Greece	*−16.7*	*−0.8*	*−1.4*	*0*	*−0.1*
Spain	−12.7	−0.4	−4.0	0	−0.2
France	−16.9	−3.6	−3.8	−0.2	−2.4
Ireland	−6.1	−2.8	−5.4	−0.2	−0.8
Italy	−19.4	−0.5	−2.0	0	−0.1
Luxembourg	−16.6	−6.0	−4.1	−0.3	0
Netherlands	−14.7	−3.4	−4.3	−1.4	−0.7
Austria	−15.6	−6.7	−2.9	0	−0.5
Portugal	−11.1	−0.9	−2.5	−0.3	−0.2
Finland	−12.4	−5.6	−11.3	−0.5	−2.8
UK	−14.0	−4.3	−3.9		−3.8
Average	−14.4	−3.3	−4.3	−0.3	−1.1

Source: De Neubourg et al. (2007).

of the Bank of Greece where it is reported that the 13.4 per cent of GDP spending on pensions contributes 19.3 per cent to poverty reduction while the 14.5 per cent dedicated to all other forms of social spending reduced poverty by only 3 per cent (Bank of Greece 2012, Table VII, p. 88).

Although unemployment benefits may have a bigger impact on poverty reduction in the future, given the recent surge in unemployment rates, only about one-third of those unemployed receive some kind of unemployment benefit, about €471 per month for up to one year, which has now been reduced by 22 per cent in line with the government's reduction of minimum wages against the prevailing collective agreement.

As part of the adjustment programme, in February 2012 the government reduced the gross monthly minimum wage in the private sector that was collectively agreed between employers' and workers' organizations in July 2010 (that is, *after* the initial adjustment programme was agreed between the government and the Troika). The reduction was from €751 per month to €586 per month for those above the age of 24 (equivalent to 22 per cent) and to €510 per month for those under 25 years of age (equivalent to 32 per cent).

The level of unemployment benefit will be reduced accordingly. For the

Table 7.7 Changes in poverty rates by employment of head of household, Greece, 2009–2010 (%)

Employment status	2009	2010	Change
Unemployed	51.1	63.7	12.6
Pensioners	24.7	29.1	4.3
Private sector self-employed	16.6	21.3	4.7
Private sector employee	12.7	16.4	3.7
Private sector professional	3.8	3.7	−0.1
Public sector/SOEs	0.3	1.4	1.1

Note: Poverty line set at 60 per cent of 2009 income adjusted for inflation (€570 in 2009 and €597 in 2010).

Source: Adapted from Matsaganis and Leventi (2011).

already unemployed, the level of unemployment benefit will be reduced to 60 per cent of the minimum wage (€360 per month augmented by 10 per cent for every child), while for the newly unemployed it has yet to be determined but is expected to be around 50–55 per cent of the minimum wage (Table 7.6).

The role of pensions and unemployment benefits in poverty reduction is confirmed in Table 7.7. Poverty is highest among families headed by pensioners, along with those headed by unemployed persons. And despite the already high rates of poverty among those two groups, poverty in these two groups increased most together with private sector employees. The table also suggests, as mentioned earlier, that public sector employment is an indirect form of social protection in Greece.

The total effects on poverty are not reflected in the above statistics as the increase in the share of the population living at risk of poverty or social exclusion was not significant during the first two years of the crisis. The share was estimated to be 27.6 per cent in 2009 and 27.7 per cent in 2010 (compared to the EU27 average of 23.4 per cent). However, for 2011 the estimated figure rose sharply above 33 per cent (Eurostat 2012).

6.2 Recession Effects

The effects of the adjustment programme can be separated into two: (i) the direct ones, such as those arising from reducing pay, downsizing employment and adjusting pensions; and (ii) the indirect, such as those from the induced recession due to lower spending by the government, declining consumption by households and subdued production in the private sector. In fact, cumulative reduction in real GDP by approximately 20 per cent since 2008 is likely to shadow many other effects.

Although it is difficult to establish these two effects separately in practice – especially in the case of Greece – because of lack of data, some early estimates, albeit tentative, are available and suggest that the recession-induced social effects can prove to be more important in the long run than the adjustment measures. For example, the change in the ratio between the income share of the wealthiest 20 per cent of the population and the income share of the poorest 20 per cent (known as S80/S20) was estimated to have declined from 6.1 to 6 due to the adjustment measures but the recession-induced effect increased it to 6.2 (Matsaganis and Leventi 2011).

6.3 Revenues

Finally, in assessing the adjustment programme one should go beyond what the government pays and examine also what it collects. In this respect there has been an unprecedented drive to increase public revenues. There have been many changes in, as well as additions to, revenue-raising measures aiming to broaden the tax base, reduce evasion and increase tax rates. Most new revenue measures have been regressive, such as the reduction in non-taxable income, increases in indirect taxes, imposition of a solidarity tax and the introduction of a property surcharge, which is a tax on practically all taxpayers (including the unemployed) plus significant increases in user fees (for example, for electricity and health services).

The way the budget deficit was to be reduced gave more emphasis on elusive revenue increases than expenditure cuts.[30] This departs from the lessons learnt from the long experience of implementing structural adjustment programmes which suggest that most of the narrowing of the fiscal gap should come from predictable expenditure cuts rather than certain increases in revenues, especially when the shadow economy is significant (as in the case of Greece where it is estimated to be of the order of 23 per cent).

Failing to follow the lessons from the international experience, the economy has provided the answer to the adjustment programme: revenues in 2011 were expected to be €58 billion and actual revenues are estimated to be €53.3 billion. The difference is more than the cuts in the health sector and 13 times more than the €350 million savings Greece had to commit to as a condition for receiving the second bailout package of €130 billion by

March 2012 and avoid default. This condition was met by imposing last-minute further cuts on pensions.

6.4 Social Dialogue

The measures were introduced without any serious involvement of the social partners. On the contrary, the adjustment programme changed the nature of industrial relations. According to the IMF (2012a):

> If the ongoing social dialogue is unsuccessful in identifying concrete solutions, then to achieve this goal the government will take legislative measures in the urgent public interest to allow wage and non-wage costs to adjust as needed. (p. 122) . . . Given that the outcome of the social dialogue to promote employment and competitiveness fell short of expectations, the government will take measures to foster a rapid adjustment of labour costs . . . At the same time, the government will promote smooth wage bargaining at the various levels. (p. 176)

The changes introduced following the 2010 crisis have fundamentally changed the bargaining structure in Greece (as well as individual contracts).[31] Until then, the framework for negotiations was provided by legislation passed back in the 1990s through which conciliation, mediation and arbitration played an important role (Fulton 2011).

The last national collective agreement was negotiated between and concluded by employers and workers in July 2010 after long discussions. Following that agreement and in view of the crisis, the GSEE (General Confederation of Workers) agreed to a pay freeze until 2012, and any increases thereafter would not exceed the average inflation forecast for the EU. This agreement provided for a binding ceiling for all agreements at both industry and company levels rather than the more conventional setting of a floor upon which other agreements could build.

The basic structure of Greek collective bargaining changed further in December 2010 through new legislation. Rather than company-level bargaining by law only being able to improve on national- and industry-level agreements, company negotiators can now agree lower conditions than those set at national-and industry-levels. The possibility of extending industry-level agreements to employers who had not signed them has also been abolished.

Finally, the possibility of either employers or unions calling for arbitration have been eliminated and now both must agree to seek arbitration. The government says this 'provides symmetric access for all parties', but it weakens the position of the unions. And as mentioned earlier, by act of

Table 7.8 Strikes by sector, Greece, January 2011–April 2012

Sector	No. of strikes	Sector	No. of strikes
Public transport	102	General strikes – public sector	30
Public hospitals	68	General strikes – private sector	16
Pharmacies	27	Private sector (others)	84
Education	38	All workers militant front	12
Local/regional governments	31	People in uniform	22
Lawyers	95	Ministry of Finance	11
Social security funds	3	Ministry of Infrastructure	8
SOEs	27	Ministry of Culture (museums)	20
Mass media	208	Ministry of the Interior	1
Agricultural sector	7	Others (sectoral unions)	28

Total number of strikes: 838
Average number of strikes per month: 52.4
Average number of general strikes per month: 2.9

Source: Authors' calculations based on www.apergies.gr.

parliament the national minimum wage was reduced by 22 per cent for adult workers (above the age of 25) and by 32 per cent for those under that age. The new rates are to be applied automatically to sectoral agreements that are not agreed within three months after their expiry. Thus, social dialogue and collective bargaining are for the time being under the unilateral control of the government.

6.5 Strikes

There are no official records on strike activity. A rough estimate based on the reported monthly incidence (not duration) of strikes suggests that there were as many as 838 strikes between January 2011 and April 2012, ranging from a low of nine strikes in August 2011 to more than 110 in October 2011. Included in these figures are 46 general strikes by the private sector (16) and the public sector (30) (Table 7.8).

These figures suggest that the average monthly number of strikes has been around just over 52. This surely underestimates the true number. Moreover, this estimate excludes other types of protest (such as road closures, demonstrations and so on).

7. CONCLUDING REMARKS AND POLICY DIRECTIONS

It cannot be disputed that the Greek public sector required wide-ranging reforms. However, the reforms have been subordinated to a structural adjustment programme that has been, in turn, subordinated to the need to save the euro and placate the international markets. Effectively, Greece has been treated for illiquidity while it was insolvent.

Leaving aside this misdiagnosis, the programme was spasmodic and sporadic while it ignored the weak implementation capacity and relied on undue optimism that defied the international experience in terms of how much the public sector can adjust and how long it can take. For example, only 15,000 of the much anticipated reduction of 150,000 jobs in the public sector are likely to come from dismissals[32] – the rest would come from gradual attrition given the protection granted to public sector workers by the Constitution. The point here is not that the constitutional provision is right or wrong: it is that it was not taken into account in the initial design of the programme.

These considerations apply *a fortiori* in the case of managing the structural adjustment programme which, unsurprisingly, has been readjusted at least four times in a period of less than two years. In any case, international experience – and that of the IMF, too – clearly recognizes that adjustment programmes need to be sustainable and socially acceptable. Even the representative of Greek employers commented

> The achievement of the fiscal targets in 2010 and 2011 appears to range from doubtful to impossible . . . If the Mnemonio leads to national divisions, change will become impossible and bankruptcy unavoidable . . . Collective agreements . . . are useful [and] a way to avoid conflict . . . Let's leave companies and workers to communicate between themselves and find their own solutions . . . What we support is derived from Europe, not some African countries . . . Europe is envied globally for its system of social protection.[33]

The lessons from the shock therapy approach that was applied to Africa three decades ago seem to have been forgotten in the case of Greece.

A critical condition for adjustment to succeed is to preserve the drivers of economic growth. This is clearly recognized at European level in the attempt to bring the increased debt that resulted from the effort to rescue the financial sector after 2008 back to the pre-crisis level. However, in the case of Greece, real GDP has fallen by approximately 20 per cent since 2008 and has yet to bottom out. Unemployment, which was below 8 (7.7) per cent in 2008, has now increased to nearly

23 (22.6) per cent, thus depressing aggregate demand. These effects have now started to look like those that prevailed in the United States in the Great Depression of the 1930s. Debt sustainability is not expected to be achieved before 2022, if then. In the meantime, seniority payments provided in *collective agreements* have been frozen by law and will be allowed to be reactivated when the unemployment rate falls below 10 per cent. Youth unemployment alone stands at 52.7 per cent, and recent ILO research indicates that the time taken for youth employment to recover from earlier crises is on average 11 years in countries where the pre-crisis level was attained, while in many it only achieved a new trough (ILO 2010).

The Greek structural adjustment programme (and within it, public sector adjustment) lacked three key ingredients that have emerged from international experience:

1. a clean and coherent strategy (was it a programme for Greece or for the euro?);
2. sound technical foundations (was the policy mix and its timing appropriate for illiquidity or insolvency?); and
3. social acceptance (has there been dialogue among the social partners and ownership of the reform agenda?).

One can probably be more lenient on the lack of a clear strategy when one is not sure about the nature and size of the problem and its future course. However, from an *economic perspective*, while fiscal crises must bridge the gap between public expenditures and taxes, they also need to:

- preserve productive and infrastructure investments to enable the resumption of economic growth;
- tax production and economic activities least and last; and
- include measures that protect the vulnerable.

None of these conditions are evident in the case of Greece. Both citizens and employers are complaining about the 32 taxes that have been introduced or expanded since 2009. Although Greece has been labelled a 'special case' among policymakers in Europe, its case may become 'general' as the need for bailouts and adjustments may well be repeated (and soon) in some other countries located along the Mediterranean coast or among the more recent members of the enlarged EU that have economic and institutional characteristics similar to those of Greece (Tzannatos 2012).

In this respect it might be useful for the countries under stress (and also for the benefit of their creditors, too) to take into account the following:

- Assess what drivers for economic growth will remain by following alternative policy scenarios.
- Examine whether a country is a high-cost economy or simply a high *labour cost* economy.
- In the case of a high labour cost economy, check whether this is because of (a) public sector pay and employment policies, in which case focusing just on public sector reforms may well address the bulk of the problems or (b) inflexibility in the private labour market.
- If the economy is a high-cost economy, not just because of public sector size/pay/benefits but because of limited capacity and weak institutions and, more importantly, because of cronyism and corruption, the adjustment programme should take into account that institution building for capacity, transparency and accountability takes time and even well-designed programmes will falter in implementation.
- If the size of the shadow economy is significant, then the adjustment programme should also take this into account. The targeting of formal sector employees in Greece by the adjustment programme shows that the old habit of 'flexibilizing' the visible part of labour by bypassing even collective agreements freely concluded between employers and workers is yet another arithmetical exercise that ignores the macroeconomic implications where production is dominated by micro and small enterprises and the shadow economy is large (Schneider 2010, 2011; Tzannatos and Monogios 2011).
- Assuming that the previous conditions are justified, the mix, intensity, sequencing and timing of adjustment measures should be realistic, meaning that they should make use of the large accumulated experience with adjustment programmes, for example, that the deficit and debt would be reduced in a more sustainable manner through expenditure cuts than tax increases.
- Both in the case of expenditure cuts and also revenue raising, the composition of measures is important, for example, which expenditures to reduce and what taxes to raise. To this end, a thorough review of public spending should be institutionalized and conducted concurrently within the medium-term fiscal strategy and the budget framework.

- The social impact of adjustment should be taken into account. It is not a matter of philanthropy but an internationally recognized fact that conserving the social fabric leads to productivity gains, increases social acceptance and creates a more equitable distribution of opportunities.

In this context, it goes without saying that the negative lessons from public sector adjustment in Greece, as discussed in this chapter, reflect a situation that needs to be transformed in accordance with the positive messages presented in other chapters in this volume: employment adjustment should be based on competencies and needs (unlike the mechanical reductions implemented in Greece), wage adjustment should be progressive (unlike the horizontal approach adopted by Greece), reforms should be decided after social dialogue (unlike the unilateral decisions introduced by the Greek government), social services and poverty reduction measures should be preserved (unlike the case of health and pension reforms in Greece), public sector adjustment should not call into question the role of the public sector (especially in productive investments and for preserving the drivers of economic growth), a social safety floor should be established for the protection of the poor and most vulnerable especially in times of distress and a long-term horizon should be adopted (instead of changing the programme before its previous version has even been implemented).

NOTES

* The views expressed are those of the authors and do not necessarily represent those of their respective organisations. The authors thank, with the usual disclaimer, Michael Ben-Gad, Angelos James, Phokion Kolaitis, Daniel Vaughan-Whitehead and the authors of this volume for their comments.

1. In a study of 133 adjustment programmes supported by the International Monetary Fund (IMF), the IMF's independent evaluation office found that policymakers consistently underestimated the adverse effects of rigid spending cuts on economic growth. See IMF (2003), Lindner (2012) and IMF (2012b). In the case of Greece, the expectation of turnaround of the economy by 2012 has been met with unemployment rising to 26.8 per cent (and youth unemployment to 56.6 per cent – both the highest in Europe) by the time this paper went to press (January 2013). Greece is entering its sixth consecutive year of recession, surpassing that of Argentina from 2001 to 2005.
2. The writing of this chapter was completed amidst evolving and uncertain conditions in Greece on the basis of incomplete data and frequently updated official reports (including two 'Mnemonia' (Memoranda of Understanding between the Greek government and its lenders, the so-called 'Troika' that includes the IMF, the European Commission and the European Central Bank), one Medium-Term Fiscal Strategy, five reviews by the IMF and another five by the EU, more than 150 implementing laws (including no fewer than four on public sector pay) plus many still pending – although announced –

expenditure cuts and revenue increases). At this point in time (June 2012) this chapter should be considered as work in progress and some of the findings may be subject to changes.

3. OECD (2011a) also states 'The inconsistency in public employment statistics has been long noticed but has persisted. It is one indication (among many) of the imperative necessity of improving the statistical coverage of the public sector' (p. 72). The statistics quoted below are primarily derived from this source and OECD (2011b).
4. Ministry of Administrative Reform and e-Governance, adapted from OECD (2011a).
5. OECD (2011b) though this is because of the long hours worked in the private sector in Greece.
6. Unsurprisingly, the definition of competencies is a constant and considerable activity for both the executive and the legislature. For example, between 1996 and 2011 there were 2,890 competency changes for the central government through laws, 11,018 through presidential decrees and 3,191 through ministerial decrees, that is, on average 1,140 changes of government competencies per year. See OECD (2011a).
7. Unreferenced estimate cited in IMF (2011a) which also states that the unadjusted premium was 32 per cent.
8. Mnemonio 2 (2012) cites this figure as a target to be achieved in line with *the most efficient* OECD countries.
9. The basic salary can at times be less than half of total earnings.
10. Officially, these figures have been neither confirmed nor disputed.
11. A total of 15,000 redundant staff were to be transferred to the labour reserve in the course of 2012, in connection with the identification of entities or units to be closed or downsized. Staff in the labour reserve will be paid at 60 per cent of their basic wage (excluding overtime and other extra payments) for no more than 12 months, after which they will be dismissed. This period of 12 months may be extended to 24 months for staff close to retirement. Payments to staff while in the labour reserve are considered part of their severance payments (Mnemonio 2, 2012: 9).
12. There was an extra monthly payment in December and ½ monthly salaries paid at Easter and in the summer.
13. This exercise is to be repeated in summer 2012.
14. These figures also include recipients of social benefits such as blind beneficiaries who, upon cross-checking, were found to hold professional driving licences. The latest account of the Ministry of Labour and Social Security reports revealed more than 200,000 fraudulent cases for benefit payments in the last two years, costing the budget between €700 million to €1 billion/year.
15. In 2008 there were almost 15 nurses for every 1,000 citizens in Finland, Iceland, Ireland and Switzerland with slightly lower rates in Denmark and Norway. Greece had the second lowest rate (5 nurses per 1,000 inhabitants) after Turkey.
16. Certain groups, especially certain establishment elites, were accorded 'hotel' treatment, including abroad.
17. This is higher only than in Australia (5.7 per cent) and Poland, Chile, the Republic of Korea and Mexico where public funding is around 4 per cent or less (OECD 2010).
18. The countries with lower increases in health expenditure were Poland, Mexico, Slovakia and the Republic of Korea.
19. These savings are anticipated from a reduction in overtime pay for doctors by €50 million and family allowances by €43 million.
20. Nonetheless, these figures have not been formally confirmed.
21. The study examined Austria, the Czech Republic, Finland, Greece, Hungary, Ireland, Lithuania, the Netherlands, Romania and the United Kingdom. It also found that the countries facing the most severe financial reversals of fortune had bigger rises in suicides, ranging from 13 per cent in Ireland to more than 17 per cent in Latvia.
22. 'Polytechnics' in Greece are universities and on average more rigorous than the latter.
23. Suffice to say that up to now only one university in the country has offered international graduate courses.

24. Authors' compilation based on information provided by the Ministry of Education.
25. Ironically, Law 1268 (enacted by the Socialists in 1982 under Andreas Papandreou the father) was replaced by Law 4009 (also enacted by the Socialists under George Papandreou the son).
26. Following ratification of the law, a significant number of schools and universities around the country were occupied by protesting students. The protests gained momentum, resulting in widespread and extensive damage to many establishments, including infrastructure, computers and equipment.
27. For a more detailed presentation of reforms in each of these areas, see Tzannatos and Monogios (2011).
28. Greeks work more than 42 hours/week compared to the EU27 average of less than 38 hours. The average retirement age in Greece (including the early retirement provisions for civil servants and employees in SOEs) was higher than the average in the EU25. The OECD reports that in 2009 the average effective retirement age for Greek men was 61.9 years (compared to 61.8 for German men and 59.1 for French men) and for Greek women 59.6 years (compared to 60.5 for German women and 59.7 for French women). According to The Economist (2011) the average age of retirement of Greek workers is 59.1 years compared, for example, to 61.8 years in Germany and 62.1 years in the Netherlands.
29. Similar results are reported in Ziomas et al. (2009).
30. Mnemonio 1 (2010). This was reversed in Mnemonio 2 (2012) attesting once more to the poor design of the programme in the first instance.
31. With regard to individual contracts, the length of the probation period for a newly hired worker was increased from two to 12 months; the maximum period for termination notices was reduced from 42 to six months; the limit for collective redundancies (for example, in a company with 250 employees) was raised from five to 12 workers; and the overtime premium was reduced by 20 per cent. See Bank of Greece (2012: 70–74).
32. Interview given by E. Venizelos, Leader of the Socialist Party and former Minister of Economy and Finance, to Elli Stae, Greek ERT (Greek Radio and Television), 2 May 2012.
33. Press conference by Dimitris Daskalopoulos, Chairman of the Board of Directors, Hellenic Federation of Enterprises, 16 November 2010.

REFERENCES

Ammerman, P. (2011), 'Public sector employment in Greece – myths and realities', 21 September. Available at: http://www.philip-atticus.com/2011/09/public-sector-employment-in-greece.html (accessed October 2011).

Avgenakis, E. (2011), 'Dramatic increase in the number of suicides due to the economic crisis and rumours of the operation of networks of usurers and blackmailers', Reference number: 16171, Hellenic Parliament, Athens.

Bank of Greece (2012), Governor's Annual Report 2012 (in Greek).

De Neubourg, C., J. Castonguay and K. Roelen (2007), 'Social safety nets and lessons from the European experience', SP Discussion Paper No. 0718, Social Protection and Labor, World Bank, Washington, DC.

Economou, M., M. Madianos, C. Theleritis, L.E. Peppou and C.N. Stefanis (2011), 'Increased suicidality amid economic crisis in Greece', *The Lancet*, **378** (9801) (22 October), 1459.

ESDY (Ethniki Sholi Demosias Ygeias) (2006), *Study of the Health Level and Evaluation of Health Services in Greece*, Athens: National School of Public Health.

ESDY (Ethniki Sholi Demosias Ygeias) (2011), *Evaluation Study of Health Services*, Athens: National School of Public Health.
European Commission (2011), *The Economic Adjustment Programme for Greece, Fourth Review*, Spring, Brussels: European Commission, 2011.
European Monitoring Centre for Drugs and Drug Addiction (2010), *Annual Report on the State of the Drugs and Alcohol Problems*, Athens: Greek Documentation and Monitoring Centre for Drugs.
Eurostat (2009), News release 182, 'GDP per inhabitant in purchasing power standards', 15 December.
Eurostat (2012), News release 21, 'At risk of poverty or social exclusion in the EU27', 8 February.
Fulton, L. (2011), *Worker Representation in Europe*, Labour Research Department and ETUI (online publication).
Hellastat (2010), *Sector Study: Health Services*, Athens: Hellastat.
International Labour Office (ILO) (2010), 'World of work report', Geneva: ILO.
International Labour Office (ILO) (2011), 'Report on the high level mission to Greece', September, p. 34, Geneva: ILO.
International Monetary Fund (IMF) (2003), *Fiscal Adjustment in IMF-supported Programs*, Independent Evaluation Office, Washington, DC: IMF.
International Monetary Fund (IMF) (2011a), *Greece: Fourth Review under the Stand-by Arrangement and Request for Modification and Waiver of Applicability of Performance Criteria*, Country Report No. 11/175, Washington, DC, July.
International Monetary Fund (IMF) (2011b), *Greece: Fifth Review under the Stand-by Arrangement, Rephasing and Request for Waivers of Nonobservance of Performance Criteria*, Press Release on the Executive Board Discussion and Statement by the Executive Director for Greece, IMF Country Report No. 11/351, Washington, DC, December.
International Monetary Fund (IMF) (2012a), *Greece: Request for Extended Arrangement Under the Extended Fund Facility – Staff Report*, Staff Supplement, Country Report No. 12/57, Washington, DC, 9 March.
International Monetary Fund (IMF) (2012b), *World Economic Outlook: Coping with High Debt and Sluggish Growth*, October, Washington, DC: IMF.
Katsadoros, D., E. Bekiari, K. Karydi et al. (2011), 'Suicide helpline 1018: characteristics of callers for January–December 2010', 21st Panhellenic Conference of Psychiatry, Athens, 5–7 May.
Kentikelenis, A., M. Karanikolos, I. Papanicolas, S. Basu, M. McKee and D. Stuckler (2011), 'Health effects of financial crisis: omens of a Greek tragedy', *The Lancet*, published online, 10 October.
Lindner, F. (2012), 'Europe is in dire need of lazy spendthrifts', *The Guardian*, 18 February.
Loverdos, A. (2011), 'A response to question by Member of Parliament', Reference number: 56885, Ministry of Health and Social Solidarity, Athens.
Martins, J., R. Boarini, H. Strauss and C. de la Maisonneuve (2009), 'The policy determinants of investment in tertiary education', *OECD Journal: Economic Studies*, Vol. 2009, No.1 (Working Papers, No. 576, 2007), OECD, Paris.
Matsaganis M. and C. Leventi (2011), 'Inequality, poverty and the crisis in Greece', Presentation at ETUI Monthly Forum, Brussels, 26 September.
Ministry of Finance (2011), *Hellenic National Reform Programme 2011–2014*, Athens: MoF, Hellenic Republic.

Ministry of Health (2011), Αποτελέματα Ηλεκτνικών Δημοπρασιών της ΕΠΥ (Results of e-auctions by the Committee on Health Supplies), 18 November.
Mitrakos, T., P. Tsakloglou and I. Cholezas (2010), 'Determinants of hourly wages in the Greek labour market (with emphasis on the wages of tertiary education graduates)', *Economic Bulletin of the Bank of Greece*, **34**, 7–42 (in Greek).
Mnemonio 1 (2010), *Greek Government Gazette*, **1** (65) (May).
Mnemonio 2 (2012), *Greek Government Gazette*, **1** (28) (February).
Monogios, Y. and P. Korliras (2012), 'Debt sustainability revisited', International Papers in Political Economy, Palgrave Macmillan (May).
Monogios, Y. and Z. Tzannatos (forthcoming), *The Inter-temporal Inconsistency of Budget Execution in Greece: Secular Trends and Crises*, Athens: KEPE (Centre for Planning and Economic Research).
Organisation for Economic Co-operation and Development (OECD) (2008), *Education at a Glance 2008*, Paris: OECD.
Organisation for Economic Co-operation and Development (OECD) (2010), *Fiscal Consolidation Survey*, Paris: OECD.
Organisation for Economic Co-operation and Development (OECD) (2011a), *Public Governance Reviews. 'Greece: Review of the Central Administration'*, December, Paris: OECD.
Organisation for Economic Co-operation and Development (OECD) (2011b), *Economic Surveys: Greece*, August, Paris: OECD.
Organisation for Economic Co-operation and Development (OECD) (2011c), *Strong Performers and Successful Reformers in Education: Education Policy Advice for Greece*, Paris: OECD.
Schneider, F. (2010), 'The influence of public institutions on the shadow economy: an empirical investigation for OECD countries', *Review of Law and Economics*, **6** (3): 441–68.
Schneider, F. (2011), 'The shadow economy in Europe, 2011: using electronic payment systems to combat the shadow economy', Johannes Kepler University for AT Kearney.
Stuckler, D., S. Basu, M. Suhrcke, A. Coutts and M. McKee (2011a), 'Effects of the 2008 recession on health: a first look at European data', *The Lancet*, **378** (9 July): 124–5.
Stuckler, D., S. Basu, M. Suhrcke, A. Coutts and M. McKee (2011b), 'The public health effect of economic crises and alternative policy responses in Europe: an empirical analysis', *The Lancet* **374** (9686): (8 July), 315–23.
Telloglou, T. and M. Kakaounaki (2011), 'Three weeks and one night on duty', in A. Papahelas, T. Telloglou and S. Papaioannou (eds), Folders, Greece: Skai TV Channel.
The Economist (2010), 'Greece: not a simple fable about ants and crickets', *The Economist*, 8 May. Available at: http://www.economist.com/blogs/charlemagne/2010/03/empathy_short_supply.
The Economist (2011), 'Special Report on Pensions', *The Economist*, 9 April, p. 5.
The Economist Intelligence Unit (2005), *Quality of Life Index 2005*. Available at: www.economist.com.
Triantafyllou, K. and C. Angelopoulou (2011), 'IMF and the European co-workers attack public health in Greece', *The Lancet*, **378** (9801), 1459–60.
Tsimas, P. (2011), 'Erevna', Mega TV Channel, Greece.
Tzannatos, Z. (2012), 'The EUROMED economies in early-2010s: two coasts in

crisis', in S. Calleya and M. Wohlfeld (eds), *Changes and Opportunities in the Emerging Mediterranean*, Valetta, Malta: Gutenberg Press, pp. 133–59.

Tzannatos, Z. and Y. Monogios (2011), 'Report on Greece', paper presented at the workshop 'Adjustments in the Public Sector in Europe: Scope, Effects and Policy Issues', ILO, Geneva, 19 November.

United Nations Development Programme (UNDP) (2010), *Human Development Report 2010, The Real Wealth of Nations: Pathways to Human Development*, New York: UNDP.

Ziomas, D., N. Bouzas and N. Spyroglou (2009), *Greece: Minimum Income Schemes*, EC, DG Employment, Social Affairs and Equal Opportunities, April.

8. Hungary: Public sector labour market from crisis to crisis

Szilvia Altwicker-Hámori and János Köllő

1. INTRODUCTION

As a combined result of falling tax revenues, the implementation of automatic stabilizers and fiscal expansion, several EU member states had accumulated huge budget deficits by the end of 2009. Increased current deficits and growing public debts require major cuts in public expenditure and public sector downsizing throughout Europe. Despite a number of similarities, however, Hungary's road to fiscal turmoil differs from the majority in several ways.

Since the mid-1980s, the Hungarian economy has had an inclination to rush into severe external and internal imbalances, which has brought the country to the verge of financial collapse at least five times in the past 22 years (1989, 1995, 2006, 2008 and 2011). The stabilization packages addressing these crises were regularly followed by episodes of fiscal expansion, which drove the economy to the next crisis and renewed austerity measures. The latest wave of restrictive measures started in 2006, preventing the budget deficit from growing substantially during the crisis. Fiscal stability was achieved with the help of an IMF–EU stand-by loan and major cuts in social expenditure, public investment and public sector wages, among other things. The austerity measures of Gordon Bajnai's government included the abolition of the thirteenth-month wage and pensions in the public sector, the abolition of the Swiss indexation of pensions, a scenario of increasing the retirement age from 62 to 65 years, reducing paid leave for mothers from three to two years, cutting the flat-rate, per-child family allowance and curtailing subsidies and allowances for housing, heating, travel and farming. As a result, the budget deficit grew by a mere 0.2 percentage points, from 3.6 to 3.8 per cent in 2009.

A failed attempt to speed up the economy by means of tax cuts by the Fidesz government, which took office in May 2010, led to increasingly aggravating fiscal problems in 2011. In 2010, GDP grew by 1.3 per cent and the estimate for 2011 is still only 1.7 per cent. In 2012, GDP is expected to fall by at least 0.5 per cent. The current deficit was kept under control by levying 'crisis taxes' on the financial sector, telecommunications, energy and large retail trade companies, while the public debt was temporarily reduced by the 'nationalization' of 12 years of private pension savings. The unorthodox measures of the so-called 'economic freedom fight' severely damaged the country's reliability in the eyes of investors, increased its country-risk indicators high above the regional average and pushed the interest rate on Hungarian government bonds to the vicinity of 10 per cent by the end of 2011. The government contacted the IMF again in November 2011.

Currently, both the EU (Ecofin and the European Central Bank) and the IMF consider Hungary's fiscal policy to be unsustainable and are calling for austerity measures and structural reforms as a condition of support. They also demand the withdrawal of several legal acts which encroach upon the autonomy of the central bank, call into question the security of private contracts, contradict the principle of *nulla poena sine lege*, reduce the transparency of fiscal policy and threaten government control over the judiciary and the media. The forthcoming austerity measures will inevitably affect public sector jobs and wages.

The chapter begins with an overview of the measures taken (Section 2) and discusses how public sector workers are affected by them (Section 3). It addresses emergency steps and reforms in public education and health care through case studies in Section 4. Section 5 discusses policy issues and Section 6 concludes. The discussion of the crisis and its aftermath is preceded by a concise introduction to the characteristics of the Hungarian public sector.

Past developments are followed until May 2010 or January–March 2011 using micro-data from the Wage Survey (WS) and the Labour Force Survey (LFS) on wages and employment, respectively. Aggregate figures are added using published statistics relating to 2011 and early 2012. Current developments and future plans are discussed on the basis of media reports, internet sources and legislative documents (nearly all of them in Hungarian). We must add the caveat that, given decision-making patterns in contemporary Hungary, which are best characterized by the fact that the government issued and/or sent to the parliament for approval a daily average of more than three acts, decrees and resolutions in 2011,[1] the plans that were introduced are volatile, their technical details are often unclear and few are based on publicly available *ex ante* impact evaluations. Forecasting is always difficult but it is nearly impossible in the Hungarian case.

2. PUBLIC SECTOR ADJUSTMENTS

2.1 Size and Characteristics of the Hungarian Public Sector

Hungarian law distinguishes employees under the scope of the Labour Code from civil servants (*köztisztviselő*) and public employees (*közalkalmazott*), who are subject to special rules. Another dividing line separates those who work in state-run institutions and state-owned firms from workers employed by private businesses. A third distinction sets apart state-dominated sectors and predominantly privately run industries. Finally, there is a grey area around the public sector, a multitude of private businesses fully dependent on state-run institutions that perform outsourced activities or deliver goods and services exclusively for government orders.

While the numbers of those who work for the public sector vary with the definitions of 'civil service' and 'employment' (Table 8.1) they do not fall very far from each other and suggest that about 26–30 per cent of employees and roughly one-quarter of all employed persons work for the public sector.

The size of the grey area around the public sector is even more difficult to estimate. Using LFS data, Elek and Szabó (2011) find that in 1998–2002 about 40 per cent of the shifts from the public to the private sector involved no change in the respondent's job, which hints at large-scale outsourcing. In 2002–08, this type of 'apparent outflows' already accounted for a much lower proportion within total outflows. The number of government-dependent private businesses is impossible to assess.

Within the public sector, public administration and education each have about a 37 per cent share, while health and social services account for 26 per cent. Local government employs 57 per cent of the public sector's workforce but the central government's institutions in public administration constitute one of the largest branches within the sector. International comparative data in OECD (2011) suggest that in both 2000 and 2008 the Hungarian public sector was fairly large in relative terms, the fifth largest in Europe after the northern countries and France.

The conditions of employment differ from those in the private sector in several ways. The Acts on Civil Servants and Public Employees (first issued in 1992) prescribe special rules for firing and hiring. Civil servants are required to pass an examination in order to be appointed and/or confirmed, and both them and public employees are entitled to extended periods of notice and severance payments (up to 20 months' salary for public employees and a maximum of about 15 months' pay for civil servants) in the case of dismissal.[2] Public employees are allowed to join trade unions and set up within-institution consultative bodies analogous to

Table 8.1 The public sector's share in total and dependent employment, Hungary, 2011Q1

	% of total employment	% of dependent employment	Period
Establishment-based data			
Civil servants and public employees	n.a.	29.7[a]	2010
Civil servants and public employees	n.a.	27.3[b]	2009
LFS data			
Employed in a state-owned establishment (state-owned firm or public institution)[c]	26.4	31.6	2011Q1
Employed in a state-owned institution within public administration, education, health or social services	23.1	26.5	2011Q1

Sources:

(a) Central Statistical Office (CSO), www.ksh.hu Stadat 2.1.29.2. downloaded 2011.11.06. The establishment-based data relate to public institutions and firms employing 5 or more workers. Civil servants and public employees working in public institutions employing less than 5 workers are, therefore, excluded.

(b) Wage Survey 2009, based on the sum of weights calculated by the Employment Office.

(c) LFS, authors' calculation. Employment defined according to the ILO–OECD guidelines. Dependent employment includes workers employed in firms with fewer than 5 employees.

work councils (*közalkalmazotti tanács*), which provide further protection against job loss, at least potentially. In 2004, the fraction of workers covered by collective agreements amounted to 50 per cent in education and 53 per cent in health in contrast to a 40 per cent national average. The share of employees represented by establishment-level works councils were 51 and 41 per cent, respectively, compared to a 36 per cent national average (Fazekas and Koltay 2005: 339 and 351).

Public sector jobs are well protected but this statement requires qualification. Elek and Szabó (2011) find that while the risk of becoming unemployed is about three times lower in the public sector, those actually losing their job have a lower probability of finding a new one. Using LFS data from 1998 to 2008 and a discrete time hazard model they estimate that the relative risks of re-employment do not differ substantially by sector of origin in the case of unskilled workers (odds ratios above 0.93) but skilled job seekers coming from the public sector are significantly worse off than their counterparts from the private sector (odds ratios of 0.49 and 0.54 for workers with secondary and higher education, respectively).

In the public and private sectors wages are set according to wage grids determined by the aforementioned laws and updated (or not) by the government. The grids define wage brackets for civil servants and minimum salaries for public employees, taking into account educational attainment, skill requirements and tenure in the civil service. The wage grid sets linear age–earnings paths for public employees unless they augment their formal educational attainment and/or shift to jobs with higher-skill requirements during their service. Employers are allowed to pay more than the base wage depending on their financial capacity and the worker's merits.

High-skilled professionals having their first job in the public sector often have formal or informal secondary sources of income. Formal secondary job holding is exceptional among public sector workers without a university diploma but it amounts to about 5 per cent in public administration, 6 per cent in education and 8 per cent in health among professionals, according to LFS data from 2011. Many skilled public sector employees also have private businesses but the amounts earned via business contracts are unknown.[3] Physicians earn more than double their official salary in the form of gratuities, on average, as discussed in detail in Section 4.

2.2 Nature, Scale and Timing of Public Sector Adjustments

Thus far, the burden of adjustment has fallen almost entirely on wages. The elimination of the thirteenth-month wage was among the first measures taken as early as 2009. Furthermore, the wage grid has not been adjusted for inflation since January 2008. The minimum wage also fell in real terms in 2009–10 as shown in the brief overview presented in Table 8.2. In order to assess the magnitude of change it is useful to recall the pre-crisis evolution of public sector wages. The public/private wage gap has displayed large fluctuations in the past 20 years, between –25 and +15 percentage points.

As shown in Figure 8.1, the public sector's relative wage controlled for gender, experience, education and region fell from about 5 per cent below the private sector's level to –25 per cent during the stabilization programme of 1995–96 (the 'Bokros package'). A period of slow recovery in 1997–2000 was followed by a series of spectacular rises resulting from one-off government decisions.

First, Viktor Orbán's first government almost doubled the minimum wage, raising it from 25,500 HUF on 31 December 2000 to 50,000 HUF on 1 January 2002.[4] The public sector was strongly affected by the hike: at the time of the decision over 60 per cent of the public employees without college or university diploma earned less than 50,000 HUF compared to 40 per cent in the private sector, according to WS data.

Table 8.2 Measures affecting public sector wages, Hungary, 2008–2012

Basic wage	The wage grid for civil servants and public employees has not been adjusted for inflation since January 2008. The monthly base salaries of civil servants were limited to a maximum of HUF 2 million (or about €6,700) in 2010
Bonuses	The thirteenth-month salaries for civil servants and public employees were abolished in 2009
Minimum wage	The minimum wage increased slightly in 2009 (3.6%) and 2010 (2.8%) and more substantially in 2011 (6.1%) and 2012 (19.2%). In real terms, the changes amounted to –1.9, –1.8, 2.1 and 13%. In 2012, the minimum wage was increased to compensate for the fall in the net earnings of low-wage workers due to changes in personal income tax

Note: Estimates from benchmark Mincer equations (log wage regressed on experience, experience squared, years in school, a female dummy and a public sector dummy). The log point estimates of the gap (b) are converted to percentage points differentials (*d*) as $d = 100e^{\beta}$.

Source: Wage Surveys, 1986, 1989 and 1992–2010.

Figure 8.1 Regression-adjusted public–private wage gap, Hungary, 1985–2010 (percentage points)

Second, just before the elections of May 2002, the government substantially raised the pay of civil servants, which increased the real average wage by 17 per cent in the public sector as a whole as opposed to 7 per cent growth in the private sector.

Third, and most importantly, the socialist government taking office in May 2002 increased the base salary of public employees by 50 per cent, with the supporting votes of the opposition, sticking to its pre-election promises. The pay rise implied a 29 per cent jump in the average wage of public employees in real terms between May 2002 and 2003, as compared to 'only' an 11 per cent rise in the private sector. The public sector wage penalty (–6 per cent in 2002) changed into a substantial premium of 11 per cent in 2003 and 15 per cent in 2004.

The advantage, however, disappeared in the course of only three years. On the one hand, as shown in Telegdy (2011), pay rises in the public sector had a strong spillover effect: in those occupations where workers can move between the two sectors, private sector wages grew significantly faster after 2003. On the other hand, the huge internal and external deficits accumulated by 2006 required a new wave of austerity measures, which brought the public sector's wage advantage down to zero by May 2007.

The abolition of the thirteenth-month salary of civil servants and public employees in 2009 implied an immediate 12 percentage point decrease in the sector's relative wage. Furthermore, the base salaries of civil servants and public employees were practically frozen at their 2008 level until recently. These measures brought the public sector penalty back to a low of –12 per cent, a level unprecedented since 1999.

The enormous fluctuations in the level of public sector pay had virtually no effect on within-sector relative wages until 2008–10. This is shown by the shifts in the age–earnings profiles by skill groups in Figure 8.2. The profiles of skilled civil servants remained practically unchanged until 2008 but older workers were slightly more affected by the cuts in 2009–10. The case was different at lower-skilled levels. In 2001, the age–wage profile was practically flat. In 2001–04, the wages of young unskilled workers grew by a lower rate, which restored an upward-sloping age–earnings profile. The crisis brought about a dramatic, 25 percentage point fall in the relative wages of unskilled public sector employees, with younger workers being slightly more affected.

Compared to wages, public sector employment changed little until recently (Figure 8.3). The size of the public sector grew substantially in the early transition period, when several tasks previously performed by the Party apparatus and state-owned firms were transferred to what we call the public sector today. This expansion was halted by the Bokros package, which brought about a 10 per cent fall in public sector employment. After 2000, the public sector started to grow again, until 2006, when budget deficits reached 10 per cent of GDP, enforcing job cuts.

Perhaps surprisingly, public sector employment followed a downward trend only until 2008, the first year of the international financial crisis, while it grew in 2009–10. Recent developments are summarized in Table 8.3.[5] On the whole, public sector employment *grew* substantially, by 4.7 per cent between January–March 2008 and 2010 and fell only slightly, by 1.7 per cent, between January–March 2010 and 2011.

The growth rate in 2009 was particularly large in public administration, education and outpatient social services, and was probably explained by the expansion of public works schemes. According to the Budapest Institute (2011) the annual average stock of participants employed by local governments in public works programmes increased by 40,000 (from 20,000 to 60,000) in this period, which roughly corresponds to the net growth in total public sector employment. Despite cuts in some branches, the public sector as a whole employed more people in January–March 2011 than three years earlier, by 3 per cent, which compares to a 4.8 per cent employment loss in the private sector.

The expectations concerning future developments are less promising – some recently decided measures in public administration and higher education threaten large-scale dismissals. The plan to further cut employment in public administration by 30,000 or about 13 per cent in 2011[6] clearly failed: in January–November 2011 employment was lower by only 1.3 per cent compared to the same period of 2010 (KSH 2012, public works participants excluded). Large-scale dismissals will probably take place within the framework of the forthcoming restructuring of public administration, which will shift a part of local government authority from the community to the micro-region level.

As far as higher education is concerned, in January 2012, just four weeks before the deadline for applications to colleges, the government decreased the number of state-funded places for first-graders from 53,500 (2011) to 29,570 (2012). A further 15,500 freshmen are expected to pay 50 per cent of the tuition fees, which had been determined by the government for each field of study.[7] The final decision on quotas by field of study was made personally by Prime Minister Viktor Orbán.[8] Preference was given to science, engineering, sports and a newly founded School of Public Administration as opposed to social sciences and humanities. The state-funded quotas were cut more in fields in which students' propensity to pay tuition fees was higher in the past but the quotas for economics (including business) and law were particularly severely cut, from 4,900 to 250 and from 800 to 100, respectively. As a second step, still in January 2012, the number of fully and partly state-financed places was determined by the state Secretariat of Education for each field of study within each college/university.[9] The reduction of state support resulted in a 30 per cent drop in applications, which will force the affected universities to lay off professors and staff and/or further decrease their wages.

Age-earnings profiles: tertiary education

2001 and 2004

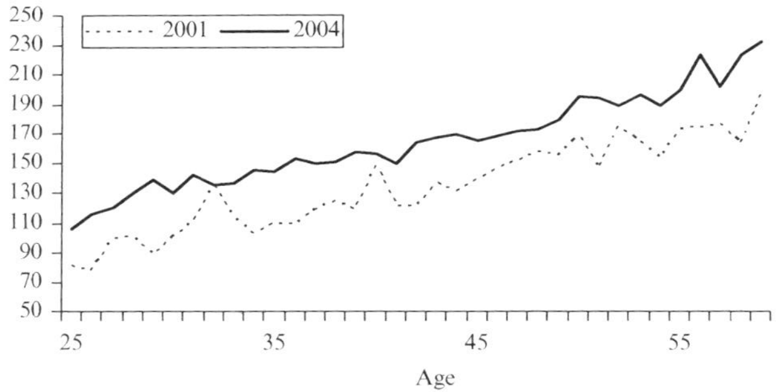

2004, 2008 and 2010

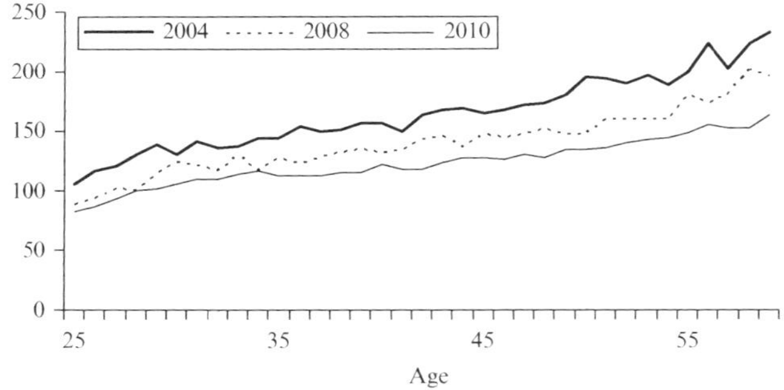

Age-earnings profiles: secondary education

2001 and 2004

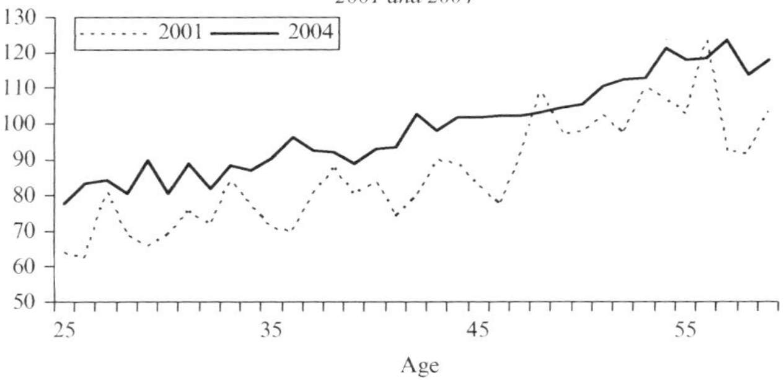

2004, 2008 and 2010

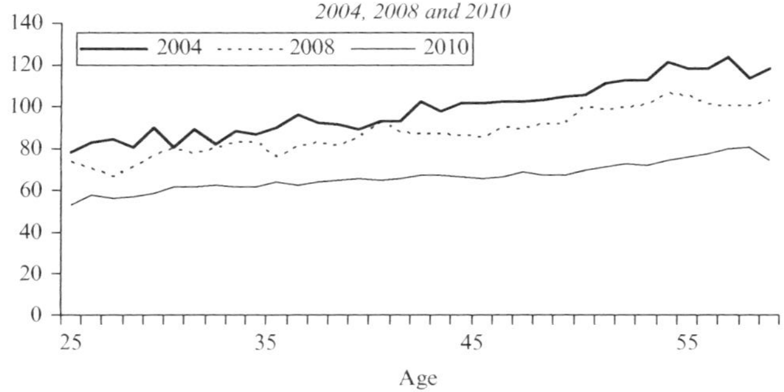

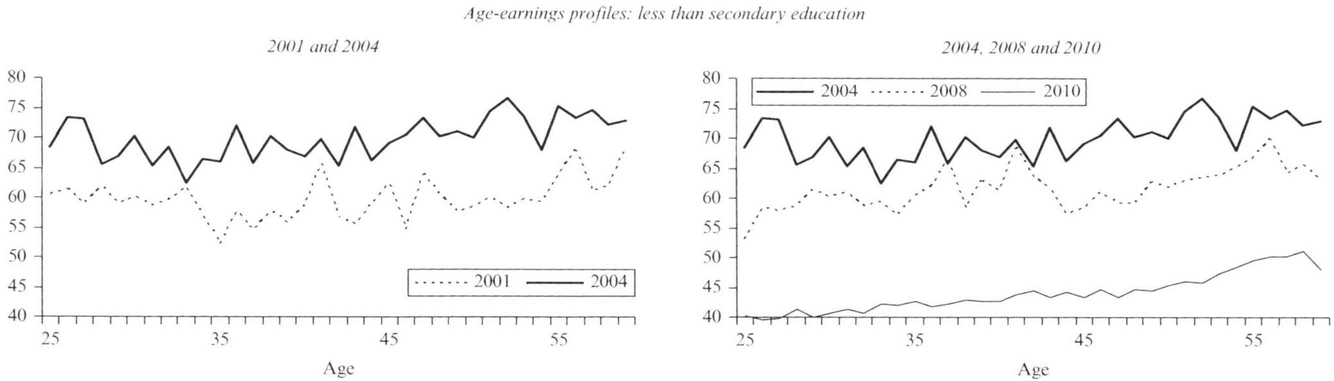

Note: The figures show earnings by single year of age. National average wage = 1.0. Individual wages are compared to the national average wage rather than to the earnings of private sector workers of similar age and education. This is why the profiles are upward sloping rather than U-shaped.

Source: Wage Surveys, 2001, 2004 and 2008.

Figure 8.2 Age–earnings profiles of civil servants and public employees, Hungary, 2001, 2004, 2008 and 2010

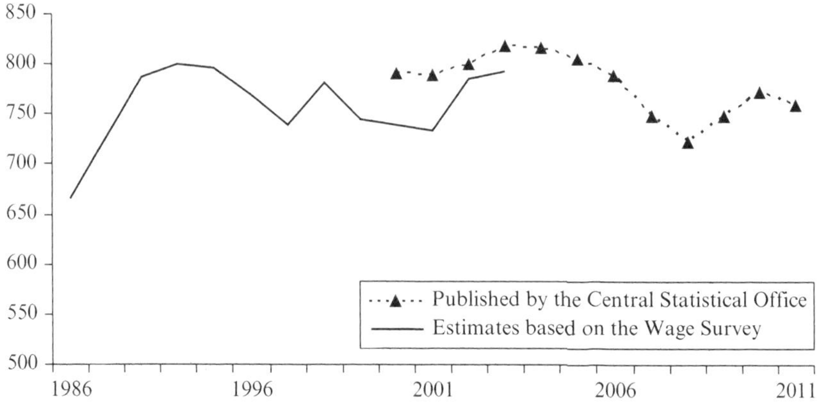

Source: CSO-Stadat and Wage Surveys.

Figure 8.3 Employment in the public sector, 1986–2011 (headcount, thousand)

Table 8.3 Employment in branches dominated by the public sector, Hungary, 2008–2011 (numbers and index 2008=100)

	Numbers				Index			
	2008	2009	2010	2011	2008	2009	2010	2011
Public admin.	273.6	282.8	298.6	283.0	100	103.4	109.1	103.4
Education	313.4	304.4	326.3	320.8	100	97.1	104.1	102.3
Health	161.2	157.9	159.1	165.4	100	98.0	98.7	102.6
Social 1[a]	57.2	50.6	58.4	54.4	100	88.4	102.0	95.0
Social 2[a]	28.0	28.0	30.1	34.9	100	100.0	107.2	124.6
Total public[b]	833.5	823.8	872.4	858.6	100	98.8	104.7	103.0
Total private	3,010.6	2,940.2	2,846.8	2,866.7	100	97.7	94.6	95.2
	3,844.2	3,764.1	3,719.2	3,725.3	100	97.9	96.7	96.9

Notes:

a. Social 1: social care, inpatient services. Social 2: social care, outpatient services.

b. Employment in state-owned enterprises and institutions outside the indicated branches is accounted as part of the private sector. Includes participants in public works programmes.

Source: Authors' calculation from the Labour Force Surveys of the first quarter of each year.

3. EFFECTS OF THE ADJUSTMENTS

In this section, we give a brief overview of the impact of adjustments on wages and non-wage amenities with special emphasis on how the overall position of women, heavily overrepresented in the public sector, is affected.

We start with Table 8.4, which presents data on two wage measures. Full-time equivalent (FTE) monthly earnings correspond to what the CSO and the Employment Office publish. Denoting a worker's observed earnings during the month with w and his/her paid hours with h the FTE measure is computed as $168 \cdot (w/h)$, in other words, hourly earnings times the paid hours of a full-time, full-month employee. This measure

Table 8.4 Nominal and real wages, Hungary, 2008–2010[a]

	Civil servants	Judges, attorneys	Public employees	Non-profits	Public sector	Private sector	Total
FTE average monthly earnings (thousand HUF)[b]							
2008	283.3	388.4	192.3	176.4	209.5	189.6	195.6
2010	272.0	314.3	195.7	162.7	189.6	201.1	202.7
Actual average monthly earnings (thousand HUF)							
2008	282.6	386.1	186.2	163.4	203.7	185.3	190.9
2010	267.5	311.0	184.2	148.4	185.3	189.2	191.2
Ratio of actual to FTE earnings (%)							
2008	99.7	99.4	96.8	92.6	97.2	97.7	97.6
2010	98.4	99.0	94.2	91.2	95.0	94.1	94.3
Change of nominal earnings 2008–10 (%)							
FTE	−4.0	−19.1	1.8	−7.7	−9.4	6.1	3.6
Actual	−5.3	−19.4	−1.0	−9.2	−9.0	2.1	0.2
Change of real earnings 2008–2010 (%)[c]							
FTE	−11.5	−25.4	−6.2	−14.9	−16.5	−2.2	−4.5
Actual	−12.7	−25.7	−8.8	−16.3	−16.1	−5.9	−7.6

Notes:
Number of observations: 218,323 in 2008 and 245,484 in 2010. The data exclude the participants of public works programmes.

a. The economy-wide nominal average wage grew by 3.6 % (from 195,643 HUF to 202,729 HUF) according to the Wage Survey. The establishment-based CSO figures hint at lower wage increase (2.8 %, from 195,824 HUF to 201,255 HUF) in the same period. See http://portal.ksh.hu/pls/ksh/docs/hun/xstadat/ xstadat_evkozi/e_qli007c.html.
b. Actual earnings during May (w) adjusted for the number of paid hours (h). The FTE figure is computed as $(w/h)*168$, i.e., hourly earnings times hours worked by a full-time, full-month employee.
c. Consumer prices increased by 8.47 % between May 2008 and May 2010. See http:// portal.ksh.hu /pls/ksh/docs/hun/xstadat/xstadat_evkozi/e_qsf001.html.

Source: Wage Surveys 2008, 2010, authors' calculations.

Table 8.5 Incidence of low pay: percentage earning less than two-thirds of the median wage, Hungary, 2008 and 2010

Level of education:	Less than secondary		Secondary (matura)		Higher (college, university)		Total	
	2008	2010	2008	2010	2008	2010	2008	2010
Civil servants	36.1	54.8	4.3	6.1	0.7	0.2	6.7	5.0
Public employees	17.3	23.2	5.1	3.0	0.2	0.1	5.9	3.8
Non-profits	50.4	78.2	18.5	28.1	3.8	2.7	25.4	35.1
Public sector	23.7	41.6	5.7	7.4	0.6	0.3	7.7	8.1
Private sector	38.1	38.4	20.8	27.5	7.1	9.7	27.3	25.9
Total	35.7	39.1	15.9	24.2	3.8	5.2	21.4	21.5

Note: Number of observations: 218,323 in 2008 and 245,484 in 2010. For the size of the particular groups see Table 8.5. The data exclude the participants of public works programmes.

Source: Wage Surveys 2008, 2010, authors' calculations.

overestimates the earnings of workers who worked less than 168 hours in the reference month in a given job and did not work the rest of the month. By contrast, actual observed wages tend to underestimate the monthly earnings of workers who worked less than 168 hours in one job but worked the rest of the month in another job. Furthermore, the FTE wage indicator measures the hypothetical full-time, full-month earnings of part-timers rather than what they actually make during the reference month. The larger the share of part-timers and the more workers lose their jobs the wider the gap between the two wage measures.

As shown in Table 8.4, wages fell even in nominal terms in the Hungarian public sector between 2008 and 2010. In real terms, public sector wages fell by 16–17 per cent as opposed to –2.2 per cent (FTE earnings) and –5.9 per cent (actual earnings) in the private sector. Civil servants, judges and attorneys and the employees of non-profit organizations were particularly severely affected. The ratio of actual to FTE earnings fell in nearly all segments of the economy, hinting at a decrease in working hours (see later) and increased labour turnover.

The data in Table 8.5 suggest that the earnings of many unskilled public sector workers sank below the low-wage threshold by May 2010, when more than half of the unskilled civil servants and over three-quarters of the unskilled non-profit employees earned less than two-thirds of the median wage. The fraction of low-paid workers grew less among unskilled public employees, while the low-wage share of their private sector counterparts

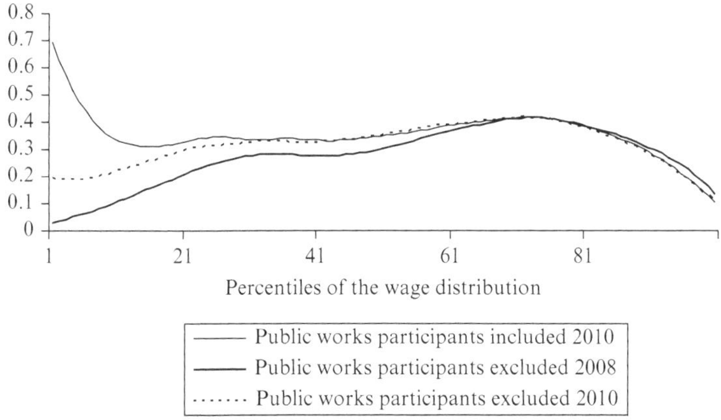

Note: The curves have been smoothed with locally weighted non-linear regression.

Source: Wage Surveys May 2008, May 2010.

Figure 8.4 Share of public sector workers in percentiles of the wage distribution, Hungary, 2008 and 2010

remained virtually constant. In the category of employees with secondary school background low-wage employment became more prevalent in the private and non-profit sectors. Earnings below two-thirds of the median were and remained exceptional among high-skilled public sector employees.[10]

The crisis brought about substantial changes in the position of the public sector within the wage distribution (Figure 8.4). In 2008, the public sector was strongly underrepresented in the lower tiers of the distribution, while in 2010 its share already amounted to 20–30 per cent in the 1st–20th percentiles. This change resulted from wage cuts in the public sector, as well as the loss of low-wage jobs in the private sector. If we include public works participants (for whom wage data became available in 2010) we find that the public sector became the dominant provider of jobs in the 1st–10th percentiles of the wage distribution.

Table 8.6 gives an overview of how working time and some other non-wage characteristics changed in public administration, education, health and two types of social services. The data suggest that the usual weekly working time fell slightly but the share of part-timers grew significantly (relative to the base-period average of 5.8 per cent). A crisis can be expected to have both negative and positive effects on the part-time share: marginal workers such as part-timers face higher risk of dismissal (negative), employers may terminate full-time jobs and create part-time ones

Table 8.6 *Changes in selected indicators of the private and public sectors, Hungary, 2008Q1 and 2011Q1 (percentage points)*

	Private sector	Public admin	Education	Health	Social inpatient	Social outpatient
Usual weekly working time (hours)	–0.5	–0.9	–1.5	–0.2	–0.2	–0.5
Part-time job	1.8	2.9	1.8	3.4	0.4	4.5
Evening work*	10.9	8.6	3.1	14.3	11.8	7.7
Night work*	4.8	6.3	1.0	9.3	8.0	3.2
Saturday work*	8.3	6.3	2.3	13.6	12.2	5.2
Sunday work*	6.2	4.8	2.0	12.9	12.5	3.0
Temporary agency work contract	0.2	0.5	–0.1	0.1	0.5	1.0
Fixed-term contract	0.7	1.4	1.5	0.1	–0.4	–2.1

Note: * At least occasionally.

Source: LFS 2011Q1, authors' calculation.

(positive) and they may formally reclassify full-timers in order to be able to pay less than the mandatory minimum wage (positive). It seems that in the Hungarian public sector the last two effects have dominated.

While total working time did not change dramatically, its distribution across days did: the proportion of employees working in the evening, at night and at the weekend increased substantially everywhere except for education (for obvious reasons). The move toward 'atypical' work schedules was monotonous after a jump in January 2009, when employers were given increased authority to determine the distribution of working hours over an extended period.

The share of fixed-term contracts did not change markedly, nor did the share of agency work. However, similar to the case of part-timers, we only observe the net effect of positive and negative forces, and in the case of agency work reporting errors may also bias the observations: it is likely that many LFS respondents with agency contracts reported that they worked for a certain enterprise rather than for an agency.

The past, ongoing and forthcoming adjustments affect nearly all groups within the public sector, from university professors to janitors in the kindergartens. It seems too early to try to assess how wider social groups will be affected, with the possible exceptions of the unskilled, who experienced

Table 8.7 *Women's share in public sector employment, by education, Hungary, 2009 (%)*

	Primary	Vocational	Secondary	Higher
Public administration				
Share	71.1	47.8	80.6	63.4
Relative to women's share in total employment	1.33	1.54	1.39	1.12
Public education				
Share	92.3	71.6	81.1	81.6
Relative to women's share in total employment	1.73	2.31	1.40	1.44
Higher education				
Share	73.1	40.9	80.1	44.3
Relative to women's share in total employment	1.37	1.32	1.38	0.78
Health and social services				
Share	76.4	76.0	81.3	74.0
Relative to women's share in total employment	1.43	2.45	1.40	1.31

Note: Public sector 1986: employees in the given sector. 2009: civil servants and public employees in the given sector.

Source: Wage Surveys 1986, 2009.

particularly severe wage losses (as was shown in Figure 8.2) and women, who are highly overrepresented in the public sector.

The public sector currently employs 36 per cent of the female labour force as opposed to only 18 per cent of males (LFS data, 2011Q1). With only a few exceptions, women's share exceeds two-thirds of the unskilled workforce, and the female share is also very high among medium-skilled employees in public administration and health (Table 8.7). The female share is again high among workers with tertiary education, with the exception of higher education. Women were overrepresented in all branch education cells except for high-skilled employees in higher education. Subsequently, women's overall earning position is strongly affected by wage developments in the public sector.

Under state socialism, men and women were paid very different wages: women's disadvantage, controlled for education and experience, amounted to 30 per cent in the 'private sector' (state-owned enterprises) and 20 per cent in the public sector. The wage disadvantage diminished rapidly in the early years of the transition in both sectors,

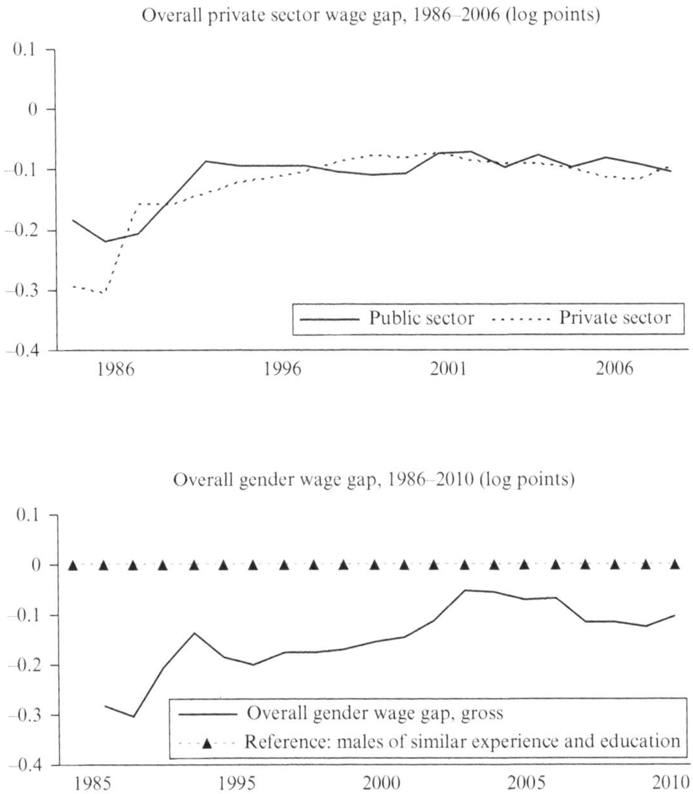

Note: Coefficients of the female dummy in benchmark Mincer equations (log gross wage regressed on a female dummy, experience, experience squared and years in school) estimated sector by sector in the upper panels and for entire samples in the lower panel.

Source: Wage Surveys 1986, 1989, 1992 and annually since 1994, authors' calculations.

Figure 8.5 The regression-adjusted gender wage gap, Hungary, 1986–2010 (log points)

and settled at similar levels, falling between 7 and 11 per cent after 1994 (Figure 8.5).

However, the large changes in the public sector's relative wage, on one hand, and women's strong exposure to these changes, on the other, had a decisive impact on the overall gender wage gap. The second panel of Figure 8.5 clearly shows that the movement towards a narrower gender gap was interrupted by the austerity measures of 1995–98 and 2006–10.

In fact, as shown by the bottom panel, there was a very strong relation-

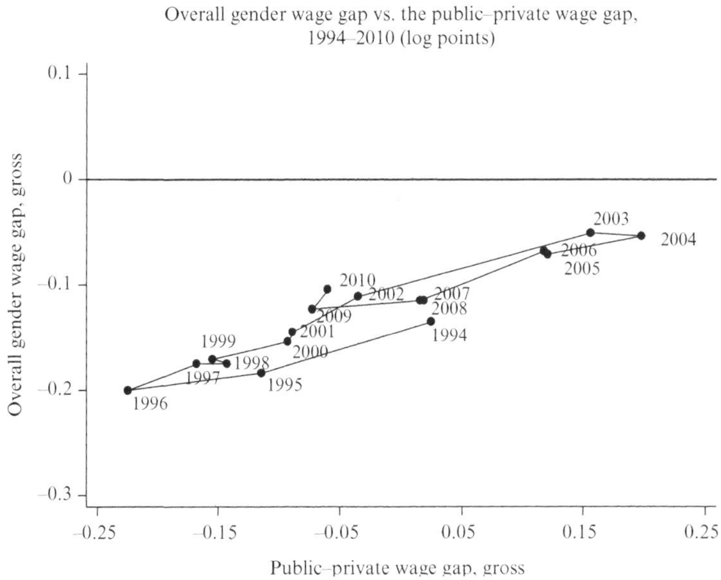

Figure 8.5 (continued)

ship between the overall gender gap and the public–private gap, at least after 1994 when the within-sector pay differentials settled. The points are located on an upward-sloping line, which suggests that a 1 log point decrease in the public sector's relative wage increased the overall gender wage gap by 0.36 log points. Even in the absence of discrimination, women as a group suffer more from the public sector wage cuts and they will also be strongly affected by the forthcoming wave of dismissals. Furthermore, given the patterns of dividing household duties, women are also worse affected by the spread of work at the weekend, in the evening and during the night.

4. REFORMS AND EMERGENCY ACTIONS: CASE STUDIES IN EDUCATION AND HEALTH CARE

In this section we give an overview of actions and plans affecting two major branches of the public sector. The nature and gravity of the problems of the public sector differ widely across the branches. Public administration foresees major employment cuts and fundamental reorganization but the details of the short-run plans and structural reforms are not yet known. Higher education is already affected by budget cuts and restrictions on the state-funded quotas of students but the labour market outcomes remain unpredictable. We therefore discuss developments in two other sectors, health and public education, in more detail.

Health care was severely affected by the doctors' struggle for higher wages in 2011, similar to several other countries in the region. We summarize the events and outcomes (until April 2012) of this conflict with an eye to their fiscal implications and links to bribery in the health sector. Education is a sphere in which the government has already initiated structural reforms affecting all areas, ranging from school governance and finance to teachers' legal standing, the structure of the education system, the curriculum and tuition. We try to summarize our understanding of the ongoing reform in Subsection 4.2.

4.1 Case Study 1: Doctors' Pay – A Year of Exit, Voice and Loyalty

Throughout Central and Eastern Europe, doctors keep fighting for substantial wage increases and many are leaving their home country for better pay and working conditions in Western and Northern Europe. Thousands of Czech, Slovak and Hungarian doctors and residents have deposited notices of resignation and/or went on strike in 2011, as did their Polish counterparts a few years earlier. While reliable statistics are hard to find, the available sources report a growing number of emigrants from the region. In Romania, almost 10 per cent of doctors have emigrated since 2007, according to Holt (2010). In Hungary, 500 to 600 doctors left annually in 2004–08, which compares to 750–800 graduates per year (Kőműves 2008) and the figures have since been on the rise. In 2011, 100 doctors per month applied for a certificate of goodwill required for working abroad (Balázs 2012).[11] In the Czech Republic, about 250 doctors leave annually, according to the Chamber of Physicians' officials (Holt 2010).

The Czech, Hungarian and Slovak governments seemed to give in, promising pay rises. They fall short of doctors' demands but are likely to improve relative wages substantially in the near future. In exchange, doctors' organizations suspended their plans for massive strikes that would paralyse the health service.

In this subsection we summarize a year of doctors' unrest in Hungary, starting with radical demands on the part of young residents, and ending (thus far) with peaceful negotiations between the professional organizations and the government. A unique feature of the Hungarian version of the story is that the issue of informal earnings was openly included in the debate, at least to begin with. Furthermore, the fiscal vulnerability of the Hungarian economy makes a mutually satisfactory compromise difficult to achieve, which highlights the conflict between welfare and fiscal considerations inherent in this debate everywhere.

4.1.1 Challenges

To begin with, while the low official wages of doctors and nurses has been a matter of debate for several decades in Hungary, no open conflicts emerged before the end of 2010, the birth of what was called the 'Green Cross Movement'. In 2010, a group of young doctors started a movement to abolish gratuities in the health service, on one hand, and a substantial rise in doctors' and nurses' official wages, on the other. A green cross badge on their coats indicated that they were unwilling to accept gratuities. In exchange, they required the doubling of their starting salaries. The proposal was supported by the overwhelming majority of young doctors but strongly opposed by the Chamber of Physicians and other medical organizations dominated by older doctors, who receive the bulk of gratuities.

Several factors seem to explain why the Green Cross Movement, organized by the Residents' Federation, appeared and why it happened at the end of 2010.

First, young doctors' pay is indeed miserable: at age 35 it falls short of half of the wage paid to a tertiary-educated worker of similar age in the private sector. At this age, a doctor's wage advantage over secondary school graduates amounts to only 28 percentage points as opposed to the 159 percentage points average on the part of college/university graduates in the private sector.

Second, the Hungarian health system has been severely infected with under-the-counter payments since the 1950s, when private practice was prohibited and doctors' relative earnings fell substantially. Private payments in the form of tips and gratuities gradually became a part of doctors' income and their official wages were step-by-step adjusted for that. Bognár et al. (1999) estimated that in the late 1990s general practitioners, specialists and hospital doctors received about 160 per cent of their official salaries, on average, in the form of gratuities. In other words, they received only about 40 per cent of their total labour income in the form of a salary. Hungary is by no means unique in this respect. Cases of massive under-the-counter payments have been reported in several countries of the region, including Poland (Chawla et al. 1998), Bulgaria (Delcheva et al. 1997), Russia (Sabirianova-Peter and Zelenska 2011), Albania (Burak and Vian 2007) and Greece (Liaropoulos et al. 2008). Young doctors obviously benefit less from the under-the-counter payments and, as newcomers to an opaque system, they are also more likely to suffer from the mutually humiliating practice of giving and accepting such payments. Their low pay prospects and need to accept gratuities, in an era of improving outside options thanks to Hungary's accession to the EU, drove many of them to join the Green Cross Movement.

Note: The points of the curves show three-cohort moving averages. 'High-skilled' stands for employees with college/university diploma. 'Medical' stands for doctors and other high-skilled personnel in medical occupations.

Source: Wage Surveys 2008, 2010.

Figure 8.6 Wages of high-skilled medical workers relative to the wages of high-skilled employees of similar age in the private sector, Hungary, 2008 and 2010 (%)

Third, the existence of similar problems and actions in Poland, the Czech Republic and Slovakia gave impetus to the Hungarian movement. The striking similarity in the demands and actions (such as the depositing of notices of resignation) clearly indicated that physicians' organizations had learned from each other in the region.

Last but not least, Hungarian doctors have suffered a huge wage loss since the start of the crisis (Figure 8.6). The wage cuts have affected older doctors most: their official earnings fell from about 90 to 70 per cent of the private sector wage, while younger doctors experienced a 10 percentage point decrease. Beginners were least affected but their level of pay sank markedly, too, without the option of increased compensation 'under the counter'.

Leading doctors represented by the Hungarian Chamber of Physicians (MOK), the Hungarian Federation of Physicians (MOSZ) and the Hospital Federation (KSZ) rejected the idea of increasing only residents' wages and directly connecting the issue of pay rises with the fight against informal earnings. After several months of stalemate and informal negotiations, in autumn 2011 the Residents' Federation started action for a general pay rise for doctors, adopting the method used in the Czech

Republic and Slovakia (depositing notices of resignation), and this time avoiding the issues of tips and gratuities, on one hand, and nurses' wages on the other. By the end of the year, nearly 2,600 notices were collected, with a warning to activate them in January 2012 unless an agreement was reached.[12] Under pressure of militant action at home, and probably aroused by the escalation of a similar conflict in Slovakia, the government started negotiations with the residents' movement, which was joined by MOK, MOSZ, KSZ and other professional associations and unions. However, it soon became clear that the Hungarian government cannot solve the problem by way of a one-time, significant pay rise, as happened in fiscally healthy Poland in 2006.

4.1.2 Costs of raising doctors' pay

The Residents' Federation is asking for an after-tax monthly salary of 200,000 HUF (€667) for a young doctor and 300,000 HUF (€1,000) for a specialist.[13] Other organizations including MOSZ are asking for a 100,000 HUF rise for doctors and 50,000 HUF for nurses and other skilled employees, while some of the negotiating parties joined in the hope of a medium-run scenario of gradual pay increases.

Rough calculations based on published wage data[14] and renewed tax rules suggest that achieving the Resident Federation's target would require a pay rise of about 35–45 per cent (after tax). A similarly calculated rate for a specialist falls within the range of 46–53 per cent. Hungarian doctors are demanding a substantial rise, but it is within the realm of feasibility: it corresponds roughly to the 40 per cent pay rise that Polish doctors received in 2006 (Holt 2010). The required amounts also fall short of what unions asked for in neighbouring Slovakia at the end of 2011 (claims of €1,200–€2,350 a month).[15] In December 2011, the government made it clear that an additional burden close to 100 billion HUF (€330 million) is beyond the country's current fiscal capacity and offered negotiations on smaller initial increases and a medium-term scenario of major future adjustments.

4.1.3 Responses

The immediate measures included the year-end payment of 7–70 thousand HUF in December 2011 as an additional duty allowance, with a promise to make it regular in the future.[16] More importantly, it was agreed that the intakes from some newly introduced taxes on unhealthy food (popularly known as the 'crisps tax' or 'hamburger tax') will be spent on pay rises in the health sector. An expected 15 billion HUF from this source supplemented by a similar amount saved by means of restructuring medical services would bring the annual extra expenditure in the vicinity of 30 billion HUF, certainly less than the amount required to accommodate the originally proposed wage levels.[17] Similar to Slovakia and the Czech Republic,[18] the negotiations ended with an agreement on a medium-run scenario rather than an immediate, substantial rise. In March 2012 the parties agreed on a package of 30 billion HUF to be spent on pay rises for hospital doctors, specialists and skilled assistants. The current wage increases fill about one-third of the gap between actual earnings and the target set by the medical unions and chambers. While the open conflicts are over for the time being, the doctors' fight for higher wages has raised a series of questions for policymaking.

4.1.4 Policy issues

In principle, a rise in medical wages might be financed from external resources but the idea of creating resources other than general budget expenditure does not seem to be popular among doctors and the general public. A recent opinion poll suggests that 88 per cent of the population supports an increase in doctors' wages, with one-third advocating a 50 per cent rise and 11 per cent proposing a doubling of doctors' salaries.[19] However, the vast majority (over 80 per cent) of this very same population voted for the abolition of copayments for general practitioner appointments (about €1 per visit) and a charge for hospital stays (€2 per day) in a referendum in 2008. The fact that the referendum was initiated by the now governing Fidesz party makes it nearly impossible for the cabinet to reintroduce copayments. The medical organizations rather propose the redirection of resources from investment to wages, shifting the burden of non-wage expenditure from the health budget to the general budget of local authorities and allowing private payments for purposes other than hotel services (jumping the queue for operations, for instance).

Solving the problem of low pay in the health sector in Hungary and other former socialist countries requires urgent action on the part of the governments but most are – and will continue to be in the near future – unable to finance a substantial rise in medical wages. The current and prospective wage levels are insufficient to contain emigration to Western Europe, which further deepens the fiscal burden through fruitless – at least for the time being – outlays on expensive medical training. The exodus of young doctors continues and there are plans to try to halt it by means of legal restrictions, although this will be difficult in practice: an act on higher education prescribes that doctors working less than 12 years in Hungary in the first 20 years of their career are required to pay back the full cost of their training, totalling about 15 million HUF or €50,000.

Equally important, the current agreements in Hungary and elsewhere are unlikely to foster developments towards a transparent health-care system. The issue of a possible trade-off between higher medical wages and lower informal payments has almost disappeared from the debate in Hungary. The sources we could find on Slovakia and the Czech Republic are also silent on the problem of under-the-counter payments and its relationship to official wages. While such a trade-off is relevant for the general taxpayer, not the budget itself, a credible programme might convince the public that additional tax revenues are required to finance the way out of the current, deeply unsatisfactory system. The chances of strong popular pressure for such a programme are weakened by the fact that in Hungary informal payments for health care are highly regressive (Szende and Culyer 2006).

4.2 Case Study 2: Public Education: Turning the Clock Back?

As in the rest of the sector, the burden of adjustment to the crisis has fallen entirely on wages in public education. The average wages of teachers with college/university qualifications fell by 2.1 per cent in nominal terms and 9.8 per cent in real value between May 2008 and 2010.[20] In 2008, a 40-year-old teacher earned 43 per cent of what a similarly aged and educated employee made in the private sector. The pay cuts of 2009–10 brought this ratio down to only 38 per cent, according to Wage Survey data. However, low pay in education is part of a broader set of long-term deficiencies which call for structural reform. In this subsection we summarize the main challenges and the government's reform proposals.

At first sight, recent developments resemble the case discussed in the previous section: teachers and doctors share a common fate of being poorly paid, especially in the middle of their career, and the problem has become more acute during the crisis. However, the policy implications of low pay are rather different in the two professions. EU accession markedly improved the outside options of doctors. The resulting shortages of physicians are immediately perceived by the public, requiring urgent action on the part of the government, while the potentially worsening quality of teachers does not necessitate emergency steps. The risk of open 'teacher shortages' is minimal since the pupil/teacher ratios in Hungarian primary and secondary schools are among the lowest in the OECD (2010b). Low pay in education is part of a broader set of long-run deficiencies, which call for structural reforms.

4.2.1 Challenges

A series of school-based tests of literacy and numeracy have drawn attention to the worsening quality of Hungarian education in the past two decades: at least until 2006 the country performed worse and worse at the PISA tests and lost its once outstanding position in students' mathematical comprehension. The knowledge acquired in Hungarian schools is difficult to transform into practical skills, as suggested by the available adult literacy test results. (For a concise overview of Hungarians' test performance over time, see Fazekas et al. 2009). Furthermore, the education system is the least successful within the OECD in moderating initial inequalities: the correlation between parental background and student performance is nowhere as strong as in Hungary (Jenkins et al. 2008). The children of low-educated parents tend to leave school with poor basic competencies, mostly to become unemployed in an economy in which the employment rate of prime-age adults with primary education or less is below 35 per cent.

The system's inability and/or unwillingness to deal with low achievers is manifested in many ways. Public education is highly 'segregated' (Kertesi and Kézdi 2010). Hungary has the highest between-schools to total variance ratio in student performance (OECD 2007) and Csapó et al. (2009) demonstrate that a large part of what seems to be within-school variance actually comes from between-class and between-premises variance. 'Segregation' has evolved as a natural consequence of the *laissez-faire* regulations laid down at the fall of state socialism. Apart from a short period (2005–09), children were allowed to apply to primary schools outside their districts, and schools were permitted to admit children applying from elsewhere conditional on having admitted local applicants. Schools are administered by more than 3,000 local governments, while the number of actual school districts (municipalities connected by daily commuting) barely exceeds 150, the number of NUTS-4 regions. The fact that there is no responsible actor at the level of school districts proper makes efficient action against 'segregation' difficult (Varga 2009). The practice of routing disadvantaged children to particular schools and classes affects the Roma minority disproportionately. (The share of Roma among the children of low-educated parents amounts to 37 percent, according to Kertesi and Kézdi 2011.) Havas and Liskó (2006) estimate that while there was a twofold increase in the share of Roma children in primary schools between 1980 and 2003, the number of 100 per cent Roma classes grew by a factor of eight. Furthermore, they found the share of Roma children to be 30 per cent in normal classes, 15 per cent in special classes for high achievers and 70 per cent in special classes for low achievers.

The socialist governments in office between 2002 and 2010 made some efforts at reducing 'segregation' by setting municipality-level upper limits to the between-school variance in the share of disadvantaged pupils. They supported several programmes of 'integrated' education and allocated more resources to schools dealing with disadvantaged children. In 2005–09, they prohibited formal entrance exams at primary schools and prescribed that priority should be given to children from a school's own district, in the first place, and socially disadvantaged children from other districts, in the second. Other applicants could be admitted on the basis of a random draw. They also made efforts at narrowing the quality gap between vocational secondary schools and apprentice-based vocational training by putting more emphasis on the development of basic competencies and increasing the duration of training in the latter. (See Kézdi et al. 2009 and Liskó 2009 on the deficiencies of Hungarian vocational training.) All of these regulations and programmes have been withdrawn by the Fidesz government.

The education system's deficiencies are further aggravated – and partly explained – by the patterns of teacher selection and teacher training. Varga (2007) demonstrates that the screening process for teachers is characterized by negative selection at every stage. Teaching majors are chosen by worse-than-average students as measured by their secondary school performance. Those who enter a teaching career are recruited disproportionately from training institutions and educational tracks of worse than average quality and the graduates from such colleges are also more likely to remain teachers in the long run. Teacher training is provided in 33 colleges and universities (offering 130 different majors) run without any kind of external outcome assessment (Kárpáti 2009).[21] As much as 80 per cent of the professors in the teacher training system as analysed in Tóth (2008) have no publications at all, less than 2 per cent have 10 or more publications and 90 per cent have zero citations, which provides indirect evidence of the quality of many of these institutions.

4.2.2 Responses

The Fidesz-led government that came to power in 2010 launched a new act on public education at the end of 2011.[22] The leading theme in the reform is centralization – of school finance, school governance and the curriculum. Schools will be owned and financed by central government. Those run by foundations have to reach agreement with the ministry on both their curriculums and possible financial support. The fate of schools run by churches – outside a list of 14 'certified churches' (as approved in a new Act on Church Affairs) – is uncertain, while approved church schools will be financed like the public ones. The act fails to define the principles of school finance, which was previously based on pupil quotas (in most cases supplemented by local governments).[23] Headteachers will be appointed by the government, and their discretion over the curriculum and employment matters will be limited.

A new National Curriculum will be developed in the coming years and it has been announced that schools will be allowed a maximum of 10 per cent 'deviation' from its detailed guidelines in terms of the content and sequencing of tuition (there is no operational definition of how such 'deviation' will be determined or quantified). The plan to centralize the issue of textbooks, and a radical reduction in their variety, was recently cancelled but without publicly revising the idea itself. Teachers' wages will be set centrally, as will working time. On top of a minimum of 22 hours per week to be spent in the classroom (and a maximum of four further hours of overtime) teachers have to stay in the school building for a further six to 10 hours. The schedule is to be set centrally but the content of activity will be determined by headteachers.

Teacher training is returning to the pre-Bologna system, that is, continuous five-year training for secondary school teachers (except for vocational training school teachers, who train for only four years) and four-year training for primary school teachers. Already in 2012, the state-funded quotas in teacher training were set by the government for each field of study within each college/university. The principles of determining the quotas across teacher training institutions have not been published.

The issue of dealing with disadvantaged and/or poor-performing pupils is also addressed in the reforms. The underlying idea is easy to identify on the basis of press releases by the decision-makers and their actual resolutions: catching-up is best accomplished by separate tracks for high and low achievers rather than by 'integrated' education. The plan to launch special classes for primary school entrants in need of further development before joining a 'normal' class was finally dropped, but a programme for post-graduate courses to assist low performers (so that they can continue their studies or enter the labour market) was maintained (the so-called Híd [bridge] Programme). The act puts in perspective the advent of 100 per cent Roma schools. Within schools, the reform returns to the practice of separating poor performers by compelling them to repeat grades, which was previously abolished for the first to fourth grades.

Separation based on performance and, in effect, social background will be further enhanced by a major restriction of places in secondary schools in favour of vocational training. The share of uncertified vocational schools will increase from 23 to 35 per cent at the secondary level. The duration of training will be shortened to three years (wherever it previously lasted for four years), and significantly less time (a maximum of 30 per cent) will be devoted to general education and the development of basic competences. To make this reform compatible with regulations on school leaving age, the age floor for compulsory school attendance was decreased from 18 to 16 years. The curriculum will be geared towards the development of practical skills from age 15 and will not prepare the students for the Matura examination required for further studies.

One of the few objectives the reform seeks to achieve by means of incentives rather than prescriptions and prohibition is improving teacher selection by way of offering a 'teaching career model', which sets age–wage profiles for five categories of teachers and conditions for moving from one category to the other.[24] Graduates are required to spend one year teaching as residents and pass an entry exam to become a teacher. Older teachers may apply for the positions of 'master teacher' and 'teacher-researcher'.

The transformation of public education is undoubtedly a 'structural reform', at least as fundamental as the shift away from the highly centralized and curriculum-oriented state socialist education system more than 20 years ago. Unsurprisingly, almost every element of the reform has been criticized by teacher organizations, academics and a sizeable part of the general public.

4.2.3 Policy debates

First, criticisms have been directed towards the recentralization of the school system, the restrictions imposed on schools' choice of their curriculum and the allocation of resources without clear rules. Further components, such as choosing between compulsory Bible classes and 'ethics' classes, which incidentally forces parents and children to reveal their cultural and political preferences, are also under attack.

Second, many experts warn of the risks of shortening the duration of public education in general, especially for disadvantaged children. As a result of this part of the plan, the average completed school years of the younger generation can be expected to fall and the share of students passing the Matura, making them eligible for higher education, will decrease substantially. Observers familiar with international comparative data note that the share of 26–35 year olds (out of school) with a college or university diploma is still only 25.5 per cent in Hungary (LFS data, 2011Q1), well below the Lisbon target of 40 per cent.

Third, there is considerable criticism of the fact that the vast majority of vocational school students and graduates lack the basic skills required at work, many of them are in unskilled jobs and the wage returns to those educated at this type of school are minimal. The government argues that Hungary needs a 'German-type dual training system' but any formal similarity between the present and planned Hungarian education and training regime and those of Germany and several other Northern European countries is misleading. Denmark, for instance, operates a three-year dual system of apprentice-based vocational training (Cort 2002) but it develops the basic competences of the students much more efficiently than Hungarian training schools. A comparison of data from the International Adult Literacy Survey (IALS) suggests that Danish vocational school graduates have more years in school, perform better in skills tests and significantly fewer have severe problems in reading, writing and arithmetic.

As many as 65 per cent of them speak English in contrast to only 0.8 per cent of Hungarians. Danish former apprentices have much higher employment rates and relative wages, they are twice as likely as Hungarians to be upwardly mobile, and perform a much wider variety of tasks involving literacy at work. They are also three times as likely as Hungarians to participate in retraining and to change jobs (Köllő 2011). It is fairly unlikely, the critics say, that the proposed reforms – such as the shortening of training and the radical cut in hours devoted to the development of basic competencies – will move Hungary in the direction of Denmark.

Last but not least, the reform has been criticized for a lack of integration efforts. Criticisms refer to a significant improvement in PISA test performance in 2009, especially at the bottom of the performance ranking, suggesting that the move towards a less 'segregated' school system was not entirely mistaken, despite its many failures (compare OECD 2007 and OECD 2010a). The decrease of the school leaving age from 18 to 16 years and the setting up of a separate track for drop-outs (Híd Programme), which provides no qualifications whatsoever, are unlikely to result in a higher employment rate for the unskilled. Instead, the argument goes, schools may use this framework to legally get rid of 'over-age' pupils, who then predictably become unemployed, as do the vast majority of the unskilled adults in the country.

5. POLICY ISSUES

The overall effects of the crisis, the challenges in health care and the reforms in education pose a series of questions addressed in the public debates, at least in the form of parallel monologues. In this section we touch upon two general issues arising from what was described in previous sections: the potential problems resulting from a wide gap between private and public sector wages and the way in which decisions are made in contemporary Hungary.

5.1 Low Pay in the Public Sector

Public sector wages have fallen significantly since 2006 and lag substantially behind private sector earnings. Furthermore, the linear wage grids for skilled public employees imply that their relative age–earnings profile is U-shaped. The reason is that the actual experience–wage profiles of skilled private sector workers are strongly non-linear: their wages grow rapidly in the first 20 years of service and flatten out later. Currently, young and old public sector workers with a college/university background earn about 20–25 per cent less than their counterparts in the private sector, but 35–45-year-olds make less than half of what workers of similar age and educational background make in the private sector. The enhanced U-shaped age–wage profile implies that young public sector workers foresee a monotonous decline in their relative earnings in the first 15 years of their career, which decreases the value of choosing a public sector job, barring some very myopic and very far-sighted persons.

The usual argument against these concerns is that skilled workers' scope for leaving the public sector is strongly limited and thus low wages do not necessarily imply shortages and/or a fall in the quality of services. The argument, however, is not particularly strong. First, the skills of teachers, lawyers, economists and engineers are highly convertible and the outside options of medical workers have also improved substantially in the past few years.[25] Second, low expected pay reduces the number of college applicants in the respective fields of study. Third, low wages constrain the public sector in hiring high-quality workers from the private sector.

Preliminary results from ongoing research suggest that higher wages in the public sector improved the quality of inflows from the private sector. Figure 8.7 measures quality in terms of the regression-adjusted wages of private sector employees who left for a public sector job in the following year. The idea is based on Borjas (2002). In an administrative dataset comprising 50 per cent of the labour force in 1997–2008 the annual log wages of private sector workers were regressed on days worked, a dummy for 365 days in the same job, gender, age, a proxy of educational attainment and a dummy for those who left the private sector for a public sector job in year $t + 1$.

Figure 8.7 suggests that in 2002–05, when the public sector paid high wages, it could attract better workers, who were paid a positive residual wage in their private sector jobs. In other years (except in the election year of 1998) the private sector hired workers with negative residual wages.[26] While further research is required to support this claim, the results warn that pushing the relative wages of public sector workers deep below the private sector mean is likely to have a negative impact on quality.

The U-shape of the wage path results from a technical error (the neglect of how private sector wages grow with tenure), but it is still difficult to repair. The earnings path is relatively easy to correct in good times by means of higher pay rises for younger workers and lower for older workers. In bad times, a rise in the relative wages of 30–40-year-olds can be financed only from savings on the salaries of the oldest and youngest workers. A crisis is clearly not the ideal time to start such a reform.[27]

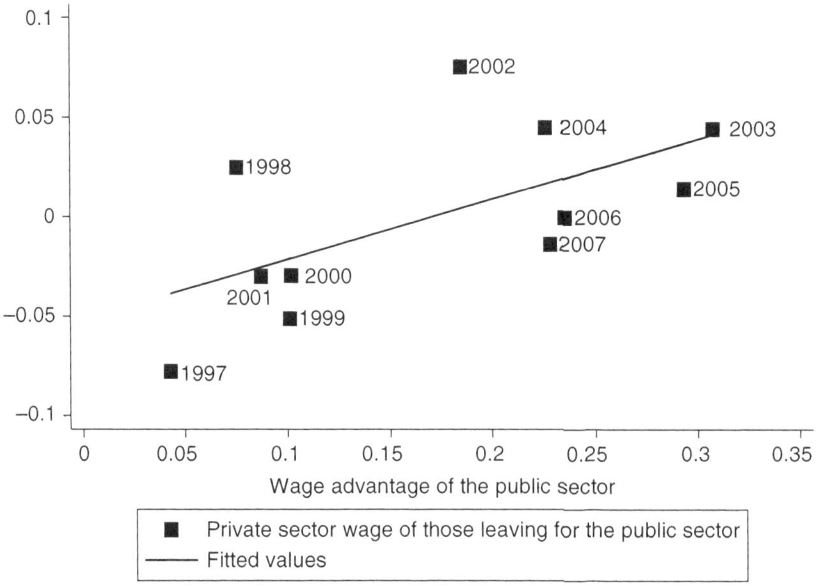

Note: 1998 and 2002 were election years bringing about changes in the governing party.

Source: Data from the National Pension Insurance Directorate (ONYF), authors' calculation.

Figure 8.7 Relative wages of private sector workers leaving for the public sector versus the public–private wage gap, Hungary

5.2 Social Dialogue and Conflicts

Fidesz's landslide victory in the 2010 elections (54 per cent of the votes) gave it a two-thirds majority in the parliament. In the wake of this, Prime Minister Viktor Orbán has often expressed the view that a government with such a super-majority evidently represents both employers and employees, making the existing bodies of social dialogue unnecessary.[28]

The most important social dialogue body, the Council for Interest Reconciliation (Érdekegyeztető Tanács, ÉT) was dissolved in May 2001, after almost 20 years, and replaced by the National Economic and Social Council (NGTT), a consultative body comprising representatives of chambers, unions, civil organizations, government-approved churches and delegates of the Academy of Sciences, the Rectors' Conference and the Association of Hungarian Economists. The chambers and unions represented in ÉT bargained about the minimum wage, as well as the recommended benchmarks for average wage increases in the private sector. The

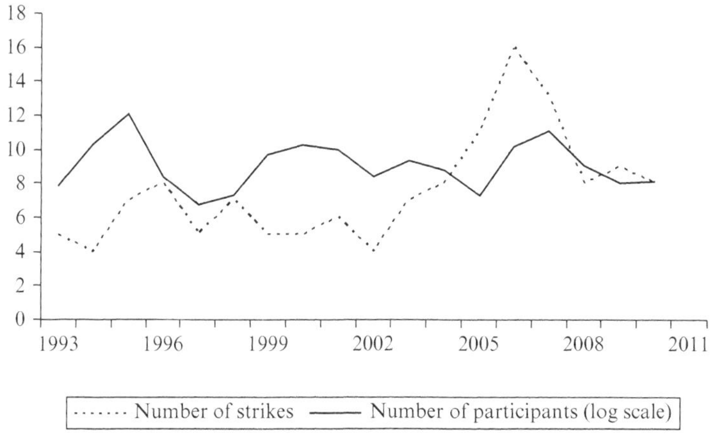

Note: The log scale compresses the range of fluctuations in strike participants. When reading the figure, 8 is the logarithm of 2,981, 11 is the logarithm of 59,874 and 12 is the logarithm of 162,755.

Source: Fazckas and Kézdi (2012).

Figure 8.8 Strikes in Hungary, 1993–2010

government was legally obliged to consider the outcome of their discussions. By contrast, the NGTT is intended to discuss a variety of yet undefined issues and the government is not obliged to observe the outcomes or consult about them. The NGTT has 32 members, in contrast to the ÉT's 16, making a focused debate and compromise more difficult to achieve.

Workers' representation has been weakened in other ways. Regulations imposing the compulsory establishment of work councils (Üzemi Tanács) were dropped from the new Labour Code in December 2011. The right to strike was curtailed by requiring prior agreement between employers and employees on 'adequate services'.

Unlike in Greece, Italy, Spain, Portugal and Romania, the severe wage cuts and the threat of dismissals have not yet provoked massive protests in Hungary. As shown in Figure 8.8, the number of strikes fell from 16 in 2006 to eight in 2008–10 and the number of participants decreased from an average of 32,000 in 2006–08 to 3,200 in 2009–10.[29] Demonstrations are part of the Budapest landscape but most of them concern political rather than economic issues. Noteworthy exceptions are a series of demonstrations held by the police, fire service personnel and professional soldiers protesting against reform of their early retirement schemes (2011) and a Fidesz-organized march against Hungary's alleged 'colonization' by the EU and the IMF in January 2012.

6. CONCLUSIONS

The short-run implications of the austerity measures for public sector workers are relatively easy to summarize: most have been able to retain their jobs until recently but they have lost 10 to 35 per cent of their earnings in real terms. Low-skilled, low-wage workers were hit hardest (as shown in Figure 8.2 and Table 8.6) but their high-skilled counterparts started from relatively lower wage levels compared to similar employees in the private sector (Figures 8.2, 8.6 and 8.7).

Reactions to these wage losses have been moderate, so far, given the scarcity of private sector job openings for the majority of public sector workers. Doctors are an important exception and it seems that their 'revolts' in several new EU countries mark the end of a long period of underpayment in health care. The near future will certainly bring massive layoffs in public administration and higher education but public education might also be affected. Downsizing is likely to affect the skilled labour force and will further adversely affect the position of women.

The long-term implications of the ongoing and planned reforms are more difficult to predict, given the patterns of policymaking in contemporary Hungary. The formal mandate of the government is strong, policymaking is strongly centralized and therefore unpredictable. (See Fukuyama 2010a and 2012b; Kornai 2012; on the nature of the contemporary Hungarian political system.) How the government's entitlements will be used in the future is an open question and so is the readiness of the public to accept unnegotiated decisions.

Further uncertainties arise from the fact that some important proposals are in preparation (for example, in health care and public administration), while others are simply unprecedented in contemporary Europe. It would be hard to find research results, for example, on how a rapid shift to extreme centralization affects employment in public and higher education, or how shortening the duration of education and lowering the school leaving age are felt in the classroom and elsewhere.

NOTES

1. See: http://jogiq.com/orszaggyules_elfogadott_torvenyek_2011/.
2. See detailed descriptions in www.kozszolga.hu. The amounts will be cut in 2012 according to government plans.
3. The tax system historically has encouraged firms to conclude business contracts (as opposed to employment contracts) for services provided by professionals employed elsewhere and for tasks beyond their employees' standard workplace duties. However, the scope for arbitrage was substantially narrowed in the past few years.

4. See Kertesi and Köllő (2003) on the motives and aftermath of this decision.
5. The CSO's establishment-base data are uninformative because of changes in the industrial classification. Therefore we use LFS data, which are less reliable and fail to distinguish civil servants and public employees from employees under the Labour Code. We use first quarter data because the last wave available for us is from 2011Q1.
6. See, for instance: http://www.bloomberg.com/news/2010-10-30/hungary-s-2011-budget-calls-for-government-job-cuts-pension-fund-income.html.
7. See: eduline.hu/erettsegi_felveteli/2012/1/20/Itt_vannak_a_2012es_keretszamok_egyetemekre_7B0URX.
8. See: www.origo.hu/itthon/20111230-uj-keretszamok-es-osztondij-a-felsooktatasban.html and other media reports on 30 December 2011.
9. See: www.origo.hu/itthon/20110504-a-felsooktatas-atalakitasarol-szolo-kormanyzati-terv.html.
10. A relatively high incidence of low pay for skilled employees in the private sector is explained mainly by wage underreporting, as shown in Elek et al. (2012)
11. The number of physicians making preparations for working abroad is lower than the number of those considering emigration but exceeds the number of those who will actually leave the country.
12. See: www.nepszava.hu/articles/article.php?id=501126 (accessed 26 January 2012).
13. See: mandiner.hu/cikk/20111229_rezidensszovetseg_megfontolando_ajanlatot_kapott_az_orvostarsadalom An exchange rate of 300 HUF/€ is applied.
14. See: portal.ksh.hu/pls/ksh/docs/hun/xstadat/xstadat_evkozi/e_qli015c.html.
15. See: www.parameter.sk/rovat/belfold/2011/11/10/1900-euroval-novelne-az-orvosok-atlagberet-szakszervezet.
16. See: index.hu/belfold/2011/11/25/haromhavi_potlek_lesz_az_egeszsegugyben/.
17. See: www.mellekhatas.hu/index.php?p=news&index.php?p=news&act=show&cid=10632; www.szakszervezetek.hu/index.php/hirek/5994-beremelest-koevetelnek-az-egeszseguegyi-dolgozok; www.medicalonline.hu/eu_politika/cikk/konfliktusok_forrasa_lehet_a_bertargyalas.
18. See: www.wageindicator.org/main/collective-bargaining/2009/czech-republic-doctors-win-substantial-pay-increase-march-6-201; mindennapi.hu/cikk/hirsor/nem-sokaig-maradtak-tavol-a-szlovak-orvosok/2011-12-03/10320.
19. See: www.vg.hu/vallalatok/egeszsegugy/no-az-orvos-es-apolohiany-323968.
20. Authors' calculation using the Wage Surveys of 2008 and 2010.
21. Furthermore, despite the fact that Hungary has an all-encompassing, regular survey of student competencies, the data are not used for the evaluation of teachers and their colleges/universities.
22. The Act (Köznevelési Törvény) was adopted in December 2011.
23. To be more precise, local governments received quotas depending on the number of school-aged children, and were free to spend the state support for whatever purpose. However, most of them had to supplement the state quotas in order to keep their schools running.
24. A general pay rise of 50–70 per cent, without staff and working-time cuts, has also been promised verbally, but without saying where the resources would come from.
25. More than 60 per cent of the college and university graduates with a teacher's diploma work in professions other than teaching, as shown in Varga (2005).
26. Note that the level and (partly) the dynamics of the public/private wage gap is different from that presented in Figure 8.2, for at least two reasons: first, the data used here relate to annual earnings affected by days in work during the year; second, the data comprise micro-firm employees and persons employed by sole proprietors.
27. Indeed, as demonstrated in Varga (2011), the 'career model' proposed by the Fidesz government for teachers will not change the shape of their age–wage profile and will not yield higher life-cycle incomes except for a predictably small number of 'master teachers' and 'teacher-researchers'. With the survival of the U-shaped wage profile it

is unlikely that the profession will be chosen by better students. The well-performing school systems usually do not spend more on teacher salaries than Hungary but several of them (including Finland, the Netherlands, Australia and New Zealand) substantially reduced the gap between starting and maximum salaries (Barber and Mourshed 2007).

28. See http://index.hu/gazdasag/magyar/2011/06/15/oet_hatter/?rnd=37, for instance.
29. This, in fact, is consistent with the classic theory of strikes which suggests that strike activity should be more intense in upswings than during downturns (Hicks 1966: 136–57).

REFERENCES

Balázs, P. (2012), 'The number of doctors and the effect of physicians' migration on Hungary' (in Hungarian), *Orvosi Hetilap*, **153** (7), 250–56.

Barber, M. and M. Mourshed (2007), *How the World's Best Performing School Systems Come Out on Top*, New York: McKinsey & Company.

Bognár, L., R. Gál and J. Kornai (1999), *Gratuities in Hungarian Health Services* (in Hungarian), Budapest: TÁRKI.

Borjas, G.J. (2002), 'The wage structure and the sorting of workers into the public sector', NBER Working Paper 9313, National Bureau of Economic Research.

Budapest Institute (2011), 'Targeting, take-up and effect on long-term unemployment of expanding public works programmes' (in Hungarian), Budapest Institute for Public Policy and Hétfa Research Institute, March.

Burak, L.J. and T. Vian (2007), 'Examining and predicting under-the-table payments for health care in Albania: an application of the theory of planned behavior', *Journal of Applied Social Psychology*, **37**, 1060–76.

Chawla, M., P. Berman and D. Kawiorska (1998), 'Financing health services in Poland: new evidence on private expenditures', *Health Economics*, **7** (4) (June), 337–46.

Cort, P. (2002), 'Vocational education and training in Denmark', CEDEFOP Panorama Series, Office for Official Publications of the European Communities, Luxembourg. Available at: http://www.cedefop.europa.eu/EN/Files/5130_en.pdf (accessed 11 November 2012).

Csapó, B., G. Molnár and L. Kinyó (2009), 'A magyar oktatási rendszer szelektivitása a nemzetközi vizsgálatok tükrében' (Analysis of the selectiveness of the Hungarian education system in an international context), *Iskolakultúra*, **4**, 3–13.

Delcheva E., D. Balabanova and M. McKee (1997), 'Under-the-counter payments for health care: evidence from Bulgaria', *Health Policy*, **42**, 89–100.

Elek, P., J. Köllő, B. Reizer and P.A. Szabó (2012), 'Detecting wage under-reporting using a double hurdle model', in H. Lehmann and K. Tatsiramos (eds), *Informal Employment in Emerging and Transition Economies*, Research in Labor Economics, Vol. 4, Bingley, UK: Emerald Books, pp 135–66.

Elek, P. and P.A. Szabó (2011), 'Analyzing flows out of the public sector in Hungary', Institute of Economics of the Hungarian Academy of Sciences, Budapest, mimeo.

Fazekas, K. and G. Kézdi (eds) (2012), *The Hungarian Labour Market: Review and Analysis*, Budapest: MTA KTI and OFA.

Fazekas, K., J. Köllő and J. Varga (2009), 'Introduction', in K. Fazekas, J. Köllő and J. Varga (eds), *Green Book for the Renewal of Public Education in Hungary*, Budapest: Ecostat.

Fazekas, K. and J. Koltay (eds) (2005), *The Hungarian Labour Market: Review and Analysis*, Budapest: OFA.

Fukuyama, F. (2012a), 'Do institutions really matter?'. Available at: http://blogs.the-american-interest.com/fukuyama/2012/01/23/do-institutions-really-matter/ (accessed 3 March 2012).

Fukuyama, F. (2012b), 'What's wrong with Hungary?'. Available at: http://blogs.the-american-interest.com/fukuyama/2012/02/06/whats-wrong-with-hungary/ (accessed 3 March 2012).

Havas, G. and I. Liskó (2006), 'Óvodától a szakmáig' (From kindergarten to vocational education), Budapest: Oktatáskutató Intézet – Új Mandátum.

Hicks, J.R. (1966), *The Theory of Wages*, 2nd edn, New York: St. Martin's Press.

Holt, E. (2010), 'Doctors in Eastern Europe prepare to walk out over pay', *The Lancet*, **376** (9737) (24 July), 221–2.

Jenkins, S.P, J. Micklewright and S.V. Schnepf (2008), 'Social segregation in secondary schools: how does England compare with other countries?', *Oxford Review of Education*, **34** (1), 21–38.

Kárpáti, A. (2009), 'Teacher training and professional development', in K. Fazekas, J. Köllő and J. Varga (eds), *Green Book for the Renewal of Public Education in Hungary*, Budapest: Ecostat, pp 203–26.

Kertesi, G. and G. Kézdi (2010), 'Segregation of primary schools in Hungary. A descriptive study using data from the National Assessment of Basic Competencies of 2006', in K. Fazekas, A. Lovász and Á. Telegdy (eds), *The Hungarian Labour Market 2010*, Budapest: IE HAS, Hungarian Employment Foundation, pp. 519–25.

Kertesi, G. and G. Kézdi (2011), 'The Roma/non-Roma test score gap in Hungary', *American Economic Review*, **101** (3), 519–25 (with online appendix).

Kertesi, G. and J. Köllő (2003), 'Fighting low equilibria by doubling the minimum wage – Hungary's experiment', IZA Discussion Paper No. 970, Bonn.

Kézdi, G., J. Köllő and J. Varga (2009), 'The failures of "uncertified" vocational training', in K. Fazekas and J. Köllő (eds), *The Hungarian Labour Market: Review and Analysis*, Budapest: OFA and IEHAS, pp. 95–143.

Köllő, J. (2011), 'A német rendszerű duális képzésről' (On German-type vocational training). Available at: http://www.szuveren.hu/vendeglap/kollo-janos/a-nemet-rendszeru-dualis-kepzesrol (accessed 14 April 2012).

Kőműves, A. (2008), 'Hungary's doctor shortage. Low pay at home, plus poor prospects and conditions, spur hundreds of physicians each year to seek work elsewhere in the EU'. Available at: http://www.businessweek.com/globalbiz/content/dec2008/gb20081217_057023.htm/ (accessed 4 February 2012).

Kornai, J. (2012), 'Centralization and the capitalist market economy', English translation of 'Központosítás és kapitalista piacgazdaság', *Népszabadság Online*, 30 January. Available at: http://themonkeycage.org/wp content/uploads/2012/02/Kornai_2012_I_30.pdf (accessed 3 March 2012).

KSH (2012), *Gyorstájékoztató*, No. 12, 20 January, Központi Statisztikai Hivatal, Budapest.

Liaropoulos, L. D. Kaitelidou, M. Theodorou and T. Katostaras (2008), 'Informal payments in public hospitals in Greece', *Health Policy*, **87**, 72–81.

Liskó, I. (2009), 'Szakképzés és lemorzsolódás' (Vocational training and drop-

outs), in K. Fazekas, J. Köllő and J. Varga (eds), *Green Book for the Renewal of Public Education in Hungary*, Budapest: Ecostat, pp. 105–30.
OECD (2007), *PISA 2006 Science Competencies for Tomorrow's World*, Paris: OECD.
OECD (2010a), *PISA 2009 Results: Overcoming Social Background: Equity in Learning Opportunities and Outcomes* (Volume II), Paris: OECD.
OECD (2010b), *Education at a Glance*, Paris: OECD.
OECD (2011), *Government at a Glance*, Paris: OECD.
Sabirianova-Peter, K. and T. Zelenska (2011), 'The price of the Hippocratic oath: determinants of bribery in Russian health care', paper presented at the IZA/World Bank Workshop Institutions and Informal Employment in Emerging and Transition Economies, IZA, Bonn, 9–11 June.
Szende, A. and A.J. Culyer (2006), 'The inequity of informal payments for health care: the case of Hungary', *Health Policy*, **75**, 262–71.
Telegdy, Á. (2011), 'Public–private wage spillovers' (in Hungarian), paper presented at the Annual Meeting of the Labor Economics Commission of the Hungarian Academy of Sciences, Szirák, 5 November.
Tóth, I.J. (2008), *A magyar neveléstudomány tudományos aktivitásának felmérése empirikus eszközökkel. Kutatási záró tanulmány* (An empirical investigation into Hungarian research activities in education science. Project report), manuscript, Wargo Közgazdasági Elemző- és Piackutató Intézet, Budapest. Available at: http://www.wargo.hu/kutatasok/letoltes/pedagogia_2008_tanulmany_080517.pdf (accessed 4 February 2012).
Varga, J. (2005), 'A pegagógus szakokra jelentkezők és a pedagóguspályán elhelyezkedők jellemzői' (The characteristics of the applicants to teacher training and the graduates working as teachers), in Z. Hermann (ed.), *Hatékonysági problémák a közoktatásban* (The problems of efficiency in public education), Budapest: Országos Közoktatási Intézet, pp. 117–42.
Varga, J. (2007), 'Kiből lesz ma tanár: a tanári pálya választásának empirikus elemzése' (Who are becoming teachers? An empirical analysis of choosing teaching as a profession), *Közgazdasági Szemle* (July–August), 609–27.
Varga, J. (2009), 'Institutional structure and funding in education', in K. Fazekas, J. Köllő and J. Varga (eds), *Green Book for the Renewal of Public Education in Hungary*, Budapest: Ecostat, pp. 245–68.
Varga, J. (2011), 'Pedagógus életpálya' (Teachers' careers), Szakmai Műhelysorozat, MTA Közoktatási Elnöki Bizottsága – TÁRKI-TUDOK, 9 February. Available at: http://www.tarki-tudok.hu/files/vargajulia_feb9.pdf (accessed 9 July 2012).

9. Cautious adjustment in a context of economic collapse: The public sector in the Irish crises

Philip O'Connell

1. INTRODUCTION

The Irish economy moved into a long and deep recession in the first half of 2008. This chapter examines the nature of that crisis, outlines the austerity programme that was adopted in response to the crisis and traces the impact of austerity on the public sector in Ireland. It draws on two case studies – restructuring of services to the unemployed and cutbacks in the education system – to illustrate different aspects of the response to crisis.

1.1 The Irish Public Sector

The broad public sector in Ireland consists of a core civil service and a wider public service. The civil service comprises the permanent staff of 15 government departments and certain specialized agencies or offices. The wider public service generally consists of specialized staff, such as teachers, doctors, the police and the armed forces. The main subsectors within the broader public service include: health, education, commercial and non-commercial state-sponsored bodies, local authorities and regional bodies, Garda Síochána (police) and defence forces.

In 2008, total public expenditure was €68.7 billion, accounting for 44 per cent of gross national product (GNP). By 2011, following a series of crises in the state and economy, virtually the same level of public expenditure accounted for almost 55 per cent of GNP (Table 9.1).

Over the 2008–11 period total employment in the public service fell from 427,300 to 392,300, although its share of total employment, which had contracted sharply in the interim, had increased from 25 to almost 26 per cent.

Table 9.1 Expenditure and employment in the public sector, Ireland, 2008 and 2011

	2008	2011
Public expenditure (€m)	68,721	68,704
Public expenditure (% of GNP)	44.4	54.6
Public employment (1,000)	427.3	392.3
Public employment (% of total)	24.9	25.8

2. FIVE CRISES

There were five key elements to the crisis that erupted in the Irish state and economy, beginning in 2008: the bursting of the property bubble; the banking collapse; the contraction in economic activity; the fiscal crisis of the state; and mass unemployment.

2.1 Property Crash

Following a long and sustained inflation in property prices over the course of the previous decade, the Irish property bubble burst. Figure 9.1 shows private residential house prices increasing steadily by over four times from 1996 through 2007, and then falling rapidly by 40 per cent over the next three years.

2.2 Banking Collapse

The property bubble had been facilitated by lax lending practices overseen by 'light-touch' regulation that followed an international pattern of neo-liberal-inspired withdrawal of the state from banking supervision. Irish banks were exposed not only to the domestic residential and property bubbles, but also shifts in the international economy because the Irish banks, and Anglo Irish Bank in particular, had borrowed abroad profligately to speculate in both domestic and international markets. In the aftermath of the Lehman Brothers collapse, two Irish banks have failed (Anglo Irish Bank and Irish National). Another, Allied Irish Bank, has been fully taken over by the state and the only other major player, Bank of Ireland, required substantial recapitalization by the state.

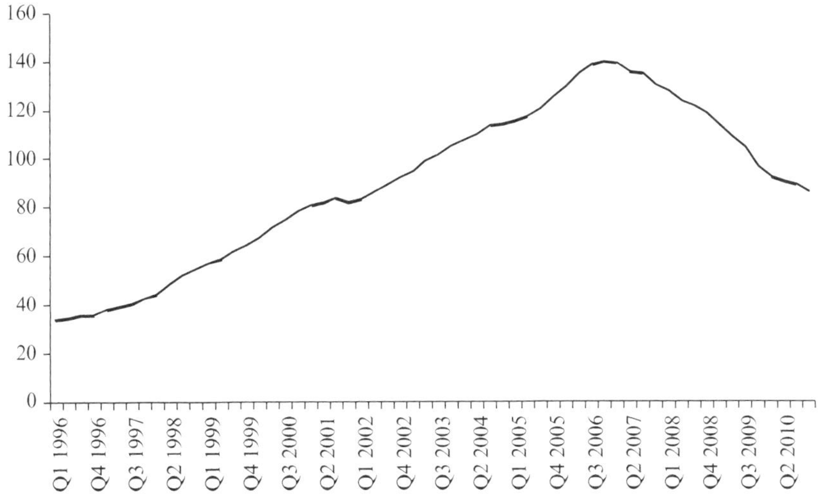

Figure 9.1 Index of house prices, Ireland, 1996–2010

2.3 Economic Contraction

The Irish economy moved into recession in the first half of 2008, leading to a dramatic deterioration in labour market conditions. GNP contracted by 3.5 per cent in 2008 and by almost 10 per cent in 2009. The economy grew by just 0.3 per cent in 2010 (Duffy et al. 2011). There was still contraction in 2011 and the most optimistic accounts point to extremely sluggish growth in 2012.

2.4 Mass Unemployment

As the Irish economy moved into recession in the first half of 2008, the slowdown was initially apparent in the construction sector, which had become bloated over the previous five years: in 2007 it accounted for over 20 per cent of male workers. The recession led to a dramatic and very rapid deterioration in labour market conditions. Employment losses have been concentrated in construction and related sectors, but are nevertheless widespread across the private sector.

Total employment fell by almost 174,000 (8.2 per cent) in the 12 months between the second quarter of 2008 and the second quarter of 2009, and by another 130,000 in the following two years. This represented a cumulative decline in employment of about 14 per cent over the three years.

Unemployment increased from less than 5 per cent at the beginning

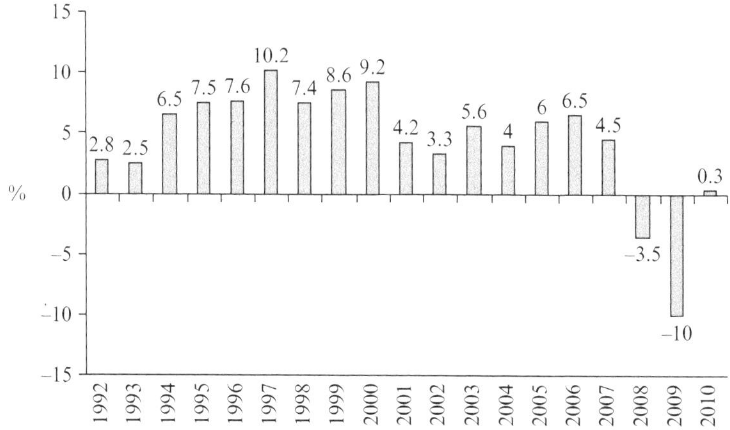

Figure 9.2 GNP growth rate, Ireland, 1992–2010

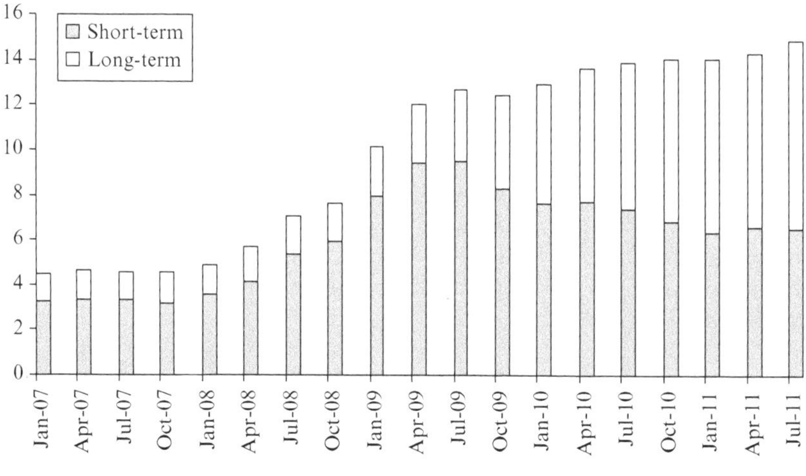

Source: Author's construction from the Quarterly National Household Survey, CSO.

Figure 9.3 Long- and short-term unemployment, Ireland, 2007–2011 (%)

of 2008 to 14.3 per cent in the second quarter of 2011. Long-term unemployment increased very rapidly as the recession took hold and persisted (Figure 9.3). By 2011, over half of those unemployed have been in that state for over one year. In response to the labour market decline emigration has increased, immigration declined, and Ireland returned to net emigration in 2009 for the first time since the mid-1990s.

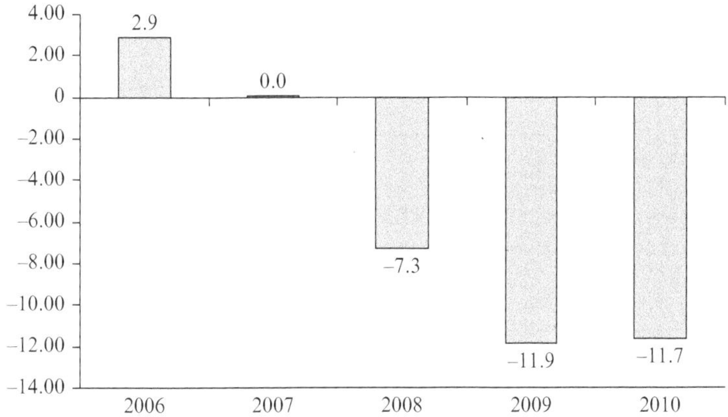

Figure 9.4 Fiscal balance (excluding banks), Ireland, 2006–2010

2.5 Fiscal Crisis of the State

There are two distinct factors underlying the fiscal crisis of the Irish state: financing day-to-day activities and the cost of the bank crisis. First, lower economic activity and employment, combined with overreliance on property-related taxes during the boom, which were used to fund rapid increases in expenditure, have led to a dramatic shortfall of government revenue over expenditure. Figure 9.4 shows that the general government balance, excluding the cost of recapitalizing the banks, and thus relating to financing of day-to-day current and capital expenditures, fell to –7.3 per cent of GDP in 2008, and to just under 12 per cent in both 2009 and 2010.

In September 2008, in the face of growing pressure on Anglo Irish Bank, then the most obvious casualty of the domestic and international downturns, the government took the momentous step of guaranteeing almost all Irish bank liabilities and recapitalizing the banks with public funds. It was a calamitous decision that reflected the close ties between bankers, property developers and the ruling Fianna Fail party and exposed the incompetence and lack of technical expertise of civil servants and financial regulators. Table 9.2 shows the public finances, observed in 2008 and 2009, and forecast for 2010 and 2011, and reveals the impact of the private banking collapse on the public finances.

The general government balance fell to –14.3 per cent of GDP in 2009 and –32 per cent in 2010, a truly dramatic figure. Of course, about two-thirds of this is a one-off extraordinary item related to the banking bailout. The cost of the bank bailout added 2.5 per cent to the government deficit in 2009, over 20 per cent in 2010 and an estimated 5 per cent in 2011.

Table 9.2 Public finances, Ireland, 2009 and 2010 and forecast 2011, 2012

	2009	2010	2011*	2012*
Exchequer balance (€bn)	–24.6	–18.7	–17.3	–14.5
General government balance (€bn)	–23.0	–49.9	–22.4	–11.4
General government balance (% of GDP)	–14.3	–32.0	–14.2	–7.1
Excluding one-off bank bailout monies (% of GDP)	–11.8	–11.5	–9.3	–7.1
General government debt (% of GDP)	65.2	94.9	104.0	109.0

Note: * Forecast.

Source: Duffy et al. (2011).

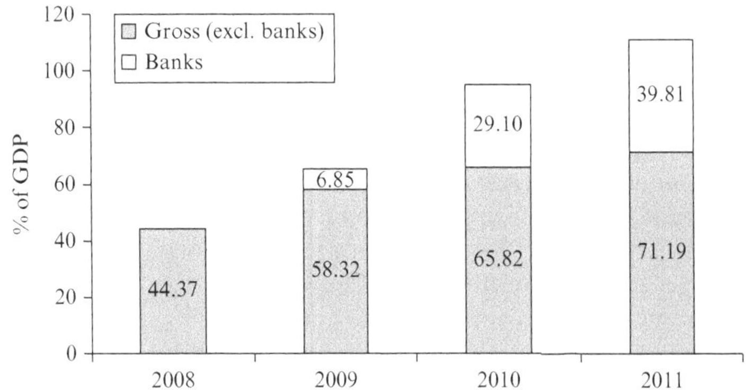

Figure 9.5 Government debt, Ireland, 2008–2011

Figure 9.5 tracks the impact of the Irish bank bailout on government debt. In 2008, at the onset of the recession, government debt stood at a modest 44 per cent of GDP. By 2010, total government debt had risen to 95 per cent of GDP, and almost 30 per cent related to the bank bailout. By 2011, government debt was over 110 per cent of GDP: almost 40 per cent relates to bank debt.

In response to the severe fiscal crisis, the government introduced a series of expenditure cuts as well as tax increases and a levy on public sector incomes. In November 2010 with mounting pressure from international financial markets, the Irish state applied for financial assistance from the IMF, the EU and the ECB (the Troika). Financial pledges of €85 billion, including €17.5 billion of Irish state resources (mainly from the public

Table 9.3 The €30 billion austerity package, Ireland, 2008–2014

	2008–10	2011	2012	2013	2014	2011–14
Revenue (€bn)	5.6	1.4	1.5	1.1	1.1	5.1
Expenditure (€bn)	9.2	3.9	2.1	2.0	2.0	10.0
Total (€bn)	14.7	5.3	3.6	3.1	3.1	15.1
% of 2010 GDP	10	3	2	2	2	10

pension reserve fund) were made to cover the combined bank liabilities (now taken into sovereign debt), the cost of bank recapitalizations and the ongoing fiscal deficit. Further severe austerity measures and far-reaching economic reforms are being implemented over the next four years, driven by the requirements of the Troika.

2.6 Austerity

In the face of the fiscal crisis of the state, the Irish government embarked on a severe austerity programme to restore balance to the public finances with the aim of reducing the headline fiscal balance from over 12 per cent of GDP in 2008 to less than 3 per cent in 2015. Table 9.3 provides a summary outline of the austerity package: a total adjustment of €30 billion, entailing about €19 billion in expenditure cuts and €11 billion in tax increases (Bergin et al. 2011). The cumulative effects of this austerity package represent 20 per cent of GDP in 2010. In the initial phase of the austerity package, 2008–10, more or less before the arrival of the Troika, adjustments amounting to almost €15 billion or 10 per cent of GDP were achieved. The second half of the austerity programme, of the same order of magnitude, is to be implemented over 2011–15, under the supervision of the Troika.

The measures implemented from late 2008 have entailed a combination of major changes in the tax and welfare systems and cuts in the number and pay of public servants.

2.7 Public Sector Adjustments

Attempts to modernize the Irish Public Service date back to the 1994 Strategic Management Initiative (SMI) which set out a broad agenda for change, primarily in the Civil Service, although it was intended to impact across the entire Public Service. In 1996, a blueprint for reform in the Civil Service was outlined in 'Delivering Better Government'. It set out a vision of a Civil Service as a high performance, open and flexible organization with a mission and culture of quality service to government and to the public, and making the maximum contribution to national social and economic development and to competitiveness (Department of the Taoiseach 1996). Various initiatives were subsequently advanced in human resource management, customer service improvements, financial management systems, regulatory reform and e-government. The OECD Review of the Irish Public Service *Towards an Integrated Public Service* was published in 2008. The OECD noted that Ireland was facing a more complex environment, with increased expectations for effective service delivery. The report concluded that the public sector in Ireland had evolved in an uncoordinated manner without a strategic vision and with poor competence at senior level, limited performance review and accountability.

In the wake of the OECD Review, a task force was established in 2008 which issued its report 'Transforming Public Services – Citizen Centred – Performance Focused' which set out a new agenda for change. Progress on the reform agenda has been slow and achievements limited and, arguably, the reform initiatives have been overtaken by the events and conditions of economic and social crises since 2008. However, the broad thrust of reform – to achieve greater efficiency and effectiveness in the public sector – is a key element of the Public Service Agreement 2010–2014 (known as the Croke Park Agreement referring to the conference venue at Croke Park football stadium) agreed between government and the Irish Congress of Trade Unions June 2010. The Croke Park Agreement represents an agreed agenda for change across the public service and provides a framework within which greater efficiency can be secured in exchange for guarantees on future pay levels and security of employment.

2.8 Public Sector Pay Bill

Reducing the public sector pay bill has been a central element of the austerity package. Table 9.4 shows the development of public pay and pensions from 2001 to 2011. There was strong growth up to 2008, and the pay and pensions bill grew by 84 per cent in nominal terms in 2001–08. Growth was particularly strong in 2002–03, which coincides with a package of public sector wage increases under the 'Benchmarking' process, an innovation of social partnership to facilitate wage gains in the public sector relative to the private sector (Kelly et al. 2009). The pay and pensions bill fell by 1.5 per cent between 2008 and 2009 and by 7.4 per cent over the following 12 months.

Pay and pensions accounted for 8.7 per cent of GDP in 2001 and had climbed to 10.4 per cent by 2008. However, even with cuts in the nominal value of the pay and pensions bill, its share of GDP, then falling, increased to 11.6 per cent in 2009 and stood at 11 per cent in 2011. In nominal terms,

Table 9.4 Exchequer pay and pensions, Ireland, 2001–2011

	€m	% change	% of GDP
2001	10,186	–	8.7
2002	11,489	12.8	8.8
2003	12,773	11.2	9.2
2004	13,746	7.6	9.3
2005	14,973	8.9	9.3
2006	16,218	8.3	9.1
2007	17,600	8.5	9.3
2008	18,753	6.6	10.4
2009	18,478	–1.5	11.6
2010	17,112	–7.4	10.7
2011	17,127	0.1	11.0

Source: Department of Finance, various years, 'Analysis of Exchequer Pay and Pensions Bill'.

the public sector pay and pensions bill fell by €1.6 billion between 2008 and 2011; this can be compared with the overall cut of €13 billion in total public expenditure in those years.

The public sector pay bill is a function of both pay rates and numbers. Both were cut after 2008.

2.9 Numbers

No public servants with permanent contracts have been fired. However, some temporary contracts have not been renewed. Reductions in the number of public sector workers have been achieved by means of a series of voluntary incentivized redundancy and early retirement packages. From May to September 2009, public service employees aged 50 years and over by 1 September 2009 who had already accrued entitlement to preserved superannuation benefits under a public service scheme, and who had not yet reached normal preserved pension age, could apply for the Incentivized Early Retirement Scheme. The scheme allowed those opting for early retirement to receive their pension entitlements immediately without actuarial reduction – on the basis of service already accrued.

The voluntary redundancy scheme was targeted specifically at management, administrative and support workers in the health service. Implemented in November 2009, it offered the equivalent of five weeks' pay per year of service plus a lump sum. For example, a middle-rank administrator on a salary of €50,000 per annum, and with 25 years of

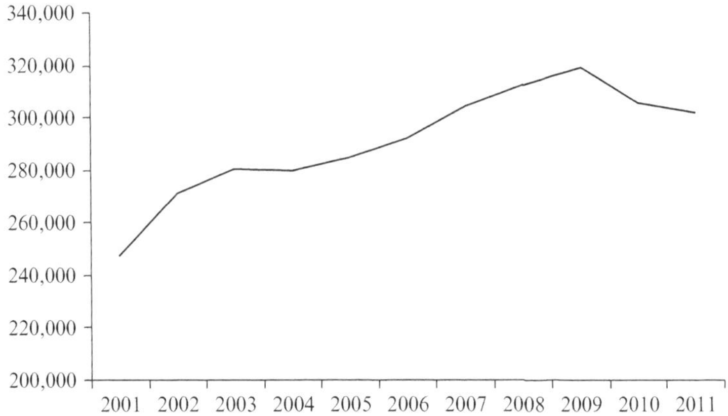

Figure 9.6 *Number employed (whole-time equivalent) in the public sector, Ireland, 2001–2011*

service, would receive a €100,000 gratuity on severance, plus a deferred lump sum of €47,000 on reaching the minimum retirement age for his or her post (typically 60–65 years of age).[1]

Figure 9.6 shows total numbers employed (whole-time equivalent) in the public sector in 2001–11. The total increased from 247,000 in 2001 to a high of 319,000 in 2009, about a 30 per cent rise. It has subsequently fallen by an estimated almost 17,000, a reduction of about 5 per cent, between 2009 and 2011.

Table 9.5 shows substantial differences in trends over time in public sector employment. Health and education both grew very strongly between 2001

Table 9.5 *Number employed (whole-time equivalent) in the public sector, Ireland, 2001, 2009 and 2011*

	2001	2009	2011	Change 2001–09	Change 2009–11	Change 2009–11
	Number			%	Number	%
Health	81,513	111,770	105,300	37.1	–6,470	–5.8
Education	67,845	94,880	93,300	39.8	–1,580	–1.7
Civil service	34,068	39,129	37,300	14.9	–1,829	–4.7
Security	24,439	26,524	24,250	8.5	–2,274	–8.6
State bodies	10,388	12,354	11,200	18.9	–1,154	–9.3
Local authorities	29,090	34,179	30,750	17.5	–3,429	–10.0
Total public service	247,343	318,836	302,100	28.9	–16,736	–5.2

and 2009; health sector employment then fell by almost 6 per cent, education by less than 2 per cent. However, part of the fall under the 'Health' heading related to the transfer of about 1,000 staff from the Health Services Executive to the Civil Service in the Department of Social Protection. Significant staff cuts also took place in local authorities of 3,400 (10 per cent), and relatively, if not numerically, in non-commercial state bodies (9 per cent). In this respect, the staff cuts fell proportionately most heavily on areas of the public sector more peripheral from the core civil and public service. In relation to state bodies, this followed an explicit rationalization agenda to counteract a perceived growth in such 'quangos' during the boom.

It is difficult to track the gender impact of public sector staff cuts in the absence of accurate data. Table 9.6 shows employment by NACE sectors, by gender. Unfortunately, the principal Irish labour force survey, the Quarterly National Household Survey, does not distinguish explicitly between public and private sectors. We can, however, make some inferences about the general trends by focusing on particular sectors. First, from the peak of the boom in the third quarter of 2007 to the second quarter of 2011, total male employment fell by far more than did female employment, –21 versus –8 per cent. This was mainly because most of the job losses were from the bloated construction sector and to a lesser extent, manufacturing industry, both of which mainly employed men.

In predominantly public sectors, male employment increased by 9,400 in education and health and remained static in public administration and defence. Women's employment in public administration fell by 7,200, but increased by 11,200 in education and by 13,500 in health, a net gain of 27,000 jobs.

2.10 Wages and Pensions

There has been a good deal of controversy over public sector wages in recent years. Public sector pay is of policy interest because it is financed out of taxation of the private sector. An additional issue in the Irish case has been a decline in international competitiveness since about 2002. Public sector wages can affect wages in the private sector through demonstration effects (where private sector workers seek to emulate pay increases in the public sector) or crowding-out effects (where private sector employers compete for labour with the public sector).

In Ireland, it has been argued that public sector pay got out of line with pay in the private sector during the boom. Two factors are believed to have been important. First, national pay agreements negotiated under the social partnership process, which had been in continuous operation since the previous economic crisis in 1987, were implemented almost universally

Table 9.6 Employment by NACE sector and gender, Ireland, 2007–2011

		2007 Q3	2011 Q2	Change	% change
Males					
A	Agriculture, forestry and fishing	100.3	76.7	–23.6	–23.5
B–E	Industry	222.1	164.8	–57.3	–25.8
F	Construction	254.9	98.1	–156.8	–61.5
G	Wholesale and retail trade; repair of motor vehicles and motorcycles	152.6	136.2	–16.4	–10.7
H	Transport and storage	76.3	77.5	1.2	1.6
I	Accommodation and food service activities	57.5	46.4	–11.1	–19.3
J	Information and communication	45.5	52.4	6.9	15.2
K–L	Financial, insurance and real estate activities	43.3	48.6	5.3	12.2
M	Professional, scientific and technical activities	67.0	62.5	–4.5	–6.7
N	Administrative and support service activities	40.8	32.4	–8.4	–20.6
O	Public administration and defence; compulsory social security	51.9	51.9	0.0	0.0
P	Education	35.0	37.6	2.6	7.4
Q	Human health and social work activities	39.2	46.0	6.8	17.3
R–U	Other NACE activities	39.4	38.9	–0.5	–1.3
Total males		*1,225.9*	*970.0*	–255.9	–20.9
Females					
A	Agriculture, forestry and fishing	11.4	9.1	–2.3	–20.2
B–E	Industry	83.5	69.0	–14.5	–17.4
F	Construction	13.3	7.6	–5.7	–42.9
G	Wholesale and retail trade; repair of motor vehicles and motorcycles	154.3	129.4	–24.9	–16.1
H	Transport and storage	15.9	17.2	1.3	8.2
I	Accommodation and food service activities	80.3	60.8	–19.5	–24.3
J	Information and communication	21.0	22.5	1.5	7.1
K–L	Financial, insurance and real estate activities	61.8	55.3	–6.5	–10.5
M	Professional, scientific and technical activities	46.9	39.3	–7.6	–16.2
N	Administrative and support service activities	41.9	33.8	–8.1	–19.3
O	Public administration and defence; compulsory social security	55.5	48.3	–7.2	–13.0

Table 9.6 (continued)

		2007 Q3	2011 Q2	Change	% change
P	Education	97.7	108.9	11.2	11.5
Q	Human health and social work activities	178.4	191.9	13.5	7.6
R–U	Other NACE activities	62.1	58.3	–3.8	–6.1
Total females		*923.9*	*851.3*	–72.6	–7.9
All persons					
A	Agriculture, forestry and fishing	111.7	85.8	–25.9	–23.2
B–E	Industry	305.6	233.7	–71.9	–23.5
F	Construction	268.2	105.7	–162.5	–60.6
G	Wholesale and retail trade; repair of motor vehicles and motorcycles	306.9	265.6	–41.3	–13.5
H	Transport and storage	92.2	94.7	2.5	2.7
I	Accommodation and food service activities	137.8	107.2	–30.6	–22.2
J	Information and communication	66.5	74.9	8.4	12.6
K–L	Financial, insurance and real estate activities	105.1	103.9	–1.2	–1.1
M	Professional, scientific and technical activities	113.9	101.8	–12.1	–10.6
N	Administrative and support service activities	82.7	66.1	–16.6	–20.1
O	Public administration and defence; compulsory social security	107.4	100.2	–7.2	–6.7
P	Education	132.7	146.5	13.8	10.4
Q	Human health and social work activities	217.6	237.9	20.3	9.3
R–U	Other NACE activities	101.6	97.2	–4.4	–4.3
Total persons		*2,149.8*	*1,821.3*	–328.5	–15.3

Source: CSO, various years, Quarterly National Household Survey. See www.cso.ie.

in the public sector, which is heavily unionized, but only patchily in the private sector.[2] Second, the benchmarking process, which was initiated on the assumption that public sector pay had fallen behind that in the private sector, recommended awards ranging between 2 and 27 per cent, and averaging 9 per cent (Public Service Benchmarking Body 2002). Higher-level public servants received similar awards in a separate related award process (Review Body on Higher Remuneration in the Public Sector 2005). The Benchmarking Report produced no evidence to support the assumption that public sector wages had fallen behind, and ignored research demonstrating that public sector workers enjoyed a wage premium before the benchmarking process (Boyle et al. 2004).

Subsequent papers by Kelly et al. (2009) and McGuinness et al. (2010) have shown that the public sector pay gap rose sharply between 2003 and 2006, by about 12 percentage points, to between 22 and 26 per cent, depending on the estimation procedure. The public sector premium was highest for those in the lower income deciles. These public sector premia in Ireland are substantially higher than those found in other countries. This debate on public sector pay formed part of the debate on policy formation in response to the crisis. Given that spending on public sector pay and pensions represents a substantial component of total public expenditure, another element of that debate related to a trade-off between cuts in public sector employment versus pay.

In March 2009 a pay increase scheduled under the then current national wage agreement was cancelled. At the same time, a public sector pension levy was announced. The first €15,000 of earnings were exempt and the levy was then charged as follows: 5 per cent on the next €5,000 of earnings, 10 per cent on earnings between €20,000 and €60,000 and 10.5 per cent on earnings above €60,000.

In December 2009, wage cuts were introduced. Effective 1 January 2010, all public salaries were reduced as follows: 5 per cent on the first €30,000 of salary, 7.5 per cent on the next €40,000 and 10 per cent on the next €55,000. This generated cuts ranging between 5 and just under 8 per cent of salaries up to €125,000. Salaries up to €165,000 were cut by 8 per cent, salaries up to €200,000 by 12 per cent, and salaries above €200,000 by 15 per cent. These pay cuts were applied generally throughout the public service, although senior civil servants argued for special treatment and their pay cut was reduced to about 3 per cent. In December 2010, in an effort to secure a structural reduction in pay rates, the Department of Finance announced that new entrants to the public service would be appointed at salary scales that had been reduced by 10 per cent of the scales relating to incumbents. Given the moratorium on public sector recruitment, it will take some time for the impact of this measure to become apparent.

Perhaps the most idiosyncratic element of the pay cuts in Ireland was the case of judges. In a somewhat controversial interpretation of the Constitution, which stipulates that the salaries of serving judges should not be reduced by government, the Attorney General determined that the pay cuts applicable throughout the public service should not be applied to the judicial service. About three-quarters of serving judges undertook to take voluntary pay cuts of a similar order of magnitude to the cuts imposed at similar salary levels elsewhere in the public sector. The

Table 9.7 Wage developments, public and private sectors, Ireland, 2008–2011

	Average hourly pay	% change	Average weekly pay	% change	Hours worked
Public					
2008	29.2		930.5		31.9
2009	29.9	2.4	947.9	1.9	31.7
2010	28.6	–4.3	903.1	–4.7	31.6
2011*	28.6	0.0	892.3	–1.2	31.1
Private					
2008	19.3		636.9		33.0
2009	19.5	1.0	622.7	–2.2	32.0
2010	19.5	0.0	616.6	–1.0	31.7
2011*	19.4	–0.5	610.3	–1.0	31.6

Note: * 2011 data based on three quarters – 2011, Q1–Q3.

Source: CSO, 2011, Survey on Earnings Hours and Employment Costs (EHECS).

situation was finally resolved when the newly elected government in 2011 held a referendum to amend the Constitution to permit cutting judicial pay in line with practice elsewhere in the public sector. Notwithstanding opposition from judicial quarters, the referendum was passed with an 80 per cent majority in October 2011. Overall, the pay cuts were projected to lead to annual savings of over €1 billion.

Information on the impact of the public sector pay cuts is limited. Preliminary analysis of the most recent National Employment Survey data relating to 2009, which are consistent with the data used by Kelly et al. (2009) to assess the growth in the wage gap between 2003 and 2006, suggest that the public/private sector wage gap had not fallen by 2009. However, this is prior to the imposition of cuts in gross pay implemented in 2010. One of the effects of the austerity programme has been the cessation of the National Employment Survey since 2009, so unfortunately we can no longer draw on this source to compare public with private sector pay during this key period of policy change.

Table 9.7, showing CSO estimates of average earnings in the public and private sectors, suggests that hourly wages in the public sector fell by 4.3 per cent, and weekly earnings by slightly more, in 2010. This coincides with the wage cuts implemented in January of that year. These data refer to gross earnings, so do not take account of the impact of the pension levy on disposable incomes imposed since 2009.

It should be noted in this context that adjustment to the crisis differed between the public and private sectors. In the public sector we have seen wage cutting, but modest cuts in employment. In the private sector, employment contracted by about 16 per cent and average working time also contracted. So while there may have been a very modest cut in hourly pay in 2011 in the private sector, most of the decline in earnings was due to cuts in working time, leading to falls in weekly earnings in each year of 2009–11.

Callan et al. (2010) examine the distributional implications of both the pension levy and the wage cuts using survey data and a tax-benefit simulation model. Compared with a counterfactual wage freeze, they found that the combined effects of the levy and wage cuts on households containing public sector workers were to reduce disposable income by about 1 per cent for households in the lowest four income deciles, and that the losses gradually increased to about 3 per cent for the top decile. Callan et al. (2012: 51) show that the public sector pay cuts have had a progressive impact – as expected, given that the cuts were designed to increase with income:

> The public sector pay cuts make little difference to low income households, but reduced the income of higher income households. While the results are broadly similar – least impact on low income households, and the greatest impact on high income households – it is noteworthy that the tax/welfare measures alone led to a reduction in income of about 7 per cent for the middle income deciles (deciles 4, 5, 6 and 7). Inclusion of the public sector pay cuts means that losses rise with income over these deciles.

Callan et al. also show that the scale of the adjustment undertaken by Ireland is substantially greater than that for a range of countries in their analysis (Estonia, Greece, Spain, Portugal and the United Kingdom) and that the distributional impact of the policy changes in Ireland has been among the most progressive.

More generally, however, the most recent Irish results from the EU Survey of Income and Living Conditions (SILC), relating to 2010 (CSO 2012), show that there were marked increases in poverty and inequality as the crisis deepened between 2009 and 2010. For example, the 'at risk of poverty rate' – referring to the proportion of households with disposable income falling below 60 per cent of the median – increased from 14.1 per cent in 2009 to 15.8 per cent in 2010. Moreover, the average income of individuals in the highest income quintile was 5.5 times that of those in the lowest income quintile, up from a ratio of 4.3 one year previously.

2.11 Working Conditions

The Changing Workplace Survey conducted among a sample of 5,000 employees in mid-2009 allows us to gain some insight into the immediate

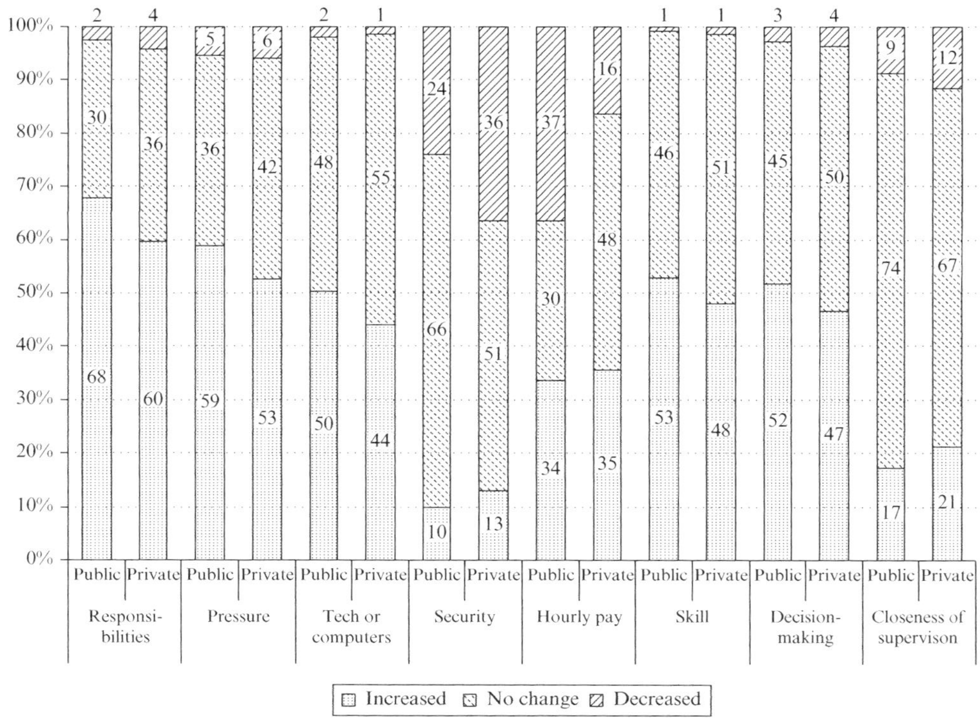

Source: O'Connell et al. (2010).

Figure 9.7 Experience of change in job tasks/conditions in past two years, Ireland, 2009

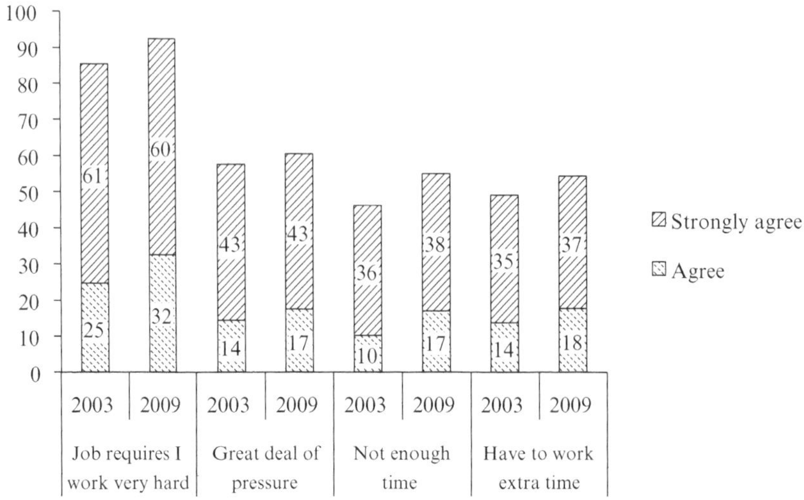

Sources: Special analysis of O' Connell et al. (2004, 2010).

Figure 9.8 Experience of work pressure, public employees, Ireland, 2003 and 2009

impact on working conditions as the crisis developed (O'Connell et al. 2010). A greater share of public sector than private sector workers reported that their responsibilities and work pressure had increased during the previous two years. Public sector workers were substantially more likely to report that their pay had fallen than private sector workers (37 per cent versus 16 per cent), although private sector workers were more likely to report that their job security had deteriorated.

We can also draw upon The Changing Workplace Survey conducted in 2003 (O'Connell et al. 2004) to examine change over time in working conditions Figure 9.8 compares reported aspects of work pressure among public sector workers in 2003 during the boom and 2009 during the crisis. All indicators of work pressure increased somewhat over the period. In particular, the proportion of public sector workers reporting that they worked very hard increased from 86 per cent in 2003 to 92 per cent in 2009. About 46 per cent of workers reported that they did not have enough time to do everything in their job in 2003, but this increased to 55 per cent in 2009.

The 2009 data on work pressure were collected prior to the implementation of the moratorium in public sector recruitment and the contraction in public sector employment between 2009 and 2011 (see Table 9.5, above), so it is to be expected that work pressure increased subsequently in the effort to provide public services with reduced staff numbers.

2.12 Industrial Relations

Industrial relations were dominated by centralized wage bargaining under tripartite social partnership arrangements for over two decades, from 1987 to the onset of the present crisis. Indeed, Irish social partnership was developed as a strategic response to the fiscal and economic crisis of the 1980s, and initially entailed an exchange of wage restraint and industrial peace for state commitment to reduce income tax (McGuinness et al. 2010). In early 2009, employers and the government declined to pay the increases due under the then current National Agreement, 'Towards 2016', which had been negotiated in September 2009, on the basis of inability to pay. The fiscal crisis continued to intensify throughout 2009, leading to the imposition of direct income levies on all employees, as well as the pension levy on all public sector workers, and cutbacks in entitlements to health services.

In this context of a growing fiscal crisis, the public sector unions held a one-day strike and street protests in November 2009, in anticipation of harsh measures in the next budget. They also developed a proposal, within the social partnership process, for short time working in the public sector (entailing 12 days' unpaid leave for public sector workers) plus flexibility over work practices to achieve cost savings. The proposal found some favour in the cabinet, but was eventually rejected following a revolt of government backbench legislators. Dellepiane and Hardiman (2012: 28) argue that 'government chose not to follow the social partnership route of gradual efficiency-based cost recovery'. Instead, the pay cuts were introduced from 1 January 2010, along with a moratorium on recruitment to the public sector and the rationalization of state agencies.

At that point social partnership collapsed and social dialogue between government and unions ceased. Rigney (2012: 9) argues:

> [T]he social partnership process had been atrophying since the inception of the crisis, and was being blamed by some conservative commentators as one of the causes of the crisis. The unions had been in a position of having access without influence for some time. The central forum for deliberative social dialogue, the national economic and social council had been effectively stood down by the government, its term of office having expired, and the council never met during much of the crisis period.

In this context, it could be argued that the conduct of industrial relations in the public sector has been remarkably peaceful, given the cancellation

Table 9.8 Industrial disputes, Ireland, 2007–2011

	Disputes	Workers	Days lost
2007	6	1,436	6,038
2008	12	356	4,147
2009	168	278,228	329,593
2010	14	511	6,602
2011	8	1,384	3,695

Source: CSO (2012), *Industrial Disputes Quarter 4, 2011*.

of the award under the national wage agreement and the imposition of the pension levy in 2009, the pay cuts in 2010 and the moratorium on public sector recruitment. In fact, the early period of adjustment in late 2009 was marked by a number of industrial disputes, strikes and protests against the wage freeze and pension levy (Table 9.8).

The number of workers involved in industrial disputes rose massively to 278,000 in 2009, up from just 356 in the previous year. The vast majority of the days lost to disputes were related to one-day strikes in the public sector in the final quarter of 2009, and industrial peace returned in 2010, and was subsequently maintained.

In spring 2010 the public sector unions and the government re-engaged in dialogue and the Public Service Agreement 2010–2014 (Croke Park Agreement) was negotiated between the government and the unions. The government undertook not to implement any further pay cuts for four years and stated that there would be no compulsory redundancies.

The main elements of the agreement are as follows:

- no further pay cuts until at least 2014;
- no change in the arrangements for indexation of pensions for public service pensioners and serving public servants at least until 2014;
- significant cost saving across the public service;
- review of extent of savings generated to be held in spring 2011 to determine if scope exists for any reimbursement of pay cuts;
- substantial reduction in public service numbers in years ahead;
- no compulsory redundancies but flexible redeployment arrangements;
- unified public service labour market to be created;
- merit-based promotion;
- promotion and incremental progression based on performance; and
- industrial peace clause.

The Croke Park Agreement was formally endorsed in June 2010 by the Irish Congress of Trade Unions. A significant minority – seven trade unions representing some teachers, nurses, lower-paid public servants and others – voted against the agreement, although most subsequently accepted it. In addition to agreeing the basis for cost cutting through acceptance of pay cuts and staffing reductions, the agreement provides for the achievement of increased productivity and improved services through revised work practices, organizational restructuring and redeployment of staff across the public sector.

The agreement provides for an annual review focusing on the sustainable savings generated from its implementation. The first annual review was published in June 2011 covering the 12 months to the end of March 2011. The Implementation Body noted that the Exchequer pay bill fell from a peak of €17.5 billion in 2009 to €15.7 billion in 2010, or €15 billion, when the effect of the pension-related deduction was factored in, representing a 14.4 per cent reduction. A further reduction to €14.8 billion was estimated for 2011, representing a 15.5 per cent fall from peak by the end of 2011. The provisional gross Exchequer-funded public service pay bill cost for 2010 was €15.9 billion. The estimate for the gross Exchequer-funded public service pay bill in 2011 was €15.7 billion. Therefore, the minimum savings target for the Exchequer-funded public service pay bill would be €220 million for 2011, with a further saving of some €28 million in the local government pay bill, which is funded differently.

The review established that estimated sustainable pay bill savings in the order of €289 million had been achieved during the review period. The saving was driven primarily by a 5,349 reduction in staff numbers but also other factors such as reductions in overtime costs (down 5.2 per cent) and pay bill savings accruing from changed work practices and rationalization.

The review concluded that the level of sustainable savings delivered during the first year of the agreement had exceeded the targeted savings for the public service pay bill in 2011. The review also found that public service bodies had generated significant non-pay cost savings through better use of resources – reorganizing work and achieving greater internal efficiencies, property rationalization, reducing the costs of purchasing goods and services and changes in the way services are delivered.

Non-pay savings (exhaustively detailed in the report) amounted to over €300 million. The report also provides some examples of initiatives taken by public bodies which have led to costs of €85.7 million being avoided which would otherwise have been incurred. The review concluded that, in the first year of the four-year agreement:

- numbers had fallen substantially, more quickly than previously estimated, and services had been maintained and in some cases expanded and productivity increased;
- the cost of delivering public services had fallen in a sustainable way, primarily through reducing headcount across the public service, enabling the state to meet its external economic and fiscal commitments; and
- thousands of staff had been redeployed, including across functional boundaries which helped to meet two challenges: avoiding gaps in service as numbers reduced and changing the way in which public services are delivered to citizens and business.

The review also noted that industrial peace was maintained across the public service during this period: this is not insignificant when contrasted with the escalating industrial unrest in the months preceding the agreement.

3. CASE STUDIES

3.1 Case Study 1: Restructuring Services to the Unemployed

A major restructuring of services to the unemployed has been in progress since 2010. This represents the beginning of the development of a strategic response to mass unemployment, and the staff redeployments involved in this restructuring can be seen as taking advantage of the flexibility in the Croke Park Agreement.

The Department of Social Protection (DSP) is to take a greater role in providing activation services for the unemployed, as well as for its more traditional role in paying unemployment-related income supports. This is similar to the role adopted by social welfare authorities in other countries and consistent with the conclusions of the OECD Report on the need to combine income support and activation policies in Ireland (Grubb et al. 2009). The reform also addresses some of the problems highlighted in an evaluation of activation measures implemented under the Irish National Employment Action Plan (NEAP), which found that up to half of potentially eligible clients who might have received job search assistance under the NEAP fell through the net and received no assistance, while those who did receive activation assistance were less likely to exit unemployment, an effect that was attributed to a reduction in job search in the absence of regular monitoring or sanctions (McGuinness et al. 2011b).

The restructuring and reform process also takes place in the context of the fiscal and unemployment crises. Unemployment increased from less than 5 per cent of the labour force at the beginning of 2008 to over 14 per cent in 2011. The Live Register, which measures claimants of unemployment related-payments (Jobseeker's Benefit or Allowance) and part-time, casual and seasonal workers, increased from 290,000 in 2009 to 440,000 in 2012. This has led to a dramatic increase in the numbers of claims processed by the DSP in a relatively short period of time. The number of recipients of Jobseeker's Benefit and Jobseeker's Allowance increased from 139,000 in 2007 to over 385,000 in 2010, and expenditure on these jobseeker payments increased from €1.4 billion to €4.1 billion over the same period (Department of Social Protection 2011b).

3.1.1 Scheduling a new activation regime at the DSP

The project plan for the National Employment and Entitlements Service (NEES) was approved by government in June 2011 (Department of Social Protection 2011a). The establishment of the NEES is a key commitment under the terms of the Memorandum of Understanding with the EU/IMF/ECB (Troika). Central to the reform and restructuring process is the integration of the income support services with employment activation services within the DSP. From January 2012, the DSP is to take a greater role in providing activation services for the unemployed, as well as for its more traditional role in paying benefits. Second, the DSP is to implement a new case management system with a strong focus on activation, rather than just income support. Third, the Social Welfare (Miscellaneous Provisions) Act 2010 provides for sanctions to be applied to unemployed persons on the Live Register unreasonably refusing to participate in training, education and employment offered by facilitators within the DSP. Fourth, the DSP has begun to implement a profiling system for the unemployed, developed in collaboration between the Department and ESRI researchers (O'Connell et al. 2009). Profiling is a statistically based system for the early identification of those with a high probability of becoming long-term unemployed at the time they first become unemployed. It allows for a ranking of jobseeker claimants according to their likelihood of long-term unemployment, and provides the capacity to target resources on those who most need, and can benefit from, activation measures.

In February 2012, the DSP launched Pathways to Work, its new integrated service. At the core of the new policy document is a commitment to reducing long-term unemployment. Pathways to Work is based on five strands:

- more regular and ongoing engagement with the unemployed;
- greater targeting of activation places and opportunities;

- incentivizing the take-up of opportunities;
- incentivizing employers to provide more jobs for people who are unemployed; and
- reforming institutions to deliver better services to people who are unemployed.

Profiling of clients to enable early identification of those at high risk of long-term unemployment is to be extended to half of all local offices by the end of May 2012 and to encompass virtually all new claimants by the end of 2012. Group engagement will also be made available, as appropriate, to all people profiled as at moderate risk of long-term unemployment and those who have been on the Live Register for at least three months The Department is to ensure that those most at risk of long-term unemployment, such as those previously employed in the construction and retail sectors, will be a specific focus of activation interventions and education and training opportunities. A new fully integrated 'one-stop-shop' service is to be piloted from four office locations in May of 2012 and extended to a further 10 offices by the end of the year.

Restructuring of services to the unemployed has entailed a series of organizational mergers. During 2011, about 1,000 personnel from the Community Welfare Service (CWS) were transferred from the Health Services Executive to the DSP and became full staff members of the Department in October 2011. While the principal focus of the CWS has historically been on income support on a personalized basis, it is planned to automate standard welfare claim processing, integrate the CWS functions with mainstream DSP functions and free former CWS staff to take on the role of NEES case management and activation.

Under the reform, FÁS, the national training and employment authority, is to be abolished and its functions dispersed. About 700 FÁS staff working in its Employment Services division were transferred to the DSP in January 2012, and the training function is to be taken over by the Department of Education and Skills. These staff are expected to bring core competencies in job placement and advice to be applied to the new activation regime. Several hundred civil servants were also transferred to the DSP from other government departments in order to cope with the increased workload resulting from the unemployment crisis, such that total staff increased from about 4,900 in 2008 to almost 7,000 in 2012.

3.1.2 Resolving industrial relations issues

Redeployment of staff and reorganization of working practices can thus be seen as one of the positive outcomes of the Croke Park Agreement, which facilitates the development of a strategic response to the unemployment crisis. The organizational merger has had to overcome a number of complex industrial relations issues. Many of the incoming staff made a transition from public to civil servant, and in the process, resigned from public service unions such as Services Industrial Professional and Technical Union (SIPTU) or IMPACT, and joined the mainstream civil service unions – the Public Service Executive Union, or the Association of Higher Civil and Public Servants (AHCPS) in the case of more senior grades. Pay scales in FÁS and the CWS each differed from standard civil service scales in the DSP – most were higher for equivalent grades – and enjoyed different terms and conditions. Following extensive negotiations and arbitration, individual officers held on to existing terms on a personal basis. This generates inequalities between staff that have come from different organizations now working side by side and engaged in similar functions, but with different pay and conditions. These differentials are regarded as posing a challenge for both management and unions and are expected to take some time to work their way through the system.

3.1.3 Lack of resources and potential mismatch between capacity and demand

Concerns have been expressed by representatives of unemployed groups about the numerical and technical capacity of the DSP to deliver the new activation regime. These concerns would appear to be warranted. Grubb et al. (2009) argued that the public employment system did not have sufficient staff to implement a system of frequent and regular monitoring interactions with the unemployed. While staff numbers at the DSP have recently been augmented by the transfer of 1,700 staff from FÁS and the CWS, it is unlikely that the Department has expanded its capacity sufficiently to implement a much enhanced activation role to a greatly enlarged clientele, given that the Live Register increased from about 290,000 at the start of 2009 to over 440,000 in 2012. This suggests that the ratio of jobseekers to case workers will remain far higher than in countries with serious activation systems. It is also likely that the enhanced activation regime will result in an intensification of work pressure on front-line staff at the DSP. Moreover, it is doubtful whether the majority of incoming staff possess the appropriate mix of technical and interpersonal skills to implement a novel and interventionist activation regime on a clientele that has been largely left to its own devices for the first three years of the crisis. It is not clear at this stage in the development of NEES and Pathways whether adequate resources have been set aside for a training regime to bridge such a skills gap.

It has also been observed that in the absence of numerical and/or technical capacity, to assist, encourage and guide jobseekers through both job searching and through a complex system of active labour market provision, private firms specializing in recruitment and personnel should be contracted to provide these services (Dan O'Brien, *Irish Times*, 2 March 2012). Concerns have also been raised about the quality and relevance of training for unemployed workers: effective training is an essential component of an activation system, and much of the training available to the unemployed has been found to be ineffective in helping them return to work (McGuinness et al. 2011a).

The development of a more active system of engagement with the unemployed represents a strategic response aimed at reducing the incidence of long-term unemployment. That strategic response has been facilitated by the Croke Park Agreement, which allowed for redeployment of staff from other agencies and some reform of work practices. Nevertheless, the potential effectiveness of the new activation regime appears to be compromised by the absence of frequent and regular monitoring, and by lack of capacity, both numerical and technical, to implement a sufficiently interventionist activation system. Given these caveats, it is clear that the implications of policy restructuring both for those implementing the reformed system, as well as for their unemployed clients, remain uncertain.

3.2 Case Study 2: Cutbacks in Education

The Department of Education and Skills had a gross current budget in 2011 of €8.7 billion; 77 per cent of this expenditure was public sector pay and pensions. It covered approximately one-third of the public service with 103,000 full-time equivalent public servants. This represents about 16 per cent of government expenditure or 4.7 per cent of GDP, which lags some way behind the OECD average of 6.2 per cent (Figure 9.9).

Total public expenditure on education, in nominal terms, increased €4.2 billion in 2000 to a high of €9.4 billion in 2009 before falling to €8.9 billion in 2011. Consumer prices increased by 29 percent over 2000–09 and increased by about 1.5 percent over the next two years The education sector pay bill increased from €3.8 billion in 2000 to €6.7 billion in 2009, or by almost 14 per cent per annum. Over the same period, the non-pay bill increased by over 10 per cent per annum, while capital expenditure increased by less than 5 per cent per annum. The pay bill fell by 3.5 per cent from its peak of €6.7 billion in 2009 to €6.5 billion in 2011. The non-pay bill fell by 5 per cent from its peak of €2 billion in 2008 to €1.9 billion in 2011; capital expenditure fell by 40 per cent to €0.5 billion over the same period. Thus, between 2008–09 and 2011, roughly half of the cutbacks in the education sector were achieved through cutbacks in the pay bill and about half through cuts in capital expenditure.

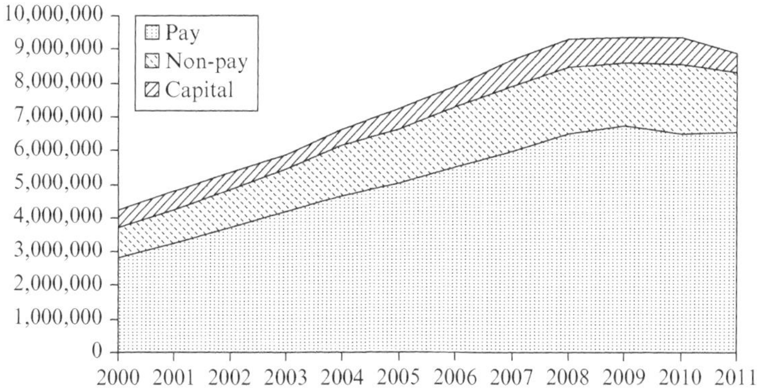

Source: Department of Public Expenditure and Reform: www.per.gov.ie.

Figure 9.9 Expenditure on education, current and capital, Ireland, 2000–2011

Most of the cuts in the pay bill can be attributed to the public sector wage cut implemented in January 2010 and to a range of productivity-enhancing measures in the Croke Park Agreement. The agreement includes a specific 'Educational Sectoral Agreement' that covers a range of measures designed 'to facilitate the most effective and efficient use of resources and to maximize the quality of educational delivery'. These measures include provisions to increase the number of working hours across the education system, as well as greater flexibility in scheduling and in redeployment of surplus teachers. Specifically, the agreement provides for the following:

- 33,000 primary teachers are to work an additional hour per week (36 in a full year);
- 27,000 post-primary teachers are to work an additional hour per week, accumulating to 33 additional hours per school year without diminishing tuition time;
- 9,500 academic staff in institutes of technology and universities are to work an additional 26–35 hours per year;
- redeployment procedures at primary level have been implemented with some 850 surplus teachers redeployed;
- new redeployment procedures for secondary level teachers have been implemented, resulting in the elimination of a surplus of some 200 teachers;
- greater flexibility in the deployment of Special Needs Assistants

(SNAs) and greater discretion in the deployment of SNAs during non-instruction days; and
- a reduction of 2,000 posts of responsibility in primary and post-primary schools. These posts broadly equate to promotional posts in teaching and their number is expected to continue to decline in line with a moratorium on recruitment.

In addition to the wage cuts, a wide range of cuts have been imposed across the education system.

In primary education, the main cuts since 2008 have entailed an increase in the pupil/teacher ratio from 27:1 to 28:1; cuts in funding for disadvantaged schools; cuts in support for special needs education and in language support for schools with higher proportions of immigrant children; cuts in capitation grants for operational and maintenance functions; cuts in material and equipment funding and in certain book grants schemes; and cuts to school transport services.

At secondary level, the main cuts since 2008 have included an increase in the pupil/teacher ratio from 18:1 to 19:1; a reduction in the number of teachers; a moratorium on posts of responsibility relating to in-school management; the withdrawal of resource teachers for members of the Travelling Community;[3] cuts to school funding; and cuts to school transport services. The cutbacks have resulted in the reduction of about 1,000 teachers in secondary-level schools and in reduced choice of subjects for students, particularly in smaller schools. There have also been losses in English-language teachers in schools with significant immigrant pupil numbers.

At tertiary level, the cutbacks have included cuts in staffing numbers across the universities of 3 per cent in 2009 and 2010 and a moratorium on recruitment in 2009–10, followed in 2011 by the imposition of an employment control framework that restricts recruitment and promotions. These staff cuts have occurred despite increases in student numbers at tertiary level. Students' registration fees were increased to €2,000 per annum, student maintenance grants were cut and a series of further increases are planned over the coming years.

Many of the cutbacks, including those affecting teachers and other staff in the education sector, have been accomplished without negotiation between social partners. This represents a dramatic departure from practice prior to the crisis and from the Croke Park Agreement. For example, while the latter was ratified by the Irish Congress of Trade Unions in June 2010, it was accepted by the Irish Federation of University Teachers only in June 2011.

Discussions between the Department of Education and Skills and the three main teachers' unions on school staffing in the context of ongoing cutbacks were initiated in June 2011. The talks resulted from a commitment undertaken the previous year for the Department to consult the education partners to provide them with a chance to identify a range of cost-cutting measures for government to consider. However, it had been stated that if 'alternative feasible measures to deliver these savings cannot be identified, appropriate increases in the classroom teacher allocation schedule will be introduced'. All the teachers' unions were opposed to further cuts in staffing, citing large average class sizes at primary level in Ireland and the likelihood that vulnerable, marginalized, socially disadvantaged and less academically able students would be adversely affected.

However, following the Budget for 2011, the Department of Education and Skills in January 2012 issued a circular stating that special allowances for teachers with additional qualifications would no longer be paid to new entrants to the profession. This circular was issued without negotiations or consultation with teachers' unions (ASTI 2012).

3.2.1 The effects of education cutbacks

Cutbacks to education have been controversial. A decision to cut special needs assistants was overturned while cuts in the numbers of additional teachers at officially designated socially disadvantaged schools have been postponed, pending a review. Both of these policy shifts followed protests by parents and teachers. This may be why the main strategy has been to increase class sizes across all education sectors. An increase in class size may be the most effective means of cutting education spending, outside of further pay cuts. However, Irish classrooms are already large by European standards. Larger classes reduce employment opportunities for teachers and can increase work pressure. The Irish National Teachers' Organization argues that Irish classes are already among the largest in Europe and that younger children do less well in large classes.

A survey of principals of second-level schools conducted on behalf of the Association of Secondary Teachers in Ireland (ASTI) in 2012 found that almost half of schools have already dropped subjects from their Leaving Certificate programme as a result of cutbacks implemented since 2009 and almost two-thirds are considering such cuts after Budget 2012. Second-level schools in the survey have lost an average of 1.6 full-time teaching posts as a result of cuts in teacher numbers and pastoral care and administration are the functional areas most affected. The ASTI argue that fewer teachers results in less subject choice and a narrower range of pastoral services. This may have a negative impact on less academically oriented students. Indeed, as Smyth and McCoy (2009) argue, many of the cutbacks erode provision for socially disadvantaged students, and may have a greater negative impact on such students. This can have the long-term effect of exacerbating social inequalities in Irish society. According to the ASTI, the main problems are: pressure on the school curriculum and the learning environment due to staffing restrictions; damage to administrative capacity of schools from the moratorium on posts; and increasing numbers of parents experiencing difficulties in meeting the costs of education. The ASTI also noted that one of the most significant budget cuts in 2012, the allocation of career guidance posts, is equivalent to an increase in the pupil–teacher ratio of 0.8. As a result, schools will be faced with the stark choice of either curtailing guidance and counselling services to students, or dropping subjects and/or special programmes to assist less academically able students (ASTI 2012). One potential danger of the reduction in guidance and counselling provision is that it may lead to increased drop-out and early school leaving (Teachers' Union of Ireland 2011) with career-long implications particularly for socially disadvantaged and less academically gifted students.

4. CONCLUSIONS

Since 2008, Ireland has experienced a most extraordinary and severe set of interrelated crises, including the bursting of the property bubble; the banking collapse; the deep contraction in economic activity; the fiscal crisis of the state; and mass unemployment. The principal response adopted by the Irish state to that crisis has entailed an orthodox deficit reduction strategy, focusing on the fiscal crisis, driven by international bond markets and, since 2010, by the terms of the IMF/EU/ECB emergency loan programme. The broad parameters of the resulting austerity package entail reducing the fiscal deficit by about €30 billion or 20 per cent of GDP (at its 2010 value), comprising revenue raising of about €11 billion and spending cuts of €19 billion between 2008 and 2014. The deficit reduction strategy thus entails a dramatic contraction of the Irish state and in the scale and nature of its activities.

A key strategy in the austerity programme has been to reduce the public sector pay bill. The public pay bill is a function of both public employment levels and pay rates and this chapter outlines how both were cut after 2008. The numbers employed in the public sector, broadly defined, fell by about 5 per cent between 2009 and 2011, having grown by almost 30 per cent over the previous decade. Average earnings in the public sector fell by almost 5 per cent in 2010 and by another 1.2 per cent in 2011. This would have offset rapid growth in average pay in the public sector during the boom years, and the evidence suggests that the public sector pay premium had grown to much higher levels in Ireland than could be found elsewhere in Europe immediately prior to the crisis. Additional adjustments to public sector net earnings were implemented in the form of a pension levy applied exclusively to public sector workers in recognition of comparatively beneficial pension arrangements available to public sector workers.

Tripartite social partnership arrangements for centralized wage bargaining dominated industrial relations for the two decades prior to the crisis. But social partnership may also have serious unintended consequences. As Dellepiane and Hardiman (2012) argue, in Ireland, the insider power of the public sector and the low levels of unionization of the private sector, especially in the exporting sector, may have distorted wage structures. This may have had the consequence of public sector wages increasing out of line with the private sector (Kelly et al. 2009; McGuinness et al. 2010). Social partnership can be seen as a casualty of the crisis in Ireland. In 2009, employers and the government declined to pay wage increases due under the then current National Wage Agreement. With the imposition of pay cuts in 2010, social partnership collapsed and social dialogue ceased. While both the pension levy and the pay cuts were designed to be progressive, taking more from the top of the earnings distribution than the bottom, in the main, this would not appear to have been due to the influence of the trade union movement. It may simply have been well-informed and strategic policymaking: fairness, even in pay cuts, may have more legitimacy than pay cuts that are perceived to fall unfairly.

What is perhaps most surprising, particularly in a comparative context, has been the relatively peacefulness of industrial relations during this traumatic period. Following a sudden and sharp increase in strike days in November 2009, mainly due to a one-day public sector strike to protest against the pension levy and the wage freeze (the refusal to pay the increase under the 2008 National Wage Agreement), the number of industrial disputes tapered off to their previous levels of passivity. There was no surge in strikes protesting the pay cuts imposed in January 2010, which may also have reflected public opinion about the issue of public sector pay. Later that year the Croke Park Agreement was negotiated between government and public sector unions, and stipulated commitments to flexibility in industrial relations and no strikes in exchange for commitments to no further wage cuts and no compulsory redundancies. The debate continues as to whether the Croke Park Agreement represents part of the solution to Ireland's fiscal crisis, in delivering productivity-enhancing reforms in exchange for guarantees on jobs and pay; or part of the problem, in so far as it maintains relatively advantageous pay rates and a sluggish pace of reform.

The case studies in the education sector and in services to the unemployed show that the impact of the Croke Park deal has differed across the two sectors. Arguably, in the policy area of services to unemployed workers, the agreement has made possible redeployment of staff and flexible reorganization of working arrangements that have facilitated the development of an important series of strategic reforms to the system. The impact of those reforms in terms of both the quality of the service to unemployed clients, and on workers implementing the system, remains uncertain, not least because of capacity constraints remaining in the system. In the education sector, the principal impact would seem to have been in productivity: working time has been increased, while pay has been cut. This productivity gain has been combined with myriad cutbacks in services and facilities and there is concern that the impact of the cuts may fall most heavily on socially disadvantaged and less academically able students, with the potential to aggravate social inequality over the longer term. Thus, in education, the austerity programme may have achieved productivity gains and cost cutting without, or even at the expense of, a strategic approach to educational reform.

NOTES

1. HSE HR Circular 011/2010 at http://www.hse.ie/go/exitschemes.
2. See McGuinness et al. (2010) for an analysis of the impact of wage-bargaining regimes in the private sector.
3. Travellers are a traditionally nomadic people of ethnic Irish identity who maintain a separate set of traditions. They have a history of educational, labour market and social disadvantage.

REFERENCES

Association of Secondary Teachers in Ireland (ASTI) (2011), 'What price education, one year on', Dublin: ASTI. Available at: http://www.asti.ie/fileadmin/user_upload/Documents/Campaigns/Budget/one_year_on.pdf (accessed 24 October 2012).

Association of Secondary Teachers in Ireland (ASTI) (2012), *ASTI*, **30** (2) (March).

Barrett, A., D. Duffy and C. O'Sullivan (2011), *Quarterly Economic Commentary*. Summer 2011, Dublin: ESRI.

Bergin, A., J. FitzGerald, I. Kearney and C. O'Sullivan (2011), 'The Irish fiscal crisis', *National Institute Economic Review*, **217**, R47–R59.

Boyle, G., R. McElligot and J. O'Leary (2004), 'Public–private wage differentials in Ireland, 1994–2001', *ESRI Quarterly Economic Commentary*, Special issue, Summer, Dublin: ESRI.

Callan, T., C. Keane, M. Savage and J. Walsh (2012), 'Distributional impact of tax, welfare and public sector pay policies: 2009–2012', *Quarterly Economic Commentary*, Winter 2011/Spring 2012: 45–56.

Callan, T., B. Nolan and J. Walsh (2010), 'The economic crisis, public sector pay and the income distribution', IZA DP 4948, Bonn.

Central Statistics Office (CSO) (2012), *Survey of Income and Living Conditions (SILC), 2010*, Dublin: Stationery Office.

Central Statistics Office (CSO) (various dates), *Live Register*. Available at: www.cso.ie.

Dellepiane, S. and N. Hardiman (2012), 'The new politics of austerity: fiscal response to the economic crisis in Ireland and Spain', UCD Geary Institute Discussion Paper, Dublin.

Department of Finance (2011), 'Budgetary and economic statistics', Department of Finance, Dublin. Available at: http://www.finance.gov.ie/documents/guidelines/BESSept2011.pdf (accessed 24 October 2012).

Department of Social Protection (DSP) (2011a), 'Project Plan for the Development and Implementation of the National Employment and Entitlements Service', Department of Social Protection, Dublin. Available at: http://www.welfare.ie/EN/AboutUs/Documents/NEES.pdf (accessed 24 October 2012).

Department of Social Protection (DSP) (2011b), Statistical Information on Social Welfare Services 2010. Available at: http://www.welfare.ie/EN/Policy/ResearchSurveysAndStatistics/Documents/2010stats.pdf (accessed 24 October 2012).

Department of the Taoiseach (1996), 'Delivering better government: Second report to government of the Co-ordinating Group of Secretaries – A programme of change for the Irish civil service', Government of Ireland, Dublin.

Duffy, D., J. Dukan and C. O'Sullivan (2011), *Quarterly Economic Commentary*, Winter 2011/Spring 2012, Dublin: ESRI.

Durkan, J., D. Duffy and C. O'Sullivan (2011), *Quarterly Economic Commentary*, Summer 2011, Dublin: ESRI.

Grubb, D., S. Singh and P. Tergeist (2009), 'Activation policies in Ireland', OECD Social, Employment and Migration Working Papers No. 75, 8 January.

Kearney, I. (2011), 'Setting the context', presentation to OECD LEED Conference 'Building Quality Jobs in the Recovery', Dublin, 13 October.

Kelly, E., S. McGuinness and P. O'Connell (2009), 'Benchmarking, social partnership and higher remuneration: wage settling institutions and the public–private sector wage gap in Ireland', *Economic and Social Review*, **40** (3) (Autumn), 339–70.

McGuinness, S., E. Kelly and P. O'Connell (2010), 'The impact of wage bargaining regime on firm-level competitiveness and wage inequality: the case of Ireland', *Industrial Relations: A Journal of Economy and Society*, **49** (4) (October), 593–615.

McGuinness, S., E. Kelly and P. O'Connell (2011a), 'One dummy won't get it: the impact of training programme type and duration on the employment chances of the unemployed in Ireland', ESRI Working Paper 410, Dublin.

McGuinness, S., P. O'Connell, E. Kelly and J. Walsh (2011b), *Activation in Ireland: An Evaluation of the National Employment Action Plan*, ESRI Research Series 20, Dublin: ESRI.

O'Connell, P., S. McGuinness, E. Kelly and J. Walsh (2009), *National Profiling of the Unemployed in Ireland*, ESRI Research Series 10, Dublin: ESRI.

O'Connell, P., H. Russell, W. Watson and D. Byrne (2010), *The Changing*

Workplace: A Survey of Employees' Views and Experiences, 2009, Dublin: National Centre for Partnership and Performance.
O'Connell, P., H. Russell, J. Williams and S. Blackwell (2004), *The Changing Workplace: A Survey of Employees' Views and Experiences, 2003*, Dublin: National Centre for Partnership and Performance.
OECD (2008), *Towards an Integrated Public Service*, Paris: OECD.
Public Service Benchmarking Body (2002), *Report of the Public Service Benchmarking Body*, Dublin: The Stationery Office, June.
Review Body on Higher Remuneration in the Public Sector (2005), *Report No. 40 to the Minister for Finance*, Dublin: Stationery Office.
Rigney, P. (2012), *The Impact of Anti-crisis Measures and the Social and Employment Situation: Ireland*, Dublin: Irish Congress of Trade Unions.
Smyth, E. and S. McCoy (2009), *Investing in Education: Combating Educational Disadvantage*, ESRI Research Series 6, Dublin: ESRI.
Teachers' Union of Ireland (2012), *TUI News*, February.

10. The Netherlands: Wage cuts no longer a constructive option

Wiemer Salverda*

1. INTRODUCTION

In the financial crisis many countries are taking policy measures aimed at lowering the wage bill of the public sector, often by drastically lowering pay rates. The Netherlands has gone down that road before. During the deep recession of 1980–85 nominal public sector pay rates were one-sidedly lowered by 3 per cent in 1984 and 'frozen' for most of the 1980s. That percentage may seem benign with hindsight, but at that time it was unique and high inflation affected purchasing power more strongly. It meant a one-time lowering of actual individual earnings and a permanent lowering of wage scales, but individual pay kept moving up because of tenure and did not necessarily remain frozen. In the end, the one-sided nature of the system of public sector wage negotiations was done away with – after unions had appealed to the ILO – while at the same time 12 decentralized wage agreements were instituted across the public sector in 1993 (Osmani 2011: 8).

In the current crisis, public sector pay has been treated differently, and so far no pay cuts have been enforced though there have been suggestions and proposals for a freeze. That may be a matter of time – this took four years from the start of the recession in the 1980s. Currently, wage negotiations are long-drawn-out without reaching a conclusion, or their conclusion has been moderate or unsuccessful. Thus in practice there has already been a freeze of wage rates.

In various countries the (un)fairness of public sector pay relative to the private sector is used as an argument in support of cuts. In the Dutch policy debate of the 1980s the stress was on competitiveness more than on fairness. The pay cut was deemed to reduce gross (labour) costs in the private sector by enabling lower taxes. This resulted from a political debate about the size and growth of the public sector relative to GDP that had sprung from the recessions of the early and mid-1970s. The wage measure also fitted the customary first Dutch response to economic problems: wage moderation. That obsession certainly seems less pronounced this time and arguments of public–private (un)fairness are heard much less than elsewhere. Even for occupational pensions – which are entirely based on capital funding – the debate is addressing the economy as a whole without any specific focus on public sector pensions.

This chapter considers the current situation, compares this to the previous experience of public sector adjustment, and scrutinizes the latter's long-run effects. The rest of this section defines the public sector, while Section 2 discusses its economic importance and adjustments. Section 3 develops a longer-run view on employment and pay in the public sector in comparison with the private sector, and lays the main foundation for the argument that there is now little scope for downward public sector pay adjustment. The section consecutively deals with employment (level and structure), wage negotiations, average earnings (level and structure), and public–private wage differentials for individuals controlling for the differences in personal and job characteristics between the two sectors. Section 4 studies the developments since the start of the financial crisis in 2008 and discusses current and future policymaking concerning adjustments in the public sector, which are increasingly trending towards austerity. Section 5 presents two case studies, one concentrating on the long-run effects of the pay policies of the 1980s, illustrated by the educational system, and the other focusing on wage formation in health care. Section 6 concludes.

1.1 Defining the Public Sector

A precise definition is not trivial. Over time the boundaries of the public sector have shifted – as the privatization of Post and Telecom may illustrate – and there are also large international differences in drawing the boundaries. The definition can be formal, based on the legal status of the public servant, or substantive, based on the sector's role in the economy. Starting from the former would miss the point. Legal status has become less important even in its traditional territory, and the public sector has expanded into fields where that status is of little importance. Instead, we choose the economic argument as a point of departure and define the public sector as including the government – central and local, with armed forces and social security services – the educational system, and health care[1] and social services. Not included in the public sector but in the private sector are public utilities and publicly owned enterprises (for example, railways). These have a tradition of catering to private demand and operating without subsidies and are at arm's length from the government, especially with regard to their personnel policies as they have their own collective labour agreements. The educational sector, by contrast, depends fully on public funding though the educational organizations are mostly private. Until the decentralization of wage negotiations of 1993 all wages were negotiated between the Ministry of Education and the unions. Since then this has increasingly been done between unions and employer associations founded by the individual institutions. Nowadays, the institutions range from organizations running (a number of) primary or secondary schools, to individual polytechnics and universities and associations for secondary vocational schools, polytechnics and universities. Responsibilities have been transferred increasingly from the ministry to the institutions, under the control of inspectorates. By contrast, health care has historically been fully privately organized and most of the higher-level medical profession is still self-employed in spite of the fact that since the introduction of the new obligatory health insurance system (ZVW) in 2006, health care has been almost fully publicly financed – or at least statistically classified as such because the ZVW financing is classified as a type of social security scheme. This classification may be overdone but it is also clear that health-care organizations are non-profit and do not operate as private sector firms.[2] Contrary to education the self-employed (doctors) have a crucial position in health care, but the focus of this chapter is employees. Their wages are privately negotiated between employers and unions in health care, though, as we shall see below, largely under the influence of the wage negotiations for government and education. The inclusion of education or health in the public sector affects its level and evolution very significantly and therefore a distinction is made between the three sectors throughout the chapter when possible and relevant.

2. THE ECONOMIC IMPORTANCE OF THE PUBLIC SECTOR

We start with the aggregate picture of the importance of the public sector in the national economy since 1970 (Figure 10.1). This long-run perspective covers the prelude to the serious recession of the 1980s to enable a better evaluation of its effects. The size of public sector spending reached a maximum in the early 1980s with a total of 60 per cent of GDP – up from 44 per cent in 1970 for structural and cyclical reasons. Then a slow decline set in which was amplified in the 1990s and was back at the initial level of 1970 by the year 2000. There it has largely remained until the financial crisis pushed it again to over 50 per cent. Public sector gross income from taxation and other sources also grew and fell though somewhat less than expenditures. Virtually all years have had a budget deficit[3] but this was clearly bigger when the sector was larger in the 1980s, and again recently with the

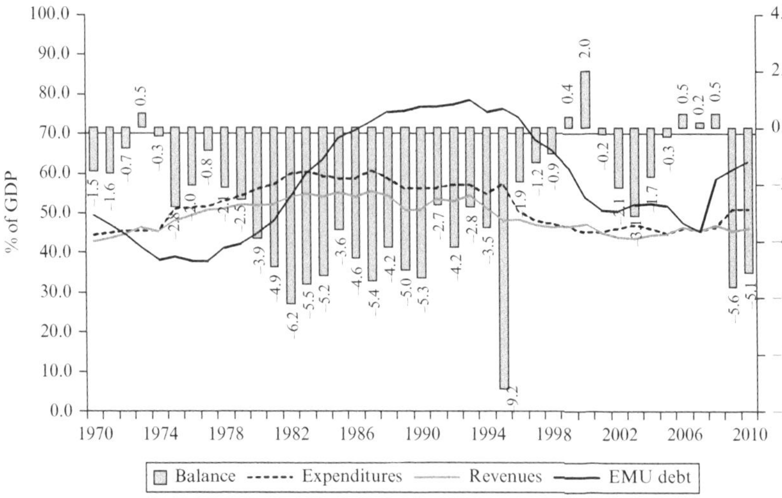

Source: CPB.

Figure 10.1 Public sector spending, income, deficits and debt, Netherlands, 1970–2010 (% of GDP)

sudden expansion of the deficit in 2009 and 2010. Consequently, government debt has risen sharply and doubled from the mid-1970s to the 1990s, reaching a maximum of 80 per cent of GDP. The level of debt was pushed down tremendously (45 per cent) until the onset of the financial crisis, when it shot up again, by 16 percentage points. Half of this increase was due to state guarantees given to the financial sector in 2008–09. In sum, the Dutch public sector has clearly undergone huge adjustments since the 1980s.

A breakdown of public spending (Figure 10.2) indicates the importance of transfers to households. These include financial transfers and services provided in-kind. Transfers are responsible for most of the growth in total public sector spending of the 1970s, its high level in the 1980s, the subsequent decline, and the recent increase. This volatility contrasts with the stability (around 17 per cent) of current direct public spending. This includes public sector wages, which secularly declined from 14 per cent of GDP in the 1970s to 9 per cent in the mid-2000s, followed by a 2 percentage point increase during the financial crisis. The gap that opened up between total direct spending and the wage bill (4 to 8 per cent) may partly reflect the effect of outsourcing. Ever since 1980 public investments have been less than 4 per cent of GDP. Unsurprisingly, given the evolution of debt, interest payments reached a maximum in the early 1990s of 6.2 per cent of GDP. In recent years those payments have remained low at

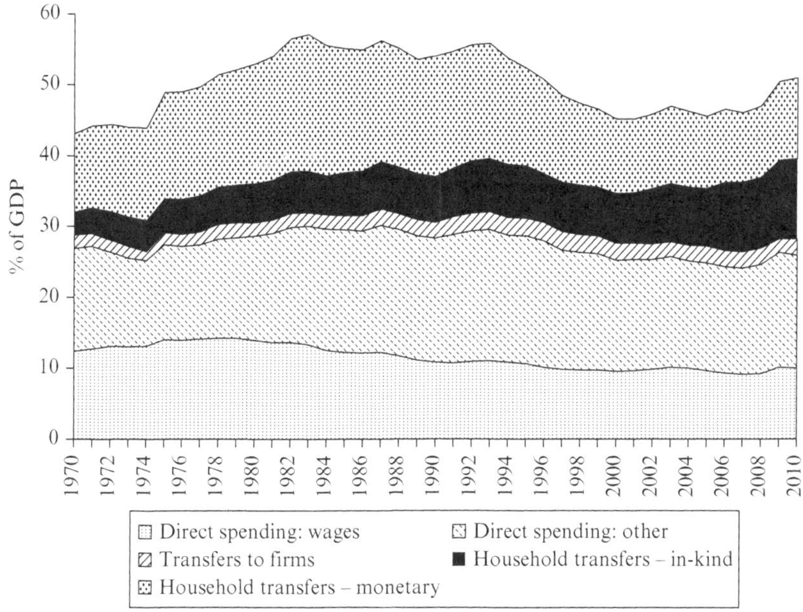

Source: CPB.

Figure 10.2 Split of total gross public sector spending, Netherlands, 1970–2010 (% of GDP)

around 2 per cent of GDP, perhaps because part of the new debt relates to guarantees instead of actual spending.

In the breakdown of transfers by social security, education and health care (Figure 10.3), the last two have climbed from 37 per cent of total transfers in the 1980s to 55 per cent currently. Health-care spending more than tripled to over 10 per cent of GDP and more than one-third of all transfers. Spending on education tended to decline in spite of the strong increase in educational participation. Social security spending is more volatile. It has borne the brunt of declining public spending since the 1980s. Between 1999 and 2008 it fell beneath its initial level of the 1970s (11 to 12 per cent). During the financial crisis, however, all three categories have contributed to the rise in spending, including education though that rose less. More than before health spending now seems to be part of the automatic stabilizers of the economy: from 2008 to 2010 spending rose by 1.5 per cent of GDP or 15 per cent of the starting level.

In-kind transfers, shown separately, increased strongly from 3 to 11 per cent of GDP, or 17 to 42 per cent of total transfers. The in-kind provi-

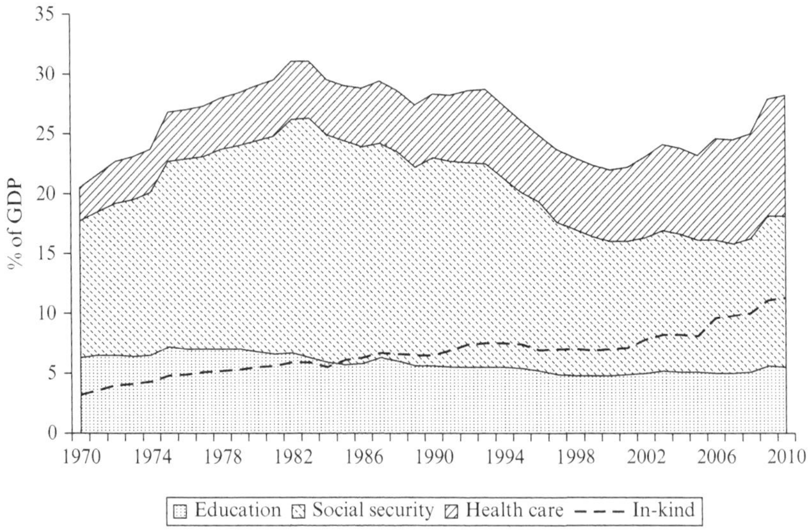

Source: CPB.

Figure 10.3 Split of total public sector transfers, Netherlands, 1970–2010 (% of GDP)

sion by means of public services implies that part of private household consumption runs to private markets via the public sector, for example, health care, while another part is directly produced by the public sector itself, for example, education. Such provisions differ significantly between countries, depending on the financing mechanism. Where most if not all is private, as in the United States, the services are considered part of private consumption. Where this is not the case or less, as in the Netherlands, these services should be taken into account when considering public and private consumption. They are paid from public funds but ultimately privately consumed. A good example is provided by the recent ZVW act for health-care insurance: households pay an insurance premium to private insurers as well as a contribution through the tax system. The latter is used, first, to even out risks between insurers, who are obliged to accept any risk for a uniform set of care provisions and may vary their premiums between narrowly prescribed boundaries only aimed at ruling out risk selection. Second, the tax contribution is used for the compensation of effects on low-income households resulting from the uniform premium. Thus the market that actually provides the service is private, but the financing comprises four financial flows of which three go through the public purse. National Accounts statistics classify this as a social security scheme and attribute it to the public sector. However, the National Accounts also distinguish 'actual individual consumption' as a part of government consumption. The public share in total private household consumption has secularly increased and almost doubled from 14 per cent in 1970 to 27 per cent in 2010. Half of this increase is concentrated in the 2000s. Thus consumption as a percentage of GDP has remained roughly unchanged, particularly during the first years of the financial crisis when a decline in market consumption was more than compensated by an increase in public consumption. Because of this much increased importance of the public channel in private consumption, austerity measures risk affecting households more strongly now than in earlier times.

3. EMPLOYMENT AND PAY

This chapter addresses the core issue of public sector adjustment which concerns pay and employment in comparison to the private sector. Four steps consecutively discuss the level and structure of employment, of collectively negotiated pay, of actual earnings, and of earnings corrected for employee differences relative to the private sector.

3.1 Employment: Growth, Especially among Women

Between 1970 and 2010 the number of people working in the public sector grew from 1 to 2.3 million and their share in employment increased from 19 to 27 per cent (Table 10.1). Average hours per employee fell by more than one-quarter, mostly before 1990. They are below the private sector average as they declined more strongly because females' role grew and their average hours fell somewhat more. The public sector share in hours worked grew from 18 to 24 per cent. However, public sector growth ran virtually parallel to the significant expansion of services in the private sector, except for the last few years. Over 2008–11 public sector employment grew by 156,000 heads while private sector heads fell by 206,000 (of which 116,000 were in services).

Table 10.1 depicts this development with a breakdown by gender and the three public subsectors. Female employment shows a substantial upward trend and their employment share within the public sector grew from 44 to 67 per cent. This is exactly the opposite of the private sector, where men make up two-thirds of all employed persons. Female growth is particularly important for the recent increase in public employment since 2008: 134,000 out of the additional 156,000 were women. The breakdown by subsector shows that the inclusion of health care doubles the size of the public sector – certainly a non-trivial effect. Interestingly, a decline

Table 10.1 Public sector employment by subsector and gender, Netherlands, 1970–2011

	1970	1975	1980	1985	1990	1995	2000	2005	2008	2010	2011
Aggregate numbers											
Public sector total											
Persons (×1,000)	1,032	1,254	1,427	1,514	1,618	1,676	1,839	2,090	2,181	2,311	2,337
Annual hours/ person	1,712	1,533	1,474	1,413	1,352	1,328	1,284	1,267	1,267	1,251	1,250
% of private	91	89	90	88	87	85	84	85	86	85	85
% of total employment, and female within-sector %											
Public sector total											
Total	19	22	24	25	24	23	23	25	25	27	27
% female	44	48	50	51	53	59	62	66	66	67	67
Government											
Total	7	7	8	8	8	7	6	6	6	6	6
% female	13	15	17	20	23	29	33	36	36	37	38
Education											
Total	5	6	6	6	6	5	5	6	5	6	6
% female	42	43	43	44	44	53	55	58	58	59	59
Health care											
Total	7	9	10	11	11	11	12	14	14	15	16
% Female	78	79	80	79	80	81	80	82	81	81	81

Source: CBS, Arbeidsrekeningen.

is found in the share of government (8 to 6 per cent) after an initial rise; at the same time the share of education has remained largely unchanged. Unsurprisingly, the evolution of employment reflects that of expenditures (Figure 10.2: government wage bill; Figure 10.3: health and education transfers). The role of women is much larger than for men in health care, about equal in education, and smaller though quickly growing in government. Since 2008 all three subsectors have shown employment growth (education +1.5 per cent; government +3.1 per cent) but health care (+11.0 per cent) contributed 134,000 to the additional 156,000.

Table 10.2 adds important current detail. In the public sector older workers, substantial part-time jobs, large organizations, and especially high-educated workers are considerably overrepresented compared to the private sector. Ethnic minorities – more often young and less educated – are strongly underrepresented. There are substantial differences in composition between the three public subsectors, not only between health care and the other two but equally between government and education. In

Table 10.2 Employment composition, pay and labour conditions by sector, Netherlands, 2010 (percentage of within-sector employment)

	Private sector[a]	Public sector			
		Total	Government	Education	Health care
Age[b]					
15–24	21	11	6	8	13
25–49	58	58	61	55	59
50–65	20	31	33	37	27
Ethnicity[c]					
Non-Western	13	8	8	6	8
Weekly working hours					
<12	16	10	2	9	14
12–20	9	15	5	14	19
20–35	21	40	25	40	46
35+	54	35	69	36	21
Organization size					
<10	16	4	0	2	6
10–100	33	8	2	9	9
100+	51	89	98	89	85
Flexible contract[d]	13	4	0	2	6
Irregular hours[d]	7	20	11	1	33
Seniority <1.5 year[d]	27	18	10	24	19
Educational level[b]					
Low	28	11	12	6	13
Intermediate	44	40	43	18	48
High	27	48	43	76	38
Occupational level[d]					
1	9	3	2	1	3
2	28	13	15	5	16
3	38	36	39	11	46
4	17	31	23	60	22
5	7	15	18	21	12
Low pay incidence					
≤ *100% minimum wage*	4.9	3.9	2.8	2.3	5.2
≤ *130% minimum wage*	20.3	10.5	5.2	5.6	15.6
Labour conditions					
High work speed	34.4		31.3	30.0	33.4
Too much work	42.1		40.6	51.0	43.6
Computer work	3.8		5.3	3.7	2.8
Accidents	0.13		0.11	0.07	0.18

Table 10.2 (continued)

	Private sector[a]	Public sector			
		Total	Government	Education	Health care
Satisfied with					
Labour conditions	77.2		83.6	79.2	78.9
Work	78.8		82.2	82.6	82.8

Notes: Computer work: daily hours; accidents: per employee. [a] Not private sector but total economy for labour conditions and satisfaction; [b] 2009; [c] 2008; [d] 2005.

Sources: Netherlands Working Conditions Survey (NEA) CBS/TNO; Employment and Earnings Statistics (SWL), CBS, and *Werkgelegenheid en minimumloon*; Enquête Werkgelegenheid en Lonen (EWL), CBS for 2005; Enquête Beroepsbevolking (EBB), CBS and *Polisadministratie* for 2008.

government the employment structure is tilted towards full-time workers and large organizations, and in education towards low-seniority, high-educated, and higher-level occupations. Health-care employees, by contrast, much more often work irregular hours and less than 20 hours and in intermediate-level occupations, also compared to the private sector. Youths and the low educated are overrepresented in health care compared to government and education but not compared to the private sector. Non-Western ethnicity is equally underrepresented across the three subsectors.

Health-care employees are paid the statutory minimum wage slightly more often than in the private sector and roughly twice as often as in government or education. The minimum wage applies to all employees and is indexed by collectively negotiated wage rates (Salverda 2010). It has not been frozen or lowered during the financial crisis so far but has followed the statutory trend of wage rates. The incidence of low pay, which could be estimated only as 130 per cent of the minimum wage,[4] is twice as high in the private sector as in the public sector. Here health care lags the private sector but is at three times the level of government and education. The table also highlights a few labour conditions, leaving out the physical ones – some of which are actually rather important in health care – and compares the public subsectors with the overall economy. Work speed is slightly below average but the workload is clearly higher in education. In government people work much longer hours at the computer screen. Health care has an above-average incidence of accidents at work. Employees in the public sector seem to be more satisfied with their working conditions and the nature of their work, but the national average is already high at 77–79 per cent.

3.2 Negotiated Pay: Towards Decentralization

When considering pay we need to distinguish between collectively negotiated rates, which stipulate the general framework, and individual earnings, which depend on a worker's position in the system of wage rates and his/her tenure profile, and on the individual's working time. Decisions about pay used to be taken unilaterally by the state, albeit after talks with the unions. The government endorsed the trend of private sector wage negotiations until the early 1980s. Years of freezes and protest[5] followed, and in 1988 it was finally agreed that mutual agreement in wage negotiations would replace unilateralism. In 1993 decentralized collective negotiations and labour agreements were established for eight public subsectors, such as central government, municipalities and education. This number expanded to 14 after a further split within the educational subsector. As a result, wage developments have diverged. For each agreement there is a separate representation of relevant public sector employers. On the workers' side there is a limited number of unions, mostly represented in all negotiations. Union density among public sector employees exceeds that in the private sector, as in many other countries. In 1970 almost two-thirds of civil servants were a union member (ICTWSS database), but that fell to 35 per cent in 1995 and 25 per cent in 2011 (CBS 2011).[6] Though the level is still higher in the public sector the decline seems to have been slightly faster. Private sector union density is now 18 per cent.

Of the current 2.3 million public sector employees, one million are covered by these 14 'pure' public sector agreements. Most of the rest are in a category of labour agreements for 'subsidized sectors', which has been distinguished since the 1980s when the government for the first time explicitly targeted also those with its wage policy (see Case Study 2). These sectors were considered 'followers of the trend', meaning that they will take the development of the pure public sector agreements as their point of reference. Health care is the most important of those, with 1.1 million employees.[7] This strong effect is an important argument of principle to include the health-care subsector in this study of the public sector.

Figure 10.4 presents the resulting real wage rates. Before 1980 developments were mostly in parallel, although the purchasing power of public sector wages had already started to decline after 1978. The rates are on an hourly basis including annual benefits such as a thirteenth month and after deflation for consumer prices. Education together with government is indicated separately from health care as, unfortunately, we cannot combine these into a single statistic for the public sector. Immediately from 1980 a large gap opened up to the private sector which kept increasing until 1985. By then government and education rates had lagged 19

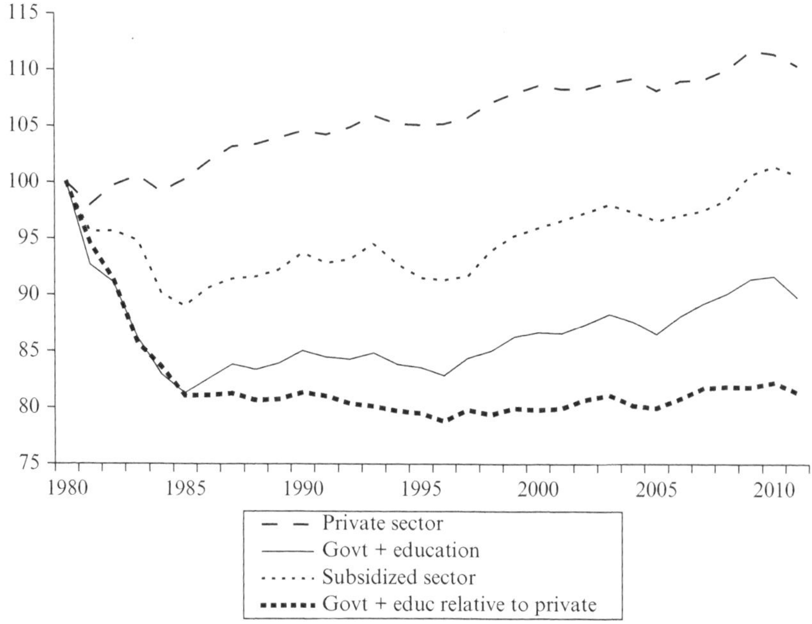

Source: CBS, *CAO-lonen* (Regelingslonen).

Note: 1980 = 100.

Figure 10.4 *Negotiated real hourly rates by sector, Netherlands, 1980–2011*

per cent behind prices and private sector rates, while for health care the gap was 11 per cent. The latter, clearly under the influence of government policy, confirms the argument for including health care in the public sector. Since 1985 the three have again largely moved in parallel to one another and the gap to the private sector has remained unchanged. In real terms these rates have moved up only very gradually (+11 per cent on balance), with clear cyclical effects in the 1990s and 2000s.[8]

Figure 10.5 shows the annual changes in real wage rates for the private sector and the three public subsectors since 1990, when a distinction between education and government became available. Although the long-run trend is much the same, temporary deviations are likely when agreements are concluded for more than one year and renewal is needed at a time of downturn and postponed. Clearly, each downturn (1990s, 2000s and now) affects real wage rates negatively and more so for the public subsectors. The first years of the current crisis, 2008 and 2009, showed

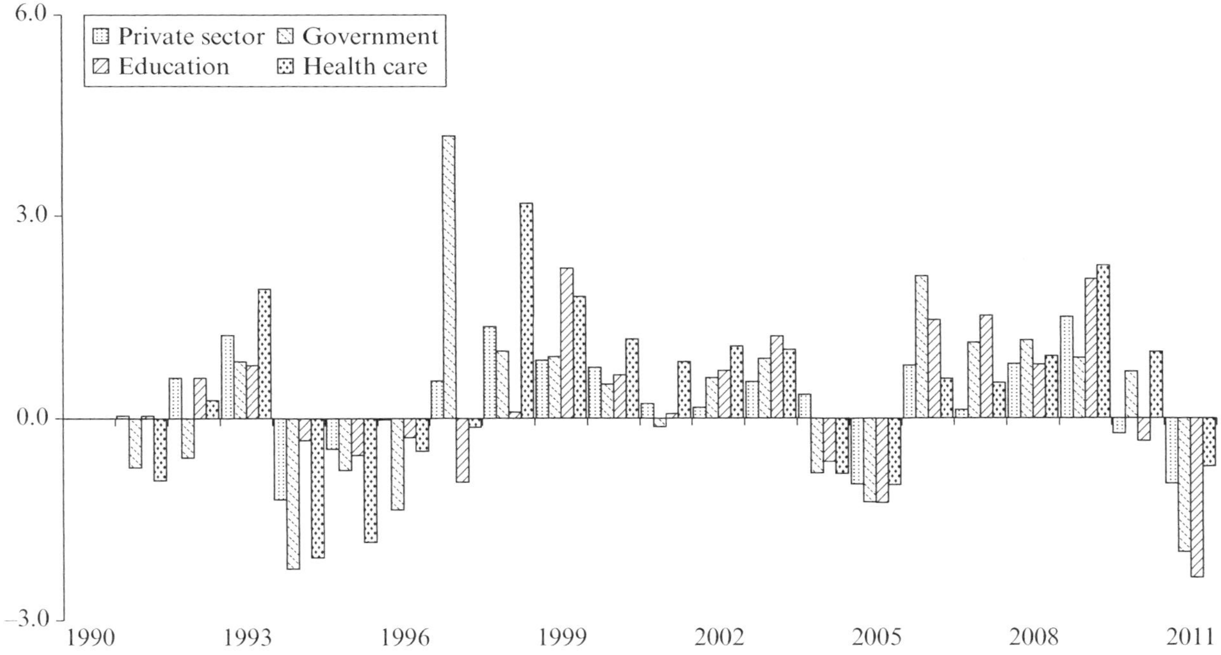

Note: 2000 = 100.

Source: CBS, *CAO-lonen.*

Figure 10.5 Negotiated real hourly rates by sector, Netherlands, 1990–2011

significant real growth[9] but rates have started moving down in 2010 for the private sector and for education. They fell in 2011 for all four (sub) sectors, in particular for education (–2.4 per cent) and government (–2.0 per cent). For health care they increased up to 2010 and fell slightly in 2011 (–0.7 per cent). Behind this lies the non-renewal of important collective labour agreements. In government and education in 2011 only three new agreements were concluded (municipalities, provinces and polytechnics) while one older agreement (academic hospitals) stipulated a rise in 2011; the 10 remaining agreements had expired and were not renewed (BZK 2011, Tables 4.3–16). By contrast, in health care most agreements have not expired and are being renegotiated (website of main union Abvakabo FNV). Thus, although there has been formal equivalence of the unions as a negotiating partner for public sector wage agreements since the end of the 1980s employers can still have the upper hand by refusing to strike a deal, which normally implies that the existing agreement stays in force and wages remain unchanged. Naturally, this is no different in the private sector in principle, although in practice it seems otherwise.

3.3 Earnings: Losing Ground with the Private Sector

Negotiated wages differ from actual earnings. In cross-section the latter depend on how workers are distributed over the range of wage rates, while over time their developments may also diverge because individuals move along tenure scales. The annual increase in wage rates is an index number on a fixed basis; average earnings have no such fixed basis and are sensitive to composition shifts in any direction: gender, age, education, occupational level, industry, employment contract, and tenure. For example, the average may actually move up during recessions if the least paid lose their job.

Figure 10.6 shows the developments of hourly earnings for the public (sub)sector(s) compared to the private sector. Hourly earnings as a concept corrects for differences in hours of work or in parts of the year worked and best indicates the differences in rewards. They are taken on an annual basis and include bonuses such as the thirteenth month, which has been gradually introduced in many public sector agreements over the 2000s. The purchasing power of national average pay rose by 84 per cent – mostly during the 1970s (+56 per cent). Earnings in education lagged substantially behind and fell from 66 per cent above the private sector in 1970 to 20 per cent above in the mid-1980s. After an initial rise, government relative earnings also fell considerably from the mid-1970s until the late 1980s. Since then the levels in these two subsectors have been 20–25 per cent above the private sector average. By contrast, health-care earnings have been below the private sector after an initial fall in the 1970s. The public sector as a whole has been

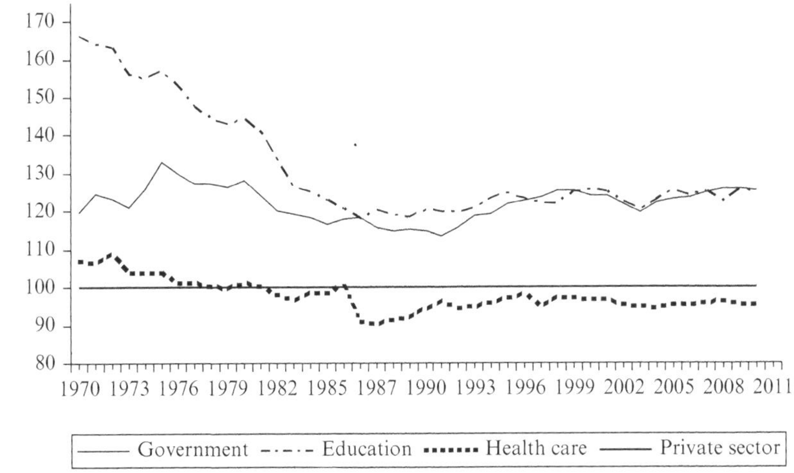

Note: Private sector average hourly wage = 100.

Source: 1970–1987 EU-KLEMS Growth and Productivity Accounts, available at: www.euklems.net; 1987–2010 CBS, *Arbeidsrekeningen*.

Figure 10.6 Public (sub)sector average hourly earnings, Netherlands, 1970–2010 (% of private sector)

paid some 10 per cent above the private sector since the end of the 1980s. The recent recession years show little deviation from the long-run stability.

Table 10.3 depicts the structure of earnings following Table 10.1. Unfortunately, information is not available for educational attainment, ethnicity, or occupational level. The position of older workers and full-time workers (35+) is very similar within the two sectors. Surprisingly, that also holds across organization size despite its very different importance in the two sectors. Also the gross, uncontrolled gender pay gap is of a comparable order of magnitude (22–24 per cent). However, the relative situation of young workers, workers on flexible contracts, and part-time jobs is rather more uneven in the private sector. Health-care hourly earnings resemble the subsectors of government and education more for youth, small and part-time jobs, and flexible contracts. By contrast, health-care outcomes are closer to private sector levels for females and prime-age and older workers, and larger organizations. Differences between government and education concern men, older workers, small and part-time jobs, and flexible contracts – here education exceeds government. Government has an advantage in medium-sized organizations.

These data relate to gross earnings as received by the employee includ-

Table 10.3 Average hourly earnings, Netherlands, 2009 (relative to within-sector average)

	Private sector	Public sector			
		Total	Government	Education	Health care
Gender					
Men	108	116	104	110	127
Women	82	91	93	92	93
Age					
15–24	45	53	52	53	55
25–49	105	99	98	95	102
50–65	119	117	113	118	116
Weekly working hours					
<12	61	91	82	92	96
12–20	68	88	84	94	90
20–35	86	96	96	103	95
35+	107	107	101	99	112
Organization size					
<10	103	104	–	94	113
10–100	94	92	97	89	97
100+	103	100	100	101	100
Flexible contract*	45	67	57	71	72

Note: * 2005.

Sources: CBS, Statistiek Werkgelegenheid en Lonen SWL, and Enquête Werkgelegenheid and Lonen EWL for 2005.

ing tax and contributions paid by the employee. Employer contributions are not included though these are particularly important for pensions. However, public–private differences for employer contributions have been much mitigated between 1995 and 2011: the employer share in gross labour costs grew from 13 to 21 per cent in the private sector, and from 18 to 24 per cent in the public sector.[10] In addition, secondary labour conditions such as for childcare or parental or care leave may be more favourable in the public sector. At the same time there are special bonuses in the private sector.

3.4 Earnings Differentials: Lower Disparity but Pay Penalty in the Public Sector

It is impossible to infer from these average earnings whether the characteristics that have been mentioned so far actually carry a pay premium in the public sector or not, because workforce composition is obviously an important determinant of these averages, as, for example, a higher employment share of high educated will lead to a higher average wage. Instead we should consider earnings differentials after correcting for composition differences. The public sector is often said to have a more compressed earnings distribution and this is commonly attributed to a relatively better treatment of low-educated employees, whose average earnings we do not know, unfortunately. Also no recent statistical information is available for the distribution of hourly earnings, while annual earnings risk is grossly misleading because they incorporate the significant variation in working hours. However, micro data (which will be used below) indicate that the distribution is indeed narrower in the public sector.

Figure 10.7 shows public and private sector hourly earnings at the same percentiles of the within-sector distributions.[11] At the bottom end, the fifth percentile of the distribution, public sector hourly earnings are 79 per cent above the private sector. The gap shrinks rapidly when moving up the distribution: 55 per cent at the 10th percentile, 36 per cent at the 25th percentile, 18 at the 50th percentile, and 11–10 per cent at the 75th and 90th percentiles. Ultimately, at the 95th percentile (the bottom of the top 5 per cent) it is the other way around. Here private sector earnings exceed those in the public sector by 6 per cent. At the mean, public earnings are 10 per cent above private earnings, in agreement with what was said before. Evidently, the private sector has a much longer tail of low pay than the public sector, the former's 25th percentile wage (€13) being similar to the latter's 10th percentile. The ratio of 90th to 10th percentile, often used as an indicator of wage inequality, is 4.1 in the private sector compared to 2.6 in the public sector. Notably, these results are still uncontrolled for compositional differences between the sectors.

Research by Berkhout et al. (2006) for 2004 is the latest and most extensive study of earnings differentials between the two sectors.[12] Berkhout and Salverda (2012) have extended the approach to 2009 and also gone back in time to 1979 using a somewhat restricted model that can be applied to the entire period given data limitations. It controls for those differences and highlights the effects on earnings of individual characteristics of employees (for example, gender, age, education) and their jobs (for example, working hours, occupational level), in isolation from the effects of the other characteristics.[13] On the basis of these estimations, an Oaxaca decomposition between the two sectors identifies the contributions made by the compositional differences. The unexplained residual of the earnings equations that remains after deducting the compositional effect indicates the specific contribution of each sector, that is, the controlled differential or the pay penalty or advantage of the public compared to the private sector.

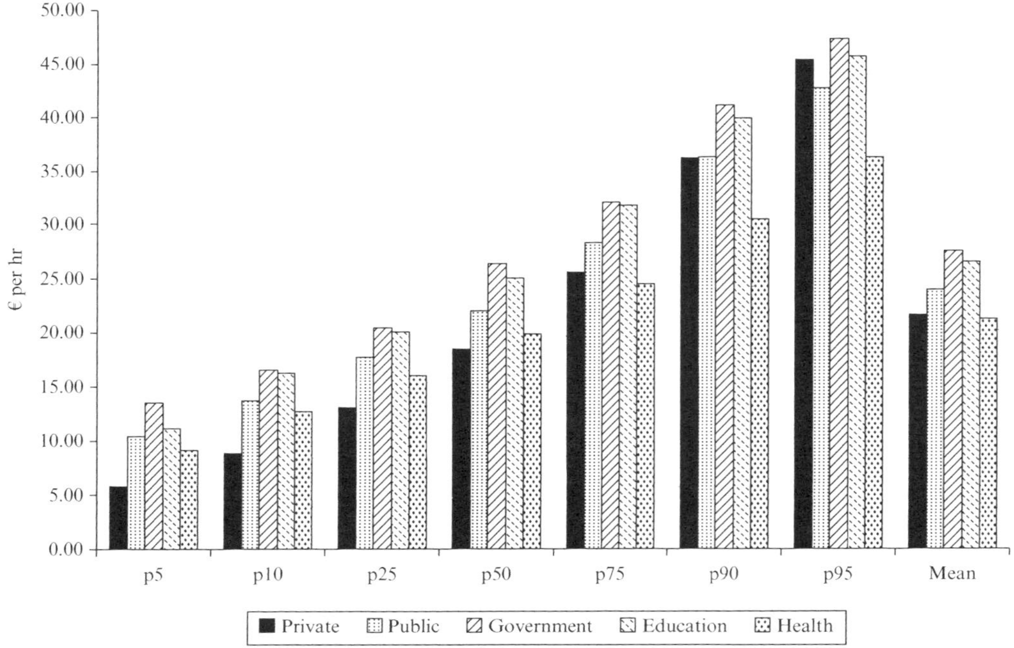

Note: Private sector percentile level = 100.

Source: Berkhout et al. (2006, Table 3.1).

Figure 10.7 Comparative earnings distributions by sector, Netherlands, 2009 (private sector level = 100)

Table 10.4 Pay differentials of public to private sector by subsector, gender and education, Netherlands, 2009 (%)

	Observed difference (raw pay gap)	Composition effect	Controlled differential
Total public sector	16.1	20.3	–4.2
Government	25.7	31.2	–5.6
Education	29.3	32.0	–2.7
Health care	5.2	9.5	–4.3

Note: Controls of the underlying wage regressions are: various subsectors also in the private sector, age and age squared interacted with educational attainment, and individual years of age from 16 to 22, type of contract (full-time, part-time, flexible, so far all interacted with gender, ethnicity, seniority, occupational level and category (technical, administrative, managing), (ir)regular working hours, and size of organization. R^2's are 0.63 (private) and 0.50 (public); tested for heteroscedasticity.

Source: Berkhout et al. (2006).

Table 10.4 mentions for the latest year first the gross observed difference between the two sectors, followed by the contribution of the diverging composition after the many characteristics have been accounted for. Third is the remaining effect which can be interpreted as the public–private difference in pay for the same personal and job characteristics. The public sector as a whole suffers a pay penalty (–4.2 per cent) compared to the private sector. All three public subsectors carry a significant pay penalty, ranging from –2.7 to –5.6 per cent. At a more detailed level, full-time workers are at a disadvantage in the public sector; part-time workers have a very sizeable raw premium which is entirely explained by compositional differences.

The table confirms the common observation that women are doing relatively better in the public sector. Men suffer a pay penalty at all levels of educational attainment, while women do so with tertiary education only. There is a clear gradient of the premium/penalty by level of educational attainment. The best educated face a strong penalty in the public sector. The two panels of Figure 10.8 illustrate the effects of gender and educational attainment, respectively, between the two sectors with the help of age–earnings profiles simulated for the average population in terms of all characteristics except age and the shown variables. Private sector men have a pay advantage over the public sector for most of the age range (Panel A), while public sector women have it for all ages. The average gender gap within the private sector (–16 per cent) appears to be twice as large as in the public sector (–8 per cent). As a result, the public pay premium largely rests on this difference; therefore the male penalty may reflect the situa-

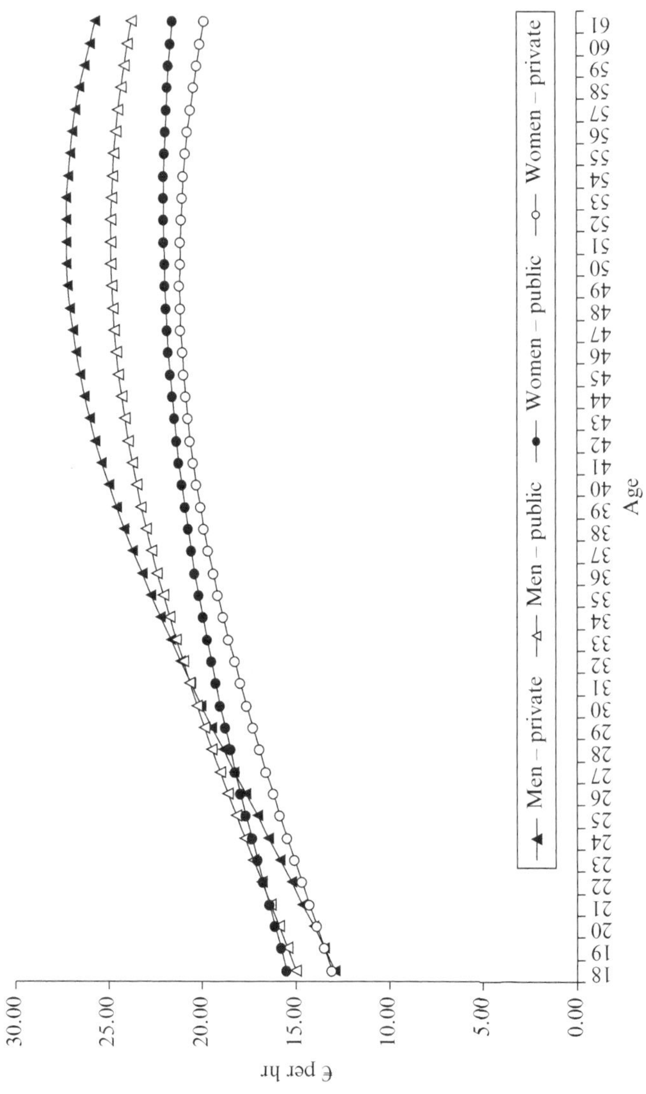
€ per hr
30.00
25.00
20.00
15.00
10.00
5.00
0.00
Age
18 19 20 21 22 23 24 25 26 27 28 29 30 31 32 33 34 35 36 37 38 39 40 41 42 43 44 45 46 47 48 49 50 51 52 53 54 55 56 57 58 59 60 61
Men – private
Men – public
Women – public
Women – private

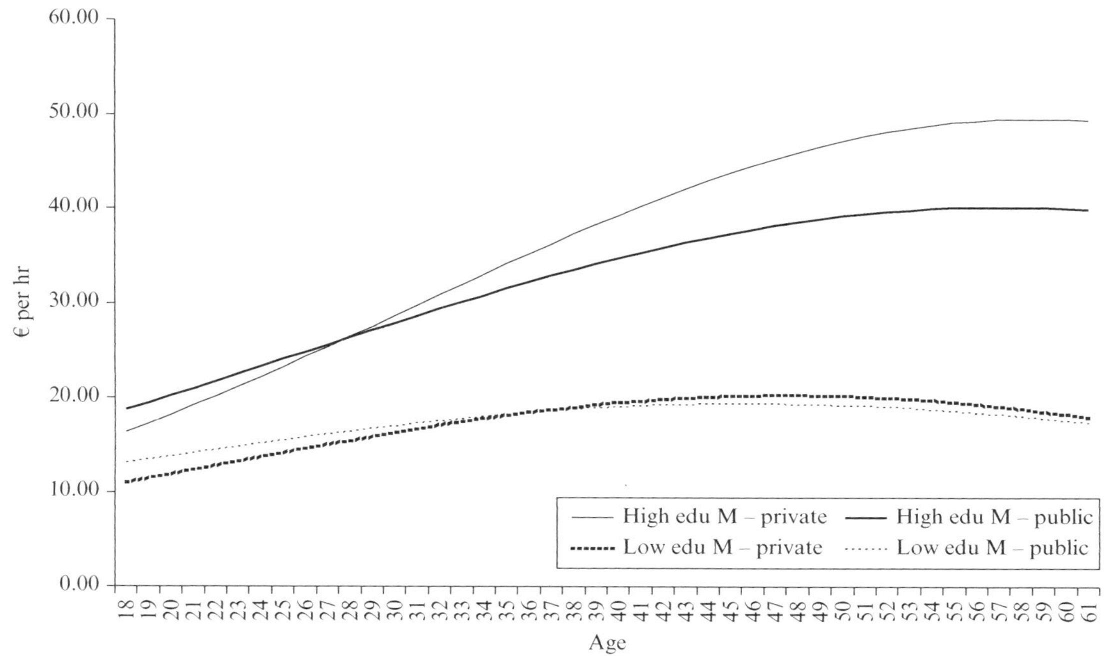

Source: Berkhout and Salverda (2012).

Figure 10.8 Age–earnings profiles, private and public sectors, Netherlands, 2009

Table 10.5 Pay differentials between public and private sectors by subsector, gender and education, Netherlands, 1979–2004 (%)

	1979	1989	1996	2002	2004	2009
Pay gap (raw)	15	8	17	16	11	12
Differentials (controlled)						
Total	4	**–7**	0	**0**	**–3**	**–2**
Government	7	**–9**	1	3	–1	**–3**
Education	6	**–5**	0	**–6**	**–9**	**–2**
Health care	**–1**	**–7**	–2	0	–2	**–1**
Males	4	**–12**	**–6**	**–5**	**–10**	**–10**
Elementary			3	2	**–5**	**–4**
Junior secondary			0	1	0	**–1**
Senior secondary			**–2**	**0**	**–5**	**–3**
Bachelor			**–10**	**–11**	**–14**	**–17**
Master			**–15**	**–12**	**–16**	**–18**
Females	4	–2	5	3	1	3
Elementary			11	7	9	22
Junior secondary			9	6	7	9
Senior secondary			4	7	9	5
Bachelor			4	0	**–2**	**0**
Master			5	**–7**	**–4**	**–2**

Note: Missing data for education in 1979 and 1989.

Source: Berkhout and Salverda (2012).

tion better. For males only, Panel B shows the profiles for the least and the best educated. The former do slightly better in the public sector at first, up to the mid-30s, but then the situation is reversed, although the difference remains small. The best educated in the public sector do better only up to the mid-20s but then the best educated in the private sector continue to rise to almost the highest age and reach a substantial premium, while public sector men plateau at the age of 50. For the least educated, earnings start to decline from the age of 50 in both sectors.

Finally, Table 10.5 indicates the evolution of the public–private differential over the long term since 1979 (penalties in bold). It shows a clear decline and ultimately disappearance (–2 per cent) of the initial pay advantage (+4 percent) of working in the public sector in general. This is a two-step process: a steep policy-wrought fall in the 1980s, when a 7 per cent premium shifted to a 6 per cent penalty, followed by some recovery until 1996 (a neutral 0 per cent premium) and ending with a more gradual decline to –2 per cent perhaps partly masked by the growing role of women. Among the three public subsectors, government shows the largest fall, from the initial highest premium (7 per cent) to the lowest (–9 per cent), and subsequently recovered to a slight premium in 1996. Education fell less, though still substantially (+6 to –5 per cent), but never really recovered. Health care, the third subsector, shares the decline of the 1980s and subsequent recovery and ends roughly on par with the private sector, with a slight pay penalty only. After the decline of the 1980s, male workers never recovered and have been facing an increasing penalty ever since. Over time, this has spread from the best to the least educated. Female workers regained a premium and ended somewhat above par. Also among them the best educated have suffered a penalty and premiums have declined at lower levels of education.

The upshot of this is that at the aggregate level, public sector pay has already been structurally aligned with the private sector. This may have gone too far as working in the public sector now carries a non-trivial pay penalty, with a steep educational gradient, and any future adjustment, aimed at maintaining the attractiveness of public sector jobs in labour market competition, might actually have to consider pay increases for the better educated.

4. THE FINANCIAL CRISIS SINCE THE FIRST QUARTER OF 2008 AND AUSTERITY POLICY

This sections considers the recent evolution of the economy and the public sector in more (quarterly) detail, and then presents the policy debate concerning public sector employment and pay in a double perspective: the short run of the current situation and the long run of the sector's role in the economy – a split that characterizes the debate in many countries.

4.1 Recent Developments

Real GDP per capita of the working-age population reached its peak in the first quarter of 2008 and subsequently declined under the influence of the financial crisis. First, it fell continuously to a trough of minus 5.2 per cent in the second quarter of 2009, then it recovered gradually until the second quarter of 2011 to a level still 1.1 per cent below the peak. After that it lost again, down to 2.0 per cent below the peak in the first quarter of 2012, four years after the start. The cumulative loss over 16 quarters since the start is 9.8 per cent of the 'peak-year' GDP, measured as four times the first quarter of 2008. There is no sign of recovery in 2012, the latest CPB official forecast being for a year-on-year decline by 0.75 per cent.

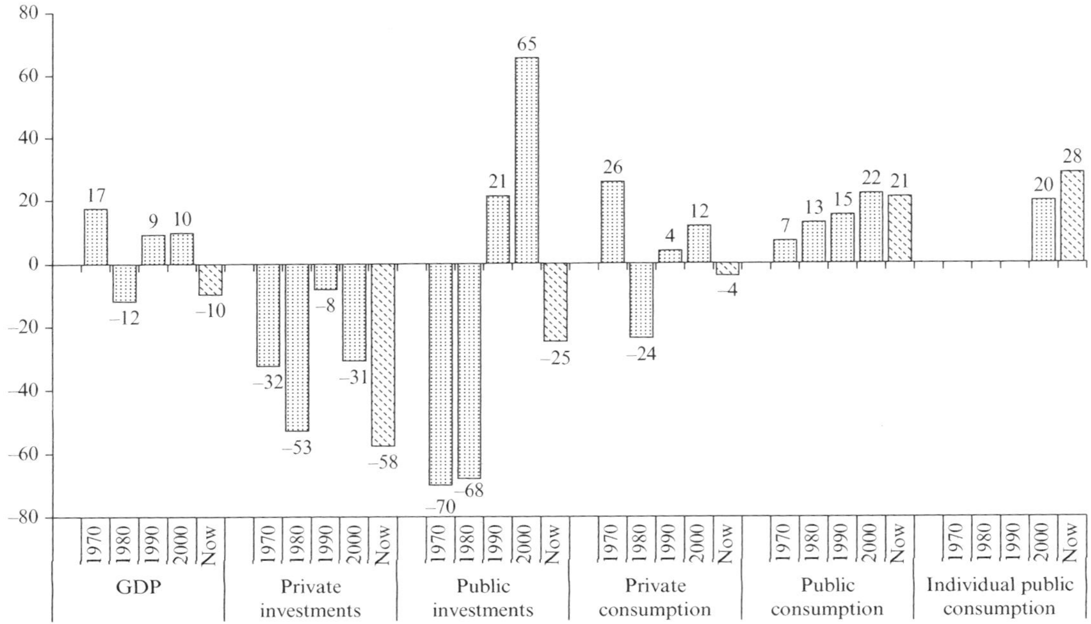

Note: Calculation based on volume figures in prices of 2005 and per capita.

Source: OECD *Economic Outlook* for earlier recessions; CBS *Quarterly Accounts* for current recession.

*Figure 10.9 Dutch recessions, cumulative volume effects, Netherlands, 2008Q1–2012Q1 (% of 'peak year' = 4 * 2008Q1)*

Figure 10.9 compares the current recession (diagonally shaded bars) with four preceding downturns, indicating cumulative effects over equally long periods of 16 quarters from the start.[14] During the recessions of the 1970s, 1990s, and 2000s (all short-lived in terms of GDP) 16 quarters led well into the ensuing upturn and brought per capita GDP significantly above the preceding peak level. Clearly, in terms of GDP the current recession (–10 per cent) is the most serious together with that of the early 1980s (–12 per cent), which hit the Netherlands more strongly than many other countries. Four other important economic aggregates are also shown in the figure. Private investments have shrunk (–58 per cent) more seriously than in the 1980s (–49 per cent). The current 25 per cent decline in public sector investment is radically less than in the 1970s and 1980s when its fall exceeded 60 per cent; it differs strongly, however, from the steep growth of the 1990s and 2000s. Private household consumption's cumulative decline by 4 per cent is in the same negative direction as the 1980s but not nearly as drastic as it was then (–24 per cent); however, the decline seems to be gaining speed currently and, again, the decrease contrasts with growth in the 2000s (+12 per cent). At the same time government consumption shows strong growth (+21 per cent), which is more than on any previous occasion. This growth has undoubtedly helped to mitigate the effects of the recession (see Case Study 2 on health spending).

If expressed comparably as percentages of ('peak year') GDP their estimated cumulative contributions during the current crisis so far are strongly negative for private investments (–9 per cent), less for private consumption (–2 per cent) and public investments (–1 per cent), and considerably positive for public consumption (+5 per cent). The latter has counteracted one-third of the current decline.

The decline in employee numbers has lagged GDP decline by one year and so far has fallen cumulatively by only 2.9 per cent per capita. Cumulative hours worked per capita provide a sharper picture, falling slowly from the very start by a total of 7.4 per cent. These aggregate employment effects seem relatively mild compared to the 10 per cent cumulative fall of GDP. Because the lower employment levels endure, they will gradually close in on the GDP loss and may not remain so benign much longer.[15]

Importantly, disaggregate employment effects look very different: the private sector lost and the public sector gained (Table 10.6).[16] After four years the private sector employment level was 3.5 per cent lower and public sector employment was 5.7 per cent higher (see Panel A). Cumulatively, the private sector lost 10 per cent of jobs and 16 per cent of hours worked and the public sector gained 16 per cent in numbers and 18 per cent in hours (Panel B).[17] Unsurprisingly, the sectors' shares in total

Table 10.6 Employment and earnings changes by sector, over the financial crisis, Netherlands, 2008Q1–2012Q1 (employees only)

	Total	Private sector	Public sector			
			Total	Government	Education	Health care
A. Level change 2008Q1 to 2012Q1, seasonally corrected						
Jobs[a]	–0.9	–3.5	5.7	–0.6	0.8	10.2
Hours worked	–1.9	–4.8	6.6	2.2	2.0	11.3
Persons[b]	–1.0	–3.6	5.5	–0.4	1.2	9.9
Men	–3.8	–4.5	–0.7	–2.1	–2.8	5.1
Women	–2.4	–2.1	8.7	3.7	4.5	10.9
B. Cumulative employment effects: sum of 16 quarterly levels compared to 2008Q1 peak year						
Jobs[a]	–2.9	–10.1	15.6	7.0	7.1	22.5
Hours worked	–7.4	–16.1	18.2	12.2	7.6	26.7
C. Shifts in employment shares: 2012Q1 distribution compared to 2008Q1						
Jobs[a]		–1.9	1.9	0.1	0.2	1.6
Hours worked		–2.3	2.3	0.4	0.3	1.6
D. Level changes by type of contract: 2010 labour volume compared to 2008[c]						
Total	–2.0	–4.8	4.8	5.6	2.6	5.4
Permanent	–2.3	–4.6	2.8	5.2	2.3	1.7
Fixed term	–1.0	–5.4	13.4	7.2	4.1	19.9
E. Level changes in average hourly earnings: 2012Q1 compared to 2008Q1						
Nominal	7.6	7.8	6.1	5.0	8.1	7.0
Real	0.2	0.4	–1.2	–2.2	0.7	–0.4

Notes:
a. Persons may have more than one job, therefore the effect on jobs differs from that on persons in work; for the latter, no seasonally corrected information is available.
b. Persons not seasonally corrected (but unnecessary as same quarters are compared).
c. Incidence of fixed-term work may be overestimated in private sector and underestimated in public sector as all temp agency work is allocated to the private sector; differences to the 3-year evolution may be limited.

Source: CBS, Labour Accounts.

employment have moved in opposite directions by around two percentage points (Panel C).

All three public subsectors show some job growth but the main contribution is from health care with a cumulative increase of 22 per cent in heads and 27 per cent in hours. It is responsible for most of the shift in the public sector employment share (85 per cent for heads, more than 70 per cent for hours). However, growth has stopped for education and government in 2010, followed by a 0.5 and 3.5 per cent decline in hours, respectively, up to early 2012. A split by gender in Panel A suggests that total female employment grew only because of a substantial increase in the public sector (8.7 per cent). Male employment grew in health care but declined in government and education.

Panel D shows the evolution of permanent and temporary contracts. For lack of more recent and quarterly data the annual level of 2010 is compared to that of 2008. The two sectors clearly diverge. In the private sector permanent and temporary contracts suffer a decline of almost equal size. By contrast, both types increase in the public sector but temporary contracts do much faster. Temporary-contract growth is strongly (80 per cent) concentrated in health care, and extends a pre-existing trend that pushed temporary numbers up by more than 50 per cent between 2006 and 2008.

Finally, Panel E sheds light on the development of hourly earnings. In the private sector they have increased nominally albeit only very slightly (+0.4 per cent), while they have declined in the public sector (–1.2 per cent), particularly in the government subsector. Note that this concerns averages that are sensitive to composition changes, which gather importance over the four-year period. In particular, a shrinking share of young people in employment may invoke a rise in the average; while they play a larger role in the private sector the upward effect of their disappearance from employment may be stronger there. The increasing role of women may have a mitigating effect but it is difficult to fathom the relevance for the sectoral comparison: the possibly larger individual effects in the private sector (Figure 10.8 upper panel) may be counteracted by the smaller share of women in the sector's employment. Real earnings – deflated by CPI – have increased in the private sector and decreased in the public sector except in education.

4.2 Policy Debate: Wage Cuts Not Considered a Viable Option

In adjusting the public sector workforce and wage bill, three issues are at play: the level and evolution of pay, the nature of the employment contract and the number of jobs in conjunction with the organization of the public services and their productivity. Naturally, there are other important options for policymaking concerning the public budget and public services which are not focused on the wage bill but on other public spending, such as subsidies and social security, or public revenues, such as from taxation. It is beyond this contribution to discuss those.

So far the policy debate has been less obsessed with pay, real wage moderation – for the public sector as much as the private sector – than usual, moderation commonly being the first response when confronted with an economic downturn. The change is difficult to explain though one may speculate that, first, the startling origin of the crisis in the operations at the heart of the globalized capitalist economy, the international financial sector, instead of in wage growth resulting from strong labour demand, together with, second, the preceding structural lowering of the wage share and the concomitant increase in the profit share, as well as, third, the novel environment of a monetary union,[18] may have something to do with it. In any case, the depth and duration of the crisis have taken policymakers by surprise both at the start in 2008–09 and again with the second dip in 2011–12.

This abstention from explicit wage moderation holds in general but also in particular with respect to the public sector. Nevertheless, the government has tried to freeze wage rates. It can be relatively easily accomplished (simply refusing to enter wage negotiations) and has a quick short-term effect – at least in comparison to projected wage increases. The government's forecaster CPB has opposed special short-run wage moderation for fear of deflation in a situation of mass (worldwide) overcapacity and the negative effects that deflation will have on debt (CPB 2009: 21; TV interview CPB director Teulings of 17 March 2009). The CPB expected the labour market to bring wage developments in line with the productivity effects of the crisis in the medium term. Also, in early 2009 a civil servants' task force, which was free to assemble any proposals for possible government budget cuts, did not suggest a lowering of salaries. Finally, those responsible for personnel management in the public sector fear what they have called the 'big exit'. The ageing of the public workforce – in 2008 35 per cent were aged 50 and over – and the negative effects of unattractive labour conditions (wage level and nature of the work) on younger employees and labour supply motivated the expectation that 70 per cent of all employees in government and education (30 per cent retirement, 40 per cent job mobility) will leave and need replacement by the year 2020. As labour conditions are already seen as lagging the private sector – particularly for the high educated – a specific lowering of public sector pay is not a helpful perspective (BZK 2011: 23). In other words, public sector wages are no longer considered as needing downward adjustment. One may surmise that the alignment already brought about between public and private sector rules out the option of making special cuts in public sector pay.

Obviously, if pay is no longer an important option this constrains austerity measures in one direction and puts the limelight of public sector adjustment on the level and composition of employment. At the parliamentary elections of June 2010 eight out of nine political parties proposed in their programmes for the 2011–15 period a reduction in the number of people employed by the public sector, varying from 18,000 to 48,000 on top of an already projected decrease (–40,000) in government and education (CPB et al., 2010, Table 2.3). Fewer parties proposed such a decline also for health care, between –15,000 and –50,000, aimed at reducing a projected increase (+150,000) and thus still leaving a net increase. The government established on the basis of these elections decided in its coalition programme to cut employment in government by 61,000 up to 2015.[19] A decrease (1–3 per cent) has already started to materialize in 2011 in government and also in education, which was thought to be exempted. The more benign treatment of health care may point to another potential constraint on austerity. ZVW-based health care covers the entire population and cuts may therefore provoke strong opposition. After the fall of the government in early April 2012 a temporary parliamentary coalition agreed on increased budget cuts aimed at lowering the budget deficit to 3 per cent of GDP in 2013, in line with European rules. However, the new coalition has done away with various cuts that had been decided by the previous coalition but will now no longer be pursued (Netherlands Government 2012). In addition it is only a voting coalition and no new government has been established – instead, the September 2012 elections had clear results in terms of voting, but no government and no agreed programme as yet. The temporary coalition's plan regarding health care comprises implicit, unequal tax rises, such as augmented own risk and own direct financial contributions to certain treatments, which are generating strong public debate. Consequently, the current situation lends significant uncertainty to the exact nature of the cuts that will be made in the end.

A serious reduction in the size of public sector employment requires that either certain tasks be reduced or productivity increased. For realizing the latter, the simplest idea is to assume an annual productivity increase and adopt that in the budgeting.[20] A deeper option concerns adapting the organizational set-up of the public sector. The Netherlands seems to be at the forefront of policy analysis here. At the country's request, the OECD has undertaken the study 'Public Administration after "New Public Management"' (2010). Although the size of Dutch public sector employment is modest in international comparison, a relatively large share of it seems to be devoted to administrative tasks instead of policymaking: 83 per cent at central government and 47 per cent at local government (BZK 2011, 10ff). This comprises, for example, the Tax and Customs Administration, Prisons, and the Public Employment and Unemployment Benefit administration UWV. The three taken together make up 42 per cent of central government employment. One option ventilated in the policy debate is to entirely close down UWV. Naturally, the tasks will not disappear, but these would be deemed to go to local government. In recent decades many tasks have already shifted to that level while budgets were reduced at the same time. It remains to be seen where this debate will lead and how the quality of the services can still be guaranteed.

In the meantime, the lack of general policy measures regarding pay together with the decentralized nature of public sector wage negotiations in combination with the focus on specific measures targeting public sector employment, may explain the absence of general strikes and worker manifestations. Instead focused manifestations have taken place, the most important of which have been in education: a strike in secondary schools against a proposed change in teachers' working hours and holiday entitlements (26 January 2012, 21,000 teachers), and a national manifestation protesting against a €300 million cut in the special teaching to special-needs pupils in secondary education (6 March 2012, 50,000 teachers), An ongoing series of actions protesting against the proposed €1 billion budget cut of WSWs, which provide 100,000 jobs for vulnerable groups, through a reduction by 70,000 places and a shifting of the remaining 30,000 places from the responsibility of central government to that of municipalities. In WSWs people are employees and represented by trade unions. This is part of a more general change in labour market provisions which is aimed at moving people with partial capacities out of assistance and WSWs towards the labour market for obtaining an income. According to the protests, it is fully unrealistic to expect the labour market to cater for these vulnerable groups, who as a result will lose much of their income.

Finally, when going the way of such employment reductions, short-run savings for the public budget are substantially reduced by the obligation for public sector employers to pay unemployment benefits to the persons involved in involuntary layoffs. The previous government intended to change the contractual conditions of employees in government and education, aiming to reduce such entitlements and also increase the possible savings in the short run (Regeerakkoord VVD-CDA 2010 financial appendix, 5). However, such changes have been on the agenda for decades.

The end result seems to be that the decentralization of wage bargaining within the public sector, together with the decentralization of governance responsibilities for public services (for example, to individual schools) and social provisions (to municipalities) makes it much harder to oppose budget cuts and to do so in a way perceptible at the national level where political sensitivities may be greatest. At the same time, it may be legally more difficult to endorse such cuts.

5. TWO CASE STUDIES OF PAY CUTS

During the major recession of 1980–85 important changes were made to the wage structure in education and to wage negotiations in health care. These provide interesting illustrations of how the public sector has come to adjust (wage) costs in these two important subsectors and of the effects of such a process. For education we focus on the long-run effects of wage changes, while for health care we also address government interference in private-party prerogatives. It seems important to see what lessons can be drawn from 30 years of experience of public sector adjustments.

5.1 Case Study 1: Long-run Effects of Wage Adjustment in Education[21]

5.1.1 The reforms

Before the bargaining decentralization of 1993 negotiations in education were held between the Ministry of Education and the unions within the framework of a single structure covering all personnel in primary and secondary education and in polytechnics (part of tertiary education).[22] In 1982, in the midst of the recession, the government launched a plan for structural reform of the structure (HOS) aimed at moving away from a strong grading according to parts of the educational system and educational qualifications of the teacher. A function-based structure was proposed where job requirements would determine pay, also no longer in conjunction with age but with experience and tenure on the job. This would strengthen equal pay for equal work, bring the educational wage structure in line with that of the civil service, lower average labour costs, and make the future educational budget more predictable as additional qualifications obtained by the teachers would no longer influence pay. After two years of negotiations, the major unions agreed to a change that would be budgetary neutral at the time of introduction – allowing compensating measures for incumbent teachers – but generate structural budget savings in the future. In 1985 the basics of HOS were implemented.

As the new system would be less strongly graded by qualifications, many incumbent teachers would receive a pay increase – particularly in primary education, junior secondary education, and vocational senior secondary education. For other incumbents, measures were taken to protect their wage–career prospects, up to a point. However, the position of the first-graded teachers (with an academic degree) was diminished, especially through the introduction of lower scales, presented as a lengthening of the tenure path by means of a downward extension.[23] The original first-grade pay scale would now relate to a specified senior function and could no longer be reached automatically. In addition, budget neutrality applied to the situation that teachers' pay had already undergone a special reduction targeting all teaching salaries (WIISO) by 1.85 per cent as of 1 January 1983. This was meant as an austerity measure reaping the benefits of proposed structural salary changes[24] and a general lowering by a nominal

3 per cent of all public sector pay as of 1 January 1984. Public spending on education declined relatively rapidly from 6.7 per cent of GDP in 1982 to 5.7 per cent in 1985.

5.1.2 Increased inequality and strikes

Although the new system abolished unequal pay for equal work as a result of individual qualifications, it established a new inequality between incumbent teachers and the 'post-HOS' new entrants, who experienced this as particularly unfair because the pay gap could be wide (25–30 per cent). The significant increase in new entrants' numbers led to many protests, initiated outside the unions which, after all, were partners to the agreement. Protests succeeded in putting the issue on the political agenda and various reparations were made (for example, higher starting salaries in 1992 with some compensation over 1985–92, shorter tenure scales in 2002). However, not all problems were solved, witness, first, that even 15 years later, in 2000, the national Equal Treatment Commission (CGB 2000) concluded that female re-entrants had been discriminated since the introduction of the new system in 1985, partly also because of the protection given to incumbents at the time of the HOS introduction. Second, even more recently, the ultimate repair – re-establishing the automatic tenure for first-graders up to the top scale, albeit conditionally – was agreed for the year 2014, closing the circle 30 years after the start.

5.1.3 Less attractive conditions and lower quality

The pay restructuring has made working in education less attractive, especially to the academically educated, and thus the average level of teacher qualifications has declined. This, together with the abolition of incentives of the old structure for individual human capital investments, is seen as contributing to a decline in the quality of educational output, among a host of other reforms that have taken place since the 1980s, such as, for example, the decentralization of budget spending to the schools[25] and the drastic changes made one-sidedly by government to the curriculum and the organizational set-up of secondary education.

The conclusion of this is that though at present in various countries many may prefer the long-run perspective of structural reform over that of short-run austerity, one has to be very careful as the nature of the structural change may actually be affected by the context of austerity. This may affect the workplace (equal treatment) but also the output (quality). In this case, a structural reform may soon run into difficulties while the remedy may take a long time.

5.2 Case Study 2: Government Interference in Private Wage Setting in Health Care[26]

5.2.1 A sector in competition with the private sector

Traditionally, the largest part of the health-care sector is financed from public funding, mainly social security funds,[27] but at the same time all health-care producers (hospitals, general practitioners and so on) are legally private parties. This implies a labour market exclusively populated by private employers and suppliers of labour, and operating in a way fully comparable with the private sector. Notably, wages are the largest category of spending in the subsector, comprising more than half of all gross production costs – a share more than twice as high as in the private sector. Clearly, this situation of direct public–private interaction can lead to a conflict of interests in times of economic recession, when a government would aim to restrain or cut public spending, including for social security and subsidies.

5.2.2 Wages: a target of government policy

Such a conflict arose during the recession of the early 1980s, and it particularly involved employees and their unions as wage formation in health care became a direct target of government policy making. In 1979 the government introduced a temporary ad hoc law (TWACS) obliging organizations receiving subsidies or social contributions to endorse in their wage bargaining the pay developments of central government civil servants, which were legally decided unilaterally by the government – with the strongly negative results shown in Figure 10.4. First enacted to run until the end of 1980, the TWACS duration was extended four times[28] and it finally expired at the end of 1985, to be replaced by a new law (WAGGS) which was made permanent in 1988. As an ultimate remedy, this law allowed the government to undo the results of wage negotiations and impose a return to the previous situation. WAGGS made the criterion for selecting organizations subject to this regulation more general,[29] and though in principle the criterion was narrowed down from any financial contribution from government to an 'important' contribution, it also became clear that this meant important not only relative to the organization finances but also to the absolute amount of public funds involved.

5.2.3 Wage bargaining undermined

From the very start of the law-making process in 1979 (TWACS), the main trade union confederation FNV protested against this as a violation of free collective bargaining under two ILO Conventions, the Freedom of Association and Protection of the Right to Organise Convention, 1948 (No. 87) and the Right to Organise and Collective Bargaining Convention, 1949 (No. 98), and brought this to the attention of the ILO. The Netherlands Socioeconomic Council subscribed to this view in its advice to the government of 1983 (SER 1983). A mission sent by the ILO in early 1984 considered TWACS a violation of Convention No. 87. In 1988 the three major trade union confederations FNV, CNV and MHP jointly lodged a formal complaint against WAGGS with the ILO's Freedom of Association Committee. In 1989, the ILO concluded that WAGGS violates Convention No. 87, for three reasons. First, the ultimate remedy is a direct violation, despite the fact that it had not been applied; second, the extended duration of the law is at odds with the prerequisite of compelling reasons of national interest; and third, wage outcomes in health care have actually been affected, as seen in Figure 10.4. In 1990–91, the government made noises about dropping the ultimate remedy. It asked the SER for new advice which in 1992 proposed dropping the ultimate remedy and made a number of suggestions for a comprehensive way of dealing with the problem of conflicting public–private interests. In the meantime the applicability of WAGGS was gradually reduced quantitatively by concluding specific budgetary agreements with certain sectors. WAGGS was terminated in 1995 and replaced by a complex set of rules (OVA) on how the relevant budget available for wage bargaining will be determined by the government and communicated to the employers. The starting point of OVA would be the trend of private sector wage agreements corrected for wage drift and desired productivity growth. The latter was dropped during the first few years after various (legal) conflicts arose and finally, in 1999 a Covenant was concluded between the associations of healthcare organizations and the government which has remained in force until today, although in 2007 another legal case was needed to prevent a budget reduction.

As we have seen, wage rates have developed very much in parallel between government, education, health care and the private sector over the past two decades. However, the effect of abolishing TWACS and WAGGS may become visible in the current situation. Recently, healthcare wage rates have developed more favourably than for government and education, as OVA rules still allowed significant budgetary increases.[30] The upshot is that wage adjustments in the public sector cannot be made indiscriminately but have to account for diverging legal obligations. The final conclusion is that the views of the ILO do matter even if it takes a long time to take a government to task for violating ILO Conventions – even for cases which seem more nuanced than the common violations of trade union rights.

6. CONCLUSIONS

The public sector is defined here as including health care (employees only), government and education. Under government pressure, health-care wage formation has run increasingly parallel to government and education since the recession of the early 1980s. It is an important argument for including health care in the public sector concept, despite the fact that it is entirely operated by private institutions. Health-care finance was traditionally not exclusively run through social security (ZFW and AWBZ) but has come fully under the sway of public sector finances since the new national health-care insurance system (ZVW) was introduced in 2006. Because of its sheer size including or excluding health care has a major effect on the comparison of the public and private sectors, as the specifications presented throughout the chapter can show.

In recent decades, the public sector has grown significantly in size relative to the private sector, although structurally at the same pace as private sector services. However, virtually all of that relative increase has been in money benefits and in-kind public services provided to private households. Thus the public channel to individual consumption has become significantly more important. Potentially, this broadens the effects of austerity measures on the population and the opposition to them. Public sector employment has mirrored this development: the quantitative importance of public sector basics, that is government, has hardly changed since 1970; education has shown a slight increase at best; health-care employment, by contrast, has expanded enormously. Naturally, the composition of the public sector workforce is affected by the inclusion of health care. Women, older workers, part-time jobs, the highly educated, higher job levels, large organizations, and irregular hours are strongly overrepresented in the public sector, while, by contrast, young people, ethnic minorities, flexible employment contracts, small jobs, and minimum wage earners are overrepresented in the private sector.

Public sector wage bargaining generally follows the trend of the private sector, with the important exception of the 1980s when, in the wake of the severe recession, wage rates suffered a policy-wrought permanent decline by 20 per cent in government and education and 10 per cent in health care. Average (unadjusted) actual earnings in government and education have remained 19–22 per cent above those in the private sector, those of health care slightly below. However, after correction for the important public–private differences in employment composition, working in the public sector appears to carry a pay penalty. The public sector pay advantage that existed at the end of the 1970s has been more than taken away. The penalty is particularly significant for the highly educated and, unsurprisingly, also for the educational subsector. The low educated are on a par with the private sector (Figure 10.8, lower panel).

Fundamentally, pay has already been aligned between the two sectors and there is no longer an economic need for downward public sector pay adjustments. Key public sector personnel policymakers are keen to ensure that public sector jobs remain attractive to labour supply as they fear that 70 per cent of the public workforce will have to be replaced over the current decade because of ageing and job mobility. Nevertheless, negotiated wages have been falling in real terms recently, to varying degrees (government –1.3 per cent, education –2.7 per cent, health care –0.8 per cent), as a result of the non-renewal of important collective agreements in education and government and modest renewals in health care. Non-renewal amounts to a nominal wage freeze. However, to date the differences with the private sector (–1.2 per cent) have been small. These developments may explain why there has been little taste for lowering public sector pay in the current financial crisis. However, at the time of writing after the downfall of the coalition government, the parliamentary majority which rapidly agreed on a set of budget cuts has included a nominal two-year (2012–13) wage freeze in government and education, considering this an inescapable measure to satisfy the Eurozone's 3 per cent deficit rule. It remains to be seen, however, how this freeze can be squared with the formal termination of one-sided wage determination in 1988 and the decentralization of public sector wage bargaining to 14 separate agreements, which imply that nowadays the government is the employer of its own civil servants only.

The policy discussion has structurally focused on shrinking and reorganizing public sector employment, aimed at reducing the wage bill while simultaneously stimulating the effectiveness and productivity growth of public services and improving the attractiveness of public sector jobs to the labour supply. To enhance the budgetary savings from the implied redundancies, the government intends to reduce the entitlements of employees in government and education to a say in the process of reorganization as well as to unemployment benefit. However, reorganizing employment is a more complex and longer-drawn-out process of taking specific measures, especially as many responsibilities have been or are being decentralized to municipalities, individual institutions, and also to separate wage-bargaining forums. This decentralization is a second type of public sector adjustment that has already been pursued extensively over the 1990s and 2000s. At the same time, it lends a nitty-gritty character to the opposition mounted to such measures. As a result, the opposition can often no longer be consolidated at the national level, where the public debate and political sensitivities may be stronger than at decentralized levels.

In addition, the lessons of the previous deep recession in the Netherlands of 1980–85 seem to be that various measures that were considered to be structural may actually have been affected by their short-run context of austerity necessitating long-run repair efforts. Wage cuts made in education over 1980–85 are still being put right to this very day. The government's infringement of wage-bargaining rights in health care from 1979 onwards met its nemesis in 1995 as a result of appeals to the ILO conventions on freedom of association. As a consequence, wage bargaining in health care has become less susceptible to government pressure legally and current outcomes do indeed exceed those of government and education. Furthermore, the newly agreed wage freeze does not apply to health care.

Finally, the general appetite for lowering wages is surprisingly weak, despite the strong effects of the crisis on the Dutch economy – with a renewed recession in the second half of 2011 – and the burden of public debt that was incurred by bailing out the country's relatively large financial sector. This reticence is based on past experience and motivated by the shrinking of demand more broadly, far beyond the Dutch economy, and fears of deflation which can aggravate the problems of debt.

NOTES

* I am particularly grateful to Ernest Berkhout at SEO Economic Research for our joint work on pay differentials (see Berkhout and Salverda 2012).

1. Including social services throughout the chapter except for the discussion of ZVW in the case study.
2. Berkhout et al. (2010) and De Mooij et al. (2010) leave out health care but include education. By contrast, Heyma et al. (2004) and Berkhout et al. (2006) include health care.
3. The exceptionally large deficit of 1996 is due to a capital-account transaction underlying the privatization of the public sector pension fund ABP.
4. 130 per cent of the adult minimum wage is close to the common low-pay threshold (two-thirds of median wage). The incidence is underestimated to the extent that for young people the reference is youth minimum wages which are well below the threshold.
5. The legal right to strike was given to public sector workers by the government in the 1980s, and formally granted to all workers by the Supreme Court of the Netherlands in 1986 on the basis of the European Social Charter.
6. The absolute number of members fell by 5 per cent while that of employees grew by more than 30 per cent. Union density differs among government (34 per cent), education (30 per cent) and health (18 per cent). The growing importance of health lowers the aggregate public sector rate. Figures for 1995 and 2010 exclude people working less than 12 hours per week.
7. These agreements also cover 200,000 employees outside our definition of the public sector. Within the public sector a remaining 145,000 employees are covered by private sector agreements.
8. If we focus on real monthly wages, disregarding the effect of shortening working hours, the decline has been larger (government + education –22 per cent; health –14 per cent) and purchasing power has grown only half as much (4–5 per cent), mostly between 1985 and 1990 while it has remained virtually unchanged since 1990 (+1 per cent). Thus any productivity gain has gone to the employer.

9. Wage negotiations take the CPB's economic forecasts of prices and productivity as a point of departure. In 2009 prices lagged expectations substantially. Salverda (2009) discusses the mechanism in more detail.
10. Calculated from seasonally adjusted total wages and the volume of hours worked in CBS, Arbeidsrekeningen.
11. The data treat security (not shown) separately from government. They make up about one-quarter of government as a whole. Their bottom-half earnings are relatively high.
12. CPB (2011) largely depends on this and similar research, and the most recent data used relate to 2005.
13. The level of individual hourly earnings is explained from personal and job characteristics with multivariate regression in the two sectors separately. An innovation in the modelling is to pay special attention to the strong rise in earnings that occurs over the short age range from 15 to 22 years, due to the Dutch system of youth minimum wage. This prevents a mistaken projection on higher years of age. It is also important because young people have a much smaller presence in the public sector.
14. Preceding peaks were: 1971Q1, 1979Q2, 1994Q4 and 1999Q4.
15. One lesson may be that GDP decline is a less than adequate measure of economic downturns (see Salverda 2011).
16. We disregard the per capita effect as that would be the same for all sectors.
17. Note that this excludes the self-employed, all in the private sector. Their numbers grew by 1.4 per cent, their hours by 1 per cent.
18. Note that the Netherlands, like Germany, is on the surplus side of intra-EU imbalances of international trade (20 per cent of GDP in 2011), while it has a strong deficit with the rest of the world (12 per cent). Over 2008Q1–2012Q1 the cumulative volume of exports fell by 9 per cent of peak year and imports declined by 2 per cent (CBS, international trade statistics).
19. See: http://www.nu.nl/economie/2345587/overheidstekort-daalt-werkloosheid-stijgt-bij-nieuw-kabinet.html. Half of those are sought in sheltered workplaces (WSWs) – note that these are operated by local government with the financial support of central government.
20. Compare OECD (2011: 78). However, productivity cuts in government wage budgeting (OVA) for health care met with much opposition and were soon abolished (see Case Study 2, below).
21. An interview with a senior union official who took part in the negotiations of the 1980s is gratefully acknowledged.
22. Only the universities were excepted, most of which were public sector institutions by law and applied the general rules of the civil service. The distinction is reflected in the fact that not teachers' unions but civil servants' unions organize university staff.
23. These teachers were mostly organized by a smaller crafts trade union organizing a special category of workers; in 1997 it merged with the major union.
24. The WIISO reduction was to be decreased gradually over time when the budgetary results of the new pay structure would come into effect. WIISO included university teaching staff whose pay was also subject to a restructuring.
25. Leading, *inter alia*, to a much larger spending on non-teaching staff at primary and secondary schools (Onderwijsraad 2006: 46).
26. Most of the process is described in SER (1992). See also SER (1983).
27. AWBZ: national social security covering heavy long-term health expenditures, and ZFW: obligatory employee social insurance for the private sector below an earnings threshold. In 2006 ZFW was replaced by ZVW obliging all inhabitants to take basic health insurance from private insurers, who are forbidden to select by risks, and to pay social contributions enabling the evening of risks between insurers and transfers to household mitigating the income effects of the single basic insurance premium.
28. To 30 June 1982, 30 June 1984, 31 March 1985, and 31 December 1985.
29. TWACS was originally thought to apply to about 0.5 million employees; WAGGS may actually have applied to three times as many.
30. 2009 to 2012: 3.42, 1.75, 3.11, and 1.75 per cent, respectively (ggzbeleid.nl/ova).

REFERENCES

Berkhout, E., A. Heyma and W. Salverda (2006), 'Beloningsverschillen tussen de marktsector encollectieve sector in 2004', Rapport 889, SEO Economisch Onderzoek, Amsterdam.

Berkhout, E., S. van der Werf and A. Heyma (2010), 'Het verdiende loon? Loonontwikkeling overheidswerknemers vergeleken met de marktsector', Rapport 2010-39, SEO Economisch Onderzoek, Amsterdam.

Berkhout, E., and W. Salverda (2012), 'Development of the public–private wage differential in the Netherlands between 1979 and 2009', AIAS Working Paper 126, SEO Economic Research and AIAS, Amsterdam.

BZK (2011), *Trendnota Arbeidszaken 2011*, Ministry of the Interior, The Hague.

CBS (Statistics Netherlands) (2010), *Organisatiegraad van werknemers 1995–2010*, Available at: http://www.cbs.nl/nl-NL/menu/themas/arbeid-sociale-zekerheid/cijfers/incidenteel/maatwerk/2010-organisatiegraad-werknemers-cm.htm.

CBS (Statistics Netherlands) (2011), *Special Tables on Union Density 1995–2010*. Available at: www.cbs.nl/nl-NL/menu/themas/arbeid-sociale-zekerheid/cijfers/incidenteel/maatwerk/2010-organisatiegraad-werknemers-cm.htm.

CGB (Commissie Gelijke Behandeling) (2000), *Inschalingsystematiek in het Onderwijs en HOS-regeling nadelig voor Herintredende Vrouwen*, Oordeel 2000–2009, Utrecht.

CPB (Centraal Planbureau) (2009), *Centraal Economisch Plan 2009*, The Hague.

CPB (Centraal Planbureau) (2011), 'Loongebouw overheid en mobiliteit', Notitie 1 November 2011, The Hague.

CPB (Centraal Planbureau) and Planbureau voor de Leefomgeving (2010), *Keuzes in kaart 2011–2015*, The Hague.

De Mooij, M., I. Bottelberghs, M. Goedhuys, J. van den Tillaart and C. Wagner (2010), *Gelijk loon voor Gelijk Werk? Banen en Lonen bij Overheid en Bedrijfsleven, 2008*, Den Haag/Heerlen: CBS.

Heyma, A., E. Berkhout, M. Biermans and W. Salverda (2004), *Beloningsverschillen Marktsector en Collectieve Sector 2001*, Report to the Ministry of the Interior, The Hague.

ICTWSS: Data Base on Institutional Characteristics of Trade Unions, Wage Setting, State Intervention and Social Pacts, 1960–2010 (Jelle Visser). Available at: http://www.aiasbase.nl/208.

Netherlands Government (2012), Voorjaarsnota, The Hague. Available at: http://www.rijksoverheid.nl/documenten-en-publicaties/kamerstukken/2012/05/25/voorjaarsnota-2012.html.

OECD (2010), *Value for Money in Government: Public Administration after 'New Public Management'*, Paris: OECD.

OECD (2011), *Value for Money in Government: The Netherlands 2010*, Paris: OECD.

Onderwijsraad (2006), *Waardering voor het Leraarschap*, The Hague.

Osmani, M. (2010), 'Gevolgen van normalisatie. Een onderzoek naar de gevolgen van normalisering van het ambtenarenrecht op het gebied van ontslag voor de sector onderwijs', Thesis, University of Applied Sciences, Utrecht.

Regeerakkoord VVD-CDA (2010), *Vrijheid en Verantwoordelijkheid*, The Hague.

Salverda, W. (2009), 'The bite and effects of wage bargaining in the Netherlands 1995–2005', in M. Keune and B. Galgóczi (eds), *Wages and Wage Bargaining in Europe: Developments since the Mid-1990s*, Brussels: ETUI, pp. 225–54.

Salverda, W. (2010), 'The Dutch minimum wage: minimum wage fall shifts focus to part-time jobs', in D. Vaughan-Whitehead (ed.), *The Minimum Wage Revisited in the Enlarged EU: Issues and Challenges*, Cheltenham, UK and Northampton, MA, USA: Edward Elgar and Geneva: ILO, pp. 299–339.
Salverda, W. (2011), 'The Netherlands: is the impact of the financial crisis on inequalities different from in the past?', in D. Vaughan-Whitehead (ed.), *Work Inequalities in the Crisis: Evidence from Europe*, Cheltenham, UK and Northampton, MA, USA: Edward Elgar and Geneva: ILO, pp. 355–96.
SER (Socioeconomic Council) (1983), 'Advies loonvoming in niet op winst gerichte sector', Advice No. 83/21, The Hague.
SER (Socioeconomic Council) (1992), 'Advies arbeidsvoorwaardenvorming in de g+g sector', Advice No. 92/01, The Hague.

11. Portugal: Structural reforms interrupted by austerity

Helena Rato

1. INTRODUCTION

Employment in Portugal's public administration registered huge growth in the second half of the 1970s, mainly due to decolonization, as the public administration was used to integrating people coming from the former Portuguese colonies, and democratization, which involved the improvement of the welfare state as well as local government. From 1984 onwards civil service employment continued to increase, largely driven by the obligations arising from EEC membership and subsequent implementation of EU policies.

In the 1990s, restructuring the public administration became part of the government's policy agenda, aimed at increasing efficiency and improving the quality of public services in line with New Public Management theories. The improvement of human capital was thus one of the main drivers of public administration reform early in the new millennium. But when Portugal was put under an EU excessive deficit procedure in 2005, the focus of its policy agenda had to be changed in order to reduce the structural deficit. Initially, the Portuguese government tried to conciliate restrictive budgetary measures with economic development within public administration structural reform programmes. In the context of the financial and sovereign debt crises, however, this attempt was not successful and thus there was a drift towards increasingly restrictive adjustment programmes.

All the variables that shape employment conditions in the Portuguese public administration are determined by laws that define public employees' status and so their rights and duties. Therefore, policy measures specifically addressed to public administration within the framework of Portugal's structural adjustment policy must be supported by laws. Accordingly, changes in public employees' status must be analysed in order to understand how structural adjustment policy has affected public employment.

The scope of Portuguese public administration is very large and is composed of three categories: direct state administration, indirect state administration and autonomous administration.

Direct state administration is composed of all public bodies directly dependent on the government. They are integrated into the organic structure of ministries. Public education, excluding universities, the National Health Service (NHS), excluding public hospitals, public security forces and the armed forces are included in the direct state administration.

The indirect state administration is composed of public entities that have legal responsibility as well as administrative and financial autonomy. However, the heads of these entities are appointed by line ministers and have to take direction from ministers. Public institutes, public agencies, public universities, regulatory entities, public hospitals, including those managed by private entities, as well as public enterprises belong in this category.

Autonomous administration also has legal responsibility and administrative and financial autonomy, and is entitled to define its own objectives and public policies. The autonomous regions (Azores and Madeira islands), local administration (municipalities and parishes) and non-profit public associations, such as professional bodies, also belong in this category.

Until 2005 there was no reliable statistical information on employment in Portuguese public administration. Since then there has been significant progress in this regard, although shortcomings remain, including the lack of statistics related to gender equality. In any case, the lack of information is wider for autonomous administration and it is discontinuous. That is why this chapter centres on central public administration, which accounts for 80 per cent of total public employment and represents 13.4 per cent of all employees. Central public administration comprises direct and indirect state administration. The latter accounts for 36.5 per cent of employment in central public administration.[1]

Central public administration employees are much more highly qualified than others. Regarding educational level, 55 per cent of public employees have academic degrees, as against only 17 per cent in the private sector. On the other hand, 64 per cent of private employees have an elementary educational level as against 23 per cent in central public administration. Such a difference is explained both by the high share of education and health care in public employment, together representing 66 per cent, and by higher feminization rates with regard to employees with a high educational level. In 2010, the percentage of women with academic degrees was 62 and 22 per cent in the public and private sectors, respectively, as against 40 and 13 per cent for men.

Section 2 provides a broad description of structural adjustment as a nationwide policy and its evolution since it was decided to pursue both structural reforms and growth on the basis of austerity. Sections 3 and 4 focus on specific measures concerning the public administration and their effects on employment in both quantitative and qualitative terms. Section 5 presents case studies on health care and education, whose feminization rates are particularly high and which have been especially affected by the deterioration of public employment. Finally, Section 6 presents conclusions.

2. STRUCTURAL ADJUSTMENT POLICIES IN PUBLIC ADMINISTRATION

2.1 Overall Characterization of Portuguese Structural Adjustment Policies

Structural adjustment policies aimed at reducing the structural deficit in public finance commenced in 2005 when the 2005–09 Stability and Growth Programme (SGP) was launched, following Portugal's application to the EU to be placed under an excessive deficit procedure.

Since then we can distinguish two different periods with regard to policy strategy. During the first, from 2005 to 2009, policies to reduce the structural deficit were part of a more comprehensive policy also oriented towards economic growth and technological development. However, due to the 2008 international financial crisis, the goal of reducing the structural deficit was not achieved and structural adjustment programmes have been redirected within the framework of a decision-making process that can best be described as 'playing it by ear'. Since 2010, adjustment policies have been focused on reducing the structural deficit. The situation was worsened more recently by the sovereign debt crisis that put Portugal at the mercy of rating agencies and speculators, pushing the country into adopting radical austerity policies.

2.1.1 First stability and growth programmes (2005–2009)

The first SGPs were characterized by a strong focus on developing information and communication technologies (ICTs), as well as strong investment in human capital improvement with the purpose of increasing productivity and national competitiveness.

This policy perspective was also applied to structural reform of public administration, inspired by New Public Management principles in order to increase efficiency by reducing bureaucracy and emulating systems in the private sector.

The development policy was intended to boost technological innovation, as well as growth and employment, particularly through the promotion of R&D and the creation of specific programmes geared to career upgrading.

Moreover, with regard to budgetary consolidation, direct and indirect taxes were increased in order to reduce the budget deficit. However, as the results of these measures were poor the 2005–09 SGP was supplemented by new measures, including the restructuring of the public education, health-care and justice services.

The effects of the US subprime crisis and the sustained rise in the price of oil spoiled the positive effects of the first SGP and some planned policy reforms were not implemented, such as the creation of shared public administration services aimed at centralizing procurement and logistics or the abolition of public bodies under the banner of resizing public administration. However, application of the 'one-for-two' rule when replacing public employees, mainly due to retirement, contributed to reducing public employment.

Table 11.1 presents the policy measures of the 2005 to 2009 Stability and Growth Programmes (SGPs) as well as their chronological sequence, both for development and budgetary consolidation.

2.1.2 Stability and growth programmes in 2010

The downturn in the economy in 2009 led to a new generation of SGPs in the course of 2010. These programmes are 'new generation' because they focus almost exclusively on austerity measures, unlike previous programmes which sought to balance stability and growth, even though GDP growth was –2.7 per cent in 2009 and unemployment rose to 9.5 per cent.

Given the severity of the announced austerity measures in the context of economic recession, trade unions, political parties, mass media and social non-governmental organizations (NGOs) became aware of the threat posed by the SGPs to Portugal's social cohesion. The policy shift and increasing popular opposition to it, as well as the deterioration of the sovereign debt crisis explain the ineffectiveness of policy measures and thus the almost continuous review of the SGPs. Indeed, in the course of 2010 there were four sequential programmes. The last one was approved in December 2010 by the parliament as the 2011 budgetary law. Nevertheless, pursuant to the Troika Memorandum, a new SGP was presented to parliament in March 2011. When it was not approved the government resigned, triggering a general election.

The 2010 SGP focused on increasing taxes and cutting tax deductions and fiscal benefits on the government revenue side. Table 11.2 summarizes the measures applied. Measures specifically concerning public administration are presented in Section 3.

Table 11.1 Evolution of stability and growth programmes, Portugal, 2005–2011

SGP (2005–2009) (June 2005)	SGP (2006–2010) (December 2005)	SGP (2007–2011) (December 2007)	SGP (2008–2011) (January 2009)
Approved plan for restructuring public administration	Convergence of social protection in public administration with private sector regulations	Restructuring of school network by closing schools in rural areas and integrating primary schools in vertical clusters	Implementation of new public employment regime
Plan against fraud and tax evasion	Beginning of reform of public health-care subsystems	Closure of small hospitals and concentration of emergency departments in large urban centres	Reform of retirement pension system – by introducing a weighting coefficient related to life expectation increase
Studies to change public employment regime	Continuation of the action lines set out in June 2005	Privatization of public hospital management	Increase of NHS fees
'One-for-two' replacement rate of public employees	Public support for training in R&D and ICT	Reduction of drug costs	Improvement of e-administration
Higher taxes on petroleum products and tobacco	Investment in human capital in public administration	Elimination of police and gendarmerie stations when acting in the same area	
Annual incomes above €60,000 taxed at 42%	Implementation of the 'new opportunities' programme to improve employability of young people	Abolition of public bodies	
Approved national plan for growth and employment		Continuation of action lines set out in June 2005	
Launch of the technology plan focused on information and knowledge development			
Distribution of computers in school network			

Source: Stability and Growth Programmes, from June 2005 to January 2009; Programme for Restructuring Central Public Administration, PRACE, 2005.

Table 11.2 Overview of major austerity measures and their impact, 2010 SGP, Portugal

Policies	Measures	Impacts
Tax increase	Increase of 2.5% on profits over €2,000 Increase of 2% VAT (as average) Individual incomes exceeding €150,000 per year taxed at 45%	Tax evasion and rising prices Decrease in net income of highly qualified employees
Tax deduction and fiscal benefits	Cuts in tax deductions for retirement pensions above €22,500 per year End of tax deduction for life insurance and on personnel accidents Reduction of tax benefits for the replacement of polluting cars	Impoverishment of middle-class families Insurance industry has less revenues and so pays less taxes Failure to comply with EU guidelines on pollution
Reduction of social spending	Freeze of social support index at €419.22 Cuts in child benefits Cuts in unemployment benefits for those who reject paid employment between 10 and 25% above the allowance	Impoverishment of the poorest Degradation of wages Degradation of pensions
	Cuts in retirement pensions by applying a new method of calculation	Impoverishment of the elderly
Autonomous regions development	Cuts in financial transfers from central government to the regions by €2.5 million	Impoverishment of autonomous regions Risk of failure of investment plans and EU programmes
Development of municipalities	Cuts in financial transfers to municipalities by €100 million Imposition of the zero borrowing rule	Impoverishment of municipalities Risk of failure of investment plans and EU programmes, leading to rising unemployment, especially in the hinterland

Table 11.2 (continued)

Policies	Measures	Impacts
Military expenditure	40% reduction in military expenditure and limits on outsourcing	Reduction of external balance deficit but difficulties for domestic armaments factories Malaise in military forces
Public investment	Freeze of investments in high-speed trains and on a new airport near Lisbon	Bankruptcies in construction industry Increase in unemployment
Public administration	Measures and impacts are presented in Section 3	

Source: Stability and Growth Programmes, 2010–2013, March 2013.

2.1.3 Structural adjustment in accordance with the Troika Memorandum

After the June 2011 elections a centre–right[2] coalition took office. This government continued to follow policies determined by the Troika Memorandum (Agreement on austerity measures and structural reforms) since the coalition parties had already signed the commitment in May 2011 during the election campaign.

Accordingly, the 2012 state budget law is focused on austerity measures aimed at reducing the public deficit and subordinating structural reforms to that objective. On the economic growth side the government intends to increase productivity by increasing workloads without additional pay and replacing overtime payments by working-time accounts. This measure will therefore eventually result in merely arithmetical productivity growth.

The Troika Memorandum contains 208 measures and various submeasures covering: budgetary policy, the regulation and supervision of the financial industry, structural fiscal measures, the labour market, energy, transport and communications, the housing market and the judicial system. All measures must be implemented by June 2014.

3. EFFECTS OF POLICY MEASURES TARGETED AT PUBLIC ADMINISTRATION

Austerity measures applied to the public administration concern employment, in both quantitative and qualitative terms. The first generation of structural adjustment programmes were aimed at changing the public employment regime to emulate the private employment regime and reducing the volume of public employment. However, since 2010, adjustment measures have been aimed at cutting public expenditure not only by reducing employment but above all by cutting wages, overtime and other compensation and social benefits, including pensions. This might damage public administration performance and the working conditions of public employees.

3.1 Downsizing Public Employment: From Structural Reforms to Unemployment

One of the major structural reforms in public administration concerns the public employment regime, which started in 2006[3] with the introduction of the possibility of dismissing public employees engaged after that date and the setting up of a special mobility scheme. The most important change occurred in 2008[4] when about 80 per cent of public employees with permanent jobs were transferred to public functions with open-ended contracts. According to the law these public employees continued to be protected from dismissal, but could be put into 'special mobility', which involves cuts in basic pay. The apparent contradiction between this and the dismissal regime regarding public employees engaged after 2006 was clarified in 2009,[5] when it was specified that the latter would be subject to the rules of private sector unemployment, even on open-ended contracts.[6] Moreover, since 2008 it has been possible to dismiss a public employee on the grounds of unsuitability for the job.[7]

Downsizing follows structural reform through the abolition and merger of public bodies, although to date downsizing by means of special mobility measures or by dismissal has not been much used. Only 1,211 public employees had been put in special mobility[8] by June 2011, 51 per cent of them women. However, according to statistics provided by the Institute of Employment and Vocational Training (IEFP) public sector unemployment[9] began to increase from 2009 on.

The evolution of unemployment by public sector occupational category from 2009 to 2011 is shown in Table 11.3. It should be noted that for health care and education, unemployment data concern both the public and private sectors. However, considering that in Portugal most health-care and education services are provided by the public sector we can assume that Table 11.3 is representative with regard to the unemployment development of public employees in these sectors, especially as most private education and health-care institutions are funded by the public sector in various ways.

Table 11.3 Unemployed in public functions enrolled in IEFP centres, by occupation, Portugal, 2009–2011

Occupations	2009*	2011*	Rate of increase % (2011/2009)
Senior public administration	113	151	33.6
Highly qualified health professionals	2,668	2,947	10.5
Other health professionals	2,218	2,565	15.6
Teachers in secondary and higher education	2,246	2,963	31.9
Other professionals of education	2,387	3,030	26.9
Total public unemployed by occupation	9,632	11,656	21.0
Total Portuguese unemployment	472,873	496,326	4.5

Note: * Data for first six months.

Source: Faro (2011: 13).

Table 11.3 shows that over the past two years unemployment in public sector occupations has grown at a rate of 21 per cent, much higher than the growth rate of total unemployment, although unemployment in public sector occupations represented only 2 per cent of total unemployment in June 2011 (IEFP). However, if social protection activities[10] are considered, then public sector unemployment reaches 35,145 in June 2011, in other words, 7 per cent of total unemployment.

Despite the increasing public unemployment, the adjustment measures that have contributed most to reducing total public employment were carried out by freezing recruitment, applying the one-for-two rule and pushing public employees into early retirement. Some of these measures were applied at the same time.

In fact, the freeze on recruitment was imposed long before the SGPs namely since 1984,[11] but at that time military and police personnel, as well as university lecturers, teachers and other educational employees were not included in the freeze. The one-for-two rule means that for every two employees who leave the public administration only one new one can be recruited. However, as public services complained that they were suffering shortages in highly qualified staff the Council of Ministers passed a resolution[12] to allow the replacement of outgoing staff in justified cases but subject to the Ministry of Finance and Public Administration's agreement. In fact, in line with the Troika requirements, the hiring freeze is now being applied to every job category in central public administration.

Retirement among public employees has increased sharply since 2005,

Table 11.4 Growth rate of retired public employees by income levels, Portugal, 2005–2010

Period	Up to €750	€750–€1,500	€1,500–€3,000	Above €3,000	All levels
2005/07	–0.4	7.1	17.0	20.3	6.4
2007/08	–0.9	5.1	16.7	15.5	5.7
2008/09	–1.0	5.9	17.2	24.8	6.5
2009/10	0.1	4.8	13.6	22.2	5.8
2005/10	–0.8	16.0	44.8	58.0	16.4

Source: PORDATA, www.pordata.pt/.

especially at the highest income levels (Table 11.4). The average age of these retirees is below 60. Thus it is highly likely that early retirement is significant. Although no statistical data are available, there are reports that support our hypothesis. For example, the media[13] recently reported that in 2011 early retirement in public administration increased by 13 per cent. This is due to changes in retirement conditions and pensions, leading to a gradual increase in the retirement age and reducing the monetary value of pensions.

Table 11.4 also shows that the highest growth rates regarding public employees' retirement occurred at the higher remuneration levels, which correspond to the most highly qualified staff. This was particularly noticeable in the health sector and forced the Ministry of Health to hire foreign doctors,[14] most of them from Latin America and Spain. With regard to Latin America, intergovernmental agreements allow reductions in doctors' remuneration; in any case, these doctors are not considered public employees.

Briefly, the one-for-two rule and the increase in early retirement among public employees is the major cause of the downsizing of the public administration, which was particularly high in health care during 2005–11 (Table 11.5). However, the data provided by the Public Employment Observatory probably do not take into account the unemployment of health care and education professionals with short-term contracts, whose situation is explained in the case studies.

3.2 Cutting Wages and Other Payments

In addition to wages, public employees receive payments related to their overall income. At this point we shall analyse the most common payments: overtime, travel allowances, meal allowances and family allowances. Table 11.6 presents an overview of cuts in wages and other payments, enabling us to draw the following conclusions. Although the cuts affecting lower-paid public employees can be considered tough due to their

Table 11.5 Rates of employment growth in the central public administration, by sector, Portugal, 2005–2011

Period	Education (%)	Health (%)	Other sectors[a] (%)	All sectors[c] (%)
2005/07	–2.0	–11.2	–9.2	–6.5
2007/08	1.0	–3.5	–2.6	–1.2
2008/09	2.1	–2.8	–1.3	0.0
2009/10	–1.9	–4.2	–1.0	–2.0
2010/11[a]	–0.2	–2.2	–1.0	–0.9
2005/11[b]	–1.2	–21.9	–14.4	–10.3

Notes:
a. 30 June 2011.
b. All central public administration, excluding education and health.
c. All central public administration.

Source: BOEP – Public Employment Observatory.

low wage level, wage inequality was reduced by 4 per cent because of the falling purchasing power of public employees at the middle and upper-middle levels. It can therefore be concluded that the adjustment reforms are leading to a widespread impoverishment of public employees, which necessarily has depressive effects on the economy.

3.2.1 Wage downsizing in public administration

Portugal's adjustment policy with regard to public employees' wages, which began long before the implementation of the SGPs, has been geared towards lowering real wages based on the argument that public wages are higher than private ones. The same argument is used to justify the current structural adjustment policies, although there is no evidence to prove this. Indeed, there are no statistics on average public wages nor is there a comparative study of public wages in relation to private ones by occupational category. Some evidence was collected by the General Directorate of Public Administration when it commissioned a study from Deloitte in 2006, but the study results were never disclosed. In order to assess lost public employee purchasing power in comparison to employees in the private sector it is necessary to look at wage policy in the public administration before 2005. Moreover, the assessment of such policy highlights the negative effects of cutting other payments.

In Portugal, the minimum wage was first established in 1974 (Table 11.7). Since then there have been two minimum wages, one for public administration and the other for the private sector, which is considered the national minimum wage. At present (mid-2012), the minimum

Table 11.6 Overview of wage adjustments and cuts in other payments, Portugal, 2010–2012

Very low paid – up to €485	Low paid – €485 to €1,000	Middle level – €1,000 to €1,500	Upper levels
Wage freeze and cut in Christmas bonus (decrease of real wage of 7.5%)	Wage freeze, cut in Christmas and holiday bonuses (decrease of real wage by 10.6%, on average)	Wage freeze, cut in Christmas and holiday bonuses (decrease of real wage by 12.6 to 24.6%)	Top managers – cut in nominal wage, cut in Christmas and holiday bonuses (decrease of real wage of 31.6%) Other public employees – real wage cut by 28.6%
Freeze in meal allowance, subsidies for risky and dangerous activities	Freeze in meal allowance, subsidies for risky and dangerous activities	Freeze in meal allowance, subsidies for risky and dangerous activities	Freeze in meal allowance, subsidies for risky and dangerous activities
Lower payments for overtime and lower pension entitlements	Lower payments for overtime and lower pension entitlements	Lower payments for overtime and lower pension entitlements	Lower payments for overtime and lower pension entitlements
Cuts in family allowances	Cuts in family allowances, abolition of allowances for wages above €628	n.a. Decrease of per diem and travel allowances from 15 to 20%	n.a. Decrease of per diem and travel allowances by 20%

Source: Portuguese Budget Laws, 2010, 2011 and 2012.

wage is €485 while the minimum wage for public administration is €343.28, both at current prices.

Public employees' wage rises are determined each year by the budget law; they are not determined by collective bargaining, as in the private sector. The wages of the various grades of public employees have been referenced since 1989 against a scale on which 100 corresponds to the minimum wage in public administration. This means that the evolution

Table 11.7 Wage gap, Portugal, 1974–2007 (€ at 1990 constant prices)

Year	National minimum wage	Public administration minimum wage*
1974	181.47	181.92
1989	173.71	195.18
2000	198.22	181.39
2005	198.82	168.29
2006	199.57	166.49
2007	202.99	164.58

Note: * General employment regime for public administration.

Source: Actualizações (2007), STAL Newsletters (Union of Local Public Administrations' workers), July.

Table 11.8 Growth rate of wages in the public administration and in the private sector compared to the CPI, Portugal, 2000–2009

Year	Public administration wages		Private sector wages		CPI (%)
	Nominal (%)	Real (%)	Nominal (%)	Real (%)	
2000	2.5	–0.4	5.1	+2.2	2.9
2001	3.7	–0.7	3.7	–0.7	4.4
2002	2.8	–0.8	2.7	–0.9	3.6
2003[a]	1.5	–1.8	3.1	–0.2	3.3
2004[b]	2.0	–0.4	3.0	+0.6	2.4
2005	2.2	–0.1	4.5	+2.2	2.3
2006	1.5	–1.6	3.1	0.0	3.1
2007	1.5	–1.0	3.9	+1.4	2.5
2008	2.1	–0.5	3.3	+0.7	2.6
2009	2.9	+3.7	3.3	+4.1	–0.8
2000–09	22.7	–3.6	35.7	9.4	26.3

Notes:
a. Wages above €1,008.7 saw no increase.
b. Wages above €1,024.09 saw no increase.

Source: Government ordinances, Annual Reports of Bank of Portugal and INE (National Institute of Statistics).

of wages for all public employees is determined by the minimum wage for public administration.

This system has resulted in the deterioration of public employees' real wages in relation to the private sector (Table 11.8) due to the continuous degradation of the public administration's minimum wage. According to

Table 11.9 Scale of state budget pay cut for public employees by remuneration levels, Portugal, 2011

Remuneration levels	Pay cut
Up to €1,500	Wage freeze
Above €1,500 and up to €2,000	3.5%
Above €2,000 and up to €4,200	From 3.8% to 9.98%
Above €4,200	10%

Source: www.WEB-EMPREGO.com and Law 55-A/2010, Articles 19 and 22.

Table 11.7, from 1989 to 2007, the minimum wage in public administration lost 15.7 per cent of its purchasing power, while national minimum wage gained 16.9 per cent in purchasing power. Thus the loss of purchasing power of the minimum wage in public administration with regard to the national minimum wage was 30 per cent. Concerning public administration maximum wages the loss of purchasing power was 7.5 per cent and thus the public administration wage gap increased by 8.2 per cent.

On average, during 2000–09, public administration wages lost 3.6 per cent of their purchasing power, but compared to the average private sector wage the loss was 13 per cent (Table 11.8). Moreover, senior officials and upper wage categories lost more than 3.6 per cent because their wages were frozen in 2003 and 2004. More precisely, senior officials and upper categories experienced a cumulative loss of purchasing power of 5.1 and 7.1 per cent, respectively.

Later, in 2010, public administration wages were frozen which corresponded to a real wage decrease of 2.5 per cent as the consumer price index (CPI) rose to 2.5 per cent. Moreover, the gross fixed monthly pay of top public managers[15] was cut by 5 per cent. The state budget for 2011 went further regarding public administration wage cuts, imposing a decrease of between 3.5 and 10 per cent of public employees' wages above €1,500. Table 11.9 shows the scale of the pay cuts. The aim was to achieve a reduction of state expenditure on public employees' wages of 5 per cent and according to the Directorate for Public Administration, 54 per cent of central public administration employees were affected by the cut.

On 7 September 2011, the parliament approved Law 49/2011 establishing an extraordinary tax of 3.5 per cent on the annual gross income of all individuals earning above the minimum wage (€485). In the case of private employees and pensioners the extraordinary tax was paid in full in December 2011. Briefly, all employees and retirees subject to additional tax of 3.5 per cent lost 7.1 per cent of their real income as in 2011 the CPI rose by 3.6 per cent.

Table 11.10 Purchasing power loss of public employees by monthly income group, Portugal, 2010–2011

Up to €485	From €485 to €1,500	Above €1,500	Top managers
7.1%	10.6%	From 13.6 to 20.6%	25.6%

Source: Author's calculation based on laws mentioned above and INE data.

Table 11.10 shows the loss of purchasing power suffered by public employees in 2010–11 by monthly income groups, taking into account (Table 11.9), the extraordinary tax of 3.5 per cent and consumer prices.

Recently, the 2012 Portuguese budget law[16] laid down further cuts in public employees' wages as follows: suspension of thirteenth- and fourteenth-month payments, which correspond to holiday and Christmas bonuses, of all public employees whose monthly wage is above €1,100; for public employees with monthly wages between €600 and €1,100 the suspension of these bonuses is partial, increasing progressively to a maximum of a 50 per cent pay cut according to a specific mathematical formula.[17] In short, the best-qualified public employees will have a nominal wage cut of 14 per cent, but the real wage cut will be above 16 per cent.[18]

3.2.2 Reduction of overtime pay and compensatory rest

The 2012 budget law also introduced cuts in paid overtime for public employees. For the first hour of overtime additional pay remains 25 per cent, but for the subsequent hours this payment falls from 50 to 37.5 per cent. Moreover, there is no longer a distinction between day and night overtime, as under the previous law.[19] As a consequence, the additional payment for the first hour of overtime at night falls from 60 to 25 per cent and the additional payment for subsequent night hours falls from 90 to 37.5 per cent. Regarding overtime on holidays or weekly rest days the additional pay falls from 100 to 50 per cent.

These changes are particularly damaging for health-care workers and security employees, especially because they are forced to do overtime due to the labour shortages caused by recruitment freezes in these sectors. For instance, the doctors' and nurses' associations are currently demanding the recruitment of new graduates. About 50 per cent of health-care workers[20] are affected by the new rules on overtime, leading to a loss of monthly income. Doctors' unions are also very concerned about cuts in compensatory rest due to emergency work and they have brought an injunction before the Administrative Court. After the threat of an overtime ban by doctors' unions in February 2012, the Ministry of Health appeared to back off, but the situation remains uncertain. As for the nurses' union one of the main slogans of the 22 March general strike was 'unpaid labour is slave labour'.

This is also the understanding of police officers' unions regarding compulsory work on compensatory rest days. They have therefore complained to the European Court of Human Rights. In the metropolitan area of Lisbon some police officers have rejected the rotas assigned to them, arguing that it prevented them from enjoying a family life (a right under European law) since most of them come from regions far away from Lisbon.

3.2.3 Cuts in compensatory supplements

In addition to the basic wage and overtime pay some public employees are eligible for compensatory supplements, including housing allowances, subsidies for risk, unhealthy and dangerous activities, and per diem and travel allowances. Every public employee enjoys a meal allowance.

All these allowances were frozen in August 2005–December 2007, but they were upgraded by an increase similar to the basic wage increase in 2008 and 2009. However, they have now all been frozen again except per diem and travel allowances,[21] which were reduced by 20 per cent for public employees whose basic wage is above €1,336 and by 15 per cent for other public employees.

3.2.4 Cuts in family allowances

Under Portuguese law, family allowances are monthly payments to help families to feed and educate their children (including prenatal allowance). Family allowances are structured in five levels in relation to average family monthly income per capita. The first level corresponds to income under half the Social Support Index (SSI), that is, €209.61, while the fifth is between two-and-a-half SSI and five times SSI, that is, between €1,048 and €2,096. Allowances decrease in accordance with family income and are higher for children under one year old. Prenatal allowances are similar to family allowances for children under one.

In 2008, the first two family income levels (up to €419.22) benefited from an extraordinary increase in allowances of 25 per cent. This increase was justified because of the impact of the crisis on the poorest. The highest family allowance therefore reached €174.72 a month and covered children under one year old and pregnant women whose average monthly family income was less than €209.61.

However, under the austerity measures of the 2010–13 SGP that was approved in September 2010, the extraordinary increase of 25 per cent at the first two levels of family allowance was cancelled and families with an average monthly income above €628 are no longer entitled to it.[22]

Policy measures on family allowances were applied to the overall population resident in Portugal, both nationals and foreigners, and therefore they were not specific to public employees. Moreover, statistics about public employees receiving family allowances are not available. However, by studying the specific case of the Instituto Nacional de Administração (INA) it is possible to assess the percentage of central public administration employees affected by family allowances cuts.

INA[23] was a public institute integrated within the structure of the Ministry of Finance and was devoted to developing human capital in the central public administration. INA staff included 118 employees and 11 managers. Most INA employees were integrated into the general career structure of the public administration, although some employees were on ICT and research career paths. Before cuts in family allowances imposed by the 2010 laws, 25 per cent of INA's employees received family allowances. At present (mid-2012), the figure is 7 per cent, a decrease of 18 percentage points. INA's employees who continue to receive family allowance are at levels 2 and 3, which correspond to a monthly average family income of less than €628.

3.3 Curtailing Social Protection and Creating Inequalities in Public Employment

Adjustment reforms to social protection are aimed at bringing the public administration closer to the general system applied in the private sector. The reforms cover old-age pension entitlements, dismissal conditions and health protection. The adjustment process was initiated in 2006[24] by applying the general private system to newly recruited public employees and convergence rules to public employees recruited before 2006. Consequently, public employees were split into two groups with regard to social protection.

For employees engaged in public administration after 2006 the general conditions are 65 years old and 40 years of contributions, while for public employees engaged before 2006 the criteria are 60 years old and 36 years of contributions. However, the application of convergence rules means that the two systems will be subject to the same criteria by 2013.

The calculation of retirement pensions was also changed,[25] in accordance with two different methods: one for public employees engaged after 2006 and another for those engaged before 2006. In brief, for the former the private pensions method is applied which is less favourable to retirees than the public administration method and for the latter, pensions are based on the average of two items, (i) years worked before 2006, which corresponds to 90 per cent of the reference wage and (ii) years worked after 2006, using the same valuation method as the private sector. More problematic for both groups is the sustainability coefficient linked to the increase in life expectancy, which is aimed at reducing the value of pensions. In 2008, the sustainability coefficient was 0.56 per cent but now (2012) it is 3.92 per cent, which means a cut in pensions in the same proportion. This is a very important issue because it has contributed to the increase in early retirement and, subsequently, to the downsizing of public employment.

Concerning conditions and rights in case of dismissal there are three different groups. Public employees engaged after 2006 can be dismissed because of job mismatch, disciplinary reasons or job extinction, as well as because of the expiry of fixed- or variable-term contracts. In contrast, civil servants under the tenure regime[26] cannot be dismissed, only suspended for disciplinary reasons and public employees engaged before 2006 and with an open-ended labour contract can be put in special mobility if they are considered unproductive or surplus to requirements. This diversity has been established by a number of different laws.[27]

The special mobility regime has three phases. The first phase lasts 60 days and is considered a transitional phase from one job to another. During this phase, public employees continue to receive their basic wage. The second phase lasts for more 10 months and is called the requalification phase because it is assumed that public employees will receive appropriate training. By 2012 during the qualification phase public employees should receive five-sixths of their basic wage,[28] but that has now[29] been reduced to two-thirds. That decrease corresponds to a wage cut of 14 percentage points: that is, from 80 to 66 per cent of the basic wage. The compensation phase is the third and final phase which is not subject to limits until the retirement of the beneficiary, who until 2012 received two-thirds of his or her basic wage. Under the 2012 budget law this has been reduced to one-half, corresponding to a 16 percentage point reduction, from 66 to 50 per cent.

Public employees who can be dismissed are subject to general unemployment rules, which follow the Troika Memorandum approved in 2011 by the government: unemployment benefits last 18 months and amount to 65 per cent of the monthly average wage for the last 12 months with a 10 per cent cut after the six first months. Besides that, unemployment benefits cannot exceed €1,047.5, corresponding to 2.5 times the SSI.

Another difference between public employees in the convergent system and in the general social protection regime concerns health: the first group benefits from its own health system (ADSE), while the other is covered only by the NHS. However, public employees in the convergent system have to pay 1.5 per cent of their basic wages into ADSE and 11 per cent into their pension fund, while public employees in the general system have to pay only 11 per cent of their basic wages for social protection.

3.4 Hindering Promotion and Pay-level Progression

Promotion involves moving up from one occupational category to a higher one in terms of technical or functional responsibilities and therefore better paid, while pay progression involves moving up to a higher pay level within the same category.

The system of promotions and pay progression was also changed by the 2008 structural reform of the public employment regime.[30] Under the old regime progression was granted to civil servants with a good performance assessment, every three years, while promotion was subject to public application for a vacant post. This system was conducive to career progression but few promotions and so the government decided to freeze progression in 2005.

Under the new system, general conditions for promotion by public tender have not changed. However, a new promotion system was created based on performance assessment, subject to strict criteria and quotas: only public employees performing well over five years can move up to a higher pay level. This period falls to three years for employees performing very well but the assignment of such evaluations cannot exceed a quota of 25 per cent. In both cases the period of progression can be reduced at the will of the top management, provided there are funds available, but at best progression never occurs in less than two years.

Moreover, it should be noted that progression to an upper salary grade corresponds to a monthly increase of €51.5 for public employees,[31] except for senior categories whose monthly compensation increase can reach €260.

In order to assess the impact of these changes a study was undertaken[32] on 2008 and 2009 data for four ministries[33] representing about 25 per cent of public employment in the central public administration. According to the study only 7.3 and 9 per cent of public employees, respectively, moved up to a higher wage level in 2008 and 2009. Nevertheless, considering that such a move is rewarded by a monthly wage increase of at least €51.5 and extrapolating the former percentages to all employees of the central public administration, the increase in payroll for a period of 14 months accounted for about 8 per cent of spending on central public administration in 2008 and 2009.

The 2011 budget law[34] prohibited any wage increase on the basis of either performance assessment or public tender. Consequently, career progressions were frozen, although it was expected that performance points would be accumulated, to come into effect once the government's financial difficulties were resolved. The budget law for 2012[35] maintained the ban on career progression.

4. QUALITY OF PUBLIC EMPLOYMENT IN PUBLIC ADMINISTRATION

With regard to quality of employment, the major factors to be considered are job security, upward mobility and career development, progression in pay levels by professional merit, social security, working hours that allow for harmonization of work and family life and confidence that labour rights will be respected.

All these factors taken together embody an 'implicit' labour contract based on expectations about career development and confidence in the enjoyment of labour rights that were assured at recruitment time. The curtailment of public employees' rights, which is being gradually and unilaterally undertaken by legislators and policymakers, generates feelings of unfairness, perplexity and fear, disturbing psychological equilibrium.

4.1 End of Job Security

The common conception of job security in public administration is a job for life. That was the situation in Portuguese public administration until 2008, when 76.8 per cent of public employees enjoyed civil servant status with permanent appointments. However, job security has since been seriously damaged by structural reforms in public employment.

First, about 80 per cent of civil servants with permanent appointments were transferred to public functions with an open-ended contract. These public employees can be put in special mobility, which implies wage cuts, as explained in Subsection 3.2.5. Moreover, any public employee engaged before 2006 can be dismissed.[36] The second big change concerns the stability of employment in public bodies. Until 2008 the composition of such personnel was permanent in terms of both numbers and careers. Since then, however, staff have to be updated every year according to needs and budgetary resources. Subsequently, there has been an increase in fixed-term contracts by 195 per cent.

Reforms of the public employment regime also include the establishment of new rules for labour contracts. Of particular importance is the possibility to suspend a labour contract[37] due to the illness of an employee, as well as dismissal on the grounds of job unsuitability for public employees engaged after 2006. Briefly, at present there are three groups of public

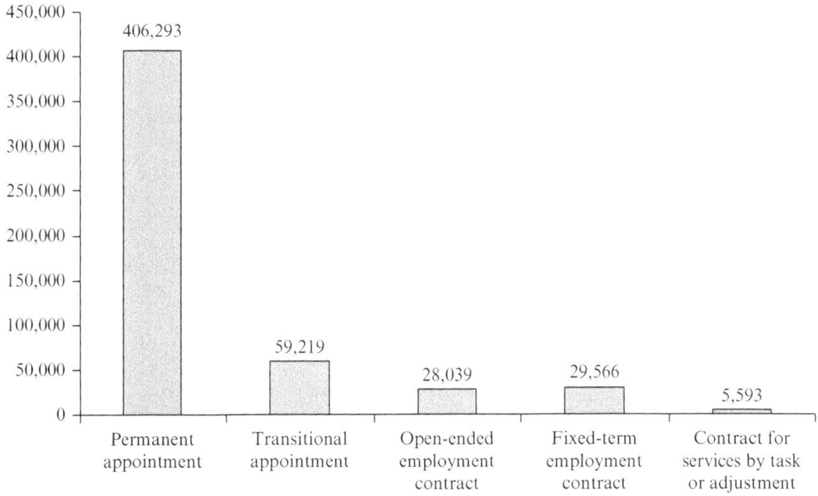

Source: PORDATA – Database of Portugal Contemporâneo, Fundação Francisco Manuel dos Santos.

Figure 11.1 Central public employment by type of contract, Portugal, 2008

employees with regard to job security: those who retain the status of civil servants and so enjoy permanent appointment (15.1 per cent); those who have public function employment contracts covered by the system of special mobility, which at worst leads to a 50 per cent cut in basic pay (64.7 per cent); and those who joined the public administration after January 2006 and can be dismissed.

Figures 11.1 and 11.2 show the effects of the reform on the composition of public employees' status in labour contract terms.

4.2 Freezing Career Development and Improving Outsourcing of Training

In Portugal's public administration, career development has two interrelated components, training and promotion to higher categories.

Training for public administration employees is governed by law[38] and considered as both a duty and a right aiming to 'qualify, dignify, motivate and professionalize the human resources of the public administration by applying a coherent and appropriate policy on careers, salaries and training'. Training for public employees used to be free of charge and supported by the state budget. In 2009,[39] the general government budget paid 67 per cent of total training costs, while public

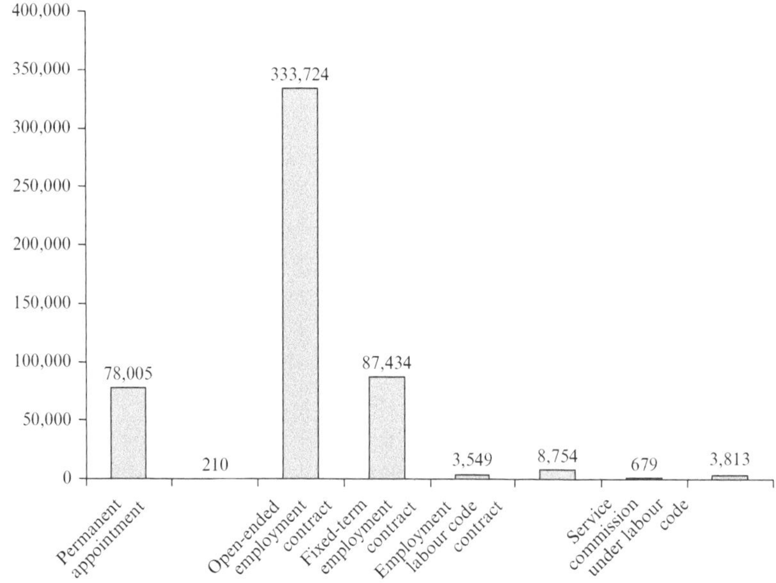

Source: PORDATA – Database of Portugal Contemporâneo, Fundação Francisco Manuel dos Santos.

Figure 11.2 Central public employment by type of contract, Portugal, 2010

entities' own revenues covered 14.5 per cent and European funds only 7.8 per cent.

In order to meet public training objectives two central public bodies have been specifically created. One[40] was INA: Instituto Nacional de Administração (National Institute for Administration) designed in 1979 for central public administration, which was developing activities in training but also research, consultancy and international cooperation. These activities were its main source of revenue and customers were mainly other public bodies. However, government budgetary restrictions brought about a serious decrease in attendance at INA training courses, as well as in consultancy projects, which led to INA's financial asphyxiation. Consequently, as already mentioned, INA was abolished, resulting in a directorate more suited to the management of public employees' mobility, which is expected to increase sharply due to the policy of downsizing public employment.

Figure 11.3 shows the evolution of INA training volumes[41] since 1998, which was the year when vocational training for the public administration was regulated. Higher growth rates correspond to the years when

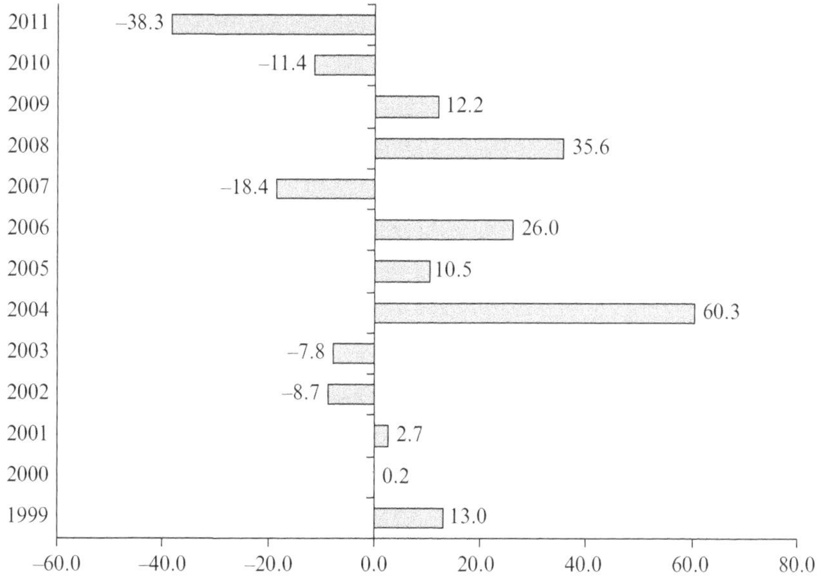

Source: INA Annual Reports.

Figure 11.3 INA training volumes, Portugal, 1999–2011

important structural reforms were implemented, concerning performance assessment, change of professional and career status of public employees and professionalization of public managers. The austerity years strongly decreased the volume of training provided by INA.

Recently, the finance minister announced the creation of the Alliance for the Promotion of Excellence in Public Administration in partnership with institutes and universities providing business courses. Under the agreement, there will be 650 vacancies for the academic year 2012–13 for public employees, who will enjoy an 80 per cent discount on tuition fees. This measure therefore ends the principle of free public training and there are concerns about its effectiveness when promotions by merit are frozen.

4.3 Less Social Security

This topic has already been well developed in the section on the main policy measures concerning public administration. At this point we shall emphasize the most relevant issues.

Social security for public employees is one area that has experienced particularly profound changes since 2005 due to the policy of convergence of specific social protection for public employees with the general social security system. One consequence of this policy is that now there are two groups of public employees: those who are already in the general regime and those who are in the convergent regime.

The first group, which includes all employees joining the public administration after 2006 or with fixed-term contracts, is subject to the unemployment rules[42] of the private sector. Accordingly these public employees are entitled to unemployment benefits only if they have paid social security contributions for at least 360 days in the previous 24 months. This condition is particularly unfair to public employees with temporary or fixed-term contracts, which do not ensure the fulfilment of those rules. In such cases, public unemployed workers can only apply for a kind of unemployment benefit which may be lower than the social minimum of €419.22, while unemployment benefits can reach €1,048.

The period during which unemployed workers are entitled to receive unemployment or social security benefits[43] depends on age and years of contribution.

Social protection of public employees under the convergence regime was described in Subsection 3.3. Accordingly, it is important to emphasize the situation of public employees pushed into the regime of special mobility who can be moved to jobs far from home or receive only 50 per cent of their basic pay after 12 months in mobility.

The health protection system has also been changed. Public employees engaged after 2006 are covered by the Portuguese NHS but they no longer enjoy the public employees' health system (ADSE) which offers more benefits than the NHS, particularly in terms of reimbursement of health expenses as well as freedom of choice with regard to medical care. However, monthly contributions to the system have increased by 0.5 per cent, while the scope and reimbursement of health expenses have been reduced.

4.4 Hampering Harmonization of Work and Family Life

Working hours constitute a major driver of the harmonization of work and family life. The situation of public administration with regard to working hours continues to be 'privileged' compared to the private sector, where workload can reach 60 hours per week, although not exceeding an average limit of 50 hours for a continuous period of two months.[44] In contrast, working hours in the public administration continue to be regulated by specific legislation[45] that maintains a workload of 35 hours per week and 7 hours a day and does not allow work to begin before 8am and to end after 8pm. Moreover, this legislation only allows two hours of overtime per day and a total of 100 hours per year.

Nevertheless, in certain areas of the Portuguese public administration there is a trend towards increasing workload without compensation as a result of the freeze in recruitment and dismissal of employees under fixed-term contracts or service contracts. This applies to teachers, health-care personnel and public security forces.

In the case of teachers the problem stems from the fact that there was a reduction of working time for lesson preparation and administrative tasks in order to increase the number of teaching hours.

For health-care personnel, the issue is the limits imposed on compensatory rest due to overtime. Moreover, some doctors and nurses may not be able to take compensatory rest due to staff shortages. This situation is particularly acute during summer holidays.

With regard to the security forces, changes in working hours prevent them from having consecutive days of compensatory rest, which is particularly harmful to personnel who are on duty away from their families.

5. CASE STUDIES ON HEALTH CARE AND EDUCATION

5.1 Case Study 1: Adjustments in the National Health Service – Wide Range of Adverse Effects

Today, health is a major concern among the population who are worried about the future of the NHS. The NHS was set up after the revolution of 25 April 1974 along the lines of the English NHS, and has performed very well. Infant mortality fell from 55.5 per thousand births in 1975 to 3.3 in 2011 and subsequently, life expectation rose from 67 to 79 years. Such an impressive performance was due to high investment in maternal and child health, as well as the establishment of health centres all over the country to ensure health-care accessibility to the hinterland population. Of course, health-care improvement is also due to the extension of sanitation throughout the country, in which democratically elected local governments have played a leading role.

During the same period, however, the fertility rate decreased by 50 per cent and now stands at 1.36 births per woman of childbearing age. There has therefore been a strong increase in the aged population and demographic desertification, especially in rural areas. Nevertheless, health costs per capita and per year are low, below €1,900 according to the OECD, representing 11.3 per cent of GDP, the same percentage as in Switzerland.

Structural reforms in the health system began in 2008 with the purpose of streamlining costs by concentrating resources. Dozens of health facilities have been closed, including some maternity hospitals. The World Health Organization (WHO) criteria were used to justify the reforms, and accessibility to health care was ensured by free transport. Since 2011 the structural reform has been deepened by continued closure of health facilities, ending free transport for non-urgent patients whose minimum monthly income is above €628.5 and increasing health-care fees. The last two measures have been strongly contested by patient groups, leading the Ministry of Health to consider extending free transport to certain types of patients, such as for cancer and renal impairment, and to enlarge the list of diseases free of health charges.

At the same time, the closure of health facilities has led to the clogging up of emergency units and increased waiting lists by 10 per cent, especially in surgery,[46] cardiology and imaging tests, which represents a setback in relation to 2008 performance levels.

5.1.1 Working conditions

Deteriorating conditions of access to health care can lead to increased violence against health professionals, which saw an average growth of 65 per cent between 2007 and 2010.[47] According to the Ministry of Health, nurses are the main victims of such violence (71 per cent), followed by doctors (20 per cent).

Like other public service employees, health professionals are also subject to a freeze on recruitment and promotions, and have also suffered pay cuts. In turn, a recruitment freeze in the face of rising demand for increasingly concentrated medical care has led to an increase in short-term contracts and widespread overtime, particularly in hospitals. Overtime pay thus makes up a significant proportion of spending on NHS employees (16 per cent in January 2012), leading the government to decide to reduce overtime pay as well as compensatory rest by applying rules[48] laid down in the 2012 budget law.

This matter has given rise to strong protests from doctors and nurses, especially since there is often a delay in overtime payments. In the face of these protests the minister of health has prevaricated, sometimes calling into question cuts in overtime pay, sometimes emphasizing the need for it. Meanwhile, as health services are subject to budget cuts, the payment of overtime has been delayed or reduced. Consequently, some health professionals refuse to work overtime, forcing some health facilities to reduce patient care.

Dialogue between doctors and the Ministry of Health became difficult. At a press conference[49] the Association of Physicians denounced the fact that the Ministry of Health intends to impose the criterion of the lowest price for hiring and asserted that achieving such a purpose would lead to the destruction of physicians' careers and collective bargaining, which would impair quality care for patients. At this press conference the Association of Physicians announced its support for the strike announced by doctors' unions, which took place on 11 and 12 July 2012. On 15 October 2012, a general agreement was signed by the Ministry of Health and doctor's unions, concerning overtime pay, working time, career progression and recruitment of young doctors.

5.1.2 Unemployment and Emigration of Health Professionals

The NHS overtime issue is mainly due to a lack of health-care professionals. In response the government has stepped up the immigration of doctors and nurses in recent years. Thus, between 2000 and 2002 the number of immigrant nurses rose from 666 to 1,966 and, in 2009, according to the Chairman of the College of Physicians,[50] 11 per cent of registered physicians were immigrants. With regard to nurses, in 2010 the Health Ministry estimated that there was a shortage of 3,500 nurses in 50 hospitals, which is particularly evident in primary and continued health care.

Nevertheless, nurses' unemployment is spreading. This is essentially female unemployment as 81 per cent of Portuguese nurses are women. At present, nurses' unemployment rate is 20 per cent, 50 per cent among newly qualified nurses, which led the Chair of the Nurses' College to request an interview with the President of the Republic. Moreover, according to the Nurses' College precarious employment is high among nurses who have graduated since 2009, as 23 per cent have fixed-term contracts, 19 per cent work under service contracts and 4 per cent are trainees undergoing internships. This situation is causing great dismay with some 40 per cent of young graduate nurses envisaging leaving the profession.

Another problem is the recent surge in the emigration of Portuguese nurses, mainly to the United Kingdom, France, Norway and Switzerland. Such emigration is increasing by 7.7 per cent a year.[51]

5.2 Case Study 2: Reform in Education Interrupted by Budgetary Restrictions

Education is the main public employer in Portugal, accounting for 43 per cent of central government employees in 2011. More than 80 per cent of these employees – about 176,000 persons – are in primary and secondary education, with feminization rates of 89 and 71 per cent, respectively. Education accounts for 13.1 per cent of public expenditure – that is, about 5 per cent of GDP – in recent years. According to the Bank of Portugal (Alves et al. 2010), however, the return on investment in education is very high, resulting in an increase in wage differentials of 30 per cent for men and 35 per cent for women, between 1995 and 2006. Moreover, between 1992 and 2010 the dropout rate fell from 50 per cent to 28.7 per cent (by gender, the dropout rate is now 32.7 per cent for men and 24.6 per cent for women). However, Portuguese dropout rates are still far above the EU27 average of 14 per cent.

From 2005 to 2010, structural adjustment reform of education followed two main lines: closing schools and improving the school network. The main goals set for the closure of schools were improving teaching quality and rationalizing resources and school closures have to meet the following criteria: less than 21 students, a single teacher and high rates of student failure. According to these criteria most schools to be closed were located in rural areas where the population is ageing and so the main problem to be solved was children's transport, which was left to the municipalities. Rationalization of resources has also led to grouping schools in clusters in which the school head carries out the integrated management of all resources. Measures against dropping include special remedial programmes for students and support for disabled students, as well as the development of extra-curricular activities, mainly in IT, arts and sports. Social assistance for needy students also increased by 56 per cent between 2000 and 2010.[52] Furthermore, in 2009, a programme was launched for secondary schools concerning energy efficiency, IT equipment and sports, as well as building enlargement in order to accommodate new students due to the raising of the compulsory school leaving age from 15 to 18 years.

In this first phase, cuts in education expenditure were based on the rationalization of resources, as described above. However, since 2011, budget constraints have resulted in a deterioration of employment conditions for education professionals which calls into question the continuation of programmes aimed at reducing the dropout rate. At the same time, the rehabilitation programme for secondary schools was suspended, which has created difficulties for the private companies involved, thus contributing rising unemployment. On the other hand, budget cuts imposed on municipalities has increased their indebtedness. In February 2012, the debts of municipalities to the bus companies that transport schoolchildren was €80 million and they are now threatening to halt this service, which would affect about 400,000 students.

The 2012 budget contained education cuts of 18.4 per cent, reducing public expenditure on education from 5 to 3.8 per cent of GDP. This cut is particularly worrying given that there is increasing demand for state schools because private schools are becoming too expensive. Currently, the most pressing case concerns preschool education where the state covers less than 50 per cent of requirements.

With regard to universities, the most evident impact of budgetary restrictions is a 30 per cent decrease in scholarships and cuts of up to 50 per cent in allocated scholarships, while 16,000 university students – about 4 per cent – have resorted to bank loans, for which the state is guarantor. Moreover, fellowships to doctoral students have decreased by 16 per cent. Another critical situation concerns PhDs who, for lack of labour market opportunities, have survived by means of postdoctoral fellowships. However, the nominal value of the latter has been frozen since 2002 and the non-renewal of fellowships is now feared.

5.2.1 Increased unemployment among teachers

Education professionals have also been affected by freezes on recruitment and promotion, as well as by wage cuts applied to all public administration employees. In addition, however, there is a high degree of job insecurity in education due to the frequency of fixed-term contracts.

In 2010, 25 per cent of preschool, primary and secondary school teachers had fixed-term contracts, while among other education professionals the figure was 12 per cent. Teachers with fixed-term contracts are selected every year by competitive tendering. This system results in a high turnover of teachers, which affects their training and professional improvement, but it has been used to reduce the unemployment rate of young, newly graduated teachers.

However, reforms in education, with the closure of schools, the concentration of management in groups of schools and, more recently, curriculum reforms, which suppressed ICT learning beyond the ninth grade and merged some study areas (such as biology/physics/chemistry and history/geography), as well as increasing class sizes[53] to 30, created surpluses of teachers, which has increased unemployment among teachers on fixed-term contracts. Since 2009, teachers' unemployment has grown by 225 per cent, 120 per cent in the past year.[54] Most of these unemployed teachers are women (71 per cent) and 44 per cent of unemployed teachers live in the north of Portugal.

For the school year in progress (2011–12) 27,000 teachers were appointed on fixed-term contracts, as against 48,000 in 2009–10. At present, teachers not placed immediately become part of a reserve who can be called on at any time. In this case the term of the labour contract is less than one year and some teachers have contracts for only one month, successively renewed on the same terms. This practice is particularly harmful because it prevents teachers from accessing both unemployment benefits and social unemployment, for which the qualification periods are a consecutive 450[55] and 180 days of paid work, respectively.

5.2.2 Deteriorating working conditions

At the same time, teachers' workload is higher because there are fewer teachers on fixed-term contracts, teachers' early retirement[56] is increasing, despite the monetary penalties, and the Ministry of Education has decided that teachers' working hours should not include lesson preparation or pedagogic or management activities in order to be entirely devoted to direct teaching in class. Teachers are thus complaining that they have to work overtime for free, since overtime work is not officially allowed.

In order to assess the impact of austerity measures on teachers' daily lives, interviews were conducted in two schools, selected on the basis of the socioeconomic diversity of the area where they are located and their level of education: Miraflores secondary school and Quinta da Medideira school.

5.2.3 Vocational training halted in Miraflores secondary school

Miraflores secondary school is located in the Municipality of Oeiras, close to Lisbon, and ranks second in the Portuguese ranking of household purchasing power. The school is attended by 800 students who come from middle- and upper-class families, but also from some poorer families. School staff consists of 170 professionals, of whom 130 are teachers. The feminization rate among teachers is 78 per cent and for support staff 93 per cent. Most staff (81 per cent) are above 40 years of age. The school works day and evening shifts. Day shifts are for secondary compulsory education, from the seventh to the twelfth grades and evening shifts are dedicated to vocational courses for students of compulsory school age and who are at risk of dropping out, as well as for adults within the New Opportunities Programme.[57] Vocational courses for the former have a strong technological and artistic dimension. Therefore it is the thematic educational diversity provided by Miraflores school that justifies the high pupil–teacher ratio, one for every seven students.

In this school, austerity measures are particularly affecting the vocational education provided in evening shifts due to the decrease of student enrolment, which is attributed to discouragement caused by the difficulty of getting a job. With regard to vocational courses for adults, the government has announced the suspension of the New Opportunities Programme for evaluation. Consequently, the school no longer needs teachers with fixed-term contracts, while the decreased workload of teachers with open-ended contracts causes them to fear that they will be put in special mobility. This situation is made worse by the suppression and merging of some courses following the curriculum reform of regular education. There is therefore an ambiance of anxiety and fear among teachers that inclines them towards social protest. However, many are tired or sceptical regarding trade unions and the oldest among them prefer early retirement.

5.2.4 Excessive workload and unpaid overtime in Quinta da Medideira primary school

Quinta da Medideira school is located in Seixal Municipality on the south bank of the River Tagus and connected to Lisbon by two bridges. Formerly one of the most industrialized areas of Portugal, Seixal is now a depressed region because of deindustrialization and it is 34th in the Portuguese ranking of household purchasing power. Currently, 60 per cent of employment is in services, but from 2008 to 2011 Seixal's population decreased by 10 per cent as a result of increasing unemployment, especially among young people. Quinta da Medideira is a primary school and kindergarten. In the primary school there are 152 children and in the kindergarten 75. The school is integrated into the structural teaching system, that is, it accepts children with special needs. School staff comprise 10 full-time teachers, seven at the primary school and three in the kindergarten, which corresponds to child/teacher ratios of 22:1 and 25:1, respectively. All these teachers are paid by the Ministry of Education, together with a full-time special educator for children with special needs and a school librarian for two days a week. Regarding support staff there are two speech specialists, two psychologists and two psychomotor specialists working a few hours a week, paid by the municipality, which also pays two permanent assistants. Another three auxiliary workers are paid by the local permanent office.

The effects of the austerity measures on the Medideira school are quite different from those reported by Miraflores school. One major problem at Medideira is the excessive workload of all staff due to the suppression of fixed-term contracts, including highly skilled professionals for children with special needs. This situation has forced teachers to undertake not only teaching, but also extra-curricular activities and management, leading them to work unpaid as the Ministry of Education has suspended overtime pay. Moreover, teachers dealing with children with special needs have also seen resources cut. The staff also suffer from poor working conditions due to poor school facilities, lack of materials and poverty among most of the children. For instance, the playground is not safe; the floor of the courtyard is of beaten earth and turns into mud when it rains; 50 per cent of children receive subsidized meals from the City Council. The City Council also pays school electricity and water costs, provides school supplies and consumables and ensures the transport of children with special needs, cleaning, the management of school equipment and minor repairs. It also ensures meals for all children during teaching breaks or school holidays. Accordingly, teachers are very worried about the funding cuts to municipalities announced by the government.

6. CONCLUSIONS AND PROSPECTS

Portugal risks succumbing to the vicious circle of recession and austerity. Indeed, the austerity policy, which has been progressively more pronounced since 2010, has been justified as necessary for achieving balanced public accounts, external debt reduction, productivity growth, job creation and improved social justice.

However, results point to the ineffectiveness of these measures and the subsequent worsening of the problems that were intended to be solved. Moreover, some macro indicators show that the austerity measures are imposing a very high social burden and are increasing impoverishment. The following indicators[58] are particularly worth highlighting, either because they are official or because of the insight they provide into how dramatic the social crisis may be:

- *Unemployment rate* 7.6 per cent in 2005, but in March 2012 it stood at 15 per cent; from 2010 to 2012 unemployed people granted unemployment benefit decreased by 5.7 per cent.
- *Youth unemployment rate* 16 per cent in 2005; 36.6 per cent in June 2012.
- *Inflation rate* 2.2 per cent in 2005, but 3.6 per cent in March 2012.
- *Impoverishment rate* 19.4 per cent of the population in 2005; 25 per cent in 2010, but 37 per cent in single parent families.
- *Child deprivation rate* (2009) 27.9 per cent.
- *Child deprivation rate in jobless households* (2009) 73.6 per cent.
- *Emigration* 150,000 Portuguese emigrated in 2011; graduate emigration rate grew by 27 per cent.
- *Bankruptcy ordered by courts* Growth of 350.6 per cent from 2007 to 2011; the percentage of this accounted for by individuals rose from 21.4 to 56.5 per cent during the same period.
- *Public revenues* For the two first months of 2012, tax revenues fell by 5.3 per cent; the major decrease was in corporate tax, which fell by 46 per cent.
- *Unemployment benefits* During the same period public expenditure grew by 18 per cent.
- *GDP growth rate* Forecasts point to –3.5 per cent in 2012.

The worsening poverty is leading to hunger among the population, a situation that has been condemned by NGOs, such as Portuguese Caritas.[59] On 16 October 2011 the President of the Food Banks' Federation against Hunger, Isabel Jonet, said in an interview with TSF radio that there is a new class of poor people who have jobs but whose wages do not allow them to cover household expenses. On 18 March 2012, the President of the Council for Refugees, Teresa Tito de Morais, said in an interview on RTP (public TV channel) that the Council had no funds to feed refugees in shelters and so appealed to the Portuguese people for their help.

With regard to employees of public administration and despite reforms undertaken since 2006 to bring about the convergence of the public employment regime with the private one, the idea that public employees have privileged status and so are at least partly responsible for the public accounts deficit continued to be promulgated. This partly explains the weak contestation of austerity measures applied specifically to public employees.

Meanwhile, austerity measures applied to public employees are strongly affecting them and society as a whole. The downsizing of public facilities aimed at reducing public expenditure is threatening to accelerate the human desertification of rural areas, which will only increase inequalities in regional development. This policy in the specific case of health care is hindering access, aggravated by the recent cuts in free patient transport.

The downsizing of public employment is being implemented by means of a number of measures, such as reform of the public employment regime which introduced the possibility of dismissing public employees or subjecting them to special mobility measures; reform of pension entitlements which has led to lower pensions; and application of the one-for-two rule and the freeze of new recruitments. These measures as a whole have depleted the human capital of public administration, both by the early retirement of the most experienced staff and by preventing young graduates from joining the public administration. Consequently, unemployment and emigration have been increasing sharply among the best-qualified young people.

The emigration of highly qualified Portuguese is also a consequence of cuts in public wages, overtime and other compensatory pay, reducing the purchasing power of public employees to very low levels, without any expectation of change. Moreover, the sharp drop in purchasing power is also a factor in worsening the recession, as public employees represent about 17 per cent[60] of overall employment.

Another important issue to be considered is decision-making and implementation of public employment reform. Since 2005 the public administration has undergone huge reforms that have drastically changed the rules of organizational management. These changes were particularly dramatic for public employees because they affected their employment and daily lives. However, perhaps the greatest drama stems from the fact that some changes have been contradictory. As an example, the introduction of the career development system, which had been justified by the goal of promoting merit recognition, was followed two years later by a freeze on all promotion. Moreover, policymakers have sought to blacken the name of civil servants by blaming them for public waste in order to justify restrictive measures on public employees' labour rights. Thus, public employees feel neglected by the government, which is their employer, personally impugned and helpless against losses of quality of life.

There has therefore been a breakdown of the implicit contract between the government as employer and public employees. On the side of public employees that breakdown is leading to severe insecurity, discouragement and even lack of faith in the rule of law and also in the European project.

If current policy continues unabated, the prospects are bleak and may even result in the paralysis of the public administration through the joint effects of lack of resources and the increasing resistance of public employees, even though collective protest has so far been weak, possibly because the trade unions are not united.

We therefore need a shift in policy towards sustainable development involving job creation, especially for qualified young people and safeguarding the ethical values inherent in democracy. Among these values is social solidarity, labour rights and equal opportunities in access to health care, education, culture and mobility.

With regard to the public administration there is a strong need to return to a policy of development and promotion of human capital in order to successfully fight tax fraud and corruption and to effectively supervise the economic agents – the banks – who ultimately caused the crisis. The process of policy decision-making must be transparent and aim at involving the citizens at whom the policies are directed and the public employees who will implement them. These are principles of good governance and are embodied in the United Nations' Millennium Declaration, to whose implementation all the governments of the world – including Portugal – committed themselves in September 2000.

NOTES

1. DGAEP, information provided by DGAEP (General Department for Public Employment of the Finance Ministry), March 2012, reporting up to June 2011.
2. Social Democratic Party (PSD) and Democratic and Social Centre-Popular Party (CDS-PP).
3. Law 60-A/2005 of 30 December.
4. Law 12-A/2008 of 27 February.
5. Law 4/2009 of 29 January.

6. Briefly, there are two groups of public employees, namely those engaged after 2006, who can be dismissed whatever kind of contract they have and those engaged before 2006 who have an open-ended labour contract and can only be put in special mobility.
7. Law 59/2008 of 11 September.
8. Data provided by DGAEP.
9. Public unemployment concerns all public sectors while special mobility concerns only central public administration.
10. As the IEFP uses NACE classification it is not possible to distinguish public and private sector employees in these activities. However, many of these activities carried out by the private sector receive public financial support.
11. Decree-law 41/1984 of 3 February.
12. RCM 38/2006 of 30 March.
13. This information was attributed to the Ministry of Finance by *Jornal Económico*.
14. According to the Chairman of the Physicians' Association, 11 per cent of those enrolled in it are foreigners (Diário de Notícias, 1 September 2009).
15. Law 12-A/2010 of 30 June.
16. Law 64-B/2011.
17. Bonus to be paid = 1,320 – 1.2 × monthly wage.
18. According to the January projections of the Bank of Portugal the growth rate of consumer prices will be 3.2 per cent in 2012.
19. Decree-law 259/1998 of 18 August.
20. Monitoring tables of the Central Health System Administration (ACSS), www.acss.min-saude.pt.
21. Decree-law 137/ 2010.
22. Decree-law 116/2010 of 22 October and Portaria 1113/2010 of 28 October.
23. The Institute was closed down by Decree-law 48/2012 under the programme to downsize Portugal's central public administration.
24. Law 60/2005 of 29 December.
25. In fact, since 1993 there have been successive changes in the calculation of pensions, with the introduction of weighting factors for different periods of years worked; all these amendments have contributed to reducing pensions.
26. This status was retained only for the following public functions: missions of the permanent Armed Forces; state representation abroad; information security; criminal investigation; public security and inspection.
27. Law 12-A/2008 of 27 February; Law 59/2008 of 11 September; Law 4/2009 of 29 January.
28. Law 53/2006 of 7 December.
29. Law 64-B/2011 or 2012 budget law.
30. Law 12-A/2008 of 27 February.
31. Portaria 1553-C/2008, of 31 December.
32. The study was carried out by INA's research team under the coordination of Cesar Madureira.
33. Agriculture, Rural Development and Fisheries; Public Works, Transport and Communications; Health; Employment and Social Solidarity.
34. Law 55-A/2010 of 31 December.
35. Law 64-B/2011 of 30 December.
36. Law 60/2005 of 29 December and Law 4/2009 of 29 January.
37. Law 59/2008 of 11 September, articles 232 and 259.
38. Decree-law 50/1998 of 11 March.
39. DGAEP, Relatório de Actividades de Formação da Administração Pública 2009.
40. The other is Fundação CEFA, which is dedicated to training employees in local public administration.
41. The volume of training is the sum for all courses of the value obtained by multiplying the number of trainees by training hours in each course.
42. Decree-law 64/2012 of 15 March.

43. This allowance can be granted after unemployment benefit expires, in other words, 540 days at the most.
44. Tripartite agreement between the Portuguese government, employers and the UGT (União Geral dos Trabalhadores) signed on 17 January 2012.
45. Decree-law 259/1998 of 18 August.
46. Statements of former Secretary of State for Health and of the Chairman of the College of Physicians.
47. Evaluation of the Health Ministry (Relatório de Avaliação dos Episódios de Violência contra Profissionais de Saúde, 2010, www.dgs.pt).
48. See paragraph (b), Section 2, Part II.
49. Newsletter of the Southern Regional Doctors' Association, year 13, no.175, 15 June 2012.
50. Diário de Notícias (1 September 2009).
51. Nurses' College News (10 April 2012).
52. Between 1990 and 2010 the increase was 398 per cent.
53. In 2009, the average number of pupils per teacher was quite low: 12 for primary and 10 for secondary education.
54. According IEFP (Employment and Training Institute) data.
55. After 1 June 2012, this period will be 360 days (Decree-law 64/2012 of 15 May).
56. Recently (Decree-law 85-A/2012, of 5 April) the government decided to freeze early retirement for persons under the general social security regime which also concerns public employees engaged after 1 January 2006.
57. This programme was an initiative of the previous government (2005–10) aimed at improving adult qualifications in academic and professional terms, including validation and recognition of formal and informal skills.
58. Main sources: National Institute of Statistics (INE), Bank of Portugal, EU-SILC 2010, European Anti Poverty Network (EAPN), Employment Office (IEFP) UNICEF (2012).
59. Social network of the Catholic Church.
60. Including central, local and regional public administration.

REFERENCES

Alves, N., M. Centeno and A. Novo (2010), 'O investimento em Educação em Portugal, retornos e heterogeneidades', Banco de Portugal, Boletim da Primavera.

Carmo, R.M. do (2011), *Desigualdades em Portugal: Problemas e propostas*, Lisbon: Edições 70.

Faro, A.C. (2011), 'Situação do Mercado de Emprego – Relatório Semestral – 1.º semestre de 2010', Instituto do Emprego e Formação Profissional, I.P., Lisbon.

Kovács, I. (2004), 'Emprego flexível em Portugal, Dossiê novas realidades do trabalho – Brasil e Portugal', Sociologias no. 12, Porto Alegre, July/December. Available at: http:/www.scielo.br/scielo.php?pid= S1517-45222004000200003&script=sci_arttext.

Observatório Português dos Sistemas de Saúde (2012), 'Crise & Saúde, Um País em Sofrimento', Relatório da Primavera 2012, versão provisória.

Quinta, P.J.C. da (n.d.), 'Evolução e Caracterização da Administração Pública Portuguesa', Proelium, *Revista da Academia Militar*, No. 10: 185–229.

UNICEF (2012), 'Report Card 10: Measuring Child Poverty', 28 May.

Laws, Decrees and Programmes

Acordo colectivo de trabalho n.º 1/2009 DR, 2.ª Série, N.º 188, de 27 de Setembro de 2009 (collective agreement for public employment union).

Actualizações 2007, Boletim STAL, revista de ideias e Estudos, n.º 27, Julho de 2007.

Conta Geral do Estado, Ministério das Finanças e da Administração Pública, Direcção-Geral do Tesouro, Volume I, 2011 (overview of Portuguese state accounting).

Decreto-Lei 41/1984 DR n.º 29, Suplemento, Série I, 1984-02-03.

Decreto-Lei 50/1998 DR n.º 59, Série I-A,1998-03-11.

Decreto-Lei 259/1998 DR n.º 189, Série I-A, 1998-08-18.

Decreto-Lei 48/2012 DR n.º 43, Série I, 2012-02-29.

Decreto-Lei 64/2012 DR n.º 54, Série I, 2012-03-15.

Decreto-Lei 85-A/2012 DR n.º 69, Série I, 2012-04-05.

Decreto-Lei 116/2010 DR n.º 206, Série I, 2010-10-22.

Decreto-Lei 137/2010 DR n.º 250, Série I, 2010-12-28.

Lei 60/2005 DR n.º 249, Suplemento, Série I-A, 2005-12-29.

Lei 60-A/2005 n.º 250, Suplemento, Série I-A, 2005-12-30.

Lei 53/2006 DR n.º 235, Série I, 2006-12-07.

Lei 12-A/2008 DR n.º 41, Suplemento, Série I, 2008-02-27.

Lei 59/2008 DR n.º 176, Série I, 2008-09-11.

Lei 4/2009 DR n.º 20, Série I, 2009-01-29.

Lei 12-A/2010 DR n.º 125, Suplemento, Série I, 2010-06-30.

Lei 55-A/2010 DR n.º 253, Suplemento, Série I, 2010-12-31.

Lei 49/2011 DR n.º 172, Série I, 2011-09-07.

Lei 64-B/2011 n.º 250, Suplemento, Série I, 2011-12-30.

Plano de Redução da Administração Central do Estado (PREMAC), Ministério das Finanças, Gabinete do secretário de Estado da Administração Pública, Setembro 2011 (plan for reducing central state administration).

Portaria 1113/2010 DR n.º 210, Série I, 2010-10-28.

Portaria 1553-C/2010 DR n.º 252, 4.º Suplemento, Série I, 2008-12-31.

Programa de Estabilidade e Crescimento (Stability and Growth Programme), 2005–2009, Ministério das Finanças e da Administração Pública, República Portuguesa, Actualização Dezembro de 2005.

Programa de Estabilidade e Crescimento (Stability and Growth Programme) 2006–2010, Ministério das Finanças e da Administração Pública, República Portuguesa, Actualização Dezembro de 2006.

Programa de Estabilidade e Crescimento (Stability and Growth Programme) 2007–2011, Ministério das Finanças e da Administração Pública, República Portuguesa, Actualização Dezembro de 2007.

Programa de Estabilidade e Crescimento (Stability and Growth Programme) 2008–2011, Ministério das Finanças e da Administração Pública, República Portuguesa, Actualização Janeiro de 2009.

Programa de Estabilidade e Crescimento (Stability and Growth Programme) 2010–2013, Ministério das Finanças e da Administração Pública, República Portuguesa, Março de 2010.

Programa de Estabilidade e Crescimento (Stability and Growth Programme) 2011–2014, Ministério das Finanças e da Administração Pública, República Portuguesa, Março de 2011.

Programa de Reestruturação da Administração Pública Central (PRACE), Resolução de Conselho de Ministros nº 124/2005, 04 de Agosto de 2005 (programme for restructuring central public administration).
Regulamento de extensão do acordo colectivo de trabalho, DR, 2.ª Série, n.º 42-1.º Suplemento, de 02 de Maio de 2010 (additional rules to the acordo colectivo).
Resolução Conselho de Ministros (RCM) 38/2006 DR n.º 76, Série I-B, 2006-04-18.
Trabalho Extraordinário, Trabalho Nocturno e Horário Flexível, SNESup, available at: http://www.snesup.pt/htmls/EkpVEZpyyEZdFyFCUI.shtml (information on nurses' working conditions).

12. Romania: A country under permanent public sector reform

Valentina Vasile

1. INTRODUCTION

During the political and economic transition in Romania, the public sector underwent continuous reform, ranging from measures required to adjust the government sector to the market economy, to those to meet the demands of EU accession, and finally to measures to overcome the crisis. Public sector employment increased significantly, with jobs paid from the state budget increasing from about 800,000 at the beginning of the transition to almost 1.4 million before the crisis, then decreasing again to below 1.2 million. The public sector concentrates about 21 per cent of the labour force and its total wage fund represents about 25 per cent of budgetary expenditure (Voinea et al. 2010).[1]

The institutional structure has followed the same path of repeated change, with increases in the number of ministries, agencies and so on and then their restructuring and merging during the crisis.

During the crisis, a mix of quantitative adjustments and structural reforms has been implemented in the public sector, some aimed at improving efficiency and others part of the restrictive IMF package. The result is that Romania has been characterized by continuous reforms in the public sector, not all with positive outcomes.[2]

The chapter proceeds as follows. Section 2 discusses public sector adjustments. Section 3 analyses the effects of the anti-crisis measures. Section 4 presents two case studies, the first on comprehensive education reform and the second on wage reform. Section 5 addresses policy issues, and Section 6 presents the conclusions.

2. PUBLIC SECTOR ADJUSTMENTS

2.1 Main Features of the Current Public Sector Adjustment

The main changes in the public sector in recent years have been concentrated on two aspects: institutional reform and policies for better use of the workforce. The main purpose was to create a well-performing state sector which would be able to meet economic and social exigencies with adequate services.

2.1.1 Short history of public sector reform

The main drivers of the public sector reform are the following: (i) transition to a market economy and the need to adjust the state; (ii) institutional reform for adjustment to EU structures; (iii) crisis response to quantitative adjustments – reducing expenditure; (iv) making state structures efficient and improving public management – emphasis on qualitative reforms aimed at making public services more modern and efficient; (v) redefining the state economic sector: its size and types of activities, including privatization/outsourcing of public utilities; and (vi) redesigning the social responsibility of the state in response to demographic ageing (pension and health-care reforms and labour force mobility – employment policy on young people and those returning from abroad).

The economic and social context represented a permanent factor both stimulating and hindering reforms in the public sector. The dynamics of the economy supported diversification of the state's activities and the employment increase in the public sector, but the lack of sustainable economic growth increased budgetary deficits, and the financial crisis, even if it did not affect Romania immediately, substantially depressed domestic demand for goods and services. As a result, economic recovery started in Romania later than in other EU member states, that is, in the last part of 2010, and continued in 2011, at a slowed down rate in the fourth quarter of 2011 and the first quarter of 2012 (Figure 12.1).

State budget expenditure for 2008–12 is shown in Figure 12.2.

Other factors causing inconsistency and/or delays in the public sector reform were: (i) low wages (minimum wage of €137, the lowest level in the EU27, and average gross income of €450 per month); (ii) demographic ageing (a high economic dependency index of old people – around 22 per cent) and labour force mobility (more than 2.5 million workers abroad); (iii) a large share of informal employment (around one-third) and a dual payment system; (iv) high and slowly decreasing level of poverty (around 40 per cent of the population face the risk of poverty or social exclusion according to Eurostat); (v) wage polarization, high differentials by

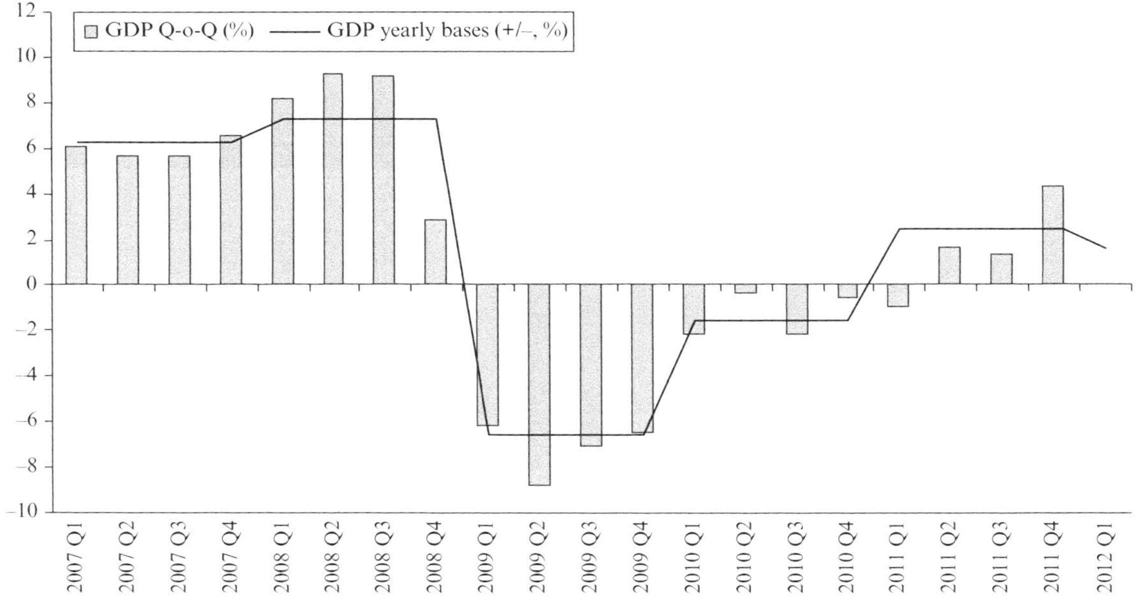

Source: National Institute for Statistics, NIS Tempo online, available at: http://www.insse.ro/cms/rw/pages/index.ro.do.

Figure 12.1 Development of GDP, Romania, 2007–2011

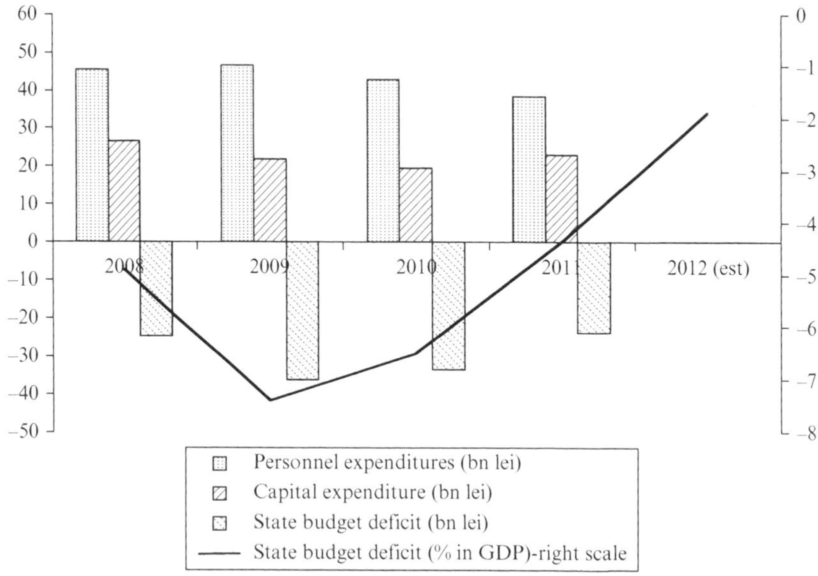

Source: Ministry of Finance, NBR Bulletin, INS Press release, available at: http://www.mfinante.ro/execbug.html?pagina=domenii.

Figure 12.2 State budget expenditure, Romania, 2008–2012

economic activity, including the public sector; high taxes, especially from the employers' point of view; (vi) a weak/low-performance wage payment system which preserves old inequities and generates new ones, based mainly on the effective implementation of wage policy; (vii) labour market flexibility measures in the new Labour Code, promoting temporary and part-time contracts, modular working time and so on, and the reform of social dialogue institutions by increasing the profitability threshold, renouncing the collective agreement at national level and eliminating the automatic *erga omnes* extensions at the sectoral level.

2.1.2 Institutional restructuring until 2009

Reform of state institutions followed naturally on the redefinition and reorganization of the role and involvement of the state in the economy and efforts to make it more efficient. Central and local administrative structures were permanently reorganized and modernized and state institutions as economic agents (autonomous administrations and national companies) were diminished by reorganization and privatization. Up to 2008 changes in the structure of state institutions depended on the requirements of modernizing the state and were made gradually, as the demand for specific services was defined. During the crisis, a general reorganization of public authorities and institutions has been pursued (Law 329/2009[3]). In a first phase in 2009–10, reform and reorganization of the public sector were aimed at public sector management, the payment of employees' wages, and education and health reform. In 2011, the reforms continued, with the emphasis on pension reform, the second round of wage reform, continuation of the public sector cuts and reorganization of social benefits.[4]

The end of 2009 represented the most important stage of the quantitative reform. Reorganization took one of the following forms: (i) doing away with the public authority or institution, as a result of absorption by another public authority or institution; (ii) absorption by a newly established department in other public authorities or institutions; (iii) merger and constitution of a new legal entity; (iv) division and takeover by two or several existing entities; (v) lowering employment grades in public authorities or institutions; and (vi) changing the financial system of some public authorities or institutions by transferring incomes to and financing expenditure from the state budget. The number of agencies and other state institutions was reduced by half, but the number of employees cut was much lower (in a first stage, along with the institutional reorganization 10,000 jobs were cut).

2.1.3 Adjustments during the extended crisis period

The year 2010 represented the second stage of economic contraction, when GDP decreased by 1.6 per cent, after a fall of 6.6 per cent in 2009. The economic turnaround was modest, starting in the fourth quarter of 2010, with oscillations during 2011, and was achieved particularly by exports, because domestic demand decreased significantly due to the strict austerity measures implemented in 2010. Remittances decreased from €6.6 billion in 2008 to €4.4 billion in 2009 and only €3.8 billion in 2010. Gross fixed capital formation diminished by 13.1 per cent in 2010 as against 2009. The public debt increased significantly during the crisis, rising to 34.3 per cent of GDP in 2011 (ESA95) from 23.8 per cent in 2009 due to continued economic contraction and budget deficit decreasing from 9 per cent of GDP in 2009 to 6.9 per cent in 2010 and 4.9 per cent in 2011 (ESA95).[5] Government debt represents over 90 per cent of the total.

Average employment was 4,238,000 in 2010, decreasing further in 2011 to below 4.2 million due to continuing economic decline and staff cuts in the public sector. In 2010, the gross wage in the total economy was 1,937 lei, an increase of 2.5 per cent against 2009, but decreased in 2011, in both nominal and real terms.

The 2012 budget was based on economic growth between 1.8 and 2.3

per cent and did not include wage and pension increases. Thus, staff expenditure is slowly increasing in 2012, to 6.7 per cent of GDP, from 6.6 per cent in 2011, 8.2 per cent in 2010 and 9.2 per cent in 2009 (GR 2012).[6] The general consolidated budget has a nominal deficit of 11.2 billion lei, representing 1.9 per cent of GDP by the cash methodology and less than 3 per cent according to European standards.[7] Budgetary expenditure is estimated to be 35.6 per cent of GDP, as against 38.7 per cent in 2011, and the investments represent 6.8 per cent of GDP, subsidies decreasing below 1 per cent of GDP. The government will cease to pay the thirteenth-month wage and meal, gift and holiday vouchers to the employees of public institutions by 2014. It will also halt bonuses to budgetary personnel and other incentives. Overtime is not paid but compensated by free time. Estimated savings are 9.1 billion lei in 2012 and 9.6 billion lei in 2013.[8]

2.2 Employment in the Public Sector

In Romania, there are two categories of budgetary personnel: (i) public sector employees – health care and social assistance, education, public administration and defence – whose wages are paid from the state budget; and (ii) employees of autonomous administrations, national and other state-owned companies, subsidized directly or indirectly from the budget. Data are provided by the National Institute for Statistics based on the Labour Force Survey (LFS) and CANE Rev. 2 activity classification and from periodical reporting to the Ministry of Finance, in which case data are organized by legal entities in the public sector. The main data in this chapter are based on the LFS and data publicly available from the Ministry of Finance.

2.2.1 Employment development based on LFS data

As for employment, an oscillating evolution is seen from about 1.25 million people in the mid-1990s to over 1.3 million in 2002, with considerable yearly variations, decreasing up to 2007 and then significantly increasing even during the crisis period, according to LFS data and CANE Rev. 2 from 1.26 million, in the third quarter of 2008 to 1.32 million in the third quarter of 2011.[9]

Around 11.5–14.5 per cent of total employment is in the public sector (Figure 12.3). During the crisis period, due to a more marked decrease in employment in the private sector, the share of the public sector in total employment increased to 13.8–14.6 per cent.

In the national economy, women's employment (Figures 12.4–6) represents 47.1 per cent, but in the public sector it is higher: in administration around 55 per cent, in education 70 per cent and in health care 80 per cent.

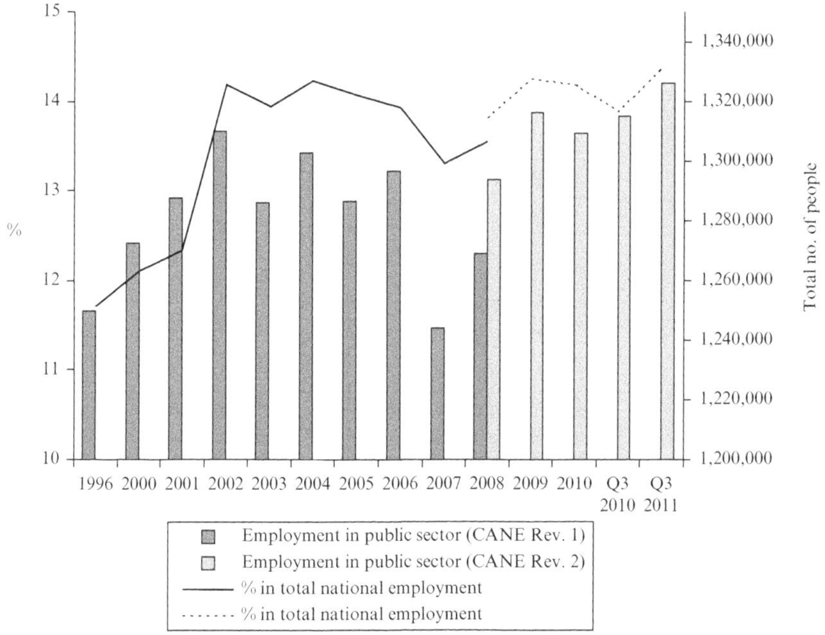

Source: LFS.

Figure 12.3 Employment in the public sector, Romania, 1996–2011 (total and as a percentage of national employment)

In public administration, women are better represented with differences at central/local level, depending on specific activities (police, armed forces and defence, in general, as well as the judiciary, prison guards and diplomatic services have a high proportion of men).

In central government, there are fewer women than men, but there is a high density of women employees in education, health care and social services.

Detailed analyses by gender differences highlight the following: (i) the presence of women in the labour market decreased slightly in 2009 as against 2004 (from 46.4 to 45.1 per cent) due to the extension of the initial education period and the more favourable conditions for giving birth (higher benefits for mothers and economic growth); (ii) single mothers earn less because they allot more time to the family, preferring private part-time jobs. This feminization of the public sector depends on activities in the public sector, so that in total the share of women's employment decreased faster than at national level, from 54 per cent in 2000 to 40 per

Source: LFS.

Figure 12.4 Women in employment, Romania, 1996–2011 (% of public sector in the total economy)

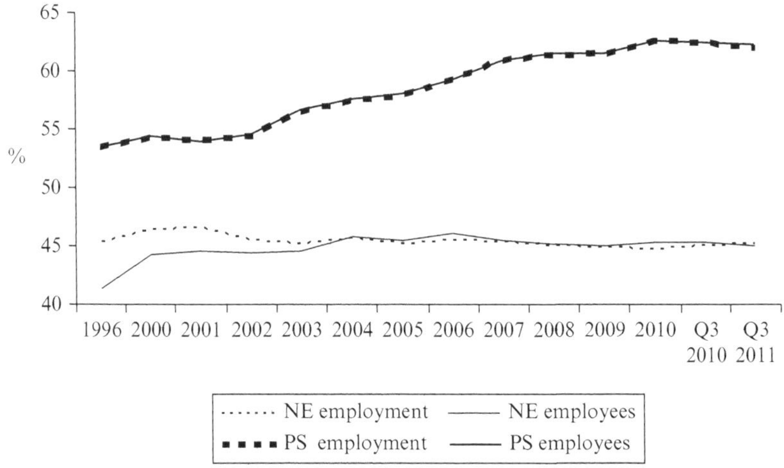

Note: NE = national economy level; PS = public sector.

Source: LFS.

Figure 12.5 Women' share of employment and employees – national economy vs. public sector, Romania, 1996–2011

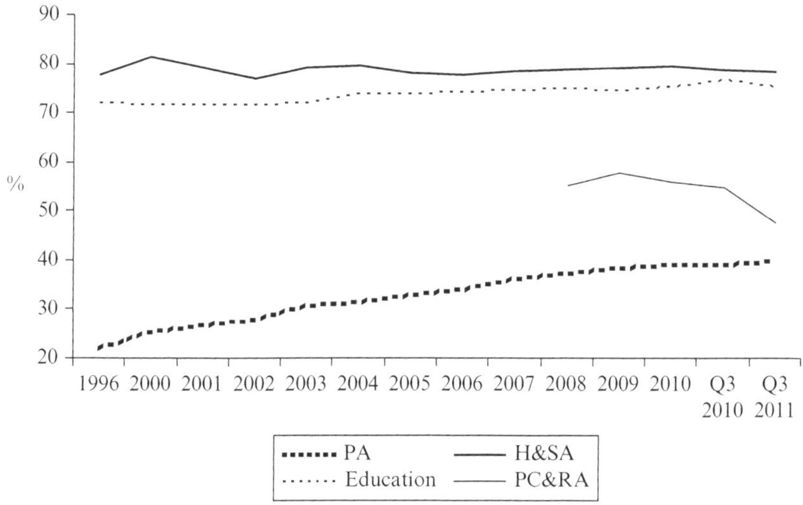

Note: PA = public administration; H&SA = health and social assistance; PC&RA = performances, cultural and recreational activities.

Source: LFS.

Figure 12.6 Women as a proportion of employees – public sector, Romania, 1996–2011

cent in 2011 (third quarter). Feminization increased by about 1 percentage point, whereas at the level of the public sector the increase is about 8 percentage points. By activities in the public sector, women account for about 40 per cent in public administration and in cultural and recreation activities, and over 70 per cent in education and health care.

With regard to public sector activities (Figure 12.7), public administration employment represents about 5 per cent, education and health care about 4 per cent and cultural–recreation activities about 0.6 per cent. With regard to total employment volume by activities, we noticed a contraction of the public administration sector and an increase in the health and social assistance sector.

Employees in the public sector, even though significantly reduced in number as a result of restructuring, remain the preponderant labour force category, with significant differentiation by activity. They represent almost all active people in public administration and defence, and about 99.5 per cent in education, 97 per cent in health and 96 per cent in culture and recreation. The largest decreases in number of employees were recorded in 2010 and in the first nine months of 2011. The trend will

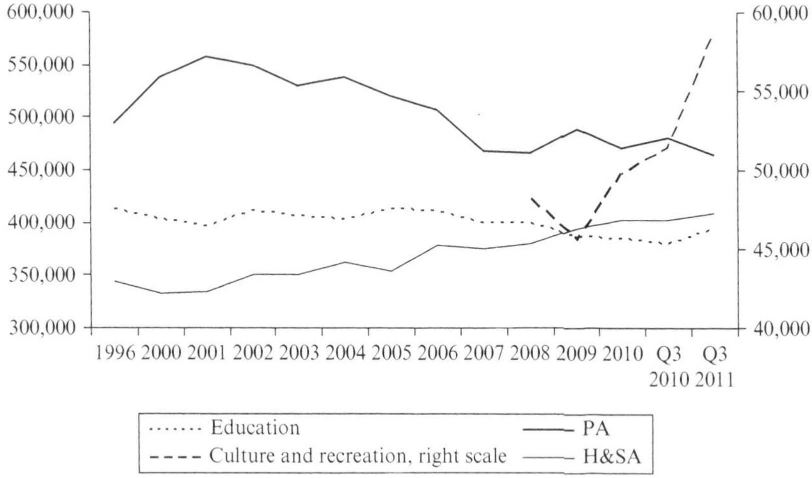

Note: PA = public administration; H&SA = health and social assistance.

Source: LFS.

Figure 12.7 Employment in the public sector by main activities (number of persons)

continue in 2012, albeit smaller. At the national level (Figure 12.8), the crisis effect on decreasing the number of employees was more significant in the first period (2009): in 2011 it registered a slight increase. In December 2011 as against September 2008, when it was acknowledged officially for the first time that Romania was in crisis, employment was reduced by 552,600 at national level and by 97,400 in the public sector. The most significant decreases were recorded in health (36,500) and education (34,600). As against September 2008, the public sector employment cut was 9.3 per cent, lower than at national level (13.7 per cent).

The variation in the number of employees (Table 12.1) during the crisis was more intense in public administration and health. Thus, there was a decrease of 14.6 per cent in culture and recreation, 9.8 per cent in health, 8.6 per cent in education and 8.4 per cent in public administration. The wage employment decrease was twice as high in 2010 as against 2009 (almost 70,000 in 2010 against 36,600 in 2009) and in 2011 the layoffs continued, so that by the end of December there were almost 152,000 fewer employees.

It should be noted that the share by activities changed slightly in favour of education and diminished in health and public administration. We cannot say that these reductions have generated more efficient reallocation of human resources in the public sector as there is a significant

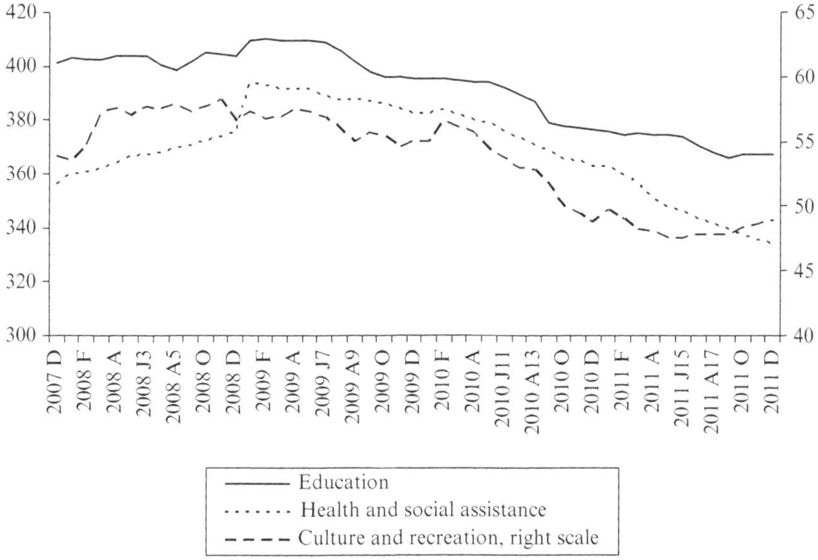

Source: Monthly Statistical Bulletin.

Figure 12.8 Employment, Romania, 2007–2011 (end of month –'000)

shortage of personnel in fields such as health (nurses, physicians for some specializations) and there is still overemployment in some public administrative structures. Such qualitative adjustments are intended for 2012, but it is only by replacement through natural wastage at a rate of one for seven, which is less likely to generate real and useful resizing and reshaping at a performance/efficient employment level and structure. Recruitment continues to be blocked, hence important qualitative adjustments cannot be made and qualitative restructuring of the public sector is again being postponed. Also, the decrease in the number of employees registered in local public administration units are also found in activities with a secondary character, such as cultural, sports and recreation activities, landscaping and services for buildings, agriculture, waste management, decontamination, construction, transport and warehousing, electric and thermal power, gas, hot water generation and supply, air conditioning, rentals of real estate, by externalizing some services and concession of others to private entities. On the other hand, transfers from central to local administration took place in the decentralization of some state services (schools, hospitals). In 2012, personnel reductions continue, but at a slower pace and only in some fields. The personnel cuts in the budgetary

Table 12.1 Number of employees, Romania, 2009–2011

	Jan. 2009		2009	2010	2011	Dec. 2011		Dec. 2011 –Jan. 2009
	'000	%	'000	'000	'000	'000	%	'000
Public administration and defence; social insurance in the public sector	237.9	21.66	–8.5	–25.2	–8	196.2	20.73	–41.7
Education	409.7	37.30	–14.6	–18.5	–9.2	367.4	38.81	–42.3
Health and social assistance	393.6	35.83	–11.2	–19.8	–28.4	334.2	35.31	–59.4
Performances, cultural and recreational activities	57.3	5.22	–2.3	–6.3	0.1	48.8	5.16	–8.5
Total public sector	1,098.5	100	–36.6	–69.8	–45.5	946.6	100	–151.9
Total economy	4,807.5		–439.8	–266.1	70.5	4,172.1		–635.4

Source: Author's calculation based on National Institute of Statistics (NIS) data, *Monthly Statistical Bulletin*.

system, with a 120,000 target in 2012, are directed especially at local administration, central administration and the Ministry of the Interior.[10] In health care, there will be no cuts and as a novelty for 2012 it is expected that the number of community social workers and sanitary mediators will be increased.

Based on the Family Budget Survey for 2004–09, employment in state-owned companies had decreased – from 20 to 15.5 per cent due to privatization.

Reform of the state sector of the economy continues, but employment in companies that are majority or wholly state owned is being done piecemeal, similar to wage policy. The measures for reducing employment include unpaid leave for several days per month, technical unemployment or layoffs. Gradual reductions are also applied, as formerly by agreement with the IMF. The 2012 objectives are: continuing the wind-up of entities in the mining industry, restructuring and reorganizing some national companies in transport and telecommunications. Thus, state-owned companies are to undergo a new wave of layoffs, including about 1,100 employees of the Romanian Railway Company (CFR)[11] by the end of March, 618 from the Romanian Post[12] (who are currently in technical unemployment and earning 75 per cent of the normal wage, the number of employees being currently about 35,000). The Petrila, Uricani and Paroşeni mines are to be closed and about 2,400 people will be dismissed in the next five years.[13] Those who are laid off will receive compensation.[14]

If we analyse the average number of employees, by gender (Table 12.2) we note that the reduction has been more significant for men at national level and in public administration and higher for women in the public sector as a whole based on the cuts in education (reform at pre-university level) and health care (migration of nurses and medical specialists).

By ownership (Table 12.3), the number and share of employees in private entities is increasing in education and health, men being more numerous than women. In education, almost 7 per cent of employees work in private entities, over 18 per cent in health and social assistance and more than one-third in cultural and recreation activities. In entities with joint ownership, employees are more numerous in cultural and recreation activities.

Although still small, private and joint ownership are gaining ground in activities such as health and education, including participation of foreign capital. This structure underwent further changes in 2011 and some are continuing in 2012, the main reasons are: (i) externalizing some activities; (ii) increasing social capital or selling shares to the private sector in some economic entities of the state; (iii) decentralizing some activities and transfer to local community management; (iv) reduction in number of employees as a result of austerity/anti-crisis measures; and (v) development of some new institutions based on foreign direct investment (FDI) and/or domestic private investments (private education institutions, health and social assistance centres or culture, arts and recreation entities).

2.2.2 Skill/educational composition of the public sector

The public sector employs twice as many university graduates as the private sector (about 40 per cent against about 20 per cent, respectively) and as a trend, the share of higher education employees (any education above high-school) is increasing for both ownership forms (Figure 12.9).

With respect to lifelong learning, only 1.8 per cent of employees benefited in 2009 from continuing vocational training, with regular courses at intervals below one year (1.5 per cent in 2004–07). Employment for

Table 12.2 Average number of employees, by activity and by gender, Romania, 2008–2010 ('000; %)

Activity (CANE Rev. 2 sections)	Total			Men			Women					
	2008	2009	2010	2008	2009	2010	2008	%	2009	%	2010	%
Total	5,046	4,774	4,376	2,723	2,542	2,291	2,323	46.0	2,232	46.8	2,085	47.6
Total public sector	997	1,053	1,009	305	326	315	692	69.4	727	69.0	694	68.8
% of public sector in total	19.8	22.1	23.1	11.2	12.8	13.7	29.8		32.6		33.3	
Public admin./defence; public sector social insurance*	213	225	210	96	103	95	117	54.9	122	54.2	115	54.8
Education	394	394	380	121	121	122	273	69.3	273	69.3	258	67.9
Health and social assistance	350	378	366	71	77	74	279	79.7	301	79.6	292	79.8
Culture and recreation	40	56	53	17	25	24	23	57.5	31	55.4	29	54.7

Note: * Excluding armed forces and similar staff (Ministry of National Defence, Ministry of Administration and Interior Romanian Intelligence Service).

Source: Labour Cost Survey.

Table 12.3 Distribution of employees by type of ownership of the job, by gender, Romania, 2008–2011 (share of total, %)

	2008Q3		2009Q3		2010Q3		2011Q3	
	Public	Private	Public	Private	Public	Private	Public	Private
Total employees	26.66	70.82	27.35	70.59	27.78	70.09	26.71	71.33
Education	94.38	4.54	93.78	5.83	93.10	6.81	92.76	6.83
Health and social assistance	80.99	18.36	81.02	18.45	82.15	17.36	81.44	18.35
Culture and recreation	–	–	68.42	30.97	55.13	41.81	50.24	49.09
Women total	30.73	67.60	31.37	66.93	32.49	65.88	31.29	67.14
Education	95.60	3.20	95.00	4.52	93.06	6.90	92.96	6.63
Health and social assistance	81.50	17.73	80.23	19.08	83.76	15.74	81.46	18.27
Culture and recreation	–	–	71.07	–	59.68	34.74	63.35	36.19

Note: The entities in central and local public administration pertain entirely to the public sector.

Source: LFS, quarterly.

replacement jobs and new job creation by modernization or the development of new job fields is increasing employment based on higher educational levels and new competencies, in both the private and public sectors. At national level, the population with a low educational level represents about 37 per cent of the total and that with secondary educational level exceeds half, while individuals with higher education account for less than 12 per cent. Women represented the majority of higher education graduates (51.5 per cent) and men the majority of secondary-level graduates (52.9 per cent) in the third quarter of 2011.

Occupational groups reflect the specific features of activities in the public sector and the increase in the share of the employed receiving specialized education:

- Men are predominant in the group of members of legislative bodies, and of executive and high officials in the public administration, which employed about 11 per cent in the third quarter of 2008, and

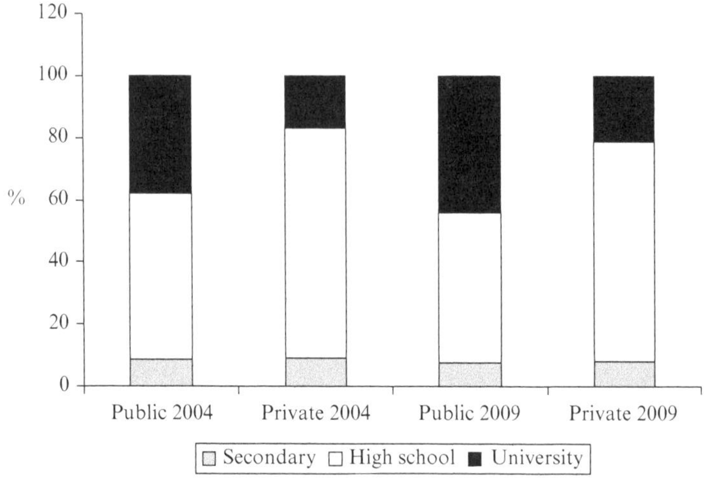

Source: 'Wages in the public sector vs. private sector', National Trade Union Block (BNS), financed by ESF, SOP-HRD, Bucharest 2010. Available at: http://www.bns.ro/wps/wcm/connect/d3eef05f-017d-42ea-bc73-0991dbdcf9f1/Salarizarea+in+sectorul+public+vs.privat.pdf?MOD=AJPERES&CACHEID=d3eef05-017d-42ea-bc73-0991dbdcf9f1.

Figure 12.9 Employment by education level, Romania, 2004 and 2009

7 per cent in the third quarter of 2011; women are more numerous in the group of experts, whose share is increasing slightly and the groups with secondary and lower training are decreasing.

- Experts in intellectual occupations represent almost one-quarter of those with a higher education in public administration and cultural and recreation activities, and are increasing against 2008, growing from 46 to 74 per cent in education and from 22 per cent to almost 49 per cent in health, based on the significant reduction of those with secondary education (technicians, foremen).

2.3 Wages and Labour Costs

2.3.1 Public sector wage policies in the crisis

The public sector is an important actor in national wage determination and dynamics. The wages of employees of state-owned companies are generally above those in the private sector. This trend was already identified in 1995 and becomes more significant after 2000. Thus, a job with a state-owned company ensured a wage 6 per cent higher than in a comparable private company. The wage differentiation originates in the relatively higher education level in the public sector than in the private sector, and in

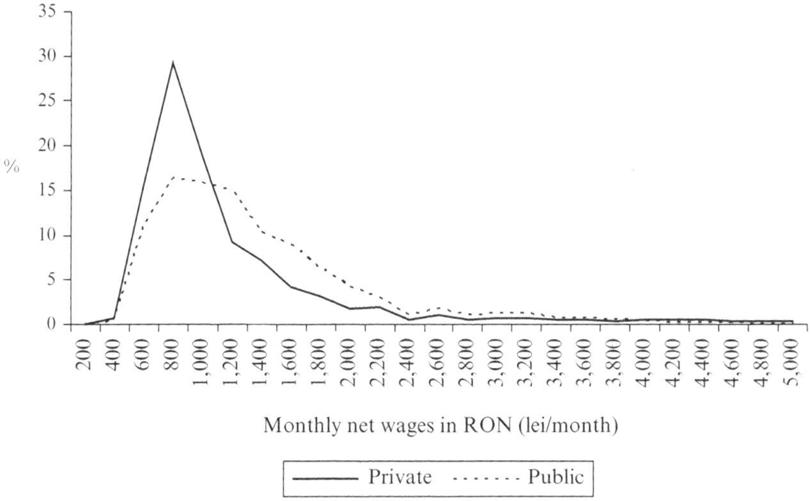

Source: 'RO Competitiveness 2.0', White Paper on National Economic Competitiveness for Romania. 2011, Aspen Institute, www.aspeninstitute.ro.

Figure 12.10 *Wage disparities: distribution of net wages, Romania, mid-2010 (% of total)*

the length of service, in other words, experience and career advancement are more certain in the public sector. Moreover, wages – at least officially – are relatively higher in the public sector, especially in the lower part of the payroll grid because the supplementary 'envelope' payments that are widespread in the private sector are not possible in the public sector.

Public sector wage policy during the crisis has aimed at reforming the grid with the purpose of improving the coherence of the entire public sector and has achieved budget savings, curbing total personnel expenditure by wage cost reductions associated with layoffs.

Wage inequality is more significant in the public sector than in the private sector (Figure 12.10). First, this may represent underreporting in the latter, while all jobs are formal – and thus with clear wage levels – in the former. Second, it reflects better wages at the bottom – at least until 2009 – but also much higher wages at the top. Employees' distribution places about 60 per cent of those working in the private sector under 1,000 lei and only 40 per cent of employees in the public sector. If we consider employees' distribution by income brackets, there are twice as many workers earning the minimum wage in the private as in the public sector.

The public sector pays low wages to a lesser extent than the private sector (Voinea et al. 2011):[15] 78 per cent of the employees with wages in the first two deciles work in private companies, against only 12.2 per cent in the public sector. The main reasons are: (i) the characteristics of some economic activities in which productivity depends on low labour costs; (ii) the share of the informal economy in the private sector; and (iii) the higher average of the education level in the public sector.

The earnings gap between activities in the public sector emerged in 2006–10, when the new basic wages were established and the share of bonuses was limited to 30 per cent.

By major occupation groups, wages are comparatively higher for activities in the public sector against the national average and for the groups GM5–GM9, in particular based on the working programme which generates the payment of supplementary hours or special working conditions when the time and frequency of labour is different (working on holidays, shifts or evening/night work). Wage differences by educational level demonstrate that a university graduate earns 10 per cent less in the state sector than in the private one. The public sector employs more experienced people (30 years or more) and fewer people lacking experience (less than 10 years of experience). An employee with less than five years' experience earns 15 per cent less in the state sector than in the private sector.[16] Inequalities in the public sector deepened in 2007–09 (Table 12.4).

The differences between the coefficients for men and women indicate that an additional year of education advantages women to a higher extent than men. In other words, the positive impact on the wage is higher for women than for men (Voinea et al. 2011).[17] The wage provided for one year of education is lower in the public sector than in the construction or financial sectors. Differences in payments for one year of formalized education are greater in the private sector, where the wages are higher. In general, men's wages are up to 25 per cent higher for the same qualifications even if they have a smaller number of schooling years.

3. EFFECTS OF THE ANTI-CRISIS MEASURES

The mix of structural reforms in the public sector are concentrated on improving efficiency and making the adjustments for financial sustainability compatible with the IMF. To date, most of the policy measures have been focused on short-term financial effects, delaying or halting structural reforms (Table 12.5). The economic and social effects of the extreme quantitative adjustments enacted mainly in 2010 have blocked any qualitative, medium- or long-term approach to the structural/qualitative reform,

Table 12.4 Net average wages, by activity, Romania, 2009

	Net average wages lei/ month (1)	Average years of education (2)	Ratio 3 = 1/2
Public sector			
Public administration and defence, social assistance in the public sector	1,276	12.83	99.45
Education	1,184	13.68	86.56
Health and social assistance	1,084	12.49	86.79
Other activities			
Activities of extraterritorial organizations and organisms	2,243	14.54	154.24
Transport, storage and communication	1,985	11.4	174.14
Financial activities, banking and insurance	1,568	14.49	108.18
Construction	988	10.12	97.62
Processing industry	905	10.58	85.50

Source: 'Employment quality and employment on low wages', BNS, ESF, SOP-HRD Project 'Office for labour market monitoring and job quality', 2011, p. 31, http://www.observator-bns.ro.

increasing tensions between these two types of reform and leading to adverse responses from social actors.

The effects of the crisis on public sector employment and wages have been both quantitative and qualitative, few of them positive, most negative. The expected positive qualitative outcomes were, in fact, few and sometimes transformed into adverse ones, leading to further costly measures.

The main characteristics of the anti-crisis responses are that they have induced higher tensions and their real implications are controversial; many consider them less economically and more politically oriented. The general effects of the reforms can be summarized as follows:

- increased pressure on social services due to rising unemployment and forced retirement;
- public sector employment less attractive because of the freeze on career advancement, lower wages than in the private sector and significantly poorer job quality and working conditions;

Table 12.5 Main policy measures and effects, Romania, 2010–2012

Measures	Effects
Administrative reorganization of public entities by reducing number of agencies and structural reorganization (141 agencies) – layoffs and forced retirement	Job cuts and employment structural changes (educational level and age groups) Forced retirement of people over the statutory retirement age
Limitation of entry into the public sector – one-for-seven replacement rate through re-employment	Reducing job vacancy rate Lower employment flexibility (fixed/temporary or part-time contracts)
Wage cut of 25% and payment reform in the public sector	Decreasing average level of education due to reduced attractiveness of employment for young graduates, especially the highly skilled Real wages decreasing by 4.5% in 2011 as against 2008
Personnel expenditure reductions (from 9.4% in 2009 to 6.6% in 2011 and 6.7% in 2012)	No overtime pay, increasing work intensity
Employees over standard retirement age can accumulate wages from public employment with a pension if the pension level is under the average gross wage	Decreasing number of employees in the public sector
Restructuring of 67 hospitals	Decreasing number of employees and labour expenditure cuts from health-care system
Increasing social contributions at the level of January 2008 and extending contribution categories (self-employed, some liberal professions); reducing tax deductions on property	Decreasing nominal incomes of teachers, researchers, artists, actors etc.
Introducing personnel standards in public and central administration	Employment decrease of more than 200,000 (as of January 2012, 14.5% of total jobs in December 2008 have been lost)

- gradual ageing of the employment structure and a decrease in the average educational level, with deficits in particular professions and specializations because young graduates are less inclined to enter the public sector;
- increasing poverty risk for an increased proportion of low paid; and
- elimination of social dialogue at national level and decreasing importance of negotiations in the public sector (wages are no longer negotiated in the public sector, being regulated annually by special legislation).

The main problems that the public sector has to deal with are loss of service quality and a potential increase in corruption. The crisis has diminished the infusion of young and relatively well-educated personnel by restrictive employment (one new recruit for every seven persons leaving), low wages and lack of career advancement prospects. Some poorly remunerated jobs in the public sector have been shed by the layoffs during the crisis, based on agency reorganization subordinate to the government, but the wage level is generally lower than in the private sector, with a minimum wage below national level. This does not generate the necessary synergies for qualitatively improved public services or capacity development needed to take advantage of structural funds and other EU funds. Furthermore, the lower remuneration level in Romania (lowest wages in EU27) has increased labour migration among specialists from the public sector, mainly doctors and nurses, aggravating the relevant structural deficits in health care.

3.1 Some Macroeconomic Effects of Public Sector Adjustment

Cutting expenditure and employment in the public sector in response to the crisis has created a Keynesian savings paradox (1936)[18] and the impact on budget incomes was much lower than expected. Because of the lower incomes of a large share of employees paid from the state budget, demand for current goods and household services was reduced drastically. This pushed up unemployment and reduced tax revenues to the local and central state budget.

The annualized impact of the 25 per cent cut in public sector wages in 2010 was calculated to have led to a 4.5 per cent drop in aggregate consumption and hence a 2.7 per cent drop in GDP. After the second quarter of 2010 showed modest growth and signs of a potential recovery, the economy plunged back into a negative territory following the implementation of the austerity measures, and stayed there for the rest of 2010, which ended in economic contraction.[19] The contraction in economic activity (or

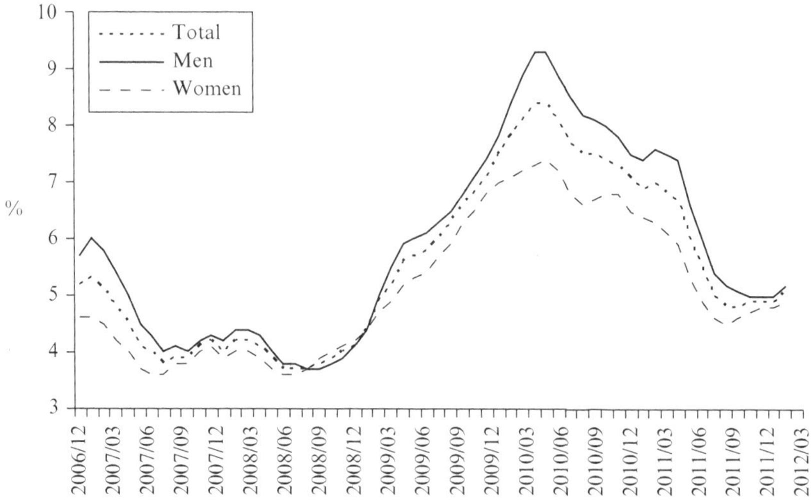

Source: Monthly Statistical Bulletin.

Figure 12.11 Registered unemployment rate, Romania, 2006–2011

temporary winding-up or bankruptcy) and the restructuring of the public sector increased the unemployment rate. However, official statistics on the number of registered unemployed do not fully reflect this process, for several reasons:

1. The accumulation of functions in the public sector: some laid-off employees also have a second job in the public or private sector.
2. Some of those laid off did not register as unemployed for various reasons: they had no right to benefit and thought that they could find another job themselves, or were re-employed in the private sector. Some may have left to work abroad.
3. Retirement of those who met the age conditions but continued to work, in particular in education, health care and cultural activities.

In the first three months of 2009, when the first measures for public sector layoffs were implemented, fewer than 22,000 people were registered with the territorial Labour Offices out of a total of 513,621 registered unemployed on 31 March 2009 (Figure 12.11).[20] For 2010, in the additional Letter of Intent to the IMF agreement, the government undertook to limit public sector personnel to 1.29 million employees until the beginning of 2011, which represented a laying off of 70,000 budget-

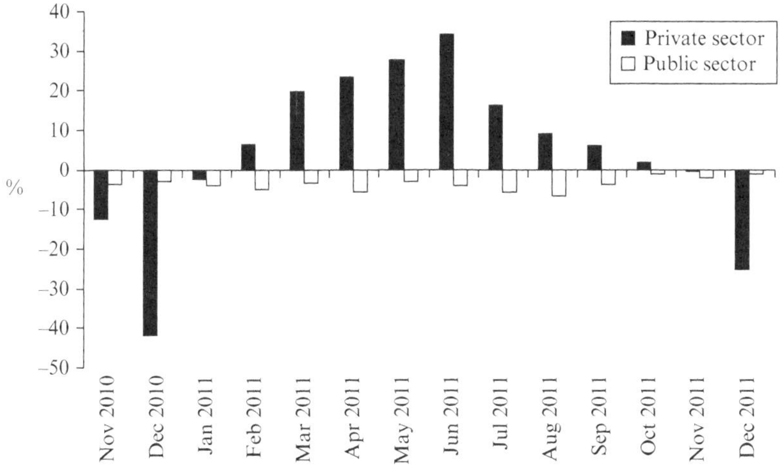

Source: Businessday.ro, based on NIS data, report no. 12.

Figure 12.12 Proportion of employees in the public sector, Romania, 2010–2011

ary employees, a little more than 5 per cent of the whole.[21] In 2011, the public sector job cuts continued, at between 1.2 per cent and 6.6 per cent a month.

In accordance with NIS data, by the end of December 2011, the number of public sector employees and in companies with at least four employees reached 4,172,100, the decrease being generated by the public sector cuts and seasonal developments in construction and agriculture (Figure 12.12). In the public sector – public administration, health care and education – employment decreased in November 2011 to under 900,000 for the first time in the past five years, declining throughout the year (by December 2011 as against December 2010 the number of employees had fallen by 45,600, 8,000 in administration, 9,200 in education and 28,400 in health care). Thus, in the budgetary sector, in December 2011 there were 196,200 employees in administration, 367,400 in education and 334,200 in health care. This represents a loss of 143,400 employees compared to January 2009. At the same time, layoffs were much heavier in the private sector.

In 2008–09 private sector layoffs occurred in the upper half of the income distribution. In the public sector, the ratio D90/D10 has also declined but remained at a high level, the reason being the strongly asymmetrical income distribution. As seen earlier, inequality is higher in the

Table 12.6 Inequality in the public and private sectors, Romania, 2004–2009

	2004		2007		2008		2009	
	Private	Public	Private	Public	Private	Public	Private	Public
p90/p10	3.016	3.466	3.133	3.634	3	3.452	2.757	3.283
p90/p50	1.985	1.949	1.967	1.973	1.92	1.854	1.807	1.799
p10/p50	0.658	0.562	0.628	0.543	0.640	0.537	0.655	0.548
Relative mean deviation (%)	20.07	19.91	19.48	20.19	19.20	20.01	18.14	18.74
Gini (%)	27.69	27.56	27.19	29.13	26.65	27.96	25.30	26.18

Source: Studiu salarizare bugetari.pdf, BNS, p. 21, http://www.observator-bns.ro.

Table 12.7 Gender pay gap by ownership, Romania, 2008–2010 (estimated data, unadjusted, Eurostat methodology)

Type of ownership	2008	2009	2010
Public	11.8	13.2	17.8
Private	12.8	10.3	14.6

Source: Labour Cost Survey and Survey on Wage Structure, 2006.

public sector than in the private, and the diminution trend is thus slower in the public sector (Table 12.6).

3.1.1 Gender pay gap and the share of low-paid employees in the public sector increased

The gender pay gap increased during the crisis period from 7.8 per cent in 2008 to 8.4 per cent in 2009 and 12.6 per cent in 2010. If we estimate the gender pay gap based on Eurostat methodology, a strong increase is found in all ownership types during the crisis, with an increase of 4 percentage points in both the private and public sectors (Table 12.7).

The proportion of women receiving low wages is higher than that of men, and there are also differences between branches. The distribution of employees by gross wage brackets computed based on the annual October Wage Survey highlights an increase in the share of those receiving low wages due to the concentration of the distribution by brackets under the average wage (Table 12.8).

Table 12.8 *Minimum and average gross wage and structure of employees by gross wage brackets, in October each year, Romania, 2008–2010*

Gross wage bracket	2008			2009			2010		
	Total	Men	Women	Total	Men	Women	Total	Men	Women
Minimum wage		540 lei			600 lei			600 lei	
up to 1000	39.9	38.5	41.6	37.1	36.0	38.5	39.9	37.6	42.7
1001–1500	21.2	21.1	21.2	21.8	21.5	22.2	21.9	20.8	23.0
1501–2000	14.8	15.3	14.1	14.8	14.9	14.6	14.2	14.7	13.7
Average gross wage in October	1,694	1,758	1,620	1,791	1,865	1,709	1,721	1,830	1,600
Over 2001	24.1	25.1	23.1	26.3	27.6	24.7	24.0	26.9	20.6
Average gross wage in October – public sector									
Public administration and defence	1,808	1,867	1,763	1,716	1,789	1,663	1,512	1,568	1,473
Education	2,025	2,228	1,936	2,085	2,268	2,004	1,625	1,784	1,555
Health and social assistance	2,068	2,344	1,990	2,057	2,279	1,998	1,571	1,768	1,515
Culture and recreation	–	–	–	1,701	1,802	1,620	1,402	1,454	1,364

Source: Wage Survey, October each year.

The wage distribution above the average level shows that women have been harder hit by the crisis than men, also for employee groups with higher incomes.

3.1.2 Labour cost indices

In the crisis the tax wedge on labour costs has increased, from 41.0 per cent in 2008 to 43.1 per cent in 2009 and 43.3 in 2010 (Romanian Statistical Yearbook). Labour costs in the total economy increased, in particular due to non-wage labour costs in 2009 against 2008 and decreased slightly during 2010. In the public sector,[22] where wage cuts have been considerable and affected all budgetary employees (save for national companies with 100 per cent/majority state capital), the reduction of wage costs started in mid-2009. In the fourth quarter of 2010, compared with the crisis start in Romania (fourth quarter of 2008) the index of wage expenditure was 73.49 per cent for health, 75.95 per cent for education and 77.61 per cent for public administration and defence, as well as 80.38 per cent for cultural and recreational activities.

This decrease in the index was attenuated partially by the preponderant layoff of low-wage personnel, who also benefited from the fiscal deductibility of 250 lei on computing the tax on wages for wage earnings of up to 1,000 lei a month. As a result, the index of non-salary expenditures decreased more slowly due to two factors: on one hand, the maintenance in the public sector of those with relatively higher wages who benefited from increased tax deductions and, on the other, due to the increase in the tax wedge, as previously mentioned.

3.1.3 Decreasing interest in lifelong learning

Interest in lifelong learning is currently marginal, even though legislation and/or collective agreements provide for mandatory periodical vocational training to increase competences and performance (Labour Code[23]). As compared to the situation at European level, Romania has made little progress, with only 1.3 per cent of the total adult population aged 25 to 64 participating in education and training, as compared to 9.1 per cent at EU27 level. Women's participation is slightly higher (Table 12.9).

Financial restrictions represent the main obstacle to continuing training, in other words, insufficient resources, even though such expenditure is tax deductible. Companies resort to training only as a last resort, largely because they face skills deficits on the labour market. On-the-job training is strictly specialized, adapted to the features of the company and workplace. Expenditure allocated for vocational training oscillates between 0.1 and 0.3 per cent of the average monthly labour cost, both

Table 12.9 Lifelong learning: percentage of adult population aged 25 to 64 participating in education and training, by gender, Romania, 2000–2010

Year	EU27 total	Romania total	Men		Women	
			EU27 men	Romania men	EU27 women	Romania women
2000	7.1	0.9	6.7	0.9	7.6	0.8
2001	7.1	1.0	6.6	1.1	7.6	1.0
2002	7.2	1.0	6.6	1.0	7.8	1.0
2003	8.5	1.1	7.9	1.1	9.0	1.2
2004	9.2	1.5	8.5	1.5	9.9	1.4
2005	9.6	1.6	8.8	1.5	10.4	1.6
2006	9.5	1.3	8.6	1.3	10.4	1.3
2007	9.3	1.3	8.4	1.2	10.2	1.4
2008	9.4	1.5	8.5	1.3	10.2	1.6
2009	9.3	1.5	8.4	1.3	10.2	1.6
2010	9.1	1.3	8.3	1.2	10.0	1.4
2011	8.9	1.6	8.2	1.6	9.6	1.5

Source: Eurostat database.

at national level and, more specifically, in the public sector, although in absolute terms they are two to three times lower in the public sector (Table 12.10).

In the public sector, training has a higher priority in public administration where, in 2008, allocations were about 2.5 times higher than in education and health care, the amounts decreasing gradually during the crisis to under 1 per cent in education and on average 2–2.5 lei per month and per employee, against almost 5 lei at national level.

3.2 Microeconomic Effects

3.2.1 Massive employment cuts

The number of jobs in the budgetary sector and in services of national and local public interest has continuously increased during the transition, especially in the past decade, owing to economic growth after 2004.[24] The number of jobs increased to 1.4 million in December 2008. The highest increase took place at the local authority level (approximately 90,000), to which about 50,000 were added in central administration. From 2009, as a result of the authorities' efforts regarding fiscal adjustment, the number of jobs in the budgetary sector was constantly

Table 12.10 Labour expenditure on vocational training and as a percentage of average monthly labour costs per employee, Romania, 2000–2010

	2000		2007		2008		2009		2010	
	Lei	%	Lei	%	Lei	%	Lei	%	Lei	%
Total	8.69	0.2	5.50	0.3	6.89	0.3	4.85	0.2	4.95	0.2
Public administration	4.35	0.1	7.44	0.3	6.13	0.2	2.82	0.1	2.65	0.1
Education	<3.86	<0.1	2.08	0.1	2.69	0.1	2.84	0.1	<2.45	<0.1
Health and social assistance	<3.86	<0.1	1.88	0.1	2.54	0.1	2.73	0.1	2.48	0.1
Culture and recreation							2.23	0.1	2.00	0.1

Source: Labour Cost Survey.

reduced by freezing vacancies (from May 2009), by layoffs and/or retirement (Table 12.11).

Over 50 per cent of job reductions in the government sector took place at local level (approximately 76,000), most of them in pre-university education. In the health-care sector, about 33,000 jobs were cut. In 2011, most job cuts took place in the Ministry of the Interior (10,000) by reorganizing some institutions and reducing the number of jobs in some administrative structures. In December 2011, the total number of jobs decreased to 1,196,067, making a total job cut of 200,262 in the public sector. In 2012, public sector jobs are estimated to decrease further as the replacement rate of one new job for seven departures (applied since 2009) is maintained. However, there are also modest increases in some institutions, with 30 new jobs at the Court of Accounts and 10 at the National Integrity Agency and the Competition Council (Figure 12.13).

In 2012, the state will also take action in state-owned companies, similar to 2011, in two respects: (a) maintaining the job freeze and subjecting all job increases to government approval; and (b) granting wage increases only if profits were reported in 2011, but not higher than forecast inflation (3 per cent). The government reached agreement with the IMF that the wage policy of autonomous/national companies will be established annually, by law.

The 'number of state employees shall reach 1.1 million by the end of 2012'.[25]

Table 12.11 Job developments in the public sector, Romania, 2008–2010

	Dec. 2008	Dec. 2010	Difference	
			Number	%
Total no. of jobs	1,398,757	1,266,550	–132,207	–9.45
A. Central administration	694,995	639,722	–55,273	–7.95
1. State budget, of which:	338,727	334,533	–4,194	–1.24
Ministry of Administration and Interior	146,955	147,822	867	–1.16
Ministry of Defence	79,666	79,210	–456	–0.57
Ministry of Public Finances	33,716	31,210	–2,506	–7.43
Ministry of Justice	13,558	15,053	1,495	11.03
Other ministries	64,832	61,238	–3,594	–5.54
2. Self-financed institutions, of which:	304,132	260,001	–44,131	–14.51
Health-care institutions	209,273	176,638	–32,635	–15.59
State higher education institutions	68,095	68,229	134	0.20
3. Institutions financed by the social insurance budgets	52,136	45,188	–6,948	–13.33
B. Local administration, of which:	703,762	626,828	–76,934	–10.93
Pre-university education	332,952	303,477	–29,475	–8.85
Local executive authorities	310,912	264,382	–46,530	–14.97

Note: For reasons of comparability health institutions were included in central administration, although part of them were transferred to local subordination during 2010 (Government Emergency Ordinance No. 48/2010 containing amendments and additions to some regulations in the field of health within the framework of decentralization).

Source: Ministry of Public Finance, Annual Report: Macroeconomic and Budgetary Developments and Perspectives, March 2011, Fiscal Council, p. 20.

3.2.2 Job vacancies fall

From 2008 up to the present, the number of job vacancies has fallen continuously (Figure 12.14). The institutional reorganization of public sector activities was aimed in a first stage to block and then to reduce job vacancies. Re-employment to fill natural/normal vacancies (retirement, resignations and so on) was allowed, but only in a proportion of one for

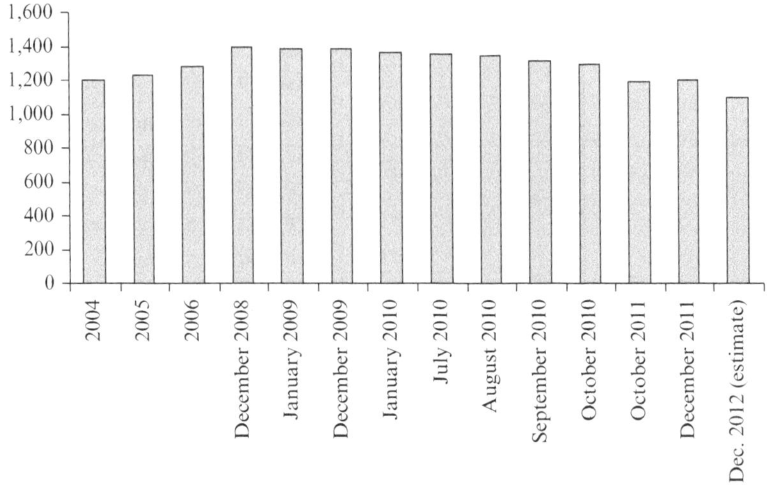

Source: INS, Tempo online.

Figure 12.13 Job evolution in the public sector, Romania, 2004–2011

seven, while particular positions could be filled with special approval from the government.

As compared with previous periods, health and social assistance registered the most significant diminution of job vacancies: 7,800 job vacancies representing more than two-thirds (67.5 per cent) of the number of job vacancies that were reduced that year in the entire economy. Government Resolution No. 286/2011 generated employment for temporary jobs and in some cases, allowed for job advancement.

3.2.3 Working hours: overtime hours no longer remunerated

Another quantitative factor that led to cuts in personnel expenditure was the ban on payments for supplementary hours. The job cut was not associated with a reduction in the workload, which was redistributed between the remaining employees, without wage bonuses or other additional payments. If supplementary hours were necessary, they were no longer paid during the crisis, but compensated with free time. In some cases there was additional work at home: in 2010, about 34 per cent of public sector employees also worked at home, as compared to 18 per cent of private sector employees.[26] To a certain extent, this also resulted in work intensification by eliminating time losses during normal working hours and also increased job discipline, improved the organization of activities at the workplace. This is also why layoffs did not trigger a corresponding working-time increase.

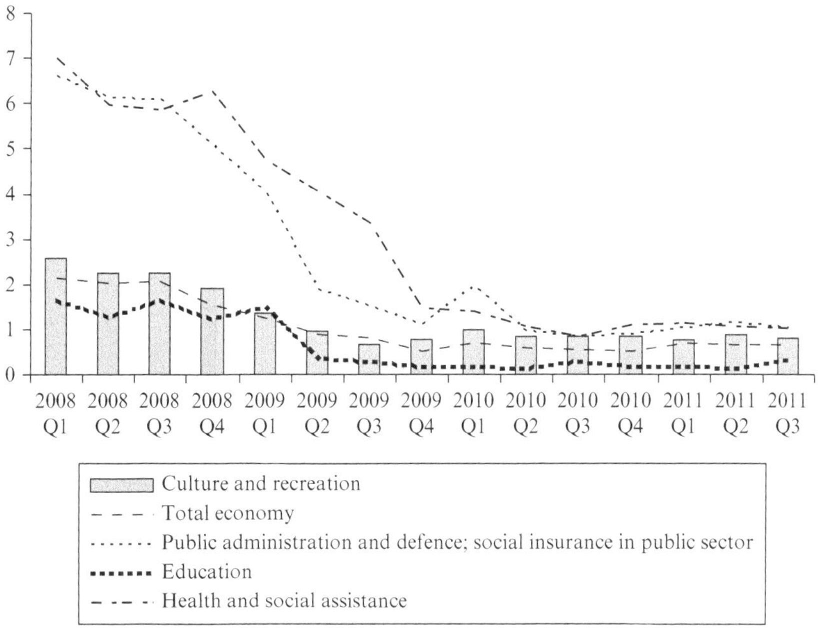

Source: Ministry of Finance; IMF staff estimates.

Figure 12.14 Job vacancy rate, Romania, 2008–2011

The average working week (main job) at national level in the third quarter of 2011 was 40.5 hours, a slight increase on the previous period. In the public sector, employees in education work less than the national average and employees in health care more. The system of wards and shifts in health care means that people sometimes work longer than their regular hours. The lack of payment for supplementary hours imposes constraints on their use.

3.2.4 Employment flexibility – more temporary and part-time workers in the public sector

In Romania, part-time and fixed-term contracts are relatively poorly developed, particularly in the public sector. They have decreased during the crisis, although they are more frequent in education (Figure 12.15). Note that most public sector employees working part-time are in public administration and education, while in health care the number is falling (Figure 12.16). During the crisis, contrary to developments at national level, the number of those working part-time in the public sector fell

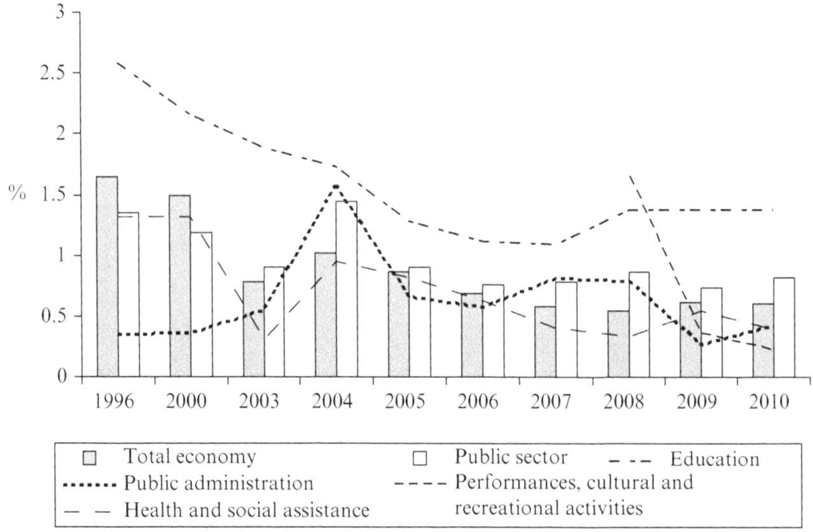

Source: NIS Tempo online.

Figure 12.15 Part-time employment, Romania, 1996–2010 (% of total employees)

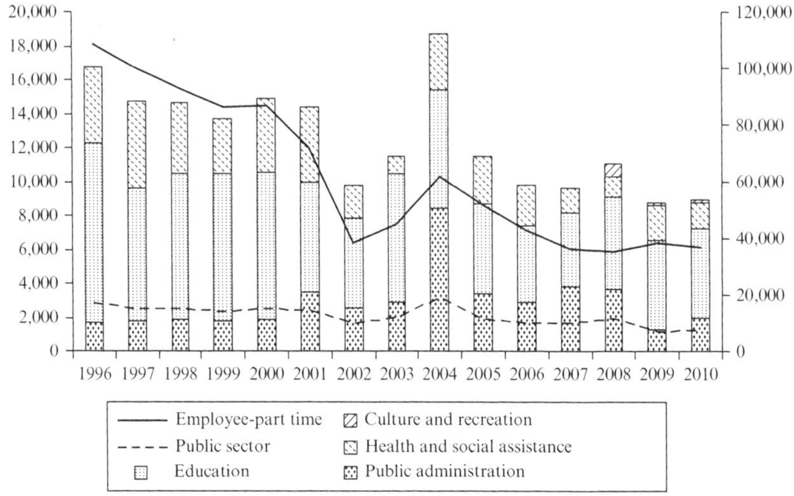

Source: NIS Tempo online.

Figure 12.16 Part-time employment, Romania, 1996–2010 (number of persons)

due to the first wave of layoffs, but then increased for the following reasons:

- Part-time employment is allowed under certain conditions for work that cannot be distributed among the remaining personnel.
- Access to European funds, changes to the Labour Code and digitalization of the monitoring of labour contracts enables the registration of several part-time contracts for the same person, besides the full-time period contract also at the same entity. At the same time, the possibility of accumulating activities is limited in particular for public sector workers who besides their main job are permitted to get involved only in teaching.
- Limiting the maximum working week provided for in the Labour Code to 48 hours for each employer for four consecutive months at the most makes it possible to perform different activities with several employers (research/education, medical practice/education, cultural activities/education and so on).
- There is also a practice of accumulating one contract or several part-time as employee and/or self-employed in some professions (accountant, evaluator, liquidator, art restorer, artist and so on).

Access to structural funds has triggered: (a) an increase in limited duration contracts either full- or part-time and (b) limitation of public sector employment by curbing recruitment, allowing registration only of those already in the system.

3.2.5 A shift in the age structure

The employment cuts combined with compulsory retirement on reaching a certain age has shifted the age structure in the public sector towards younger workers, but not necessarily better-trained and specialized personnel, due to the low wages. The working-age population in total employment is increasing in the economy as a whole, which exemplifies the trend of active ageing, but in the public sector it is falling slightly, due to the limits imposed on remaining employees after reaching pension age. Even here some exceptions are allowed for highly qualified personnel in education, health care and culture, but they are paid part-time or for determined periods (in education also per hour). Remaining employees are obliged to retire. As a result, the following age features appear in the public sector:

- Public sector employment has a younger age structure than in the economy as a whole.

- A shift is discernible with regard to the employment of young people who have a higher education, with the share of those aged 15–24 years in the public sector decreasing from 6.8 per cent of total employment at national level in 2008 to below 5 per cent in 2011, due to an increase in the 24–34-year age group.
- The employment of those aged 25–44 years is increasing to the detriment of those aged over 45 years.
- The youngest age structure is developing in public administration, while the oldest is in education.

3.3 Severe Reduction of Social Dialogue in the Public Sector

Freedom of association is almost universally permitted for both career civil servants and contractual employees in Romania since 2003. Trade union density is higher in the public sector, between 55 and 70 per cent in central government (EIRO: European Industrial Relations Observatory, national contribution, 2006). Until 2010 trade unions in the public sector were part of the representative bodies and participated in national bargaining. However, important reforms were introduced in 2011 that seriously reduced the scope of social dialogue with most elements being decided by legislation. The new Law on Social Dialogue (Act 62 of 10 May 2011) regulates only sectoral agreements and stepped up the representativeness conditions. Social dialogue in the public sector is organized at institution, group and activity levels. Collective agreements cannot include clauses on financial rights or in-kind rights other than those provided for under the legislation on the relevant personnel category. Negotiations take place after the approval of income and expenditure budgets. Wages are laid down by law, within precise limits and cannot be the object of negotiations (they cannot be changed by collective agreement).

The trade union movement has been weakened over time, also due to excessive fragmentation (for instance, among public officials there are over 20 trade union federations[27]), the preponderance of tripartite dialogue and the prevalence of wage claims, as a rule during the run-up to the state budget for the next year while other working conditions are often neglected, even though the rate of labour accidents is high. Working under stressful conditions and unhealthy working regimes are two other factors in the public sector that seem to be neglected in the social dialogue process.

The high union density in the public sector is sustained by the practice of automatically retaining payroll contributions.[28] The real number of trade union members remains another unknown element, the data being based on trade union leaders' declarations and not official statistics. At national

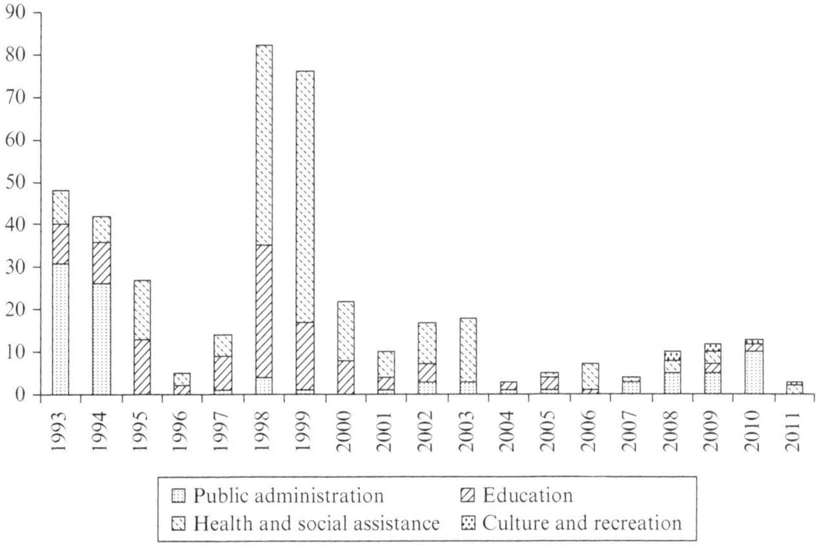

Source: Ministry of Labour, Family and Equal Opportunities.

Figure 12.17 Conflicts of interest in the public sector, Romania, 1993–2011

level, trade unions talk about 50 per cent trade union representation (from about 83 per cent at the beginning of the 1980s), and 90 per cent among public sector employees.[29]

Even though Romania has a high trade union density (two or three times higher than in Hungary, Poland or the Czech Republic), protest rallies barely gather more than a few tens of thousands, at best. In 2009, when the most serious economic downturn in Romania's recent history was recorded, there were only 92 conflicts of interest, as compared to the peak year 1999 when 653 were recorded. In the public sector there were just 12 (five in the public administration, three in health and two each in education and cultural–recreational activities), as compared to 76 in 1999 (one in public administration, 16 in education and 59 in health care). The lack of willingness to engage in such events led to a decrease in the number of participants by 16.7 times for general issues and by 8.3 times in the public sector (2010 against 1999). During the crisis period, in 2008–11 there were only 38 conflicts of interest (in 2011 just three), with only 31,525 participants (Figure 12.17).

During the crisis rallies were organized, but the outcomes were poor or non-existent and the number of participants fell rapidly.

Social dialogue has been reformed again and the new legislation is more restrictive as regards employees' benefits, and is aimed at reining in the trade union movement. The Law on Social Dialogue No. 62/2011 modifies collective negotiations and industrial relations and unifies the regulations regarding employers' organizations, trade unions, social dialogue and collective labour contracts, the setting up of the National Tripartite Council for Social Dialogue and the organization and functioning of the Economic and Social Council. The major elements of this social dialogue reform – that directly hurts the public sector functioning – include the increase in the representativeness threshold for trade unions and employers' organizations, elimination of the collective agreement at national level and of the *erga omnes* automatic extensions at sectoral level.

4. CASE STUDIES

Romania entered the crisis against a background of public sector reforms. The reform of public expenditure in 2009 and 2010 and thereafter fiscal consolidation for 2011 and 2012 have represented the major objectives behind the recent reforms. Currently, these measures are continuing, with annual adjustments and completion measures that sometimes contradict the general principles of structural adjustment. We shall see below the nature and effects of these reforms in one important sector, education, before analysing in more detail in a second case study the overall scope and effects of the wage reform process in the public sector.

4.1 Case Study 1: Comprehensive Education Reform

4.1.1 The context: the need for reforms in a low participatory system

Reform of the national education system was necessary for at least the following reasons: to develop a modern system, focused on skills and competences; to increase the quality of education; to render more flexible the educational path and development of open vocational routes; to increase access to education; and to provide student finance and decentralization in secondary education. Participation in education in Romania is among the lowest in Europe, involving only 54.8 per cent of women and 48.8 per cent of men.[30] Education reform started in the second half of the 1990s with a general revision of secondary education (curriculum changes, new education programmes, more labour market-oriented education, vocational education (Vasile et al. 2007)[31]). At the university level, the Bologna system was adopted. Furthermore, the National Pact on Education was signed, whose main purpose was to modernize the education system and institutions in 2008–13 in order to increase the competitiveness of Romanian schools at international level. It was agreed that the education reform should contribute to fiscal consolidation while improving the productivity of the future workforce through better training.[32]

The whole system was thus reorganized[33] to better accommodate it to the current requirements of the knowledge-based society and to smart, sustainable and inclusive growth. The main objectives of the new Law on National Education are: education based on individual educational routes; a modern curriculum oriented to skills and competences needed in the labour market; changing early education into a public good and guaranteeing unrestricted access to 10 years' compulsory education; decentralization of financial, curricular and human resources; promoting student financing;[34] involvement of civil society as responsible partners in education; autonomy of educational entities supported by the local community; hierarchy of universities and their specialization (some concentrating on BAs, others on MAs and others still on doctoral studies and research); and adopting a Charter of Rights and Liberties in education, which would guarantee access to quality education. In order to narrow the gaps in the quality of education, some priority areas will be defined and lifelong learning will be made the backbone of the education system (the proposed target by 2013 is to have annual continuing training for 12 per cent of the active labour force and to finalize the National Qualification Framework to make it compatible with the European one). The Law on National Education provides for the allocation of at least 6 per cent of GDP for education every year, although the financial constraints will limit it at a much lower rate, namely 4.25 per cent in 2007 and even 3.1 per cent of GDP in 2009.

4.1.2 Effects of quantitative adjustment: opposing structural needs?

University education has been hardest hit by job and spending cuts. This was visible in areas and sectors, with higher education in Romania being characterized by excessive differentiation of academic specialization and a dispersion of resources (human, material and financial).

University education in 2010–11 was hit hard by the adjustments:

1. the total number of educational institutions fell to 108 (compared to 121 in 1999–2000) of which 52 are private (63 in 1999–2000);
2. the total number of students also fell to 673,000, down from over 907,000 in 2007–08;
3. at the same time the number of students per teacher increased to 22.6 compared to 14.1 in 1989–90;
4. over 191,000 graduates (26,000 in 1990–91, 68,000 in 1999–2000); and

5. according to the Academic Ranking of World Universities, as of 2011 there was no Romanian university in the top 500 universities worldwide. We must add that the education system in Romania lacks benchmarks for measuring quality and efficiency so that it is difficult to measure other adverse effects expected with regard to quality (GR 2011).[35]

The first interim evaluation is expected in 2015, but we can synthesize the preliminary results, mainly based on the evaluation of trade union leaders. They consider that even though reform was necessary, most of the provisions were not related to Romanian realities/peculiarities, especially its real potential of infrastructure and personnel. No statistical data are available but, based on interviews among teaching university staff we can present some qualitative assessments in Table 12.12.

On the whole, these measures are aimed at promoting higher standards, but with fewer benefits. Also, the re-employment restriction of one for seven will create significant structural deficits with regard to professions and qualifications. The main effect of these measures in the long term will be the reduction of human resources in education, mainly due to the insufficient attractiveness of employment in education because of low wages and teacher status. During the crisis the total number of university teaching staff was reduced from 31,964 in 2007–08 to 29,746 in 2010–11, although the proportion was lower than in education as a whole, at 7 per cent as against 8.6 per cent (Figure 12.18).

The expected results from a human resources perspective are as follows: increasing the relevance of education and training by streamlining towards skills formation; opening up schools to the community and business environment; development of vocational education and training; stimulating lifelong learning; and improving teachers' performance in education and research (National Reform Programme 2011–2013, Government of Romania). The establishment of the National Register of Qualifications in Higher Education and of a Single Register and its connection to labour market demand will increase graduates' employability. All these measures will increase the attractiveness of schools not only for students but also for teachers, and will re-establish – at least partially – teachers' social status. At the same time, public expenditure on education will be used more judiciously for allocating both employment and professional degrees, but also for performance-based pay (Figure 12.19).

In higher education, career advancement has become a key issue for all teaching staff because of the very restrictive criteria for personal and institutional evaluation based on high-quality outcomes from teaching and research; appointment as reader or full professor requires certification from the National Council of University Titles. Diplomas and certificates

Table 12.12 Main changes in university education, Romania

Measures	Main expected results
Nationwide standard wage for teachers	Cuts in personnel expenditure Very low pay considering new quality standards (private sector more attractive for similar professions) Future staff deficit likely
Increase in statutory teaching hours per person, with professional grades	Personnel expenditure reduction, increasing productivity
Ceiling on working hours at maximum twice full-time employment in all teaching jobs in all universities	Personnel expenditure reduction, increasing quality Limited income from teaching Multiple employment including informal employment
University ranking and different student financing according to type of university (education, research, etc.)	Wage differences between institutions for same qualifications
New evaluation and career advancement standards, very restrictive system for career advancement for university staff – very high standards	Increase excellence in teaching, more difficult access to highest professional positions Lower wages – very low pay considering new quality standards (private sector more attractive for similar professions)
Reduction in number of students financed from state budget	Lower total expenditures on education Changes in employment in particular fields and professional specializations – related to number of students financed from public funds and also limitation of total number of students who must pay for education

Table 12.12 (continued)

Measures	Main expected results
Restricted access to teaching careers – initial training of teachers will include BA studies in a related qualification, a two-year MA in teaching and one-year vocational traineeship	Quality and selective employment
Very restricted criteria for applying for RDI national funds	Selective access to supplementary sources of income for teachers
Limited active ageing – only for full professors and payment by hours worked, not a contract, although they will receive a pension	Compulsory retirement at standard age Lower payment for the same work
A 25% wage cut for all public sector workers	Reducing expenditure on personnel in education – some teachers contested this decision and, as according to a court ruling, they should recover 33.4% of their monthly pay, but the government has postponed reimbursement

Source: Author's synthesis based on national legislation and preliminary evaluation of the trade unions and other stakeholders.

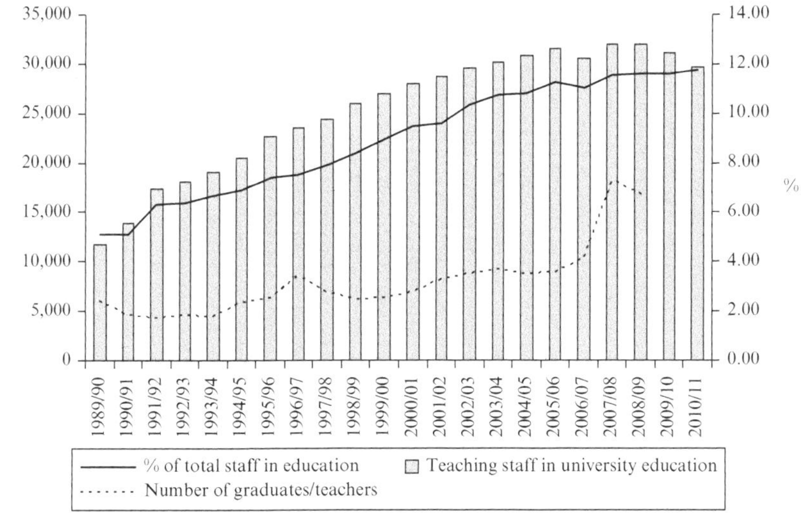

Source: NIS data, *Romanian Statistical Yearbook* (RSY), 1990–2010.

Figure 12.18 Employment in university education, Romania, 1989–2011

based on new evaluation criteria to promote international excellence and the profile of the didactic and research activity of university teaching staff. Also, access to additional financing or supplementary incomes for teaching staff by basic research contracts financed by the national Research Development and Innovation (RDI) programme depends on new extremely restrictive excellence criteria designed to stimulate the continuing professional training of teaching staff and increase their international visibility by articles and books published abroad.

Another qualitative standard is aimed at ensuring that leadership, mentoring and management positions in education are occupied by teachers who have completed an accredited training programme in education management (a National Body of Experts on Education Management will be established by selection, based on competition). The most important expected positive results are: changing the structure of specialization and degrees in science (closer to occupational demands in the labour market). New regulations in the Labour Code and pension law will bring about a rejuvenation of staff in the national education system and employment forms will become more flexible, as will work duration.

From a teaching staff point of view, this new education reform may stress some important aspects, both quantitative and qualitative, but its implementation during the crisis, with the main focus on levels of

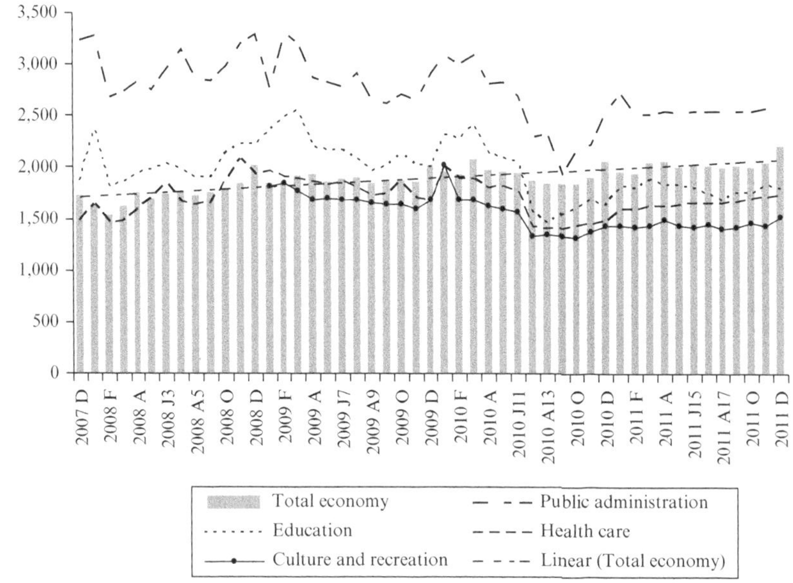

Source: NIS data, RSY, 1990–2010.

Figure 12.19 Monthly gross wages in education and other sectors, Romania, 2007–2011

employment and public expenditure, could have adverse effects, such as emigration of experts into the business sector or to other countries for professional development; faster ageing of human resources and bigger shortages of specialists, stimulating multiple employment and informal supplementary incomes, thereby harming teaching quality. The sporadic implementation of reform in response to the crisis, focused mainly on the lack of financial resources will hinder coherence and boost inequalities.

The risks currently being highlighted are:

- Unattractiveness of jobs in education due to low wages and current low social status of teachers.
- Risk of staff deficits in some fields for some teaching ranks (reader, professor) due to inadequate promotion prospects, the difficulty of developing a professional career and the relatively long period required for reaching minimum standards for career advancement.
- Risk of underfinancing the education system, both from public funds (allocation of at least 6 per cent of GDP is difficult to ensure and insufficient for the required modernization of the system and

proper performance) and attracting additional funds from research projects, the conditions for obtaining national funds being currently more restrictive than those for accessing international funds (for example, FP7, SEE Program).

Due to the brief implementation period, the first outcomes are still being measured, but expectations are high because this reform was expected to re-establish quality and competitiveness in the entire education system. However, the quantitative adjustments may lead in the opposite direction.

4.2 Case Study 2: Wage Reform Frozen because of Quantitative Adjustment

4.2.1 The context before the reforms

Before wage reform, the basic wages of budgetary sector personnel were determined by 39 normative deeds, as follows: (a) between a minimum and maximum limit for contractual staff in the budgetary sector and military personnel; (b) specific values for length of service for staff in the education sector; (c) single levels for public positions; and (d) varying levels for public officials. The use of these systems led to over 400 wage levels that can no longer be related to the initial hierarchy of positions and fields of activity. As a result, the ratio between the minimum and the maximum wage in the budgetary sector is 1/29. The main characteristics of the public sector pay system before the new legislation were as follows:

1. There was no unified wage scale and there were many laws regulating wages in different parts of the system.
2. A large part of gross income was based on bonuses and premiums. The abundance of bonuses and other benefits and their generosity (some are up to 75 per cent of the basic wage: for instance, the bonus for managing European funds) can increase earnings several times greater than the basic wage (on average, in 2008 bonuses represented 51 per cent of gross earnings).
3. Disparities in pay between positions with similar skills and responsibility in public sector activities.
4. Increased non-wage compensation: meal vouchers, holiday vouchers.
5. Seniority more important than performance.
6. Wage increase not based on productivity, political interference undermines competitive recruitment and pay.

The main issue generating wage reform in the public sector was the poor functioning of the labour market, particularly with regard to wage coherence in the system. The measures to improve labour market flexibility and the business environment implemented through the National Reform Programme 2011–13 (NRP) during 2007–10 had limited effects, but continue to represent a priority for 2011–13.[36]

4.2.2 Wage policy during the crisis: mainly quantitative adjustments

During the crisis, wage policy focused especially on savings related to wage expenditure and was associated with layoffs or technical unemployment. In the private sector, mainly bonuses and other wage advantages provided for in individual labour contracts or bargained in collective agreements were cut and/or layoffs were implemented, doubling the unemployment rate.

For public employees the crisis measures with regard to wages were as follows:

- For employees of national companies with individual labour contracts, this contract was renegotiated and, in some situations, layoffs were implemented and some re-employment but with diminished wages (especially for people in managerial positions in 2009).
- The wages of the heads of government agencies were reduced several times, setting a ceiling of 4,800 lei a month (around €1,100)[37] in 2009.
- Payment was ceased or bonuses reduced (starting from 2009).
- Overtime was no longer paid but compensated with free time and applied for the whole period.
- It was recommended to reduce labour duration or unpaid furlough, equivalent to 10 working days for each employee in November–December 2009.
- Restructuring of the wage system was implemented: unified law on wages for budgetary personnel applicable as of 2010 for new entrants and with annual re-evaluation of wage policy (level, dynamics and structure).

4.2.3 Wage reform: for a unified framework in the public sector

The unified wage law was considered both a response to wage reform and an anti-crisis measure (Figure 12.20).

Two significant stages are distinguished with regard to the payment of budgetary personnel during the crisis:

- In 2008–09 the provisions of Law 154/1998 were implemented, with subsequent additions in which payroll grids were laid down for various fields of activity, including coefficients and algorithms

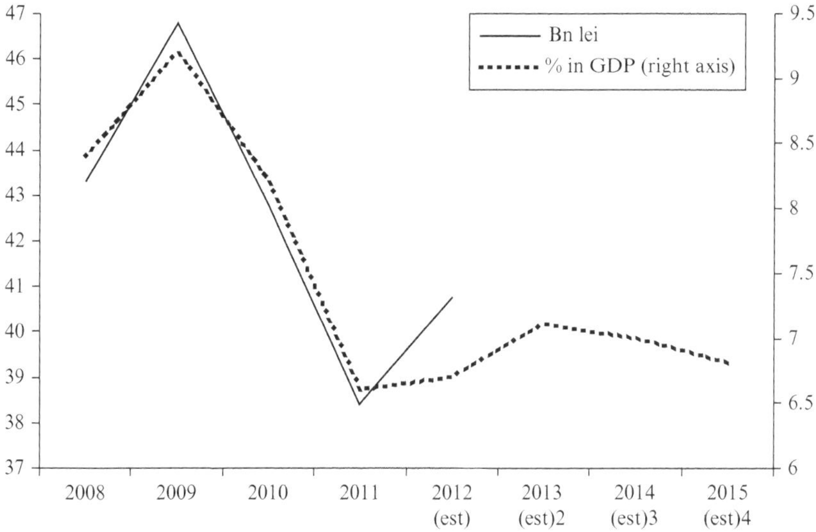

Source: Romanian Government, Reforms 2009–12, AP/R/8/2012, 27 March 2012.

Figure 12.20 Main effects of the wage reform: reduction in labour expenditure, Romania, 2008–2012

for payment. Each year, the general payment policy for the public sector was regulated by ordinances which aimed mainly at indexing wages and the value of the starting coefficient or new instalments were stipulated on wage brackets and fields.

- On 1 January 2011 a wage reform in the public sector was initiated. Basic wages were determined in jobs grouped into seven occupational families: administration, health, education, justice, culture, diplomacy and defence, public order and national security.

The objectives of Framework Law No. 284/2010 were: (a) to harmonize the wage system of budgetary sector personnel in accordance with importance, accountability, complexity of activity and level of studies required;[38] (b) to establish basic wages as the main element of wage earnings (establishing an equitable income structure in which basic wages start from the hierarchy coefficients and are complemented by bonuses of up to 30 per cent, depending on the characteristics of the activity (contents and importance of delivered work), working conditions and other established criteria; (c) to establish a hierarchy of basic wages both between fields of activity and in the same field, having as background job evaluation based on seven criteria agreed in the Bipartite Commission;[39] (d) to ensure the transparency of the mechanism for determining the basic wage; (e) to simplify the wage system by reducing the number of professional ranks and degrees to a maximum of three for each position[40] as against five at present for the majority of contractual positions. Promotion to immediately higher professional ranks and degrees, when there are no provisions in this respect in the specific statutes may be done every three years, depending on individual professional performances, assessed with the qualifications 'very good' at least twice in the past three years; and (f) to establish the wage differential depending on the level of studies – hence, the minimum hierarchy coefficients have the following values: 1.00 for unskilled workers without bonuses and 1.10 with bonuses; 1.20 for high-school studies; 1.30 for short-term higher education; 1.75 for higher education; and (g) differentiation of basic wages depending on the level at which the activity is delivered: central, territorial and local. Thereby, the inequities in the system will be reduced with respect to payments for equal or equivalent work, and reducing the ratio between maximum and minimum wages from 1 to 12. Wage increases will be more dynamic for low wages and will take into account macroeconomic indicators and the development of social indicators.

By eliminating excessive wages, in particular in companies wholly or partially state owned (national companies and autonomous companies), and promoting performance, management also aims to reduce losses and gain savings for the state budget. Based on the new payroll grid and complying with the principle of obtained wage rights, the position after the introduction of the new wage (to which are added bonuses) against the grid in the Framework Law shows instances in which wages were superior to those in the new grid and others in which they were lower. The financial restrictions did not allow for wage increases for those receiving wages under the level of the new grid, save for the exceptional cases of those who were under the minimum wage in the economy.

4.2.4 A progressive implementation of the law

Because it was not possible to apply the new grid immediately and as a whole, it was agreed that the steps to be taken in the wage system would be stipulated yearly by special laws, until integration has taken place in the new grid, both for those already in the system and for new entrants. Thus, special enforcement laws were approved which will be applied gradually, initially in 2010–15, by strictly remaining within the framework of total wage expenditure as a proportion of GDP (which is expected to diminish to 6 per cent by 2015). The period of implementation for the law will be determined by the period in which there will be differences between wage earnings and earnings that would result from applying the reference coefficients, being directly influenced by the financial resources allocated to personnel spending in the budgetary sector.

The Unified Wage Law (UWL) approved in 2009 and amended in 2010 (Law 284/2010) has as its main purpose to create performance equilibrias among different jobs in the public sector and to establish wage equity for equivalent jobs. In order to accomplish a comprehensive restructuring of public employment and pay, the main expected result was to create an adequate pay scale and structure of gross income for all people paid from the state budget (public servants and contractual employees). The UWL also aims to improve the simplicity, transparency and fairness of public compensation. In principle, trade unions agreed with the wage reform of personnel paid from the state budget and agreed to be part of the negotiations. Bargaining with unions to lay down equivalences for the social partners lasted nine months but without reaching agreement.[41] The law was eventually imposed by the government. Implementation of the UWL through special annual legislation will contribute to medium-term fiscal sustainability. The full wage scale will apply to all personnel after gradual implementation and in accordance with the availability of financial resources. The wage inequities and discrepancies created in the pre-crisis period will be partially reversed over time in line with a major improvement in the fiscal balance.

The legislation for implementing the UWL is based on the following principles:

- It will ensure compliance with the quantitative targets for the public wage bill included in the unified public wage law and the proposed changes will be fully funded.
- It will ensure that the new salary grading structure is simplified and that pay will be linked to job responsibility and qualifications. The new pay system will be benchmarked in relation to private sector wages (through a salary survey) to ensure that public pay is broadly aligned with actual labour market conditions, in accordance with affordability constraints.

Implementation of the UWL was set for 2010. A special annual law regulates wages for personnel employed before 2010 in accordance with economic dynamics and budgetary constraints. Since January 2010 the annual pay law for simplifying the structure of gross earnings has been implemented by limiting the possibility of providing bonuses/premiums and so on to a maximum 30 per cent of the basic wage. The 'new' basic wage includes: basic wage, management bonus and merit wage (if it was not suspended in 2009). Gross earnings include a 'compensatory amount' comprising, for example, a bonus for having obtained a doctorate and other specific bonuses provided by law. Actually, due to this stage, the total gross wage from 31 December 2009 remains at the same level in January 2010, without being influenced by the provisions of the UWL. The only wage change involving a decrease with regard to the new grid involves bonuses paid to the highest-ranking personages, the president, ministers and managers of national companies, for whom corresponding amounts were determined according to the function hierarchy in the grid.

4.2.5 Flaws in the new law

The political opposition considers that wage reductions for ministers were only a 'stunt' which only introduces anomalies into the system (for instance, the wages of ministers are reduced more than some of their advisers, sometimes even by several times). This political stunt has had the effect of exacerbating, not repairing, the inequities in the system. It has forced state employees to adjust, to carry out additional work in the private system on the unregistered labour market and poor quality and performance in public offices have remained the same or even increased. Corruption and influence peddling have not diminished. In conclusion, it may be said that the system did not become sounder, but quite the contrary! Romania, by reducing wages, achieved low-level equalization (Keynes 1936; Stiglitz 2008) by uniform wage cuts in the budgetary system. After this measure (associated also with a 5 percentage point growth in VAT to 24 per cent) the economy re-entered recession.

4.2.6 From 2010: cuts along new recession further postponing law enforcement

On 1 January 2011, the basic wage and the compensatory amount, reduced by 25 per cent since July 2010 and indexed by 15 per cent, was laid down as the 'new basic wage'.[42] Employment has a corresponding category and rank under the law, but without applying the wage coefficient provided for by the framework law (differentiating from 1 to 12). In practice, from the wages viewpoint, the reform is still not being enforced: the wages currently paid are those from 2008 reduced by the non-uniform elimination of some bonuses, then cut by the globally applied 25 per cent and, as of 1 January 2011, indexed by 15 per cent, again applied proportionally for all. Hence, the structural adjustment of wages provided for in the UWL is not applied either for those already employed or for newly employed personnel. For people newly employed in similar positions to existing ones, the wages granted are at the level of those applied for comparable positions in each public institution. Only if employment is in a new position that did not exist in the wage grid is account taken of the new grid. If the level of current wages is compared with the corresponding wage level of the Framework Law there are some situations in which wages are higher and others in which they are lower, hence the differences and inequities remained or were even increased by eliminating bonus differentiation in various parts of the public sector in 2009. Currently, there are no other legal proposals or regulations in preparation in the field of wages for employees paid from the state budget.

In 2012, implementation in stages of the Framework Law will continue with successive increases of the basic wage and of military wages, depending also on monthly employment bonuses to reach the payment level established in the annexes to the law. The reference value corresponding to the hierarchy coefficient of 1.00 is maintained at the level of 600 lei.

Anti-crisis wage measures are aimed at laying down in personnel expenditure a ceiling for the general consolidated budget (Law No. 275/2010 on indicators specified in the fiscal budgetary framework). Wage austerity was associated with personnel cuts and a certain employment flexibility provided for by the new changes to the Labour Code (Table 12.13).

In 2012, the nominal wages of budgetary personnel will be gradually restored but staff cuts from the state apparatus will continue at the same 1 to 7 ratio, but in a differentiated way (IMF, Letter of Intent[43]). Wage expenditure will be reduced below 7 per cent of GDP in 2011–12 (from 9.2 per cent in 2009 and 8.2 per cent in 2010), and the difference from the initial deduction of 25 per cent will be restored in three stages (2011 January, 15 per cent, June 2012, 8 per cent and 7.4 per cent in December 2012). Recently, the government acknowledged that the uniform and sudden wage cut of 25 per cent, by suppressing consumption, has slowed down economic recovery. In the first quarter of 2012, Romania registered a technical recession and some additional policy measures will be introduced to stimulate investment.

In parallel, efforts to reduce personnel expenditure will continue on the basis of the existing replacement policy of one for seven, but based on a more flexible formula to eliminate blockages in sectors with personnel deficits. In some cases, such as health care, the ratio will be lower and additional employment of medical staff will be approved at hospitals' special request. The implementation of all the above normative acts involved not much reform of the wage system, but rather real wage reductions. It is in this sense that institutional reforms on wages did not make much progress but were eaten up by more short-term budgetary considerations (Figure 12.21).

Table 12.13 Adjustment measures in the public wage system because of the crisis, Romania, 2009–2014

Measures[a]	Implementation	Impact
Ceiling for personnel expenditure	9.2% of GDP in 2009, 6.6% in 2011, 6.7% in 2012, 7.1% in 2013 and 6.8% in 2014	Layoffs; mandatory retirement at statutory age; limited access to employment for pensioners Minimum wages in public sector below national level: 2009 – similar; 2010–11 – public 600 lei/private 670 lei; 2012 – public 600 lei/private 700 lei
Wage decreases	April 2009 – elimination of most bonuses August 2009 – further cuts in additional payments and bonuses Jan 2010 – consolidate bonuses into basic wage July 2010 – 25% cut from July to December[b]	Decreases and inverts the pay gap by property form Increases the proportion of people on low incomes (no transparency, no statistical data) Increases poverty among lower qualified personnel in the public sector No real coherence in the system, more confusing in the implementation period (gradual implementation– insufficient resources) – increased inequities Specialists leave the system: private sector or emigration (medical staff – specialists and nurses) Employment deficit and overemployment No stimulus for graduates to develop a career in public sector
Wage level recovery	2011 – pay on average will be increased by 15% over the year, restoring part of the 25% cut imposed in July 2010	Restoration of the purchasing power of wages and stimulate recovery of consumption level before 25% wage cut No qualitative adjustments – uniform cut + uniform increase to recover 2010 level

	2012 – 8% increase from June and 7.4% from December to restore July 2010 nominal level (because of inflation, real wages decreased)	
13th-month pay	2009 – partial payments 2010 – no payments 2011–14 – no payments	Lower incomes
Granting benefits, bonuses and holiday and lunch vouchers	2009 – yes 2010 – present – no	Lower incomes
Compensating activities outside normal working hours exclusively by free hours	2009–12 – yes 2013–14 (fiscal strategy) – yes	Increasing productivity Lower incomes Work intensity (increased social productivity but less work quality
Unpaid leave	2009 – yes 2 weeks (Oct–Dec) 2009–14 – no	Reducing monthly earnings, lower public expenditure
Prohibiting combining pension with wage from the state if the pension exceeds a certain ceiling	2009 – no 2010–14 – yes	Decreasing reemployment, reducing share of older personnel in the public sector Restricted active ageing

Notes:

a. There were also other measures that were initially considered but abandoned thereafter, such as: imposing a solidarity tax of 90 per cent on wages higher than 8,000 lei (it was not applied; instead, a solidarity fund was instituted to which anyone could contribute on a voluntary basis with the purpose of diminishing budgetary expenditures: the fund did not attract much money); and reducing wages for members of the government by 20 per cent in the period 1 August 2009–31 December 2009, but the measure was not adopted.

b. In 2005–08, spending on public wages and pensions nearly doubled and public wage growth outpaced growth in private wages. A cut of 25 per cent in personnel compensation would result in compensation falling to between 2007 and 2008 levels in nominal terms and the 2006 level as a percentage of GDP (IMF Country Report No. 10/227, July 2010, p. 15).

Source: Author's synthesis based on national legislation and official documents and reports related to policy measures during crisis period.

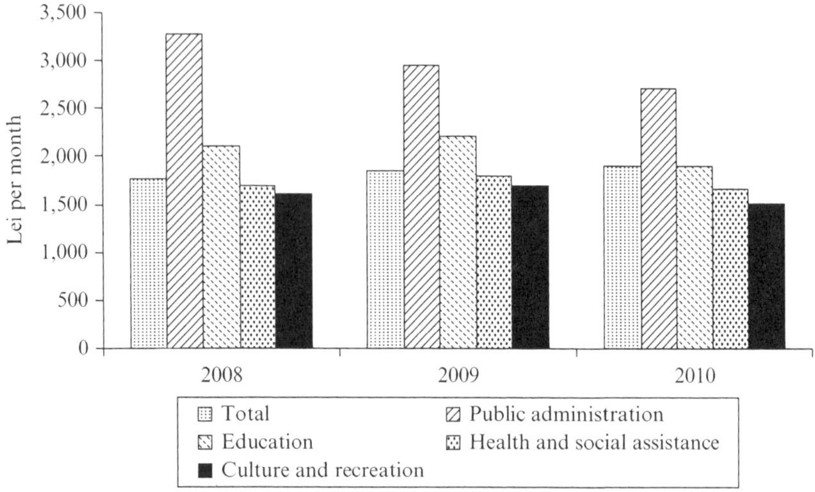

Source: Romanian Government, Reforms 2009–12, AP/R/8/2012, 27 March 2012.

Figure 12.21 Main effects of the wage reform: gross salary per employee (lei/month), Romania, 2008–2010

4.2.7 Conclusion

The implementation of wage legislation in the public sector during the crisis can be summed up as follows: (i) the positive outcome is that they helped to reduce labour expenditure and maintain the limits agreed under the IMF agreement; in particular bonuses were limited to a maximum 30 per cent of gross earnings; (ii) on the other hand, the uniform wage cut and then restoration has hindered the attainment of reform objectives, except for the lowest wages which were allowed to increase, even if in the meantime the minimum wage in the private sector increased[44] – while the one in the public sector remained frozen – and thus increased inequalities between the two sectors; as a result the attractiveness of public sector employment has decreased for experts and highly qualified staff who are better paid in the private sector in equivalent jobs; finally, career advancement was blocked and thus better prospects for future jobs. In practical terms, registration in the pay grid of all budgetary employees was postponed and the current remuneration system is only transitional (Figure 12.22).

In conclusion, the main policy measures with regard to public sector wages not only led to a serious loss for public sector employees, in terms of both pay and quality of working conditions and job prospects, but they also limited progress on more wage structure reforms. They finally

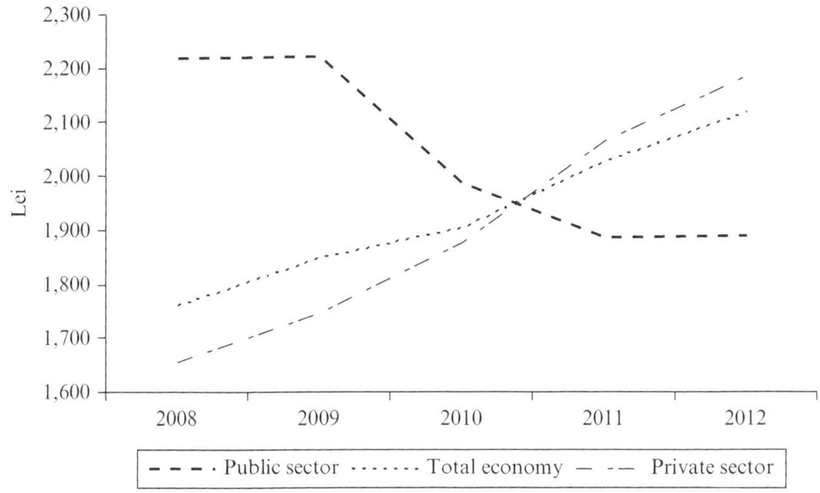

Source: Romanian Government, Reforms 2009–2012, AP/R/8/2012, 27 March 2012.

Figure 12.22 Main effects of the wage reform: pay gap, Romania, 2008–2012

contributed to sharply reducing consumption, with severe effects on budget revenues.

5. POLICY ISSUES

In Romania, public sector adjustment has been a combination of adjustments in response to ongoing structural changes in transition to a competitive model and due to the impact of the crisis on the Romanian economy and public finance sustainability. In some cases, the structural reforms were halted or delayed, as anti-crisis measures were applied.

In the 2000s, up to 2008, but in particular after 2004 budgetary expenditure increased due to wage increases and material and current capital expenditure. Election years saw significant wage and pension increases, the minimum pension of 350 lei per month was instituted and also the minimum wage increased. During this period, progressive taxation was eliminated and the shift was made to a flat rate of 16 per cent. The informal economy did not compress to the expected size, budgetary incomes being lower than expectations. The budgetary deficit increased. The anti-crisis programme was implemented with the aid of the international financial institutions, involving measures to reduce the oversized budgetary apparatus, accompanied by severe wage restrictions which were uniformly enforced.

Reforms in various areas of the public sector continued and took the form of severe austerity, sometimes affecting the principles and initial purpose of the reforms. The targets of reform at the beginning of the crisis were: the pension system (finalizing the reform of pillar I, PAYG, and in 2008 implementing the compulsory private pensions pillar by transfer from contributions to the public system), university education (Bologna system implementation) and health-care modernization (investments in hospitals, modernization of the subsidized drugs system, development of health programmes for chronic diseases and so on).

The crisis generated a series of adjustment measures, such as:

1. reform of state agencies, including reorganization, restructuring and winding-up/mergers;
2. decentralization and externalization of some common services, transfer to local administration of some responsibilities, such as schools, hospitals, structures of the Ministry of the Interior;
3. introducing cost standards for all public sector activities, shifting to financing on a pupil/student basis;
4. reorganizing rural schools and hospital institutions by closing some of them;
5. wage reform in the public sector by merging the existing wage systems and creating a single wage grid, also rationalizing bonuses, limiting other wage benefits/non-salary benefits, merging the special pensions system into the general public system, recalculating pensions for some categories of pensioners (from the ministries of Defence, of the Interior, of Justice) and increasing the retirement age;
6. cutting employment in all sectors by internal reorganization and eliminating overemployment; and
7. cutting wages by 25 per cent and other monetary benefits (payment for childcare for children up to two years of age) and freezing pensions.

In the short term, the aim was to reduce labour expenditure by means of cutting employment (with the restriction of one new recruit for every seven departures), blocking existing vacancies, cutting wages and eliminating bonuses:

8. involuntary leave; and
9. compulsory retirement on reaching the standard pension age and a ban on combining a pension with wages over a certain pension level.

Job cuts were accompanied by the redistribution of work tasks to the remaining personnel, thus intensifying work, without payment for extra hours, but rather free time. For those who sought to supplement their incomes, the choice was between multiple part-time jobs or work in the informal labour market.

The emigration or shift to the private sector of well-qualified health-care professionals has intensified (doctors, nurses); research and staff deficits are increasing in education (lack of teachers in rural areas); and graduates are, among other things, finding employment in areas different from their specialization. Also, so-called 'envelope wages' are paid, along with dual – formal/informal – employment.

New recruitment to the public sector is allowed only for unique jobs and with special approval, although the wages are unattractive to more highly qualified personnel. In practice, a decapitalization of human resources is taking place, the quality and, implicitly, the performance of the labour force is decreasing and those who remain find their career advancement blocked.

6. CONCLUSIONS

In response to the economic crisis, the reform emphasis in the public sector shifted to quantitative adjustments and qualitative reform slowed down. On one hand, the crisis represents an opportunity for public finance reform.[45] On the other, there are significant differences between expectations and real effects with regard to both structural reforms and reforms instigated in response to the crisis. Policymakers focus all their attention on introducing programmes and strategies in the hope that something will work, while actual outcomes are neglected and implementation lacks transparency, and available data are sporadic and not comparable, making it difficult for experts to carry out analyses.

The public sector needs structural reforms, but in combination with anti-crisis measures they have generated adverse effects so that some of them have even been halted. Continued reform is necessary, but if it is to be sustainable and its proper objectives are to be attained it must be uncoupled from uniform anti-crisis measures (across-the-board job and wage cuts, freezing career advancement and new recruitment on a one-for-seven basis, regardless of qualitative criteria, such as particular needs and the stage reached by reform hitherto). Moreover, the reform framework must be reconceived in some fields (performance in higher education, access to national funds to support research, ensuring the financial sustainability of the public pension system and reorganizing health care).

The effects of the austerity measures on the state budget have fallen short of expectations and indeed have led to numerous adverse effects: insufficient budget revenues, reduction of domestic demand for goods and services, deteriorating quality of public services, preponderance of cosmetic adjustments rather than substantive ones, continuing inequities in employment and wage policy in the public sector and mismanagement of youth employment and active ageing. The financial support provided by the IMF loan has sustained some adjustments, but has done little towards exiting the recession and has not supported small entrepreneurs.

The impact of public sector wage cuts in 2010 not only deepened some inequalities within the public sector, but in December 2010 the public–private wage relationship was reversed in favour of the average wage in the private sector, which now exceeds the average wage in the public sector. The overall impact of the 25 per cent wage cut on the state budget has been much lower than had been hoped: only 0.55 per cent of GDP as against 1.4 per cent estimated for June–December 2010.[46] The uniform 25 per cent wage cut in the public sector encouraged people to leave for the private sector in some trades/professions and reduce the attractiveness of the public sector for young graduates with a university education in favour of the private sector or working abroad, with significantly higher wages, but in many cases in jobs for which the person concerned did not study or train. The wage cut for about one-quarter of the employed population in Romania curbed consumption. It also pushed people into the informal economy. The increase of the minimum wage during the crisis from 540 lei in October 2008 to 700 lei in 2012 and maintenance of the minimum wage in the public sector at 600 lei on one hand, generated a slight increase in the private sector of envelope payments and multiple employment of those in the public sector (to supplement their incomes, especially in the informal economy, thereby boosting fraud and corruption) and, on the other, stimulated emigration by the highly qualified (doctors and nurses from the health sector, young graduates and so on).

The anti-crisis measures emphasized short-term effects at the expense of sustainable improvements (compulsory minimum taxation, increasing duty and prices for basic goods, allotment of public expenditure to secondary objectives such as swimming pools, sports facilities and so on, as well as expensive road infrastructure).

Adjustments pertaining to human resources in the public sector were based on formal and quantitative criteria and did not aim at qualitative development.

The job replacement rate of one for seven and the blocking of career advancement during the crisis reduced the attractiveness of public sector employment for highly qualified people. These measures also do not permit the employer – at institutions financed partly/entirely from the state budget – to improve labour performance. Furthermore, the one-for-seven ratio and blocking of vacancies have maintained the shortcomings of structural reallocation, limited the number of young people and experts who can enter the system (also due to the unattractive wage levels), maintained overemployment in the central administration, decentralized and reallocated entities in education and health, created personnel deficits at local level and generated adverse social effects (limiting school access for children from rural areas, reducing access to emergency medical assistance). The lack of financial resources contracted vocational training in the public sector and transferred the task of training for career development to the individual (expenditure on lifelong learning remain the smallest in the EU27, at 1.3–1.5 per cent and only 0.1–0.2 per cent of labour force costs are for vocational training, as most people receive minimal training on the job).

The trade union movement, in all its forms, is extremely weak. Dialogue with the state is formal and changes to the legislation on social dialogue have led to the elimination of national social dialogue and restriction of the extension of negotiated provisions, while representativeness criteria were tightened up. The profile of the union movement has decreased and members have lost confidence in it, rendering them unwilling to participate in industrial action.

Working conditions have become more precarious and stress has increased dramatically. The workload for those who remain after job cuts has increased and the digitalization of public services has not simplified the system but the reverse. Perceptions of the role and efficiency of the public sector have worsened and it is seen as providing inadequate, poor-quality services riddled with influence peddling and red tape, not to mention corruption, particularly with regard to the payment of fines and penalties by the business sector but also, in general, taxpayers.

At present, the main risk is that 2012, as an election year, will create new dysfunctionalities and further deepen inequities – also from the viewpoint of public sector employment in jobs created for political clients with high and even very high wages.

NOTES

1. Source: http://www.observator-bns.ro/.
2. The IMF recognized the failure of the recovery programme in Romania, see http://www.zf.ro/eveniment/fmi-recunoaste-esecul-programmeului-de-finantare-cu-romania-marea-dezamagire-este-ca-economia-nu-si-a-revenit-7900793.
3. Law 329/5.11.2009 on the reorganization of some public authorities and institutions,

cutting public expenditure, supporting the business environment and complying with the framework agreements concluded with the European Commission and the IMF in force as of 12 November 2009. The law regulates measures for: (a) the reorganization of 141 public authorities and institutions; (b) reducing personnel expenditure in the budgetary system; (c) restrictions on supplementing pensions with wage incomes from public sector activities; (d) financial–budgetary discipline at the level of autonomous/national companies or trading companies of which the state is the majority owner; and (e) supporting the business environment to overcome financial difficulties. The measures aimed at reducing the effects of the crisis are included in the Memorandum of Understanding between the European Community and Romania, concluded in Bucharest and Brussels on 23 June 2009 and the Stand-by Agreement concluded between Romania and the IMF.

4. See: http://www.wall-street.ro/articol/Economie/91881/Restructurarea-sectorului-public-si-adoptarea-de-reforme-trebuie-sa-continue.html.
5. See: http://discutii.mfinante.ro/static/10/Mfp/buletin/executii/informare_investitori_februarie.pdf.
6. Fiscal budgetary strategy 2013–15, Romanian Government, based on Eurostat fiscal notification, 23 April 2012.
7. See: http://www.zf.ro/companii/buget-2012-venituri-de-195-3-mld-lei-cheltuieli-de-206-5-mld-lei-si-deficit-de-11-2-mld-lei-8965592.
8. See: http://www.realitatea.net/guvernul-taie-tichetele-de-masa-si-primele-si-blocheaza-angajarile-pana-in-2014_860920.html.
9. The information regarding the 'budgetary sector' must be carefully analysed because the data refer to statistics from economic activities (aggregated after the homogeneous activity) in accordance with CANE 2 Rev. 2 by: public administration, education, health and social assistance (including private sector for education – about 3 per cent, about 5 per cent for health and social assistance), excluding military and assimilated personnel (MApN: Ministry of National Defence; SRI: Romanian Intelligence Service; MAI: Ministry of Administration and Interior; and so on). These statistics do not take into account the financing form, their purpose being to supply information by economic activities according to CANE Rev. 2.
10. Traian Basescu, see: http://www.ziare.com/basescu/criza/basescu-explica-reducerile-de-personal-din-2012-statul-se-sufoca-din-cauza-aparatului-de-stat-1135930 (24 November 2011).
11. The government agreed with the IMF in December 2011 to continue layoffs within railway companies, to impose four days of unpaid leave on employees of the Railway Interventions Company and to close all routes that cannot be sold by tender and to conclude public–private partnership contracts for commercial premises belonging to CFR.
12. By reducing the number of post offices to less than 5,700 from the 7,100 existing in 2011. At the same time, the state will reduce its participation to 51 per cent (as against 75 per cent currently) through takeover by a strategic investor. (According to data from the relevant ministry, representatives of the national postal operators from Austria, Belgium, Germany, Italy, the United Kingdom and Sweden have shown an interest in becoming shareholders in Romanian Post.)
13. These layoffs were agreed with the IMF. Decision 2010/787/EU of the Council regarding state aid for facilitating the winding up of non-competitive coal mines allows public authorities to grant, under certain conditions, assistance in the coal industry, with the purpose of facilitating closing uncompetitive coal mines by December 2018. The measure is in accordance with EU norms regarding state aid that provides for the progressive reductions of aid to cover production costs. Romania undertook to enforce completion measures for diminishing the social and environmental impact of closure. The National Coal Company JSC Petrosani is a state-owned enterprise and the only company in Romania producing coal. Currently, it has seven production units, and three of them which are regarded as uncompetitive will be closed: Petrila, by the end of

2015, and Uricani and Paroşeni by the end of 2017. Romania will spend grant public aid of 1.17 billion lei (about €270 million). See: http://www.realitatea.net/romania-va-cheltui-270-milioane-de-euro-pentru-inchiderea-a-trei-mine-de-carbune_916121.html (25 February 2012).

14. Source: http://www.realitatea.net/concedieri-masive-in-sectorul-bugetar-4-000-de-oameni-raman-fara-locuri-de-munca-video_916337.html (25 February 2012).
15. Low wages are insufficient for maintaining a household. The minimum consumption basket for 2011 was based on the last calculation carried out in 2003 by the National Institute of Statistics, updated with inflation. It resulted in a current value of the minimum basket of a household of 980.5 RON. Calculations indicate that 31 per cent of wages do not cover the subsistence minimum: http://www.observator-bns.ro.
16. The Office for Monitoring Labour Market and Job Quality, a labour market research institution established by BNS within a project financed by ESF, SOP-HRD: http://www.observator-bns.ro.
17. 'Employment quality and employment on low wages', BNS, ESF, SOP-HRD, Bucharest, 2011, p. 36.
18. The more a country tries to make savings, the less revenue it receives and the fewer resources it has for such savings.
19. However, the economic crisis reduced household consumption by 10 per cent in 2009 and by about 3 per cent in 2010. Pro-cyclicality has been a constant feature of Romania's macroeconomic policy mix. In 2005–08, loose fiscal and budgetary policy poured gasoline onto a raging fire. Then, since the election year of 2009, when most of the IMF money was spent just to buy time, Romania has been implementing pro-cyclical tightening. Instead of focusing on economic growth and adopting prudent fiscal and budgetary rules that would ensure growth and result in a lower deficit, the government targeted a lower budget deficit as its primary goal. See White Paper on National Economic Competitiveness for Romania, Part I, Aspen Institute, Romania, http://www.aspeninstitute.ro/Upload/887238c7-508c-4e3d-9098-e540711796da.pdf, http://www.aspeninstitute.ro/articole/562/Aspen-Romania-White-Paper-on-Competitiveness.html.
20. See: http://www.ziare.com/articole/someri+sector+public.
21. See: http://www.business24.ro/fmi/stiri-fmi/guvernul-s-a-angajat-sa-reduca-personalul-din-sectorul-public-cu-70-000-salariati-in-acest-an-1475242.
22. Information about the 'budgetary sector' should be used cautiously because the data refer to statistics from economic activities (aggregated by homogeneous activity), according to CANE Rev. 2, for public administration, education and health care, as well as health care and social assistance (including the private sector for education, about 3 per cent, and health care and social assistance, about 5 per cent), excluding military and auxiliary personnel (MApN, SRI, MAI). These statistics do not take into account the financing form, their purpose being to provide information on economic activities according to CANE Rev. 2. Information according to financing form is managed by the Ministry of Public Finance, in accordance with the provisions of Government Emergency Ordinance no. 48/2005, with subsequent additions and amendments.
23. Republished 1 Official Bulletin No. 345 – 18/05/2011 Art. 194. – (1) Employers have a duty to ensure participation in vocational training programmes for all employees, as follows: (a) at least once every two years, if they have at least 21 employees; (b) at least once every three years, if they have under 21 employees. (2) The expenditures on participation in vocational training programmes, ensured according to the conditions of para. (1) are borne by the employers. Art. 195. (1) Employers with legal personality with more than 20 employees work out annually and apply vocational training plans by consultation with the trade unions, or as the case may be, the employees' representatives. (2) The vocational training plan elaborated according to the provisions of para. (1) becomes an annex to the collective agreement concluded at workplace level.

24. See: http://www.pressnet.ro/numarul-de-posturi-ocupate-in-sectorul-bugetar-in-crestere-cu-238-668-de-posturi-in-perioada-2006-2008.
25. Basescu explains the personnel reduction in 'The state chokes because of the state apparatus', available at: http://www.ziare.com/basescu/criza/basescu-explica-reducerile-de-personal-din-2012-statul-se-sufoca-din-cauza-aparatului-de-stat-1135930.
26. Work and Romanians, perceptions of work in Romania, IRES. Available at: http://www.ires.com.ro/articol/54/munca-si-romanii--percepții,-pareri,-analize, http://www.ires.com.ro/uploads/articole/raport_munca_si_romanii.pdf.
27. See: http://cursdeguvernare.ro/umbra-sindicatelor-si-dialogul-social-mimat.html.
28. This is a continuation of the model from the communist period: but the prohibition on retaining contributions from pay laid down by Order of the Ministry of Education will substantially reduce the number of members, the trade union rate being currently 85 per cent (according to the leaders of the trade union federations).
29. See: http://www.finantistii.ro/sindicate/sindicatele-din-invatamant-au-ramas-fara-pusculita-70288/.
30. According to Eurydice, Key Data on Education in Europe 2009.
31. V. Vasile (coordinator), G. Zaman, S. Pert and F. Zarojanu (2007), 'Restructuring Romania's education system considering its development from a domestic market perspective and impact on RDI', Study no. 2, Project SPOS 2007 – Strategy and Policy Studies, European Institute of Romania, available at: http://www.ier.ro/index.php/site/page/strategy_and_policy_studies.
32. IMF Country Report No. 10/227, July 2010.
33. Parliament passed the Law on National Education, No.1/2011 on December 2010, and the act entered into force on 10 February 2011.
34. The World Bank has supported measures to increase the fiscal savings and improve the quality and access to education services, namely the capita financing starting with school year 2010–11 (the measure is piloted in eight counties, accounting for 20 per cent of total student enrolment). In addition the Bank has supported the government programme in education through an investment operation targeting the rehabilitation of schools in rural areas.
35. The main problems of Romanian higher education are as follows: (a) a poor correlation between higher education qualifications and labour market requirements; (b) small-scale transfer of higher education research to the economy; and (c) too strong a theoretical component, which does not provide graduates with practical skills and competencies (Romania: National Reform Programme 2011–2013, p. 116).
36. See Chapter 5 and Chapter 6, Section 6.1 of the NRP 2011–2013.
37. The wages of state company managers were reduced to the level of a secretary of state, from 20,000–28,000 lei to 4,800 lei, and the pay of the heads of autonomous administrations subordinated to the local and county councils will have a ceiling equivalent to the wage of a council vice-president of 3–4,000 lei. Managers of state companies hitherto have received monthly wages of between 20,000 lei, at the Romanian Civil Aeronautics Authority and the Romanian Car Registry, 27,000 lei, at Hidroeletrica and 28,000 lei at Romgaz. The pay of the members of administration boards at state companies and autonomous administrations was drastically cut, from 20 per cent of the wages of their managers to just 1 per cent. If they do not accept the new ceiling – Prime Minister Emil Boc stated – they will be replaced with persons for whom membership of an administration board is an attraction in itself (see: http://www.mediafax.ro/social/salariile-directorilor-de-companii-de-stat-reduse-la-maximum-4-800-lei-3679592).
38. The hierarchy system is based on seven criteria: knowledge and experience; complexity, creativity and diversity of activities; judgement and impact of decisions; influence, coordination and supervision; contacts and communication; labour conditions; and incompatibilities and special regimes.
39. Bipartite commission, based on the provisions of Art. 42 of Framework Law No. 330/2009.

40. Within each rank or professional degree the basic wage differential is established on five levels, corresponding to the five brackets of length of service, except for public positions where three professional ranks and three wage levels are used.
41. In a first stage, the equivalence of budgetary positions on three levels was determined and then by negotiation the functions of the institutions within the system were placed on the grid. Because the necessary budgetary funds in accordance with the negotiated wage grid exceeded the forecast availability for wage expenditure, the maximum/minimum ratio was reduced from 15 to 12 and the representatives of the Ministry of Labour have unilaterally decreased the coefficients on the grid for some positions (initially by up to 40 per cent, and the procedure was repeated afterwards for the grids of some other ministries, the direction of the changes being to increase the value of coefficients – for instance, for justice – but also to reduce them – for health, research, education), an issue that stirred trade union discontent. After repeated discussion rounds, the positions' equivalence disappeared (according to the trade unions the inequities became sharper even compared to the current situation) and a grid was implemented by gathering up the positions in the lower half. Differences of opinion meant that after nine months of negotiations an acceptable wage grid could not be established by the social partners.
42. The 25 per cent wage cut in 2010 was combined with layoffs in the public sector, which allowed for a partial restitution to the budget of 2011 (by an increase of 15 per cent). In real terms, due to inflation, wages continued to decrease for personnel paid from the state budget.
43. See: http://www.finantistii.ro/macroeconomie/scrisoarea-de-intentie-cu-fmi-fara-angajari-si-cresteri-de-salarii-sau-pensii-69493/.
44. As the basis for determining the value of the grid coefficient, a minimum wage level is determined that will not be identical with the minimum wage in the economy; instead, it will represent only the minimum wage in the budgetary sector, to which bonuses will be added. As a result, this minimum level may differ from the one in the private sector, similar to the practice applied in previous years when the value of the coefficient 1 in the public sector was inferior to the level of the minimum wage in the economy (370 lei/month compared to a minimum wage of 390 lei/month, equivalent to 170 working hours). The value of the hierarchy coefficient 1 is determined by law each year (705 lei in 2010, 765 lei in 2011, 845 lei in 2012, 935 lei in 2013, 1,015 lei in 2014 and 1,100 lei in 2015, without reference to the minimum wage in the economy, but the 25 per cent wage cut reduced its level to the current 600 lei).
45. Preparation of the Fiscal Budgetary Strategy for 2011–13 took place at the intersection of an economic crisis, administrative deficiencies in urgent need of reform and restructuring of the economy, public finances and the public sector. Though this will require long-term austerity measures it will lay the foundations for sustainable economic growth, increase the capacity of the Romanian economy to face global competition, attract FDI and create jobs. See: STRATEGIA_FB_27 sept.pdf, p 7.
46. Starting from public sector wages totalling 9.5 per cent of GDP in 2009, it was estimated that the 25 per cent wage cut over the first seven months would yield savings of 1.4 per cent of GDP. But the payment of taxes on wages associated with the effect resulting from the VAT increase from 19 to 24 per cent will diminish savings by 0.65 of a percentage point (from 1.4 to 0.75 per cent of GDP) and a cumulated annual decrease of 0.32 per cent of GDP of VAT cashing, respectively, 0.18 per cent for 7 months (with an income elasticity of 60 per cent and a share of total consumption of 33 per cent) (calculations by BNS, 'Wage study for budgetary personnel', PDF, BNS, p. 21, available at: http://www.observator-bns.ro.

REFERENCES

GR (2011), 'National Reform Programme (2011–2013)', Government of Romania, available at: http://ec.europa.eu/europe2020/pdf/nrp/nrp_romania_en.pdf.

GR (2012), 'Strategia fiscal bugetară pentru perioada 2013–2015', Government of Romania, available at: http://discutii.mfinante.ro/static/10/Mfp/strategbug/STRATEGIA_2013_2015_29mai2012_anexe.pdf.

Keynes, J.M. (1936), *The General Theory of Employment, Interest and Money*, Cambridge: Macmillan/Cambridge University Press for the Royal Economic Society.

Stiglitz, J. (2008), 'The triumphant return of John Maynard Keynes', Project Syndicate, 5 December, available at: http://www.project-syndicate.org/commentary/the-trumphant-return-of-john-maynard-keynes.

Vasile, V., G. Zaman, S. Pert and F. Zarojanu (2007), 'Restructuring Romania's education system considering the evolutions from the domestic market perspective and impact on RDI progress', Study No. 2, Project SPOS 2007 – Strategy and Policy Studies, European Institute of Romania, available at: http://www.ier.ro/documente/spos2007_en/Spos2007_studiu_2_en.pdf.

Voinea, L., F. Mihăescu, N. Mardari, F. Lucidi, S. Sansonetti, M. Castagnola, A. Veraschagina and G. Fiorani (2010), 'Salarizarea in sectorul public vs. sectorul privat', Biroul pentru observarea pieței muncii și a calitații locurilor de muncă, SOP-DRU 2007–2013 project, Blocul National Sindical, available at: http://ftp.bns.ro/observator/studiu_salarizare_bugetari_convertit.pdf.

Voinea, L., N. Mardari, R. Filip, V. Voineagu, V. Duma and M. Jifcu (2011), 'Calitatea ocupării şi angajarea cu salarii mici', Biroul pentru observarea pieței muncii şi a calitații locurilor de muncă, SOP-DRU 2007–2013 project, Blocul National Sindical, available at: http://ftp.bns.ro/observator/studiu_ocupare_convertit.pdf.

13. Those were the days, my friend: The public sector and the economic crisis in Spain

Rafael Muñoz de Bustillo and José-Ignacio Antón

1. INTRODUCTION

After more than a decade leading employment creation in the European Union (EU), in 2008 Spain was hit by the international financial crisis, which quickly turned into a severe economic recession. The advent of the international turbulence added to the bursting of the housing bubble and the end of easy and cheap credit in an economy with a large current account deficit. The consequences have been devastating: GDP experienced a fall of 4 per cent from 2008 to 2010, employment declined by more than 10 per cent and, in the context of a growing labour force, unemployment climbed from barely 8 per cent in 2007 to 22 per cent by the end of 2011.

After some initial countercyclical measures in line with Keynesian prescriptions, in the middle of 2010 the Spanish government changed the course of its economic policy and embarked on a process of fiscal consolidation, a move partly associated with pressures from the European Central Bank and the 'international financial markets'.

The aim of this chapter is to describe in detail the main features of the Spanish public sector, particularly those related to employment and how the economic crisis and the subsequent spending cuts have affected both the level and quality of employment and the provision of public goods by the state. With that aim, the chapter unfolds as follows. After a brief presentation of the main features of the Spanish public sector in Section 2, Section 3 focuses on the characteristics of public sector employment. Section 4, the core of the chapter, deals with the implications of the crisis and the process of fiscal consolidation for the delivery of public services, employment and industrial relations in the public administration. Section 5 illuminates this process by means of two case studies centred on two of the sectors most affected by the spending cuts: health care and education. The final section summarizes the main conclusions.

2. OVERVIEW OF SPANISH PUBLIC SECTOR EMPLOYMENT

The first defining characteristic of the Spanish sector is its smaller size compared to European counterparts. With public spending of 38.4 per cent of GDP in 2006, just before the crisis, Spain had one of the lowest levels of government expenditure in the EU. After the increase in public spending relative to GDP associated with the fall in national income and the rise in both discretionary expenditure and that linked to the action of automatic stabilizers, the level of government spending climbed to 45 per cent, still below the 50.3 per cent EU average. This helps to explain why public employment represents 13 per cent of total employment in 2005, before the crisis, slightly below the OECD average. This figure was one of the lowest in the EU, similar to the Netherlands and the Czech Republic and above only Germany, Slovakia and Austria.

The second idiosyncrasy of the Spanish public sector is the intense and rapid decentralization of the public sector from the central government to the regions (*Comunidades Autónomas*).[1] This process has resulted in an abrupt reduction in employment in the central administration over the past two decades, mainly in favour of the regions, which manage a significant part of welfare state services, such as education and health care. By the end of this process, Spanish regional governments contributed almost 56 per cent of total public employment compared to slightly over 18 per cent on the part of central administration and social services and 21 per cent on the part of local authorities.

According to data from the Spanish Labour Force Survey (LFS), public employment played a very minor role in the employment growth experienced in Spain in the decade prior to the crisis: from the second quarter of 1996 to the second quarter of 2008, public employment rose by 31 per cent, whereas the number of people employed in the private sector increased by more than 65 per cent. During the crisis, from the second quarter of 2008 to the second quarter of 2011, while private sector employment decreased by roughly 10 per cent, the number of public employees experienced a growth of 10 per cent. This explains why the public employment ratio went from 14.4 to 17.6 per cent during this period. Since then, the impact of the measures taken to reduce public expenditure has led to a reduction of 3.6 per cent in total public employment (second quarter of 2012).

A last important feature of public employment in Spain is its unequal distribution across Spanish territory. In some regions, such as Catalonia or the Balearic Islands, public employment is well under the average, while in others – notably in Extremadura – it contributes roughly to a quarter of total employment. In fact, unsurprisingly, on average, less-developed regions – in terms of per capita GDP – have higher rates of public employment. The reason behind such unequal incidence of public employment across all regions is the existence of universal social rights in areas such as health or education that warrant the public provision of certain services independently of the market and the level of regional economic development.

3. CHARACTERISTICS OF PUBLIC SECTOR EMPLOYMENT

3.1 Work Contracts

Theoretically, most employment in the public sector should be permanent as, traditionally, public employees are *funcionarios* (civil servants) who join the public sector by an open process of selection based on competitive examinations. In practice, a sizeable proportion of public employees – around a quarter – have fixed-term contracts. In fact, due to the downward impact on employment of the economic crisis, and the reliance of firms on the non-renewal of temporary contracts as a mean of adjustment (Muñoz de Bustillo and Antón 2011), by 2011 both public and private sector had similar rates of temporary employment (24 and 25 per cent, respectively).

From a gender perspective, in the public sector, in sharp contrast to the private sector where the share of men and women with fixed-term contracts is similar (especially after the crisis), women have a higher rate of temporary employment. In 2011, male public employees had a temporary employment rate of 18.5 per cent compared with 29 per cent of their female colleagues (thus, 55 per cent higher among women). This difference was even greater during the first year of the crisis, when one-third of women in public employment had a fixed-term contract. The adjustment process pursued in the public sector and involving non-renewal of temporary contracts thus hurt more women than men. As a result, women are underrepresented in the group of public sector employees with the highest employment protection, civil servants. The higher female temporary employment rate is partly explained by the high use of fixed-term contracts in education and health, activities with a high female presence.

3.2 Job Quality

Using data from the 2006–10 waves of the Quality of Work Life Survey (QWLS), comprising information (35 variables) on overall job satisfaction, wage, work organization, work environment, labour relations, working-time arrangements, health and safety conditions and training opportunities, we find that public employees show a higher level of overall satisfaction and higher satisfaction with working-time arrangements, even after controlling for different covariates. Other differences worth mentioning are the following: (a) better training opportunities for public employees;[2] (b) lower satisfaction with work organization among public sector workers, although the difference is explained mainly by observable characteristics; (c) lower satisfaction among the same types of employees, with variables related to work environment, such as air conditioning or space; (d) differences in labour relations are tiny, particularly when controlling for observable characteristics; and (e) in terms of health and safety conditions, public employees seem to experience a higher level of risk at their job, while, at the same time, they report being less satisfied with health and safety conditions and equipment than their private sector counterparts. We might conclude that, on average, public sector employees enjoy better working conditions in terms of working time and flexibility, and training. Therefore a reduction in public employment will have a negative impact on the overall level of job quality.

3.3 Gender and Age Distribution

Due to the increase in women's labour force participation over the past two decades, women have constantly gained share of total employment in both the private and public sectors. Nevertheless, this tendency has been slightly stronger in the public sector than in the private one: according to LFS data, in the former, the share of female employment went from 34 per cent in the second quarter of 1987 to 54.1 per cent of total employment in the second quarter of 2011, while in the latter – excluding self-employment – during the same period, the share of females evolved from 27.1 to 45.5 per cent. Women have accounted for more than half of total public employment since 2003.[3] Furthermore, around 21 per cent of total female employment is in the public sector (compared to 15 per cent in the case of men). This fact has important implications when discussing the impact of fiscal consolidation on public employment: it is likely that an overall downsizing of public employment is having a higher than average impact on women.

Public employment is also idiosyncratic in terms of age distribution, having an older workforce, with a higher proportion of workers from 45 to 49 years old compared to 30 to 34 years of age in the private sector. The difference is particularly significant at both extremes of the age range, with a very low proportion of public employees below 25 years of age (2.6 compared to 7.2 per cent in the private sector) and a much higher proportion of older (55 and over) workers: 18.3 per cent in the public sector compared to 9.5 per cent in the private sector. These differences are explained by the higher rate of dismissal of older workers in the private sector (probably related to their higher wages and declining productivity) and by the higher educational requirements and longer process of selection (*oposiciones*) of public employment.

3.4 Pay

The structure of pay in Spanish public administration and the differences from the private sector are studied using the Continuous Sample of Working Histories 2009 (CSWH 2009), an administrative register based on social security records.

First, we address the issue of the differences in average pay, dispersion of earnings and incidence of low pay between public and private sector workers. According to the database mentioned above, in 2009 the mean and median wages in the public sector were roughly 16 and 31 per cent higher, respectively, than in the private sector, while the dispersion of hourly pay was substantially lower among the former, as suggested by the standard deviation and the Gini and Theil indexes (Table 13.1). The different percentile ratios show that the source of this lower dispersion is not in the lower part of the earnings distribution: in fact, all the ratios presented in the table are fairly similar or even smaller in the private sector (for example, p50/p10), with the exception of p90/p50, indicating that the differences in dispersion against the private sector have to do with the upper part of the wage scale, that is, the differences in terms of earnings within each sector between employees with high and those with medium earnings. Using the well-known additive decomposability of the Theil index, it is possible to determine that more than 99 per cent of total wage dispersion is associated with within-sector inequality, that is, the average gap between public and private sector employees plays a marginal role in explaining earnings inequality in Spain.[4] Therefore, as long as pay inequality is lower among public employees, in principle, and without knowing the distribution of job cuts across the earnings distribution, one can speculate that an overall downsizing of public sector jobs will contribute to increasing wage inequality. Finally, the incidence of low pay, in terms of both monthly and hourly wages, is higher in the private sector (almost 30 and 20 per cent, respectively) than in the public sector (roughly, 10 and 13 per cent, respectively).

Table 13.1 Main descriptive statistics of hourly gross earnings, private and public sectors, Spain, 2009

	Private sector	Public sector
Mean hourly gross earnings (€)	11.900	13.900
Median hourly gross earnings (€)	9.100	11.900
Standard deviation of earnings (€)	16.700	10.400
p90/p10	4.240	4.300
p90/p50	2.220	1.900
p50/p10	1.910	2.260
Gini index	0.357	0.315
Theil index	0.285	0.185
% of low-paid employees (gross monthly earnings)	28.600	10.700
% of low-paid employees (gross hourly earnings)	19.600	12.600

Source: Authors' analysis from the Continuous Sample of Working Histories 2009 with tax information.

Second, using the same data source, we explore the earnings gap between public and private employees. Particularly, we explore which part of the gap is not explained by differences in the basic observable characteristics of the workers. In order to do so, we apply the well-known Oaxaca–Blinder decomposition (Oaxaca 1973; Blinder 1973). This strategy requires selecting a reference group whose returns to human capital endowments are considered standard. Since from a theoretical perspective it is more appropriate to refer to the earnings gap as a public sector wage premium rather than unfavourable treatment of private workers, private employees are chosen as reference. With this methodology the total gap can be decomposed into a gap explained by characteristics ($\Delta^{\text{explained}}$) and another unexplained by such endowments, or due to differences in returns to them ($\Delta^{\text{unexplained}}$). The first component refers to earnings differences observed if both types of worker had the same characteristics and public sector employees were paid like their private counterparts, whereas the second has to do with the differential observed if workers employed by private firms had the same observable endowments as employees holding public jobs.

In addition, using the same strategy, we explore in which sectors male–female wage gaps not explained by differences in productivity are narrower. In this case, it is reasonable to consider that the reference group, which defines the returns to observable characteristics considered as standard, are male workers.

The results of the decomposition of the hourly gross wage gap between public and private employees indicate an earnings differential in favour of public sector employees of 19.4 per cent on average, 17 per cent among men and 29.5 per cent among women; 31 and 65 per cent of such differentials are not due to observable characteristics and can be attributed to more favourable treatment for public sector employees. As long as most hiring in the public sector is regulated by rigid, public, open and often widely known administrative procedures – for example, competitive examinations – the room for discriminatory practices against women in the sector is smaller, which can explain why women in the private sector face a much larger disadvantage than their male counterparts.

This finding is complemented by the results of the decomposition of the gender pay gap in both types of employment. The gap in the public sector is roughly 19 per cent and it complies entirely with differences in returns to observable characteristics, while the differential rises to more than 31 per cent in the case of private firms, 23 percentage points of which are not associated with human capital and firm characteristics but differences in returns to such observable endowments. Therefore, although the unexplained gender differential in the public sector is definitely wide, it is below the level of the gap in the private sector, giving some support to the theoretical explanation suggested above based on the smaller likelihood of discrimination in the public sector. Therefore, as long as the gender gap is narrower in the public than in the private sector, an overall cut in public employment – even if equally distributed between sexes and sectors of activity – is likely to result in greater earnings differentials by sex.

A further step is to study how these average gaps evolve across earnings distributions, a task that can be accomplished by applying the Machado–Mata decomposition (Machado and Mata 2005), an econometric technique based on quantile regressions that allows the gap not explained by human capital and other observable characteristics to be computed. Although the details of this technique are not presented here for brevity, we refer to the main results: (a) the public sector wage premium decreases along the wage distribution and is higher for low-skilled than for high-skilled workers, for which the premium is even negative. For example, after controlling for observable characteristics, the wage premium is null at the 90th percentile (around –13 per cent for men and +11 per cent for women); (b) the disadvantage faced by women is larger in the private sector across practically the whole earnings distribution; this gap is wider at the lower and upper tails in the private sector, while it is roughly steadily decreasing along the earnings distribution of public sector employees. This applies to both the raw gap and the differences detected after controlling for observable characteristics, suggesting that cuts in public employment will contribute to achieving not only worse distributional outcomes but also worse results in terms of equality of opportunities, as long as employment in this sector, where gaps not explained by human capital characteristics are lower (and, hence, equality of opportunities might be considered greater), is downsized.

4. FROM THE FINANCIAL TO THE FISCAL CRISIS: THE IMPACT OF THE CRISIS ON THE SPANISH PUBLIC SECTOR

4.1 General Overview

As we have argued elsewhere (Muñoz de Bustillo and Antón 2011), the government has followed two very distinctive types of economic policy during the present economic crisis. In the first stage of the crisis the government applied the classic Keynesian recipe, compensating for the decrease of effective demand that followed the financial crisis, the bursting of the construction bubble and the credit crunch, with an increase in public expenditure. Simultaneously, the drop in GDP and the heavy reliance of the tax system on the taxation of revenue related to the construction industry led to a significant drop in public revenues of 6 percentage points from 2007 to 2009. As a result of the combined impact of both tendencies (see Figure 13.1), the public balance went from a surplus of 1.9 per cent in 2007 to a deficit of 11.2 per cent in 2009.

In 2010, the financial crisis suddenly evolved into a debt crisis and the concerns of the government turned from fighting the drop in effective demand to adopting whatever measures were necessary (and demanded by EU institutions, the IMF and the international financial markets) to reduce the public deficit up to 4 per cent of GDP in 2012 and 3 per cent in 2013. The combined impact of the actions taken on the expenditure and revenue sides enabled a reduction of the public deficit by almost 3 percentage points in two years, but also led to a sharp reduction of demand at a moment when the public sector, together with exports, was the only actor capable of sustaining and improving the effective demand needed to pull the economy out of virtual stagnation.[5] In 2011, public consumption decreased by 2.2 per cent, while exports – the only component of aggregate demand with a positive contribution to GDP – increased by 9 per cent. In spite of this harsh programme of fiscal consolidation, the deficit at the end of 2011 reached 8.5 per cent of GDP, far above the 6 per cent

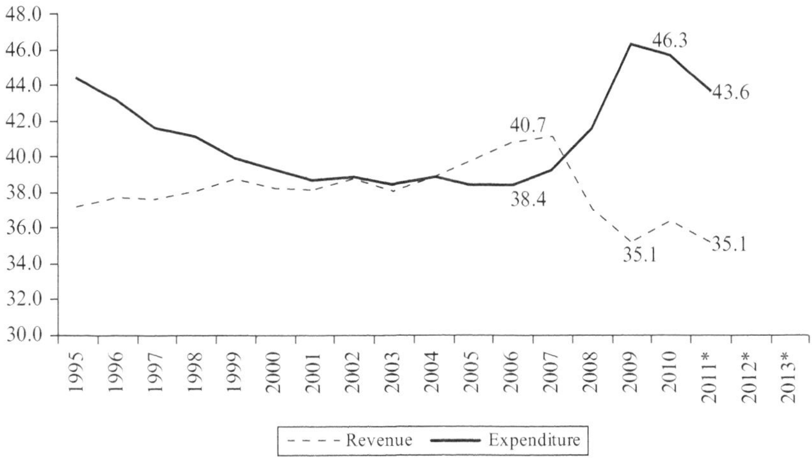

Figure 13.1 Public budget balance, revenue and expenditure, Spain, 1995–2011

target. According to the Bank of Spain, 90 per cent of the deviation from the target was associated with tax revenues, as a result of the stagnation of the economy, since public spending was even lower than budgeted despite the unexpected increase of the interest rate paid on public debt issues (Banco de España 2012). Nevertheless, the European Central Bank and the European Commission have, so far, shown no mercy, not taking into consideration 'mitigating circumstances' and have severely reproved Spain's 'misbehaviour' and lack of compromise and seriousness and have argued that fiscal consolidation is indispensable. In response, the government has renewed its compromise with austerity and has promised to make additional cuts in order to achieve deficits of 5.3 per cent in 2012 and 3 per cent in 2013 (Figure 13.2). According to the IMF, it is unlikely that such adjustment is feasible in the current context of depression and considers that the 3 per cent objective could be accomplished only by 2018. This process of fiscal retrenchment planned by Spanish authorities entails that all regions in 2012 must achieve a fiscal deficit of, at most, 1.5 per cent of their regional GDPs (against an estimate of over 3 per cent in 2011). Such reduction of the deficit means a reduction of the budgeted expenditure for 2012 of more than €14 billion. In addition, at the end of April 2012, the central government passed a law on budget stability stating that, from 2020, all public administrations will have to present a zero budget deficit, irrespective of economic conditions, and that the central government will be able to take the control of regional administrations if they do not meet central fiscal objectives.

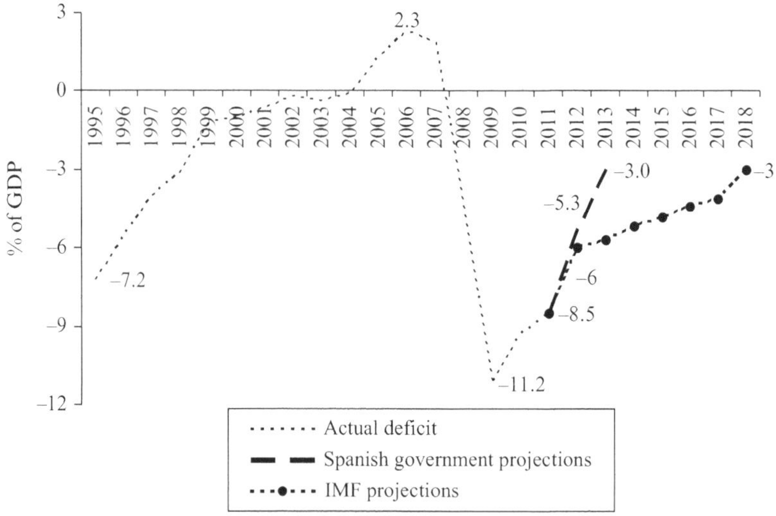

Sources: Authors' analysis of expenditure, revenue and budget balance data from Eurostat (1995–10), Bank of Spain database, forecast budget balance data from the Spanish government (2012–13) and the IMF (2012–18).

Figure 13.2 Public budget balance, actual deficit and projections, Spain, 1995–2018

4.2 Allocation of Spending Cuts

Spain is a much more decentralized state than most developed countries. According to OECD statistics, public spending in Spain was roughly 46 per cent of GDP in 2009, of which 51 per cent was accounted for by the central state, 35 per cent by the autonomous communities and 14 per cent by local governments. Therefore, in order to assess how the reduction of spending is affecting the different areas of the public sector, one needs to look at the budgets of the various components.[6] In Spain, the central state is responsible for some public goods (defence and in part, security forces and justice) and part of social spending, mainly pensions and unemployment benefits. Regional governments or autonomous communities have competences in health and education, among others, thereby concentrating a very important share of public social expenditure. Finally, local governments administer local public goods (water supply, street lighting, garbage collection and so on) and in some cases (large municipalities) in some autonomous communities local government provides some types of social assistance and childcare facilities. In

Table 13.2 Evolution of central state budget during the crisis, Spain, 2008–2012 (annual real rate of growth

	2008	2009	2010	2011	2012
1. General public services (justice, defence, security, etc.)	8.6	−0.8	−2.8	−11.5	−9.2
2. Social protection (pensions, employment, housing)	3.6	10.3	7.6	−6.1	−3.9
Unemployment	4.9	24.6	56.1	−4.5	−5.5
3. Health	1.5	4.6	−1.6	−11.1	−6.8
4. Education	13.9	2.2	1.6	−10.8	−21.9
5. Culture	4.1	0.8	−8.7	−6.2	−15.1
6. (2–5) Social expenditure	3.8	11.2	12.1	−6.0	−4.3
7. Economic affairs (infrastructure, R&D, agriculture, industry, etc.)	4.2	−1.4	−1.0	−19.6	−17.0
8. General expenditure (including debt)	2.9	1.6	12.9	−29.3	13.8
Total	3.8	5.3	7.2	−15.0	−1.3

Note: The annual rate of growth is computed as the difference between nominal rate of growth and rate of growth of the consumer price index (CPI). All figures correspond to authorized spending.

Source: Authors' analysis of data from the Spanish Ministry of Budget and Public Administration (www.sgpg.pap.meh.es/sitios/sgpg/es-ES/Presupuestos/).

each case, figures come from the different budgetary information available when writing this chapter.

4.2.1 Central state

In keeping with the evolution of the Spanish deficit presented above, central state budget data (Table 13.2) reflect an increase in real total expenditure in almost all categories until 2009 (except defence). In contrast, after the economic policy turnaround in May 2010 from expansive fiscal policies to immediate fiscal consolidation, the budget was severely cut: in 2011, total spending was reduced by 15 per cent and social spending decreased by 6 per cent, with cuts even affecting unemployment benefits and pensions. The 11 and 10 per cent declines in health and education spending, respectively, are in principle less relevant, as long as competences in these areas are in the hands of regional governments, so state action in these fields is limited to regulation and some research institutes. In 2012, although central government spending is planned to diminish only by 1.3 per cent, the budget also reflects relevant decreases in all areas except for general expenditure, because of the increase in the transfers to regional and local administrations and debt service.

4.2.2 Autonomous Communities

As already mentioned, regional governments in Spain play an important role in terms of public spending, particularly in social areas, as they have assumed competences in health, education and social exclusion, among others. According to the authors' one-by-one analyses of regional budgets from 2009 to 2012 several conclusions can be drawn. First, regional budgets for 2009, elaborated in 2008, the year in which employment and economic activity began to decline, were clearly expansive and in most cases the growth of social spending was similar to the overall increase in budget resources. In the second place, cuts began in many autonomous communities in 2010, but they were not generalized and, in many cases, they did not affect social expenditure and education. However, all budgets were reduced in 2011 and almost the same applied to 2012.[7] In this case, resources allocated to social protection, health and education not only experienced reductions but also, in some regions, the cuts were even larger than in total expenditure. Although it is difficult to summarize the budget information of 17 regions, some examples might be illustrative: even without taking into account the additional cuts that regions are currently accomplishing in order to adapt to the lower transfers from central government, between 2010 and 2012, 12 out of 16 regions cut their budgets by more than 10 per cent, another two by less than 10 per cent, two increased the budget and the remaining one (Asturias), which is in the middle of a political crisis, is currently preparing the budget for 2012. Social spending was reduced in all the 16 regions (excluding Asturias, which will follow a similar pattern), with 10 of them imposing cuts of 10 per cent or more. Regarding health and education, the pattern was very similar: all the regions on which data are available reduced their spending from 2010 to 2012 in these areas, with 10 and 13 regions reporting cuts of more than 10 per cent in health and in education spending, respectively. In sum, regional governments, which are responsible for around 35 per cent of total public spending and most in-kind welfare benefits, have implemented contractive fiscal policies since 2010, with social areas (social protection, health and education) being affected along similar lines to total budget resources. Moreover, as already mentioned, the central state budget for 2012, approved at the end of June, involves lower transfers to regional governments, thus imposing additional spending cuts (and tax rises), which most autonomous communities are working on right now. Nevertheless, there are even more clouds on the horizon: according to most predictions, even with all these measures, Spain is not likely to meet the deficit target and new cuts might be necessary.

4.2.3 Local governments

The evolution of the local administration budget in Spain from 2008 to 2011 reveals that fiscal adjustment has affected local budgets in a similar fashion to other levels of government. From 2008 to 2009, local budgets were expansive, but that trend reversed from 2009. From 2009 to 2011, local public spending fell by 11.3 per cent, with a reduction in health spending by 29 per cent (it is not possible to calculate the change in the other kinds of spending because of a change in the classification of local spending from 2009 to 2010). From 2010 to 2011, local budgets were decreased by 12.1 per cent, with reductions of 12 per cent in social protection, 6.6 per cent in health and 14.3 per cent in education spending. Overall, the figures discussed above suggest that the crisis has also negatively affected the resources of municipalities and councils.

Three messages arise from this subsection, necessarily riddled with budgetary statistics: first, after a very brief Keynesian interlude, all Spanish administrations followed contractive fiscal policies; second, the aim was to accomplish fiscal consolidation mainly by spending cuts; and third, social spending was not safeguarded from such reductions: in fact, in most cases, the spending cuts have affected social areas in a similar way to – if not more than – total expenditure.

4.3 Impact on Pay, Employment and Working Conditions of Public Employees

4.3.1 Impact on pay

According to data from the National Statistics Institute and the Bank of Spain, for most of the decade before the crisis, public wages experienced a negative evolution in real terms (a decrease of 7 per cent between 1996 and 2003) or were stagnant (from 2004 to 2006), with a 1.1 per cent increase in 2007 and a 0.6 per cent decrease in 2009. Once the crisis began, only in 2009 can we see a significant increase in the real wage, the result of the unexpected drop in the CPI. The following year, 2010, the government announced a token wage increase of 0.3 per cent agreed with the trade unions in September 2010, but then unilaterally decided a 5 per cent decrease in nominal wages for 2011. This cut was applied progressively, from 0.56 to 7 per cent.[8] In 2011 and 2012, and also for budgetary reasons, nominal wages were frozen.

During the same period (2010–11), according to data from collective agreements, private real wages remained virtually stagnant. As a result of these dynamics, the estimated earnings differential in favour of public employees (19 per cent in 2009) would be around 9 per cent in 2011, less than half the original differential, wiping out most of the unexplained gap – in other words, not corresponding to differences in human capital – estimated at 12 percentage points. Furthermore, as the nominal wage reduction of public employees has been progressive and the wage premium is lower for high-skilled public employees, it is safe to conclude that for the higher quintile, on average, the gap might even be negative now.[9]

Adding to such a general wage reduction for all public employees, several autonomous regions have passed wage cuts for their employees, for example, Castile-La Mancha (3 per cent), Catalonia (3 per cent annual summer bonus in 2011 and 2 per cent annual Christmas bonus plus another 2 per cent in 2012) or the Valencia Autonomous Community (reduction of specific wage complements for health – 50 per cent – and education employees). The former region also approved a reduction of working time in 2012, with a proportional reduction of wages for temporary public employees (excluding education and health) of 25 per cent. The same policy will be applied by Catalonia, in this case by 15 per cent, to temporary public employees working in 'non-essential services', affecting around 7,000 people, most of them in low-skilled jobs and already with low wages.

4.3.2 Impact on employment

The start of the debt crisis and the change from an expansionary to a contractive fiscal policy affected not only the wages of public employees, but also the level of public employment. While in 2008 public sector recruitment amounted to almost 36,000 jobs a year, in 2011 the number was reduced to slightly over 15,000. In 2010 and 2011 the replacement rate (percentage of vacancies, mostly as a result of retirement, covered by new public employees) was reduced to 10 per cent. In December 2011, the new conservative government announced that, irrespective of the number of retired public employees, there will be no new hirings in the public sector in 2012, with the exception of the armed and security forces, education and health, where only 10 per cent of retired workers will be replaced. As already mentioned, in less than one year public employment decreased by 3.6 per cent, and the trend is expected to continue in the near future, often involving termination of the contracts of temporary public employees.

During the crisis, numerous reports have been published questioning whether there are too many public employees in the public administration. Although as shown by Navarro and Tur (2009), such reports often do not bear close examination, the idea has caught on with the public, and the reduction of public employment has become a commonplace when discussing possible strategies of fiscal consolidation.

4.3.3 Impact on working conditions

In order to analyse the evolution of working conditions among public workers during the crisis we have estimated three different models using the data of the 2007 and 2010 waves of QWLS mentioned in Subsection 3.2. For reasons of space, only the main results of the analyses are summarized here.

1. With the crisis the working conditions of public employees have deteriorated in nine out of 35 of the attributes considered: satisfaction with wage, stress, physical effort, sex, age, ethnic and disability discrimination, the existence of bullying at the firm and satisfaction with working time flexibility. The remaining attributes show no change, except in overall satisfaction and self-fulfilment, with a positive change.
2. Such variations are not driven by compositional effects. After controlling for human capital endowments and sectoral features there is not only a deterioration in most of the above-mentioned working conditions, but in some cases where no change was detected without controls (monotony and satisfaction with job stability) a worsening is observed after controlling for workers' observable characteristics.
3. The crisis affected both private and public working conditions in roughly the same way, that is, the evolution of working conditions in the private and public sectors has been roughly similar and deterioration of some job features has been common.[10]

More recently, after a string of working-time increases by various autonomous communities, at the end of 2011 the national government decreed an increase of 2.5 hours of the weekly working time of public employees, from 35 to 37.5. This 7.1 per cent increase in working time was equivalent to a reduction of the hourly wage of 6.6 per cent, further eroding the existing wage premium at the turn of 2012. However, that is not the only change in working conditions taking place at the time of writing. For example, among the measures approved by the new conservative government on 30 December 2011, we find the elimination of public administration contributions to employees' complementary pension funds (0.3 per cent of all wages). In the same spirit, the regional government of Madrid has decided to eliminate the wage supplement that regional employees receive in the case of sick leave. According to national legislation, when on sick leave, from the fourth to the fifteenth day workers receive 60 per cent of their wages. Hitherto, the regional government had supplemented the amount up to 100 per cent of the wage. From 2012 the regional government has dropped the supplement (except in the case of work accidents or maternity). A similar policy has been 'temporarily' adopted for 2012 by the government of the Basque Country, the Valencia Community and Galicia.[11] Galicia will reduce the number of *moscosos* (days that can be freely used by public employees) from nine to six per year. In March 2012 the government of Catalonia approved a non-negotiated plan to unilaterally change working conditions (geographical reallocation, changes in working time and so on), affecting 45,000 public employees. Finally, in April 2012, the national government decreed an increase in the classroom hours of university (under some circumstances) and non-university teachers.

4.3.4 Impact on social dialogue

Social dialogue in the public administration was one of the first casualties of the second stage of the economic crisis. In 2009, conscious of the difficult public finance situation, the major trade unions signed an agreement fixing the wage increase of public employees at a token 0.3 per cent for 2010. As mentioned earlier, six months later the government unilaterally broke the agreement and applied an average 5 per cent nominal wage reduction to all public sector employees. This policy was accompanied by a general and harsh public opinion campaign questioning the job performed by public employees, their 'unjustifiable' ('privileged') working conditions and their surplus number. All these elements further worsened the relations between the social partners in the public sector. In order to counter these attitudes, the major trade unions have launched several campaigns to defend the role played by public employees in modern societies. The reduction of public expenditure and other reforms have been met by an unprecedented number of strikes and demonstrations: 2011 witnessed a series of demonstrations in defence of public services and public employment in general or in defence of specific groups of public employees, such as teachers, health professionals and so on. These rallies, national and regional, started with the public employees' strike on 8 June 2010, and include a general strike against the labour market reforms and the reduction of public expenditure on 29 September 2011. In 2012, the campaign has continued, culminating in a general strike on 29 March.

The unions have also been the target of an intensive public opinion campaign, picturing them as parasites on the labour market and public spending and the cause of many of the problems in the labour market. The focus of this campaign has been their lack of representativeness of the workforce and their dependence on public subsidies.[12] It really does not matter that these claims can be proven false. For example, trade unions received €16 million from the public administration (the same amount as employers' organizations), which makes up only 4 per cent of their budget, while 90 per cent of employees participate in union elections (a turnout much higher than in general, regional, local and European elections). What is important is that the campaign has had an impact on public opinion, sharply reducing the level of trust in workers' representatives, and weakening their role in the public sector and society more generally. For instance, according to data from the Latinobarometer, the share of the adult population reporting no confidence in trade unions rose from 22 per cent in 2004 to 42 per cent in 2010.[13] Furthermore, the president of the employers' organization himself recognized, in an interview in a national newspaper, the existence of a public opinion campaign against trade unions (*El Mundo*, 4 March 2012).

Finally, as part of the package approved by the central government on 30 December 2011 and probably as a consequence of the public opinion campaign mentioned above, subsidies to trade unions, employers' associations and political parties are to be reduced by 20 per cent in 2012. This process of revising the role of social dialogue in public administration and the reduction of public expenditure has also affected the number of public employees that benefit from full release from their duties in public administration in order to perform trade union duties full-time. Under Spanish law, members of works councils and union delegates have the right to use a certain number of hours (from 15 hours per month in firms with up to 100 employees to 40 hours in firms with more than 751 workers) for union activities. In turn, these hours can be accumulated (if laid down in the Collective Agreement) for a single person who can be fully 'liberated' (*liberados sindicales* in the argot) from his or her usual work for the firm and thus work full-time for the union. In the past, different levels of public administration have reached agreement with the trade unions to increase the number of union hours in order to increase the role and participation of unions in different institutions. For example, in the region of Castile and Leon the number of hours granted per delegate was 45, while in Madrid it was 70. The need to reduce public expenditure and the often confrontational (in the sense of non-passive) attitude of the unions to such reductions has led to a reversal of the previously positive stance on the part of the public administration with regard to the role of the trade unions in public administration affairs.[14] As a result, different administrations have unilaterally limited the number of these union hours to the legal minimum (reduction of 35 per cent in Galicia in health and education, 63 per cent in Castile-La Mancha, 70 per cent in the Balearic Islands and 66 per cent in Madrid, for example).

4.4 Summary and Implications

Concluding this section, Table 13.3 presents a summary of the main measures taken to reduce the public deficit as well as their implications both

Table 13.3 Main public sector policy changes, Spain, 2010–2012

Policy change	Declared aim	Level affected	Impact on public employment	General
5% wage cut for public sector employees in 2010 Wage freeze in 2011 Wage freeze in 2012*	Fiscal consolidation through the reduction of public expenditure Reduction of public deficit	S, R, L	Reduction of wages. Further decreases in 2012 in selected autonomous communities (3% in Castile-La Mancha, 25% for temporary employees in Valencia Community – with proportional reduction in working time, etc.)	The increase in public sector wages is one of the variables considered when negotiating collective agreements in the private sector. The reduction + freeze of public wages will influence downwards private sector wage agreements
Virtual freeze of new hiring. Replacement rate of 10% only in police, education and health, 2012*	Fiscal consolidation through the reduction of public expenditure Reduction of public deficit	S,R,L	Reduction of public employment Increase in the workload of remaining public employees	Likely reduction of quality of public services: longer waiting time, higher number of students per class, phase out of some local services, etc.
Increase of working time of public employees from 35 to 37.5 hours per week*	Reduction in labour costs Reduction of public deficit	S, R, L	Reduction of hiring, longer hours, lower take-home pay for some workers (in health, for example) through a decrease in overtime pay Deterioration of work–life balance Reduction of public employment hourly wage premium	

Elimination of the contribution of the public administration to occupational pension plans*	Fiscal consolidation (0.3% of total labour costs for the public administration in 2011)	S, R, L	Reduction of social benefits of public employees	
Increase in classroom hours of non-university teachers and number of students per class*	Reduction of hiring Reduction of public deficit	S, N	Longer class hours, less time for other teaching-related tasks, less personalized attention to students	Likely reduction of the quality of education
Reduction of other benefits related to sickness leave and other social programmes	Fiscal consolidation of the autonomous regions	R	Reduction of social benefits of public employees	
Reform of pension system	Reduction of future expenditure on pensions	N	Raising standard retirement age by 2 years (from 65 to 67) Stringent requirements for full pensions	
Freeze of minimum wage in 2012*	To reduce labour costs and facilitate employment	N		Increase in the number of low wage workers as real minimum wage will be reduced
Delay until Jan. 2013 of approved (Equality Law of 2007) increase in paternity leave to 4 weeks*	Reduction of expenditure Reduction of public deficit	N		Deterioration of employment conditions Step back in gender equality fight Deterioration of work–life balance
Non-renewal of youth emancipation subsidy for new claimants*	Reduction of expenditure Reduction of public deficit	N		Young people planning to leave the parental home (the subsidy consists of €210 per month to pay the rent) Means tested

Table 13.3 (continued)

Policy change	Declared aim	Level affected	Impact on public employment	General
Moratorium on the 2-year limit on temporary employment in the same job	To facilitate the permanent employment of temporary workers in the same firm during the crisis	N		Probable increase of temporary employment Reduction of employment turnover
Moratorium of one year for new claimants of the System of Attention to Dependent Persons affecting all claimants with moderate dependency*	Reduction of expenditure Reduction of public deficit	N		Around 150,000 people with moderate (type III) dependency
20% reductions of subsidies to trade union, business associations and political parties*	Reduction of expenditure Reduction of public deficit	N		Reduction of the funds available to trade unions for their activities
Temporary increase of income tax rates on labour from 0.75 % points to 7% points (over €300,000)*	Increase of revenue Reduction of public deficit	N	Further reduction in disposable income to be added to wage cuts of 2010 and wage freeze of 2011–12	Reduction in take-home pay
Temporary increase of income tax rates on capital from 2% points to 6% points (over €24,000)* This increase adds to a previous increase from 19 to 21%	Increase of revenue Reduction of public deficit	N		

Labour market reform*	To increase labour market flexibility Reduction of labour costs	N	The procedure for collective dismissals in public administration will not require previous approval of the labour authorities; it will be enough to show insufficient budget for 3 consecutive quarters	Reduction of redundancy payments, deterioration of working conditions, increase in the capacity of firms to change agreed working conditions, increase of the leverage of firms *vis-à-vis* workers, facilitation of dismissal in case of absenteeism, etc.
General reduction of expenditure in all sectors	Reduction of public deficit	N	Increase in workload of remaining public employees	Deterioration of public services, especially infrastructure, education and health. Phase-out of selected public services targeted on minorities
Increase in health-care copayments*	Increase of revenue Reduction of expenditure Reduction of public deficit	N, R		Reduction in the access to health care, regressivity of user charges, eventual negative effects on health
Increase by 33% in class hours of university teachers who do not actively carry out research work*	Reduction of expenditure Reduction of public deficit	S, N	Longer class hours, less time for research and administrative tasks	Likely reduction of the quality of education
Increase in university tuition fees*	Increase of revenue Reduction of public deficit	N		Reduction of high education students

Note: * Measure taken by the new conservative government in office since December 2012. S: Sectoral; N: National; R: Regional; L: Local.

Source: Authors' elaboration.

for public employees and for society as a whole. As can be seen, so far the adjustment has lain heavily on public employment, through a reduction in hiring, covering only a small part of the vacancies produced by retirements and quits, a reduction of wages and other social benefits previously enjoyed by public employees and an (uncompensated) increase in weekly working hours. As a result, in future the Spanish public sector will have fewer employees, with lower salaries, worse working conditions and longer working hours. Considering the important role that standard economic theory gives to incentives, it can be concluded that the deterioration of what is called in Spain *la función pública*, together with a deterioration of the public image and prestige of public employees, will probably have a negative impact in terms of the quality of public services, as well as the future capacity of public administration to attract well-qualified employees. In the short run, with a high unemployment rate and low hiring in the public sector, that might not be a problem, but a selection problem might arise should the conditions of the labour market improve in the future. Furthermore, and regardless of the incentive issue, the reduction of employment and other expenditure related to the provision of goods and services by the public sector (maintenance of infrastructure, medical equipment and so on) might directly affect the amount and quality of the goods and services produced, with obvious negative implications in terms of the well-being of the population and the future growth of the economy, as many of the services provided (notably, but not only, health, education and R&D) are related to both well-being and growth. This is especially worrying in a country such as Spain, where the welfare state is relatively undeveloped. Section 5 describes in more detail the impact and implications of the adjustment in expenditure in the areas of education and health.

Obviously, the above-mentioned problems would disappear if the Spanish public sector really were overstaffed and spendthrift. However, as shown above, comparative analysis does not back this up. Even after the abrupt and sudden increase in social expenditure as a percentage of GDP, as a result of both the increase in social expenditure (mostly explained by the increase in unemployment benefits, from 2.1 per cent in 2006 to 3.7 per cent three years later) and the reduction of GDP (3.7 per cent from 2008 to 2009), both due to the crisis, Spain dedicated 25 per cent of GDP to social expenditure in 2009 (most recent available data), well under the 29.7 per cent EU27 average. This difference can be found in all categories of social expenditure (excluding unemployment).[15] As for the alleged profligacy of the welfare system, it is important to underline that the administrative costs of running the system are also relatively low: 0.51 per cent of GDP compared to 0.87 per cent in the EU27, 1.18 per cent in Germany and 1.49 per cent in the Netherlands.

In some cases, the pay and working conditions of public employees can be favourably compared to those in the private sector. At this point, it is convenient to remind the reader that this feature, which is often considered a privilege of these workers, can also be interpreted as the result of a policy of fair wages and decent working conditions in the public sector, initiating a process by which such standards might be followed by the private sector in the near future. This is especially obvious in areas such as work–life balance, where the public sector often sets the standards that later on (either through the passing of legislation, by agreement between the social partners or by imitation) are adopted by the private sector. In this respect, it is useful to remember that, in the past, previous interventions in favour of public employees in fields such as pensions or health insurance were extended later on to all employees.

As already mentioned several times, it is likely that new adjustments in both wages and public sector jobs will be made in the near future if, as expected, Spain cannot meet the deficit target in the middle of the current economic recession.[16]

5. CASE STUDIES: THE IMPACT OF THE CRISIS AND THE ADJUSTMENT OF PUBLIC EXPENDITURE ON EDUCATION AND HEALTH

Not taking pensions into account, health and education are the two major service delivering activities of the public sector. In 2008, before the crisis, the two added up to 43 per cent of social expenditure and a similar percentage of total public employment. Moreover, competences in both areas have been transferred to the autonomous regions, making room for a range of policy responses in the wake of the crisis. Finally, in both cases we are dealing with essential public services with a profound impact on well-being, growth and inequalities. As there is no real time information on the impact of most of the cuts made in social spending, the bulk of the evidence presented in the case studies is based on new information appearing in a range of Spanish media. (For reasons of space, such sources are not detailed below but a file with all the media news is available from the authors upon request.)

5.1 Case Study 1: Adjustment in the National Health System

Since 1986, the basic structure of public health care has remained largely unchanged. It is organized as a national health service (NHS), providing universal assistance funded by general government revenues. It covers a wide set of health-care treatments and only dental care is subject to significant restrictions. In contrast to most OECD countries, the Spanish NHS is free, with copayments limited to prosthetics, spectacles, hearing aids and drugs (40 per cent, with exemptions for pensioners, chronic patients and those on a low income) until 2012. Whereas the Spanish NHS largely involves public provision of health services, the past decade has witnessed a considerable increase in the importance of publicly financed but privately produced health care, through different forms of managed care. The relevance of these new forms of health care varies widely across regions, being present to a large extent in Catalonia and in those autonomous communities with conservative governments during the past decade, particularly Madrid and Valencia. With a few exceptions, doctors working in public health care are salaried employees, paid a lump sum fixed by decree and several supplements (based on the number of patients and exclusive dedication to public health practice, among other things). From a comparative perspective, Spain allocates fewer resources to health care than the EU27 average (7.4 versus 8.4 per cent of GDP in 2009), and much less than core EU countries, such as France (9.4 per cent) and Germany (9.7 per cent). In fact, if we discount the statistical impact of the crisis and the fall in GDP, which automatically generates an increase in relative expenditure on health, the weight of public expenditure in GDP has shown remarkable stability during the 2000s, even in a period of high population growth associated with massive immigration flows.

There are two different sources of pressure on the NHS. The first is unrelated to the economic crisis, although the current economic situation has often been used as an excuse to press for reforms largely independent of the contemporary economic situation. This perspective questions whether a system of organization based mainly on public provision of medical services, by public employees, in public hospitals and health centres, is an appropriate model in terms of efficiency and cost compared to models based on managed care. The second source of pressure is directly related to the public revenue cuts (from taxes and, mainly, central state transfers) suffered by autonomous governments as result of the crisis, the level of administration in charge of the health system, which has led to systematic underfinancing of the different regional health systems and the development of a so-called 'health-care deficit'. This lack of sufficient finance has led to (a) a debate about alternative ways of financing the system and reducing the demand for health services, notably the introduction of new copayments; and (b) the reduction in the budget allocated to health services, and the corresponding deterioration of the system and worsening of working condition of health-care employees.

Regarding the first issue, the introduction of 'new' forms of managed care, the lack of transparency and the few available studies on the cost and performance of the publicly funded and privately run hospitals do not allow us to present a proper evaluation of this process. In any case, it is important to stress that these changes are not backed by previous analyses of the costs and benefits of these reforms, and even less by public discussions. On the contrary, faith in the benefits of market forces is the main driver. The empirical evidence on the performance of these new ways of organizing health care shows, at best, no improvement in terms of equity or efficiency of health-care delivery over traditional forms of organization and, in general, they seem to be more expensive.[17] In this respect, regions such as Catalonia, Madrid, Castile-La Mancha and Valencia Community, among others, are increasing their utilization of these new ways of organizing health services, whose benefits, even in terms of cost, are far from proven, without proper scrutiny and public discussion.

Regarding cuts in health services and spending themselves, there are also several lines of action. First of all, after a fierce public campaign conducted by employers' organizations, many economists and several politicians, patient cost-sharing mechanisms in health care have been reinforced. In this respect, the Catalonian government under the conservative–nationalist party Convergencia-i-Unió has approved the introduction of a new copayment in 2012 of €1 per prescription (with exceptions for those on a low income or patients suffering from chronic diseases) and, in April 2012, the central government announced new cuts of €7 billion in health spending, passing a package of measures that included the raising of drug copayments for those earning more than €18,000 per year from 40 to 50/60 per cent of the price, depending on income, applying the same system to prostheses and non-urgent health transport services and extending the cost-sharing system to pensioners (up to 10 per cent with some exceptions and a monthly cap of €18). Although it is outside the scope of this study to analyse the advantages and disadvantages of copayment, it is worth mentioning that it has proven to be inefficient as a mechanism of cost containment for different reasons related to the doctor-induced nature of demand for health services, information imperfection and regressivity arguments (Robinson 2002; Thomson et al. 2010). In addition, within the same set of measures, new requirements for foreign population to access public health services have established, de facto excluding illegal immigrants (who have been able to access the NHS since a reform carried out in 2000) from benefiting from any type of treatment except for emergency care.

In relation to the second issue, we focus mainly on the case of Catalonia, a region that made early and radical cuts in the regional health system. In 2011, the regional government passed a reduction of 6.5 per cent of the health budget. Nevertheless, the budget for 2011 included expenditures already made in 2010, so deducting such expenditures the reduction amounted to more than 15 per cent (Colom et al. 2011), leaving the health budget for 2011 in real terms at the level of 2003. The effects of these cuts detected so far include the following: (a) a freeze of renovation work or construction of new hospitals and health centres; (b) a moratorium on patients' right, recognized in 2007, to have surgery with a maximum delay of six months for 14 of the most common surgeries; such limits have been kept only for heart conditions and lumbar hernias; (c) closure of hospital wings and surgery rooms; particularly, 40 health centres and half of the intensive care units of two major hospitals were closed down during the summer (almost 11 per cent of total primary care centres) and the eight biggest hospitals of the Instituto Catalan de la Salud (ICS) were closed during Christmas (five days); and (d) after a long period of reductions of surgery waiting lists, during 2011 waiting lists increased by 42 per cent. Together with these measures, the Catalonian government is planning to sell seven hospitals and rent them back from the future owners, in what in fact is a decapitalization of the health system. An estimated 3,000 temporary health sector employees have lost their job.

All these measures are being taken regardless of the lack of convincing arguments and success stories in favour of the advantages of these types of reform (see above). Furthermore, as exemplified by a recent scandal concerning one hospital in Catalonia, this trend could lead to segregation of patients in the public system between those who can afford private health insurance and receive preferential treatment and those who rely exclusively on the public system, generating new inequalities in health care. In this respect, recently, in one privately run public hospital (La Seu d'Urgell in Lleida, Catalonia), patients were offered the possibility of skipping the surgery waiting list using their private health insurance. In those cases, the patients were operated on in the same place, by the same surgeons but in the afternoon or evening when the surgery was closed.

In other regions similar measures are being taken. For instance, in Galicia, apart from the reduction of resources devoted to health care, which has led to an increase in waiting lists, new hospitals are planned under the private finance initiative (PFI) and the process of acquisition and maintenance of medical technology is going to be contracted out, with both elements implying larger costs for the exchequer than traditional ways of managing health care.

5.2 Case Study 2: Impact of Fiscal Consolidation on Education

As in other dimensions of the welfare state, according to Eurostat data for 2008, relative public spending on education in Spain is below the EU average, with public spending in this area of 4.6 per cent of GDP, compared to 5.1 per cent for the EU27 and as much as 7.8 per cent in Denmark. This deficit is associated with lower-than-average spending on secondary and college education. The main problems of the Spanish educational system are school failure (youth not finishing mandatory secondary education), early school leaving (those not completing upper secondary education), the scant development of the vocational training system and the lack of appropriate educational itineraries for those who experience difficulties in the lower levels of schooling (Muñoz de Bustillo et al. 2009). One last feature concerns the increase in the number of foreign students since the mid-1990s, with foreigners accounting for roughly 10 per cent of non-university students (around 15 per cent in some regions).

The main measures taken up to now involve several lines of action. First, most regions (particularly Catalonia, Valencia Community and Castile-La Mancha) have implemented several changes that have severely affected the working conditions of public workers. Among others, we might mention the following: reduction in the number of teachers (in many cases, by converting full-time positions into part-time ones, which implies a reduction of total teaching hours, or establishing a moratorium in most regions on new hiring through public exams), pay decreases (by reducing specific regional wage complements), cuts in the replacement rates of sick benefits, removing the right to holiday pay for temporary workers in education, not covering temporary vacancies due to sick leave, diminishing subsidies to trade unions and limiting the number of education employees working full-time for trade unions to the minimum established by law, increase in teaching hours (one or two weekly hours depending on the region). Second, at the end of 2011, the just-elected conservative government decided that only 10 per cent of new vacancies, mainly associated with teacher retirements, would be covered. Third, in April 2012, the central government announced an additional €3 billion cut in resources devoted to education, which involves the following measures: an increase in the number of students per classroom in primary and secondary education, an increase in minimum classroom hours for non-university teachers, non-substitution of teachers on sick leave for the first two weeks, reduction of the budget devoted to teacher training, complete freeze on the expansion of the education of the under-threes, reduction of Erasmus scholarships and grants for learning foreign languages abroad, absolute prohibition on hiring new staff by universities, increase in university tuition fees from 15 to 25 per cent of total cost of tertiary education and increase in the number of teaching hours by 33 per cent for university teachers not actively involved in research work.

6. CONCLUSIONS AND POLICY ISSUES

Throughout this chapter we have pursued a double aim: first, to provide a detailed description of the Spanish public sector, with a particular focus on its employees and, second, to describe the impact of the crisis on the public sector.

The first issue that should have been made clear in these pages is that the size of the public sector in Spain, in terms of both spending and employment is smaller than in most EU member states. This feature, apart from an evident political choice, reflects the late development of the welfare state in Spain.

Second, we have characterized public employment in comparison to private sector employment. The most remarkable features of the former have to do with a higher presence of women and older workers, higher pay (and a lower gender wage gap) and better working conditions in terms of working-time arrangements.

The third message conveyed by this chapter has to do with the particular response to the crisis of the Spanish authorities and its consequences for the public sector. After a brief episode of expansionary fiscal policy, in 2010 the government embarked on fiscal consolidation at the urging of the EU authorities under the auspices of the German government. This process has mainly involved spending cuts across the board. This untidy process of spending reductions has led to a deterioration in the working conditions of public sector employees, not only through pay cuts (which might have made the public employment wage premium disappear) but also longer working hours, less employment stability, reductions in sick pay entitlements and larger workloads as a consequence of firings and non-substitution of workers on sick leave, among other things.

Fourth, despite the obvious limitations of the available data, overall, it can be said that the policy of fiscal consolidation is seriously affecting employment in key areas of the public sector. According to Spanish doctors' media statements, cuts are, to a large degree, indiscriminate and not driven by careful study of their impact and the areas in which greater inefficiencies are present. As shown throughout the chapter, and exemplified in the two case studies, the core areas of the welfare state are being affected, with significant consequences for the well-being of the

Spanish population. One important element explaining the so far relatively low level of social conflict in the face of an unemployment rate of 23 per cent is the compensatory role played by social expenditure, both monetary benefits and the public coverage of important needs (such as health care and education, including higher education). Reduction in the level or quality of these public services in a context of high unemployment would certainly have a significant impact on both well-being and social peace. The growing number of demonstrations and strikes exemplifies this risk.

At present, the outlook is not encouraging. Both central and regional governments, ruled by the same party and under pressure from the European Commission, seem strongly committed to continuing the contractionary fiscal policy, which is beginning to undermine the fundamentals of the already underdeveloped Spanish welfare state. The reasoning guiding this policy seems to be what some qualified observers, such as Paul Krugman (2010), have called the 'confidence fairy', that is, the hope that an improvement in a country's fiscal position will raise agents' expectations and confidence to such levels that this a priori contractionary policy will foster economic activity. In any case, the next few months are likely to be crucial: the government has committed itself not to exceed a fiscal deficit of 5.3 per cent of GDP at the end of 2012, irrespective of the fact that the deficit at the end of 2011 was 8.5 per cent, far above the planned 6.6 per cent. In sharp contrast to popular beliefs, as shown by comparative data, the Spanish public sector is neither overstaffed nor profligate, at least in the core areas of the welfare state. If national and European authorities continue to prioritize fiscal consolidation Spain might soon cross red lines in the maintenance of its social policy and become caught in a dynamic of deterioration and retrenchment of its far from mature welfare state, with significant implications in terms of well-being and growing inequalities.

The suicidal policy we have described is frequently presented as the only alternative. That is certainly not the case. A slower pace of deficit reduction so as not to exacerbate the crisis; a more active role on the part of the EU in the development of alternative sources of funding for member states (see, for example, Varoufakis and Holland 2011); fiscal reform to increase public revenue, including tough measures to combat fiscal fraud and evasion; a thoughtful review of public expenditure aimed at discovering inefficiencies and waste; a negotiated restructuring of core public services with the same aim but with the complicity of public employees and trade unions (who often have a better knowledge of where the inefficiencies are and whose cooperation is, in any case, a prerequisite of successful reform) are some of the courses of action needed to reconcile the maintenance of a welfare state which is backed by most of the population and coping with the crisis. These things are not just important in themselves but mutually reinforcing.

NOTES

1. In 1975, roughly 90 per cent of public spending corresponded to central administration, while in 2005 the spending of regional and local administrations comprised almost 50 per cent of the total (Alcaide 1985; OECD Statistics Database).
2. For example, according to the LFS 2009, 10 per cent of public employees enrolled in in-house training in the past year compared to 4.1 per cent of private employees.
3. Furthermore, the percentage of women in private employment has also increased in recent years because the crisis has predominantly affected male-dominated sectors, such as construction and industry.
4. The Theil index of the complete earnings distribution is 0.265, with within- and between-group components of 0.263 and 0.002, respectively.
5. This outcome was confirmed by the IMF (2011: 22), who estimate that the fiscal consolidation carried out in Spain cost the country over two points of GDP growth in 2011, most of it due to the reduction of public spending.
6. Unfortunately, consolidated data – which include the public sector as a whole avoiding the double accounting of internal transfers – are available only up to 2009.
7. Only the budget of the Canary Islands included a tiny increase in public spending (1.4 per cent), but after the approval of the central government budget in March 2012, like most regional administrations, this autonomous community had to make additional spending cuts.
8. Real Decreto-ley 8/2010, de 20 de mayo, por el que se adoptan medidas extraordinarias para la reducción del déficit público (Royal Decree-Law 8/2010 of 20 May by which extraordinary measures for the reduction of the public deficit are taken).
9. This figure is a rough calculation, not taking into account the possible wage drift of public and private employees.
10. The crisis has brought with it a relatively modest improvement in the position of public sector employees in the case of physical effort and satisfaction with health and safety. The only dimensions where there has been a deterioration of working conditions of public workers relative to their private sector counterparts are satisfaction with heating and with working time.
11. In the case of Galicia, the administration will not pay any wage for the first three days of sick leave and will supplement the social security payments only from the twenty-first day (with the exception of maternity leave, sickness due to work or work accidents).
12. According to the Quality of Working Life Survey 2010, union density 18.9 per cent in 2010 (31.5 per cent in the public sector), a figure in line with countries such as France.
13. A survey carried out by Simple Logica (a Gallup partner) a week before the general strike showed roughly 48 per cent of those interviewed against the mobilization and approximately 45 per cent in favour. Furthermore, two-thirds of those surveyed did not agree with the labour market reform, the main reason for calling the strike.
14. As examples of union resistance to the cuts, one might mention the strike by public employees in June 2010, a general strike in September 2011 and a string of strikes and demonstrations in particular sectors, notably health and education in certain regions.
15. The higher relative expenditure on unemployment, 3.67 per cent compared to 1.72 per cent in the EU27, is explained by the higher rate of unemployment in Spain, 18 versus 9 per cent in the EU27 in 2009.
16. Such a possibility was suggested by the Concluding Statement of the IMF Mission

(2012 Article IV Consultation with Spain) of 14 June. In their own words, 'To give assurance that the envisaged savings will materialize, future public wage cuts . . . could be legislated now and only cancelled if the targets are hit.'

17. See, among many others, McKee et al. (2006) and, on the British experience, Pollock et al. (1997, 2002) and Gaffney et al. (1999a, 1999b). On the Spanish case, see Martín-García and Sánchez-Bayle (2004), Puig-Junoy and Ortún (2004), Sánchez-Bayle and Martín-García (2004) and Martín-García et al. (2005).

REFERENCES

Alcaide, J. (1985), 'El comportamiento del gasto público en la OCDE y España', *Papeles de Economía Española*, **24**, 181–201.

Banco de España (2012), *Boletín Económico 04/2012*, Madrid: Banco de España.

Blinder, A.S. (1973), 'Wage discrimination: reduced form and structural estimates', *Journal of Human Resources*, **8** (4), 436–55.

Colom, A., S. Marimón and T. Tuà (2011), *Análisis del Presupuesto de salud 2011 y propuestas para mejorar el sistema público de salud*, Barcelona: Centro de Análisis y Programas Sanitarios.

Gaffney, D., A.M. Pollock, D. Price and J. Shaoul (1999a), 'NHS capital expenditure and the private finance initiative – expansion or contraction?', *British Medical Journal*, **319** (7201), 48–51.

Gaffney, D., A.M. Pollock, D. Price and J. Shaoul (1999b), 'PFI in the NHS – is there an economic case?', *British Medical Journal*, **319** (7202), 116–19.

International Monetary Fund (IMF) (2011), *Regional Economic Outlook: Europe. Navigating Stormy Waters*, Washington, DC: International Monetary Fund.

Krugman, P. (2010), 'Myths of austerity', *New York Times*, 1 July.

Machado, J. and J.A.F. Mata (2005), 'Counterfactual decomposition of changes in wage distributions using quantile regression', *Journal of Applied Econometrics*, **20** (4), 445–65.

Martín-García, M., V. Ruiz-Hervella and M. Sánchez-Bayle (2005), 'Satisfacción laboral en el personal de las fundaciones sanitarias en Galicia', *Revista de Administración Sanitaria*, **3** (2), 303–13.

Martín-García, M. and M. Sánchez-Bayle (2004), 'Nuevas formas de gestión y su impacto en las desigualdades', *Gaceta Sanitaria*, **18** (Sup. 1), 96–101.

McKee, M., N. Edwards and A. Rifat (2006), 'Public–private partnership for hospitals', *Bulletin of the World Health Organization*, **84** (11), 890–96.

Muñoz de Bustillo, R. and J.-I. Antón (2011), 'From the highest employment growth to the deepest fall: economic crisis and labour inequalities in Spain', in D. Vaughan-Whitehead (ed.), *Work Inequalities in the Crisis: Evidence from Europe*, Cheltenham, UK and Northampton, MA, USA: Edward Elgar, pp. 393–444.

Muñoz de Bustillo, R., J.-I. Antón, F.-J. Braña and E. Fernández-Macías (2009), *Abandono Escolar y Mercado de Trabajo en España*, Madrid: Ministerio de Trabajo e Inmigración.

Navarro, V. and M. Tur (2009), *El Empleo Público en España no es Excesivo. Los Errores del Informe Sobre el Coste de la Administración de la EAE Business School*, Estudios de la Fundación No. 18, December, Fundación 1° de Mayo, CC.OO.

Oaxaca, R.L. (1973), 'Male–female wage differentials in urban labor markets', *International Economic Review*, **14** (3), 673–709.
Pollock, A.M., M. Dunnigan, D. Gaffney, A. Macfarlane and F.A. Majeed (1997), 'What happens when the private sector plans hospital services for the NHS: three case studies under the private finance initiative', *British Medical Journal*, **314** (7089), 1266–71.
Pollock, A.M., J. Shaoul and N. Vickers (2002), 'Private finance and "value for money" in NHS hospitals: a policy in search of a rationale?', *British Medical Journal*, **324** (7347), 1205–09.
Puig-Junoy, J. and V. Ortún (2004), 'Cost efficiency in primary care contracting: a stochastic frontier cost function approach', *Health Economics*, **13** (12), 1149–65.
Robinson, R. (2002), 'User charges for health care', in E. Mossialos, A. Dixon, J. Figueras and J. Kutzin (eds), *Funding Health Care: Options for Europe*, Buckingham: European Observatory on Health Care Systems, pp. 161–83.
Sánchez-Bayle, M. and M. Martín-García (2004), 'Nuevas formas de gestión: las fundaciones sanitarias en Galicia', Documento de Trabajo 43/2004, Fundación Alternativas.
Thomson, S., T. Foubister and E. Mossialos (2010), 'Can user charges make health care more efficient?', *British Medical Journal*, **341** (3759), 487–89.
Varoufakis, Y. and S. Holland (2011), 'A modest proposal for overcoming the Euro crisis', Policy Note 2011/3, Levy Economics Institute of Bard College, Annandale-on-Hudson, NY.

14. Early fiscal consolidation and negotiated flexibility in Sweden: A fair way out of the crisis?

Dominique Anxo

1. INTRODUCTION

Despite a wave of privatizations and liberalization of a large part of the service sector during the 1990s, Sweden's public sector remains large, by international standards, reflecting strong public and political involvement in the provision of a wide range of services. The tendency towards retrenchment of the public sector and increased competition since the mid-1990s, common to many modern economies, have led to a decrease in public employment, but the share of public employees in total employment remains one of the highest among OECD countries (31 per cent in 2010).

During the early phase of the current crisis (2008–09), employment declined in the female-dominated public sector, in particular at the municipality and county levels, which are in charge of the provision of social services, health care, and primary and secondary education. However, the employment decline in the public sector was relatively short-lived and heavily concentrated on employees with fixed-term contracts. At the end of 2011, public sector employment was almost at the same level as before the onset of the Great Recession. The temporary impact of the crisis on public employment might be ascribed to several factors. In comparison with the 1990s' crisis, the room for manoeuvre in which to conduct a more expansive macroeconomic policy was larger than during previous economic downturns, due to healthier public finances at the start of the recession. In order to mitigate the impact of the crisis on income development and employment, in 2008–10 the Swedish government implemented a package of recovery and countercyclical measures, ranging from expansive fiscal and monetary policy to active labour market and education policy. In this context and in order to maintain and secure employment in the public sector, the government also decided to increase central government grants to local authorities, as well as investment in infrastructure. These countercyclical policy measures have certainly had an effect in limiting the fall of employment in the public sector.

This chapter is structured as follows. Section 2 describes the main features and scope of the Swedish public sector and identifies the major reforms implemented during the past two decades and their major implications. Section 3 analyses the nature of the adjustment in the public sector and the impact of the current crisis on public employment wage developments and working conditions. Section 4 illustrates the impact of the crisis on working conditions and wage development through the analysis of two case studies, the first of elderly care and the second of a local public employment office. Section 5 provides some concluding remarks.

2. PUBLIC SECTOR ADJUSTMENT

2.1 Public Sector: Definition and Scope

The public sector comprises two levels: the central government sector (state) and the local authorities. The central government includes the parliament (*Riksdag*) and governmental authorities responsible for the provision of public services, such as police, defence, the judicial system, higher education (universities and colleges), infrastructure and central administration. The central government is organized in several agencies.[1] Relatively small ministries are responsible for legislation, policymaking and control, while agencies are responsible for conducting most government activities. The central government sector refers to the operations conducted by the government administration, that is, those for which the government or the parliament has direct responsibility and are regulated by public law. Accordingly, the central government sector encompasses all government agencies, regardless of how they are financed. It also embraces public enterprises[2] (*affärsverk*) that are regulated under public law and, consequently, are considered part of the central government sector.[3] The second level comprises local government, including municipalities and county councils, responsible for education (from childcare to secondary education), health care and the care of the elderly and the disabled.

There are various methods of measuring the size of the public sector. In relation to GDP, the public sector's contribution (public consumption and investment) amounted to 31 per cent in 2009, a relatively high figure compared to many other European countries.[4] It should be noted that this contribution has remained relatively stable during the past two decades, oscillating between 29 and 32 per cent. The central government sector encompasses a relatively small part of the Swedish economy and quite a small part of the public sector. To illustrate: slightly more than 5 per cent of the labour force work for the government, while 25 per cent work for municipalities and county councils.

2.2 Main Features of the Public Employment System

In contrast to other EU member states, such as France or Germany, there is no specific employment status for civil servants, and Swedish public employees are subject to the same labour market regulations as private employees. Irrespective of sector, the legal status of employment is therefore similar and all employees, in both the private and public sectors, have legally guaranteed rights to bargaining and industrial action (strikes).

Regarding the gender composition of the workforce across sectors (see Figure 14.1), the labour market remains highly gender segregated.

In 2009, women accounted for around 70 per cent of public employment, the corresponding figure in the private sector being 35 per cent. The shares of female employees in the central government sector and local authorities at the same date were, respectively, around 50 and 80 per cent.

The level of educational attainment also differs significantly across

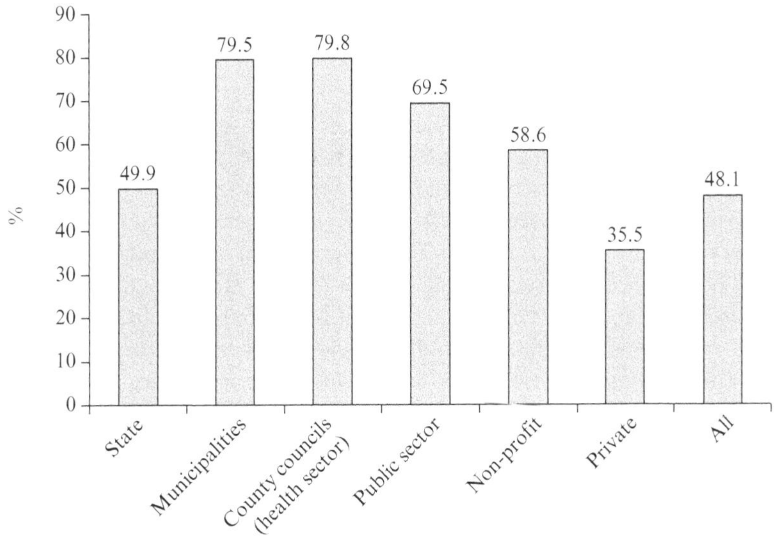

Source: Statistics Sweden (2011d).

Figure 14.1 Share of female employment by sector, Sweden, 2009

sectors. The proportion of employees in the central government sector and county councils (health sector) with a post-secondary education is much higher than in municipalities and the private sector. In 2009, 70 per cent of employees in central government and 67 per cent in county councils had a post-secondary education, while the corresponding shares for municipalities and the private sector were, respectively, 47 and 31 per cent.

Conversely, the share of employees with low educational attainment is much higher in private limited companies than in the public sector, namely 14.6 and 6.2 per cent (see Table 14.1). Also worth noting is that the share of highly educated (low-educated) employees in state- or municipality-owned companies is lower (higher) than the corresponding share in the public sector as a whole, but still higher (lower) than in private companies. Sweden therefore exhibits a higher polarization of educational attainment in the private sector. In the public sector, there is a higher incidence of employees with low and medium education in the female-dominated municipal sector.

Regarding wage differentials between the public and private sectors, the wage level in the public sector is on average lower than in the private sector. The wage premium in the private sector is particularly high among high-skilled workers. However, some wage premium in favour of the public sector remains for low-skilled/low-educated workers, but the wage premiums for this group have had a tendency to diminish over time.

As shown by Table 14.2, the adjusted gender wage gap is higher in the private sector and much lower in the public sector, in particular in municipalities. According to a recent study (Ekberg and Holmlund 2010), Sweden also experienced a reduction in the gender wage gap between 2005 and 2009. This reduction affected all industries but was particularly important in the public sector. The reduction in the gender wage gap might be ascribed to a relative increase of female educational attainment, the deregulation and privatization of part of the public sector, negotiated increases of female wages among low-skilled workers in some bargaining areas (in particular the municipal sector) and also an increase in the share of women in managerial positions.

Another interesting comparison concerns the differences in wage level between private and public providers operating in particular sectors, such as education, health care and social services. As shown by Table 14.3, in 2009 there were minimal differences in salary levels between public and private providers within education, health care and social services. Employees in compulsory and upper secondary schools had an average monthly salary of just over SEK 24,000 in both private enterprises and

Table 14.1 Educational attainment by sector and gender, Sweden, 2009 (%)

Sector	Compulsory education or lower			Secondary education			Tertiary education		
	M	W	All	M	W	All	M	W	All
Public sector			6.2			38.7			54.9
Central Government	3.2	4.5	4.1	21.6	28.5	25.4	75.1	67.0	70.2
Municipalities	8.7	7.3	8.0	39.3	47.1	45.0	52.0	45.6	46.9
County councils	3.3	2.2	2.4	23.8	32.4	30.8	73.0	65.3	66.6
Private sector			15.1			53.5			30.8
Limited companies			14.6			54.6			30.2
Other companies			20.4			52.1			26.3
State-owned companies			12.6			52.9			34.3
Local authority-owned companies			11.7			49.2			39.0
Private sector									
Manual workers	21.6	20.6		68.6	64.0		9.7	15.3	
White collar workers	7.1	6.0		45.7	41.4		51.5	48.3	

Source: Mediation Office (2011d) and Statistics Sweden (2011c).

Table 14.2 Average wage (SEK) by gender and sector; female wage as a percentage of men's, non-adjusted and adjusted (age, education, sector, occupation and working time), Sweden, 2010

Sector	Women	Men	All	Women's wage as % of men's	Women's wage as % of men's, adjusted
All sector	26,200	30,600	28,400	85.7	94.1
Private sector	26,700	30,700	29,200	87.2	92.7
Manual workers	22,100	24,600	23,800	90.0	96.0
Non-manual	29,700	37,500	34,000	79.2	90.7
Public sector	25,600	30,000	26,800	85.4	97.1
Municipalities	24,200	25,700	24,500	93.9	99.6
County councils	28,300	38,500	30,300	73.5	95.2
Central government	29,400	32,900	31,100	89.3	94.2

Source: Mediation Office (2011c).

Table 14.3 Average salary in education, health care and social services, Sweden, 2009 (SEK)

Sector	Private firms	Municipalities	County council
Primary/secondary education	24,100	24,300	–
Health care	30,400	–	29,600
Care	23,500	22,900	–

Source: Statistics Sweden (2011e).

in the municipalities (2009). Within health care, the average monthly salary was just over SEK 30,000 in private companies and just short of SEK 30,000 in the county councils. In social services the average monthly salary was SEK 23,500 in private firms and just short of SEK 23,000 in the municipalities.

In combination with deregulation of employment intermediation in the early 1990s short-term contracts and agency work have increased significantly. In the aftermath of the 1990s' recession and in relation to the deregulation of intermediation the share of fixed-term contracts increased by almost 40 per cent between 1990 and 1995. Since then and up to the current recession this share has increased continuously, reaching 17 per cent of total waged employment at the onset of the current recession. As

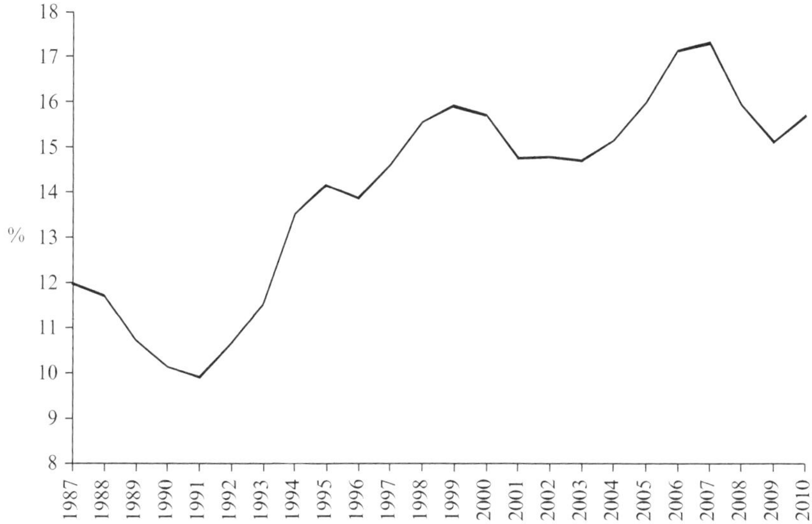

Source: Statistics Sweden (2011b).

Figure 14.2 Development of short-term contracts, Sweden, 1987–2010 (% of dependent employees)

Table 14.4 Share of short-term contracts per sector, 16–64 years old, Sweden, 2007 (%)

Sector	Men	Women	All
Central government	14.3	17.5	15.9
Local authorities	21.4	17.7	18.5
Private	13.5	21.0	16.4
All	14.5	19.3	16.9

Source: Statistics Sweden (2011b).

shown by Figure 14.2, the share of dependent employees on fixed-term contracts declined sharply during the economic crisis.

Table 14.4 displays the share of temporary contracts across broad sectors. The higher incidence of short-term contracts at the municipal level is related to the larger share of women in this sector and the higher need for substitutes linked to various forms of legal absenteeism (in particular parental leave).

2.3 Reforms of the Public Sector during the 1990s and their Implications for Public Employment

The Swedish welfare state, social protection and tax system have undergone a series of transformations and reforms since the end of the 1980s. These reforms aiming at strengthening 'work incentives' and fostering 'flexibility' could hardly be achieved without consequences perceived as 'rising inequality' (wider dispersion of wages, disposable income and wealth) and 'less security', in particular a less generous social insurance system and a weakening of employment protection regulations, implying among other things strong development of fixed-term contracts in both the private and public sectors. The structural reforms undertaken have also included a wave of deregulations, liberalization and privatizations, aimed at exposing previously protected activities to competition. The implementation of these reforms has, to a large extent, involved the dismantling of previously existing public monopolies and an increase in private for-profit suppliers. The striving for efficiency-enhancing competition has been manifested not only in a somewhat increasing role for private providers but also in organizational reforms intended to achieve more competition between different agencies within the public sector, for example between different schools, hospitals and universities, as well as productivity-enhancing organizational changes (rationalization, downsizing, management by objectives, new public management and so on).

More recently, the current right-wing government, which took office in 2006 and was re-elected in 2011, took further measures to increase the role of the private sector, establishing a choice of systems that allows service users to choose their providers among a list provided by the public authorities. Against this background a new law, the Act on System of Choice in the Public Sector (2008: 962) took effect in 2009. This act applies when a contracting public authority decides to apply a system of choice regarding services in health care and social services. According to the act, 'system of choice' means a procedure by means of which people are entitled to choose the supplier that is to perform the service and with which a contracting authority has approved and concluded a contract, within the framework of the Public Procurement Act.[5] In addition to the early waves of deregulation and privatization these reforms therefore explain part of the decline of public employment and the tendencies towards an increasing diversity of providers in social services.

Even though municipally financed services (childcare, and elementary and secondary schooling, support for the disabled, elderly care and so on) are increasingly provided by private actors the proportion of private suppliers remains, by international standards, relatively limited. As shown by

Table 14.5 Employment trends by sector in education, health care and social services, Sweden, 2000–2009 (%)

Sector	2000	2005	2007	2008	2009
Central govt	4.0	4.5	4.3	4.4	4.6
County councils	21.6	20.6	20.3	20.2	19.8
Municipalities	60.3	58.5	57.6	56.5	55.1
State-owned corporation	2.0	1.5	1.8	1.8	1.9
For-profit companies	8.7	11.4	12.7	13.9	15.3
Non-profit companies	3.5	3.5	3.3	3.3	3.3

Source: Statistics Sweden (2011d).

Table 14.6 Employment by activity within education, health care and social services, Sweden, 2009 (%)

Activity	State	County councils	Municipalities	State owned	Private firms	Non-profit
Education	10.7	0.6	70.5	1.5	11.6	5.0
Health	0.2	73.8	4.5	4.1	16.6	0.8
Elderly/disabled care	1.0	0.2	76.0	0.6	18.9	3.3
Total	4.6	19.7	55.0	1.9	15.5	3.3

Source: Statistics Sweden (2011d).

Table 14.5, the share of private employment in education, health care and social services increased from around 8 per cent in 2000 to around 15 per cent in 2009.

In 2009, the highest proportion of employees working in for-profit private companies was found in care activities (elderly care and care for the disabled) and the health sector (see Table 14.6). The share of hours by private actors increased from 7 per cent in 2000 to 12 per cent in 2010. The county councils, in charge of the administration of hospitals and health care, have not experienced the same increase. Since 2000, this share has been largely unchanged at around 10 per cent (SALAR 2011).

Despite the increase in the share of for-profit private companies operating in the welfare sector, education and social services, by international standards, Sweden still has a high level of public employment, reflecting still very strong public and political involvement in the financing and provision of a wide range of services. For crucial service activities – notably

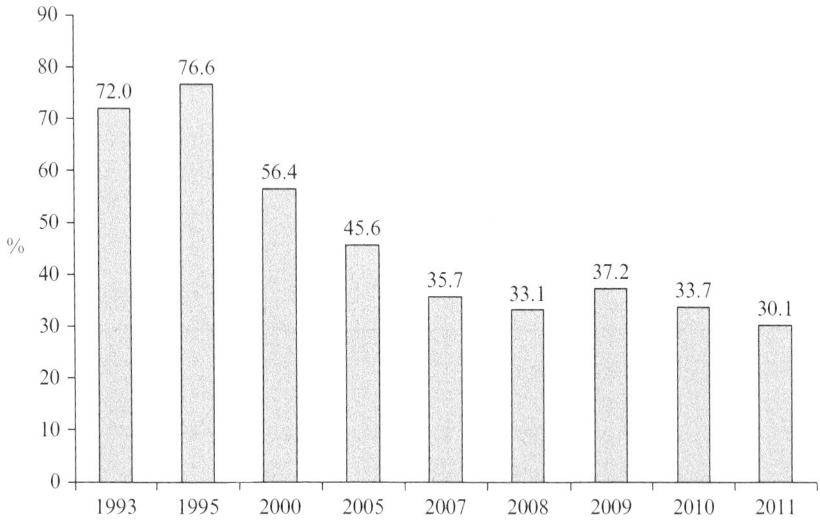

Source: NIER (2012).

Figure 14.3a Development of public debt, Sweden, 1993–2011 (% of GDP)

childcare, elderly and health care, schooling and higher education, as well as measures for the disabled – the public sector remains the main provider.

2.4 Public Finances and Sovereign Debt: Less Need for Fiscal Consolidation and Public Employment Reduction

In the wake of the deep recession of the early 1990s, the employment crisis became acute. In just three years – from 1990 to 1993 – the employment rate decreased by more than 10.5 percentage points to about 73 per cent, and the rate of open unemployment quintupled from less than 2 to almost 10 per cent of the labour force. Furthermore, the public budget deficit increased from about zero to about 14 per cent of GNP, while public debt attained 77 per cent in 1995 (see Figure 14.3a). Facing the deterioration of public finances, the various governments during the 1990s took several austerity measures to reduce the budget deficit and public debt. Several reforms were implemented implying stricter eligibility requirements and lower replacement rates in various social insurance systems (sickness, unemployment insurance, pension reforms), and various measures were taken to increase public revenues (tax increases, privatization of state owned corporations and so on).

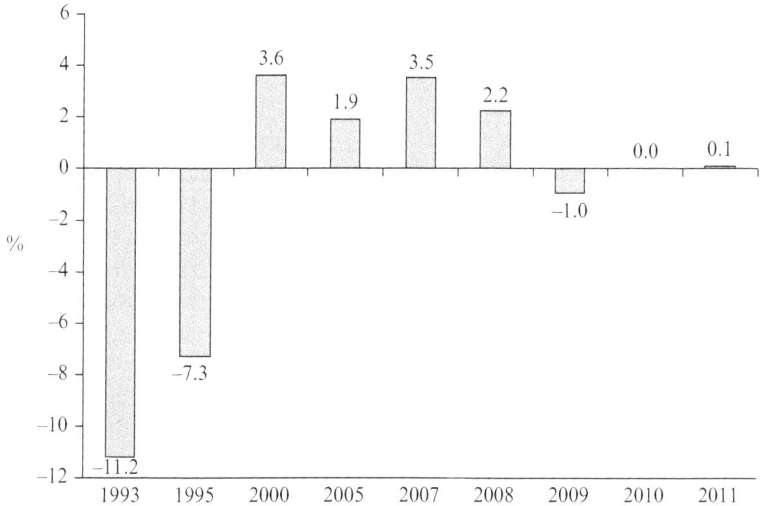

Source: NIER (2012).

Figure 14.3b Development of budget deficit, net lending as a percentage of GDP, Sweden

Generally, since the mid-1990s, both fiscal and monetary policy have become more restrictive in Sweden, leading to a historically low rate of inflation and significant improvement of public finances (see Figure 14.3b) and declining public debt. A fiscal policy framework has been gradually introduced to limit the budget deficit and improve the conditions for long-term fiscal policy sustainability. Since 2000, under the Budget Act the government must propose a net lending target (surplus target) for the general government sector. The overall principle is that the surplus target for net lending must amount to 1 per cent of GDP on average over a business cycle in accordance with the EU Stability and Growth Pact.

The reformulation of economic policy, the priority given to fighting inflation and the re-absorption of budgetary deficits also had a decisive impact on the emergence of new compromises with regard to wage formation (see Subsection 3.4). An important aspect of this development was also to re-establish the normative pace-setting role of the sector exposed to international competition, favouring wage adjustments in line with productivity development, reinforcing Sweden's competitiveness and export-led economic growth.

2.5 Impact of the Crisis on Public Finances

Due to healthier public finances at the start of the economic downturn in 2008, the room for manoeuvre for conducting a more expansionary macroeconomic policy was larger than during the previous recession, implying that the impact of the crisis on public employment has been limited and short-lived (see Anxo 2011). In connection with the 2008 crisis and expansionary fiscal policy, Swedish public finances have been somewhat weakened, even though from an international perspective the problems have been limited (see Figure 14.3b). Overall, the Swedish experience shows that strong public finances are essential to handle the challenges confronting fiscal policy, especially in a deep recession. Against this background and in light of the recent economic recovery the need for fiscal consolidation and excessive deficit procedure is limited, implying that the negative impact of restrictive fiscal policy on employment in the public sector has been and will be limited in Sweden compared to other EU member states. On the other hand, there is a risk that the above-mentioned long-term tendency towards a decline in public employment will be reinforced by the policy measures implemented by the current government. These measures, aimed at further opening up the public sector to competition, might have a detrimental effect on public employment in the future.

3. IMPACT OF PUBLIC SECTOR ADJUSTMENTS

3.1 Long-term Public Employment Trends

In 2010, private sector employment accounted for about 68 per cent and the public sector (central and local authorities) for the remaining 32 per cent of total employment in Sweden. In 1965, the corresponding shares were about 85 and 15 per cent, respectively. As shown by Figure 14.4 (upper panel), public employment increased continuously from the mid-1960s up to the early 1990s. During the same period the number of employees in local authorities increased significantly – by about 35 per cent – while the number of public employees at the central government level remained almost unchanged. To a considerable extent, the economy's good employment record during this period was clearly related to the creation of a modern welfare state, strong public involvement in the financing and provision of health care, social care and education and the related expansion of public employment. Obviously the development of public services also contributed to the strong expansion of female labour supply and the feminization of the labour force: the female participation rate

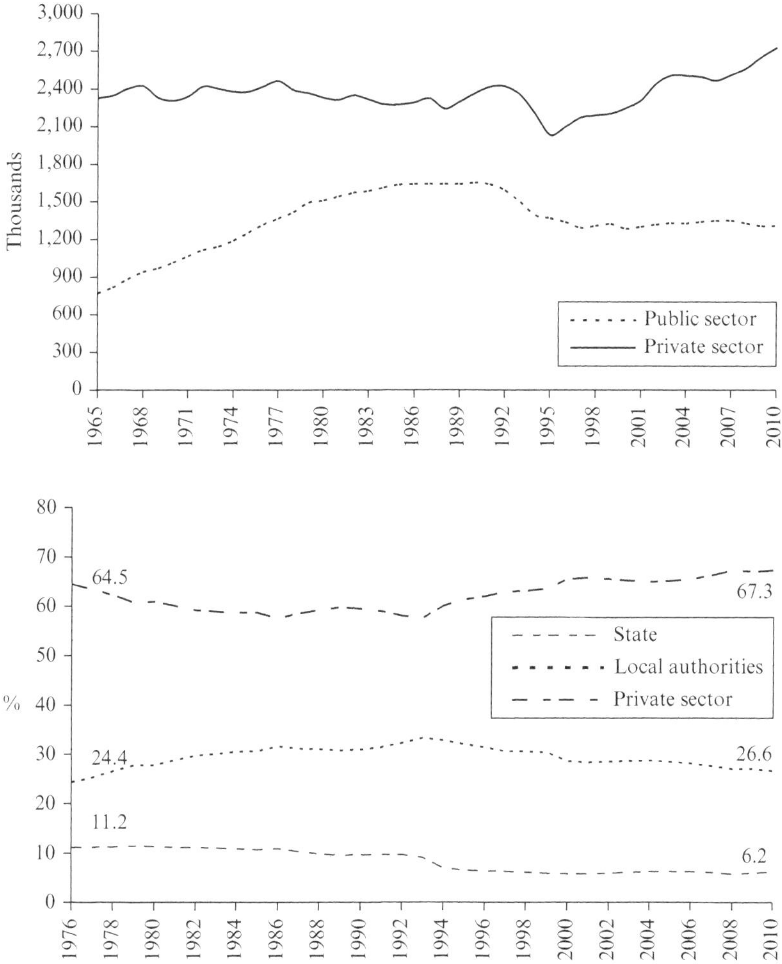

Source: Statistics Sweden (2011a).

Figure 14.4 *Employment trends in the public and private sectors, Sweden – upper panel 1965–2010, (in 1000); lower panel trends in employment share in the private sector, the state and local authorities, 1976–2010 (%)*

increased from about 67 per cent in the mid-1970s to about 78 per cent at the end of the 1980s.

In connection with the deep economic crisis in the early 1990s, however, the number of employees in both central government and local authorities fell sharply. The decline of employment in the public sector as a whole during the past decade – a reduction of 291,000 employees between 1991 and 2007 or 17.7 per cent – can be ascribed to the above-mentioned waves of liberalization/privatization, as well as rationalization and downsizing initiated in the aftermath of the deep economic crisis of the early 1990s. According to Statistics Sweden, in 2010 approximately 247,000 people were employed in the central government sector, corresponding to slightly more than 5 per cent of total employment. The municipalities and county councils jointly had more than one million employees or 24 per cent of the total number of employed persons in the country. At the same date, employment in public companies amounted to around 5 per cent of total employment.

3.2 Impact of the Crisis on Public Employment, 2008–2010

Sweden is a small, open economy, highly dependent on exports and very sensitive to variations in global demand. Sweden therefore exhibited some signs of a downturn already in early autumn 2008, with a significant decline in newly reported vacancies, while lay-off notices increased dramatically.

Despite the increased state support for local authorities in the wake of the recession, the reduction in tax revenue at the local level led to budget cuts that translated into a reduction of employment in the female-dominated public sector. The bulk of employment adjustment in the public sector was concentrated on employees with short-term contracts. Between 2007 and 2010 this share fell from 18.7 to 15.8 per cent in local authorities, from 16.5 to 15.8 per cent in the government sector and from 16.8 to 15.8 in the private sector (see Figure 14.5). Between 2008 and 2010 employment fell by 1.5 per cent in the private sector (41,800 employees) and 1.4 per cent in the public sector (19,200 employees). Almost all the reduction of public employment during the 2008–10 period can be ascribed to a reduction in the number of short-term contracts (around 95 per cent of the decline of public employment, the corresponding figure for the private sector being 37 per cent).

As far as gender is concerned, the relatively stronger impact of the crisis on male unemployment is related to the decline of employment in the male-dominated export-oriented manufacturing sector, but compared to the previous crisis (1993) the gender gap in unemployment has remained much lower this time due to the more rapid decline in public employment at the local and regional levels, despite the above-mentioned additional appropriations to local government by the central government. Globally, women account for 37 per cent of the decline in total employment (26 per

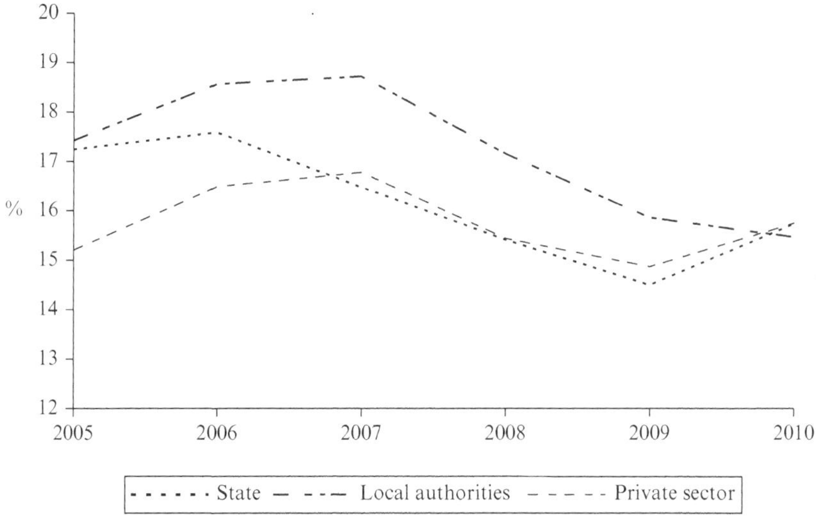

Source: Statistics Sweden (2011b).

Figure 14.5 Share of short-term contracts by sector, Sweden, 2005–2010

cent in the private sector and 98 per cent in the public sector). This result is obviously related to the strong labour market segregation by gender and also the fact that the crisis hit particularly activities and services provided by local authorities where women largely dominate. As also shown by Table 14.7, the decrease of employment in full-time equivalents (FTEs) has been lower than in headcount terms, implying that the reduction of employment in the public sector, in particular in the female-dominated local authorities, was primarily concentrated on part-time workers.

3.3 Impact of the Crisis on Working Conditions

Regarding the impact of the crisis on working conditions in the public sector, to our best knowledge, no study has been performed in Sweden due in particular to the lack of available data. An exception is the European Working Condition Survey (EWSC) conducted every five years since the 1990s by the European Foundation for the Improvement of Living and Working Conditions (Eurofound 2011). The EWCS's objective is to assess and quantify working conditions and to identify groups at risk, issues of concern and areas of progress by monitoring trends over time across European countries on a harmonized basis. In order to assess the impact of the crisis on working conditions in the Swedish public sector we used

Table 14.7 Variation of public employment, Sweden, 2008–2010 (all public employees and full-time equivalents, men and women, %)

	Men FTE	All male employees	Women FTE	All female employees	All employees	All FTE
State	–2.1	–2.2	3.8	3.6	0.7	0.8
Municipalities	–1.0	–0.5	–0.8	–1.8	–1.5	–0.9
County councils	–1.4	–2.1	–1.9	–3.2	–3.0	–1.8
Public sector	–1.4	–1.3	–0.5	–1.4	–1.4	–0.7

Source: Statistics Sweden (2011d).

the fourth and fifth EWSCs conducted, respectively, in 2005 and 2010. Our assessment is based on five dimensions: working time, work intensity, work satisfaction, work–life balance and incidence of training paid for by the employers. Tables 14.8 and 14.9 describe the evolution of these indicators between 2005 and 2010.

As shown by Table 14.8, weekly working time has slightly increased during the recession, in both the public and private sectors. Unfortunately, we cannot assess whether this increase was due to a lengthening of working time among the remaining employees or to a modification in the distribution of working time due to the fact that layoffs were concentrated on female employees with part-time contracts. There are reasons to believe that the lengthening of working time in the public sector is related to the decrease in the share of female part-timers and also to a reduction in absenteeism. The share of female part-timers in the public sector has actually declined during the past decade. As shown previously (Table 14.4) the decline of employment has also been concentrated on part-time workers. In other words, it seems that the recession did not imply a lengthening of working time for the remaining employees and that lengthening of working time is essentially due to a compositional effect. As shown by Table 14.8, work intensity declined between 2005 and 2010 in both the private and the public sector, the decline of work intensity being particularly marked among public male employees while remaining almost unchanged among female public employees. Furthermore, the extent of the work–life balance has hardly been affected by the recession. On the contrary, the share of respondents indicating that their working hours fit very well or well with their family or social commitments outside work has increased for both gender and sectors. Last but not least, the proportion of employees reporting that they were very satisfied or satisfied with their working conditions has increased during the period, irrespective of sector and gender.

Table 14.8 Weekly working time, work intensity, work satisfaction and work–life balance by gender and sectors, Sweden, 2005 and 2010 (dependent employees)

Sector	Weekly working time (hours/week)			Work intensity (0–1)			Work–life balance (%)			Work satisfaction (%)		
	M	W	All	M	W	All	M	W	All	M	W	All
Public sector 2005	39.2	35.5	36.8	0.48	0.53	0.51	84.0	75.7	79.0	85.7	78.7	81.2
Public sector 2010	39.2	36.9	37.6	0.40	0.52	0.48	92.9	86.2	88.0	91.3	84.8	86.8
Private sector 2005	40.8	34.8	38.8	0.52	0.54	0.53	82.4	81.3	82.2	87.5	86.6	87.2
Private sector 2010	41.0	36.5	39.3	0.51	0.51	0.51	85.0	88.1	86.0	89.1	87.6	88.5

Notes:
Questions: Working time: How many hours do you usually work per week in your main paid job? Work satisfaction: On the whole, are you very satisfied, satisfied, not very satisfied or not at all satisfied with working conditions in your main paid job? Share of workers that are satisfied and very satisfied.
Work–life balance: In general, do your working hours fit in with your family or social commitments outside work? Share of respondents answering well and very well.
Work intensity: Composite aggregate index (work speed and pace, tight deadlines etc.), ranging between 0 and 1.

Source: EWCS 4th and 5th waves, author's calculations based on Eurofound (2011).

Obviously, these results have to be interpreted with care since the crisis has hit in particular low-skilled and low-educated workers, as well as individuals with a weaker attachment to the labour market (fixed-term contracts and part-time workers). In other words, we cannot exclude that the absence of impact on working conditions is due to such compositional effects.

As shown by Table 14.9 the share of employees who have undergone both training and on-the-job training (OJT) paid for by the employer during the past 12 months is significantly higher in the public sector. Regarding gender disparities, the share of female employees undergoing training or OJT is higher. The incidence of training and OJT among employees in the public sector has, however, slightly decreased between 2005 and 2010, the converse being true in the private sector. The same tendencies are found regarding OJT, a slight decline in the public sector

Table 14.9 Incidence of paid or on-the-job training among dependent employees by gender and sector, Sweden, 2005 and 2010 (%)

Sector	Training paid for by the employer (%)			On-the-job training (%)		
	Men	Women	All	Men	Women	All
Public sector 2005	59.0	62.3	61.1	59.1	56.4	57.3
Public sector 2010	55.6	57.8	57.1	49.2	56.9	54.7
Private sector 2005	46.0	43.9	45.2	46.1	41.2	44.4
Private sector 2010	49.4	45.6	47.9	45.0	48.2	46.2

Notes: Questions: Paid Training: Over the last 12 months have you undergone training paid for or provided by your employer? On-the-job training: Over the last 12 months have you undergone on-the-job training?

Source: EWCS, 4th and 5th waves and own calculations, Eurofound (2011).

and an increase in the private. One tentative explanation of the contrasted impact of the crisis on training across sectors is that private firms to a larger extent than public organizations have used training in combination with various forms of short-time working or work sharing to keep employees at the company (labour hoarding).

3.4 Wage Formation in the Public Sector: Decentralization and Individualization

3.4.1 Main features and development of the wage formation and bargaining systems

In order to understand the major developments and features of the wage formation system in general and in the public sector in particular, it is necessary to take a historical perspective that stretches beyond recent years. From 1955 to 1983, the wage formation process was based on a highly centralized and coordinated bargaining system and the application of a wage norm, the so-called 'solidarity wage policy' based on fairness (equal pay for equal work irrespective of sector, firm profitability and individual performance) and efficiency (that is, a policy that fostered rationalization at the company level and promoted productivity-enhancing structural changes through the closure of unproductive plants). In 1983, Sweden experienced a breakdown of two decades of centralized and coordinated bargaining and national inter-industry agreements: from this date, collective bargaining was carried out at two levels: industry/sector and enterprise/organization.

Table 14.10 Average annual wage growth by sector, Sweden, 2005–2010 (corrected for compositional effects)

Sector	Average wage growth 2005–2010
Private sector	
Blue collar	3.4
White collar	3.3
Municipalities	3.4
County councils	3.4
State (central government)	3.6

Source: Mediation Office (2011a).

The erosion of the Swedish model of industrial relations, particularly the weakening of mechanisms for coordinating collective bargaining and the resurgence of industrial disputes during the 1980s (see Figure 14.7), high wage inflation and the explosion of unemployment during the dramatic recession of the early 1990s had a decisive impact on the emergence of new compromises on wage formation. These new compromises in both the private and public sectors implied a clear tendency to re-coordinate the wage formation system at the industry and sector levels.

In short, the spirit of these new agreements, still in force today, was to ensure industrial peace and promote more consensual industrial relations. These changes in industrial relations also re-established the pace-setting role of the sector exposed to international competition. In other words, and in contrast to the mid-1970s, public sector wages since the second half of the 1990s do not have any effects as signal setters on private sector wages. Against this background and correcting for structural effects, such as the change in the age, gender, skill and occupational composition of the labour force, Sweden during the past decade has experienced a clear convergence of wage growth across sectors (see Table 14.10).

3.4.2 Decentralization and individualization of wage formation, impact on wage dispersion and inequalities

In addition to the establishment of new procedural rules aimed at ensuring industrial peace and a re-coordination of wage bargaining at the industry sector level, since the second half of the 1990s we have also witnessed a clear tendency towards the individualization and decentralization of wage setting at the local level, in both the private and public sectors. In other words, the above-mentioned tendency to re-coordinate collective bargaining at the industry level should not be seen as a weakening of the role played by enterprise/organization-level negotiations. Wage negotiations at the local level play a central and growing role in the setting of wages, as well as in the terms and conditions of employment. In fact, enterprise/organization-level bargaining has tended to gather strength in the past decade, particularly in the public sector. The wages of a large majority of public sector employees are now set locally and largely individualized through performance monitoring, in strong contrast to the previous wage scale system based on seniority that was dominant up to the mid-1990s. The acceptance of a more individualized type of wage formation based on individual skills and performance/productivity rather than on job characteristics, as had been the case in the past with the application of the *solidaristic* wage policy, testifies to societal changes regarding wage norms and norms of fairness, among both private and public employees and their representatives.

In the central government sector (state), all agreements are currently concluded without any individual guarantees and 38 per cent of them do not include any stipulated wage increase at the central level, implying that for these bargaining areas, the wage increase is fully determined at the local/organizational level. This kind of agreement is less common at the municipality level (5 per cent of all collective agreements), the dominant wage-setting procedure being a stipulated wage increase at the central level with some individual guarantees (in 40 per cent of cases) or no individual guarantee (54 per cent). Compared to the private sector, the tendency to a decentralization and individualization of wages appears to be even more pronounced in the public sector. It should be noted, however, that the prevalence of fully individualized/performance wage formation without individual guarantee in the public sector remains higher among high-skilled/high-educated public employees than among low-skilled/low-educated public employees. To illustrate: at the local authority level, (municipalities and county councils) one major collective agreement between the Municipal Workers' Union[6] and the Association of Local Authorities covering occupations such as assistant and auxiliary nurses, home-care workers, cleaners, childcare assistants and so on includes both a wage increase at industry level and some individual wage guarantees at the local level.

The marked tendency towards decentralization, differentiation and individualization of wages and terms and conditions of employment coincides with a wider dispersion of the wage distribution (see Figure 14.6).

The increase of wage dispersion has been particularly marked for white-collar employees within both the public (state and county councils) and private sectors. As also shown by Figure 14.6, wage dispersion at the municipality level during the past decade has been almost unchanged. Part of this stability in wage dispersion might be ascribed to the above-

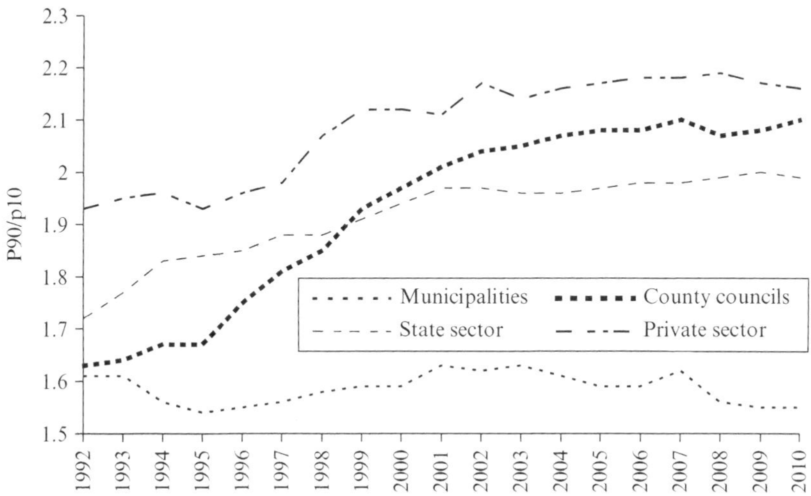

Source: Mediation Office (2011b).

Figure 14.6 Development of wage dispersion (p90/p10) in the private, state and local authority municipalities and county councils, Sweden, 1992–2010

mentioned more limited individualization in wage formation among blue-collar and low-skilled/low-educated workers in the municipal sector.

Between 1996 and 2009 the increase of wage inequality was higher for women than for men, except for blue-collar workers in the private sector. The increase in wage inequality among women was particularly marked among white-collar employees in the private sector (an increase of almost 21 per cent) but also in the state sector (+15 per cent). Part of the increase in female wage dispersion might be ascribed to a compositional effect, that is, the increase of the share of females working in the private sector (in particular, in white-collar jobs) and also to the tendency towards the individualization of wage setting, in particular in the female-dominated public sector, implying greater wage differentiation.

It should be remembered, however, that in contrast with other countries with highly decentralized and individualized bargaining systems, such as the United Kingdom, strong and powerful trade union organizations and high union density[7] at company/organization level in Sweden lead to the implementation of negotiated forms of wage individualization and differentiation. There are strong reasons to believe that the individualization and differentiation of wages will continue, that collective and undifferentiated ways of setting wages are being gradually abandoned and that individualized types of wage formation are being generalized across the whole Swedish labour market.

3.4.3 Impact of the current crisis on wage developments and industrial relations

The significant changes in the orientation of monetary policy, namely the complete autonomy of the Swedish Central Bank and the introduction of a clear inflation target (2 per cent per year, within a range of plus or minus 1 per cent) in the mid-1990s, in connection with the above-mentioned re-coordination, mechanisms in wage setting have without doubt had an impact on wage formation and wage developments. The social partners in both the private and public sectors were aware that wage developments not compatible with productivity growth and macroeconomic balance would not, as previously, be accommodated with devaluations but lead to the implementation of a restrictive monetary policy (interest rate increase) with a potential negative impact on employment and unemployment. We may argue that this reorientation of macroeconomic policy has played a crucial role in wage development as a discipline device against excessive wage increases and wage inflation, and has actually led to wage moderation (but still real wage increases), rising employment and positive development in the current account.

The experience from the deep economic crisis of the early 1990s shows that wage moderation has characterized wage developments during the second half of the 1990s and early 2000s. There were therefore strong reasons to expect that, in the wake of the current severe economic and financial crisis, wage agreements would also be concluded to preserve employment stability and limit further increases in unemployment.

The moderate outcome in terms of negotiated pay settlements during the last rounds of collective bargaining (2009–10), coupled with the weak labour market, imply that wages rose moderately in both the private and public sectors during the past two years, with a declining differential across sectors at the end of the period. The crisis also had no direct impact on industrial relations and the 2008–10 period has been characterized by industrial peace, as shown by Figure 14.7, in contrast with the situation in the second half of the 1980s and also during the previous recession (1992–95).

According to short-term wage statistics from the Mediation Office (2011a), the rate of wage increases in 2009 and 2010 was 3.3 and 2.5 per cent, respectively, for the economy as a whole (see Figure 14.8) and were significantly below those recorded in 2008 in both the private and public sectors. In our view, these developments well illustrate the extent of Swedish negotiated wage flexibility during a recession, and the willingness

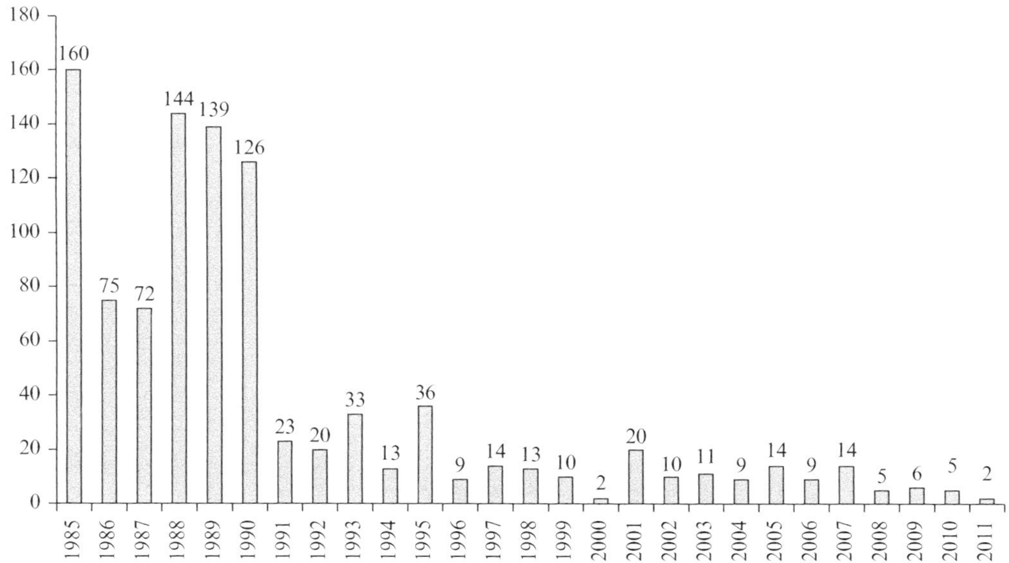

Source: Mediation Office (2011a).

Figure 14.7 Number of industrial conflicts, strikes and/or lockouts, Sweden, 1985–2011

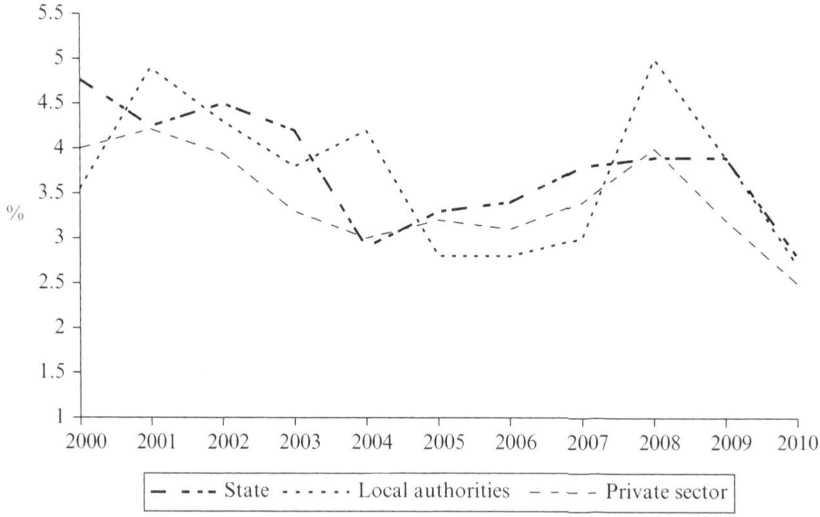

Source: Mediation Office (2011a).

Figure 14.8 Wage development by broad sectors, Sweden, 2000–2010

of the two sides of industry to share equally the burden of the crisis and limit the potential impact of the recession on employment, wage structure and inequality.

4. IMPACT OF THE CRISIS ON WORKING CONDITIONS: A CASE STUDY APPROACH

Relying on two case studies in the public sector, the main objective of this section is twofold: first, to assess the impact of the crisis on employment, wages and working conditions at the organization level and to identify the strategies used to cope with the economic downturn. Second, the selected case studies are aimed at illustrating the long-term developments in the public sector, in particular the tendency to increase competition through the outsourcing of public services, as well as the impact of the individualization of the wage and employment structure.

The two selected organizations belong to the state sector (a local public employment agency) and the municipal sector (an elderly care unit). Both organizations are located in the southern part of Sweden (Småland, city of Växjö). The choice of a local public employment service was motivated by the potential impact on caseworkers' working conditions of the increase in unemployed job seekers during the crisis. This choice was also motivated by the central stabilizing role of Sweden's active labour market policy during the recession. The choice of elderly care, in particular home care, was guided primarily by the fact that this sector underwent significant transformations implying an increasing share of for-profit private providers, increased contracting out through public procurement and privatization of some public residential elderly care. In each organization visited, semi-directed interviews were conducted with both employer and employee representatives (trade unions).[8]

4.1 Case Study 1: Home-care Reforms and their Implications – Växjö Municipality

4.1.1 Municipalities' move towards private service providers

The home-care system for elderly persons over the past decade has experienced major organizational changes regarding both the provision of services, with the expansion of private for-profit providers, and changes in work organization (rationalization of tasks). A growing share of municipalities gave up the previous system of direct administrative control of service provision and introduced a purchaser/provider system. It should be noted, however, that decisions about eligibility and the amount of care granted remain the responsibilities of local authorities. The introduction of the Act on System of Choice in the Public Sector (see Subsection 2.3, above) in 2009 implies that once the care need has been established and granted by the local authority, senior citizens may choose between public and private home-care providers or residential care. In other words, actual care services are provided by either municipal employees or independent organizations (for-profit companies) on the basis of contractual agreements. During the past decade there has been a clear tendency to reduce the number of senior citizens in residential care and a corresponding increase in home-care services. While the reallocation of resources might be partly ascribed to changes in individual preferences for being cared for at home, this development also responds to cost-minimizing considerations, the cost of home-care services being much lower than residential care. Between 2000 and 2009, the cost of elderly care fell by around 6 per cent, while the number of beneficiaries remained almost unchanged. During the past decade the share of elderly-care hours provided by private companies has increased continuously (from 7 per cent in 2000 to 19 per cent in 2009, see Hartman 2011). In 2010, the share of elderly-care employees in private companies amounted to 10.4 per cent (5.4 per cent in home-care services and 15.8 per cent in residential care).

4.1.2 A poor working environment

Regarding the development of working conditions the elderly-care sector is characterized by a relatively high share of low-skilled/low-paid workers (auxiliary and assistant nurses) and poor working environment with a high incidence of occupational diseases. The elderly-care sector has among the highest rates of sickness absenteeism. The Municipal Workers' Union (Kommunal 2009) conducted a survey among its members in elderly care in 2008 to assess the development of working conditions in this sector.[9] The questionnaire covered, among other things, issues such as trends in working time, wages and work environment. Generally, the results of the survey show a high degree of dissatisfaction despite the fact that a large majority of the elderly-care employees/auxiliary nurses were proud of their job (92 per cent of respondents). Around 49 per cent said that they could not influence their working time, 48 per cent declared that they did not earn a living wage, 45 per cent believed that they would not be able to work until retirement, 37 per cent said that they were not allowed to work full-time and 27 per cent did not consider the working conditions as 'safe/ secure'.

If the results of the survey reveal a relatively high degree of dissatisfaction regarding working conditions among auxiliary nurses in the elderly-care sector in general, one cannot infer that working conditions have deteriorated during the recession. In order to determine whether this is the case we now turn to the results of our case study.

4.1.3 Reform experience in Växjö municipality

During the past three years Växjö municipality has experienced an increase in the privatization and outsourcing of elderly care (both residential and home-care services) to private suppliers. The main motives among local politicians for increasing outsourcing and contracting out to private providers are the expected enhanced freedom of choice for senior citizens as well as the potential beneficial impact of increased competition on economic efficiency. Elected local politicians establish the selection criteria for the choice of private actors during the procurement process. In Växjö, the selection criteria of private providers are based solely on the quality of the service provided and not on price competition. The municipally conducts follow-up and evaluation studies each year to check whether these quality requirements are being respected. Currently, private for-profit companies provide around 30 per cent of residential and home-care services,[10] the remainder being provided by the municipality. In 2010, around 1,200 employees worked in the municipal elderly-care sector (1,100 auxiliary nurses and 100 nurses).

4.1.4 Age, gender and educational composition of the labour force

Regarding the age and gender composition of the labour force, a large majority of care personnel are women (90 per cent) and there is a tendency towards workforce ageing which, according to the interviewees, might create recruitment difficulties in the future. The average level of educational attainment is relatively low, since the majority of employees in home-care services are auxiliary nurses with at most secondary education. Wages are set locally, individualized and performance related, with no seniority premium. The criteria guiding the individualization and differentiation of wages have been negotiated with the trade unions. The wage among municipal auxiliary nurses ranges between SEK 18,100[11] (wage at entry) and SEK 24,500. Compared to the municipal sector, the wage level in the private sector is slightly higher among auxiliary nurses and nurses.

4.1.5 Budgetary constraints during the early phase of the crisis: implications for employment and work organization

According to the head of the elderly-care unit, in the early phase of the crisis (2008–09), due to budget constraints related to the reduction of tax revenue, the administrative department of the elderly-care unit was restructured, implying a slight decline in the number of employees (natural attrition, early retirement with no replacement). The number of municipal home-care employees has decreased during the past five years but mainly due to expansion of private providers. While it is difficult to accurately assess the employment trend for the whole elderly-care sector, the fact that personnel intensity (number of personnel per patient) is on average lower among private providers indicates that total employment might have decreased during the past three years. According to the trade union representatives interviewed as well as the head of the elderly-care unit in Växjö municipality, the increased outsourcing of home-care services to private actors was not used as a downsizing device during the crisis, but rather reflects a propensity among local politicians to expand the share of private providers and increase competition. According to both the employers and trade union representatives interviewed, the impact of the crisis on employment in the home-care sector has been limited. The main adjustment during the recession concerns wage development, the last bargaining round being characterized by wage moderation. While on average the collective agreement for auxiliary and assistant nurses concluded in 2007 – in other words, before the crisis – gave a nominal annual wage increase of around 4.2 per cent, the collective agreement signed in the aftermath of the crisis (2010–11) gave 2.2 per cent.[12] Obviously, the trade unions at the local and national levels accepted a lower wage increase in order to limit the potential negative impact of decreasing tax revenue on the employment level. But it should be stressed that the wage adjustment implies a reduction of the wage increase and not a wage freeze or wage cuts, as in other member states.

Regarding working conditions, both the trade union and employer representatives declared that the impact of the crisis has been limited. The length of working time and the volume of overtime have remained unchanged during the recession. It should be noted, however, that faced by budget constraints (diminishing tax revenues), some modifications in work organization have been introduced. According to the head of the unit, some work tasks have been rationalized and the work schedule compressed/tightened (reduction of breaks and pauses) in order to increase productivity and reduce costs. We cannot therefore exclude the possibility that work intensity increased slightly in 2008–09, especially among auxiliary nurses in the home-care sector.

4.2 Case Study 2: Local Public Employment Agency – Växjö

In order to cope with rising unemployment, the government decided in 2009 to increase the resources for active labour market policy (ALMP). The volume of participants in the various ALMP programmes was gradually increased, but compared to the previous economic downturns, the government focused more on labour supply-oriented measures, such as job matching, job search assistance, coaching and work experience schemes. In order to implement this policy, appropriation and funding were increased to local public employment agencies. In other words the reorientation of ALMP and the stronger emphasis on matching and supply-oriented measures implied a greater role for local public employment agencies.

As already mentioned, the choice of a public employment service located at Växjö in Småland was motivated by the potential impact on caseworkers' working conditions of the significant increase of unemployed job seekers in the Småland region during the crisis. Actually, the region has an industry structure characterized by medium–large export-oriented companies that were particularly hit during the recession. The development of employment at the Växjö employment agency well illustrates adjustment patterns during the crisis, reflecting the crucial stabilizing role of ALMP. The increase of resources allocated by the government implied that the number of caseworkers increased from 69 employees in January 2008 to 106 in January 2011 (112 case workers in January 2012). Compared to the home-care sector, the level of educational attainment among caseworkers is higher (requirement of at least tertiary education) and the gender distribution more even (60 per cent of female workers), but in recent years there has been a tendency towards increased feminization of the workforce. Currently, there are no employees on fixed-term contracts. Wage setting is completely individualized and based on individual performance, the criteria for wage differentiation being, as in the case of elderly care, negotiated between the employer and trade unions.

According to both the employer and trade union representatives interviewed, the crisis has not adversely affected working conditions, with regard to either workload or work intensity. The increase in the number of caseworkers during the recession, as well as the outsourcing of search and coaching activities to private actors made it possible to stabilize the number of job seekers per caseworker and stabilize the workload. Working time and the volume of overtime were not affected by the crisis. As in the care sector, the main adjustment concerned wage moderation during the last round of negotiations. Looking at the two collective agreements before and after the crisis, the annual nominal wage increase was around 2.4 per cent for 2007–09 and 1.8 per cent for 2010–12.

5. CONCLUDING REMARKS AND POLICY ISSUES

Over the past two decades, Sweden has undergone major structural and institutional changes, which explain its relatively good post-crisis performance. Both fiscal and monetary policy since the mid-1990s have become more restrictive, leading to a historically low rate of inflation, significant improvements in public finances and declining public debt. A fiscal policy framework has been gradually introduced to limit the budget deficit and improve the conditions for long-term fiscal policy sustainability. The reformulation of economic policy, the priority given to fighting inflation and the reabsorption of budget deficits also had a decisive impact on the emergence of new compromises in wage formation. Another significant aspect of this development was the re-establishment of the normative pace-setting role of the sector exposed to international competition, favouring wage adjustments in line with productivity development, reinforcing Swedish competitiveness and export-led economic growth. Confronted by the severe deterioration in the labour market and in order to mitigate the impact of the crisis on income development and employment, in 2008–10 the government implemented a package of recovery and countercyclical measures, ranging from expansionary fiscal and monetary policy to active labour market and educational policy. Due to early fiscal consolidation and therefore healthier public finances at the start of the economic downturn, the room for manoeuvre for a more expansionary macroeconomic policy was greater than during the previous recession in the early 1990s. Overall, the Swedish experience shows that strong public finances are essential to handle the challenges confronting fiscal policy, especially in a deep recession. Public finances have been somewhat weakened, even though from an international perspective the deficits have been limited. Against this background the need for further fiscal consolidation and excessive deficit procedure is limited, implying that the negative impact of restrictive fiscal policy on employment in the public sector has been modest in Sweden compared to other EU member states. In order to preserve employment stability and limit further increases in unemployment, wage moderation has also characterized recent rounds of collective bargaining (2009–10). The resulting slowdown in the rate of increase in labour costs helped to alleviate the negative effects of the recession on output and employment. The decline of public sector employment has been overwhelmingly concentrated on employees with fixed-term contracts. At the end of 2010, employment in the public sector reached more or less the same level as in the mid-2000s. The bulk of the adjustment in the public sector took the form of wage moderation, with the public sector following the same wage development as the private sector.

An analysis of the last two waves of the EWCS conducted by Eurofound in 2005 and 2010 did not reveal a significant deterioration of working conditions in the Swedish public sector in the aftermath of the recession. Working time was barely affected, work intensity remained almost unchanged and work satisfaction and work–life balance opportunities seem to have increased during the period. The only noticeable negative effect was the slight decline of the share of employees in training paid for by employers, which by international standards remains among the highest among EU member states.

The two case studies, one in a public local employment agency the other in the municipal elderly-care sector, confirm the adjustment patterns described above and the virtual absence of a negative impact of the crisis on working conditions in the public sector. The volume of employment in the two selected organizations was hardly affected by the crisis. In order to cope with the increased number of job seekers as a result of the recession, the local public employment agency received extra funding. The increase in the number of unemployed job-seekers and also the reorientation of ALMP towards matching measures and a resource boost made it possible to increase the number of caseworkers. According to both employer and trade union representatives, the crisis did not adversely affect working conditions, with regard to either workload or work intensity. The only impact of the crisis was some wage moderation during recent bargaining rounds. The same tendencies could be identified in the home-care sector in the selected municipality. If we except a minor reorganization in the administrative division of the elderly-care unit, due to the downward pressures on local government expenditure at the beginning of the recession, employment has not been affected by the crisis. Working conditions among elderly-care personnel (nurses, auxiliary nurses) were slightly affected at the beginning of the recession through rationalization, which might have increased work intensity. On the other hand, the outsourcing of activities to private providers has not been used as an instrument for downsizing but in response to a long-term trend towards increasing privatization and the outsourcing of elderly-care activities. As for the public local employment agency, the main adjustment took the form of wage moderation.

The Swedish experience shows clearly that healthy public finances and the possibility of conducting an expansionary macroeconomic policy are not only a prerequisite for mitigating and absorbing the negative impact of external macroeconomic shocks but also a good instrument for limiting the negative impact of a recession on the provision of welfare and public services. The specific features of the industrial relations system, characterized by a relative balance of power between the two sides of industry, also helps to explain why the cost of the crisis has been more evenly distributed between different socioeconomic groups. The specificity of the institutional set-up also explains why Sweden still has one of the highest levels of job quality and why the current recession has not adversely affected working conditions by means of wage cuts, longer working hours, higher workloads and increased work intensity, as it has in other EU member states.

NOTES

1. For example, the Tax Agency, the Customs Service, the Public Employment Service, government offices, the Social Insurance Agency and more than 150 other agencies.
2. For example, the Road, Rail, Civil Aviation and Maritime administrations.
3. According to national accounts and Swedish employment statistics, publicly owned companies along with the market-oriented activities that municipalities conduct are not included in the public sector. The main criteria for classification are the company's main activity (for-profit market activities) and legal form (limited companies), not ownership. Government- or municipality-owned for-profit companies are therefore not included in the public but in the private sector (SAGE 2011).
4. In 2009, the share of the public sector's value added (state and local authorities) amounted to 18 per cent (4 per cent for the state sector and 14 per cent for local authorities). At the same date public expenditures and revenues amounted to, respectively, 53 and 52 per cent of GDP.
5. The Law on Public Procurement (LOU (2007) Lagen om offentlig upphandling 2007: 1091) adopted in 2007 is based largely on the EU directive on public procurement (2004/18/EC). According to the law, the contracting authority – in other words, central and local authorities – has to treat suppliers in an equal and non-discriminatory manner.

6. The Swedish Municipal Workers' Union (*Kommunal*) is affiliated to the Swedish Trade Union Confederation LO. With around 510,000 members it is the largest union within LO.
7. Despite the recent decline, average union density in Sweden is above 70 per cent (85 per cent in the public sector), while the coverage rate of collective agreements is around 90 per cent in the private sector and 100 per cent in the public sector. It should also be noted that there is far less wage inequality in Sweden than in the United States and the United Kingdom.
8. In the local Public Employment Agency, from the employer's side, the director of the agency and the head of one unit with long experience with placements were interviewed. For the employees, two trade union representatives were interviewed. For the elderly-care unit in Växjö municipality, the head of the unit and three trade union representatives organizing the main employee groups in the sector – administration, auxiliary nurses and nurses – were interviewed.
9. The Municipal Workers' Union (Kommunal) is affiliated to the Trade Union Confederation LO. With around 510,000 members it is the largest union in LO. The survey response rate was 79.5 per cent (871 individuals).
10. Large capital venture multinational companies such as Attendo Care and Carema Care. These two companies account for 50 per cent of the market in Sweden.
11. 1 SEK = €0.11.
12. The rate of inflation was on average 1.4 per cent in 2007–09 and 1.7 per cent during 2010–11.

REFERENCES

Anxo, D. (2011), 'Negotiated flexibility in Sweden: a more egalitarian response to the crisis?', in D. Vaughan-Whitehead (ed.), *Work Inequalities in the Crisis: Evidence from Europe*, Cheltenham, UK and Northampton, MA, USA: Edward Elgar, pp. 445–76.

Ekberg, J. and L. Holmlund (2010), *Vad Säger den Officiella Lönestatistiken om Löneskillnaden Mellan Kvinnor och Män 2009?* (Wage Differential between Women and Men in 2009), Stockholm: Swedish Mediation Office.

Eurofound (2011), *Fourth and Fifth European Working Conditions Survey*, Luxembourg: European Foundation for the Improvement of Living and Working Conditions.

Hartman, L. (ed.) (2011), *Konkurrens Konsekvenser* (Consequences of Competition), Stockholm: SNS förlag.

Kommunal (2009), *Quality of Work and Services: Survey Kommunal – The Situation of the Elderly and Staff in Elderly Care*, Stockholm.

Mediation Office (2011a), *Wage Statistics*, various years, Stockholm. Available at: http://www.mi.se/ (accessed January 2012).

Mediation Office (2011b), *Avtalrörelsen och Lönebildning 2010* (Collective Bargaining Rounds and Wage Formation 2010), Stockholm. Available at: http://www.mi.se/inenglish/menu_eng_annualreport.html (accessed January 2012).

Mediation Office (2011c), *Vad Säger den Officiella Lönestatistiken om Löneskillnaden Mellan Kvinnor och män 2010?* (Gender Wage Gap, what can we Learn from Official Statistics in 2010?), Stockholm.

Mediation Office (2011d), *Röster om Lönebildning och Medling?* (Voices about Wage Setting and Mediation), Stockholm.

National Institute of Economic Research (NIER) (2012a), *Wage Formation in Sweden, Summary 2011*, Konjunkturinstitutet, Stockholm. Available at: http://www.konj.se/280.html (accessed January 2012).

SAGE (2011), 'Facts and figures about the Swedish central government sector 2008', Swedish Agency for Government Employers (SAGE), Arbetsgivarverket, Stockholm.

SALAR (2011), Economic Report (Swedish Association of Local Authorities and Regions (SKL)). Available at: http://english.skl.se/publications_and_reports (accessed January 2012).

Statistics Sweden (2011a), *Labour Force Survey*, various years, Stockholm. Available at: http://www.scb.se/Pages/Product_23262.aspx (accessed January 2012).

Statistics Sweden (2011b), National Accounts. Available at: http://www.scb.se/Pages/SubjectArea_10978.aspx (accessed January 2012).

Statistics Sweden (2011c), *Offentlig Ekonomi 2011* (Public Finances 2011). Available at: http://www.scb.se/Pages/PublishingCalendarViewInfo_259923.aspx?publobjid=15306 (accessed January 2012).

Statistics Sweden (2011d), 'Registerbaserad arbetsmarknadsstatistik (RAMS)'. Available at: http://www.scb.se/Pages/Product_7892.aspx (accessed January 2012).

Statistics Sweden (2011e), 'Financiers and providers within education, health-care and social services, 2009', Statistika meddelanden, SM_OE29SM1201, Stockholm.

15. Austerity, privatization and levelling down: Public sector reforms in the United Kingdom

Damian Grimshaw

1. INTRODUCTION

The United Kingdom is witnessing a prolonged economic depression. The level of GDP during the first quarter of 2012 was still 4 per cent lower than the pre-recession peak recorded in early 2008[1] and it is expected that the period of recovery will be the longest of any crisis since the end of the First World War (NIESR 2011). Policy reforms designed to encourage a recovery of the economy came in the wake of the financial crash of 2008–09, but were in fact steered away from attempts at reforming the evident failures in the UK's neoliberal model of finance-led capitalism; a wide-ranging government review of banking ('Project Merlin') concluded by supporting the status quo, arguing against a re-regulation of the industry and rejecting a tax on banks or on bonuses (King et al. 2012). Instead, in a context of an escalating sovereign debt crisis in Europe, a newly elected Conservative-led coalition government is arguing that economic recovery depends upon a radical reform of the state's role in delivering public services in order both to reduce the structural deficit and to open up new opportunities for private sector investment and job growth. Both claims are hotly contested. As in other European countries, attempts at fiscal consolidation are backfiring: economic growth has stalled in the six quarters since the new government came to power; levels of employment and hours worked fell during 2011 (after a modest recovery in 2010); businesses report a sustained pessimistic outlook; and unemployment among men and women has increased further to new highs.

The current public sector reforms have three characteristics: they impose a downwards quantitative adjustment in activity, involve transferring activity to the private sector and in several areas entail the ending of services provision. This chapter examines these characteristics (Section 3) and explores their consequences for employment, pay and pensions

(Section 4). In addition, two case studies (Section 5) are presented that examine the consequences of, and new tensions arising from (i) privatization of welfare-to-work services and (ii) downsizing of local government. Section 6 concludes. We begin with a critical assessment of the economic and political factors driving current reforms to shrink the state.

2. SHRINKING THE STATE: AUSTERITY CRISIS AND NEOLIBERAL IDEOLOGY

The programme of fiscal consolidation introduced in 2010 in the UK is underpinned by two interlinked visions – mainstream economic theory about the role of government budget deficits and right-wing political ideology about the appropriate role of the state in the economy. We begin by assessing the merits of these visions.

2.1 A Flawed Economic Vision

The economic argument is that unless radical fiscal consolidation is applied, the UK will witness rising interest rates on government bonds leading to larger debt, rises in interest rates and falling business confidence which in turn will crowd out private sector investment and raise the risk of a default on debt payments. Government ministers have regularly played on doomsday scenarios of the responses of credit rating agencies to justify their belief that 'there is no alternative' to fast fiscal consolidation. Until late 2011 the British public and the popular media largely supported this view, but opinions turned during 2012. The spending cuts announced in the 2010 budget set a target to balance the 'structural budget' over a six-year period – to reduce 'cyclically adjusted net borrowing' from 8.7 per cent of GDP in 2009–10 to 0.3 per cent in 2015–16 (HM Treasury 2010). Then in late 2011, the government extended the period of spending cuts by a further two years, which provided fiscal balance for a controversial decision in March 2012 to cut the top rate of tax from 50 to 45 per cent. The government has remained rigid in its approach. It argued prematurely in August 2010 that thanks to its deficit reduction plan, 'The much-needed rebalancing of our indebted economy – away from government and towards the private sector, away from consumption and towards business demand, away from imports and towards exports – is beginning' (George Osborne, August 2010).[2]

The government's economic approach is questionable on several fronts. First, it goes too far, too fast. Although the government has counted the OECD among its supporters,[3] a closer reading of OECD analyses indicates its nuanced position. In its *Economic Outlook*, the OECD identified the UK as in a potentially risky position, at the head of a sample of 12 countries with front-loaded consolidation involving the largest adjustment in spending; it argues, 'Fast consolidation has the advantage that it may reduce the overall scale of required consolidation and reassure financial markets, but it also increases the risk of adversely affecting the recovery particularly if monetary policy is constrained' (2011c: 227 and table 4.5). Furthermore, it recognizes the problem of an assumed one-way causation – that debt is necessarily the driver of slower growth rather than the other way.[4] The position of the UK government is also questioned by an IMF report (IMF 2010) which rejects the hypothesis that spending cuts are expansionary in a context of low interest rates; it states that, 'a budget cut equal to 1 per cent of GDP typically reduces domestic demand by about 1 per cent and raises the unemployment rate by 0.3 percentage points' (cited in Fontana and Sawyer 2011: 48).

Second, government estimations about the structural budget deficit rely on imprecisely justified estimates of the gap between potential and actual output. In a detailed analysis, the macroeconomist, Malcolm Sawyer (2012), shows that the Coalition government has reduced its estimate of the UK's potential output by around 6 per cent by cutting expected capital investment and assuming a higher level of 'natural unemployment'. However, Sawyer argues that it makes no sense to use a decline in the potential output of the private sector to motivate 'the knee-jerk reaction' of public spending cuts. To do so ignores the damaging impact of reduced government spending and investment on productive activity. Spending cuts will massively reduce public sector output, he argues, thereby 'compounding the losses of productive activity' (p. 215).

Third, fiscal consolidation has failed in the short to medium term and there are serious questions regarding medium-to-long-term prospects. Forecasts of GDP growth have been significantly curtailed in response to the unexpected downturn at the end of 2010 and stalled growth in 2011/early 2012. The June 2010 pre-budget forecast issued by the independent Office for Budget Responsibility (OBR) centred on estimates of GDP growth of 2.6 per cent (2011) and 2.8 per cent (2012). Within 18 months, however, by November 2011 the revised estimates were 0.9 per cent (2011) and 0.7 per cent (2012). Unemployment figures were also revised, from a forecast falling unemployment rate of 7.9 per cent in 2011 and 7.4 per cent in 2012 to a forecast rise from 8.1 per cent to 8.7 per cent (Table 15.1). In fact, the ongoing depression (the period when GDP remains below its pre-recession peak) has already exceeded in duration that experienced during the 1930–34 depression (Myers 2012). Moreover, consecutive falls in the last quarter of 2011 and first quarter of 2012 caused a double-dip

Table 15.1 Changes in official forecasts of GDP growth, employment and unemployment, UK, 2010–2013 (%)

	Percentage change in GDP				Employment, millions (unemployment rate, %)			
	2010	2011	2012	2013	2010	2011	2012	2013
Pre-budget June 2010	1.3	2.6	2.8	2.8	28.8 (8.1%)	29.0 (7.9%)	29.3 (7.4%)	29.6 (6.8%)
June 2010	1.2	2.3	2.8	2.9	28.8 (8.1%)	28.9 (8.0%)	29.2 (7.6%)	29.5 (7.0%)
Nov. 2010	1.8	2.1	2.6	2.9	29.0 (7.9%)	29.1 (8.0%)	29.3 (7.7%)	29.6 (7.2%)
March 2011	1.3	1.7	2.5	2.9	29.0 (7.9%)	29.0 (8.2%)	29.2 (8.1%)	29.5 (7.6%)
Nov. 2011	1.8	0.9	0.7	2.1	29.0 (7.9%)	29.2 (8.1%)	29.1 (8.7%)	29.2 (8.6%)

Source: 'Economic and fiscal outlook' reports of the Office for Budget Responsibility, various years, http://budgetresponsibility.independent.gov.uk/ (accessed 13 February 2012).

recession. By the end of 2011, GDP still lagged 4 percentage points below its previous peak (Figure 15.1).

A fourth problem is the rigidity of the government's economic position. All economic forecasts of GDP growth are made within a range of probabilities but the government has stuck to a rigid objective of balancing the structural deficit. The austerity measures set out in 2010 were founded on overoptimistic forecasts of economic performance yet the government refuses to budge, despite warnings. In its review of failed IMF programmes of macroeconomic reforms in 70 countries, a recent UNCTAD report argues for lessons to be learned – 'Mis-judging the effects of fiscal tightening seems to be the rule rather than the exception . . . In country after country where fiscal tightening was expected to both reduce the budget deficit and boost investment and economic growth, the opposite happened' (UNCTAD 2011: 65). The opposition Labour Party accuses the Coalition government of being 'growth-deniers':

> We have a Chancellor who believes that he can slash public spending, raise VAT and cut benefits . . . and none of this will have any impact on unemployment or growth. Against all the evidence . . . he argues the private sector will somehow rush to fill the void left by government and consumer spending.[5]

2.2 Resurgence of Neoliberal Ideology

Running parallel with the Coalition government's flawed economic vision is an ideological vision that seeks to radically reduce what is perceived to be an oversized and overcentralized public sector said to be crowding

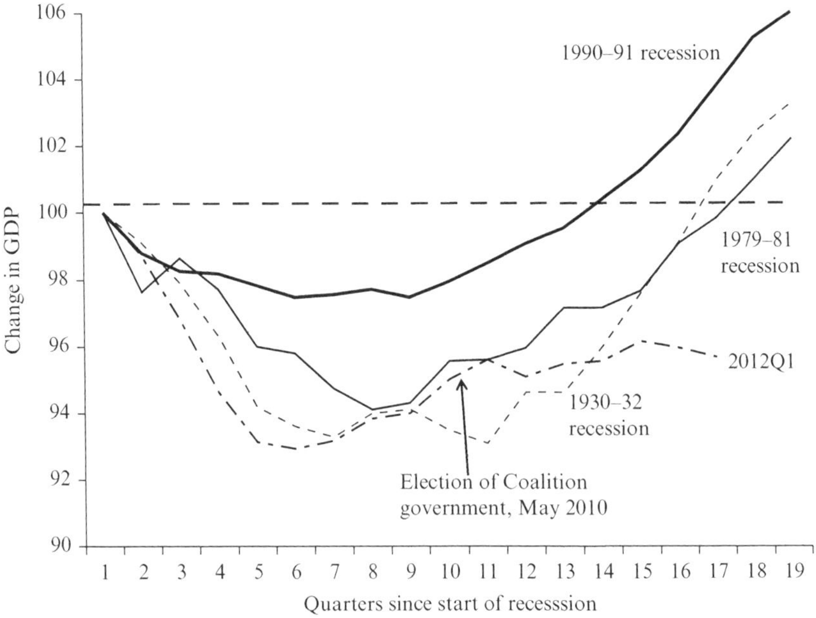

Note: The 2008–09 trend runs from 2008Q1 to 2012Q1.

Source: Office for National Statistics.

Figure 15.1 Comparison of GDP fall and recovery with previous recessions, UK

out private sector activity and supporting a unionized and 'privileged' public sector workforce. At times, the rhetoric against the public sector is tied to the state of the economy, at other times it is singled out in purely negative terms. In early 2010, David Cameron argued that 'In some parts of the country the state accounts for a bigger share of the economy than it did in the communist countries in the old eastern bloc. This is clearly unsustainable'.[6]

More generally, the spending cuts fit with the argument that the post-war welfare settlement of universal public services and benefits needs to be diminished in scale and replaced by a stronger private sector and new forms of copayments for users. Since 2010, the government and media have bombarded the public with reports of 'golden-plated' pensions and privileged employment conditions among public sector workers and have carefully constructed the impression that public spending increases during 1999–2009 under the New Labour government were wasted. Of course, it is no accident

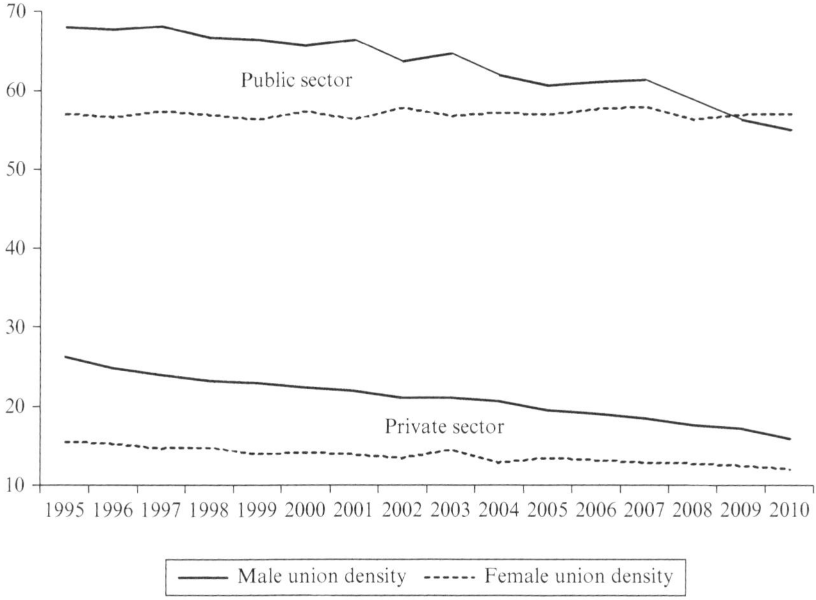

Source: ONS Labour Force Survey reported in Achur (2011).

Figure 15.2 Segmented patterns of trade union density, public and private sectors, UK, 1995–2010

that the attacks challenge trade union heartlands. More than three-fifths of union members were in the public sector in 2010 (62 per cent, up from 52 per cent in 1995) despite it accounting for less than three-tenths of total employment; levels of union density are triple (for men) and nearly five times (for women) those in the private sector (Figure 15.2).[7] Unlike other European countries, social dialogue – including a formal role for trade unions – has not been integral to the shaping of government fiscal policy. Instead, unions have exerted influence through a series of national and local protests and strike actions, as well as local negotiations with public sector employers over the design and implementation of cuts (Box 15.1).

The government has thus acted on the back of its fiscal consolidation approach to pursue a right-wing assault on the welfare state, the collective provision of public services and the jointly regulated protection of terms and conditions of employment. Even the governor of the Bank of England expressed concern about switching the blame from the banking bailout to the public sector. He told the Treasury Select Committee in 2011 that the billions spent bailing out the banks and the emphasis on public spending

BOX 15.1 EXAMPLES OF UNION PROTESTS AND STRIKE ACTIONS DURING 2011

- Rally of 300–500,000 people in London (March 2011)
- Strike by civil servants, academics and teachers (June 2011)
- 35,000 people outside the Conservative Party conference in Manchester (Oct. 2011)
- Coordinated lobby/protest of Parliament prior to budget (Oct. 2011)
- Coordinated local protests at public sector workplaces (Oct. 2011)
- Youth rally in London (Oct. 2011)
- Multiple coordinated regional protests against the pension cuts (Nov. 2011)
- Strikes over pension cuts (Nov. 2011)

cuts were the fault of the financial services sector: 'The price of this financial crisis is being borne by people who absolutely did not cause it . . . Now is the period when the cost is being paid, I'm surprised that the degree of public anger has not been greater than it has'.[8] The attack on the public sector appears to have overwhelmed all areas of government, such that the widely accepted need for a rebalancing of the economy appears in practice to involve only a downsizing of the public sector rather than expanding exports and reducing reliance on financial services. As two well-known UK social and government policy experts put it:

> Few can deny that Britain needs a new growth model but building a green economy, a greater export capacity or a larger manufacturing base is something that has to be planned and worked for over decades. It is unlikely to be delivered by massive cuts in the supporting physical and human infrastructure and investment. (Taylor-Gooby and Stoker 2011: 3)

3. THE CHARACTER OF PUBLIC SECTOR REFORMS

During the 2000s the public sector's challenge was to deliver more and better services with rising revenues. The policy approach tied higher spending with two conditions: (i) performance targets and implementation

Table 15.2 Key characteristics of public sector governance in 2000s and 2010s, UK

	2000s (New Labour government)	2010s (Conservative-led Coalition)
Public spending	Strong record of spending increases, continued during the recession – rise from 38.2 to 47.3% of GDP	Deep and sustained spending cuts, despite absence of economic recovery – forecast drop from 47.3 to 39.8% of GDP
Public–private mix trend	Continued Margaret Thatcher's programme of incremental privatization with increased outsourcing and subcontracting	Intensified approach supported by ideological stance against 'monopoly state' provision and a new presumption that all public services should be open to private sector providers
Examples	Private Finance Initiative (building programme and outsourcing of ancillary services); new privately owned Independent Treatment Centres in health services; some prisons privatized; introduction of student fees in higher education; continued privatization of social care	Privatization of health services under 'Any Willing Provider' (including private firms taking over 'failing' public hospitals); privatization of welfare-to-work programme; privatization of higher education (including tripling of fees); failed attempt to privatize English forests; 'Big Society' programme forces opening of local government services to new providers; accelerated privatization of prisons
Issues	Inefficient service procurement from private sector, spiralling costs of mega-contracts, two-tier employment conditions	Trade union protests and strikes against privatization agenda; controversial implementation of payment-by-results

of monitoring systems across different parts of the public sector; and (ii) 'quasi markets' that enforced competition among public sector providers and blurred the interface with private and voluntary sectors. Since 2010, spending cuts mean that the challenge now is to deliver the same (or less) for less money (Table 15.2). There is more focus on engaging the private sector in delivering public services. And there is a new rhetoric about moving away from centralized government control to a decentralized, local governance system with a 'big society' of voluntary and community organizations involved in public services.

Box 15.2 summarizes the composition of the public sector.

BOX 15.2 COMPOSITION OF THE UK PUBLIC SECTOR

The UK public sector encompasses both general government activities and market activities controlled by government. It is defined in the UK National Accounts following the categories set out in the 1996 regulation from the Council of the European Union. Altogether, the Office for National Statistics (October 2011) lists some 2,391 separate public sector organizations, set under four headings:

- *central government*: includes government departments, executive agencies, non-departmental public bodies and other non-market bodies controlled and mainly financed by central government;
- *local government*: includes public administration organizations that cover only a specific locality and any non-market bodies controlled and mainly financed by them;
- *public financial corporations*: market bodies operating in the financial sector controlled by either central or local government. These can include government-owned companies and trading funds; and
- *public non-financial corporations*: market bodies in the non-financial sector controlled by either central or local government.

Classification of organizations as public sector depends on government's right to exercise control. The BBC, for example, is established under Royal Charter and its governors are appointed by the Queen on advice from ministers. Another television channel, Channel 4, is also a public sector body since the board is appointed by Ofcom (the public sector regulator) subject to the approval of the government. During the crisis many banks were redefined as public sector organizations following government interventions. For example, the Northern Rock bank was classified as public sector in October 2007 since it received substantial liquidity support from the Bank of England and new clauses give government power to control its general corporate policy. The major organizations, as well as selected examples of other minor organizations, included in each category are shown below:

Central government	Local government	Public financial corporations	Public non-financial corporations
• 12 government depts • HM Treasury • HM prisons • NHS trusts • Agencies (e.g., Benefits, Food standards, Countryside, etc.) • Scotland organizations • Wales organizations • Northern Ireland *Other examples*: • BBC, Agricultural Wages Board, British Library, Gangmasters' Licensing Authority, Low Pay Commission, Medical Research Council bodies, National Audit Office, UK Film Council	• 353 councils in England • 32 councils in Scotland • 22 councils in Wales • 26 councils in N. Ireland *Other examples*: • Public–Private Partnerships Programme, Bristol port, Hull Marina, Rail for London	• Bank of England • Financial Services Authority *Banks, including*: • Northern Rock Bank • Royal Bank of Scotland • NatWest Bank • Lloyds TSB Bank • Scottish Widows' Bank • Ulster Bank	• BNFL • British Council *Others*: • Channel 4, Eurostar, Hackney Homes, London buses, London underground, Manchester airport, NHS Blood and transplant, OGC buying solutions, Partnerships UK, Post Office Counters, Remploy Ltd, Royal Mint, Stockport Homes, Yorkshire Metro

Source: ONS data 'Public sector classification guide' (October 2011, www.ons.gov.uk/classification/national-accounts-sector-classification/); Kellaway and Shanks (2006).

3.1 Deep and Fast-paced Spending Cuts

Forecast spending cuts for the five-year period from 2010 follow the pattern of previous Conservative party governments when sustained cuts reduced spending as a share of GDP by 9 percentage points (1982–89) and seven percentage points (1992–2000[9]). The current forecast cuts are estimated to reduce spending from 47.5 per cent of GDP to 39.8 per cent. While consistent with past Conservative government cuts, current plans will have a more radical impact because they follow an 11-year period of sustained growth in public spending (Figure 15.3). It is notable that public spending continued to increase as a share of GDP during the 2008–09 recession under the New Labour government. This was not simply the result of automatic stabilizers. Spending rises in education and health were especially significant, suggesting that Gordon Brown and his team were applying Keynesian demand management, albeit in a relatively weak form.[10]

Against a changed backdrop of austerity crisis during spring 2010 (including the first hints of a sovereign debt crisis in Europe and the risk of default by the government in Greece) the incoming Coalition government announced a medium-term plan of spending cuts with the goal of eliminating the structural deficit by 2015–16, which had ballooned due to both the costs of the banking bailout and adjustment of the UK's 'potential output' (see above). Tax rises play a minor role in Britain's austerity plans – outweighed by spending cuts by a factor of four to one.[11] By 2014–15 it is forecast that social security spending will have lost £4 billion in real terms, education £3 billion, defence £6 billion and local government £6 billion. In percentage terms, local government and defence are by far the most impacted; the Coalition government will cut 21 per cent from local government spending by 2014–15.

3.2 Privatization: Repeating Past Mistakes

The second feature of public sector reform is privatization (Table 15.2). Since 2010, the Coalition has sought to create open markets for procurement of public services from the private and voluntary sectors. While the foundations for marketization were laid under Margaret Thatcher and Tony Blair, especially with the privatization of elderly-care services, the private finance initiative and various forms of outsourcing of ancillary services across the public sector, current reforms promise to go much further. The 2011 White Paper states that the new privatization programme 'will switch the default from one where the state provides the service itself to one where the state commissions the service from a range

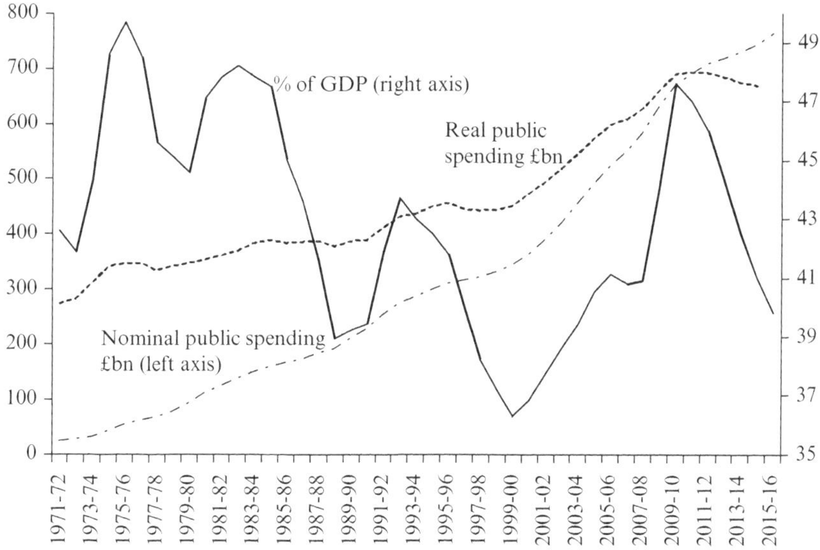

Real values, deflated by expected inflation, 2010–11	2010–11	2011–12	2012–13	2013–14	2014–15	% change in real spending
Social security	169.0	169.2	170.1	165.0	164.8	–2.5
Health	98.4	98.6	98.6	98.7	98.8	0.4
Education	51.3	49.7	49.3	48.8	48.4	–5.6
Defence	28.4	26.5	23.8	22.9	22.1	–22.2
Scotland	25.2	24.0	23.8	23.3	22.8	–9.5
Local government	26.0	25.3	23.1	22.3	20.5	–21.2
Tax credits	25.2	26.1	27.0	26.6	26.0	3.3

Sources: HM Treasury 2011 PESA data (table 4.1), www.hm-treasury.gov.uk; forecast nominal spending for 2010–11 to 2015–16 from the 2011 Budget (http://cdn.hm-treasury.gov.uk/2011budget_complete.pdf); social security forecast data from OBR fiscal supplementary tables (86.54.44.148/wordpress/docs/obr_fiscal_supplementary_tables1.xls) (accessed 13 February 2012). Author's compilation.

Figure 15.3 Long-run trend in public spending – real, nominal and as a percentage of GDP, UK, 1971–2016 (forecast from 2011)

of diverse providers' (HM Government 2011: 29[12]). In the health sector, 2012 legislation will, on one hand, establish consortia of doctors who will be responsible for commissioning services from 'any qualified provider' with the explicit aim of 'liberating provision of National Health Service services' and, on the other, expand the role of the regulatory body to ensure free competition in health service procurement. Prior to implementation, this reform faced sustained criticism in the media and opposition from *all* major professional associations and trade unions involved in health and social care. For example, Unison argues that the revised Bill:

> continues to permit competition in the health service based on price, encouraging private companies into the service to engage in a cost cutting frenzy that damages patient care. And the legislation continues to point a dagger at the NHS principles of equity and fairness, with private companies allowed to walk off with the most profitable contracts and private patients jumping the queue on NHS patients.[13]

More open commissioning of services is also being applied to a range of central and local government services where it is expected to bring 'a host of benefits' by encouraging the entry of 'new, innovative providers to compete for contracts' (ibid.: 29). In most cases, in line with EU Procurement Directives, services are advertised on the website for EU tenders.[14] Local government services are said to have strong privatization potential, including customer relations, planning, property and facilities management, back-office transactional services, housing and family support (ibid.: 30–31).

A major weakness of the privatization programme is the need for a large upfront spend to deliver the anticipated longer-term savings. The partial privatization of health services is estimated to require £600 million to £1.2 billion in redundancy costs alone associated with closures of Primary Care Trusts and Strategic Health Authorities.[15] A second problem is that forecast savings have limited supporting evidence. In the opinion of a leading expert on public policy, 'There is little systematic evidence about the overall effects of such reforms on cost saving, and certainly no consensus among policy experts or in the academic world that such reforms have significantly cut costs overall' (Hood 2010: 6). One question is the extent to which under a new regime of cost-cutting central government works harder at getting better procurement deals with the private sector, an issue that has been the object of past critical assessments (Grimshaw et al. 2002), including a recent government commissioned review (Green 2010).

Other limitations of the privatization programme include the use of 'partnership' as a model for public services procurement (Erridge and Greer 2002; Kirkpatrick 1999; Lonsdale et al. 2010). In social care, research casts doubt on whether longer-term relationships have developed; contracts continue to be short term and cost focused with limited involvement of contractors in shaping delivery (Rubery et al. 2013). In IT services procurement, public sector organizations are at risk of becoming 'locked in' with specialist providers and lack the expertise to re-specify contracts to adapt to fast-changing information and communication technologies (Grimshaw et al. 2002). Also, Private Finance Initiative partnerships do not necessarily deliver value for money: risk can be inappropriately distributed and some contracts appear to be awarded in response to lobbying of powerful private sector firms (Froud and Shaoul 2001; Crouch 2003).

4. IMPACT OF REFORMS ON PAY AND EMPLOYMENT

The reforms are different in type. Some involve a quantitative adjustment – a reduction in spending that may mean job cuts or a pay freeze. Others require qualitative change such as the redesign and streamlining of services provision or withdrawal from provision altogether. In his assessment of possible reforms, Hood (2010) distinguishes three types. First, 'resetting' existing practices includes a continuation of existing policy but with a downwards quantitative adjustment, whether in, for example, capital spending, maintenance spending or workforce labour costs. Second, 'system redesign' involves the re-engineering of existing services ostensibly to improve value for money, service quality and user experience (for example, IT projects to re-engineer the user experience, privatization, outsourcing and 'Big Society' projects). And the third type is the withdrawal of services. Each reform type has specific employment, pay and pension effects (Table 15.3). See Table 15.5 for a fuller listing of public policy reforms.

4.1 Employment Effects

Reduction in public sector employment has been a planned component of the government's austerity budgets since 2010. The 2010 budget forecast a reduction of close to 10 per cent (490,000 jobs) in public sector employment over five years (OBR 2010: table 1). Data available up to the first quarter of 2012, less than two years after the introduction of austerity measures, demonstrate that this forecast will in fact be substantially exceeded (Table 15.4). Approximately 420,000 jobs have already been cut in just eight quarters since the start of 2010, an average rate of 53,000 per quarter, and it is notable that the scale of cuts was ratcheted up in 2011 to an average 69,000 per quarter. If this average rate of job loss since early 2010 continues, then the UK will witness a net cull from the public sector

Table 15.3 Characterizing the pay and employment effects of austerity measures, UK

	1. Resetting	2. System redesign	3. Withdrawal
Definition	Downwards quantitative adjustment	Re-engineering of services to improve value for money	Elimination of services
Employment effects	Reduced employment throughout public sector exceeds original 2010 budget forecast, particularly in local/central government (to date)	Shift of jobs to 'public services industry' (private/ voluntary firms) through staff transfer (protected by TUPE*) and direct recruitment	Downsizing of workforces by collective dismissals (closed childcare centres, libraries, care homes, career services)
Pay effects	Pay freeze for all except the lowest paid who mostly receive a small flat rate supplement	Reduces likelihood of coverage by joint regulation/trade unions; efforts to level down raw wage premium and other benefits	Increased wage–income insecurity
Pension effects	Proposed rise in pension contributions/ retirement age	Switch from a final salary to a career average pension	–

Note: * Transfer of Undertakings (Protection of Employment) regulations.

Source: Author's elaboration using Hood's (2010) three categories.

of 640,000 jobs by the first quarter of 2013 and 850,000 jobs by early 2014 – that is, almost double the forecast number even before the ending of the period of austerity measures.

The largest reduction, by headcount, is in public administration (central government civil service and local government) where there has already been an 11 per cent reduction in just eight quarters – 134,000 jobs. Education has witnessed a 5 per cent cut (approximately in line with the overall 6 per cent real spending cut, Figure 15.3). And it is notable that the National Health Service (NHS) has lost 45,000 jobs, 3 per cent of the workforce. The Coalition government has repeatedly claimed that frontline health-care

Table 15.4 Trends in public sector employment, disaggregated by industry, UK, 1999–2012Q1

	Army	Police (including civilians)	Public admin.	Education	NHS	Other health & social work	Publicly owned financial corp.	Other public sector	Total public sector emp.*	% of total employment
1999	218	230	1,181	1,395	1,212	392	–	609	5,469	20.2
2000	217	229	1,187	1,450	1,239	388	–	611	5,550	20.2
2001	214	232	1,193	1,475	1,285	375	–	639	5,642	20.4
2002	214	241	1,221	1,482	1,348	368	–	656	5,749	20.6
2003	223	251	1,265	1,538	1,417	347	–	658	5,912	21.0
2004	218	266	1,278	1,575	1,475	361	–	648	6,030	21.2
2005	210	274	1,297	1,595	1,528	368	–	660	6,133	21.3
2006	204	275	1,293	1,622	1,522	361	–	631	6,096	21.0
2007	197	284	1,280	1,633	1,486	358	–	621	6,039	20.7
2008	193	287	1,236	1,641	1,506	355	–	631	6,019	20.4
2009	197	294	1,221	1,662	1,572	357	238	588	6,313	21.9
2010Q1	199	294	1,225	1,675	1,606	359	218	568	6,323	21.9
2010Q2	197	292	1,213	1,689	1,596	360	221	559	6,292	21.6
2010Q3	196	289	1,191	1,684	1,591	353	216	560	6,263	21.5
2010Q4	195	285	1,187	1,665	1,595	350	218	548	6,214	21.3

Table 15.4 (continued)

	Army	Police (including civilians)	Public admin.	Education	NHS	Other health & social work	Publicly owned financial corp.	Other public sector	Total public sector emp.*	% of total employment
2011Q1	194	282	1,176	1,652	1,591	349	213	557	6,177	21.1
2011Q2	193	277	1,133	1,632	1,565	342	214	537	6,054	20.8
2011Q3	191	271	1,117	1,603	1,557	330	207	534	5,979	20.5
2011Q4	189	267	1,102	1,595	1,561	333	212	520	5,938	20.4
2012Q1	187	262	1,091	1,600	1,561	323	202	516	5,899	20.1
Change since 2010Q1	–12	–32	–134	–75	–45	–36	–16	–52	–424	–1.8 pp
% change	–6.0	–10.9	–10.9	–4.5	–2.8	–10.0	–7.3	–9.2	–6.7	–8.3

Note: * Includes publicly owned financial corporations – Royal Bank of Scotland Group plc, Lloyds Banking Group plc and Northern Rock from 2009. Figures for 'public sector construction workers' not shown here but included in the total (42,000 in 2012Q1).

Source: ONS Public sector employment by industry, June 2012 release (www.ons.gov.uk/ons/rel/pse/public-sector employment/q1-2012/stb-pse-2012q1.html, accessed 14 February 2012).

jobs in the NHS would be protected, but survey data suggest more than half planned job cuts in early 2011 were clinical, frontline posts.[16]

The gender impact of public sector job cuts is skewed against women due to their disproportionate share of the public sector workforce. Women experienced nearly three in five of the jobs lost – amounting to 185,000 and 130,000 jobs for women and men, respectively. In fact, women's share of job cuts is marginally less than their share of public sector jobs, which has remained at around 65 per cent during 2010–11. From the end of 2009 to the third quarter of 2011, women's employment fell by 4.0 per cent and men's employment by 5.2 per cent.

Figure 15.4 displays the employment impacts by major occupational groups and by full- and part-time employment for the prior five-year period of expansion and the period of austerity. Public sector employment increased prior to 2009, especially among female full-timers, although these women experienced a polarization between growth among professional and managerial jobs and among personal service occupations but a major loss of jobs among administrative and secretarial jobs. During the period of cuts the share of job losses has been largest among female part-timers and male full-timers. Surprisingly, female part-time employment increased among the higher-paid managerial and professional and associate professional jobs by 5 per cent; also, full-time jobs increased for men and women in lower-paid sales/customer service jobs (men and women) and personal service (men) jobs.

A separate data source[17] clarifies what has happened across different subsectors (Figure 15.5). The largest single employment loss during the five quarters from early 2010 to the second quarter of 2011 was among female part-timers in education, a fall of 69,000 – likely to involve reductions in teaching assistants who provide supplementary (sometimes specialist) assistance in school classrooms. The second largest drops were shared by male and female full-timers in public administration (around 40,000 each). A third significant loss was among female part-timers in health, 36,000 employees. Again, these data show that across all four areas of the public sector, women have experienced the brunt of employment cuts. These cuts are especially significant during a period when across all sectors of the economy there has been no significant change in numbers employed. Small rises in male full- and part-time employment, along with female part-time employment have been offset by a net reduction in female full-time employment by 2.1 per cent, or 147,000. Here is further clear evidence of the unequal adverse impact of public spending job cuts on women's employment opportunities.

'System redesign' policies (Table 15.3) have generated particular types of employment effects. Programmes of outsourcing and privatization,

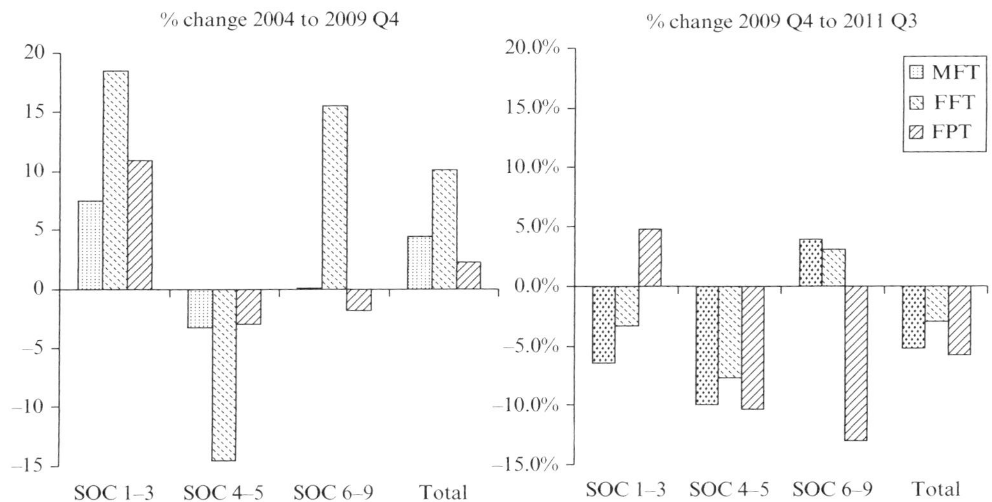

Note: SOC 1–3 includes managers and senior officials, professional occupations and associate and technical; SOC 4–5 includes administrative and secretarial and skilled trades occupations and SOC 6–9 includes personal service occupations, sales and customer service occupations and process, plant and machine operatives.

Source: LFS data (specially requested tables). Author's compilation.

Figure 15.4 Change in public sector employment by major occupational group, sex and full-time/part-time, UK, 2004–2009 and 2009–2011

transform public sector employment by blurring the boundaries with the private sector. Government websites now routinely refer to the fast-expanding 'public services industry'. Current government reforms build on previous policy but are accelerating the pace of change. There are limited publicly available data to illuminate this important policy trend.[18] One source suggests that the market for public services has expanded quickly in recent years. In 2007–08 it was estimated that the government purchased services from the private and voluntary sectors at a cost of £79 billion, double the figure spent (in real terms) in 1995–96, and estimated to account for one-third of spending on public services[19] (Julius 2008: 11–13). On the demand side, most spending is for health services (30 per cent), followed by social protection, defence and education. On the supply side, the major activities are 'managed services' (for example, running prisons, welfare-to-work services, childcare services), facilities management, ICT services and business process outsourcing (ibid.: 21).

This expanding market is forecast to support 1.3 million jobs in 2010–11 (ibid.: 18), one-fifth of the 6 million public sector workforce. Trade unions are doing their best to monitor the employment impacts of current reforms but it is difficult because of the fragmented and uncoordinated character of change. The lessons of previous evaluations of privatization and outsourcing (for example, Walsh and Davis 1993) are that reforms are likely to mean job cuts either prior to or following transfer of services to the private sector and heightened concerns over job security. Recent studies attest to the increased job churning. A 2004 National Audit Office survey of 43 public–private partnerships found that thousands of workers are routinely transferred from the public sector to the private sector contractor and then there is a rapid fallout from the workforce through voluntary quits and redundancies. The survey results show that of the 3,200 people who left after transferring from the public sector, 17 per cent were made redundant or were dismissed and 66 per cent resigned voluntarily (NAO 2008: table 6).

'Withdrawal' of public services means downsizing of employment since it cannot be achieved through natural wastage or a recruitment freeze. In local government, budgets have been cut but organizations have been granted more discretion in how to tailor services to budgets by the removal of ring-fenced services provision – such as childcare for deprived neighbourhoods, for example, or local career services for young people. Examples of abolished local services include:[20]

- *Childcare centres* Closure of 124 Sure Start centres (from 3,631 in April 2010 to 3.507 in September 2011).
- *Libraries* Withdrawal of 95 library services, which includes the closure of 33 library buildings (including 13 in Leeds and six in

Public administration, defence, social security (SIC 84)

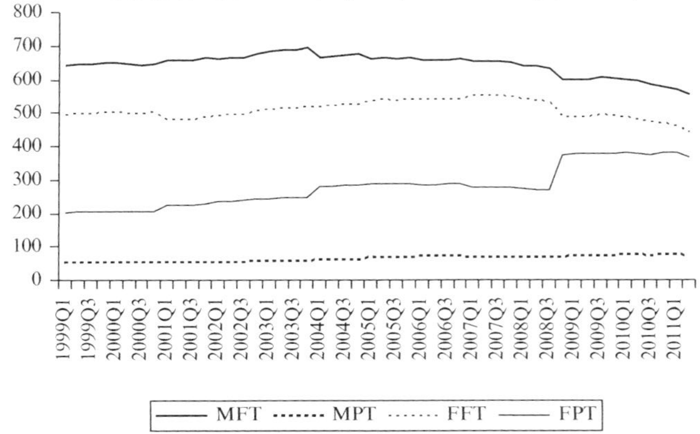

Education (SIC 85)

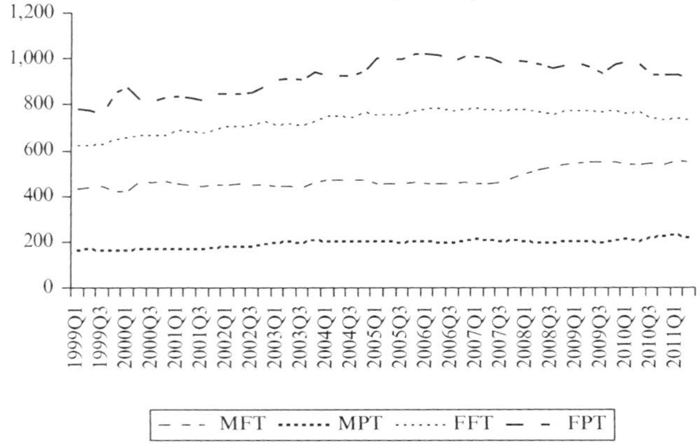

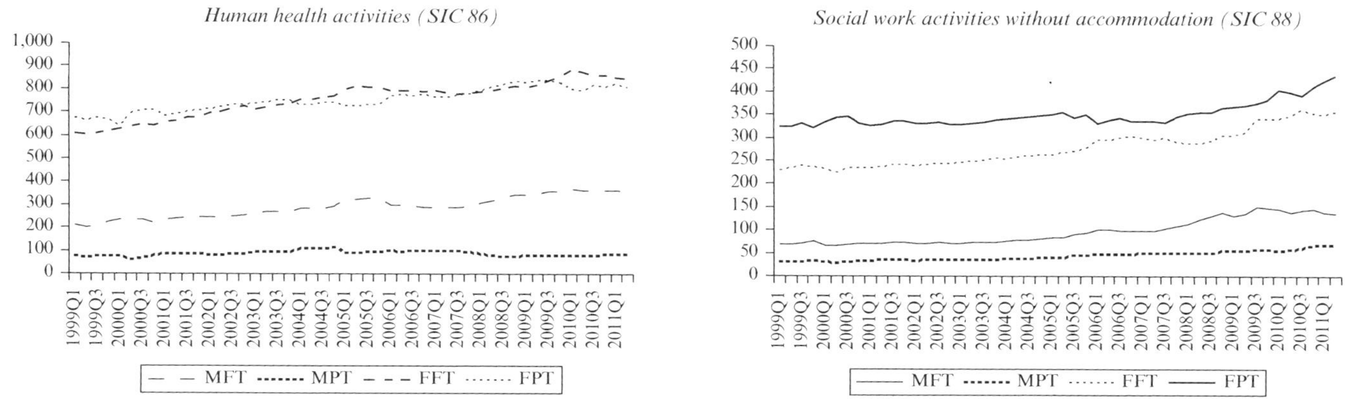

Note: The data do not separate out public sector from the small share of private sector employment.

Source: ONS jobs data, www.ons.gov.uk/ons/rel/lms/labour-market-statistics/october-2011/index-of-data-tables.html#tab-Jobs-tables.

Figure 15.5 Jobs trends in four sectors by sex and full-/part-time, UK, 1999–2011

Brent) and 43 mobile libraries, the substitution of volunteers for paid librarians in 14 library buildings and the takeover of five libraries by social enterprises or the local church.

- *Career services* An estimated 8,000 job cuts associated with cuts and closures of careers services provided by local authorities, including the closure in East Sussex, Essex and Lewisham.
- *Care homes* Six homes to close in Leeds with job cuts.

Downsizing is nevertheless a costly practice. Severance payments mean that many public sector organizations are unlikely to achieve their desired spending cuts in the short term.

4.2 Pay Effects

'Resetting' through spending cuts is also achieved by cutting the real level of public sector pay. Pay policy had already been a key focus during the recession under the New Labour government with press releases in late 2009 warning of problems of a 'culture of excess' among some higher-paid groups (senior civil servants, judges and doctors). Ignoring the recommendations of the independent senior salary pay review body, it implemented a pay freeze in 2010–11, followed by a two-year cap of 1 per cent, estimated at the time to save £3.4 billion (Table 15.5).[21]

Table 15.6 lists the main public policy changes and their impacts.

The policy of a nominal pay freeze was picked up by the coalition government and applied across all areas of the public sector for two years from 2011 to 2012. The one exception was the recommendation that a small fixed annual supplement of 'at least £250' be awarded to the lowest paid (defined as having annual earnings less than £21,000). What is interesting about the policy is that it received support by the ostensibly independent pay review bodies (separately constituted for the various professions, including teachers, health service workers, prison staff and so on), which caused an outcry from trade unions on the basis that the pay bodies had failed to question government thinking and had thereby compromised their independent status.[22] With inflation at around 6 per cent in 2011, the pay freeze (with or without the small £250 supplement) caused a significant erosion in real earnings; in the meantime, the private sector median pay settlement was around 2.5 per cent in 2011.[23]

Figure 15.6 shows trends in nominal and real median earnings in the public sector compared to the private sector for different workforce groups. The trend in real earnings tended to be flat during 2005–09, although women in public sector part-time jobs did quite well. During 2009–10, the year following the recession, the UK economy was deflation-

Table 15.5 Summary of public sector pay reforms and their effects during the crisis, UK, 2010–2012

Pay issue	Pay reform	Effects on wage levels and wage structures
Annual pay settlement	Unilateral government imposition of a 2-year freeze (most from April 2011), followed by 2-year imposed 1% limit	3% cut in public sector real earnings 2010–11; likely to be higher in 2011–12; falling real pay will continue until at least 2014–15; cut in 'raw unadjusted gap' between public and private sector
High-wage earners	High-profile independent review commissioned to examine 'culture of excess' in public sector, but no mention in 2012 budget	None to date
Low-wage earners	Government provision of £250 fixed supplement for earnings < £21k	Limited impact in reducing real pay cut among lowest paid. But not applied in local government due to refusal of employer body
Local pay	Government aims to dismantle national agreements and hopes to implement local/ regional pay	Already planned for civil service from April 2012; awaiting responses from pay review bodies for health, education, prisons. Motivated by goal to cut public wage premium (unadjusted) in regions outside London but government propaganda obscures complex issues; will increase public sector wage inequality, widen interregional income inequality and worsen pay for the lowest skilled who are least protected
Automatic pay increments (seniority)	Government pressure on pay bodies to freeze pay increments	Mixture of responses – e.g., no increments for civil servants at the Dept for Work and Pensions but honoured for prison service workers

ary (retail price inflation was around –5 per cent) and as such all workforce groups experienced rising real earnings, even male full-time workers in the private sector who were the only group to experience a cut in nominal earnings that year. But with a return to high inflation in 2010–11, all workers experienced a significant fall in real pay, ranging from a cut of

Table 15.6 Main public policy changes and their impacts on workers and citizens, UK, 2010–2012

Policy reform	Impacts on public sector workforce	Impacts on all workers	Impacts on public services and citizens
Public spending cuts (9.5% cut in departmental real expenditures; 3.3% cut in total real expenditures, 2010–11 to 2014–15)	Cuts in pay and employment, as well as reduced career prospects	Likely reduced budgets for commissioning of public services from private sector	Diminished quantity and quality of public services across all areas signifies deterioration in the social settlement for UK citizens; especially negative shock in deprived regions
Cut corporation tax to 27% (2011–12), 26% (2012–13), 25% (2013–14), 24% (2014–15)	Massive reduction in tax base (estimated £4.1bn) means less revenues to fund pay and employment	Shifts balance of tax payments from employers to workers	Likely decline in quantity resulting from reduced tax revenues
Increased tax-free income allowance from £6475 in 2010–11 to £9,205 in 2013–14	Increases net earnings for a small group of low-wage workers not in receipt of tax credits	Same impact as public sector workers	N.A.
Increased income taxes for many workers (higher share covered by the 40% income tax bracket caused by lower minimum threshold – from £37,401–150,000 in 2010–11 to £32,245–150,000 in 2013–14)	Reduced net income for middle-to-high wage earners	Same impact as public sector workers	N.A.
Reduced income tax for the highest-paid workers (£150,001+), from 50 to 45% from April 2013	Only applicable to a handful of very senior managers	Benefits many workers at the top of the pay distribution	N.A.

Public sector pay freeze, 2010–11 to 2012–13 with possible £250 supplement for lowest paid Public sector pay limit of 1%	Real wage cuts. Varied timeline of implementation; £250 for local government workers refused by employer body	Only affects public sector	Recruitment and retention problems expected – likely to aggravate management of public services delivery
Reduction* in real level of adult National Minimum Wage in 2010 (–2.3%), 2011 (–2.9%) and 2012 (forecast –1.8%)	Pulls down base rates in public sector pay agreements, especially local government where rate is lowest	Major adverse impact on minimum wage workers; reduces real living standards	Reduced wage floor likely to increase incentives to outsource public services to private sector where many firms use the minimum wage as the going rate of pay
Planned public sector workforce cuts (estimated 490,000 or 10% 2010–11 to 2015–16)	Very likely to exceed forecast 10% cut. Job cuts include 'frontline' posts in NHS. Disproportionate impact on women, local government, deprived regions	Adds to unemployment, increasing competition for job vacancies. Especially problematic in regions with a weak private sector	Worsening of public services provision, especially difficult in a period of rising poverty, homelessness, ageing population and an increase in cohort of young children
Privatization and outsourcing of public services through new programmes in health care ('Any Willing Provider'), welfare-to-work ('Work Programme'), prisons and 'failing' schools	Further cuts encouraged in public sector employment; reduced numbers with terms and conditions protected by joint employer–union regulations	New job opportunities; unions find it difficult to mobilize members in private firms providing public services; evidence of a reduced 'public service ethos' in privatized prisons (Koumenta 2011)	Likely reduction in universal provision of public services with focus among private firms on most profitable activities; already some evidence of conflicts of interest/corruption among private firm managers and shareholders; weaker democratic governance arrangements to monitor public services quality; evidence of user dissatisfaction in privatized social care for the elderly (Rubery et al. 2013)

Table 15.6 (continued)

Policy reform	Impacts on public sector workforce	Impacts on all workers	Impacts on public services and citizens
Abolition of 'two-tier code' that underpinned agreed extensions of terms and conditions to workers in private sector contractors	No immediate impact but likely medium-term impact of increased public–private gap in terms and conditions among lowest paid	Removes basis for negotiated protection of workers in private sector providers of outsourced public services	Likely to encourage higher incidence of minimum wage jobs in private sector providers of public services
High pay reforms – government departments asked to consider proposals of 2011 Hutton report	No publicized progress on issue of high pay	Only applicable to public sector	N.A.
Pension reforms include: raised employee contributions; replacing final salary scheme with average salary scheme; normal pension age aligned with state pension age; indexed to CPI	Varied agreements by subsector on details of new defined benefit schemes; national strikes over increased pension contributions and increased normal pension age rise (for many from 60 to 68); protected deals for those within 10 years of retirement	All workers affected by changes to state pension and retirement age	Radical change in intergenerational income distribution; younger workers expected 'to work longer, pay more and get less'
Review of Transfer of Undertakings (Protection of Employment) regulations (known as TUPE) with aim of abolition	Threat of driving down outsourcing costs by targeting employees' terms and conditions	Affects all workers by lowering the wage floor in public services labour market	Risks adverse impact on public services quality through lowest-cost outsourcing and worsening employment conditions

Reduced entitlement to redundancy compensation and unfair dismissal (from 2011, 24 months' tenure required instead of 12)	Increased proportion of workers with limited redundancy rights	Same impact as public sector workers	Representative of further shift towards employer-focused labour market flexibility irrespective of workers' socioeconomic needs
Abolished major £1bn Future Jobs Fund and replaced with limited spending on 'new' apprenticeships and work experience	Unlikely to have significant impact	Unlikely to have significant impact	Represents a major shift away from the active promotion of youth employment opportunities
Removed entitlement to universal child benefits from families with a higher earner from 2013	Removes significant addition to total household income where one person earns > £50k with tapered effect up to £60k	Same impact as public sector workers	Abolishes a symbolic universal right to a welfare benefit
Working tax credit cuts for low-income households: a 3-year freeze, reduction in childcare element and reduced entitlement to part-time workers with children (<24 hours)	Considerable reductions in total earnings	Same impact as public sector workers	Representative of a redistribution away from low-income households

Notes: * Adjusted by change in the retail price index for the 12 months up to October each year (ONS Statistical Bulletin, p. 24); 2012 figure based on forecast RPI of 3.6% (www.xperthr.co.uk).

Sources: HM Treasury Budget 2011, 2012 and June Budget 2010.

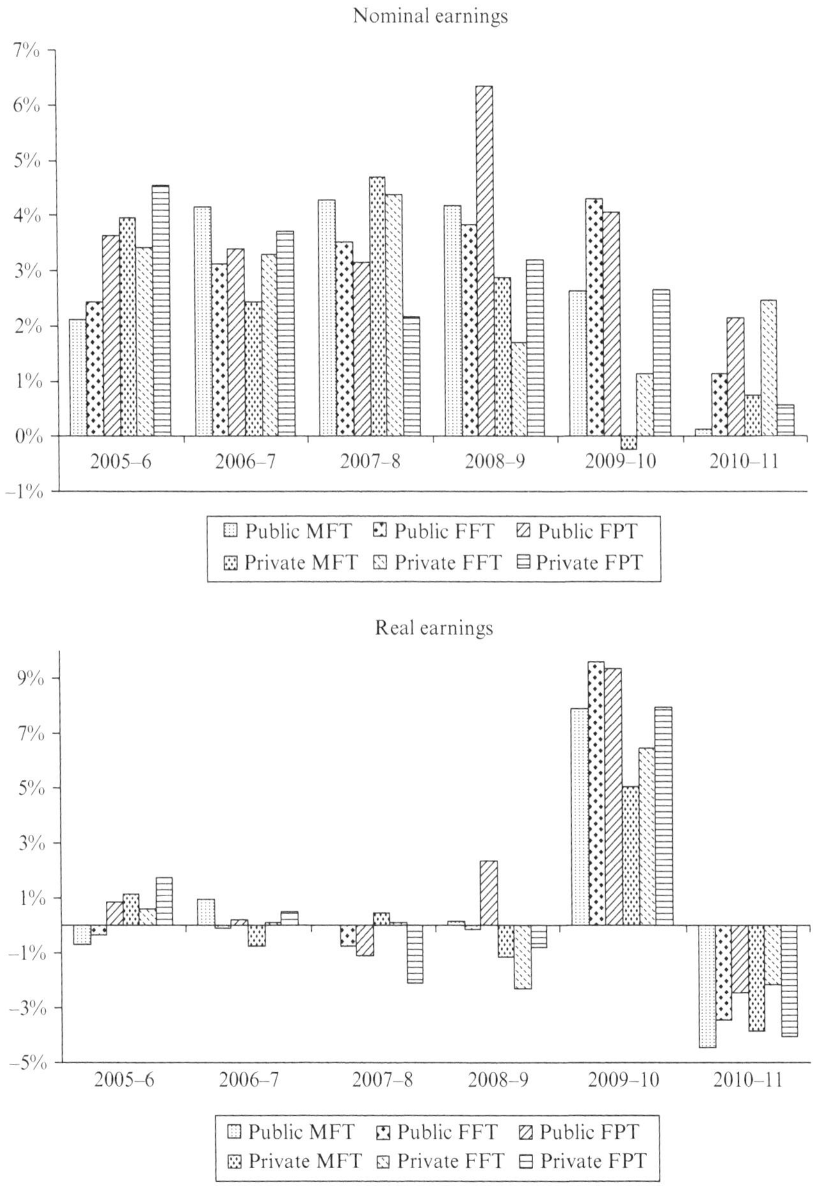

Source: Annual Survey of Hours and Earnings (ASHE) (ONS pay data). Gross hourly earnings for all employees excluding overtime.

Figure 15.6 Change in median gross hourly pay, public and private sectors, UK, 2005–2011

	Public MFT	Public FFT	Public FPT	Private MFT	Private FFT	Private FPT
2005	£13.20	£11.89	£7.99	£10.62	£8.50	£5.93
2006	£13.48	£12.18	£8.28	£11.04	£8.79	£6.20
2007	£14.04	£12.56	£8.56	£11.31	£9.08	£6.43
2008	£14.64	£13.00	£8.83	£11.84	£9.48	£6.57
2009	£15.25	£13.50	£9.39	£12.18	£9.64	£6.78
2010	£15.65	£14.08	£9.77	£12.15	£9.75	£6.96
2011	£15.67	£14.24	£9.98	£12.24	£9.99	£7.00

Figure 15.6 (continued)

2 per cent for female full-timers in the private sector to almost 5 per cent for male full-timers in the public sector.

The government's approach to pay reforms is shaped by an ideological ambition to level down what are perceived as 'privileged' conditions of employment. Much has been made of the apparent wage premium earned in the public sector. As the table of data in Figure 15.6 shows, median pay remained significantly higher in the public than the private sector during 2005–10 for men, women, full-timers and part-timers: the 'raw' public sector median pay premium in 2011 was 28 per cent (male full-time), 43 per cent (female full-time) and 43 per cent (female part-time). However, comparison of unadjusted wage levels is not appropriate under any circumstances. First, it does not account for differences in composition of workers by level of skill and qualification. Decomposition of the wage gap after controlling for differences in years of schooling, age and qualifications suggests that approximately half the premium is associated with the higher share of professionally qualified and higher-skilled employees in the public sector; in one study the raw gap was 25 percentage points and the adjusted gap 12 points (Bozio and Disney 2011); education differences are especially significant for women (Table 15.7).

Second, median private sector pay is significantly reduced by the employer practice of setting pay for low-level employees at or close to the statutory minimum wage – that is, misuse of the minimum wage as the going rate of pay instead of setting pay in line with the varying skill, qualification and performance characteristics of the job or individual. In 2011, around 6 per cent of private sector jobs were minimum wage compared to less than 1 per cent in the public sector (LPC 2011: figure 2.1). Throughout 2005–11 the bottom decile wage of female part-timers in the private sector was equivalent to the statutory minimum; in the public sector by contrast there was a premium of between 10 and 15 per cent (Table 15.8). The bulk of minimum wage jobs are in the private sectors of hospitality, retail, cleaning and social care (LPC 2011).

Table 15.7 Decomposition of the public–private sector wage gap, UK, 2009–2010

	Men	Women	All
Mean difference in wage	+0.207 (0.012)	+0.276 (0.009)	+0.246 (0.007)
Controlling for education	+0.098 (0.011)	+0.153 (0.009)	+0.124 (0.007)
Controlling for education, age, qualifications	+0.052 (0.011)	+0.096 (0.009)	+0.075 (0.007)

Note: OLS estimation on log hourly wage; control variables include public sector, age left full-time education, highest qualification, age, age squared, interactions between age/age squared/age left full-time education. Standard errors in parentheses.

Source: Bozio and Disney (2011: table 7.3) using quarterly Labour Force Survey data for 2009Q1–Q4 and 2010Q1–Q3.

Table 15.8 Comparisons of wage differentials within the public and private sectors, UK, 2005–2010

	D9/D1 Male full-time		D9/D1 Female full-time		D1/NMW Female part-time	
	Public	Private	Public	Private	Public	Private
2005	3.33	4.12	3.13	3.44	1.15	1.00
2006	3.27	4.18	3.00	3.47	1.14	1.00
2007	3.19	4.17	2.96	3.39	1.10	1.00
2008	3.13	4.24	2.95	3.44	1.10	1.00
2009	3.22	4.15	2.90	3.43	1.12	1.00
2010	3.25	4.11	2.88	3.42	1.12	1.00

Note: NMW = national minimum wage.

Source: ASHE. Author's calculations. Gross hourly earnings excluding overtime.

Third, static comparison wrongly presumes similarity of age–earnings profiles. Wages are more compressed in the public sector than the private sector for men and women (Table 15.8), suggestive of less steep age–earnings profiles; in fact, among female full-timers in the public sector, the D9–D1 differential decreased during 2005–11. One novel decomposition analysis argues that assuming individuals are forward looking, such that employment choices also account for income mobility, volatility and security, means that wage gaps ought to be computed over an individual's life cycle; the estimates suggest a public sector pay premium of 2–3 per cent and this reduces to 0 per cent for individuals with a low risk of unemployment (Postel-Vinay and Turon 2007). One factor is different returns to experience; returns in the public sector are smaller but follow a U-shape relative to the private sector – returns for men in the private sector are steeper from a lower base but then tail off sooner (ibid.). A fourth problem with government rhetoric about the public sector wage premium is that pay is only one part of the reward package. Workers in the public and private sectors have varying access to bonuses, overtime pay, fringe benefits (for example, car and travel expenses), annual leave, company share schemes and pensions.

4.3 Pension Effects

The coalition government intends to generate savings in pensions and has followed a course of first publicly attacking what it calls 'gold-plated' public sector pensions and then setting out a policy, prior to negotiations with unions, which seeks to increase workers' pension contributions and decrease the payouts, switching from a final salary scheme to a career average calculation. The proposed rises are tiered for different income groups – in 2012–13 for civil servants, teachers and health workers this means no change for incomes less than £15,000, up to 0.6 per cent rise for £15,000–£21,000 and up to 2.4 per cent for the rest. The proposed payout is known as the 'career average revalued earnings' (CARE) scheme.

Again, as with debates over pay, the government agenda is framed by an apparent ambition to downgrade the status of public sector employees. The problem with UK pensions, however, is that the bulk of private sector workers in the UK are not members of an employer-sponsored pension – less than 35 per cent compared to 85 per cent of public sector workers (Hutton 2011: 25), although membership among the lowest-paid and part-time workers is significantly lower (ibid.: chart 3H). Also, pensions paid to public sector workers are generally higher than in the private sector but are still very low: in 2009–10 the median public sector pension was around £5,600 a year and the median private sector pension for a single pensioner (sum of occupational and personal pension income) was around £3,900. In local government the average pension is just £4,200 a year and among women members of the pension scheme it is £2,870 (Unison 2011a).

A further problem confronting policymakers is that the system of contributions to pensions are very fragmented across the different public sector groups. Prior to the reforms, the teachers' pension scheme, for example, required contributions of 6.4 per cent from members and 14.1 per cent from the employers. By contrast, in the civil service scheme members contribute between 1.5 and 3.5 per cent and the employer an average rate of 19 per cent (Hutton 2011: table 3G).

Key changes include:

- The normal pension age is expected to move in line with changes in male and female state pension age: for men it increases from 65 to 66 by 2018–20, to 67 by 2034–36 and 68 by 2044–46; for women the change is more dramatic since it involves an increase from the present retirement age of 60 years.
- For teachers, from April 2012, increased contributions are broadly in line with Hutton's recommendations of tiered changes, ranging from no increase for salaries less than £15,000 and a 0.6 per cent increase for salaries of £15,000–26,000 up to a 2.4 per cent increase for salaries of more than £112,000.[24]
- Pensions to be uprated in line with earnings during the accrual phase but prices after payment (Hutton recommendation).

5. CASE STUDIES

5.1 Case Study 1: Privatizing Welfare-to-work Services

Building on earlier smaller-scale privatizations of welfare-to-work services (Box 15.3), in 2011 the Coalition government implemented the 'Work Programme', which outsources a significant proportion of job search services to the private sector and is said to be 'the centre-piece' of welfare-to-work reforms (DWP 2010: 2). The government issued 40 regional contracts to 19 organizations at a total estimated cost of £3–5 billion over five years (NAO 2012: 17). The public sector body previously charged with managing this work, Job Centre Plus, remains but in a reduced form (Figure 15.7). It is still the principal service for most adult claimants during their first 12 months, for young people for the first nine months and people on incapacity benefits the first three months. Thereafter it provides a referral service to alternative providers. It nevertheless still assumes responsibility for issuing benefit payments and applying sanctions for the entire unemployment period of claimants.

An innovative contractual feature is payment by results. Contractors are paid to find work for the unemployed on a sliding scale according to the length of time they remain in work and the unemployment group they come from. A three-tier payment system involves: an attachment fee when a user is referred; a job outcome fee (after 13 or 26 weeks in a job according to type of claimant); and a continued employment fee (every four weeks up to 18 months). The emphasis on sustained job outcomes is novel and in principle provides contractors an incentive both to ensure a good match

BOX 15.3 BACKGROUND TO THE WORK PROGRAMME, UNITED KINGDOM

It was in fact Tony Blair who endorsed the recommendations of a report commissioned from a retired City banker to examine reforms to welfare to work and who implemented these in partial form as the Flexible New Deal. The report (Freud 2007: 6) argued for privatization of job search services, replacing activities undertaken by Job Centre Plus:

> This arrangement could in principle apply to all benefit recipients, including people on incapacity benefits, lone parents and partners of benefit claimants, but excluding carers. The private and voluntary sector would be responsible for intensive case management and for providing individual, tailored help for individuals to re-engage with the labour market.

The report also set out the key principles subsequently applied in the 2010 government legislation. The contracts would: apply on a regional basis; include a payment-by-results system; and be awarded to a small number of prime contractors who would subcontract to 'an appropriate blend of subcontractors' (ibid.: 7). The 2007 report advertises the promise of a 'multi-million' market for new business providers but also carries the warning that the government must develop a world-class contracting capability to ensure its 'complex social goals were met without compromising the robustness of the outcome focus'.

The report's author, Lord Freud, collaborated closely in his new position as Minister for Welfare Reform with the current Minister for Employment to implement the £5 billion programme, live from June 2011. The government selected 19 prime contractors for 18 regional contracts organized in pairs (in 14 regions) and threes (in four regions). The government makes the bold claim that having at least two job search organizations in each region 'will ensure there is ongoing competition between providers to drive up performance' (DWP 2010: 6). Despite its aim to open up the market to voluntary and charity providers only one prime contractor is from the voluntary sector (Rehab) and one from the public sector (Newcastle College). There is also already evidence of preferred supplier status with seven contracts won by Ingeus (50 per cent owned by Deloitte), five by A4e, four by Seetec and three by Avanta, G4S and Working Links.

Sources: Various including Centre for Economic and Social Inclusion (www.cesi.org.uk/ NewPolicy/news/wp_results_april11) and the official DWP website (www.dwp.gov.uk/supplying-dwp/what-we-buy/welfare-to-work-services/work-programme/).

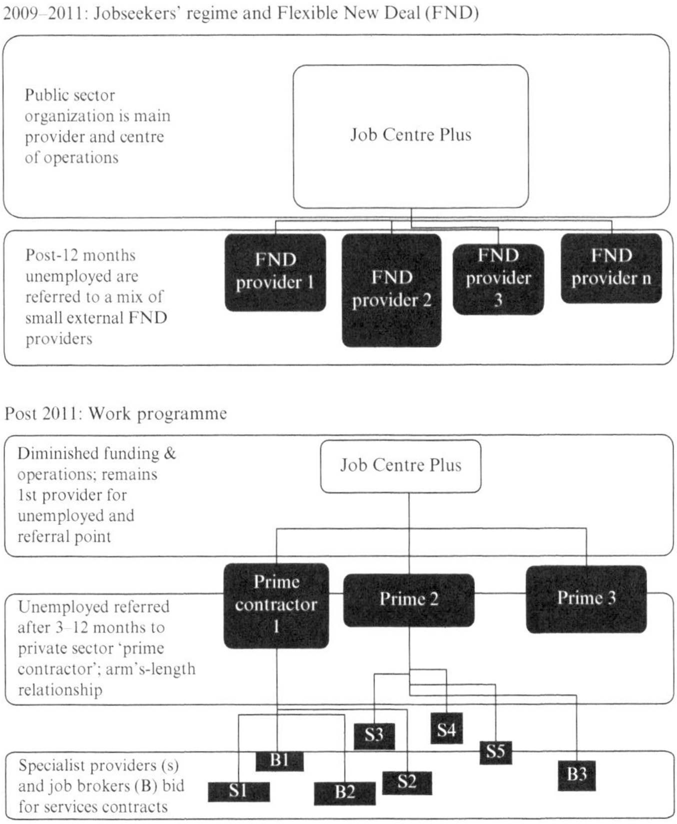

Figure 15.7 Changing the structure of welfare-to-work services provision: the new Work Programme, UK, 2011

between job seeker and job vacancy and to support the person's trajectory over a short period. In practice, the definition of continued employment is loose. It allows for discontinuous periods of employment such that the 13-week fee, for example, could be paid to the contractor for posting someone in three different jobs that sum to 13 weeks employment but with periods of job search in between:

> Churn is a feature of the labour market. I had this conversation with a job seeker who rang me up and asked 'Isn't the Work Programme about sustainable employment?'. I said, 'Yes it is. But it doesn't necessarily mean the same job. It doesn't mean we get you into the perfect job and keep you there. It might mean that over two years we get you into two or three jobs.' . . . The nature of the labour market these days is that nothing is permanent, nothing is settled. (Prime manager 3)

Differences in fees are designed to reflect savings to the government in benefit payments. For example, the total payment accrued for an unemployed person with a disability (on Employment Support Allowance benefits) is around £14,000, while for an unemployed person described as 'easy-to-help', the payment averages £4,000–7,000 (NAO 2012: figure 4). The government emphasizes the generous benefits to business the new model provides and expects contractors to make a 10 per cent return on investment. The employment minister stated, 'What we have tried to do is create a situation where our interests and the interests of providers are really aligned. They can make shedloads of money by doing the things we would absolutely love them to do'.[25]

There is insufficient space here to detail the full range of issues involved in this major area of policy reform.[26] It is also too early to provide an evaluation. Nevertheless, drawing on our interview data,[27] we briefly review three key issues where contradictions in policy and practice may undermine the performance of privatized services and may introduce new risks in sustaining the quality of welfare-to-work services.

5.1.1 Building a new workforce: transfers and redundancies

The first issue concerns the question of how private sector contractors were able, at very short notice, to establish teams of staff with the required expertise and skill to deliver complex job search services for the long-term unemployed. The new Work Programme involved cancelling the smaller FND contracts. Staff in many FND organizations were entitled to TUPE transfer rights once the new Work Programme contracts were signed. However, they had no right to choose which organization they would transfer to. In the local region investigated, transferring employees were randomly split among the three prime contractors and these contractors, in turn, allocated staff among organizations in their supply chain. There was a great deal of turbulence as a result.

From the perspective of the prime contractors, TUPE transfers meant they were forced to shoulder a fair amount of risk in taking on people potentially not equipped for the tasks required of the Work Programme. There was a strong partnership approach among public and private sector employers to avoid pre-transfer redundancies, but once transferred each contractor began a process of staff selection and redundancies:

> On our side, anyone who wanted to TUPE did TUPE. That doesn't mean to say that ultimately they kept their job because once they had TUPEd then we had to go through a process of selection. . . . We picked those staff who best matched the requirements of the Work Programme and the other people we had to let go as part of our redundancy scheme if indeed they were entitled to it because some people weren't. (Prime manager 1)

An important policy reform introduced quickly by the Coalition government when elected in 2010 was reduced rights to redundancy compensation by requiring 24 months' rather than 12 months' job tenure. This certainly facilitated the turbulent pattern of job changes sparked by the Work Programme. Many transferring staff lacked 24 months' employment experience and therefore did not qualify for redundancy compensation.

The turbulence is ongoing. One prime contractor estimates that around 30 per cent of the staff in post immediately after the transfer process subsequently exited. Nevertheless, it had not planned for the high staff attrition and nine months after the initial period of 'overstaffing' this company in fact faced a staffing shortfall.

5.1.2 Cost-led Performance Management Systems

One major rationale of government for bringing in the private sector to manage welfare-to-work services is their assumed greater expertise in performance management and ability to deliver cost savings. Prime contractors are expected both to performance manage the subcontractors in their supply chain and to performance manage their own staff. Whereas underperforming public sector organizations are slow to reform systems, so the argument goes, the private sector enacts change quickly.[28] Whether or not this is true, it raises the question as to the unintended consequences of tightly managed performance systems, particularly where it leads to the loss of organizational and individual expertise and experience in cases where underperformance results from exogenous factors.

While all prime contractors use performance management software systems that are able to scrutinize the conversion rates of unemployed referrals to job outcomes for each subcontractor (and for each individual adviser employed in the various subcontractor organizations), none accounts for differences in levels and trends in local labour market conditions. This means that job brokers[29] in high unemployment areas are evaluated against the same performance targets as job brokers in low unemployment rate localities. The ability of job brokers to 'convert' customers from unemployed to job status depends on various factors outside their control including the local unemployment rate, the entry of new employers (such as a new supermarket, for example) and competition with other job brokers for job vacancies. But is it possible to design a performance management system to account for these factors?

One prime contractor manager argued that this would be 'one level of complexity too far'. For a system designed to monitor day-to-day performance it would be difficult to know how to build in delayed knowledge about local unemployment, or to have up-to-date information on new employers in the area, and so on. Surprisingly, the view among managers was that unemployment was not the key driver of performance.

One manager did, however, point to the new problem created by privatization of welfare-to-work services where multiple job brokers now have to compete against each other in the local area for vacancies:

> Imagine a new Asda [supermarket chain] is opening, you've got every training provider, ever, and the job centre and possibly the local council that is lottery funded, all bombarding the employer saying let us help you recruit. . . . If there could be some way of making more cohesive the offer to the employer. Because eventually the employer gets fed up. (Prime manager 1)

5.1.3 Privatization and ongoing public–private sector conflicts

The effectiveness of the Work Programme depends on the overall functioning of the web of organizations and their relationships with each other. However, the policy has been controversial and has generated tensions between private sector prime contractors and the public sector Job Centre Plus (JCP) organizations. The data reveal two conflicts. First, a backlash against privatization appears to be impeding the smooth coordination of services provision across JCP and contractor organizations. JCP personnel are required to refer claimants to a prime contractor and follow up with details via a tailor-made software system. While computer-based data entry is the primary feature of the relationship, there are typically further issues to be resolved and questions arising about claimants that require either a conversation or additional exchange of data. However, staff in the private sector contractors said this additional effort could be difficult:

> In many [JCP] offices they are very reluctant to share information. Some of that is driven by data protection. Some of it is driven by Work Programme protocol. And some of it is driven by 'Why should I help you when you have got our jobs?' . . . There is a feeling among some JCP advisers that these large contractors [it] is a move to privatize some of the JCP service. (Prime manager 1)

Second, a proportion of the second tier of organizations delivering job search and specialist services for the unemployed are public sector organizations, but they now have to bend to the performance management rules of prime contractors. One prime contractor, which has four local authority organizations in its supply chain of nine job brokers, had experienced ongoing problems and was at the point of cancelling contracts with two of them just eight months into a five-year contract.

> There are some real management challenges emerging for us about how we can help . . . public sector organizations deliver better performance. In terms of performance management of staff, their speed of movement . . . their willingness to implement change. . . . We have a tremendous sense of urgency to make the Work Programme work. . . . So there is quite a clash of cultures there. (Prime manager 3)

Overall this case is illustrative of the government's ambition to privatize core areas of the public sector. It has all the hallmarks of the so-called 'modernization agenda': to bring in the large business service providers; to emphasize private sector performance management systems; and to inject turbulence in labour mobility and retention among public services workers. Moreover, the reform appears rushed, with risks to both service users (the unemployed) and the continued goodwill among managers and employees in the partner job centres.

5.2 Case Study 2: Local Government Downsizing

The second case study concerns local government. Local government merits special attention for several reasons: the Coalition government has targeted it as a primary area for spending cuts; its workforce already suffered a pay freeze in 2010, one year before the rest of the public sector; its employer association has refused to pay the £250 low-wage supplement; and it accounts for a disproportionately high share of public sector job losses. A recent Audit Commission report describes the situation in blunt terms:

> Government funding for local government will fall by 26 per cent or £5.5 billion over the period covered by the Spending Review (2011/12 to 2014/15), and councils must find most of the savings in the first two years. Because staff account for nearly half of spending by councils, workforce costs have to come down. (Audit Commission 2011: 3)

Excluding fire service staff and school teachers whose pay is negotiated separately, the local government workforce includes school support staff and social care workers, as well as employees who deliver essential local services in libraries, sport, environmental health, planning and development. It is strongly female dominated; prior to austerity (first quarter 2010) women accounted for 75 per cent of all jobs and women in part-time jobs accounted for almost half of the workforce (47 per cent). Cuts to local government spending ought therefore to be interpreted as having a direct adverse impact on women's pay and employment prospects.

5.2.1 Cutting real pay in the lowest-paid segment of the public sector

Pay for local government workers is settled through national-level collective bargaining in a forum known as the National Joint Council for Local Government Services. The main trade union representing local government workers is Unison, with around 700,000 members, along with GMB (approximately 100,000 members) and Unite (30,000). Despite national-level coverage, high trade union density and a forum for collective bargaining, unions have not been able to protect the living standards of local government workers in recent years. Moreover, the evidence suggests that the deterioration in local government pay is worse than in other areas of the public sector.

A pay freeze was imposed by employers first in 2010, again in 2011 (the year when most other public sector employers imposed the first year of a pay freeze) and for a third consecutive year in 2012. Moreover, while the Coalition government promised that low-wage public sector workers would be partially protected from the cut in real wages by the payment of a fixed annual sum of £250, this was rejected by local government employers. In their defence, the government made a controversial U-turn by arguing that in practice local government workers were in fact not necessarily eligible for the £250 because they were not directly employed by central government. At a time of high inflation, the three-year pay freeze means that local government workers' pay will have fallen by 13 per cent by the end of 2012.[30]

The size of pay cut is substantial by any standard. It is especially significant in local government because pay is low compared to other parts of the public sector (Figure 15.8). The bottom rate of pay set in the local government collective agreement in 2010–11 was just £6.30 per hour compared to the then statutory minimum wage of £5.93. The NHS pay agreement, which set a bottom rate at £7.11, has been far more effective thanks to the success of the same union, Unison, in applying a clear egalitarian pay bargaining approach (Grimshaw et al. 2010). The key difference, however, is the capacity and willingness of the NHS employers to approve of better protection for the low paid and the intransigence of the local government employer body.

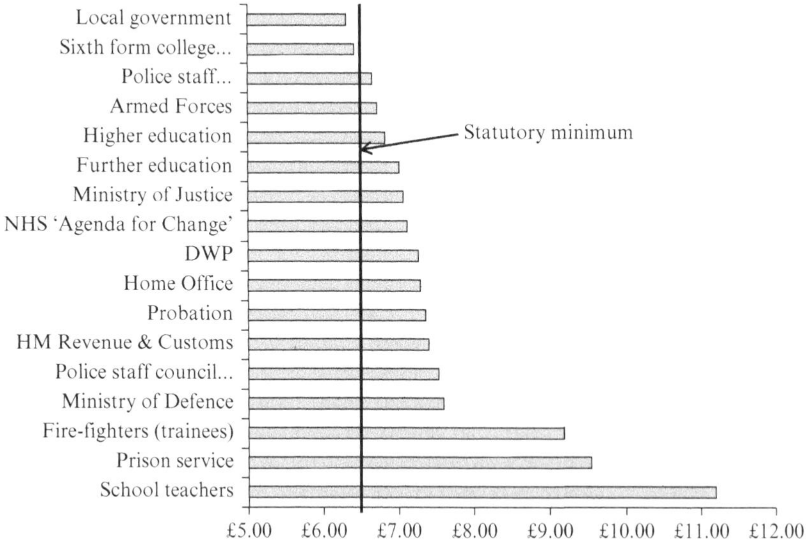

Note: Pay rates refer to individual settlements for different groups during late 2010/early 2011 with the exceptions of sixth form colleges (1 September 2011), firefighters (1 July 2011), probation (1 April 2010) and DWP (1 July 2011).

Source: Unison (2011b: table 3); author's compilation.

Figure 15.8 Minimum pay rates compared across different groups of the public sector, UK, 2010–2011

5.2.2 No trade-off with protecting jobs

Analysis of local government employment data shows that the spending cuts have had a dramatic effect on the size of the workforce. In the four years prior to 2010 local government employment fluctuated around 2.25 and 2.30 million (England and Wales only). Then, from the first quarter of 2010 it started to drop, down to 2.2 million by the start of 2011 and then further at an accelerating pace as local authorities reacted to the growing budget pressures, leading to a drop of 180,000 employees during the four quarters of 2011. The net change is an 11 per cent reduction in the local government workforce between the first quarters of 2010 and 2012.

The workforce cuts have affected women more than men because of women's overrepresentation in the sector. Two in three jobs (67 per cent) cut were women's jobs, amounting to 159,000 over the two-year period. Moreover, women in full-time jobs were more likely to be impacted than women in part-time jobs, respective cuts of 12 and 8 per cent during

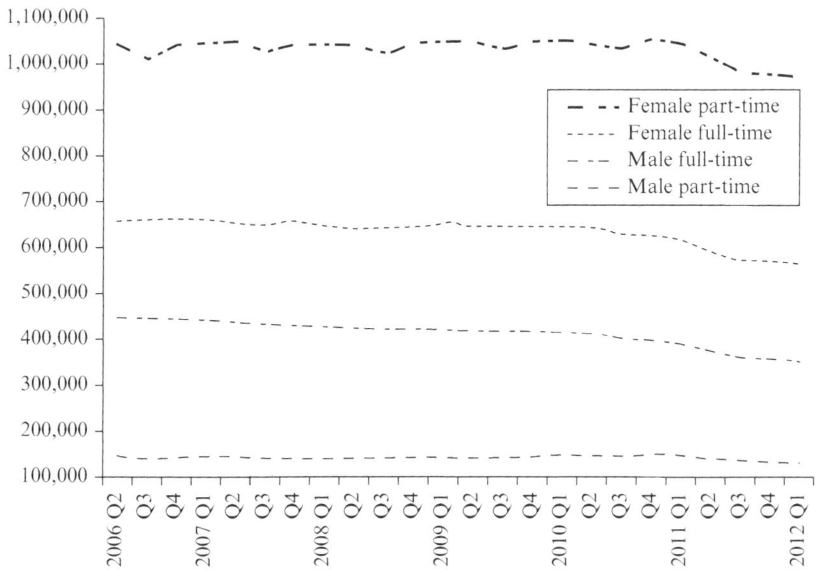

Source: ONS public sector employment data published by the Local Government Association (www.local.gov.uk/web/guest/local-government-intelligence). Author's compilation.

Figure 15.9 Job cuts in local government, by sex and full-time/part-time, 2006–2012 (England and Wales)

2010–12 (Figure 15.9). Among men, overall job losses were less but in fact the percentage cut was significant – a 15 per cent fall in male full-time employment and 11 per cent in male part-time employment, some 78,000 jobs altogether.

The unevenness of job cuts by gender and full-time/part-time is further illustrated in Figure 15.10. Given that women comprised 75 per cent of the local government workforce in 2010, they were in fact slightly underrepresented among employment losses despite experiencing the bulk of job cuts. Most jobs lost were full-time and this has caused a further increase in the representation of part-time jobs in local authorities, which by early 2012 accounted for more than half (55 per cent) of all jobs.

The overall figure of an 11 per cent job cut across England and Wales hides significant variation across different regions of the country. Job losses were unevenly distributed across regions with some evidence of a north–south divide, albeit with some exceptions to this usual trend, most notably with the South West region having experienced to date the largest job cuts (Table 15.9). Nevertheless, London and the South

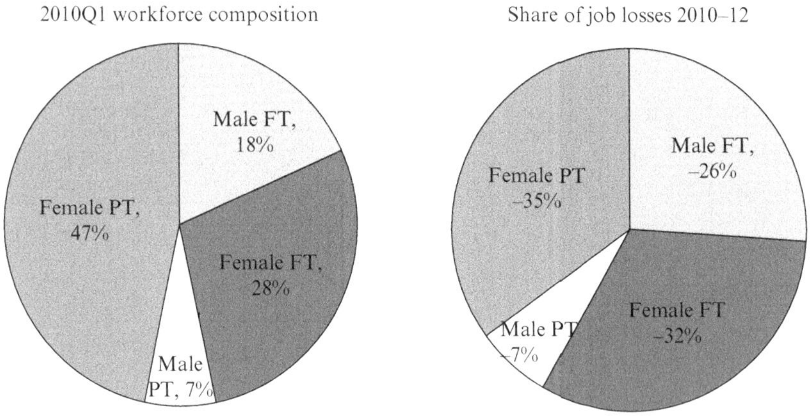

Source: Quarterly local government data from ONS, http://www.lga.gov.uk/lga/core/page.do?pageId=1955843.

Figure 15.10 Composition of local government employment losses by sex and full-time/part-time, 2010Q1 to 2012Q1 (England and Wales)

East, the two most populous southern regions, both experienced below-average job cuts in local government. Across the 10 regions in England and Wales, the reduction in numbers employed varies from 4 per cent in Wales to 19 per cent in the South West. Most regions tended to reduce the number of full-time jobs more than part-time jobs. It also appears that one region, the East Midlands, made a partial switch of male employment from full- to part-time jobs. Also, there is no common pattern in job cuts of permanent as opposed to temporary workers; it is surprising that in three regions (Wales, East Midlands and West Midlands) permanent workers were more likely to lose jobs than temporary workers.

We also know that there is strong regional variation in the spending cuts in direct proportion to the level of deprivation in localities. The recent study by Hastings et al. (2012), funded by the Joseph Rowntree Foundation, maps the level of spending cuts experienced by individual local authorities against an official index of multiple deprivation (collected by the government's Department for Communities and Local Government). It finds a striking negative correlation of –0.89 between the level of spending change during 2010–11 to 2011–12 and the index of multiple deprivation, such that larger spending cuts were experienced in localities with higher levels of multiple deprivation. The reasons for the

Table 15.9 Distribution of local government job cuts by region, UK, 2010Q1 to 2012Q1 (%)

Region	Headcount	Male FT	Female FT	Male PT	Female PT	Permanent	Temp/ Casual	F share of job losses	F share of employment in 2010
South West	–19.0	–24.8	–21.8	–25.0	–15.1	–18.9	–19.9	67.7	75.1
North East	–14.6	–15.0	–11.9	–25.6	–14.8	–8.5	–41.3	67.2	72.1
East of England	–13.9	–16.8	–13.5	–20.0	–12.4	–13.9	–13.9	70.6	76.9
North West	–11.2	–18.2	–14.0	–10.0	–6.4	–11.3	–10.7	64.1	75.2
West Midlands	–10.2	–14.2	–12.6	–10.9	–7.2	–12.0	5.8	69.6	76.4
Yorkshire & Humber	–10.0	–15.9	–11.4	–5.6	–7.7	–8.2	–19.3	67.5	75.3
London	–9.2	–10.8	–18.0	–11.4	–9.1	–8.2	–17.1	68.0	73.0
South East	–7.8	–12.7	–11.7	–2.7	–4.6	–7.8	–8.0	71.2	77.4
East Midlands	–6.8	–16.2	–11.2	1.5	–2.6	–8.0	–1.8	60.3	75.6
Wales	–3.8	–6.3	–4.1	–4.4	–2.4	–4.2	–2.6	57.1	71.9
England & Wales	–10.6	–15.0	–12.0	–10.9	–7.9	–10.3	–12.4	67.2	75.2

Source: Quarterly local government data from ONS (http://www.lga.gov.uk/lga/core/page.do?pageId=1955843).

skewed impact are complex but concern the greater dependency of poorer localities on grant income from government and their lesser ability to raise local property tax revenues, as well as the scrapping of special grants (ibid.).

In practice, approaches to downsizing are varied across local authorities. As with other public sector organizations, there is evidence of management willingness to use alternatives to compulsory redundancy, including early retirements, holding unfilled vacancies and outsourcing staff, but the practice of compulsory redundancies has nevertheless been a strong feature. An Audit Commission report (2011) suggests that local authorities are downsizing employment as part of a wider restructuring that involves reducing the number of departments, shared services between local authorities, delayering management layers and outsourcing. Alternatives to redundancies (ibid.) include the following:

- recruitment freeze (although less effective in a recession since staff turnover tends to decline);
- switching staff from full- to part-time employment, especially older staff close to retirement;
- flexible working (such as offering staff the option to work during school terms only, in exchange for a reduction in salary);
- redeploying staff (useful to fill skill needs usually filled by spending on temporary agency staff); and
- pooling and sharing of staff between councils and departments.

In sum, local government spending cuts are having a massively adverse impact on workers' pay and conditions, jobs and local services. This brief case study has not included many other challenges facing local government, such as the conditions in deprived localities, the fragility of current national pay arrangements and evidence of some local authorities cutting sickness benefits and maternity leave. A further extensive study is required to follow the current reforms. Moreover, we know little at present about the wider implications of the spending cuts on working conditions (levels of work intensity and stress for example), on changes in working hours and their relationship with less generous criteria for claiming tax credits, or about the damage to women's equality of pay and employment. Local government is without doubt the area of the public sector that is most ravaged by ongoing Coalition government spending cuts.

6. CONCLUSION

The radical public sector reforms being implemented by the Coalition government are not a solution to the UK's ongoing economic depression. Nor, in their present design, are they a constructive component in a wider effort to balance the economy towards less dependence on a bloated financial services sector, more exports and a boost to innovative, knowledge-intensive industries in manufacturing and services. The planned cuts in public spending promise to take the UK to a position where spending as a share of GDP will be lower than that in the United States within five years (Taylor-Gooby and Stoker 2011). Moreover, in qualitative terms, the cuts represent an assault on the incremental development of publicly provided services to UK citizens, and are already undermining (and conflicting with) expectations about the country's social settlement in terms of the quid pro quo between payments of taxes and social security contributions and the state's accountability for provision of universal public services of appropriate quality. The scale and speed of changes has proved to be very controversial, with public sector strikes and large-scale public protests throughout 2011 and more planned for 2012.

As the UK economy continues to falter, the economic vision underpinning reforms is being dismissed by more and more commentators as misguided. This is especially the case in regions of the UK where the public sector accounts for a high share of the economy and a very high share of local job growth. Beatty et al.'s (2011) pre-recession analysis showed that a strong public sector is especially important in local areas characterized by above-average levels of deprivation and unemployment. They show that job growth in these local regions was far more reliant on public sector than private sector employers, by a ratio, on average, of seven to two during the decade preceding the recession (ibid.: Table 15.8). As these authors put it, 'This does not augur well for an era of public spending cuts. But most particularly, the trends up to 2008 in the weaker local economies outside London do not inspire confidence that job growth in the private sector will easily take over from the public sector' (p. 20).

What is needed now are renewed critical analyses of the neoliberal principles that underpin government policy towards the downgrading of public sector employment terms and conditions and the privatization of public services provision. To some extent, the reforms continue a tradition of interventions set out by the Thatcher and Blair governments and there are already valuable critiques of privatization and the adverse consequences of outsourcing as a race to the bottom. However, a renewed critique is needed alongside a constructive framework for alternative policy interventions. Such policy actions need to address six key areas of socioeconomic need:

- the need for democratically accountable provision of public services (at national and local levels) that delivers value to economy and society;
- the need to invest in a public sector as a site of professional and knowledge-intensive services;
- the need to establish a responsive system of public sector employment that incorporates effective social dialogue with employees;
- the need to defend and reinforce the UK's tradition of using the public sector to set gender equality standards in pay and employment practices;
- the need for public sector organizations to play a core role in local regions, contributing to income generation and investment; and
- the need for decent and equal work to be a foundation stone of a renewed public sector with a reassertion of the ethics of public sector bureaucracy, a defence against the intrusion of crude private sector performance managerialism and a triumphing of equality measures and outcomes.

NOTES

1. Office for National Statistics (ONS) data show 2012 first quarter GDP was 95.6 per cent of the pre-recession peak recorded in the first quarter of 2008. Had annual growth continued its 1997–2007 trend then GDP would have been 9 per cent higher than that recorded for 2011.
2. See Osborne's full speech at www.hm-treasury.gov.uk/press_37_10.htm (accessed 13 February 2012).
3. At critical points during 2011, the OECD released favourable assessments of UK reforms. Prior to the 2011 budget, the headline statement from the OECD's UK survey was that while fiscal consolidation was 'generating headwinds for the recovery . . . inaction would have been worse. . . . Early and resolute action ensures that debt will stop growing and help contain upward pressure on interest rates' (OECD 2011a). Then, during post-budget debates in the British press, the OECD reaffirmed its support: 'The current fiscal consolidation strikes the right balance and should continue in line with the government's medium-term plan to eliminate the deficit, while allowing the automatic stabilisers to work' (OECD 2011b).
4. It argues, 'There is unfortunately a trade-off between slowing the accumulation of government debt to stave off its possible negative effect on growth, and the risks that fiscal consolidation itself may create sustained headwinds on the recovery and lead to stagnation' (OECD 2011c: 247).
5. 2010 Bloomberg lecture by Ed Balls, Shadow Chancellor, www.edballs.co.uk/blog/?p=907 (accessed 13 February 2012).
6. Reported in *The Guardian* 23 April 2010.
7. 2010 LFS data records 4,068,000 union members in the public sector (density of 56 per cent) and 2,467,000 members in the private sector (density of 14 per cent) (Achur 2011: table 1.4).
8. See: www.guardian.co.uk/business/2011/mar/01/mervyn-king-blames-banks-cuts (accessed 13 February 2012).

9. Conservative government spending cuts were controversially continued during the first two years of the Labour government, 1997–99.
10. The 2008–09 recession witnessed rises in real spending of 5.1 and 6.9 per cent in education and 3.1 and 5.0 per cent in health. This followed the pre-recession trend: during 1999–2000 to 2007–08 annual spending increases averaged 6.4 and 5.2 per cent, respectively. Data refer to 'total managed expenditures', Public Expenditures Statistical Analyses (2009, www.hm-treasury.gov.uk).
11. In the 2010 budget, forecast spending cuts accounted for 77 per cent of total planned consolidation over five years and a net tax increase of 23 per cent (HM Treasury 2010: table 1.1). The plans estimate a reduction of £128 billion by 2015–16 – spending cuts of £99 billion and a £29 billion net increase of taxes (ibid.).
12. Five principles are said to underpin current reforms: (i) increased choice; (ii) decentralized provision; (iii) a mix of providers; (iv) fair access; and (v) accountability to users and taxpayers (HM Government 2011).
13. See www.unison.org.uk/healthcare/pages_view.asp?did=13427. Government has already granted private firms the right to take over 'failing hospitals'. The first contract was agreed in November 2011 with Circle Healthcare at Hinchingbrooke hospital (*The Guardian* 11 November 2011).
14. See the Tenders Electronic Daily (http://ted.europa.eu/TED/search/) and supplement to the *Official Journal of the European Union*.
15. See the impact assessment of the Health and Social Care Bill, available at: www.miphealth.org.uk/home/Health_and_Social_Care_Bill_Note_for_the_Future_Forum_May_2011.aspx.
16. Evidence from the Royal College of Nursing's survey of 21 NHS trusts in England, reported April 2011, found that 54 per cent of approximately 10,000 planned job cuts were frontline clinical posts: www.rcn.org.uk/newsevents/news/article/uk/ more_than_half_of_nhs_ job_cuts_are_on_clinical_frontline (accessed 14 February 2012).
17. The data in Figure 15.5 do not separate out the small number of private sector employees in these four areas.
18. While the ONS redefines bailed-out banks within the National Accounts and their workforce as part of public sector employment, it would be useful if it would also categorize separately the number of workers who provide public services within public sector establishments and are employed by a private sector company reliant on public sector funding.
19. This estimation derives from total current spending excluding transfer payments, debt interest and procurement of goods (Julius 2008: 13).
20. Various newspaper clippings, plus a 2011 Unison listing, www.publiclibrariesnews.com/p/6-closed-since-1411.html and www.unison.org.uk/asppresspack/pressrelease_view.asp?id=2290 (accessed 14 February 2012).
21. Hansard's written ministerial statements, 24 March 2010, www.publications.parliament.uk/pa/cm/cmtoday/ cmwms/archive/100324.htm#hddr_15.
22. Unison said the NHS Pay Review Body was 'hidebound' by government 'diktat', the National Union of Teachers said the School Teachers' Pay Review Body had 'colluded' with ministers and the Prison Officers' Association argued the pay review body had failed in its duties by not compensating for prison officers' inability to take strike action (*Public Finance* 21 March 2011, www.publicfinance.co.uk/news/2011/).
23. In the three months to September 2011, the median private sector settlement was 2.6 per cent and that in the public sector was 0.0 per cent.
24. Sourced from www.teacherspensions.co.uk/resources/continc_calculator.htm (accessed 14 February 2012).
25. Cited in *The Guardian*, 9 November 2011.
26. For example, how is a job defined? What happens when an unemployed person takes up self-employment? Under what conditions can sanctions be applied? What are the rules defining what job and under what conditions have to be accepted, including travel time, skill match, working hours, multiple part-time positions?

27. Case study data include interviews with senior managers in three 'prime contractors' and Job Centre Plus in one UK region, an interview with a senior researcher at the Department for Work and Pensions and documentary information.
28. One prime contractor, which outsources all its welfare-to-work services and only takes charge of supply chain management, argued that the government wanted 'to outsource outsourcing'.
29. Job brokers provide the core welfare-to-work services such as job search, CV support and motivation building. Another tier of suppliers provides specialist services such as mental health services, drug and alcohol advice.
30. Annual inflation (retail price index) of 4.8 per cent (2010), 5.3 per cent (2011) (www.ONS.gov.uk) and forecast 3.6 per cent for 2012 (www.xperthr.co.uk) (accessed 30 March 2012).

REFERENCES

Achur, J. (2011), 'Trade union membership 2010', Department for Business Innovation and Skills (BIS), London: National Statistics Publication.

Audit Commission (2011), 'Work in progress: Meeting local needs with lower workforce costs', London: Audit Commission.

Beatty, C., S. Fothergill, T. Gore and R. Powell (2011), 'Tackling worklessness in Britain's weaker local economies', Sheffield Hallam University. Available at: www.shu.ac.uk/_assets/pdf/cresr-tackle-worklessness-report-nov10.pdf (accessed 23 June 2012).

Bozio, A. and R. Disney (2011), 'Public sector pay and pensions', in *The IFS Green Budget February 2011*, London: Institute for Fiscal Studies. Available at: www.ifs.org.uk (accessed 23 June 2012).

Crouch, C. (2003), *Commercialisation or Citizenship? Education Policy and the Future of Public Services*, Fabian Ideas, London: Fabian Society.

DWP (2010), 'The Work Programme Prospectus November 2010', Department for Work and Pensions, London. Available at: www.dwp.gov.uk/docs/work-prog-prospectus-v2.pdf (accessed 23 June 2012).

Erridge, A. and J. Greer (2002), 'Partnership and public procurement: building social capital through supply relations', *Public Administration*, **80** (3): 503–22.

Fontana, G. and M. Sawyer (2011), 'Fiscal austerity: lessons from recent events in the British isles', *Challenge*, March–April: 42–60.

Freud, D. (2007), 'Reducing Dependency, Increasing Opportunity: Options for the Future of Welfare to Work', Independent report to the Department for Work and Pensions. Available at: www.dwp.gov.uk/docs/welfarereview.pdf (accessed 23 June 2012).

Froud, J. and J. Shaoul (2001), 'Appraising and evaluating PFI for NHS hospitals', *Financial Accountability and Management*, **17** (3): 247–70.

Green, P. (2010), *Efficiency Review by Sir Philip Green*, HM Government: Cabinet Office.

Grimshaw, D., C. Shepherd and J. Rubery (2010), 'National report UK', Report prepared for the EC project 'Minimum Wage Systems and Changing Industrial Relations in Europe'. Available at: http://www.mbs.ac.uk/research/europeanemployment/projects/minimum-wage.aspx (accessed 23 June 2012).

Grimshaw, D., S. Vincent and H. Willmott (2002), 'Going privately: partnership and outsourcing of public sector services', *Public Administration*, **80** (3): 475–502.

Hastings, A., G. Bramley, N. Bailey, and D. Watkins (2012), 'Serving deprived economies in a recession', Phase 1 Report, Joseph Rowntree Foundation, York.

HM Government (2011), *Open Public Services White Paper*, Cm8145. Available at: www.cabinetoffice.gov.uk (accessed 23 June 2012).

HM Treasury (2010), *Budget 2010*, HC 61, June, London: The Stationery Office.

Hood, C. (2010), 'Reflections on Public Service Reform in a Cold Fiscal Climate', Report for the 2020 Public Services Trust.

Hutton, J. (2011), *Independent Public Service Pensions Commission: Final Report*, March, London: HM Treasury.

IMF (2010), *World Economic Outlook: Recovery, Risk and Rebalancing* (October), Washington, DC.

Julius, D. (2008), 'Understanding the public services industry – how big, how good, where next?', *Public Services Industry Review Report*, BERR (July). Available at: www.bis.gov.uk/files/file46965.pdf (accessed 23 June 2012).

Kellaway, M. and, H. Shanks (2006), 'National accounts classifications: public sector broadcasting', NACC decisions, NACC case 2003/27, National Statistics, London.

King, L., M. Kitson, S. Konzelmann and F. Wilkinson (2012), 'Making the same mistake again – or is *this time* different?', *Cambridge Journal of Economics*, **36** (1): 1–15.

Kirkpatrick, I. (1999), 'The worst of both worlds? Public services without markets or bureaucracy', *Public Money and Management*, October–December: 7–14.

Koumenta, M. (2011), 'Modernisation, privatisation and the public sector ethos', in D. Marden (ed.), *Employment in the Lean Years: Policy and Prospects for the Next Decade*, Oxford: Oxford University Press.

Lonsdale, C., I. Kirkpatrick, K. Hoque and A. De Ruyter (2010), 'Supplier behaviour and public contracting in the English agency nursing market', *Public Administration*, **88** (3): 800–18.

Low Pay Commission (LPC) (2011), *National Minimum Wage; Low Pay Commission Report 2011*, Cm 8023.

Myers, M. (2012), 'Economic review: April 2012', Office for National Statistics. Available at: www.ons.gov.uk/ons/dcp171766_263951.pdf (accessed 23 June 2012).

National Audit Office (NAO) (2008), 'Protecting staff in PPP/PFI deals', London: NAO.

National Audit Office (NAO) (2012), 'The introduction of the Work Programme', London: NAO.

National Institute of Economic and Social Research (NIESR) (2011), 'NIESR monthly estimates of GDP', 11 October. Available at: www.niesr.ac.uk/pdf/111011_125821.pdf (accessed 23 June 2012).

OECD (2011a), 'Launch of the OECD' economic survey of the United Kingdom'. Available at: www.oecd.org\document/42/0,3746,en_21571361_44315115_47385066_1_1_1_1,00.html (accessed 23 June 2012).

OECD (2011b), 'United Kingdom economic forecast summary'. Available at: www.oecd.org/document/60/0,3746,en_33873108_33873870_45267516_1_1_1_1,00.html (accessed 23 June 2012).

OECD (2011c), *OECD Economic Outlook*, Vol. 2011/1, Paris.

Office of Budget Responsibility (OBR) (2010), 'Further information on general government employment growth', June 2010 pre-budget and budget forecasts. Available at: http://budgetresponsibility.independent.gov.uk/ (accessed 23 June 2012).

Postel-Vinay, F. and H. Turon (2007), 'The public pay gap in Britain: Small differences that (don't?) matter', *Economic Journal*, **117** (October): 1460–503.

Rubery, J., D. Grimshaw and G. Hebson (2013), 'Exploring the limits to local authority social care commissioning: competing pressures, variable practices and unresponsive providers', *Public Administration*, forthcoming.

Sawyer, M. (2012), 'The tragedy of United Kingdom fiscal policy in the aftermath of the financial crisis', *Cambridge Journal of Economics*, **36** (1): 205–22.

Taylor-Gooby, P. and G. Stoker (2011), 'Sleepwalking through a cross-roads', mimeo. Available at: www.kent.ac.uk/sspssr/staff/academic/taylorgooby/public_spending.pdf (accessed 23 June 2012).

UNCTAD (2011), *Trade and Development Report, 2011: Post-Crisis Policy Challenges in the World Economy*, Geneva: United Nations.

Unison (2011a), *intouch*, Issue 21, summer.

Unison (2011b), 'The NJC Trade Union Side Pay Claim for 2012–13' (October). Available at: www.unison.org.uk/acrobat/NJCPayClaim_2012_13.pdf (accessed 23 June 2012).

Walsh, K. and H. Davis (1993), 'Competition and service: The impact of the Local Government Act 1988', Report prepared by Institute of Local Government Studies, University of Birmingham, for Department of the Environment, London: HMSO.

Index